MILTON

IN THE

PURITAN REVOLUTION

MILTON

IN THE

PURITAN
REVOLUTION

by

DON M. WOLFE

1963
Humanities Press
New York

First published in 1941

Copyright 1963 by
Humanities Press, Inc.
by special arrangement
with the author

Printed in U.S.A. by
NOBLE OFFSET PRINTERS, INC.
NEW YORK 3, N. Y.

TO

ANNIE CUNNINGHAM

AND

MARY STORMONT

HE lived at one of the most memorable eras in the history of mankind, at the very crisis of the great conflict between Oromasdes and Arimanes, liberty and despotism, reason and prejudice. That great battle was fought for no single generation, for no single land. The destinies of the human race were staked on the same cast with the freedom of the English people. Then were first proclaimed those mighty principles which have since worked their way into the depths of the American forests, which have aroused Greece from the slavery and degradation of two thousand years, and which, from one end of Europe to the other, have kindled an unquenchable fire in the hearts of the oppressed, and loosed the knees of the oppressors with an unwonted fear. . . .

He never came up in the rear, when the outworks had been carried and the breach entered. He pressed into the forlorn hope. . . .

There are a few characters which have stood the closest scrutiny and severest tests . . . which have been declared sterling by the general consent of mankind. . . . These great men we trust that we know how to prize; and of these was Milton. The sight of his books, the sound of his name, are pleasant to us. His thoughts resemble those celestial fruits and flowers which the Virgin Martyr of Massinger sent down from the gardens of Paradise to the earth, and which are distinguished from the productions of other soils, not only by superior bloom and sweetness, but by miraculous efficacy to invigorate and to heal. They are powerful, not only to delight, but to elevate and purify. Nor do we envy the man who can study either the life or the writings of the great poet and patriot, without aspiring to emulate, not indeed the sublime works with which his genius has enriched our literature, but the zeal with which he laboured for the public good, the fortitude with which he endured every private calamity, the lofty disdain with which he looked down on temptations and dangers, the deadly hatred which he bore to bigots and tyrants, and the faith which he so sternly kept with his country and with his fame.

—MACAULAY, "*Milton.*"

THE outstanding effect of the study of Milton's philosophy as embodied in his poetry and prose, and of the endeavor to relate him more closely to his English predecessors has been to minimize the importance of his theology in the narrower sense, and to exalt in its place, not merely his art and eloquence and imagination, but those elements of insight and reflection which he holds in common with Spenser, Hooker, Shakespeare, and Bacon— men in whose work the northern and southern currents of the age are fused in that richer and profounder creative humanism which is the special contribution of the English Renaissance. The essential character of that humanism is its assertion of the spiritual dignity of man, its recognition of the degree to which his higher destinies are in his own hands, its repudiation of the claim of his lower nature to control his higher or of any force or agency external to his own mind and will to achieve for him salvation. This humanism is sharply and irreconcilably at odds with mediæval thought. It discards, first of all, the ascetic principle and releases for enjoyment and use all the agencies of self-realizing perfection. It proposes, moreover (and this is its essential character) to achieve its goal through the study not of God but of man and it trusts the human reason as well as intuition and revealed truth as the instrument of its knowledge. It turns, therefore, to Scripture for the best record of man's nature in its relation to the God of righteousness and love, then to the *litterae humaniores* of antiquity, where it finds a wider revelation of man as an individual and a citizen, this latter source constituting no denial but a completion of the data afforded by the former.

—JAMES HOLLY HANFORD, *"Milton and the Return to Humanism."*

PREFACE

OR some years readers of Milton have felt a need for a comprehensive analysis of Milton's social ideas other than that found in Masson's exhaustive *Life*. This book attempts to meet that need, orienting Milton's political beliefs with both the historical events and the social ideas of his influential contemporaries. That Milton and his fellow rebels spoke for more than his generation is more than ever apparent today, when the most elementary freedoms for which they struggled are more sharply debated than in any decade during the past century.

The source literature interpreted, consisting mainly of the pamphlets of the Thomason Collection of the British Museum and the McAlpin Collection of Union Seminary, falls almost exclusively between 1640 and 1660. I have made little attempt to trace either the origins or the influence of Milton's political beliefs; each of these topics deserves separate and thorough consideration. In treating the main threads of Milton's social thought, I have found it necessary to retrace with differing emphasis the same sequence of events in several chapters, a procedure inevitable, as I see it, in any thorough examination of ideological topics. Since the prose contains the clearest statements of Milton's sociological beliefs, it was with some hesitation that I concluded the book with a brief analysis of the political implications of *Paradise Lost,* an analysis which cannot be construed, of course, as an unfavorable judgment of the poem as a whole. Milton was so many sided that any ultimate judgment of him requires many qualifications. Of this no man who has spent years with Milton can be unaware. Like most readers of Milton I subscribe in the main to that still timely and revealing essay, "Milton and the Return to Humanism," by James Holly Hanford (*Studies in Philology,* 1921). No book on Milton's politics can show him, however, always at his truest and his best, that is, when his

ix

rich humanistic background dominated the expression of his social ideas.

I wish to acknowledge my indebtedness to Professor Willis H. Wilcox, formerly of Davis-Elkins College, under whose instruction I was first directed to a consideration of democratic theory; to Dr. John Davis, of Southwestern, for hints on Thomas Hobbes; to Dr. James H. Hanford for suggestions on revision and method of approach; to Dr. Putnam F. Jones, of the University of Pittsburgh, for invaluable assistance in editing the original manuscript; to Dr. Theodore Calvin Pease for information concerning Leveller bibliography; to Dr. William G. Crane, for critical reading of the first chapters; to Dr. R. S. Crane for conscientious editing of the chapter on Milton and the people, which appeared originally in *Modern Philology;* to Dr. George Coffman, for suggested additions to the chapter on kingship, which appeared in *Studies in Philology;* and to Mr. and Mrs. J. C. Palamountain for invaluable suggestions for manuscript revision. I also wish to thank Miss Margery L. Allison, formerly reference librarian at the University of Pittsburgh, for frequent and valuable aid in borrowing rare books and pamphlets; the librarians of the British Museum and Jesus College, Oxford; the officials of the Public Record Office, London; Dr. William W. Rockwell and his assistants at Union Seminary Library, particularly Miss Charlotte Maupin, custodian of the McAlpin Collection, for indefatigable patience and timely assistance on many occasions; and Mary Stormont Wolfe, for many long hours of copying in the North Room and diligent correction of the proof.

D. M. W.

New York
December 15, 1940

CHRONOLOGY OF MILTON'S WRITINGS [1]

1. In tracing the development and crystallization of Milton's social ideas, one finds it imperative to keep in mind the chronology of his writings, which did not always correspond, of course, with publication dates. Except when otherwise noted, dates in the list refer to time of publication. This list is not intended to be exhaustive.
2. First published in 1870.
3. Date of entry in Stationers Register.
4. Probable date of composition.
5. Probable date of composition.
6. If Milton's condemnation of the Long Parliament is authentic, he probably wrote it in 1648. It was not published until 1681.
7. Probable date of composition. Milton had the first four books completed by the spring of 1649.

8. Thomason Catalogue, I, 786.
9. Date of composition.
10. Probable period of composition.
11. Probable date of composition.
12. Registered with the Stationers Company September 20, 1670.

CONTENTS

xiii

MILTON

IN THE

PURITAN REVOLUTION

INTRODUCTION

I N the Puritan Revolution a rising middle class of business men, their cause sustained by widespread Calvinistic teachings, their program supported by large sections of the lower middle classes and by liberal members of the aristocracy, clashed with the adherents of a declining feudal order. In its early stages the Revolution sought a limitation of monarchical power, an assurance of Parliamentary control of all major policies, and a substitution of a Presbyterian state church for the Anglican. But the middle class leaders of the Revolution, the more prosperous members of the Puritan faction, soon realized that many of their followers were pushing toward more radical objectives than they had envisioned. The war brought release of fervent democratic agitation especially in the New Model army, agitation soon regarded with horror by most of the Puritans themselves, so that by 1649 they preferred a kingly dictatorship to the strange governmental notions of Cromwell's army. Abolition of the House of Lords, annihilation of kingship, establishment of a republic—no one had dreamed in 1642 that the Revolution carried this poison in its womb. While repressing still more drastic reform programs, the Independent army made these measures dire realities, bringing surprised stares and fearful hearts to most Englishmen of the middle classes and their spokesmen, the Presbyterian clergy. Distrusted by the orthodox Puritans and the aristocracy, hated by the Leveller radicals, the Independents ruled uneasily for eleven years, upheld largely by might of the army. The orthodox Puritans welcomed with the aristocracy the reactionary Restoration of 1660, preferring to risk loss of their original objectives to support of utopian republican projects. To command any widespread popular support the extremities of the Independents had occurred too soon in what Sir Charles Firth has called "the evolution of democracy." Furthermore the implications of these

1

extremities clashed with the economic interests of the orthodox Puritans, who wanted substantial political representation of their rising commercial power. In the Revolution of 1688 they achieved in the main the aims that had agitated their fathers in 1642, reconciling themselves, it is true, to an Anglican state church, but consolidating in their own hands a preponderant share of governmental control that remains theirs to this day.

Milton was one of the many Puritans who gave his whole-hearted support to the Parliamentary cause in 1642, one of the rebel few who hailed the destruction of kingship and lords in 1649. Milton's background made him inevitably a partisan of the Parliamentary faction. A city home of Puritan inclinations, a neighborhood of wealthy merchants, a boyhood outlook of deep seriousness enhanced by Bible study, a Puritan minister in the parish pulpit, a strict Puritan master in his earliest school, two or three susceptible years at St. Paul's under the Calvinist Thomas Young, Cambridge study under Joseph Meade—these influences were decisive. But it was inevitable, too, that Milton should dissent from Puritan orthodoxy. His imagination was too intense, his confidence in his intellectual powers too deep, to be bound by Presbyterian creed. His prolonged reading of the Greek and Roman classics (a university habit which in Hobbes' view nourished the rebellion) emphasized his early love of liberty and mitigated the harshness of Calvinist discipline. Time after time he was to justify revolutionary opinions by the humanistic law of nature. But the most important factor in Milton's alliance with the Puritans was his belief in the individualistic interpretation of the Bible. Himself his own interpreter, he identified the law of nature with the law of God, unhesitatingly repudiating the religious and political teachings of his time. On Milton as on few other figures of the period, Protestant individualism stamped a revolutionary attitude, an almost reckless reforming zeal, removing him as far from the orthodox Puritan as from the staunchest royalist. The Restoration he was to regard with complacent contempt, scornful of the idolatrous multitude, secure in his republican principles.

THE PURITAN LEADER EMERGES

The typical Elizabethan leader was a landed aristocrat, a lover of adventure, a courtier, a poet, a man of much love of beauty and little interest in business. A Drake for sinking the Spaniards, a Raleigh for seeking the gold of Guiana, a Leicester for gracing Kenilworth pageantry, an Essex for fighting the Irish rebels—these were the salt of English nationalism. In the hands of their kind lay the economic power of the land. Since the dissolution of the monasteries, they had added to their estates land and buildings valued in modern terms at nearly half a billion dollars, purchased from the crown at figures dictated by necessity. Income that had formerly supported schools, succored the poor, provided hospitals, now flowed into private hands. Sheep raising proving more profitable than diversified farming, the aristocracy turned peasants off the land, inclosed many commons, "the greatest grief," said Lever, "that hath been unto the people of this realm." [1] They raised rents, dispossessed the poor, sent them swarming into the cities. One third to one fourth of the Londoners were paupers. "What say you?" cried a preacher at St. Paul's. "The poor lie under every wall, and cry under every stall, and die in the streets, in the time of the gospel." [2] To livings owned formerly by the church the Elizabethan landowners appointed clergymen of their choice. The aristocrats liked the pageantry of the church, read the Bible little, the classics often. They frequented theatres, loved music, hunting, and beautiful gardens. The Queen they revered; not often did they question her divine right to rule the land.

But the times were fashioning a new man, less appealing, more efficient, to work the will of a changing England. From 1521 to 1545 over £630,000 in gold annually had been transported from the New World to Europe; from 1556 to 1578 £440,000; from 1578 to 1600 £280,000. [3] With the sanction of Elizabeth English mariners boarded Spanish treasure ships on the high seas, and carried New World gold to London. The rich men of England organized stock companies to exploit the Americas, the Baltic, the Far East. They lent gold to craftsmen to set up their trades outside the restrictions of the gilds; they lent it to sheep raisers to market their wool in Antwerp. Shipbuilding boomed. New-type fighting ships swept fleets of Spanish galleons from the seas. The trade of England expanded at an unbelievable pace. The customs income of $50,000 in 1590 increased to $2,500,000 in 1641, indicating an enormous expansion. More conservatively Defoe estimated a 2500% increase in trade in a century. [4] The middle classes assumed new responsibilities, drew recruits from the yeomanry, grew wealthy and powerful. Their leaders travelled in Holland, France, and Italy, rubbing shoulders with Protestant merchants, learning eagerly the new business methods, carrying back to London disturbing new notions of politics and religion.

The citizen rising to new commercial power in London usually had little in common with the feudal aristocrat. He believed in hard work, a sober life, and the open Bible. He was a practical man, skilled in the arts of trade and commerce. The price of wool in Antwerp, tea in Calcutta, silver bullion in Venice; insurance rates on shipping to Constantinople; interest charges of London goldsmiths; expiration dates of patents and monopolies; probable profits in a joint-stock mining company; wages of Dutch seamen— such information marked his conversations. The average city Puritan distrusted the culture of the aristocracy, cared little for art and music, recoiled from delight in sensuous pleasure. The useful he contemplated more willingly than the beautiful. He wore plain clothes and cut his hair short. His person, like his home and his church, was usually unadorned. The shadow of Calvin, the rigor of the Old Testament, hung over the daily worship of his family circle, marked the brow of his parish minister, subdued the laughter of his children. The Bible he read diligently; but pagan and Catholic classics he distrusted. One of the liberal Puritan accusations against William Walwyn in 1649 was his familiarity with Lucian and Plutarch and Montaigne. "Go to this honest Papist, or to these innocent *Cannibals*, ye Independent Churches," replied Walwyn, "to learn civility, humanity, simplicity of heart; yea, charity and Christianity." [5] The Calvinist psychology divided into many intricate patterns, but seldom coalesced easily with spontaneous charity. In a man like Prynne, flinty and dynamic, Calvinism found a willing disciple. Over men like Saltmarsh, Walwyn, and Winstanley Calvinism gradually lost its hold, and Puritanism flowered in more lovely, if less sturdy, protagonists of change.

The Puritan brought to the political and economic struggle the energy of fanaticism. He believed in the miraculous efficacy of conversion. Once convinced of the favor of Jehovah, he resisted fearlessly the power of bishops and kings, braved the storms of the Atlantic, sang Psalms in the darkness of dungeons, charged the enemy on the field of battle with the utmost intrepidity. The presence of his God intoxicated his spirit and sustained him in the hour of trial. "Of a sanguine complexion," wrote Baxter of Harrison, "naturally of such a vivacity, hilarity and alacrity as another Man hath when he hath drunken a cup too much." [6] Bastwick and Burton suffered their ear-cropping in joyous bravery, even joviality. Whipped through the streets to the pillory, Lilburne was so exalted that he felt no pain. "It is Gods cause," he exclaimed to the crowd, "and for my part I am cheerfull and merry in the Lord." [7] It was this spirit that welded together the triumphant Puritan army. Time after time officers in prayer meeting announced a conviction that the Lord was through them outlining a portion of the divine plan. If anyone except the civilian Wildman smiled a little at these grave pronouncements, the record has not been preserved. The experience was vital in hundreds of lives, and its effect on military action often decisive.

As this commercial power increased, the sturdy Puritan business men resisted with heightened pertinacity the restrictions upon trade imposed by the crown. For many decades the granting of patents and monopolies to favorite courtiers and wealthy citizens had been a main source of the monarch's revenue; with the expansion of commerce monopolies of every kind assumed the aspect of tyranny. Elizabeth had granted patents to single persons to manufacture powder and bullet boxes; to buy linen rags and make paper; to sell foreign steel within the realm; to purchase and sell abroad ashes and old shoes; to license tanners; to brew beer for exportation; to import Irish yarn; to print the Psalms; to publish school books; to manufacture mathematical instruments. [8] A license granted by Elizabeth for trading in the "Levant Seas with currants only" brought her an income of four thousand pounds per annum. In 1604, when in recognition of the prevailing injustices a bill for free trade was considered by the House of Commons, the proponents of the bill declared that "the mass of the whole trade of all the realm is in the hands of some two hundred persons at the most, the rest serving for a shew only, and reaping small benefit." [9] The bill asserted that the two hundred members of the Merchant Adventurers controlled the sale of two thirds of the cloth of the realm, a business that would have provided work for thousands of merchants and their employees. By the law of nature, insisted the Commons, every freeman has the privilege of exercising his energies in trade. Free trade would distribute wealth, enlarge the volume of business, send traders to new markets, increase the customs.

Though the free trade bill was finally dropped, Parliament continued to express the protests of the "middle sort" of the commercial classes. James in his tactless way granted patents in reckless disregard of Puritan disfavor. The hated soap monopoly assigned to Roger Jones and Andrew Palmer in 1623 brought a mounting storm of protest. The Statute of Monopolies in 1623 reminded James that in spite of his declaration in 1610 that "all grants of monopolies and of the benefit of any penal laws, or of power to dispense with the law . . . are contrary to your Majesty's law," . . . he had continued to execute many such illegal grants.[10] In the words of Tawney: "The Puritan tradesman had seen his business ruined by a monopoly granted to a needy courtier, and cursed Laud and his Popish soap. The Puritan goldsmith or financier had found his trade as a bullion-broker hampered by the reëstablishment of the ancient office of Royal Exchanger, and secured a resolution from the House of Commons, declaring that the patent vesting it in Lord Holland and the proclamation forbidding the exchanging of gold and silver by unauthorized persons were a grievance. The Puritan money-lender had been punished by the Court of High Commission, and railed at the interference of bishops in temporal affairs. The Puritan clothier, who had suffered many things at the hands of interfering busy-bodies despatched from Whitehall to teach him his business . . . rallied to the Parliament. . . . The Puritan merchant had seen the Crown squeeze money out of his company, and threaten its monopoly by encouraging courtly interlopers to infringe its charter." [11] Living sober, industrious lives, imbued with a conviction of their personal righteousness, confident in their rising economic power, the Puritan business men resisted more and more boldly royal interference in the economic life of the nation.

The intensified commercial life in varying degrees and with diverse effects stamped its character on the minds and habits of the Puritan participants. It required ceaseless diligence and unremitting toil: the Puritans exalted the dignity of labor, lending to business activity a respect seldom accorded it by their predecessors. It severed men from traditional ties of estates and occupations: the Puritans carved out new careers unflinchingly, stressing self-reliance and the unchanging solicitude of Jehovah. It forced men into using new methods, taking new risks, breaking the old business patterns: the Puritans developed a bold flexibility of action that shattered traditions with equanimity. Expanding trade clashed with established gilds, monopolies, antagonism to usury, apprenticeship agreements, all barriers to free enterprise: the Puritans carried their grievances to Parliament, placed more and more dependence in representative resistance to the vested economic power of crown and aristocracy. The economic interests of well-to-do Puritans impelled at once a justification of democratic doctrine in political and religious activity and a renunciation of democratic tendencies in economic reform. The unorthodox Puritan Ireton, much more staunch for the republic than Cromwell, defended property rights as rigidly as any feudal barrister, while granting the difficulty of demonstrating Biblical support of his position. To Ireton property was "the most originall, the most fundamentall civil Constitution of this Kingdome"; and he opposed manhood suffrage because it might tamper with property holdings. "Why may nott those men vote against all propertie?" asked Cromwell, in support of Ireton.[12] In his most relentless and fearless castigation of monarchy, Milton set his face against "injurious alteration or circumscription of men's lands and properties." [13] Nowhere is the economic philosophy of the liberal Puritans more pointedly set forth than in *A Declaration of Congregationall Societies* (1647), in which the Independents declared that God justified differences in owner- ship and suggested that laziness was the cause of poverty. Attacking community of goods, the writers justified economic differences thus: "If this conceit of community should stand, the difference between poore and rich, borrowing and lending, buying and selling . . . would all fall; upon the foundation of which notwithstanding, God hath built many injunctions of duty unto men." [14] Walwyn, against whom the tract was written, though he was anxious for the poor to have sustenance and work, had no systematic plan for economic reorganization, and the Levellers as a group hastened to repudiate the schemes of the Diggers. Of the Puritans only Winstanley called for an economic, as well as a political and religious, revolution; and it is noteworthy that he was a failure as a business man in London before he retired to the country and began to write his socialist manifestoes. The conclusion is inescapable that the economic philosophy of the various Puritan leaders corresponded roughly to their economic positions. The Independents carried the Puritan Revolution to a position of domination, and justified their radical measures by democratic manifestoes. Yet they immediately took steps not only to safeguard the interests of the business classes but also to suppress the agitation of the Levellers for increased participation of the masses in governmental affairs.

Thus emerged the Puritan, business man, traveller, breaker of traditions, champion of free enterprise, resister of kings, supporter of Parliament, proponent of democratic ideas, protector of property interests.

DYNAMICS OF PROTESTANT INDIVIDUALISM

In the Puritan Revolution, as in no other political and economic struggle, the language of the Bible filled the speeches, letters, pamphlets, state papers, and daily conversations of the chief protagonists. Biblical sanction cloaked economic aims and obscured political issues; it clouded the purposes of the charlatan and the hypocrite; it justified the divinity of kings. But in the Scriptures lay the dynamite of revolution, too, an explosive most powerful in the hands of idealists like Milton and Roger Williams, Overton and Winstanley. Fearless soldiers like Rainsborough attacked property rights with scriptural reasoning; Milton constantly contrasted the meekness of Jesus with the pomp of kings and bishops; Overton arraigned the unchristian hatred of the Papists. When to every man the right was once granted of reading and interpreting the Bible for himself, his reflections were filled with portent for political and economic traditions. Hence the swarms of sectaries, the birth of utopias, the hasty measures of the Presbyterians to cast into the Calvinist mold the dynamic flow of Protestant reform effusions. The conflict between a democratizing Christianity and concentrated political and economic power, though resolved, as one might expect, in favor of the rich and the powerful, loosed rebellious ideology from thousands of Scripture-seeking reformers. The poor and the lowly, when they could read at all, found in the Bible ideas of society disturbingly unlike those of the prayer book and the parish minister.

I

The advent of Christianity, with its emphasis on the worth of the individual, its insistence that the commands of God are of equal importance with those of the magistrate, and its belief in the fundamental equality of all human beings before God, "a notion that has again and again proved a levelling force to which no other can be compared," [15] had given vigor and permanence to the Stoic conception of natural law and provided the broadest background for the spread of democratic ideas. The first great influence of the church for democracy, which in general was spread over the three centuries after Christ, had been the teachings of the early Christians in the face of persecution. How antagonistic these teachings were to the Roman Empire may be gathered from a review of the systematic persecution of those who placed obedience to God before the law of Rome. Such persecution had resulted only in the quickened absorption of Christian principles throughout the Roman world, and it would be difficult to overvalue such spread of Christianity as the seed from which future democratic government was to grow. But even after the identification of the Church with the Empire, and the acquisition of temporal power by the Church itself, whereby it became in part responsible for the obedience of its members to the state, the Catholic Church made its second great contribution to the growth of democratic ideas, i.e., the political philosophy of individual teachers who remained within the fold of the Church. The support which Irenaeus, Tertullian, Ambrose, Gratian, Chrysostom, Lactantius, and Isidore of Seville gave to the Stoic conception of natural law, the vigor with which Thomas Aquinas, Suarez, and Bellarmine defended the power of the people to depose a king, and the influence of Ivo of Chartres and his successors in rationalizing English civil law,—all these forces did service to the cause of democratic development which can hardly be calculated. Milton frequently refers to the church fathers as authorities for his republican principles. If, as Gooch and Borgeaud say, democracy is the child of the Reformation, not of the comparatively conservative reformers, she is the great grandchild of primitive Christianity, and the grandchild of the great Catholic political thinkers.

As the ordinary pre-Christian and pre-Stoic conception of

natural law had been that it must be subservient in practice to the written law, that the ideas of justice which the individual held must yield to the ideas of justice agreed to by his fellows, so the Church likewise had insisted that in the religious world the interpretation of truth and justice, of the natural law as seen in God, should be the function of the church rather than that of its individual members.[16] The general assumption was that in the Church religious authority was superior to that of the individual in the determination of rights and duties. It was this relation between Church government and Church member that was challenged by the reformers, Luther, Calvin, and Knox. "It belongs to each and every Christian," wrote Luther, "to know and judge of doctrine." [17] Thus Luther propounded the grounds for Protestant revolt against Protestant creeds, political and economic as well as religious.

Although Luther and Calvin prepared the way for democratic philosophy by insisting upon the right of the individual to read his own Bible and freely to inquire, and by their stand for the equality of the members as priests of God (the one principle, as Gooch remarks, leading to liberty and the other to equality in the political world), they did not stand politically for individual resistance against the state, nor did they establish a church government which was in itself democratic. Luther advised the Danish nobles and citizens at Lubeck at the time of their rebellion against Christian II to obey the king even if he were wrong; he called upon the princes to crush the peasants in the Peasant's War; and he declared it the duty of the Christian citizen to obey the constituted ruler, even a tyrannical one. Calvin likewise maintained against revolution, saying that unjust rulers were really the hand of God punishing the people for their sins, and that therefore the people were duty bound to obey even a tyrant. Calvin did modify this belief to the extent that in his opinion the people had a right to protest through their magistrates to the king. But as head of the theocracy at Geneva Calvin repudiated to Elizabeth the doctrines of Knox, and prohibited the circulation of his books.[18] As he demonstrates in the Fourth Book of his *Institutes,* Calvin had little use for the common people, depriving them of all but a theoretical power in electing the ministers of their churches.[19] In the theocracy at Geneva no one had political rights who did not attend church; heresy was punishable by the civil magistrates. Thus in four fundamental principles, Calvin differed from the Independents who were to follow him: (1) he denied toleration to non-conformists, (2) he repudiated the doctrine of separation of church and state, (3) he rejected democracy in church organization, and (4) he would hear nothing of the right to revolt against unjust rulers.

In spite of his greater liberality and respect for the commoners, John Knox differed from Calvin in only one of these four principles, the right of the people in the interest of their religion to overthrow the existing government. When Queen Mary asked, "Thinke you . . . That Subjects, having power, may resist their princes?" Knox replied, "If Princes do exceed their bounds . . . Madame, and do against that wherefore they should be obeyed, there is no doubt but they may be resisted, even by Power. . . . Their blinde zeale is nothing but a very mad phrenzie; and therefore to take the sword from them, to binde their hands, and to cast them into prison, till that they be brought to a more sober minde, is no disobedience against Princes, but just obedience, because that it agreeth with the Word of God." [20] In *A Letter to the Queen Regent of Scotland* (1556) Knox again plainly justifies religious revolution.[21] In his fifth letter, *The Admonition of John Knox to the Commonality of Scotland* (1558) Knox praises the capabilities of the church's common people. He stresses the fact that in God's eyes they are of equal value with the nobles of the land: "For albeit God hath put and ordained distinction and difference betwixt the King and his Subjects, betwixt the Rulers and the Common-people in the Regiment and Administration of Civill Policies, yet in the hope of the life to come he hath made all equall." [22] To Knox it was evident that no oath or promise could bind a people to uphold a tyrant against their interpretation of God's will. Yet when the Reformation of Scotland was finally accomplished twenty years later, the Presbyterian Church government of Scotland was hardly less aristocratic than that of Geneva, and the Scotch had hardly entertained the idea of separating the powers of the Church from the powers of the magistrate. Individualistic deviations from the Presbyterian doctrine met with sharp reproof.

II

In England, however, forces were gathering even before Elizabeth's day that carried the seeds of the social upheaval of 1642-49.

In the cities especially, where the influence of early reformers persisted among the trading classes, men deeply resented the exclusive right of the clergy to interpret Biblical teaching and the church's antagonism toward any English translation of the Bible. In 1514 Richard Hunne, a well-to-do London tailor who had refused to pay a fee to the church for the burial of his child, was one day found dead in the Lollards' Tower, his body hanging from a beam in his cell. When a copy of Wyclif's Bible was discovered among his belongings, Hunne was burned in Smithfield as a heretic. So intense was the anger of the Londoners that the coroner and his jury returned a verdict of murder against the Chancellor of the Bishop of London.[23] The intellectuals of the day supported the intense desire of laymen to read the Bible in English. "I entirely dissent," said Erasmus, "from those who are unwilling that the sacred Scriptures should be read by the unlearned translated into their vulgar tongue, as though Christ had taught such subtleties that they can scarcely be understood even by a few theologians, or as though the strength of the Christian religion consisted in men's ignorance of it. The mysteries of kings it may be safer to conceal, but Christ wished His mysteries to be published as openly as possible." [24] Erasmus' edition of the Greek New Testament (1516) inspired Tyndale to complete an English translation, the first edition of which was smuggled into England in bales of merchandise in 1525. In vain Henry ordered them burned and Bishop Tunstall denounced them as heretical and seductive; in vain did Henry's persecution drag the learned Tyndale to the flames. When, only two years later, Henry ordered English Bibles (really Tyndale's translation) to be placed in the choirs of every parish church in England, he accelerated the inevitable. From this time forward the revolutionary ideas inherent in individualistic interpretation gained new impetus. In the words of Trevelyan: "The effect of the continual domestic study of the book upon the national character, imagination and intelligence for nearly three centuries to come, was greater than that of any literary movement in our annals. . . . Indeed it created the habit of reading and reflection in whole classes of the community." [25] In such reflection did the Puritans find justification for resistance to bishops and kings.

III

When Elizabeth ascended the English throne in 1558, the national English Church, as established by Mary Tudor, was Catholic. The rural districts leaning to Catholicism and the towns to Protestantism, Elizabeth compromised by establishing the Anglican Church, retaining some of the forms of Catholicism, but abolishing others. All might believe as they liked, provided they worshipped regularly according to the Episcopalian forms.[26] But a number of Protestants within the Church, imbued with the teachings of Calvin, could not accept the Anglican ceremonies; they wished to purify the church of the last vestiges of Catholic ritual, and of such symbols as surplices, hoods, square caps, signs of the cross, crucifixes, and chasubles. Elizabeth, however, was determined. Upon her accession she had issued a proclamation forbidding preaching, directed not only against unlicensed Puritan preachers, but also against nonconformists within the ministry.[27] In 1561 her ecclesiastical commissioners embarked upon the ambitious scheme of voiding all the preaching licenses of the land, requiring all who wanted to be licensed anew to promise strict conformity in ceremony and dress.[28] For refusal to conform Thomas Sampson, dean of Christ Church, and Lawrence Humphreys, president of Magdalen College, were thrown into prison; and many men of high position felt the sting of the commissioners' power. For refusing to wear the required apparel thirty-eight of a hundred London clergy were suspended from the ministry.[29] "We may not use anything that is repugnant to Christian liberty," wrote the thirty-eight, in their manifesto, "nor maintain an opinion of holiness where none is; nor consent to idolatry, nor deny the truth, nor discourage the godly, and encourage the wicked; nor destroy the Church of God, which we are bound to edify . . . all which we should do, if we should consent to wear the outward and ministering garments of the pope's church." [30] Many ejected ministers went up and down the land, preaching, said Bishop Jewel, "as if they were apostles." They spoke not to comfort and sustain, but to arouse and exhort. Often distrustful of loveliness in church arch or glorious window or organ note, they wished to substitute the sermon for the old worship, relying upon that individualistic interpretation that was to bring forth so many rebellions **against rebels** in the decades to follow.

In 1572 the Puritans, after Elizabeth had stopped the passage of several bills on their behalf, sought redress from a sympathetic House of Commons. The famous *An Admonition to Parliament*, filled with spirited, driving phraseology, was the first open appeal for civil protection of the Puritans against Elizabeth and her bishops. In *An Admonition* the authors Wilcox and Field prayed for the establishment of a church government modelled after the primitive church. "We in England are so far off," they wrote, "from having a church rightly reformed, according to the prescript of Gods worde, that as yet we are scarce come to the outward face of the same." [31] At the differences between the primitive and the English churches Field and Wilcox aimed their most ringing sentences: "Then the ministers were preachers, now bare readers. . . . In those days knowne by voice, learning and doctrine: now they must be discerned from other by popish and Antichristian apparel, as cap, gown, tippet, etc. Then, as God gave utterance, they preached the word only: Now they read homilies, articles, injunctions, etc. Then it was painfull: now gainfull." Bitter were the Puritan complaints about the restrictions on preaching: "By the word of God, it is an offyce of preachyng, they make it an office of reading: Christe sayde goe preache, they in mockery give them the Bible, and authoritie to preache, and yet suffer them not, except that they have new licences. So that they make the chefest part which is preching, but an accessory." The authors advocated the abolition of episcopal authority superior to that of minister, the approval by each congregation of any minister presiding over it, the abolition of pluralities, advowsons, patronage, impropriations, involved ritual at burials and weddings, saints' days, private communion. The commissary's court, complains the *Admonition*, is "but a pettie little stinking ditche," the archbishop's court a "filthy quagmire." Devoid of learned meanderings, it spoke the blunt language of the man on the street. No document of the day summarized more trenchantly the essential conflicts that seventy years later were to fill the pages of Milton, Bastwick, and Burton, and find resolution in the Puritan Revolution. Despite Elizabeth's censors the *Admonition* ran through at least four editions, and the imprisonment of the authors enhanced its popularity. Their defence of their position, as presented in their prison conversation with Archbishop Parker's chaplain Pearson, is an illuminating document.

"We wrote a book in time of parliament," said Field, "justly craving a redress and reformation of many abuses, for which we are thus imprisoned and uncourteously treated." [32]

The most prominent intellectual to protest against Elizabeth's high church policies was Thomas Cartright, professor of divinity at Cambridge. Cartright wanted a church such as Knox had established in Scotland, a church governed by a series of assemblies, one above the other, but all directly or indirectly elected by the members themselves. Deprived of his professorship for publishing his beliefs, and then banished from the university, Cartright migrated to Antwerp, where he became pastor of a congregation of English merchants. In 1572 he returned to England and toward the end of the year published, in support of Field and Wilcox, *A Second Admonition to Parliament*. Though less appealing than *An Admonition*, it too summarizes the main currents of the rising Puritan protest. Cartright pleads with Elizabeth to allow the Puritans "freely to discusse all things as they are set forthe in the woorde of God." [33] Not once but several times he insists emphatically on the right of free inquiry: "It is allowed and commaunded to Christian men, to trie all things, and to holde that whiche is good, whosoever forbidde withoute exception, Prince, or other." [34] He appeals for variation in ceremonies according to congregation preferences, as among French and Swiss Protestants; for levelling of ranks and orders among the clergy; congregational approval of all ministers; the abolition of university degrees as a ministerial attainment; a preaching, not a reading, clergy; drastic penalties for usury; succor for the poor: "I would, we wold in some part, in this our great wealth and abundance remember the care for the pore (our owne brethren, our owne fleshe)"; [35] hospitality to strangers from abroad. Cartright's *Second Admonition* and his replies to Whitgift became cardinal planks in the Puritan platform; soon other men came forward boldly, too, pledging themselves to stand for true reformation. On August 5, 1573, Bishop Sandys wrote to Burghley and Leicester as follows:

Theese tymes have altered opinions. Suche as preached disretlie the last yeare now labour by raylinge to feede the fansies of the people. . . . The deceiptfull diuell enemie to religion hath so poured oute the poison of sedicion . . . that it is hard to tell whome a man may truste. . . . Certaine men of sundrie callings are as it were in commission together to procure hands to Mr. Cartright's booke and promesse to stande in the defence thereof unto death. . . . The citie will neuer be quiet untill theese authors of sedicion who are now estemed as godds, as Fielde, Wilcocks, Cartright, and other, be farre removed from the Citie. The people resorte unto them as in poperie they were wonte to runne on pilgrimage.[86]

In the 1580's Puritanism's boldest, most effective pamphleteer was Martin Marprelate, a man of exuberant humor and intense zeal, still unidentified, but surely an intellectual ancestor of Richard Overton. No Calvinist at heart, Marprelate; and had he written half a century later, he certainly would have found himself pilloried in passage after passage of Edwards' *Gangraena*. Against the bishops he loosed alternately satire and blazing indignation:

It is no marvel that his Honour could obtain this small suit at your graceless hands. . . . Remember your brother Haman. Do you think there is never a Mordecai to step to our gracious Esther, for preserving the lives of her faithfullest and best subjects, whom you so mortally hate and bitterly persecute? I hope you have not long to reign. . . .

And . . . [we are] likely to have no redress, seeing our impudent, shameless, and wainscot-faced Bishops, like beasts, contrary to the knowledge of all men, and against their own consciences, dare in the ears of her Majesty affirm all to be well, where there is nothing but sores and blisters; yea, where the grief is even deadly at the heart. . . .[87]

Carnal and senseless beasts, who are not ashamed to prefer the outward estate of men before the glory of Christ's kingdom.[88]

Marprelate denounced the destruction of Puritan printing presses and the leniency shown to Papist pamphleteers; he taunted Whitgift for his inability to cope with Cartright's manifestoes; he declared his undying antagonism to the episcopal hierarchy, while publishing his conditions of peace. "Leave you your wickedness," he concluded, "and I'll leave the revealing of your knaveries." [39] No reformer typified more forcefully than Marprelate the relentless driving power of Puritan convictions. He taunted the bishops: "What though I were hanged, do you think your cause shall be the better? For the day that you hang Martin, assure yourselves there will be twenty Martins spring in my place." [40]

In passage after passage Marprelate protested the loyalty of the Puritans to the queen, contrasting their sober patriotism with the machinations of the bishops. But Puritanism, as Elizabeth had recognized and Cartright had hinted, was rapidly becoming a threat to kingly power. Elizabeth warned James that the Puritans "wold have no kings but a presbitrye." "Yea, looke we wel unto them," she wrote to him. "Whan the have made in our peoples hartz a doubt of our religion, and that we erre if the say so, what perilous issue this may make I rather think than mynde to write. I pray you stop the mouthes . . . of suche ministers as dare presume to make oraison in their pulpitz for the persecuted in Ingland of the gospel." [41] Resistance to bishops was resistance to the crown. No longer was the church an independent hierarchy, a counterbalancing force that upon occasion had tipped the scales in the cause of the commoner. The state and the church now being inseparable, a heretic was a traitor; offenses against the church were offenses against the state. As head of the church Elizabeth claimed the exclusive right to deal with the Puritan resisters; on this assumption she had effectually prevented the passage of several bills mitigating the severity of ecclesiastical discipline and ceremonies. If allowed to preach, what peculiar ideas of government might even a thousand Puritans impress upon the masses? Such a policy had made inevitable the *Admonitions*. If Elizabeth was to support the bishops with the weight of her secular authority, the Puritans had to rest on their constitutional privileges of appeal to Parliament and public opinion.

In Cartright's "whosoever forbidde . . . Prince, or other" Elizabeth, James, and Charles I might well have read the need for royal caution. Puritan individualism was driving slowly but inevitably toward open conflict with regal power.

IV

The determined agitation of the Puritans under James, as under Elizabeth, brought upon their heads only intensified persecution. The *Millenary Petition* (1603), representing the views of perhaps a thousand of the nine thousand clergymen of the national church, was a moderate plea for modifications of ceremony and discipline, appointment of able preachers, limitation of benefices, and stricter observance of the Sabbath. But James rightly saw in Puritanism an ultimate threat to his own power. He dashed the hopes of the petitioners at the Hampton Court Conference, saying, "If this be all your party hath to say, I will make them conform themselves, or else I will harrie them out of the land, or else do worse, only hang them, that's all." [42] He visualized the political effect of a more democratic church organization when he burst out angrily: "A Scottish presbytery . . . agreeth with a monarchy as God with the Devil. Then Jack and Tom and Will and Dick shall meet, and at their pleasure censure me and my Council and all their proceedings." [43] In his *Proclamation Enjoining Conformity* (1604) James declared that "what untractable men do not perform upon admonition they must be compelled unto by authority," and claimed for himself the supreme power in such matters "by God's ordinance." [44] The king's assumption of dictatorial power over church affairs brought a sharp pronouncement from the Commons that "your Majesty should be misinformed if any man should deliver that the Kings of England have any absolute power in themselves either to alter Religion (which God defend should be in the power of any mortal man whatsoever), or make any laws concerning the same otherwise than as in temporal causes, by consent of Parliament." [45] His harsh measures against the Puritans brought a protest from the House in the *Petition concerning Religion* (1610), which deplored the removal of ministers for refusal to conform to the required ceremonies, the toleration of pluralists, and the severity of ecclesiastical censures. But James was obdurate. In his *Directions to Preachers* (1622) he warned against "unprofitable, unsound, seditious, and dangerous doctrines," [46] limited strictly the topics of sermons, and admonished all clergymen to refrain from discussion of the powers of the crown and differences between monarch and people. The *Directions* reveal at once James' determination to make the church support his claims to divine right and his fear that the preaching Puritans would lend to resistance the sanction of Scripture.

V

In the dynamic surge of individualistic reflection and discussion, nothing was more uncertain than unanimity of opinion. Each man brought to his Bible the shadow of his wealth or his poverty, the teachings of his parents, the stamp of his community opinion, the influences of his teachers and friends; and the sayings of the Bible marked no two minds alike. Puritanism was already giving birth to rebels and heretics as inimical to the Puritans as the hated prelates.

On one difference between the Puritans and the Separatists Roger Williams later wrote as follows: "Such as have separated, have been lookt at by the Bishops and theirs, as known and professed enemies: wheras the Puritans profest subjection, and have submitted to the Bishops, their Courts, their officers . . . and yet (as the Bishops have well known) with no greater affection, then the Israelites bare their Egyptian cruel Taskmasters." [47] Marprelate himself was too daring for the sober Puritans; they recognized in him a mind that Calvinism could not bound. His secular spirit ran too free. "The Puritans are angry with me," he wrote; "I mean the Puritan preachers. And why? Because I am too open; because I jest. . . . I am plain; I must needs call a spade a spade; a pope a pope." [48] Cartright, in a letter to Burghley, disavowed any hand in the Marprelate tracts, testifying to his "mislike and sorrow for such kind of disordered proceeding." [49]

Another rebel was Robert Browne, leader of the first separatists, forerunner of John Robinson, Roger Williams, Milton, Hugh Peters, and the fearful Independent sectaries of Cromwell's army. A Cambridge man of large intellectual endowments, but fiery, unpredictable temperament, Browne even as a young man was persecuted for his unorthodox opinions, and afterwards boasted that "he had been committed to *thirty-two* prisons, in some of which he could not see his hand at noon day." [50] To Browne the purification of the Church of England was an impossible compromise. He propounded the heresy that the church should be entirely free of the magistrate's coercion or support. Each congregation, Browne maintained, should be the supreme judge of its own theological and disciplinary decisions, cooperating voluntarily with other congregations of like beliefs. Repudiating a professional ministry, Browne and his followers insisted that any man chosen by the congregation might serve as its pastor. How fully these ideas anticipated the spirit of the Independency of Milton's day, and of Milton's own concepts as revealed in *Christian Doctrine*, may be suggested by the following passages from Browne's *A Treatise of Reformation without Tarrying for Anie* (1582):

It is the conscience and not the power of man that will driue vs to seeke the Lordes kingdome.
_____
Goe to therefore, and the outwarde power and ciuil forcings, let vs leaue to the Magistrates: to rule the common wealth in all outwarde ius-

Penry, "the meeting in woods, in caves, in mountains . . . is a part of the cross of the gospel . . . The question should not so much be, *where* we meet, as *what we do* at our meetings." [53] Changing their meeting place from week to week to escape the bishops' officers, the London congregation of Brownists was finally discovered one Sabbath at Islington, and fifty-six members thrust into prison. Many of them died after long and barbarous imprisonment, and three leaders, Henry Barrow, John Greenwood, and John Penry, were executed at Tyburn.

In the fearless fanaticism of these men seethed a revolutionary explosiveness destined a half century later to rock the foundations of England's social order. In one of his hearings before the archbishop Barrow denounced him to his face as "a monster! a miserable compound," and added, "I know not what to make of him. He is neither ecclesiastical or civil; even that second beast spoken of in the Revelation." [54] A contemporary satirist wrote, "The laws that maintain the archbishops and bishops, are no more to be accounted of than the laws maintaining the stews." [55] In the primitive Christians the rebel Puritans pictured their ideal of evangelistic persuasion. "We have the example of the Primitive Churches for our patterns and warrant," wrote Barrow, "which sued not to courts and parliaments, nor waited upon princes' pleasures." [56] The petition that brought Penry to the gibbet, though he protested his loyalty to the queen, shows the radical implications of the Brownist reforming zeal:

The last days of your reign are turned rather against Jesus Christ and his Gospel, than to the maintenance of the same.

I have great cause of complaint, Madam; nay, the Lord and his Church have cause to complain of your government: not so much for any outward injury . . . as because we your subjects this day are not permitted to serve our God, under your government, according to his word. . . .

If we had had Queen Mary's days, I think that we should have had as flourishing a Church this day, as ever any. For it is well known, that there was then in London under the burden, and elsewhere in exile, more flourishing churches than any now tolerated by your authority.

Now whereas we should have your help, both to join ourselves with the true Church, and reject the false, and all the ordinances thereof, we are in your kingdom permitted to do nothing; but accounted seditious, if we affirm either the one or the other of the former points. And therefore,

Madam, you are not so much an adversary unto us poor men, as unto Christ Jesus, and the wealth of his kingdom. . . .

When any are called for this cause before your Council, or the Judges of the land within your land, they must take this as granted, once for all, that the uprightness of their cause will profit them nothing, if the law of the land be against the same. . . .

This know, Madam, that he that hath made you and me, hath as great authority to send me of his message unto you, as he had to place you over me.[57]

Throwing off at last the contradiction of loyalty to the queen and resistance to the bishops, Penry stamps almost every word of this remarkable document with a democratic coloring antagonistic to kingship itself. In it no obsequious bows, no compliments, no poetic titles: only a blunt "Madam." On Elizabeth, not on her bishops, Penry lays the blame for the failure of reformation. The smouldering zeal of the Bible-reading fanatic has momentarily overwhelmed traditional awe of royalty, swept away deference to a popular dictator, set down in equal colloquy queen and commoner. In the last statement of his petition ("This know, Madam, that he that hath made you and me"), which alone under shadow of hanging Penry was willing to recant, one may discern the democratic impetus of Puritanism. A Cromwell stiff-backed before Charles, a haughty, hat-wearing Lilburne before the lords, a stubborn Everard proclaiming to Fairfax the rights of the Diggers, a Milton spitting defiance at an enveloping Restoration—these men, like Penry, drew from the Bible the dynamite of rebellion and the cobweb visions of utopia.

VI

Soon after the execution of Barrow, Penry, and Greenwood began the Separatist exodus to Holland, a movement that was to continue until the very opening of the Civil War, leavening scores of minds with a more drastic religious and political radicalism than they had known in England; then, being reversed, injecting into the conflict leadership in the Independent cause. Holland was then the most tolerant country in the world. Since 1578 Amsterdam had permitted freedom of worship to all, even Catholics and Anabaptists; it encouraged the migration of the English Protestants, finding them intelligent and industrious workers. Already Jacobus Arminius, whose reasoning was to capture the profound respect of John Milton, had challenged Calvin's wholesale damnation by predestination; every man, he insisted, as Milton was to believe, might choose the path of salvation. At the University of Leyden Arminius' pupil Episcopius carried on daily debates against the strict followers of Calvin; and sects and heresies began to flourish. To the orthodox English clergy Amsterdam was a shocking place. Joseph Hall, Milton's future antagonist, remonstrated with the exiles in horrified accents: "Compare the place you have left, with that you have chosen . . . Lo there, a common harbour of all opinions, of all heresies; if not a mixture: here, you drew in the free and clear air of the Gospel, without that odious composition of Judaism, Arianism, Anabaptism: there you live in the stench of these, and more! You are unworthy of pity, if you approve your misery." [58] Yet there was a limit to the patience of Holland's own orthodox clergy, with whom even John Robinson sympathized in their distrust of the Arminians. In 1619 sentence of banishment was pronounced upon Episcopius and his followers; two hundred remonstrant ministers were removed from their posts; and their advocate, the distinguished statesman Barneveldt, was executed for treason.[59]

The Separatists in Holland, like the Puritans in England, soon felt the disintegrating effect of Protestant intellectual methods. From 1600, when the Amsterdam church was probably first organized, until 1610, three rebellious groups seceded from the church and organized congregations of their own. The first discontented group withdrew in protest over the fine dress of the minister's wife. Johnson, the pastor, was required, after many attempts to reconcile the two factions, to excommunicate his father and brother. The next secession was of far deeper doctrinal significance. John Smyth, who had been pastor of a Separatist church in Lincolnshire, who had gone into exile and joined the Amsterdam congregation in 1606, found himself differing from Johnson and Ainsworth on theories of baptism. Smyth was a restless sectarian who never let down his anchor; at the end of his life he could not conscientiously join any church. Ainsworth's comments are worthy of record, possibly more commendatory than he intended: "In three sundry books he hath showed himself of three several religions." [60] "I had experience, in former dealing with Mr. Smyth, of his unstayedness, that would not stand to the things which himself had written." [61] Robinson wrote: "His instability and wantonness of wit is his sin and our cross." [62] According to Robinson, to organize a new church Smyth baptized himself and his friend, Helwys.[63] Helwys returned to England and organized what may have been the first Anabaptist congregation of purely English origin. After the withdrawal of Helwys and Smyth still a third division disturbed the peace of the Amsterdam congregation. Johnson and Ainsworth differed over the power of the elders and that of the congregation, Ainsworth contending for the "Popular cause." "The whole church," wrote Ainsworth, "is a kingdom of priests, that is, of *ministers;* who are to be guided and governed by their officers, called also *ministers* in more special manner." [64] Thus the Separatists at Amsterdam, sincere and vehement, quarreled among themselves; and their arguments foreshadowed a thousand pleas and counterpleas of the 1640's.

In 1608, after harrowing persecution following abortive escapes from the English coast, a little band of Separatist farmers, with their wives and children, joined the Amsterdam congregation. About a year later, disturbed by the dissensions of the Amsterdam church, they removed to Leyden where they were to remain until they set sail for the New World in 1620. Unused to the commercial ways of the Dutch cities, untrained in handicrafts or professions (only two had possessed property in England), the little band faced hardships fearlessly but realistically. "Though they saw faire, and bewtifull cities, flowing with abundance of all sorts of welth and riches," wrote Bradford, "yet it was not longe before they saw the grimme and grisly face of povertie coming upon them like an armed man." [65] Unlike the brethren at Amsterdam, the church at Leyden lived harmoniously, "with a single hartedness and sinceir affection one towards another, that they came as near the primative patterne of the first churches, as any other church of these later times have done." [66] Bradford attributed their harmony in large part to Robinson's leadership, which followed the Pilgrims to the New World. "His love was greate towards them, and his care was all ways bente for their best good, both for soule and body; for besides his singular abilities in devine things (wherin he excelled) he was also very able to give directions in civill affaires, and to foresee dangers and inconveniences; by which means he was very helpfull to their outward estates, and so was every way as a commone father unto them." [67] Even Baillie praised Robinson as "a man of excellent parts . . .

the most learned, polished, and modest spirit that ever separated from the Church of England." [68]

Robinson's Calvinism suffered continuous adulteration from his broad humanistic learning and his eager drinkings of the New Testament. Though no revolutionary like John Smyth or Roger Williams, he set forth ideas of church democracy which were to form a springboard for social action in the Puritan Revolution. Like Milton after him, he stoutly upheld the capacity of church members to choose their own ministers. Is not everyone, he asked Bernard, capable of finding wisdom in the Bible? Are the members less likely to err than the officers? The evils of the church have in the past sprung from the governors, not from the people. "Nothing," he told Bernard, "hath more in former days advanced, nor doth at this day uphold the throne of Antichrist, than the people's discharging themselves of the care of public affairs in the church, on the one side: and the priests, and prelates arrogating all to themselves on the other side." [69] The church government, wrote Robinson, compounded monarchical, aristocratic, and democratic types of government in Christ, the eldership, and the congregation. But any believer may be a spiritual leader: "Every one is made a king, priest, and prophet, not only to himself but to every other, yea to the whole." [70] In a letter written to his little flock upon their departure to the New World, Robinson admonished them to choose leaders by their true worth only, and to honor the magistrate's authority, represented by "how meane persons soever." [71] Had he assumed leadership in the Plymouth Colony, Robinson, like many another liberal Puritan, might have turned to persecution of dissenters or justification of theocratic rule. But from the ferment of equalitarian agitation centered around Robinson's Separatist principles were to emerge the Baptists, the Independents, and those political and economic democrats, the Levellers and the Diggers. No sooner had the Puritans set up ideological fences than the Separatists forthwith began to batter them down; in like manner the Baptists broke from the Separatists, and Levellers were to break away from Independency into a broader revolutionary activity. In the dynamics of Protestant individualism, the crude realities of social experiments were constantly giving birth to new utopias.

VII

Meanwhile the revolt of Smyth and Helwys, and the subsequent founding of Baptist congregations in London, had evoked intellectual patterns that were to mark the minds of some of the most resolute and heretical participants of the Puritan Revolution. "I am no anabaptist, I thank God," [72] Greenwood had exclaimed, unwilling, like all the sectarian leaders, to welcome the extreme positions to which their own pointed the way. As often the more liberal, and the less prosperous, Puritans withdrew into Separatism or semi-Separatism, so the least Calvinistic and the poorer Separatists turned to Anabaptism. "No man," wrote Lamb, "can be true to the principles of Independents and Brownists, but they must turn Anabaptists." [73] Pagit recorded the inevitable tendency: "Out of a few members in the Brownist's churches, more fell to Anabaptism than out of many thousand members of the Presbyterian churches amongst the Dutch." [74] The Baptists welcomed the possibility of universal redemption, leaned heavily on the charity of the New Testament, denounced the whole theory of original sin. Such a creed, unlike variations of Calvinism, hardened reluctantly into a mold of absolute truth. Taunted for changing his principles so rapidly, Smyth replied: "I professe I haue changed, and shall be readie still to change, for the better: and if it be ther glorie to be peremptorie and immutable, in their articles of Religion, they may enioye that glorie without my envie." [75] Smyth knew the apparent inconstancy of intense spiritual growth, the rapid rebellions against former tenets inherent in Protestant individualism. In the last months of his life his sympathy both for all precipitant pilgrims and, on the other hand, conservatives shackled, as he thought, by ignorance, loomed larger than theological considerations. Where love flowed freely, he thought, who was to damn his brother? *The Last Booke of John Smith,* written in the last stages of consumption, is the testament of a spirit less dogmatic than Roger Williams, more gentle and forgiving than Milton, more mature and fearless than Robinson. "If a synne of ignorance make a man an Anti-Christian," he wrote, "then I demaunde wher shall wee finde a Christian." He retracted his anger, his persecuting manner, not his ideas: "All those bitinge and bitter words. . . . I vtterly retract and revoke, as not being of the spirit of Christ. . . . I retract not for that it is wholly false,

but for that it is wholly censorious and criticall: and for that therein
the contention for outward matters, which are of inferiour note, hath
broken the rules of loue and charitie, which is the superiour law:" [76]
In Smyth Walwyn would have recognized a kindred spirit sloughing
off what he called the attributes of the superstitious Christian.

Most despised of all English sects, the Baptists were possibly
the first to ask for toleration, not only for themselves, as did the
Separatists, but for all other strange Gospel-searchers. In their one
hundred *Propositions and conclusions* Smyth's Amsterdam congregations included an uncompromising tolerationist demand roundly
condemned by Robinson: "The magistrate is not by vertue of his
office to meddle with religion, or matters of conscience, to force and
compell men to this or that form of doctrine: but to leaue Christian religion free, to euery mans conscience. . . . If the magistrate
will follow Christ . . . he must loue his enemies and not kill them
. . . he must feed them and giue thē drinke, not imprison them:
banish them: dismember them." [77] In *A Short Declaration of the
mistery of iniquity* (1612) Thomas Helwys braved the wrath of
James and the bishops to declare: "Mens religion to God, is betwixt
God and themselves; the King shall not answer for it, neither may
the King be judg between God and man. Let them be heretickes,
Turcks, Jewes, or what soever it apperteynes not to the earthly
power to punish them in the least measure." [78] In 1614 appeared
Leonard Busher's *Religions Peace,* Baptist forerunner of the extreme
tolerationist views of the 1640's, anticipating by thirty years the
leading ideas of *The Bloudy Tenent.* A poor man, Busher complained
of the lack of money necessary to print for the truth. "We that
have most truth, are most persecuted." Provided that they cite
proofs from the Scriptures only, Busher asked that "it be lawful for
every person or persons, yea, Jews and papists, to write, dispute,
confer and reason, print and publish any matter touching religion,
either for or against whomsoever." [79] Like Milton after him, Busher
welcomed the printing of heresies and the open grappling of falsehood and truth: "And you shall understand, that errors being
brought to the light of the word of God, will vanish as darkness before the light of a torch. Even as the chaff before the wind cannot
stand, so error before truth cannot abide." [80] To Busher utopia
inevitably would follow the free searching of the Bible, with no more
burning and hanging for differences of faith, no more executions for

theft, or oppression of the poor "by usury and little wages," or forced marriages, or whoredom. "Then shall not the poor, lame, sick, and weak ones, be stocked and whipped; neither shall the poor, stranger, fatherless, and widows be driven to beg from place to place." [81] Busher's remarkable tract was followed in 1615 by *Persecution for Religion Judg'd and Condemned* and in 1620 by *A Most Humble Supplication,* Baptist manifestoes pleading for liberty of conscience, Jews and papists not excepted. To the latter tract, which may have been written by John Murton, Williams gives high praise in *The Bloudy Tenent.* He had heard that the author wrote the treatise in milk on the paper stoppers of his milk bottles, writing that became legible when held to the fire: "It was in *milke,* soft, meeke, peaceable and gentle, tending both to the *peace* of *soules,* and the *peace* of *States* and Kingdomes." [82]

The dynamics of the Baptist creed could not, of course, achieve a stability free from political and economic implications. Toleration of religious ideas inevitably carried with it examination of social heresies, especially among the poorer classes. As the Civil War progressed, secular freedoms loomed larger and larger, and democratic agitation rose in mighty surges, particularly rampant in the New Model army. From the ranks of the Baptists sprang many of the radicals of Cromwell's army and a large number of the Leveller rank and file. Prominent army Baptists were Thomas Harrison, Robert Bennet, Robert Overton, Charles Howard, Robert Lilburne, John Hutchinson, Richard Deane, Henry Danvers, John Desborough, William Allen, Richard Lawrence. Ludlow alone at one time commanded twenty-five regimental Baptist officers.[83] The army printer, Henry Hills, was a Baptist. The establishment of Baptist churches frequently followed the movements of the preaching officers and soldiers. A number of the Leveller agitators in 1647 were Baptists. In the breaks between the Independents and the Levellers the Baptists also divided, the more mystical and evangelistic ones siding with Cromwell and Ireton, the secularly minded with the Levellers. Until this break the Anabaptist churches in London had supported the Leveller manifestoes. Among Lilburne's earliest friends in London had been the Baptists William Kiffin and Thomas Patience. Richard Overton may have been a friend of Thomas Helwys; he was possibly the author of an early Baptist manifesto.[84] But by 1649 some of the Baptists had become prosperous, influential citizens, skeptical of the wisdom of the radical Leveller demands. Baptist leaders, among them Kiffin, joined with friends of John Goodwin to discredit William Walwyn, Lilburne's colleague, as an atheistic heretic favorable to communism.[85] But to many Leveller Baptists this time-tested strategy proved ineffective. In them rebellious Puritanism had reached an outpost of rational secularism, an inevitable outcome of the workings of Protestant intellectual methods in the minds of the most radical reformers.

VIII

The little band of Pilgrims that settled in Plymouth in 1620 was not tainted with Anabaptist notions. In the wilderness they hoped to preserve the purity of their semi-Separatist creed without fostering more schisms and heresies and losing the precious harmony that had marked the years at Leyden. When Roger Williams settled among them, they received him cordially, and valued his teachings; but seeing soon that his restless queries might bring divisions, they willingly let him depart.

But the colonists at Plymouth suited their ideology much more plastically to the democratizing pressure of a frontier wilderness than did the Puritans of subsequent migrations to Massachusetts Bay. The Separatists had sprung largely from the humbler ranks of English yeomanry, whereas many of the Puritans, in Cotton Mather's words, "were gentlemen of ancient and worshipful families, and ministers of the gospel then of great fame at home, and merchants, husbandmen, artificers." [86] The Pilgrims were few and poor; the Puritans many and prosperous. The Puritans under James had at times joined with the prelates in their persecution of the Separatists; but now they sought escape to America from Laud's rigid persecution of even the milder non-conformists. In twelve years (1628-1640?) 198 ships were employed to carry thousands of Puritans to New England, at a total cost, Mather estimated, of 192,000 pounds.[87] By 1640 there were perhaps 12,000 in the Massachusetts colony, about six times the population of the Plymouth settlement. In Plymouth there was little attempt to maintain the social distinctions that had prevailed in England; but Massachusetts, wrote Hutchinson, "from the beginning, endeavored to preserve two distinct ranks or orders of men, gentry and commonalty";[88] and the ministers preached that the governor and chief officers should be selected from the gentry. In Plymouth a rough civil democracy prevailed, with civil penalties, it is true, against card playing, reviling of ministers, swearing, drunkenness; but in the Massachusetts theocracy it was early decreed that only church members should vote. Hereditary distinctions the Massachusetts men believed justified both by scripture and nature. "Democracy," wrote John Cotton to Lord Say and Lord Sele, "I do not conceyve that ever God did ordeyne as a fitt govermennt eyther for church or commonwealth. If the people be governors, who shall be the governed? As for monarchy, and aristocracy, they are both of them clearly approoved, and directed in scripture, yet so as referreth the soveraignty to himselfe, and setteth up Theocracy in both, as the best forme of government." [89] Against this whole theory ran the fierce tide of Independency, of which the colony at Plymouth and the teachings of Robinson were broadly representative. Against it, too, were to run the rebellious minds of Thomas Hooker and Roger Williams, and the inexorable democratizing effects of abundant free land in the hands of the commoners.

IX

In Roger Williams, "divinely mad," "passionate and precipitate," worked a restless and questioning mind that would have been dangerous in any society. In him were compounded the rebellious notions that agitated the train of iconoclastic Bible-reading teachers from Luther to Milton and Lilburne. But for his theological training and America's economic abundance, he might have swung the full circle to the revolutionary secularism of Winstanley. From the Bible he drew forth justification for doctrines sharply inimical to most of the institutions of his day, fearlessly accepting in consequence banishment, distrust, exile, never losing his magnanimity, never showering upon people his hatred for their ideas. Finally, like Milton in the *Areopagitica*, he called for an intellectual method that would have brought in its wake perpetual attack on the *status quo* toleration of every type of religious propaganda, and an honest examination of all new religious opinions.

Promising Cambridge graduate, protégé of the great Coke, friend of Masham, St. Johns, the Barringons, Williams arrived in Massachusetts in 1631 at the age of twenty-eight. Five years later he was an exile, pushing through the wilderness with a dozen followers to a utopia where even the hated Papists might worship unmolested. Soon after his arrival at the Bay colony, when he was called to the ministry of the Boston church, Williams refused, saying that he "durst not officiate to an unseparated people, as upon examination and conference I found them to be." [90] He wished them to separate unreservedly from the Church of England. He insisted, moreover, that the magistrate had no right to punish men for Sabbath breaking, blasphemy, heresy or any breach of the First Table. To have agreed to his proposals, the Puritan fathers of the Bay would have had to uproot the whole structure of their theocratic state. On April 12, 1631, against the protests of the Boston court, Salem, which had adopted the Separatism of the Plymouth colony, received Williams as teacher. But when he preached against the tenets of the Boston church, and his full views became known, some opposition around Salem crystallized against him, and he felt constrained to remove to the Plymouth colony. Here he remained two years, holding no office, but prophesying and teaching informally, learning the ways of farming, making friends with the Indians.[91] Bradford's comments on Williams reveal even the Pilgrims' distrust of his ideas:

Mr. Roger Williams (a man godly and zealous, having many precious parts, but very unsettled in judgmente) came over first to the Massachusets, but upon some discontent left that place, and came hither, (wher he was friendly entertained, according to their poore abilitie,) and exercised his gifts amongst them, and after some time was admitted a member of the church; and his teaching well approoved, for the benefite whereof I still blese God, and am thankfull to him, even for his sharpest admonitions and reproufs, so farr as they agreed with truth. He this year begane to fall into some strang opinions, and from opinion to practise; . . . and in the end some discontente on his parte, by occasion whereof he left them some thing abruptly. Yet after wards sued for his dismission to the church of Salem, which was granted, with some caution to them concerning him, and what care they ought to have of him. But he soone fell into more things ther, both to their and the goverments troble and disturbance.[92]

Many of the Plymouth settlement did not wish Williams to leave, but Elder Brewster persuaded them to allow him to go; he was convinced that Williams "would run the same course of rigid separation and anabaptistry, which Mr. John Smith, the Se-Baptist, at Amsterdam, had done." [93] Called again to Salem, where a warm affection for him had prevailed over distrust, Williams, supported by Pastor Skelton, soon found himself in conflict with the ministers of the Bay colony, who in one of their fortnightly meetings advised Salem against calling Williams to office. He stirred deep resentment by arguing that the king's patent gave the colonists no true right to the land of the Indians. In April, 1634, when the General Court passed an order requiring all non-freeman Bay residents to take an oath pledging their loyalty to the orders of the Court, Williams led a revolt against the oath at Salem and refused to take it himself. The oath accepted the right of the Court to punish for breaches of the First Table. On September 27, 1634, Williams brought down decisive wrath upon his head by denouncing eleven sins of the Bay colony. The Council of magistrates decided to give Williams a year of probation in which to discover the errors of his preaching. His reply was more denunciation of their laws, especially one passed March 4, 1635, which required attendance at public worship and financial support of the church. He rejected a new oath of fidelity. When, under pressure of political and economic sanctions from the controlling Bay colony, Salem's loyalty to Williams began to waver, he demanded that they cease communion with the Bay churches. The Salem church, however reluctant, refused, and Williams withdrew. On October 8, 1635, after dozens of private conferences in which the religious leaders of New England tried unavailingly to convince Williams of his errors, the court convened which sentenced him to banishment. "All the ministers in the bay being desired to be present," wrote Winthrop, "he was charged with the said two letters,—that to the churches, complaining of the magistrates for injustice, extreme oppression, &c., and the other to his own church, to persuade them to renounce communion with all the churches in the bay as full of antichristian pollution, &c. He justified both these letters, and maintained all his opinions . . . Mr. Hooker was appointed to dispute with him, but could not reduce him from any of his errors." [94] Even Winthrop, of whose friendship Williams spoke with reverence until the end of his days, assented to the penalty of banishment. Hugh Peters, later an unlovely disciple of Williams' doctrines, recommended a sentence of excommunication. Upon petition Williams was granted permission to stay in the Bay colony until spring, provided he would not vent his dangerous opinions. Alarmed by Williams' project of a new colony, by his continued influence, especially with Sir Henry Vane, who had arrived a few days after his sentence of banishment, and with Winthrop himself, who had been censured by the Council for "his too much leniency to disaffected souls," Governor Haynes and his assistants resolved to force Williams upon a ship bound for England. Advised by Winthrop, Williams fled.

Choice spirit that he was, respected, even loved, by many of his antagonists, Williams had not yet freed himself from some of the narrowness of his persecuting enemies. Many of the amazing toleration principles of *The Bloudy Tenent* were not yet distilled. Some of the sins of which he accused not only the Bay colony but also the Salem church were not defects of love, but errors of dogma, with himself as the judge. At the Salem church he had refused to approve for membership anyone who would not agree to rigid separation from the Church of England. Looking upon non-separation as a sin, he refused to commune with the Salem church if they continued communion with non-separating churches. Williams' justifications of his position on separation, on which account he refused the pastorship at Boston and withdrew from both Plymouth and Salem, reflect a spiritual snobbishness unworthy of his abundant charity. He thought necessary a "separation of holy from unholy, penitent from impenitent, godly from ungodly," and even maintained that "godlie and regenerate persons . . . are not fitted to constitute the true Christian Church, untill it hath pleased God to convince their soules of the evill of the false Church, Ministry, Worship." [95] He took the side of Endecott against the wearing of veils in church; he argued that the colonists should cut the cross out of the flag.

But the soul of Roger Williams enlarged with every season; and the events were planting in his mind the seed from which were to flower the mature toleration principles of *The Bloudy Tenent*. In vain he had protested against the use of the magistrate's power to enforce religious conformity. He had watched the workings of a theocracy justifying its code, not from the parables of Jesus, but from the laws of Moses. "Persecutors," he wrote later, "seldom plead Christ, but Moses." [96] He had seen the Bay colony withhold land at Marblehead Neck to force Salem into severing his pastorship. And then, when he had fallen ill from the strain of disputations and impending sanctions, he had ceaselessly revolved the tormenting issues: "During my sicknes," he said to Cotton, "I humbly appeale unto the Father of Spirits for witnes of the upright and constant diligent search . . . made after him, in the examination of all passages, both my private disquisitions with all the chief of their Ministers, and publike agitations of points controverted: and what gracious fruit I reaped from that sicknes, I hope my soule shall never forget." [97]

In his meditations Williams was throwing off the stern code of Calvin, a psychology that was to cling so tenaciously to thousands of American colonists, bringing forth the Salem witchcraft trials, the hell of Jonathan Edwards, and the soul of Arthur Dimmesdale. Upon Williams' imagination was fastening an ideal of Jesus that was to dominate all his noblest utterances and provide a justification for the most radical doctrines of "turners of the world upside down": *"Who disdained not to enter this World in a Stable, amongst Beasts, as unworthy the society of Men: Who past through this World with the esteeme of a Mad man, a Deceiver, a Conjurer, a Traytor against Caesar, and destitute of an house wherein to rest his head: Who made choice of his first and greatest Embassadours out of Fisher-men, Tent-makers, &c. and at last chose to depart on the stage of a painfull shamefull Gibbet. If him thou seekest in these searching times, mak'st him alone thy white and soules beloved, willing to follow him . . . in doing, in suffring."* [98] Such an ideal clashed decisively with the psychology of the Massachusetts theocracy; it justified Williams in his banishment and sustained him in carrying his new doctrines to his old friends across the seas. In trailing such a vision, Williams was not alone. One finds it in the pages of Saltmarsh, Walwyn, and Winstanley, radical prophets who, like Williams, lost the vinegar of Calvin in their search for the fresh waters of the Gospel. When a revolutionary Christ beckoned them to new, impossible utopias, they charged, now blindly, now realistically, into the inexorable windmills. And the sway of this beckoning transcended economic pressures, security of loved ones, hostility of friends, fear of dungeons and gibbets. The student of economic and political forces looks in vain among familiar patterns for central explanations of seventeenth-century prophets.

As strikingly as any other figure of his day Williams embodied the sharp, seemingly precipitate intellectual transitions inherent in an explosive individualism. Converted to Puritanism at eleven, he was successively a Puritan Anglican, semi-Separatist, Separatist, and Seeker before he was thirty-five. His departure to Providence brought with it a shift in emphasis reported by Winthrop: "Having, a little before, refused communion with all, save his own wife, now he would preach and pray with all comers." [99] Williams' historical sense made him keenly aware of the rebellious extensions of Puritanism and of his own place in the process. "I beleeve that there hardly hath been a conscientious Seperatist," he wrote, "who was not first a Puritan: for . . . the grounds and principles of the Puritans against Bishops and Ceremonies . . . must necessarily, if truely followed, lead on to, and inforce a separation . . . to seek out the true way of Gods worship." [100] In *The Bloudy Tenent* he called for complete freedom of personal interpretation: "In vaine have *English Parliaments* permitted *English Bibles* in the poorest *English* houses, and the simplest man or woman to search the Scriptures, if yet against their soules perswasion from the Scripture, they should be forced . . . to beleeve as the Church beleeves." [101] To Williams the realization of the principles of primitive Christianity seemed hidden so far in the future that even the speediest advances toward it were all too slow. In the crucial decisions of his middle years he chose almost invariably the more extreme courses, painfully conscious of the penalties of retreat. Backsliding he divided for Cotton into four categories, a description of possible courses of action that reveals his prolonged wrestlings with the problem of an evolutionary religious radicalism. He shied away from even the least painful compromise: "Others, although preserved from Familisme, prophanes and persecuting of others, yet the lease of their Christian course hath withered, the later beautie and favour of their holines hath not been like their former; and they have confest & do, their sin, their weaknes, their bondage, and wish they were at liberty in their former freedom: and some have gone with little peace, but sorrow to their graves, confessing to my selfe and others, *that God never prospered them in soule or body, since they sold away his truth.*" [102] Awareness of an ever widening Reformation, so pronounced in Williams, animated also his friend Milton, who pleaded in the *Areopagitica* for an honest examination not only of all sectarian ideas but secular heresies as well. Had he not himself in a few short years passed from Puritan Anglican to Presbyterian to Independent tenets? And Lilburne, in the middle 1640's, pushed forward from one democratic demand to another, embracing eagerly a brave new world, dreading only a retreat to the old. These men knew how swiftly one outpost of liberty captures another and marches on toward the morning star of utopia.

From life in Holland and the New World emerged ideas and personalities that stamped their influence undeniably upon the Puritan Revolution. Appearing at a critical time, Williams' *The Bloudy Tenent* immediately called forth denunciations as one of the most heretical books of the time. His extreme tolerationism became the rallying cry of the army radicals. Williams was a friend of Vane, a leader of the Parliamentary Independents; friend also of Milton and Cromwell. Hugh Peters, fresh from the wilds of America, injected himself vigorously into the left-wing leadership, his counsel at times apparently weighing heavily with Cromwell himself. In the New World no social experiment seemed impossible of realization; and the contrast with the relatively static patterns of English social life weighed heavily on the minds of some exiles. "I have lived in a Countrey," Peters told the Parliament, "where seven years I never saw beggar, nor heard an oath, nor looked upon a drunkard; why should there be beggars in your *Israel* where there is so much work to do?" He rebuked the Council for its paltry relief measures: "The streets also are swarming with poor, which I refer to the Senators of this Citie, that is glorious many wayes, why should it be so beggarly in the matter of beggars." [103] New England also fostered the radicalism of Hanserd Knollys, who returned to England in 1641, served as an army chaplain, preached tirelessly for toleration, his sermons sometimes followed by riots and tumults. Neither from the frontier life of America or the free intellectual intercourse of Holland, where Lilburne himself had read the forbidden books, could English rebels emerge cold and disheartened reformers. Carrying back to England a resolute optimism in their blueprints of social betterment, they turned all their energies to the support of the left-wing adherents of the Parliamentary cause.

X

In Puritanism two powerful streams of influence, one relentlessly exploratory, the other tenaciously static, crossed and recrossed in the endless discussions that culminated in the revolutionary impetus of Cromwell's army. The original basis of Puritanism was the Protestant creed of individualistic interpretation of the Bible. Then Calvin came forth to systematize Protestantism, to lend it some of the creedal assurance that had comforted the members of the mother church. So thoroughly did he build, so logical were his conclusions, that most thoughtful people of Scotland and England were by the opening of the Civil War persuaded to the Calvinistic coloring of Protestantism. It was a faith that sustained martyrs, justified a sober, reasoned existence, exalted family life, honesty, occupational diligence. It upheld the pioneer in his wilderness sacrifices. It stood for the privileges of the sober, hard working citizens against the vested rights of the bishops and aristocracy. Here the Calvinist paused. He wished to freeze England as well as Scotland into a utopia inspired but also bound by the principles of the great Genevan, dominated by the upper middle class of clergy and prosperous Puritans.

But it was impossible to pour a dynamic individualism into a Calvinist mold. Diligent reading of the Bible, urged by all Puritans, soon serried the ranks of the disciples, breaking through the restrictive interpretations imposed by the code of Calvin. The rebels attacked the Old Testament emphasis of Calvin's theology: its stern imposition of thc Hebraic laws, its assumption of relatively infallible judgment on all the matters of personal morality, its dark absorption with sex restraints, its distrust of sensuous pleasure, its laughter-withering seriousness, its determined subordination of woman, its assumptions of spiritual superiority, its justification of persecution. Whereas the Catholic and the Anglican had accepted the whole man, his primitive instincts, his inevitable response to sensuous beauty, his imagination, his playfulness, his laughter, the Calvinist attempted to reduce man to a reasoning mechanism, rational in both response and expression. But under the long faces, the black hats, the sober clothes, in the midst of pious expression of Calvinist dogma, still beat the fires of passion, the yearning for beauty, a whole psychology of forces too powerful for Calvinism to resist or wholly degrade. Hence the long gap between Sabbath preachments and nightly yearnings, the hypocrisies, the repressions, the burning hatreds, the almost savage insistence on the letter of dogma. In their souls raged a perpetual conflict between the world of the senses and the stern discipline of an Old Testament creed futilely diluted with the tolerant charity of the Gospels. Neither the darkest recesses of the Puritan soul or its brightest will ever be probed; its complexities are too many, its variations too diverse. But in the characterizations of Hawthorne, the trial record of Anne Hutchinson, the relentless spirit of William Prynne, the subtle reticences of Cromwell, his justifications of the Drougheda massacre, the sophistry of *Walwins Wiles,* the shameful vilifications of Milton's *Pro Se Defensio,* one may meet some of the ugliest phantasms of the Puritan mind. And over much, if not all, that looms dark and forbidding, lie the shadow of Calvin and the laws of Moses.

There was, it is true, a brighter side of Calvinist orthodoxy. When Emerson wrote "Men are better than their theology," he spoke from a both practical and theoretical knowledge of the Puritan mind. Thousands of Presbyterians, while maintaining implicit faith in Calvinist theology, in practice rejected its harshest principles: their natural humanity and their sense of brotherhood were stronger than the theology of the pulpit. Often they failed to grasp the essential pessimism of the Calvinist creed, being followers rather than thinkers, lacking the theological training to follow the maze of abstractions that upheld it. Then, too, the Gospels were a continuous leavening influence that not even the sternest minister could banish even from his own meditations.

Over the lives of thousands, however, Calvinism gradually lost its power; and Puritanism, sloughing off the black terror of damnation and the rigid Old Testament creed, flowered into diverse, often contradictory, loveliness of personality and social idealism. The very root of the Protestant method, the duty of each person to interpret the Bible, undermined the tenacious grip of Calvinist dogma, loosening it bit by bit from some minds, at one lightning thrust from others. As a pure Calvinist Milton could not have conceived his divorce tracts, the *Areopagitica,* or indeed anything that he wrote thereafter. Yet he never wholly eradicated from his philosophy the shadow of Calvin, as one may read between the

lines of *Paradise Regained*. In some ways he remained till the end
of his days an Old Testament Christian, and the full freshness of
the Gospels somehow escaped him. Milton's rich contributions to
the social idealism of the period, and his fruitful explorations of
the springs of personality, derived not the slightest inspiration
from the dogma of Calvin. They evolved, rather, from his rebellious
individualism constantly at grips with the prevalent tone of Presbyterianism and from the broad humanist learning of the pagans.
As individualistic Gospel searching was the central impetus of
Milton's radicalism, both religious and political, so it also, in varying
degrees, lighted and sustained reforming fires in almost all the radicals of the time. Cromwell's sincere devotion to toleration, Rainsborough's arguments for manhood suffrage, Lockyer's unselfish
allegiance to the cause of the dispossessed, Lilburne's unswerving
expansion of democratic doctrines, Overton's relentless militancy
for Leveller principles, Walwyn's humane reasoning for the cause
of the underprivileged, Winstanley's utopia—all these had their
justification in the teachings of the Gospel. They represented the
rebellious response of idealists to the dogmatic, mothering Calvinism
that had nurtured their boyhood religious ideas. In Walwyn and
Winstanley rationalism gradually dissipated theological emphasis
on the supernatural and strengthened their faith in the social teachings of Jesus. For the earthly saving of bodies and souls they cared
much; for heavenly rewards, very little. In the divination of
theologians on the nature of life after death Winstanley read one
of the grossest tyrannies of the age. In his utopia he desired
preachers and teachers should speak only from earthly observation
and experience:

And if a man should go to imagine, what God is beyond the Creation,
or what he will be in a spiritual manifestation after a man is dead, he doth
as the proverb saith, build castles in the air, or tells us of a world beyond
the Moon, and beyond the Sun, merely to blinde the reason of man.

Ile appeal to your self this question, what other knowledge have you
of God, but what you have within the circle of the Creation?

For if the Creation in all its dimentions be the fulness of him, that fills
all with himself, and if you yourself be part of this Creation, where can
you finde God but in that line or station wherein you stand?

God manifests himself in actual knowledge, not in imagination. . . .

But when a studying imagination comes into man, which is the devil, for it is the cause of all evil, and sorrows in the world; that is he who puts out the eyes of mans Knowledg, and tells him, he must beleeve what others have writ or spoke, and most not trust to his own experience. . . .

Look likewise into the ways of all Professors, and you shall finde, That the Enjoyment of the Earth below, which you call a low and carnal Knowledg, is that, which you and all professors . . . strive and seek after.

Wherefore are you so covetous after the World, in buying and selling? counting your self a happy man, if you be rich, and a miserable man if you be poor. And though you say, *Heaven after death is a place of glory, where you shall enjoy God face to face,* yet you are loth to leave the Earth and go thither.[104]

In these lines the dynamics of Protestant individualism come to rest in a biting rationalism inimical in the utmost degree to the Calvinist coloring of the Puritan movement. Winstanley combined in his philosophy the most unconventional religious opinions with the most extreme social creed that the Puritan Revolution produced. He stood at the last outpost of a rebellious Protestantism, a queer, deranged relative of Calvinist intellects, disciple of a strange Christ, beckoning in vain toward utopian salvation.

CHAPTER I

A RADICAL SECTARY IN THE MAKING

A. ATTACK ON THE PRELATES

THE STORY of Milton's breaking away from Episcopalian, Presbyterian, and eventually from Independent church discipline is one that may be told in various forms of many seventeenth-century radicals. Like Vane, Williams, Lilburne, and Ludlow, Milton first wanted a purging of the Church of England and afterward its abolition, following far to the left the sweep of Protestant individualism. But it became more and more evident to this fringe of radical Puritans that the achievement of religious liberty could not be disentangled from opposition to the kingly rule under which they lived. Because national polity was so firmly knit with national church polity, radicalism in religion inevitably led to radicalism in varying degrees in politics. Such was Milton's own experience. Forsaking reluctantly his soaring hope of writing such poetry as his countrymen "should not willingly let . . . die," he plunged zealously into the rising whirlwind of pamphleteering. From this whirlwind no mind could have emerged unchanged, least of all one of Milton's intense and fearless imagination.

Everywhere one finds striking proof that the governments of James I and Charles I relied upon the Church of England to inculcate monarchical beliefs. The cause of the Church was the cause of Charles I; the bishops and Charles looked to each other to maintain the supremacy of the Crown in opposition to the Calvinistic Parliament. Nowhere is this more evident than in Charles' apology, *Eikon Basilike* (written by Dr. Gauden), an amazingly popular pamphlet that ran into many editions after Charles' execution: "I find it impossible for a Prince to preserve the State in quiet, unless he hath such an influence upon Church-men; and they such a dependance on Him, as may best restrain the seditious exorbitancies

41

of Ministers tongues." [1] Jeremy Taylor stated it plainly, too, arguing that it was "natural and consonant that kings should defend the
rights of the church, and the church advance the honour of kings." [2]
No one was less likely than Laud to neglect this principle of state.
The canons of 1640 specifically directed each minister of the land
to read the following sentence four times a year: "The most high
and sacred order of kings is of divine right, being the ordinance of
God himself, founded in the prime laws of nature." [3] When Laud
replaced Buckingham as Charles' chief adviser, the union of an
attempted despotism with an aristocratic church organization was
complete. With their primate at the helm of state, the twenty-four
bishops (each receiving an average of six thousand pounds annually)
assumed a secular importance hitherto seldom attained, and now
most bitterly resented by the growing urban classes.

Centralized authority marked the entire governmental structure
of the Church of England. The king appointed the primate and the
Archbishop of York. In theory he also appointed the twenty-four
diocese bishops, though Laud as chief adviser really made the
choices. In turn the bishops ordained the priests and deacons of
their respective dioceses (there were in all 9284 parish ministers).
No priest, though he might be selected by the owner of the land supporting the living, could take office without Episcopal ordination by
the diocese bishop. To check the rising Puritan clamor against his
enforced high-church ceremonies, which in the time of Elizabeth had
remained somewhat optional with each minister, Laud used his
power of appointment rigorously, substituting always for Puritan
sympathizers men of known willingness to carry out his program,
and using the civil power unhesitatingly to punish recalcitrant
priests. To suppose, however, that the vast majority of priests were
opposed to Laud's beliefs would be an error. Of the nine thousand
parish priests, Masson estimates that fully four thousand were in
agreement with Laud, and that probably 3500 desired only moderate
reforms. No more than 1500 could have wanted a completely puri-
fied ritual or the abolition of the prelates.[4]

Before Milton, with his "left hand," struck out on behalf of the
Puritan cause, a few determined and vociferous leaders had rallied
against the prelates unexpected popular support. Of these Dr. Henry
Burton, rector of St. Matthews Church in London, together with
Dr. John Bastwick of his congregation, and the tireless fanatic,

William Prynne, were for a time the most pre-eminent. As early as 1631 Prynne had attacked the Laudian tenets in his *Lame Giles His Haultings;* for his *Histrio-Mastix,* 1633, he had been condemned by the Star Chamber, degraded of his academic degrees, expelled from the legal profession, fined, and condemned to the Tower for life.[5] As a crowning ignominy, he was condemned to have his ears cut off and sit in the pillory. Two years later, Dr. Bastwick, who had been brought up as a youth to despise the Puritans, was deprived of his medical practice, fined, and imprisoned for attacking Episcopacy. His *Letany,* published in 1637, reviews the whole ground for his hatred of the prelates: "For the Prelates to say No Bishop, no King, is as great impiety, as to say no deuill, no king, which were damnable to thinke." Further, Bastwick complains, "all the Iudges, all the sheriffs, all the Mayors, all the bailiffs . . . all the Constables . . . are their lacqueis to run and goe." Even colliers had been arrested by the Archbishop for landing their barges at Westminster stairs. Furthermore, "He goeth in state . . . to Cambridge and Oxford . . . and with a rod in his hand in the schooles, to whip those naughty scholars, that will not learne well their lesson of conformity." [6]

Meanwhile Burton's sermons had aroused the bishops to punitive action. In late 1636 appeared his pamphlet, *For God, and the King,* the substance, he says, of two sermons preached on November 5 *"to teach my people obedience to both."* Bitterly he inveighs against the new rites and ceremonies, which *"doe now, not steale and creep into the Church, but . . . are violently and furiously obtruded upon Ministers and people, and that with . . . ejection out of the house and home, threatenings and thundrings to the refusers, who do not yeeld conformity unto them."* [7] On February 1 following, Laud having brought charges against him before the High Commission, Burton's doors were broken open, his papers rifled, and himself taken into custody. Prosecuted, with Prynne and Bastwick, in the Star Chamber, Burton was condemned on June 14; he was deprived of his benefice, fined 5000 pounds (which were never exacted), degraded from the ministry and his academic degrees (from St. John's, Cambridge, he had received the M.A.); condemned to be set in the pillory at Westminster and his ears cut off; and to be perpetually imprisoned at Lancaster Castle without access to wife or friends, or use of pen, ink, and paper.[8] Prynne and Bastwick received similar sentences. To the Star Chamber Laud spoke in part as follows: "I humbly give you hearty thanks for your just and honourable censure upon these men, and for your unanimous dislike of them." [9] The sentences were duly carried out, Prynne's ear-stumps being sawed instead of cut off, and Burton's ears being shaved so closely that the temporal artery was cut, and blood "gushed forth in torrents upon the scaffold." [10] In his *Narration* Burton gives thanks repeatedly for the courage which upheld him through this and later ordeals. At the pillory he said, in part, "I was never in such a pulpit before. Little do you know what fruit God is able to produce from this dry tree. Through these holes (meaning the pillory) God can bring light to his church." [11]

To what extent the three men had crystallized popular sentiment appeared on July 28, when Burton, his ears partially healed, was taken from the Fleet to be lodged at Lancaster Castle. More than one hundred thousand people lined the streets to acclaim him.[12] "On the day appointed," Burton writes, "I passed on horseback from the Fleet through Smithfield, where for throng of people all along, I could not passe, but very slowly, though the Keeper hastened all he could, who fretted to see so many thousands all the way we went, he reckoning the number to be forty thousand. By the way so many taking me by the hand, pressed the very blood out at my fingers ends, but with another minde then the great ones drew the blood out at mine eares." [13] Over three years later, when the Long Parliament in one of its first acts ordered the three men released, Burton was received with every demonstration of joy, ten thousand people escorting him from Charing Cross to London. Along the way bells pealed, and "the poore people brought forth whole baskets of Rosemary and Bayes, to furnish every one in the traine." [14]

When the Long Parliament met on November 3, 1640, the rising tide of Puritan feeling burst out anew, demanding more peremptorily than ever redress of church grievances.[15] On December 11, fifteen hundred London citizens appeared at the House with a petition signed by fifteen thousand, beseeching that the Episcopal church government "with all its dependencies, roots and branches, may be abolished, and all laws in their behalf made void," and listing twenty-eight grievances against the prelates.[16] Among other petitions, some of them for the maintenance of the Episcopacy,

Parliament received *A very considerable and lamentable Petition*, praying that "Prelacy may be totally Abolished, and . . . the Voteing of the Popish Lords removed out of the House of Peers"; [17] *The Humble Petition of divers Knights, Esquires . . . of the Countie Palatine of Lancaster*, "for expunging out of the Church innovations, and confining Church men to their proper functions." [18] Burton, Prynne, and Bastwick resumed their agitation with confident zeal, Burton's congregation receiving their earless pastor as a triumphant witness for the faith.

Nor had Parliament been slow to act. Strafford they had immediately retained and lodged in the Tower; and Laud was to follow soon after. Victims of the Star Chamber had been released and voted compensation, and Laud's canons voided. On March 30 had been introduced the Bishops' Exclusion Bill, a measure that would have excluded the bishops and clergy from all state offices and employment, limited the power of the bishops in ecclesiastical affairs, and greatly reduced the revenues of Deans and Chapters.[19] At first rejected and later passed by the Lords (it became law February 13, 1641–42), this bill revealed unmistakably the sharp sentiment of the middle classes; but a more radical measure was to follow. The Root-and-Branch Bill, which would have abolished all ecclesiastical orders above the rank of parish minister, was introduced by Sir Robert Deering at the request of Cromwell, Haselrig, and Vane. Possibly to their surprise, the Bill passed, on May 27, not only the first but the second reading. Though there it halted, to be postponed for action and finally dropped by mutual consent at the opening of the Civil War in 1642, the Root-and-Branch Bill was a significant indication of the determination of the radicals to effect fundamental changes in the traditional social structure.

*   *   *   *   *   *

It was not until this point that Milton's pamphleteering career began; for him cannot be claimed the distinction of leading the church reformers of his day. In his own words the story runs as follows:

The vigour of the parliament had begun to humble the pride of the bishops. As long as the liberty of speech was no longer subject to control, all mouths began to be opened against the bishops; some complained of the vices of the individuals, others of those of the order. They said that

it was unjust that they alone should differ from the model of other reformed churches; that the government of the church should be according
to the pattern of other churches, and particularly the word of God. This
awakened all my attention and my zeal. I saw that a way was opening for
the establishment of real liberty; that the foundation was laying for the
deliverance of man from the yoke of slavery and superstition; that the
principles of religion, which were the first objects of our care, would exert
a salutary influence on the manners and constitution of the republic; and
as I had from my youth studied the distinctions between religious and civil
rights, I perceived that if I ever wished to be of use, I ought at least not to
be wanting to my country, to the church, and to so many of my fellow-
Christians, in a crisis of so much danger.[20]

It were sad for me if I should draw back; for me especially, now
when all men offer their aid to . . . the church, to whose service, by the
intention of my parents and friends, I was destined of a child, and in
mine own resolutions: till coming to some maturity of years, and perceiving what tyranny had invaded the church, that he who would take orders
must subscribe slave, and take an oath withal, which, unless he took with a
conscience that would retch, he either must straight perjure, or split his
faith; I thought it better to preserve a blameless silence. . . Howsoever,
thus church-outed by the prelates, hence may appear the right I have to
meddle in these matters.[21]

Though it was evident to all that Charles and the prelates upheld
each other in their war on the Puritans, Charles against the power
of Parliament and the bishops against the recalcitrant clergy, neither
Milton nor any one of his fellow pamphleteers had yet ventured
to attack Episcopacy as a tyrannical adjunct to the Crown. Indeed,
one of Milton's main counts against the prelates is that they have
weakened the monarch's prestige: "Monarchy is made up of two
parts, the liberty of the subject, and the supremacy of the king.
I begin at the root. See what gentle and benign fathers they have
been to our liberty! . . . These devout prelates . . . have not
ceased . . . to trample under foot all the most sacred and lifeblood
laws, statutes, and acts of parliament, that are the holy covenant
of union and marriage between the king and his realm." [22] By their
tyrannies the bishops are undermining loyalty to the king, driving
many thousands to the wilds of America, encroaching everywhere
upon secular power and state decisions, haling freeborn Englishmen
into their courts, extorting from them fines and lip conformity.
Can such men enhance kingly glory? Finally, even in the *Reason*

of Church Government, the last of his five pamphlets against the prelates, Milton still maintains that they have weakened monarchy; comparing the King to Samson and the prelates to the Philistines, he refers to the "prelatical razor" which shaves off "all those bright and weighty tresses of his law, and just prerogatives, which were his ornament and strength," thus permitting the Philistines to "deliver him over to indirect and violent counsels." [23]

Though Milton is not yet ready to call Charles a tyrant in his own right, he does suggest, as the above passage reveals, that he is a tyrant by default to the bishops. And at the end of *The Reason of Church Government* Milton strikes his first blow at prelaty as an aid, not to monarchy, but to tyrannical monarchs. If, he says, the prelates can persuade the king to listen to their bargains, they will sell the bodies of the people as they have already done their souls. And if a tyrant should come into power, he will use the prelates as so many soldiers to overawe the people. A tyrant custom in religion breeds a tyrant custom in government, and prelaty is the "agent and minister" of tyranny.[24] From this time forth, although Milton does not attack Episcopacy directly as an aid to absolute monarchy, he couples prelaty with his attacks on Charles I.

Like Burton and Bastwick, Milton strikes telling blows at the worldliness of the bishops, a worldliness he repeatedly contrasts with the humility and poverty of Jesus and the bishops of primitive Christianity. Their stately palaces, rich foods, splendid house furnishings, servants, retinue, silken clothes—all are objects of Milton's ridicule. When a bishop substitutes "spiritual dignity for carnal precedence . . . then he degrades, then he unbishops himself; he that makes him bishop, makes him no bishop." [25] Their courts Milton repeatedly derides: "Two leeches they have that still suck and suck the kingdom—their ceremonies and their courts. . . . What a mass of money is drawn from the veins into the ulcers of the kingdom this way; their extortions, their open corruptions, the multitude of hungry and ravenous harpies." [26] The most worthy prelaty would labor humbly to teach, to restrain by spiritual admonition only, to reject secular honor and preferment, "by lowliness to confound height," content to ride upon asses. In one long and bitter sentence Milton summarizes both his hatred of the bishops and his conception of an honorable one:

He that will mould a modern bishop into a primitive, must yield him to be elected by the popular voice, undiocesed, unrevenued, unlorded, and leave him nothing but brotherly equality, matchless temperance, frequent fasting, incessant prayer and preaching, continual watchings and labours in his ministry; which what a rich booty it would be, what a plump endowment to the many-benefice-gaping-mouth of a prelate, what relish it would give to his canary-sucking and swan-eating palate, let old bishop Mountain judge for me.[27]

Again and again Milton berates the bishops for their consecrating crucifixes, images, altars, communion tables, carpets, tablecloths, not allowing the plain man to touch such objects, thinking it blasphemous for him to lay his hat on the chancel table, "whilst the obscene and surfeited priest scruples not to maw and mammoc the sacramental bread, as familiarly as his tavern biscuit." Not awe of consecrated baubles, but a cleansing of the inner self, admonishes Milton, prepares one truly for God's service. Furthermore, man under the Gospel has been exalted into fellowship with Christ, a fellowship fostered by self-reverence, not abasement: "The exclusion of Christ's people from the offices of holy discipline . . . causes the rest to have an unworthy and abject opinion of themselves." [28] St. Peter authorized all of God's people to be ministers of the Gospel. Yet the bishops would forbid them to touch the altar table.

Finally, Milton attacks the bishops for their aristocratic hierarchical organization, "an insolent preferring of yourselves above your brethren," a church government antagonistic both to the Gospel and to primitive church government. Much of the treatise *Of Prelatical Episcopacy* he devotes to proving that the bishops and presbyters of the early church had the same spiritual authority. Originally, he says, one of the apostles appointed a worthy man as head of a particular church; this man was either bishop or presbyter, the name bishop in Greek signifying that he was of the more famous presbyters, not that he had any more authority in the church government. Not of divine origin, Milton contends, prelaty grew up as a part of man's effort to organize the church; that it was at least four hundred years after the time of the apostles before any distinction arose between bishop and presbyter.[29] Such distinction, Milton insists, is contrary to the practices of Christ himself: "First, therefore, if to do the work of the gospel, Christ

our Lord took upon him the form of a servant, how can his servant
in this ministry take upon him the form of a lord?" [30] Not ordination by the bishop, but election by the people, should be the method
of appointing ministers; and highly insulting it is to a redeemed
people, however plain or uneducated, to be thought unworthy and
incapable of choosing their spiritual leaders.[31] Thus Milton stands
forth plainly for the abolition of all church officers superior to the
parish minister, and him to be elected by the people. A Root-and-
Branch man he was, as Masson says, "to the uttermost bounds
known." But to true reformation the lordly prelates still barred the
way.

In the main Milton's anti-prelatical pamphlets undoubtedly
reflect the democratic tendencies of the day. The whole population,
required by law to be present at the Sabbath ceremonies, engaged
in religious controversy. In those sections, largely rural, where high
church ceremonies had prevailed for decades, the Laudian decrees
had met with little opposition; but wherever the gradual purification of the ritual and increasing emphasis on preaching had become
the rule, congregations were bitter indeed. Crowds in the London
streets muttered against, even jostled the bishops and their trains.
In 1641 a petition of 30,000 apprentices prayed for the end of
"the insulting Domination of the Lordly Bishop of *Canterbury* and
some others." [32] On February 4, 1642, *The Humble Petition of the
Gentlewomen, Tradesmen's Wives, and many others of the Female
Sex* complained that the "superstitious Bishops are suffered to have
their Voice in the House of Peers," asking that the prelates be
abolished, and concluding with a bold claim to their right to speak
on public matters: to which petition Pym, coming to doors of the
Commons, responded graciously, commending them for their timely
appeal.[33] Many of the complaints of *The Root and Branch Petition*
of 1640 and *The Grand Remonstrance* of 1641, the latter of which
the Commons presented to Charles as their impression of the state
of the kingdom, show how closely Milton's views paralleled those
of the rising middle class:

The Root-and-Branch Petition

1. The subjecting and enthralling all ministers under them and
their authority. . . .

2. The faint-heartedness of ministers to preach the truth of God, lest
they should displease the prelates. . . .

4. The restraint of many godly and able men from the ministry, and thrusting out of many congregations their faithful, diligent and powerful ministers. . . .

13. The offices and jurisdictions of archbishops, lord bishops, deans, archdeacons. . . .

15. The standing up at *Gloria Patri* and at the reading of the Gospel, praying towards the East, the bowing at the name of Jesus, the bowing to the altar towards the East, cross in baptism, the kneeling at the Communion.

16. The turning of the Communion table altar-wise, setting images, crucifixes, and conceits over them, and tapers and books upon them, and bowing to . . . before them.

17. The christening and consecrating of churches and chapels, the consecrating fonts, tables, churchyards. . . .

23. Yea, further, the pride and ambition of the prelates being boundless, unwilling to be subject either to man or laws, they claim their office and jurisdiction *jure divino*.[34]

The Grand Remonstrance

The root of all this mischief we find to be a malignant and pernicious design of subverting the fundamental laws and principles of government. . . . The actors and promoters hereof have been:

1. The Jesuited Papists. . . .

2. The Bishops, and the corrupt part of the Clergy, who cherish formality and superstition. . . .

3. Councillors and courtiers . . . for private ends. . . .

The common principles by which they moulded and governed all their particular counsels were these:

First, to maintain continual differences and discontents between the king and the people, upon questions of prerogative and liberty. . . .

A second, to suppress the purity and power of religion. . . .

A fourth, to disaffect the King to Parliaments by slander and false imputations. . . .

The bishops and the rest of the clergy did triumph in the suspensions, excommunications, deprivations, and degradations of divers . . . ministers. . . .

We confess our intention is . . . to reduce within bounds that exhorbitant power which the prelates have assumed unto themselves.[35]

In these sentiments Puritans, Brownists, sectaries, even some of the aristocracy, joined hearts and minds. Though Milton had not, like Prynne and Bastwick and Burton, for the cause risked prison dungeons or cutting of ears, and though the whirlwind was rising when he had tilted first with prelates, his voice, if relatively uninfluential, spoke the common negative aims of multitudes of Englishmen. On the problem of state church and retention of kingship the united front against Episcopacy was to split asunder. But the cleavage had not yet appeared.

———————

Milton opposed the prelates, then, for their worldliness, their aristocratic church structure, their oblique detraction from the dignity and worth of the Christian layman and preaching minister, and their insistence on ceremonial conformity. Whether or not these charges were unfair,[36] they drove Milton from Episcopacy to Presbyterianism; and their democratic influence on Milton's politics is hardly to be denied. The writing of the pamphlets forced him to re-examine and clarify his fundamental tenets. Repeatedly he gives indications of his scorn of tradition and reliance upon personal scriptural interpretation, intellectual approaches that were to lead him to further religious and political radicalism. He berates the Episcopal apologists for "searching among verminous and polluted rags dropped overworn from the toiling shoulders of time" instead of relying upon the pure fountain of truth, the Gospel. For the "unwieldly volumes of tradition," "the wild and overgrown covert of antiquity," the "horseloads of citations and fathers" he has nothing but contempt. Such an individualistic religionist could pause, not anchor, among the orderly and disciplined Presbyterians.

B. From Presbyterianism to Independency

In his fourth anti-Episcopal pamphlet, *The Reason of Church Government*, 1642, Milton declares flatly for Presbyterian government.[37] Each parish, he says, should be in itself the unit of organization; the parishes should then organize themselves into a general assembly, which he likens to a cube of a number of equal parts, "an emblem of truth and steadfastness." The Presbyterian state church organization as proposed for England by the Scots does not exactly meet Milton's description.[37] The first unit of church government, according to the Scottish plan, was the congregational presbytery made up sometimes of only one large congregation,

sometimes of two or three associated congregations. Then followed
the classis, composed of twelve or thirteen congregations, next the
province of possibly twelve classis units, and finally the nation
as a whole. Elders from each congregation were to meet in congregational presbytery once a week and in classical presbytery once
a month. Every six months two ministers and four elders, selected
by the classical presbytery meeting as a body, were to meet in a
provincial synod; and as often as Parliament should decide, two
ministers and four elders from each provincial assembly were to
gather in a national assembly.[38] There were to be sixty provinces,
"about co-numerous with the shires, and, in most cases, identical
with them." [39] London was to be a province in itself, containing
fourteen classes. The decisions of the various assemblies pertaining
to excommunication, partaking of the sacrament, etc., were to be
binding on the members within their jurisdiction. In contrast to
this plan, Milton makes no mention of the intermediate assemblies,
but assumes that each church should have equal authority in a
national assembly: "Of such a council as this every parochial con-
sistory is a right homogeneous and constituting part, being in itself,
as it were, a little synod, and towards a general assembly moving
upon her own basis in an even and firm progression, as those smaller
squares in battle unite in one great cube, the main phalanx, an
emblem of truth and steadfastness." [40] Though Milton significantly
omits the intermediate assemblies, an omission perhaps indicative
of his distrust of any hierarchy, he bluntly declares that any right
thinking Protestant will confess Presbyterianism the "only true
church government," without "any crookedness, any wrinkle or
spot." [41]

Despite this statement Milton had become, by November, 1644,
when *Areopagitica* appeared, a bitter enemy of the Presbyterians
as the "new forcers of conscience." In these two and a half years,
amid bristling speeches, pamphlet showers, and clash of arms,
thousands of minds veered left with the Independents, disagreeing
among themselves upon the question of church government, but
united in their opposition to a Presbyterian state church. It was
inevitable that Milton should desert his Smectymnuuan friends on
this issue; indeed it is doubtful that he was ever an orthodox
believer in the organizational perfection so happily agreed upon by
the Scots. Even in *The Reason of Church Government* passages

appear that must have made Thomas Young, Milton's old teacher, shake his head dubiously. "Sects and errors . . . ," Milton writes, "God suffers to be for the glory of good men, that the world may know their true fortitude and undaunted constancy in the truth." [42] Rather than a hindrance to reformation, sects will require Christians to examine their principles and lead them to a deeper faith. Such tolerance for "fond errors" was an Independent, not a Presbyterian tenet. Milton's repeated praise of the common man's ability to select his pastor, to understand spiritual matters equally well with ministers, even to preach himself, were sentiments afterward pounced upon as ridiculous by Presbyterian apologists. "Is it fitting," lamented Edwards, "that well meaning Christians should be suffered to goe and make Churches, and then proceed to chuse whom they will for Ministers, as some Taylor, Felt-maker, Button-maker, men ignorant, and low in parts?" "They who lay hands on and make Ministers," he wrote, "should be greater in place and Authority & not lesse, as the common People be." [43]

The meeting of the Long Parliament in November, 1640, had been the signal, not only for tumultuous issuance of unorthodox pamphlets, but also for the return of leading spirits among the religious radicals who had been banished from England.[44] Already friendly to these courageous spirits, Milton knew them to be hardy Separatists, Brownists, or Independents; and he was already receptive to their intellectual influence, and to that of London sympathizers. Except for its plea for toleration of Roman Catholics, Milton would have given assent in 1641, to *The Humble Petition of the Brownists,* pleading that Arminians, Socinians, and Brownists be allowed to worship in their own congregations unmolested.[45] Had Milton read John Robinson's bold stand that churches may function without officers, and that "every one is made a king, priest, and prophet, not only to himself but to every other"? [46] If so, he would have found himself one with the Pilgrims' pastor. Though long dead, Robinson was again on men's lips. In 1639 had appeared a new edition of his *A Justification of Separation from the Church of England;* in 1641 Thomas Edwards quoted and condemned him, along with Henry Burton and his *Protestation Protested.*

In this pamphlet, parting from his famous fellow-sufferers Prynne and Bastwick, Burton declares flatly for the toleration of Independent congregations outside the national church: "Where such Congregations are erected and allowed of by a Civil State, they are both a strength and a beauty." To the kind of national church established Burton was relatively indifferent, so long as private groups might worship in their own way. If Milton had not heard Burton preach, or read his *Protestation Protested,* he had read carefully Hall's reply, entitled *A Survay of that Foolish, Seditious, Scandalous, Prophane Libell, the Protestation Protested,* a tract which Milton mentions scornfully in his last prelate pamphlet, *An Apology for Smectymnuus.* In *A Survay,* as well as in *A Modest Confutation,* Hall denounces the rabble's voice as the "hummings of a factious congregation." Is it possible that Burton would allow "the meanest chimney-sweeper amongst you his calling to preach, to expound scripture, to give the Sacraments"? [47] But in *An Apology* Milton stoutly proclaims the capacity of the meanest Christian and "plain artisan" to elect their ministers.[48] Could they possibly be as light-headed as the bungling clergy? Thus in Hall's pamphlets Burton and Milton were attacked for one of the same Independent heresies, and Hall's reply to Burton must have strengthened Milton's peculiar tenets.

A pamphlet that directly influenced Milton's Independent tendencies, perhaps more decisively than any other, was Lord Brooke's *A Discourse Opening the Nature of . . . Episcopacie* (1641). For the Puritan cause no more tolerant or persuasive voice had spoken than that of Lord Brooke. With deft and refreshingly original logic, with a subdued, even kindly, irony, he had stated his case against the prelates. Toward the end of his long tract he pleads for toleration of the Independents, characterizing them thus: "They poore men Expect a new Heaven, and a new Earth, wherein there shall neede no more Temples of stone, but all Good men shall be Prophets, Priests, and Kings. In the meantime they say Waters must flow out of bellies of all that beleeve, till . . . the Great Waters of the Sanctuary flow forth without measure. Yea, they are much encouraged from the Practise of the Church in the *Acts,* where all the members, Every believer, being scattered by persecution, went about preaching." [49] And would it really offend custom to allow them to set up their own congregations? After all, he continues, England already has *Peculiars,* that is, congregations of the Church of England traditionally free from the jurisdiction of the diocese bishop. All that the Separatists want is that *Inde-*

pendent Peculiars be permitted. "I could heartily wish," he writes, "some pitty might bee shewed to these poore mens soules." [50]

How profoundly these words appealed to Milton is revealed in his high praise of Lord Brooke in *Areopagitica,* written after Brooke's death on the battlefield: "Next to His last testament, who bequeathed love and peace to his disciples, I cannot call to mind where I have read or heard words more mild and peaceful. He there [in *A Discourse Opening the Nature of . . . Episcopacie*] exhorts us to hear with patience and humility those, however they be miscalled, that desire to live purely, in such a use of God's ordinances, as the best guidance of their conscience gives them, and to tolerate them, though in some disconformity to ourselves." [51] In Brooke's tract, which Milton must have read in 1641 or 1642, he had found, not only a reflection of his own incipient beliefs, but also a personality wholly admirable, one for whom his harsh and bitter language would have been impossible. Striking him with double force, Brooke's pamphlet provided a significant impetus to Milton's growing unorthodoxy.

Meanwhile the opening of the Great Civil War showed how generally the cleavage in religious opinions foreshadowed the political and military alliances of the day. Among the clergy the staunch Episcopalians allied themselves on the side of the king, their livings being liquidated by the predominantly Presbyterian Parliament. To Charles' side also rallied the landed gentry and the nobility, men, with notable exceptions, of the Anglican persuasion, looking distrustfully upon the beauty-hating narrowness of many Puritan minds, dreading the rising power of the business classes, and revering the traditional kingship. For Parliament's prerogatives the bulk of Presbyterians, townsmen, yeomen, and clergy, took their stand. The king, it is true, they also revered, hoping for the speedy conclusion of the war, with the king again restored to his constitutional privileges, and a Calvinistic state church supreme. For Parliament, too, came forth almost all men of more extreme and individualistic sectarian beliefs, among them to be Milton and Cromwell, men generally classified as Independents. From staunch sectarians Captain Cromwell had already picked his company of horse, trusting the steady Puritan zeal of well-fed workers and farmers to match the mettle of aristocratic training. "You must get men of a spirit," Cromwell said to Hampden, "of a spirit that is likely to go as far as gentlemen will go, or else you will be beaten still." [52] And not until Cromwell was allowed his way did the army conquer the king's cavaliers. Already the Independents were striking off on democratic tangents disturbing to the Presbyterians. "One extremitie . . . hath caused another," Edwards had written, "the Tyrannie of Episcopall government in some Bishops hath brought forth the Democracie and Independencie, the violent pressing of some pretended orders hath set many against all order." [53]

On July 1, 1643, the Westminster Assembly of Divines, instructed by Parliament to determine the true doctrine and discipline for England's state church, met for the first time. "A certain number of divines were called," Milton later wrote, "neither chosen . . . for either piety or knowledge above others left out; only as each member of parliament in his private fancy thought fit." [54] Predominantly Presbyterian, the Assembly soon made known their desire for a state church of the Scottish type. If all England would take a Covenant to support such a church, then, said the Scottish Commissioners, the Scottish army would assist Parliament in prosecuting the war. Though anxious for a civil treaty, some of the Parliamentarians hesitated to accept Presbyterianism lock, stock, and barrel, a hesitation shared by a swelling number of Independents throughout the land. Through the action of Sir Henry Vane, former governor of Massachusetts and close friend of Roger Williams, the Solemn League and Covenant were amended in Parliament, the words "according to the example of the best Reformed Churches" being changed to "according to the word of God and the best Reformed Churches." [55] The way being thus left at least partially open to Independency, most sectarian consciences found the Covenant not too reprehensible, especially since it contained some passages (for abolishing prelacy and upholding Parliament), which they could accept without question. That Milton as a London householder signed the Covenant, as required of all Englishmen over the age of eighteen, is evident from a passage in *Tetrachordon* in which he speaks of himself as "partaker of . . . your vows and solemn covenants." [56] Like Vane and Cromwell, however, Milton could have signed only with significant reservations.

More extreme sectaries than Milton, Henry Robinson and Roger Williams were quick to attack the Covenant. "I would very faine know . . .," wrote Robinson, "whether such a Covenant . . . doth

not oblige us to the same which we call Canonicall obedience . . .
nay, is it not yet worse then the vow of single life wherein all
Nunnes and *Fryers* intrap themselves?" [57] In his *Queries of Highest
Consideration* (1644) Williams asserted that no national church
could possibly be initiated without intense spiritual suffering and
persecution of earnest Christians. Where, he exhorted, can "you
now find one footstep, Print or Pattern in this Doctrine of the Son
of God, for a Nationall holy Covenant, and so consequenty [*sic*]
. . . a Nationall Church"? [58] Fairly enough, royalist pamphleteers
turned against the Presbyterians their own former arguments for
liberty of conscience, pleading for the right to worship in the traditional Episcopal manner.[59]

From the spring of 1642 until August 1, 1643, when his *Doctrine
and Discipline of Divorce* appeared, Milton had published nothing.
Nor does this pamphlet anticipate Milton's rejection of Presbyterianism. But certainly the clergy who damned his gross heresy so
piously (and on this issue he had no supporters even among the
extreme sectarians) ejected him further than ever away from his
nominal support of the Calvinist position. Cheated, as thought, of
a true marriage, supremely confident of the nobility of his motives,
he turned upon his detractors with more bitterness than upon the
prelates. Inexplicably enough no one came forth to grapple openly
with Milton's strange and ugly tenet until after the appearance of
the second edition, on February 2, 1644. But that in the meantime
some of the clergy had raised their voices in horrified accents we
know from Milton's own story in *The Judgment of Martin Bucer
Concerning Divorc*e: "I was told that . . . some of the clergy began to inveigh and exclaim on what I was credibly informed they
had not read." [60] Then it was, he adds, that he decided to sign his
name to the second edition so that his opponents might not have
to confute an anonymous pamphlet. On August 13, 1644, preaching
before both Parliament and the Westminster Assembly of Divines,
Herbert Palmer made a dramatic attack on Milton's heresy: "A
wicked booke is abroad and *uncensured*, though *deserving to be
burnt*, whose *Author* hath been so *impudent* as to *set his Name* to it,
and *dedicate it to your selves*." [61] Was it not beyond all reason,
Palmer asked, that toleration should be claimed for such damnable
ideas? Now a resolute leader of the Presbyterian faction, Prynne
succinctly dubbed Milton's theory *divorce at pleasure*.[62] In replying,

whereas Milton dismisses Palmer's attack with some contempt, he shows that Prynne's blow had touched him to the quick: "One above others, who hath suffered much and long in the defence of truth, shall after all this give her cause to leave him so destitute and so vacant of her defence." [63] In Prynne's pamphlet, as well as in Daniel Featley's *The Dippers Dipt, or the Anabaptists Duck'd and Plung'd Over Head and Eares* (February 7, 1645) and Ephraim Pagitt's *Heresiography* (May 8, 1645), Milton's heresy is coupled with Roger Williams' *Bloudy Tenent* and Richard Overton's *Mans Mortallitie* as the most outrageous of the new notions deserving suppression. If, as Masson thinks likely, Milton first made the acquaintance of Roger Williams during his stay in England from midsummer, 1643, until fall of 1644 (when Williams was long a guest at Vane's house), the two men found much in common, with Williams leading the way toward a more drastic Independency.

In the months preceding the publication of *Areopagitica* the Independent pamphleteers were clashing more and more frequently with the proponents of a Presbyterian state church. Sitting among the Westminster divines, the five dissenting brethren, Thomas Goodwin, Philip Nye, William Bridge, Jeremiah Burroughes, and Sidrach Simpson, all returned from exile for conscience's sake, had voiced their grave and moderate doubts. In *An Apologeticall Narration*, published January 4, 1644, the five had carefully explained their position, pointing out their agreement with Calvinist doctrine, but rejecting the power of discipline and excommunication lodged in the hands of synods and assemblies. Surrounding congregations in their judgment should have the restraining power of admonition only. Not opposed to public financial support, or to the magistrate's occasional interference in church matters, the brethren summed up their position as follows: "We beleeve the truth to lye and consist in a *middle way* betwixt that which is falsely charged on us, *Brownisme;* and that which is the contention of these times, the *authoritative Presbyteriall Government* in all the subordinations and proceedings of it." [64] But men like Henry Burton, Henry Robinson, and John Goodwin were much more outspoken and uncompromising. In *A Vindication of Churches Commonly Called Independent* Burton argued closely that all the churches established by the apostles had retained separate and complete authority. Robinson and Goodwin attacked the proposed state church as a forcer of conscience. In his

A Reply of two of the Brethren to M.S. Goodwin stoutly claimed that all sects and schisms should be permitted, the only condition being that they be peaceful citizens subject in all else to the civil magistrate.[65] Yes, says Goodwin, we too want religious unity. But can you attain spiritual unity by compulsion of the body? Rather, as he says, in *Theomachia,* or *The Grand Imprudence,* the use of the secular sword cuts off all hope of persuasive redemption.[66] And Henry Robinson in *John the Baptist . . . or, A Necessity for Liberty of Conscience, as the only means under Heaven to strengthen Children weake in faith,* raised the cry that was to be heard so often in the years to come: *"Tell me, Good Reader, what difference does thou make betwixt being persecuted by an Episcopall or Presbyteriall Clergie?"* With what alarm many Presbyterians read such sallies is reflected in a typical Prynne outburst: "Yea, every Heretick, Sectary, or guidy-pated Enthusiast, upon pretext of new Revelations . . . will erect new Independent Churches of their own . . . uncontroulable, unsuppressible by any Ecclesiasticall or Civill authority." [67]

Milton's denunciation of the Presbyterian program in *Aeropagitica* shows how sharply his sympathies had swerved toward the more radical thought streams of the day. In his hatred of persecution of the sects Milton was now one with Goodwin and Williams. In a time of truth seeking, he believed, the more sects, and the more freely communicated their tenets, the more glorious the victory over ignorance and superstition. What if the sectarian winds blow furiously? Truth will abide: "Let her and falsehood grapple; who ever knew truth put to the worse, in a free and open encounter?" [68] The building of true Reformation, like the building of a temple, requires not workers of a uniform skill and talent, but men of many "moderate varieties and brotherly dissimilitudes." The spreading of sects indicates merely an earnest desire to learn, and this desire begets "much arguing, much writing, many opinions; for opinion in good men is but knowledge in the making." [69] Like the noble Lord Brooke, all true believers should speak now for a brotherly Christian tolerance, hoping for many truths, long enthralled, to be rescued from the tight fist of custom and compelled conformity. But alas, just when Reformation has ousted the bishops and bids fair to raise up a more glorious life for all England, "the episcopal arts begin to bud again; the cruise of truth must run no more oil; liberty of printing must be enthralled again, under a prelatical commission of twenty [censors]; the privilege of the people nullified; and, which is worse, the freedom of learning must groan again, and to her old fetters: all this the parliament yet sitting." [70] If the prelates are gone, their narrow minds still work in Presbyterian heads. And they who once cried down the prelates now presume to sit in judgment on the life or death of a good book, to stem "the precious life-blood of a master-spirit," and forbid his immortality. Does any one have the right to sit at home in an arm chair and snuff out reason as if it were a candle? If so, if this is Reformation, it is not what John Milton meant when *he* made "covenants and protestations." [71] He calls upon all Englishmen to make in time of Reformation vital and lasting changes, not only in religion, but also in political and economic institutions.[72] For the Presbyterians to kill the flow of pamphlets is to halt the yeast of reforming zeal before it has leavened the lump.

Thus did Milton reject the plan of the Presbyterians for a settlement of England's religious difficulties. For him they had been a bitter disappointment. Not only had they begun to attack and suppress those sects for whom he had asked tolerance in *The Reason of Church Government;* and not only had their spokesmen ridiculed his learned and reasonable analyses of the divorce problem. Now they had attempted to stop all further agitation by cutting off the right of the sectarians to influence public opinion.

C. INDEPENDENCY PECULIAR

Milton had become an Independent only in the broad sense of opposition to Presbyterianism and conviction that all Protestant sects should be permitted to organize in their own way. As his religious beliefs crystallized, it is doubtful that any group of that day would have admitted him to membership. It is true that his conception of church organization proper would have been acceptable to the Congregationalists. Each church, Milton says in *Christian Doctrine,* is of right a unit in itself, electing its ministers from its members,[73] and not subject to any higher earthly power, whether an assembly or an individual.[74] He then quotes *Matthew* xviii, 20, "where two or three people are gathered together in my name, there am I in the midst of them." Such churches as wish, however, may cooperate freely and voluntarily for the common welfare.[75] But to the average

congregationalist church Milton's divorce tenets would have prohibited his membership, even if he had not revealed to them his sincere and honest belief in polygamy, which he defends at length in
Christian Doctrine.[76] Nor is it likely that many devout Independents
would have looked with favor on Milton's anti-trinitarian beliefs,
which they would have called Arian or Socinian tenets stoutly
maintained in *Christian Doctrine*,[77] and, in spite of censorship, often
suggested in *Paradise Lost*. Moreover, like Richard Overton, Milton
insisted that the soul dies with the body, to rise again at the resurrection; here was a serious heresy indeed.[78] And what of the Sabbath? On this issue also Milton would have been heretical to most
sectarian congregations: "Under the gospel no one day is appointed
for divine worship in preference to another." [79] Like the Anabaptists, Milton believed in adult baptism only;[80] but they, contrary to
his belief, allowed women to participate in church government. Like
the Quakers who were to spring up a few years hence, Milton believed in no professional ministry and no ritual; but unlike them he
maintained the efficacy and justice of war as an instrument of
Christian statesmanship. Except for antinomianism, Milton's sectarian position combined planks from most of the heretical plat-
forms of his day; yet in no one sect would his spirit have found altogether congenial company. Only in support of decentralized church
organization, detestation of tithes collected by statute, and belief
in limited toleration could Milton and the various sects have struck
a common ground. When it becomes clear that he finally ceased to
attend any church at all, and that his high reverence for himself forbade his permitting any intermediary, whether individual or institutional, between his personality and God, Milton's principle is clear:
No minister and no church has a right to intervene between God and
man. Thus his plea to the Holy Muse:

> And chiefly Thou O Spirit, that dost prefer
> Before all Temples th' upright heart and pure,
> Instruct me, for Thou know'st. . . . What in me is dark
> Illumine, what is low, raise and support.

Around the root of Milton's peculiar Independency were entwined
tenacious religious principles which were to exercise a profound influence on his political judgments. One was his decisive preference of
individual to institutional interpretation of the Scriptures, an in-

veterately stubborn reliance upon his own ability to understand the Biblical teachings. This radical principle, the match that lighted hundreds of revolutionary fires in Milton's day, justified his scornful rejection of custom and tradition in both religion and politics. It was this imperious individualism that led him away from belief in Episcopalianism, through Presbyterian church government, and finally even beyond church democracy as found in Independency, to what we might call ecclesiastical anarchy. And, as we have seen, not once did Milton hesitate to adopt a sectarian belief if he believed it founded on Scriptures, regardless of the calumny heaped on his head in consequence.

What is man's fundamental relation to God? Is God a dictatorial father, insisting upon His superior position, or a believer in substantial equality between himself and his children? For Milton these were basic considerations. He leans toward the view that men, like Christ, though in lesser degree, are sons of God, capable of approaching Him in spiritual worth. In *Christian Doctrine* Milton contends that it was man's soul, not his body, which was created in the image of God; he thus on several occasions identifies man's soul with God, and from this principle deduces the conclusion that man is by nature endowed with wisdom and holiness, with a capacity for perfectibility.[82] In *The Reason of Church Government* he writes that under the Hebrew law man was taught by the priests, scribes, and pharisees, but under the Gospel (man now being united in fellowship with Christ) he may expect a more direct communication from God, not now the Jehovah of the Hebrews, but the father of Christian sons. By the atonement, provided that men accept Christ and thus free themselves from the bondage of sin, they become "sons instead of servants, and perfect men instead of children." [83] The acceptance of Christ means regeneration both spiritual and intellectual; the regenerate are then "ingrafted in Christ," infused with "new and supernatural faculties." By such faculties men may know all that is necessary for earthly happiness and spiritual salvation. Moreover, such men are free from all earthly law; they are above the law. In *Paradise Lost* Christ speaking to God calls man "thy youngest son," a position affirmed in *Paradise Regained* by the lines: "Sons of God both Angels are and Men." [84]

Since all men equally possess free will, is it possible for all men to become equally free from earthly law, for all men by accepting

Christ equally to regenerate their minds and souls? Milton saw about him too much inequality of intellect and spirit, was too conscious of his own superiority, to accept this conclusion, a conclusion to which his belief in absolute free will might logically have led him. In *The Reason of Church Government* (1642), before he had fully avowed his belief in free will, he thinks some Christians are as "newborn babes comparatively to some that are stronger." [85] In *Christian Doctrine* Milton states plainly his concept of spiritual aristocracy: "For, as will be shown hereafter, there are some remnants of the divine image left in man, the union of which in one individual renders him more fit and disposed for the kingdom of God than another." [86] It is true that in many passages, especially in the prelate pamphlets and in *The Likeliest Means to Remove Hirelings out of the Church* (1659), Milton vigorously proclaims the capacity of the ordinary man, the uneducated, to grasp the fundamentals of Christianity. But in *Paradise Lost* he reaffirms his belief in spiritual aristocracy, from which it is not likely that he ever really parted. There Milton sees all life, vegetable, animal, and human, possessing the attributes of God in varying degrees, men rising in spiritual excellence through orders of angels and archangels through Christ to God.[87] In heaven no equality prevailed, as Satan says:

> Not equal all, yet free,
> Equally free; for Orders and Degrees
> Jar not with liberty, but well consist.[88]

Satan had been rejected from Heaven for "affecting all equality with God" and revolting against the spiritual pre-eminence of Christ. The theological framework of *Paradise Lost* thus leaves no doubt that Milton believed men, despite equal acceptance of Christ, unequal in the capacity for spiritual regeneration.

To rise even a little toward God-like perfection, depends, however, upon man's own choice. He is free to accept or reject God and his commandments. If man were not free, if he were bound by the pressure of his environment or any other force to become sinful, then God might be said to be the author of sin, since He created the universe.[89] "I made him just and right," says Milton's God in *Paradise Lost*, "sufficient to have stood, though free to fall." [90] Thus did Milton reject the harsh Calvinistic doctrine of election, by which the atonement was declared to serve for the benefit of a few only, the vast majority of men being condemned inevitably to perdition, and not being able by exertion of their will to change their status. Whereas the Calvinists had emphasized the inherent depravity of man and the changelessness of God's stern decrees, Milton, following the teachings of the Arminians, asserted man's innate nobility and made the infliction of God's wrath contingent upon man's freedom of choice.[91] From Milton's point of view all people might secure the benefits of the atonement, whereas the Calvinists would have salvation the good fortune of the elect few only.

Milton's doctrine of free will, though more humane than the Presbyterian tenet of predestination, gives a strangely harsh tinge to his political philosophy. Accepting Christ, man should be free from all temporal law; denying him, they should be subject to the temporal rule of their spiritual betters. Woe unto sinners! Yoked by passion, swayed by idolatrous king-worship, blind to the merits of godly men, responsive to evil orators, such men deserve not a government of their own choosing, but an earthly slavery. For Milton no middle ground availed. As he writes in *Defensio Secunda*: "It is not agreeable to the nature of things that such persons ever should be free. However much they may brawl about liberty, they are slaves, both at home and abroad, but without perceiving it; and when they do perceive it, like unruly horses that are impatient of the bit, they will endeavor to throw off the yoke, not from the love of genuine liberty, (which a good man only loves and knows how to obtain,) but from impulses of pride and little passions." [92] This is God's judgment of wicked men, as Milton reaffirms in *Paradise Lost*:

> Therefore since hee permits
> Within himself unworthie Powers to reign
> Over free Reason, God in Judgement just
> Subjects him from without to violent Lords.

Milton never freed himself from this essentially religious interpretation of man's political freedom. The wave of horror at the king's execution in 1649, the attacks on Cromwell, the cries for a king in 1660, the Restoration with its tyranny and its "sons of Belial flown with insolence and wine"—all these, he thought, sprang from the voluntary rejection of God's will. Upon the people, fools and slaves, God has visited his just judgment; and England, that might have been a paradise, was lost. The discrepancy between his own fortunate intellectual environment and that of England's masses seems to have had small place in Milton's meditations. Nor can we claim for him the pitying eye of Dante or the compassionate heart of his unlettered contemporary, Gerrard Winstanley.

In his doctrinal interpretation of man's right to liberty Milton parts company with more extreme democrats of the seventeenth century, the Levellers. Whereas Milton believed that simple acceptance of Christ brought not only inner liberty but political freedom and insight, John Lilburne believed that man needs to be taught political principles before he can be expected to gain his liberty. The Levellers were frankly secular in their aims; they depended upon man's reason and not upon revelation of Christian liberty to make him free upon earth.[94] Both Milton and Lilburne believed that man is perfectible; but whereas, in Milton's judgment, it is man's own fault if he is not perfected, Lilburne believed that the people cannot be expected to perfect themselves and their government without an opportunity to learn. Hence, to the last, Lilburne's faith in the sound sense of the people; and hence, at the Restoration, Milton's bitter disillusionment. Free will to Milton was not relative, depending upon a person's chance to know the truth, but absolute and unqualified. The ways of God to man are just, not the ways of man to God.

The seeds of Milton's peculiar Independency, found, as we have shown, in the midst of his attacks on the prelates, continued to grow as the Presbyterians attempted to force a state church upon England, and finally came to full light of day in *Areopagitica*. In *Christian Doctrine*, in his later pamphlets, and in *Paradise Lost* we find an elaboration and classification of his heresies, but not a fundamental departure from the principles enunciated in *Areopagitica*. Milton's hatred of conformity, his extreme and zealous individualism, had driven him far into the religious and political left-wing groups of his day. Now Milton was pushing ahead of current public opinion; he no longer represented that distrust of the prelates and their enforced ceremonies that had been so widespread, especially in English cities. Rather he was now looked upon with profound distrust by the large Presbyterian groups which controlled a substantial section of urban opinion. Numerically the Independents Milton represented were weak indeed. In 1642 they could not have counted, Masson estimates, more than eighty ministers and 23,000 members, made up mainly of the New England congregations.[95] Of 120 parish ministers in London, no more than three were suspected of Independency. By 1644 the number had increased considerably; the Anabaptists alone had fifty-four congregations in England, seven of them in London.[96] Of the New Model Army, which numbered 21,000 men, not many more than half could have been sectarians; Edward estimated that they numbered no more than a fifth or sixth. In all England in 1644, therefore, the Independents could not have numbered more than seventy or eighty thousand souls out of a total population of around four millions. True, their strength was out of all proportion to their numbers. After the battle of Marston Moor (July 2, 1644) Cromwell's star rose rapidly; on two occasions he demanded that Parliament grant toleration to the sects. What Cromwell was to the Army, Sir Henry Vane was to Parliament: a staunch and fearless Independent. And among the clergy men like John Goodwin and Henry Burton commanded respect. In his spirit of searching inquiry Milton was one with the nucleus of enlightened and determined sectarians, representing as well as anyone in England the principle Goodwin had enunciated in his *Imputatio Fidei* (1642): "If so great and considerable a part of the world as *America* is . . . was yet unknowne to all the world besides, for many generations together: well may it be conceived, not only that some, but many truths, yea and those of maine concernment and importance, may be yet unborne." Impregnated in a restless and powerful minority, this intellectual approach was destined to justify revolutionary changes in England's social and political institutions.[97]

CHAPTER II

TENDER CONSCIENCE AND MAGISTRATE'S SHADOW

URING the last four years of the Great Civil War one issue kept hardening and swelling, like ice expanding in a barrel: Should England grant toleration to the many peculiar sects and dissenting congregations? At bottom this issue helped to divide Parliament and the resolute Independent Army, burst the Commonwealth asunder, making inevitable the execution of Charles and Cromwell's military dictatorship. Differing in creed, on toleration the Army was almost unanimously insistent. After the victory at Naseby, as after Marston Moor, Cromwell's tongue was ready to speak for what lay nearest his heart. To Lenthall: "Honest men served you faithfully in this action. Sir, they are trusty; I beseech you, in the name of God, not to discourage them. . . . He that ventures his life for the liberty of his country, I wish he trust God for the liberty of his conscience." [1] Around every army campfire where voices echoed "No forcers of conscience!" Presbyterian Parliamentarians might well have lingered to ponder the strife inevitable.

Except during brief periods when Independent majorities prevailed, Parliament in these years disregarded the pleas of the tolerationists both in and out of the army. Step by step, through 1645 and 1646, Parliament had established a Presbyterian state church substantially as submitted by the Assembly of Divines. To this procedure the Independents voiced no violent protests. As yet only Roger Williams, in the van as always, had set his face against *any* state church. In 1645, it is true, John Saltmarsh in *A New Quere* gravely doubted the advisability of haste in setting up a state church: "We never read in the New Testament of a Gospel-government setled upon any that were not brought first under Gospel-obedience by power of the Word and Spirit, which thousands of Congregations in this Kingdom are not." [2] To most Independents,

67

however, the continuation of a national church seemed inevitable and necessary. They resisted heatedly only Parliament's persistent anti-tolerationist measures. When the Assembly of Divines called for the extinguishing of dozens of sectarian fires, Parliament often echoed its horror of the heretics. In the spring of 1647, the Royalist armies scattered and all England anxious for a return to peaceful ways, the Presbyterian majority in Parliament called for a disbandment of Cromwell's army with no guarantee whatever either that the arrears would be paid or that toleration would be granted the sectaries. To the army the payment of arrears (eighteen weeks for the infantry and forty-three for the horse) was a pre-eminent consideration, along with assurance of widows' and orphans' pensions and compensation for property losses; and had Parliament seen the necessity, in spite of difficulties, for raising the £330,000 to satisfy the Army's economic demands, they probably could have secured its disbandment without an assurance of toleration.[3] Regarding the Army's petitions as dangerous and mutinous, assured of the support of the London citizenry, Parliament proceeded in April and May with specific disbanding orders carrying payment of six weeks of arrears.[4] To these orders, however, the Army, despite sincere mediation on the part of Cromwell and Fairfax, refused to yield. In a series of remonstrances and representations, written by Lambert and Ireton after mass meeting of the soldiers on June 4 and 10, the Army reiterated its stand for liberty of conscience, again assuring Parliament that it had no desire to oppose or overthrow the established Presbyterian church government.[5] The army also voiced its request for the dissolution of the Parliament and the election of a new one on a wider suffrage basis. For the first time, too, it asked an unconstitutional action: the ejection from the Commons of its eleven principal Presbyterian enemies. Toward the last of June, when the eleven voluntarily withdrew, and Parliament's Commissioners were again negotiating in friendly fashion, reconcilement loomed closer. But crowds of London citizens rose in riotous protest against army influence and toleration, petitioning for thorough church establishment, support of the Covenant, protection of the king's person, and immediate disbandment of the Army.[6] More pressure from the Army, a march through the city, was followed by continued quiet negotiations. Meanwhile to Charles the officers had submitted the Army's *Heads of Proposals*, a remarkable political document representing both the democratic sentiments of the Army and its desire for practical compromise. It called for biennial Parliaments by wider suffrage; elimination of rotten Boroughs; toleration of all sects, even a limited toleration of Catholics; repeal of all laws enforcing civil penalties for ecclesiastical censure; restoration of the King; restoration of the Royalists to their civil rights and privileges; freeing of penniless debtors; vindication of the right of petition.[7] As for a state church the Army was indifferent to its establishment, provided that attendance would not be required or dissenting sects prohibited.[8] Such extreme toleration, even under pressure from the Army, Parliament could not abide. In October, 1647, it passed resolutions allowing non-conformists not Roman Catholic to worship separately, but still insisting upon compulsory attendance at state church and the prohibition of any preaching contrary to God's word! The secret treaty of Charles and the Scottish Commissioners, signed December 26, 1647, for three years assuring royal support of Presbyterian church government, and the suppression of all sects and heresies, helped to precipitate the Second Civil War. While the Independent army was crushing the royalist uprising in the summer of 1648, Parliament Presbyterians hoped fervently that Cromwell would suffer disaster. On May 2, just as the Second Civil War was opening, it passed an extreme order for the "suppression of blasphemies and heresies," providing for trials of the accused and the death penalty upon conviction and refusal publicly to recant.[8] Upon this issue, or that of Charles, which now overshadowed even toleration, the Army could temporize no longer. In March or April, 1648, after long heart-searchings and repeated prayer meetings, the officers had resolved to bring Charles "to an account for that blood he had shed and mischief he had done to his utmost against the Lord's Cause and People of these poor Nations." [9] In the Grand Remonstrance of October, 1648, the Army to Parliament formally demanded that the king be brought to justice, that future kings be elected by Parliament, that biennial Parliaments be elected by broader suffrage, that the present Parliament terminate within a reasonable time, etc.[10] In its rejection of the Army's proposals in December, Parliament probably represented the sentiment of England at large, whereas the Army, politically a century ahead of its time, was a compact and powerful minority determined to have its way. When Colonel Pride on December 6 and 7 purged Parliament of its Presbyterian members, the struggle against kingship and for toleration of the sects resolved itself into the victorious but questionable use of military power against the civil. Over the protests of Parliament and probably against the public sentiment at large, the Army had won an acceptance of the principle of toleration.

TOLERATIONIST ZEALOTS

The extreme demands of the Army for toleration represented views already formulated by the left-wing religionists of the day. As early as 1641 the *Humble Petition* prayed for right of Socinians, Arminians, Puritans, even Papists, to worship according to decree of conscience. "That which is erroneous," it concluded, "will in time appeare, and the professors of it will bee ashamed, it will perish and wither as a flower, vanish as smoake, and pass as a shadow." [11] In her reply to Edwards in 1641 Katherine Chidley had exclaimed: "Now I pray you, Master *Edwards,* would you have Magistrates, and Kings, and Princes to have more power over their subjects then over their bodies, estates, and lives? would you have them be Lords over their consciences?. . . . Where must Christ reigne then?" [12]

When Roger Williams' *The Bloudy Tenent of Persecution* appeared in 1644, the Presbyterians at once seized upon it as a tract of arch heresy. And well they might: *The Bloudy Tenent,* though somewhat loosely reasoned, contains more complete and cogent arguments for extreme toleration than any other tract of this tumultuous period. Williams points out that Christ Himself was a desperate heretic condemned by churchmen, finally crucified between two malefactors. Likewise the disciples were sectaries: *"Paul* and all true Messengers of *Jesus Christ* are esteemed seducing and seditious teachers and turners of the World upside downe." [13] If you justify persecution now, claims Williams, then these early heretics were rightfully harried. Though Jesus dwelled constantly among nonbelievers, He treated them all with love and tolerance, not with arms of steel. Because "briars, thorns, and thistles may not be in the garden of the church," Williams asks, shall we root them up? "He that is a *Briar,* that is, a *Jew,* and *Turke,* a *Pagan,* an *Anti-christian,* to day, may be (when the Word of the *Lord* runs freely) a member of *Jesus Christ* to morrow cut out of the wilde *Olive,* and planted into the true." [14] Better the ravishment of women's bodies than the rape of souls; better forced and loveless marriages than hypocritical sub-servience to a persecuting church.[15] Williams was one of the first re-formers to sense the impossibility of Protestants ever again achieving unanimity of opinion even in a broad sense; to him a dynamic and revolutionizing sectarianism boded well for a fuller application of Christian principles. Williams doubts that any church can claim perfected comprehension of the Gospel. If Paul and Jesus were to come to London, would not each sect, the papists, the prelatists, the Independents, the Presbyterians, ask them for recognition as the true church? But when one of these parties gains control of the government, "what weapons doth Christ Jesus authorize them to fight with in His cause?" [16] Thus does Williams show that however men differ, they hate to be persecuted for conscience' sake. In the midst of honest disputes and differences, toleration offers a practical working principle.

Cromwell's army was full of extreme tolerationists. Cromwell himself, Baxter reported, though ally of no sect, contended for the liberty of all. Vacancies he filled with sectaries, whether Anabaptists, Antinomians, Seekers, it made no difference, so long as they, like him and his Council, believed in liberty of conscience.[17] Though not a majority, these "proud, self-conceited, hot-headed Sectaries had got into the highest places, and were *Cromwell's* chief Favour-ites, and by their very heat and activity bore down the rest, or car-ried them along with them, and were the Soul of the Army." [18] Of all the disputes Baxter heard among the soldiers, those for extreme toleration were the most frequent and heated, the usual trend of argu-ment being that the magistrate had no authority whatever in re-ligious matters, and that every man might not only believe as he pleased, but preach his doctrine also. The numerous petitions and declarations submitted to Parliament by both officers and men show the substantial accuracy of Baxter's analysis. The famous *Heads of Proposals*, which formed the basis for numerous later demands, some among them included in editions of the *Agreement of the People*, call for a repeal of all acts compelling church attendance, reading of the prayer book, supporting the state church, or taking of the Covenant. No penalties should be imposed on those who refuse to take the Covenant, "whereby Men might be constrained to take it against their Judgments or Consciences." [19] The Paper of Proposals submitted by the agitators on November 1, 1647, contains a typical statement: "That matter of Religion, and the Ways of God's Worship are not at all intrusted by us to any Human Power, because therein we cannot exceed a Tittle of what our Consciences dictate to be the Mind of God." [20] In the *Agreement of the People* submitted to the Council of the Army on October 28, 1647, these same words had been used; the two documents are almost identical.[21] As stated in this and later *Agreements* the Levellers were indifferent as to the kind of state church instituted, "so long as it be not compulsive." Editions of the *Agreement* appearing December 11 and 15, 1648, contained the same provisions.[22] On December 21, 1648, appeared *No Papist nor Presbyterian: But the modest Proposalls of Some well-affected and Free-born People,* a pamphlet repeating some articles of the *Agreement* in different words. In this pamphlet toleration of Catholics appears as a chief tenet: "It cannot perfectly be said to be *Liberty of Conscience,* . . . that they [Catholics] or any others that weare the Title of Christians, should be excluded." [23] Though the *Agreement* presented to Parliament on January 15, 1649, excluded Catholics from toleration, the one of May 1, 1649, called for full freedom of conscience: "We do not impower . . . our . . . representatives . . . to compell . . . any person to any thing in matters of faith, Religion or Gods worship or to restrain any person from the profession of his faith, or exercise of Religion according to his Conscience." [24] Thus had the protracted and vehement discussions in the Army given rise to the extreme tolerationist views found in the Leveller *Agreements,* views inevitably coalescing with radical and revolutionary political planning. In no other army has the white heat of discussion fired so many breasts with determined revolutionary zeal, transformed so many men into prophets, ranters, and "turners of the world upside down." In this army, as in no other group of Milton's day, was given the right "to know, to utter, to argue freely according to conscience." Only through the practical exercise of this principle did the fantastic extremes of the Army visionaries finally crystallize in military control of the state.

Meanwhile the radical pamphleteers of London, fearing suppression at the hands of the Presbyterian leaders of the new state church, argued vehemently for toleration of the sects. "There have been more Books writ," said Edwards, in his first *Gangraena* (February 26, 1646), "Sermons preached, words spoken, besides plottings and actings for a Toleration, within these foure last yeers, then for all other things. Every day now brings forth Books for a Toleration. . . . Independency is become a compound of many Errors, and if Independency could once get a Toleration, wee should then see it speake out to purpose." [25] Soon to be ejected from his pulpit, Henry Burton, though old in years, still spoke with wrath and fire. In his *Vindiciae veritatis* (1645) he pressed Williams' conception of Jesus as a heretic: "You inveigh against *new truths, and new lights,* as you every where nauseously call them. . . . What say you of that precedent of the Apostles, who in the Temple daily preached a diverse doctrine, to that of the *Pharisees?* So of *John Baptist.* So of Christ." [26] In *Conformitie's Deformity* (1646) Burton argued against a state church as an enslaver of men's consciences and a disgrace to the Gospel, contending again and again that no earthly power has a right either to bind the conscience or rule the church.[27] Zealous as always, John Goodwin sent forth tract after tract, now against Edwards, now against Prynne. In *Anapologesiates Antapologias* (1646) he replies to Edwards' arguments against toleration, denying that the magistrate rightfully has any supervision whatever over the promulgation of truth or preservation from creedal delusions. For Edwards' argument that toleration means a temptation to err because man is freed from restraint, Goodwin has nothing but contempt. His reply is strikingly reminiscent of *Areopagitica*: "Is a *Toleration of errours* any other *kind of Invitation* . . . then his *Toleration* of hypocrisie, is to make men hypocrites; or then his Toleration of men to goe freely into Apothecaries shops, is a *tentation* to them to buy rats bane or other poyson to destroy their owne lives?" [28] In his *Cretensis, A Briefe Answer to an ulcerous treatise . . . Gangraena,* (1646) Goodwin replies to Edwards in a contentious and somewhat bitter manner, falling, as Milton was wont to do, from appealing constructive idealism to tirades personal and negative.

In 1645 and 1646 possibly the most colorful and resourceful tolerationist writer was Richard Overton, author of the much hated *Mans Mortallitie*. Posing as "Young Martin Mar-Priest" Overton threw aside the usual Bible-quoting methods for a sharp, witty, epithet-hurling style, dubbing the main characters of his closet farces *Sir John Presbyter* and *his superlative Holinesse, Sir Simon Synod.* The Assembly of Divines is Overton's most frequent target. In *A*

Sacred Decretall (1645), which Overton pretends has been issued by the Assembly itself, he thus characterizes the purposes and spirit of the Presbyterians:

If the *People once understand their owne Rights, and that the exaction of Tythes, is meere Theft and Robbery,* they'l have the wit . . . *to keep their owne,* cease hiring us to cheat and delude them to their faces, while they want to supply their owne necessities, and cashiere us, as they did the *Bishops;* then the Parliament will regaine their *Power,* and the People their *native Liberties* from our divine usurpation, and we shall be laid levill with the Mechannick illiterate Laicks (a wickedness not to be mentioned in the Church of God), this is MARTINS drift, that great *Anti-Clergie:* O that profane *Martin!*[29]

In *The Araignement of Mr. Persecution* (1645) Overton calls the Assembly a "gorbelly'd Idoll" and "a quagmire of croaking skip-jacke Presbyter." Next to persecution of the sects, Overton hated the tithe-gathering habit of the state clergy. Here is another vituperative, but illuminating passage:

He that lives but a small time shall surely see a *Presbyter* as fat as ever was a *Bishop;* those are enemies to all knowledge . . . all heads must be made even with the *Presbyters,* none *higher* nor none *lower,* just as *tall,* and no *taller, he that is too short must be stretched out, and he that is too long must be pared even,* least they should misse of their Prayers; *give us this day our dayly tythes;* that the *Germaine proverbe* might be fulfilled . . . 'The covetousnesse of the Preists and the mercy of God endure forever'; I would exhort them to be otherwise minded, but that I know, *venter non habet aures,* the belly hath no eares.[30]

As is apparent from the above passages, Overton was no ordinary pious Independent. Like Lilburne he had become resentful not merely of the Presbyterians alone, but of the clergy generally. In Overton's pamphlets one finds a mocking, irreligious undertone unlike Lilburne's intense, if unorthodox faith, and Walwyn's steady dependence on love and social tolerance as lubricant of human frictions.

In his constructive passages Overton's psychological and philosophical analysis of toleration problems rises to a brilliant persuasiveness. Persecution he condemns as the obstructor to all spiritual advancement. Only by degrees, in the free play of ideas, not in one great leap, can a man attain spiritual maturity. Then, still knowing only in part, a man believes what he once condemned as heresy. Such a gradual and never completed process, Overton's reasoning runs, persecution for conscience's sake can only hinder and freeze.[31] With similar incisiveness he pleads against persecution of the Catholics, an unchristian counterattack, in his opinion, on Catholic forcing of conscience. Let the Protestants know them as human beings; when they find that the Catholics are at heart as kind and good as themselves, they cannot lift up their hands against them. Here is the crux of the problem, Overton insists: failure to inquire, understand, converse, love. Become neighbors, understand each other, and you will cease to persecute. "Why should we hate and destroy one another? are we not all the creatures of one God? . . . this should provoke us to Love and peace one towards another." [32] Overton's plea for toleration of Catholics is more vigorous and wholehearted than that of any of his radical contemporaries except Roger Williams, who had even recommended that for better mutual understanding Protestants and Papists attend each others' meetings.[33] In this respect Overton shows, as we shall see, a far more humane and liberal spirit than Milton, who never overcame, even in writing his great epic, his prejudice against the Catholics.

Leader of the Levellers and friend of Overton, John Lilburne also supported the cause of toleration, though in 1645 and 1646 his pamphlets attacked mainly the prerogatives of the House of Lords and the arbitrary measures taken against him (at the instigation of Prynne) by the House of Commons. Always more secular in spirit than Burton and Goodwin, Lilburne's main interest was shifting more and more drastically to constitutional privileges, the widening of the suffrage, the curtailing of the Lords' powers, in sum to the reorganization of England's governmental structure on a more democratic basis. That Lilburne's concern for toleration, if subordinated, was still intense, is indicated by passages in *The Oppressed Mans Oppressions declared* (January 30, 1647). If Thomas Edwards claims for one magistrate the right to judge heresy, do not all magistrates at all times have the same prerogative? If so, then what of the Protestant-burning magistrates of Queen Mary's time? Them you cannot possibly condemn, runs Lilburne's argument.[34] Later, as leader of the Levellers, Lilburne supported if he did not actually write (in some editions) those sections of *An Agreement of the People* which stand unequivocally for complete toleration. Against the Presbyterian forcers of conscience, Lilburne unleashed tirades even more bitter than those of Overton, calling them "that lying, deceitfull, forsworn and bloody sect," condemning them for their "persecuting, soul-destroying, *Englands*-dividing and undoing . . . *Covenant.*" [35]

Fellow-Leveller with Overton and Lilburne, William Walwyn occupies a unique place among the tolerationists. If Professor Pease is right in his tentative surmise that Walwyn is the author of *The Brownists Humble Petition,* Walwyn anticipated by several years the extreme tolerationist views of *The Bloudy Tenent of Persecution.* Lover of Montaigne, Seneca, and Plutarch, urbane critic of Puritan theological excesses, Walwyn approached the toleration controversy with a sincere secular faith in the appeal of understanding and the efficacy of love. Alone with Lord Brooke among the tolerationists, he pamphleteered for the cause without bitterness or rancour, projecting into his tactics the principles of his creed. "God onely perswades the heart," he writes to Edwards: "compulsion and enforcement may make a confused mass of dissembling hypocrites, not a Congregation of beleevers." [36] Though a man may have all worldly comforts (as Walwyn himself had), if really conscientious he finds persecution of his faith an intolerable burden, and life thereafter sorrowful and tasteless. Of all liberties, that of conscience is to the Christian pre-eminent.[37] In *A Parable, or Consultation of Physitians upon Master Edwards* (1646) Walwyn strikes his main theme: into the labyrinth of disputes take the light of love. Whether a man's beliefs agree with yours or not, love him; love has naught to do with opinions, but with goodly conversation and manners. If a man loves you and tries to persuade you to follow his belief, and still you do not believe, can he, loving you, compel you to follow his rules? Loving, you cannot compel. Compelling, you repudiate love, Christianity itself. While knowledge is imperfect, continues Walwyn, what seems truth to one man will seem error to another, and no one can possibly be infallible in his religious perceptions. [38] In this vein Overton had written in his *The Araignement of Mr. Persecution,* and likely it is that Walwyn had been his tutor. Not until the Quakers had developed their creed of non-resistance some years later was Walwyn's ideal of brotherly controversy realized even by a small sect as a practical extension of the toleration principle.

On the Dangers of Toleration

Against the concept of toleration the Presbyterian pamphleteers waged a bitter warfare. To grant toleration meant the release of repeated numberless attacks on their cherished state church. More democratic in government, purged of its ceremonies and consecrations, the new state church could claim to represent a victory for the reforming Puritans over the prelates. The tremendous secular power of the bishops having been annihilated, no longer would it be possible to hale citizens into court for refusing to conform to the hated high-church ritual. Thus reasoning, the Presbyterians felt that a settled state church would now bring peace and harmony to England's troubled population. Why not give the state church a chance to prove its worth? Why were the Independents so certain that Presbyterianism would not in time be accepted by the whole people? Repeated attacks from the sectarians, under the protection of toleration, would mean that it had no chance to win its way.

The Presbyterians were especially fearful of tolerating unlicensed, unordained preachers, the army men in their opinion being the most dangerous of all. Baxter lamented that though at the beginning of the war an able minister had gone out with each regiment, after the battle of Edgehill they had almost all gone home, leaving the propagation of the gospel to unqualified sectarian soldiers, and showing greater reluctance to re-enter the army as the sectaries grew in power. Had the ministers not thus deserted "to an easier and quieter way of Life," the army in Baxter's judgment might have been saved for orthodoxy.[39] In their powers of disputation soldiers of weak judgment gained unwarranted confidence. To the ordinance of April 25, 1645, forbidding all but ordained ministers to preach, they paid little attention, Cromwell himself supporting them. "Are you troubled that Christ is preached?" he asked the Presbyterians. ". . . Where do you find in the Scriptures a ground to warrant such an assertion that preaching is exclusively your function?"[40] The soldiers heckled ministers, sometimes ejected them from their pulpits and preached themselves. According to Edwards Captain Pretty of Ireton's regiment once ordered a minister to stop preaching and come down from the pulpit; the minister had been drunk, he said, on Saturday night, and was therefore unworthy to preach the Gospel on Sunday morning.[41] With the people of the countryside the soldiers talked feverishly, laying down a continuous barrage of pamphlet propaganda. And the civilians, Baxter records, admiring the victorious army, were ready to accept whatever the soldiers told them.[42]

One of the main objections to toleration was that it would open the way to revolutionary ideas. This was, of course, exactly the truth. Toleration is a radical principle, radical because under its protection any religious or political concept, however strange or new, may appear, in the hands of an able disputant, plausible and workable. Thus the Presbyterians were fond of holding up the more shocking of the prevalent ideas as illustrative of the evil results of a toleration. In *A Fresh Discovery Of some Prodigious New Wandring-Blasing-Stars* (1644) Prynne points out that logically paganism, popery, and Judaism cannot be excluded if liberty of conscience prevails. If a man wishes to be an adulterer, drunkard, liar, rebel, traitor, according to his conscience, how can you consistently condemn him for it? [43] Prynne's argument may now appear disputatious hypocrisy; but his query was repeated by hundreds of Presbyterian agitators. Bastwick, in his *The Utter Routing of the whole Army of all the Independents and Sectaries* (1646), strikes a similar note, asking why prelates may not be allowed to worship again, Turks, malignants, or Papists, if a toleration is just and right.[44] To the alarmed Presbyterian clergy the results of a partial toleration already were painfully apparent: *"Schisme, Heresie, Ignorance, Prophanenesse, and Atheisme, flow in upon us, Seducers multiply, grow daring and insolent, pernicious Books poyson many souls."* [45] The Council of the City of London appealed to the Lords in May, 1646, to suppress all private congregations and schismatics, and to refuse to employ any but Presbyterians in offices of public trust. The Council was astonished to find beliefs of the most ridiculous nature boldly asserted by "swarms of sectaries, which discover themselves everywhere." [46]

The London ministers, sensing the rise in the power and popularity of the Independent clergymen, campaigned against toleration vigorously. In *A Letter of the Ministers of the City of London against Toleration*, 1646, they complained that toleration would hinder reformation, dividing the people into many factions, striking friction between England and Scotland, nullifying the Covenant, encouraging the multiplication of still more dangerous sects than then existed.[47] *Certaine Additionall Reasons,* which appeared the same day (January 1, 1646), satirically reinforced these arguments with a claim that since the Presbyterians were in the majority in the kingdom, other sects should be suppressed and toleration discontinued. There being a dearth of ministers, Independents would be employed if toleration were permitted; this would be disastrous. The author taunts the Presbyterians thus: If toleration were granted the subsistence of many ministers would be taken away: "Our Trade and living would by degrees fall to the ground by Toleration." [47] The orthodox feared that the Independent ministers would win into their congregations those men not primarily godly, but rational in outlook; thus the Presbyterian clergy would lose the honor and esteem to which they were accustomed.[48] Pressed by the radicals, the Presbyterian clergy were on the defensive; they wished to use the prestige of the Assembly of Divines and the power of the Presbyterian majority in Parliament to give them that protection against the sectaries without which the new state church could not be surely projected into the religious life of the people. But the arguments they had used against the prelates for freedom of conscience now provided the impetus for rebellion against the Presbyterian *status quo*.

The charge that toleration nullified the Covenant solemnly sworn to by all adults in 1643 was a favorite one with the Presbyterians, and rather difficult for the sectarians to dispute. The Covenant had called for not only reformation "according to the word of God and the example of the best reformed churches" but for the extirpation of "heresy, schism, profaneness, and whatsoever shall be found contrary to sound doctrine and the power of godliness." Yet the vast majority of the Independents did not now believe in extirpating any sect save Papists, and many of the soldiers were for an unlimited toleration. How, the London ministers asked, could you believe in toleration and at the same time hold to the uniformity of faith, church government, directory for worship and catechising, as called for by the Covenant? The truth was, of course, that many Independents had made mental reservations when they swore to the Covenant. Very few frankly faced the issue, as John Lilburne did, and refused to sign. Many thousands, on the other hand, had later thrown their ideas into the white hot crucible of revolutionary discussion: they emerged not only altered but far more malleable than they could have believed. To defend their opposition to the Covenant most Independents who felt the necessity of explanation simply pointed to Sir Harry Vane's insertion of the words "according to the word of God," which in their opinion were not realized in the new state church, certainly not in the extirpation of sects. In *The Smoke in the Temple,* 1646, John Saltmarsh argued with more consistency than most Independent apologists on the score of the Covenant; he insisted that each person had a right and duty to interpret his duties under the Covenant according to his own conscience. Each man was interpreter of the phrase "according to the word of God"; each man had, therefore, liberty of conscience under the Covenant. To every sect, to every variation of religious opinion the Covenant, in Saltmarsh's opinion, threw open the door.[49] The inescapable fact was, however, that the vast majority of the people interpreted the Covenant to mean Presbyterianism as embodied in the Church of Scotland.

The most widely read anti-tolerationist was of course Thomas Edwards, whose *Gangraena* appeared in three parts in 1646. In Part I Edwards lists 176 errors and heresies, and adds twenty-three in Part II, citing his sources in marginal references. Toleration to Edwards meant the unleashing of devilish forces through the kingdom. How can any one be silent, he asks, when *"our Father, our Saviour and blessed Spirit are wounded by damnable heresies and blasphemies, and many precious souls destroyed"?*[50] He complains about the preaching of illiterate mechanics, boys, and women; of the meetings of the sectaries, whereof one parish has at least eleven; of the excesses of the army preachers; of prayers offered by a minister for John Lilburne; of the revolutionary political theory being preached openly in the army; of the radical book sellers Overton and Calvert; of Overton and Walwyn, who would give all power to the House of Commons, claiming too that all people should have a voice in the selection of Parliament members; of Milton's divorce ideas; of prayers that the king be brought to judgment. All the heresy being taught so freely flows from the principle of toleration: *"The great opinion of an universall Toleration, tends to the laying all waste, and dissolution of all Religion and good manners. Now are not these Errours, Heresies and Schismes, spots and blots in our Reformation? . . . are they not the dead flies in the Apothecaries ointment, sending forth a stinking savour . . . and are not Sectaries*

*strangely suffered, connived at, keeping open meetings in the heart
of the City? yea printing with License their erroneous opinions?"* [51]
Most of the principles condemned by Edwards are commonplace
enough in the twentieth century. His method is not to confute by
logic but to condemn by mere naming, assuming that his reader
will hold up his hands in horror, as Edwards himself does, at the
end of each quotation.

Able supporters came forth to echo Edwards' pious fears. In *The
Schismatick Sifted* (1646) John Vicars called toleration a "most
damnable plea . . . the high-way to ruinate and destroy all *Religion* and *Conscience.*" [52] John Brinsley, in *Arraignment of the
Present Schism* (1646), voiced his alarm at the agitation already
caused by the sectaries; he feared that an open toleration would
mean the fall of all the orthodox churches, if not of religion itself.
Should we not strive for a blessed unity, as St. Paul urged the Co-
rinthians?[53] Jasper Maine recommended that the orthodox ministers
draw up a catechism beyond which no preacher might be permitted
to question a parishioner, all who disobey to give an account to the
magistrate.[54] Still stoutly supporting the Presbyterian cause, Herbert Palmer, in *The Duty and Honour of Church Restorers* (1646),
called for the suppression of heresies according to the Covenant,
claiming justification in the law of nature, and maintaining that
since the magistrate also has a conscience he cannot disregard it in
extirpating mischievous errors.[55] The anonymous author of *Anti-
Toleration* (1646) recommended the strict quarantining of all
seducers as the surest way to prevent the spread of schism. As with
fashions, he wrote, so with doctrines; weak human nature, especially
that of illiterate persons, is attracted to new doctrines and enticed
away by them, as a child may leave his parents for sake of an apple.
He reminds the Independents that they themselves have not always
practiced toleration, having driven Mrs. Hutchinson and other
sectaries out of New England. And has any one heard of New
England receiving the Presbyterian church as a sister government
in its midst?[56]

Though the Presbyterian arguments against toleration do not
strike the modern reader as appealingly constructive, they were much
more representative in the seventeenth century than the pleas of
tolerationists like Milton, Overton, Walwyn, and Goodwin. The Presbyterians could count upon a decisive majority in Parliament and

probably upon more than eight thousand of the nine thousand parish ministers to support their cause. Behind them, too, stood the most highly respected leaders of the Scottish nation, the aristocracy friendly to Parliament, the mass of business and professional men eager for peace and stability. To the toleration banner rallied a number of prominent sectarian clergymen, a number of zealots among their congregations, a large number of lower middle class followers of Lilburne and the Levellers, and—Cromwell's army. Had it not been for the army the Presbyterians would have succeeded in snuffing out the tolerationist pamphleteers.

MILTONIAN TOLERATION

In his early prelate tracts, while still nominally a Presbyterian and praising the Presbyterian ideal of church government, Milton had, as we know, spoken time after time for liberty of the sects. As the Presbyterians with ever sharper insistence demanded the quelling of heresy, and pointed with particular dread at the divorcers, Milton's zeal for toleration of peculiar religious ideas grew in intensity. In the *Areopagitica* his toleration had widened its base immeasurably into a secular freedom of speech and writing of profound significance. For here Milton's idealism threw off much of its religious, certainly most of its theological, overtone and attained a statesmanlike appeal of universal validity. Noble offshoot of Milton's tolerationist views, the *Areopagitica* is easily the greatest of all tolerationist pamphlets.

As Milton's tolerationist views widened, his antipathy to the Presbyterians became as bitter as that of Overton and Lilburne. By the spring and summer of 1646, goaded by fresh slurs against his divorce pamphlets, Milton's bitterness against Presbyterian intolerance was overflowing. Few lines that he ever wrote reflect a more decisive hatred:

> *On the new forcers of Conscience under the Long Parliament*
>
> Because you have thrown of your Prelate Lord,
>   And with stiff Vowes renounc'd his Liturgie
>   To seise the widdow'd whore Pluralitie
>   From them whose sin ye envi'd, not abhor'd,
> Dare ye for this adjure the Civill Sword
>   To force our Consciences that Christ set free,

And ride us with a classic Hierarchy
Taught ye by meer *A.S.* and *Rotherford?*
Men whose Life, Learning, Faith and pure intent
Would have been held in high esteem with *Paul*
Must now be nam'd and printed Hereticks
By shallow *Edwards* and Scotch what d'ye call:
But we do hope to find out all your tricks,
Your plots and packing wors then those of *Trent*
That so the Parliament
May with their wholsome and preventive Shears
Clip your Phylacteries, though bauk your Ears,
And succour our just Fears
When they shall read this clearly in your charge
New Presbyter is but *Old Priest* writ Large.[57]

As in later outbursts, Milton here shows his deep resentment of the Presbyterian attachment to their vested economic interests, their attacks on pious Independents whom he admired (no doubt including himself), but especially their binding of conscience. As for parliamentarian curbing of the Presbyterian intolerance, that was not to come until 1653, though from 1649 onward toleration broadly prevailed without express legal sanction.

When ninety Presbyterian members of the Commons were excluded by Colonel Pride on December 6 and 7, 1648, this step being necessary for the army's domination of the government, the extreme tolerationists exulted. Full liberty of conscience! The army forever! The execution of Charles was less than two months away. But in the midst of such a revolution, which was to abolish both lords and kingship, the Presbyterian ministers spoke out undauntedly and persistently against toleration, against the illegal trial of the king, against the Independents and all their principles. Intellectually narrow these ministers may have been; but their backbones were broad and stiff. On January 18, 1649, appeared *A Serious and Faithfull Representation Of the Judgments Of Ministers of the Gospell Within the Province of London*, refusing an invitation of the army officers to confer with them, this on the ground that acceptance would imply approval of the army actions. The forty-seven signers were in accord: the army had acted illegally and unjustly.[58] In *An Apologeticall Declaration Of . . . Presbyterians*, which appeared January 24, the signers lamented the opening of the door to sects and heresies: "Which doth the more sadly affect our hearts . . . because of that so eagerly endeavoured . . . Tolerating of them all [heresies] (except, in the subtill exception of theirs, of the open practise of Popery and Prelacie) as if it were that Liberty of Conscience which we have all this while engaged for." [59]

In writing *The Tenure of Kings and Magistrates,* which appeared on February 13, 1649, Milton responded vehemently to Presbyterian protests. As he says in *Defensio Secunda,* their bold attacks on the Independents had been the instigation of *The Tenure,* mainly, of course, their cries that the trial and impending execution of Charles were contrary to Christian principles. But Milton flays repeatedly their tyranny over consciences, their determination to sit in judgment over the religious opinions of their fellow citizens. Like the author of *The City-Ministers unmasked* (March 5), who couples Presbyterianism with popery and prelacy, all three depending, he says, on the power of the magistrate, persecution of every other sect, and the show of material wealth, Milton berates the Presbyterians as following in the footsteps of the persecuting prelates. Toward the end of the tract, realizing that his language against them has been harsh and bitter, he falls into a somewhat milder tone, confessing that many "faithful and good Christians" are numbered among the Presbyterians, still exhorting them, however, to mix no more in politics, and "not to compel unforcible things, in religion especially." [60] Without expanding his own views on toleration, Milton rejoices that army interference has put an end to Presbyterian domination. It is plain that he expects the Rump to confirm immediately by statute what the army has gained by force: "But now . . . their censorious domination is not suffered to be universal, *truth and conscience to be freed,* tithes and pluralities to be no more." [61] But this expectation and hope, so dear to Milton, was to suffer, like many others, a long frustration and final black-out.

Slow to act at all, the Rump finally straddled the issue. On January 6 it had received a long blast from the Scottish Commissioners protesting the measures being taken to "overturn the whole Work of Reformation, to cast off the Ministry, and introduce a Toleration of all Religions." [62] This in itself would not have affected them had not they felt it represented the feelings of the vast majority of ministers, especially those of London. With power in its hands to carry out a complete program of toleration, with the army urging action, the Rump hesitated, influenced somewhat, no doubt, by the overshadowing issue of kingship itself, soon to be abolished. On January 20 the army had presented with a petition a long draft of *An Agreement of the People,* the latter asking that a state religion be recommended but not compelled, that no one be penalized for not attending church, and that all be tolerated who professed a faith in Christ (except those who adhered to popery or prelacy).[63] Needless to say, this toleration was much more limited than that asked by the radical Levellers; but it was apparently too broad for the Rump itself. On February 17, only four days after *The Tenure* appeared, when the Rump finally answered the Declaration of the Scottish Commissioners, it incorporated a statement on toleration that must have been a shock to Milton:

> For the toleration of all religions . . . we know not whom they intend in that charge: as for the truth and power of religion it being a thing intrinsical between God and the soul . . . we conceive there is no human power of coercion thereunto . . .; but if they mean only the outward and public forms of profession or worship we know no such toleration endeavoured or intended amongst us, neither yet do we find any warrant to persecute all that do not worship God or profess to believe in the same form that we do.[64]

It is true that this statement begins and ends on a note favoring toleration; but the Rump could easily jump to the other side of the fence by virtue of the "no such toleration endeavoured or intended."

What Milton's private thoughts were on this issue during the months that followed it is difficult to say. For on March 17 he became an official of the government, attended thereafter most of the meetings of the Council of State, and acted as the pamphleteering voice of the new republic. He could hardly speak out against the Rump for not having confirmed toleration by statute; yet his next pamphlet shows that he was aware of its failure. In *Observations upon the Articles of Peace with the Irish Rebels,* which appeared May 16, 1649, Milton says to the Belfast Presbyterians that Parliament could establish universal toleration if it so wished: "Certainly were they so minded, they need not labour it, but do it, having power in their hands; and we know of no act as yet passed to that purpose." [65] But if Parliament were to establish universal toleration, Milton continues, it would be no breaking of the Covenant.

Yes, it is true that the Covenant enjoins us to quell heresy and schism; this we are endeavoring, claims Milton, but not through secular power, which has no place in these matters. From this one would conclude that though Milton wants a toleration statute, and recommends it obliquely as consisting well with the principles of the government, he is not discouraged that the Rump has not acted, being assured that persecution under the Independents cannot rear its head. He points out, however, that Parliament does not profess to tolerate atheists or malicious enemies of God and Christ;[66] thus does even Milton take refuge in the usual polemic equivocations so common among pamphleteers on the defensive.

In *Observations* Milton makes much of the tolerationist argument that the magistrate's sword should not be used against conscience: It is impossible for any power to win over a man's heart by force; any such attempt on the part of the magistrate can end only in helplessness and frustration. In matters of civil conduct, yes, the magistrate can intervene; but a man's conscience is an inviolable possession. Christ and his apostles had no power but persuasion to win the hearts of men. And when any church has sought and obtained greater protection and aid of the civil power than the apostles had, then, Milton insists, began its ruin and degeneration.[67] Our task, even according to the Covenant, is not to persecute men, but to confute their errors in relatively peaceful ways: by sound preaching, able conversing, and judging by the congregation. "For the conscience, we must have patience till it be within our verge."[68] And no minister who "understood his high calling, or sought not to erect a secular and carnal tyranny over spiritual things, would neglect this ample and sublime power conferred upon him, and come a begging to the weak hand of magistracy."[69]

As in *The Tenure* Milton is writing against Presbyterian ministers, this time of the Presbytery of Belfast. Against their argument that the Independents have broken the Covenant, Milton is particularly biting and effective, though not altogether fair. As he points out, the Covenant did not demand the extirpation of error by force; but every intelligent person who swore to the Covenant, certainly Milton himself, had realized that in the minds of Parliament extirpation of error had meant persecution of people. Against the Covenant Milton uses, however, a more appealing and constructive argument. If it involved absolute promises, then nothing whatever criminal that the king might have done would absolve people from their pledge; if, on the other hand, the promises were conditional upon the attainment of liberty both secular and religious, and these impossible so long as the king lived, then what we have done, concludes Milton, is no breach but fulfilment.[70] On this analysis such vindication as time can offer leans to Milton and the Independents: No oath, as the Quakers were afterward to assert, can have an absolute validity.

In *Observations* Milton reveals his limitations as a tolerationist: he stopped far short of the extreme views of Overton, Walwyn, and Williams. For although he makes it plain that, like Cromwell, he would let the Jews live in peace, he is bitter against the Catholics, particularly the Irish, whom he calls "a mixed rabble, part papists, part fugitives, and part savages, guilty in the highest degree of all these crimes." As in later tracts he characterizes the Catholic Church as Antichrist, and calls for war against it to a murderous end:

He . . . who makes peace with this grand enemy and persecutor of the true church, he who joins with him, strengthens him, gives him root to grow up and spread his poison, removing all opposition against him, granting him schools, abbeys, and revenues, garrisons, towns, fortresses . . . he of all true protestants may be called most justly the subverter of true religion.[71]

Here was a blind spot in Milton's mind (or a peculiar coldness of nature) that was to remain fixed until the end of his days. In his intolerance of Catholicism he was representative, not of the choice spirits of his age, but of the mass of bigoted Englishmen for whom he was later to speak such contempt. And what of the Presbyterians? Were they to be allowed henceforth to speak out from their pulpits, advising the magistrates, claiming the right to criticise openly and freely? These privileges Milton would forbid them. Teach justice and obedience, as is your duty, he admonishes them, but stay out of state disputes; preach not on alterations of government, or stir up your synods and assemblies to remonstrances and petitions.[72] Thus, his party's prestige now a primary consideration, does Milton argue against the principles of his *Areopagitica*. Though the tolerationist ideals of the army contradicted curiously their summary military action against Parliament, it cannot be claimed that on the whole they followed Milton's advice or the persecuting precedent of their enemies: After a few repressive measures they in the main allowed the Presbyterians to keep not only their pulpits and incomes, but also their liberty of conscience and freedom of speech. One cannot, of course, disclaim as persecution Cromwell's hideous massacres at Drougheda and Wexford, where defenceless women and children were butchered without mercy, outrages for which Cromwell claimed the favor of a benevolent God. Such were the fruits of Puritan intolerance, a dark hatred from which Milton's capacious spirit never quite soared free.

Though he favored repressive action against Catholics and Presbyterians, both of whom he regarded as traitorous state factions, Milton still hoped that the Rump not only would pass a toleration statute but also abolish the state church altogether, leaving the support of the ministry to voluntary contributions alone. In both these expectations he was disappointed. The Rump made no move to abolish the state church, or even to disturb the orderly procedures of the Presbyterian church government, and showed every evidence of wishing to placate Presbyterian sentiment. On toleration it struck a middle ground that pleased no one. On June 29, 1649, a bill was twice read to remove penalties for not coming to church; a first step toward toleration, this bill did not become law until September 27, 1650.[73] In August, 1649, an act was introduced for the protection of tender consciences against prevailing penalties of several laws; but this bill died in committee. In its *Declaration of the Parliament of England, in Vindication of their Proceedings*, September 28, 1649, the Rump defended its toleration policy. After complaining against Presbyterian persecution, which had used "the foul Names of Heresy, Blasphemy, and Schism" for true reforming Christianity, the *Declaration* announces the intention of Parliament to "take away all Obstructions and Hindrances to the Growth of Religion"; to consider to this end (for possible repeal) those laws now on the statute books that tender consciences have found coercive. Nevertheless, the *Declaration* continues, Parliament will not suffer liberty of conscience to be abused; it will proceed promptly and vigorously against all offenders! [74] Whether or not Rump made the latter statement with tongues in cheeks, it did take some intolerant measures in the months that followed. On February 1, 1650, it ordered a blasphemous book, *a Flying Fiery Roll*, to be burnt by the hangman;[75]

on June 14 it initiated repressive measures against the Ranters;[76] and on August 9 it threatened punishment for the expression of "several Atheisticall, blasphemous, and execrable opinions." [77] Not to be thought remiss in upholding public morality, the Rump passed acts against adultery, immodest dresses and face-painting, and profane swearing, the penalties of the latter vice ranging from thirty shillings for an earl's swearing freedom to three shillings four pence for that of a wharfman or servant![78] Aside from such individual measures, however, the Rump took no decisive action for or against the broad toleration so earnestly advocated by the Independents before Pride's Purge.

With some justice both enemies and friends of the Commonwealth accused the Independents of denying, after gaining power, that liberty of conscience they had so ardently proclaimed. Prynne wrote: *"I . . . protest against all these their proceedings . . . especially by pretended Saints, who hold forth nothing but justice, righteousness, liberty of conscience, and publick freedome in all their Remonstrances, whiles they are triumphantly trampling them all under their armed iron feet."* [79] In a temperate plea the Catholic apologist John Austin sought leniency for the Papists, pointing to the persecution and execution of the Jesuit Wright as a violation of Christian decency. Upon the scaffold, Austin relates, the officiating minister had told Wright he could still save his life if he would turn protestant; but the Jesuit resolutely preferred his faith to his life: "Against what have we . . . fought all this while," asks Austin, "but coercency in Religion . . . but *liberty of tender Consciences? is this to hold forth the truth in love? is this to instruct in meeknesse?"* [80] In the general jail delivery of consciences, are those of the Papists alone to be kept in prison? In that remarkable tolerationist tract, *Zeal Examined* (1652), the anonymous author evaluates the proposal to set up a model of Gospel ordinances as pharisaical intolerance.[81] And Roger Williams, as we shall see, looked with as much displeasure as Milton upon the proposals for propagation of the Gospel; he felt that the bloody tenet was gaining ascendancy among the Independents themselves. George Fox complained that "some are beat, and stockt, and knockt down" for conscience' sake.[82] In his *De Corpore Politico* (1652) Thomas Hobbes describes the inevitable transition toward persecution among those who proclaim liberty of conscience. First a demand also for liberty of action, and the freedom to persuade others; once this is achieved, the former sufferers want the magistrate to forbid all opinions except their own.[83] One must admit for Milton's time the general accuracy of Hobbes' analysis: the victorious Presbyterians persecuted the Independents; and the Independents, having gained the ascendancy, were unwilling to practice their more extreme ideals of toleration.

MILTON ON THE STATE CHURCH

In February, 1652, a group of fifteen Independent ministers alarmed Milton and other extreme opponents of a state church by proposing to Parliament certain measures for the propagation of the Gospel. Parliament was petitioned to set up a committee in each county to eject scandalous or disaffected ministers; to appoint, on the basis of the committees' reports, successors to the ministers thus ejected; to require every one to attend church each Sabbath, except those abstaining for conscience' sake; to require all persons not attending the state church to meet each Sabbath in public places, giving notice to the magistrates of their meetings; to prohibit people from preaching who did not believe in salvation.[84] That army officers like Whalley and Okey had concurred with the petitioners suggested that some of the leading Independents were now losing the zeal for religious freedom that had characterized their strivings before Pride's Purge. Referred finally to a committee of fourteen of which Cromwell was a member, the proposals emerged in March, 1653, substantially unchanged in meaning. The House passed a resolution "That the Magistrate hath Power, in Matters of Religion, for the Propagation of the Gospel," thus settling its determination to keep the state church.[85] The Rump approved only the first three proposals, however, these being for the maintenance of the ministry at public expense, for trial of ministerial candidates in lieu of a testimonial by "six Godly Ministers and Christians," and for the appointment of county committees to receive testimonials. The fourth article, which provided for the ejection of ministers, the Rump did not act upon, whether from tolerationist convictions, pressure of other business, or desire to postpone the issue, can hardly be determined. Only a few weeks remained before Cromwell's rough dissolution; in that time the Rump did not return to the delicate issues of the proposals.

Two of Milton's friends were closely interested in the actions of the ministers. That rigid tolerationist, John Goodwin, as he hesitatingly explains in *The Apologist Condemned* (1653), had been persuaded by Nye to subscribe to the proposals, not as approving them entirely, but as measures worthy of consideration by the committee.[86] Goodwin had been attacked satirically as a tolerationist turncoat in *An Apology for Mr. John Goodwin. Thirty Queries* (1653) and *The Apologist Condemned* vigorously reassert Goodwin's extreme tenets. In *Thirty Queries,* upholding the validity of each person's spiritual insight and right of interpretation, Goodwin asks what tests of ability to preach the early Christians had to pass. And what person can claim infallibility in spiritual matters, has been wholly free from error? Goodwin's antipathy to secular interference is pronounced in both pamphlets. Always, he claims, men in authority have been enemies of Jesus, refusing to receive the truth and purity of the Gospel,[87] possessing "an itching humor, and love to be tampering in matters of Religion . . . and to have Religions and Worships of their own calculation . . . how blind or insufficient soever they be for the managing or regulating such an affair." [88] In view of these statements it is unlikely that Goodwin had swayed very far from his persistent tolerationist zeal. A fairer antagonist than Milton, Goodwin is seldom merely contentious or personal. But in their daring and unorthodox interpretations of the Scriptures, in their assumption of every man's capacity for redemption, above all in their humane tolerationist principles, Goodwin and Milton are philosophical brothers. Though overloaded with Biblical allusions, scarcely a page of Goodwin's pamphlets lacks a sentence of twentieth-century pertinence.

Another of Milton's friends immediately concerned with the ministers' proposals was Roger Williams, who had arrived in England early in 1652. In a letter written to Winthrop in 1654 Williams shows that during his time in England he had been on familiar terms with Milton: "The Secretary of the Council, (Mr. Milton) for my Dutch I read him, read me many more languages." [89] On April 28, 1652, Williams sent forth *The Bloody Tenent Yet More Bloody,* a bold and uncompromising assertion of his principles, prefaced by an address to Parliament and followed by *An Appendix to the Cleargie of the four Great Parties.* Again, as in *The Bloudy Tenent,* Williams claims for Papist and Arminian outcasts complete freedom of conscience, praising the citizenship of conscientious Catholics, calling upon his countrymen to have full faith in Christian persuasion, none in unchristian persecution.[90] The priests of all religions he condemns as "the greatest *peace-breakers* in the *world* . . '. they . . . never rest stirring up *Princes* and people against any . . . that shall oppose their own *religion* and *conscience,* that is in plaine *English,* their *profits, honours* and *bellies.*" [91] In his address to Parliament, though he has high praise for their achievements, Williams warns them against losing their zeal in the moment of victory, allowing their former fine professions to "prove but a fading colour." [92] Let them now surpass all other statesmen in the extension of toleration to Papists, Arminians, and all other dissenters; let them guard against shipwreck of souls on the rock of the bloody tenet.

In his *Appendix to the Cleargie* Williams analyzes with styptic clarity the persecution inherent in the fifteen proposals, which demonstrate what mercy to souls, he says, may be expected from the Independents themselves. By these proposals hundreds, perhaps thousands, of Presbyterian and Episcopalian clergymen will be ejected against the consent of their parishioners and to the sorrow of a multitude of citizens. As for preaching without ordination, yes, the proposals allow it, but only upon swallowing a like bitter pill, an *approbation* in which two ministers must concur. If a man's conscience forbids him to attend the established church, the proposals permit him to worship in private, provided that he notify the magistrate; who may, no one knows how soon, become his persecutor; thus do the proposals require him to deliver himself up to his enemies, concludes Williams. To allow freedom within slavery, to use plummet, line, rule and square to circumscribe man's soaring spirit—such, Williams claims, is the contradiction of the new model.[93] All this is but "Winding Staires and back dores" to that persecution the Independents have universally deplored. Fresh from his counter-attack on John Cotton, Williams shrewdly evaluates the "Proposals" as a reflection of the Massachusetts state-and-church relationship: liberty of conscience accepted in theory and forbidden in practice. Exiled by the prelates, the Massachusetts divines had in turn harried Williams out of the land. On the unravelling of such an old pattern he could speak with special precision.

Williams was now in a solid position to aid his cause. Not only was he a close friend of Sir Harry Vane, the most powerful member of the Rump; he talked frequently with Cromwell himself. From the preface of *The Fourth Paper Presented by Maior Butler,* which appeared May 30, a month after *The Bloody Tenent Yet More Bloody,* it is evident that Williams was present at at least one meeting of the committee when the proposals of the ministers were considered. He tells of Cromwell's blunt statement to the committee: *"His Excellency with much* Christian zeal *and* affection *for his own* Conscience *professed also, That he had rather that* Mahumetanism *were permitted amongst us, then that one of Gods Children should be persecuted."* In this tract Williams again appeals directly to Parliament "to proclaim a true and absolute *Soul-freedom* to all the people of the Land impartially; so that no person be forced to *pray* nor *pay,* otherwise then as his Soul believeth and consenteth." [94]

Meanwhile Milton too had been watching anxiously the turn of events, at one with Vane and Williams in the hope for sharp resistance to the ministers' proposals. How could he help? He knew that Cromwell, who had always stood staunchly for toleration, was on the key committee and that his personal prestige might overweigh all. It is likely that he had heard of Cromwell's decisive testimony, perhaps from Williams himself. Yet in Milton's mind Cromwell's stand was still a matter of doubt. Might he not still for politic purposes maintain the state church, even deny those extreme tolerationist tenets he had often expressed in the army councils? Well, if Cromwell wavered, Harry Vane might hold him steady: in Vane no retreat on *this* principle.

To sway Cromwell toward Vane's position Milton wrote two complimentary sonnets that reflect his intense anxiety for the cause at stake. Even in the heading of the sonnet to Cromwell he shows his resolution to make his appeal unmistakable: "To the Lord Generall Cromwell May 1652. On the proposalls of certaine ministers at the Committee for Propagation of the Gospell." After complimenting Cromwell on his military and civil achievements, Milton warns that "new foes aries, threatening to bind our soules with secular chaines." Then, as though Cromwell cannot fail to want the greatest liberty of conscience, he concludes:

Helpe us to save free conscience from the paw
Of hireling wolves whose Gospell is their maw.[95]

In the sonnet to Vane Milton reserves his highest tribute for Vane's understanding of the exact relationship that should exist between church and state:

Both spirituall powre and civill, what each meanes
What severs each thou 'hast learnt, which few have don.
The bounds of either sword to thee wee ow.
Therefore on thy firme hand religion leanes
In peace, & reck'ns thee her eldest son.[95]

The sonnet to Vane was presented to him on July 8.[96] Though dictated to different amanuenses, the two poems must have been written, therefore, within a few days or weeks of each other. It is plain that Milton was recommending Vane's advice to Cromwell in the most acceptable and yet in the most unequivocal manner possible. About Cromwell, on the state church issue, Milton was beginning to have doubts. The two sonnets reflect both his fears and his hope of deliverance from England's religious perils. But his appeal, like so many others, ended in frustration: neither Milton's advice nor any other convinced Cromwell that the state church should not be maintained. The decision of the Rump of March, 1653, to use civil power to support the church could hardly have been taken without Cromwell's approval.

Milton was too keen an analyst to err in selecting Vane as the repository of tolerationist confidence. Though we have no statement from Vane himself about the ministers' proposals, his brother Charles was on the committee that protested against them, and Milton's sonnet is itself evidence that Vane was sharply antagonistic to the coercion inherent in the suggested legislation. To this day Vane's own religious views remain vague and misty; but on the question of toleration he was clear and consistent from youth to death. To Vane, as to Williams, American intolerance had been a rough, unforgettable training school. As the twenty-three year old governor of Massachusetts he had encouraged Mrs. Anne Hutchinson to expound her strange antinomian theories, half believed them himself, protected her against incipient persecution.[97] On the issue of tolerating Mrs. Hutchinson Winthrop, in April, 1637, had defeated him for the governorship; whereupon Vane returned to England. In

November Winthrop and the orthodox ministers banished Mrs. Hutchinson from Massachusetts, accusing her of "speaking in derogation of the ministers among us," breaking the peace of the state; to her objection, "That's a matter of conscience, Sir," Winthrop replied, "Your conscience you must keep or it must be kept for you." [98] The verbatim report of her examination illuminates more clearly than Winthrop's cautious journal the persecuting, witch-burning psychology against which Vane rebelled; one reads the drama even yet with shame and dismay.

Through his long leadership in the Long Parliament and after, Vane supported all extreme tolerationist measures. In *The Bloudy Tenent* Williams alludes to a "heavenly speech" on toleration, evidently by his friend Vane. Baillie regretfully reported that "the great shott of Cromwell and Vane is to have a libertie for all religions, without exceptions," [99] and that Vane "whom we trusted most, had given us many signs of his alteratione; twyce at our table prolixie, earnestlie, and passionatelie had reasoned for a full libertie of conscience to all religions." [100] In 1647 the unitarian John Bidle prefaced an explanation of his views by an appeal to Vane for help against persecution: "My adversaries . . . have . . . instigated the magistrate against me, hoping by his sword, (not that of the Spirit) to uphold their Will-worship. . . . It will be your part, Honoured Sir . . . to examine the business impartially, and to be a helper to the truth." [101] Vane rose in Parliament and moved that Bidle be freed.[102] Like Williams he was unwilling even to persecute the Catholics.[103] In *The Retired Mans Meditations* (1655), written after his forced retirement from public life, Vane insists that the magistrate "is not to intrude itself into the office and proper concerns of Christs inward Government and rule in the conscience." [104] The next year, in *A Healing Question propounded and resolved,* he inveighs again against magistrates' coercion, complaining that since the fall of the bishops and the Presbyterian persecutors, "the same spirit is apt to arise in the next sort of Clergy, that can get the ear of the Magistrate." [105] In 1659, when Vane was returned to the Commons by the electorate of Whitchurch, he spoke against the Declaration of a fast, a measure that denounced heresies and the remissness of the magistrates in controlling them: "This imposition upon consciences is, I fear, the setting up of that which you always cried out against. . . . It is a coercing of conscience." [106] That Vane's ideal of toleration was completely sincere no one has questioned. Neither king nor dictator daunted him, nor death itself. No one of the brave thousands barbarously executed for king or Parliament faced the ordeal, or defended his principles at his trial, with more extreme intrepidity than Vane.[107]

When Cromwell dissolved the Rump on April 20, 1653, Milton, since 1649 Latin Secretary to the Commonwealth, supported Cromwell rather than Vane, Bradshaw, and Overton. This we know from his continuance as Latin Secretary and from his praise of Cromwell in *A Second Defence,* wherein appears no mention of Vane. Had he felt strongly enough that Cromwell's action was tyrannical, or that from him there was no hope of disestablishment, he would have resigned his position in protest; if he was present at the Council meeting on the afternoon of April 20, when Cromwell appeared and ordered its dissolution, he might even have been impelled to support, with a firm sentence or two, his friend Bradshaw's calm defence of constitutional privilege. Much as he admired Vane and Bradshaw, however, Milton was no friend of constitutional privilege; he had approved every action of the army in forcing its will upon Parliament; he then visualized in Cromwell an instrument of divine justice deserving the powers of a dictator. Even in December, 1653, when Cromwell assumed the Protectorate for which the Instrument of Government prescribed continuance of the state church, Milton continued to support him. The Instrument of Government provided, it is true, a broader toleration of Protestant dissenters than the Rump had written into statute.[108] But Milton wanted the state church abolished altogether.

By May, 1654, Milton had discovered that even a man subject to no inner tyranny whatever may deprive others of outward liberty; his praise of Cromwell in *A Second Defence* is qualified by friendly warning, and laudation of his administration followed by a direct admonition on the question of the state church: "But if you," he says, addressing Cromwell, "who have hitherto been the patron and tutelary genius of liberty, if you, who are exceeded by no one in justice, in piety, and goodness, should hereafter invade that liberty which you have defended, your conduct must be fatally operative, not only against the cause of liberty, but of the general interests of piety and virtue. Your integrity and virtue will appear to have evaporated, your faith in religion to have been small." [109]

Two allusions in the above passage indicate that Milton is here speaking of the state church itself. The first is the words, "the general interests of piety and virtue." When we remember at this point Milton's tirades against paid religious servants of the state, we can only conclude that he believes the paid ministers of the Protectorate will cause the people to "have an abject and unworthy opinion of themselves," that the ministers will rather serve the Protectorate than the spirit of their calling. Then Cromwell's faith in religion will appear, he writes, "to have been small." Only two years before Milton had appealed to Cromwell to sever church and state; it had not been evident at that time, therefore, that Cromwell intended to maintain a union of the two, and his extreme Independency had led Milton and others to believe that he would insist as they did on complete separation. But Cromwell had struck out in the opposite direction from which Milton hoped he would follow. Parliament now being at work on the revision and acceptance of the Instrument of Government, Cromwell will be thought insincere, Milton suggests, if he insists with a number of Parliament members upon a close union of church and state. Not content with this, Milton admonishes him directly: "Then, if you [110] leave the church to its own government, and relieve yourself and other public functionaries from a charge so onerous, and so incompatible with your functions; and will no longer suffer two powers, so different as the civil and the ecclesiastical, to commit fornication together, and by their mutual and delusive aids in appearance to strengthen, but in reality to weaken and subvert, each other; if you shall remove all . . . persecution out of the church (but persecution will never cease, so long as men are bribed to preach the gospel by a mercenary salary, which is forcibly extorted, rather than gratuitously bestowed, which serves only to poison religion and to strangle truth,) you will then effectually have cast those money-changers out of the temple, who do not merely truckle with doves but with the Dove itself, with the Spirit of the Most High." [111] We cannot mistake this passage: Milton is admonishing Cromwell straightforwardly, reaffirming his belief in complete severance of religious and civil affairs, and his hatred of tithes. It is impossible, he tells Cromwell, to remove persecution out of the church as long as there is any state church at all.

In his desire for abolition of the national church, Milton repre-

sented only a small fanatical minority of the English nation. Though
in American political theory and practice the complete separation
that Milton demanded is accepted as axiomatic, public opinion in
England does not even yet support Milton's view; the national
church is still strong and powerful, its income secure, its influence
persistent. Cromwell and his officers in all their radical theorizing
had not unanimously favored the total abolition of the church. In
that remarkably complete and moderate statement of the Army's
position *A True State of the Case* (1654), the apologist affirms
that "the Body of the Army never declared themselves either
against the Magistrates power in matters of religion, or that the
Magistrate might not hold forth a publick Profession of Doctrine
and Discipline . . . but moved only for the taking away of all
Coercive power . . . and for the repealing of all Acts imposing
penalties for not coming to Church." [112] Even the Levellers, the
most truly popular party of the day, had not made disestablishment
a tenet of the many *Agreements*. To any state church "so it be not
compulsive" they were agreeable. What the army and the Levellers
did want, and certainly consistent in Cromwell's own philosophy
and practice, was the broadest possible toleration of peculiar tenets
outside the church. Milton, on the other hand, wanted both disestablishment and toleration, though on the score of toleration he
was less charitable than Cromwell and the Levellers. As the passage
Defensio Secunda indicates, Milton felt that any ministry supported
by public funds would find itself impelled to persecute its com-
petitors. In this Milton was right: even under Cromwell the national
church persecuted the strange new theorists such as seekers and
Quakers. Few pamphleteers pleaded, however, for disestablishment;
whereas hundreds demanded liberty of conscience.

Though not representative of the nation, the Barebones Parliament, like Milton, wanted to annihilate the national ministry. The
Saints held sway in Parliament from July to December, 1653,
fearless zealots like Christopher Feake preaching meanwhile to
crowded audiences at Blackfriars. The moderates in Parliament,
backed by the army, had in July succeeded in preventing a vote
on the motion to abolish tithes. But the Fifth Monarchy men would
not yield to Cromwell's desire for compromise. On November 17
Parliament resolved to abolish patronage. On December 10 they
rejected Owens' scheme for church establishment,[113] essentially

that of the "Fifteen Proposals" of 1652, a vote referred to by Roger Williams as "fifty-six against priests and tithes, opposite to the vote of fifty-four who were for them." [114] The Saints accused Cromwell of not carrying out his promise to abolish tithes; Feake called him "the most dissembling and perjured villain in the world." [115] "I am more troubled now," said Cromwell, "with the fool than with the knave." [116] Imprisoned by the officers, Feake sent letter after letter to his congregation; though praising the original purposes of the army, he complains that they have now fallen away from prayer and piety: *"But Oh!* Oh my Bowels, my Bowels! *The gradual declension and defection since* Worcester, *with what words shall I bewail it? how have all the things of Christ been neglected?"* [117] In more specific terms John Canne also accused the army leaders of losing their former zeal for reformation; whereas in the old days men asked boldly for abolition of the national ministry, now the paid ministry is defended by those who pretend to extreme nonconformity.[118] Such was the spirit that animated the Barebones Parliament; though more secular in spirit than they, Milton was in complete sympathy in their hopes for disestablishment, and certainly he shared their disappointment in Cromwell.

In *A True State of the Case* the army apologist complains against the extreme notions of the Saints: their preference for godly, poorly educated parliamentarians to men of great knowledge and ability, but uninspired; their attack on the national ministry as unchristian; their "hot men at the *Black-Fryers* Meeting, who pronounced all the Reformed Churches to be as the Out-works to Babylon"; their disclaiming persecution while demanding ejection of the whole ministry; their pleading for separation of the civil and religious powers while insisting that saints should become "Governors and Princes"; their determination to destroy property and undermine the fundamental laws of the land.[119]

Milton himself criticized the Barebones Parliament, much as he sympathized with their religious aims. In *Defensio Secunda* just preceding a panegyric of Cromwell, he dismisses the achievements of the Saints with the following: "They meet; but do nothing; and having wearied themselves with their mutual dissentions, and fully exposed their incapacity to the observations of the country, they consent to a voluntary dissolution." [120] Later he glanced at them distrustfully, saying that if civil and religious powers were separated, there would be "no more pretending to a fifth monarchie of the Saints." [121] Nevertheless Milton was in principle somewhat of a Fifth Monarchy man himself. Like them, he placed supreme emphasis on godliness, though in his ideal he had incorporated perhaps unconsciously the virtues of Greek and Roman manhood. Like the Saints, Milton believed that the good man, not the well trained man, is likely to be the better ruler.

When Milton wrote *Defensio Secunda,* the Instrument of Government was functioning as England's first written constitution; nothing could have gone into the Instrument that was not agreeable to Cromwell. Here, then, was another opportunity for Cromwell to separate the functions of church and state. This, however, Cromwell failed to do, as was to be expected from his opposition to the Barebones fanatics. The Instrument provides specifically not only for a state church, but also for the continuance of tithes until such time as maintenance "less subject to scruple and contention" could be devised. In March, 1654, the Protector issued ordinances making provision for the appointments of ministers to benefices and for the appointment of a general Commission of triers, assisted by a committee of three "godly" persons in each county, to approve all appointments to benefices. The right of patronage was upheld. Under this arrangement men of all Protestant persuasions except Anglican and Catholic might hold benefices at the will of the patrons, no ordination being required; each minister was subject, however, to possible ejection by a separate committee set up in each county, among other things for "blasphemous or atheistical opinions." [122] How objectionable all this was to Milton, who was often present at discussions of the Council of State, may be imagined. Cromwell's rejection of the Saints' policy, his acceptance of a state church in the Instrument of Government, and now his bolstering of the state church by specific ordinances—three times he had disappointed Milton on this issue. Yet that for which Milton and other liberal leaders had sought from the Rump for four years, toleration of Protestant dissenters, is inherent in the Instrument, written into statute for the first time.[123] One would have thought that the guarantee of toleration would have called forth shouts of jubilation, state church or not. But Milton makes no mention of this achievement. Only when one considers Cromwell's repeated failures from Milton's viewpoint, as against Cromwell's decisive step toward a broad toleration, can he estimate the full weight of Milton's admonitions in *Defensio Secunda.*

During the four years which remained before Cromwell's death, Milton wrote nothing further to censure his policy of a state church. But in February, 1659, less than two months before Richard Cromwell's Parliament met, Milton came forth with a pamphlet which showed, whatever his reasons had been for remaining silent, that he had lost none of his fervent conviction on the subject of the separation of civil and religious government. The full title of his most decisive argument in itself indicates his stand: *A Treatise of Civil Power in Ecclesiastical Causes; Shewing that it is not lawfull for any power on Earth to compel in matters of Religion.* The foundation upon which he builds his reasoning is this: since the Scripture is the foundation of the Protestant religion, and since Protestants agree that only the individual conscience can be the final interpreter of the Scripture, no particular church can be the final arbiter of religious belief, much less the magistrate.[124] Religion is an affair of the inner man, the spirit; not outward force can effect or change man's spiritual nature against his will; religion must be voluntary to be religion at all.[125] Furthermore, for the church to call upon the magistrate is an indication that the spiritual power of the church has dwindled to nothing; that, whereas conscience should regulate force and authority, for the magistrate to force conscience is to give material force an unnatural and unchristian superiority. To force people into the church against their beliefs is to make them hypocrites instead of honest men: "We read not that Christ ever exercised force but once, and that was to drive profane ones out of his temple, not to force them in." [126] Then Milton returns to his old theme, that under the Gospel men are free to stand upright before God and Christ; now that man is filial and not servile to God, least of all should he be servile to the magistrate. Having new Christian liberty under the Gospel, man no longer should suffer in religion "that law of terror and satisfaction belonging now only to civil crimes; and thereby in effect abolishes the gospel." [127]

But Milton is not content with establishing his arguments that individual conscience is the ultimate authority for religious belief. He proceeds to answer the argument for a state church advanced by Ireton,[128] Cromwell's son-in-law and chief lieutenant, and many ministers, including John Owen,[129] that the magistrates of Israel having had both civil and religious power, such a plan has the authority of the Bible and should be adopted. This precedent should not be followed Milton says, first, because under the law of the Old Testament, religion, engraved in stone, was followed according to the letter of the law; under the Gospel, however, religion, being of the spirit, should be obeyed according to the persuasion of the Gospel. That the magistrates of Judah were divinely taught how to enforce the law (present-day magistrates having no such aid), and magistrates used force only to inflict punishment for idolatry and for practices forbidden by the letter of Moses' law, are further reasons Milton advances for not following the example of the Hebrews: He concludes by reiterating his demand: the complete divorce of state from church.[130]

Near the date of March 3, 1660, when the land was waiting to break into open acclamation of Charles II, Milton incorporated into the first edition of his *Readie and Easie Way* a final and uncompromising demand for disestablishment. Reviewing briefly his old arguments for separation of civil and religious powers, he adds that if the state avoided interference with ecclesiastical matters, it would remove much hypocrisy and contention from public life. If churches, on the other hand, would abstain from attempting to influence state counsels, there would be less faction in choosing parliament members, less opportunity for ambitious military leaders to dissolve parliaments. In the second edition of *The Readie and Easie Way,* published in April, 1660, only two weeks before the Restoration, Milton omitted his demand for disestablishment, stressing only full liberty of conscience.[131] In the remaining fourteen years of his life he made no formal demand for abolition of the state church.

MILTON ON TITHES

Like every other institution, traditional tithing during the Civil War underwent a searching scrutiny by radical pamphleteers. Against tithes Milton directed much of his sharpest, most penetrating social criticism; and since the population at large, but especially the poor, annually felt the economic pinch of tithes,

Milton voiced a complaint much more representative than his appeals for toleration and disestablishment.

By Milton's time over one-third of all the tithes in England were in the hands of laymen: for centuries both laymen and clergy had insisted with ever increasing strictness on tithe payments as a religious and patriotic duty, although before 1200, certainly before 800, tithing in England had been neither universal nor mandatory.[132] To the ruling classes tithes gradually assumed the aspect of an important vested privilege to be properly guaranteed by civil statutes. Originally the tithe had been used for the poor and the necessary expenses of the church, being divided among the parishes of a bishopric; but between 800 and 1200, as Selden points out in *Historie of Tithes* (1618) the patron of a church assumed the right to bestow the tithe income on whom he pleased, and often on laymen.[133] Princes and bishops joined to collect tithes with the understanding that part of the tithes were to be infeudated to the princes by the church.[134] The summoner in Chaucer's "Frere's Tale" personifies the evils of enforced tithing. Bitterly Wycliffe had inveighed against tithes, pointing out that Christ and his apostles had lived from free will offerings and the labor of their hands; but now the priests persecute the poor and harry them into court; though Christ never constrained any one to give. From wicked priests the people should withdraw their tithes.[135] But Wycliffe's protests against tithes went unheeded. Kings and clergy gradually enforced payment more and more firmly. While dissolving the monasteries and appropriating to himself over one-third of all the tithes of England, Henry VIII enacted a strict law for the payment of tithes throughout his realm. Henry and his successors to the time of William III, often through estate middle men, made 5664 grants of tithes to their followers, mainly of the nobility and gentry, thus diverting to laymen much of the income originally in the possession of the church.[136] At the enormous and prolonged infeudation of tithes Selden glances distrustfully.[137] After gathering the names of the beneficiaries of Henry's rape of the church, Sir Henry Spelman so feared the wrath of the nobility and gentry that his *History of Sacrilege*, though written partly in 1632, did not appear until 1698. The startling nature of his researches was not, therefore, known to the tithe critics of Milton's day. Though Spelman wrote to prove the calamities almost invariably fell upon those to whom the tithes were diverted, thus upholding the sacred right of the church to its tenth, his book is a curious confirmation of the unobtrusive greediness of the rich and noble. Among the radical critics only Winstanley evaluated the tithes as another trump card held by the rich in the midst of political revolution. With the fall of the bishops during the Civil War the Presbyterian clergymen, even many Independents, proved themselves as eager for a guaranteed income as their predecessors. And the Parliaments of 1640–1660, responsive to economic pressure, anxious to maintain as much traditional procedure as possible in the whirl of revolutionary changes, and perplexed to find a solution to the intricate economic problem, as a whole upheld the tithe-gathering rights of both churches and lay impropriators.[137]

For the continuance of tithes writers advanced both practical and theoretical arguments. From the viewpoint of Cromwell and his fellow revolutionists, to have cut off nine thousand parish ministers from their traditional livelihood, among whom were the most talented and outspoken critics of the new regime, would have been to invite mounting bitterness among an already uneasy population. Independent leaders like Owen and Nye saw no reason for destroying the financial support of the reformed church. Though a liberal and a commonwealth man, James Harrington defended the clergy-supporting tithe.[138] The impropriations of preceding centuries made the problem immensely complicated. "Many Widdows have tithes for their Joyntures, which their parents did purchase for them," runs one plea," . . . and Orphans, tithes assigned for the raising of their portions; and younger Sons have Annuities assured out of tithes."[139] What proportion of impropriated tithes were directed thus to needy persons the pamphleteer does not reveal. Alarmed by the violent petitions against the clergy, over six thousand men of Worcester County petitioned in 1652 that tithes be maintained, insisting that a "beggarly Ministry will lose . . . much of their authority."[140] A frequent controversial thrust was that those who preach the Gospel should live from it. Prynne argued that the spiritual blessings contributed by the clergy were of more worth than the carnal gifts of tithes, and that clergymen no more than soldiers should be forced to depend upon the capricious benevolence of the people.[141] Who are the petitioners? asked Prynne, in 1659, when the Commonwealth was faltering. Almost always "poor mecanical [sic] persons, of such mean inconsiderable fortunes" that they do not have to pay tithes.[142] To John Gauden, since the New Testament does not mention tithes, it did not abrogate them; therefore they should be paid. Like Prynne, he attacked the quality of the radical pamphleteers, dismissing their conscientious scruples against paying tithes as ignorance, malice, or revengefulness.[143] By custom and tradition ministers were entitled to tithes, insisted an anonymous pamphleteer, with as much a legal right as landlords had to their rents; and to deny them tithes was to be in danger of sacrilege.[144]

Against tithing the liberal writers poured forth voluminous objections. No more than one inhabitant in a thousand is a priest, complained Lilburne; yet the priests demand a tenth of the income. Lilburne looked upon the institution of tithing as a Jewish ceremony abolished by the Gospel.[145] Overton, like many others, such as the author of *The Tender Conscience Religiously Affected* (1646), resented tithes as oppression of the poor.[146] In *The Bloudy Tenent* Williams had argued against the whole principle, contending that ministers should depend upon manual labor and free will contributions. In a very bitter vein wrote the authors of *Tythes no Maintenance for Gospel Ministers* (1652); [147] they called tithe taking an oppressive sin that cried out for vengeance; many, they complained, unable to maintain their own families, found tithes an inescapable and intolerable burden; and the priests were flinty as Egyptian taskmasters. In *The Tythe-Takers Cart Overthrown* (1652) Lupton stamps a tithe-taking minister as an utter contradiction: "Look to it well, O ye pretending Priests and Presbyters, and take no more Tythes . . . Our Saviour himself when he sent his Apostles to teach the Gospel, gave not the least direction or precept concerning Tythes; nor did the Primitive Christians demand any: And have our Ministers any juster claim or right unto Tythes then any or all these think you?" [148] Consistent with his incisive analysis of England's social structure, Gerrard Winstanley looked upon tithes as kingly thievery, bestowed in turn upon the priests to keep the poor submissive to the land-robbers:

And for their pains for thus preaching, the King established by his Laws, that they should have the tenth of the encrease of all profits from the Earth, . . . placing their freedom where he placed his own, and that is in the use of the Earth brought into their hands by the labors of the enslaved men. . . .

Then this Clergy . . . began to divine and to deceive the people by a shew of holiness . . . to tell us of a Heaven and Hell after death, which neither they nor we know what wil be.

The former hell of prisons, whips and gallows they preached to keep the people in subjection to the King: but by this divined Hell after death, they preach to keep both King and people in aw to them, to uphold their trade of Tythes and new rased Maintenance. . . .

Say they, *If the people must not work for us, and give us Tythes, but we must work for ourselves, as they do, our Freedom is lost.*[149]

If less realistic than Winstanley, the Quakers adamantly set their faces not only against tithes, but against the ministry as a profession. "Christ sent not any Teachers to sue men at Law for Tythes," wrote Fox, "or to seek for augmentations. Oh blush, and be ashamed all you teachers of England!" [150] It was Fox' habit to rise from his place in the congregation to challenge the statements of the minister. On a Sunday afternoon in 1651, when Fox heard a sermon on the free riches of the Gospel, he cried out: "Come down, thou deceiver; dost thou bid people come freely, and take of the water of life freely, and yet thou takest three hundred pounds a-year of them, for preaching the Scriptures!" [151]

In 1659, when Milton was moved to make his most extended bitter protest against tithes, dozens of pamphlets and petitions were condemning them utterly. On April 27 a petition signed by more than fifteen thousand conscientious objectors to tithes was presented to Parliament; the petitioners protested against the continued oppressions, especially lawsuits, judgments, and imprisonments for non-payment of tithes.[152] On July 18 appeared John Osborne's *An Inditement against Tythes,* one of the most thorough and convincing pamphlets in the tithe literature of the period. Approaching the problem historically, Osborne claims that no tithes were paid in England until 786, and then only in Mercia. Not before Henry VIII's time were men permitted to sue for tithes in the civil courts, no law before that time requiring tithe payment. Not until the time of Edward VI, continues Osborne, was a three-fold tithe payment demanded for failure to pay the original amount on time; and judges now interpret the laws incorrectly in favor of tithe-gatherers.[153] In the preface to Osborne's pamphlet, John Canne complains that men have been imprisoned for non-payment of a groat and tuppence tithe; that even the poor receiving alms have been forced to pay; that families have had their household goods taken from them; and that some, owing only a five- or six-pound tithe, have been forced in the end to pay seventy or eighty pounds. John Crook published his *Tythes No Property to, nor lawful maintenance for a Powerful Gospel-preaching Ministry* in 1659, and Peter Corneliszoon Plockhoy in *The Way to the Peace and Settlement of these Nations* reprinted a letter to Cromwell in which he had appealed for the nulling and voiding of tithes.[154]

Undismayed by the turbulent state of the commonwealth, Milton in August, 1659, came forth with *The Likeliest Means to Remove Hirelings Out of the Church*. Having written on persecution of conscience, he turns now, he says, to a much more dangerous custom, the hiring of ministers; for the effect of hire is to corrupt the teachers, to drive the truth from their hearts. At a propitious time, the problem of tithes being now under debate, he hastens to make his position clear. A minister is entitled, not to tithes or maintenance of any kind by the magistrate, but to free will offerings only, whether they be a tenth or a twentieth. The tithes of the Old Testament Milton sweeps aside as having been part of the Hebrew ritual abolished by the Gospel. And "Christ never claimed any such tenth as his annual due, much less resigned it to the ministers, his so officious receivers." [155] Nor did Jesus require for Himself or his disciples any income, publicly or privately, except sufficient for sustenance. Even the scribes and pharisees rather paid tithes than received them, being less covetous than our own ministers, Milton insists. For three hundred years after Christ, he continues, no mention of tithes appears, "though error by that time had brought back again priests, altars, and oblations." [156] And even the first Christian emperors did not require tithes but contributed to the clergy's needs from their own revenues. Admitting that tithes in England are of ancient practice, Milton points out that according to the canons of Ecbert and Elfric, two-thirds of the tithes were reserved for the poor, but priests of today must have all. But what should ancient English law or practice avail to those who are for true reformation? Having cast out bishops and altars, are we now to continue a worse corruption? Bitterly Milton berates the tithe-takers for "seizing of pots and pans from the poor, who have as good right to tithes as they; from some, the very beds; their suing and imprisoning, worse than when the canon-law was in force." [157] The endowment of churches Milton condemns as another drain upon the labors of the people, without their consent, to gain priests' support for kings: "Ofttimes a bribe to God or to Christ for absolution, as they were then taught, from murders, adulteries, and other heinous crimes." [158] It is utterly wrong, in Milton's view, for a government to use its power to force payment of any funds to the church, making the ministers pensioners of the state; and, being masters of their salaries likewise the molders of their opinions. "The church of Christ," writes Milton, "was founded in poverty rather than in revenues, stood purest and prospered best without them." [159]

That Milton is keenly disappointed with those Independent ministers who have supported tithes is evident in *The Likeliest Means*. To call one's church independent, and at the same time depend upon the magistrate for maintenance, is notorious inconsistency. A minister supported by the state loses inevitably his intellectual independence; and soon or late the committees that pass upon the qualifications of ministerial applicants will select those agreeable to the opinions of the magistrate.[160] Hirelings not only soon adapt themselves to the philosophy of their paymasters but to justify their positions force their new views upon others. Most of all are those hirelings to be condemned who fear that with the abolition of tithes the Gospel would fail. It is not lack of tithing that makes atheists, Milton says sharply, but the cheating, grasping clergy that control the propagation of the faith. Thus he berates them, calling up constantly the example of the impoverished apostles and teachers of their primitive church, taunting the hirelings with lack of faith in ideas, reviling them for their blasphemous mercenary spirit.

Milton's attack on tithes in *The Likeliest Means* is consistent with his life-long antagonism to a state-employed clergy. Having in his youth planned to enter the ministry, he found that by no stretching of his conscience could he take the required oath; he "thought it better to preserve a blameless silence before the sacred office of speaking, bought and begun with servitude and forswearing." [161] He felt himself "church-outed" by the prelates. Lines in "Lycidas" show how acutely he had pondered the position of the ministry, how much contempt he felt for those reaching after fat livings:

> How well could I have spar'd for thee, young swain,
> Anow of such as for their bellies sake,
> Creep and intrude, and climb into the fold?
> . . . Blind mouthes!

In the prelate pamphlets, though he does not condemn tithes utterly, he attacks time after time the greediness of the Anglicans, as he was afterward to condemn the Presbyterians. "They have fed themselves, and not their flocks," he writes in *Animadversions*.[162] Applied to the greedy clergy the word *wolves* was a favorite one with Milton. In *Defensio Secunda* he writes a bitter passage on the wolves of the church, "stuffed with tithes"; yet nothing can satisfy their rapacious cravings.[163] In *The Tenure* he calls them "ravenous wolves." [164] And in *Christian Doctrine*, where one always looks for Milton's most mature and considered opinions on church matters, he bluntly affirms that the exaction of tithes is the act of wolves, not of ministers.[165] Finally, the prophecy in *Paradise Lost* contains a typical characterization:

> Wolves shall succeed for teachers, grievous wolves.[166]

Among the tithe critics of the seventeenth century Milton assumes a place of pre-eminence. Especially in *The Likeliest Means*, where he does not feel it necessary to fill his pages with learned references to refute opponents like Prynne, his reasoning has an appeal of universal validity. For Milton was never content with the historical method, much as he felt forced to use it. In *The Likeliest Means* he reviews the history of tithes from the earliest times, citing many of the authorities used by his opponents. The Bible, the church fathers, the historians of Saxon and Norman England, these authorities he uses more skilfully than tithe-haters like Katherine Chidley and John Osborne, though Selden's learning Milton cannot match. Of the historical matter, however, Milton makes an end as soon as possible; he prefers to argue from first principles: the psychology of corruption, the effect of men's salaries on their opinions, the nature of persuasion, the contrast between the poverty of Jesus and the opulence of England's teachers. It is true that Milton's appeals for tithe-abolition went unheeded. For now, three centuries later, England still has her tithes, paid in

London on building rent, at a rate stipulated by Henry VIII.[167] American practice, on the other hand, has sustained Milton's condemnations.

Though Milton argues with all his old confidence in *The Likeliest Means,* one catches now and then a tone of weary despondency. "If I be not heard nor believed," he concludes, "the event will bear me witness to have spoken truth: and I in the mean while have borne my witness, not out of season, to the church and to my country." [168] In the years past Milton had imagined that he had placed his hand on the pulse of the people, and that they had followed his counsel. That for which he had argued, abolition of the kingship and House of Lords, freedom of the press, toleration for all Protestants, the pulling down of the prelates—all this Cromwell and the Independents had in large measure accomplished. But whereas Milton believed his pamphlets had helped to educate the people to take long steps toward liberty, Cromwell and the army had driven them forward in spite of themselves, against their choice and judgment. And now, a year after Cromwell's death, Milton had an inkling of how far he had failed to understand his countrymen, how little his pamphlets had moved them, how momentarily potent had been Cromwell's sword.

TOLERATION OF CATHOLICS

From the time of his break with the Presbyterians in 1644, Milton had championed the cause of Protestant toleration, a principle inherent, as we have shown, in Independency. But whereas the complete separation of church and state for which Milton stood implied and included toleration of Protestants (in his extreme plea in *Civil Power in Ecclesiastical Causes* he evidently found it difficult for the moment to exclude even Catholics), it is not true that complete toleration of sects meant separation of church and state. During the Commonwealth and Protectorate a state church continued to exist side by side with toleration of Protestants. But in no instance except during the time of the temporary persuasion we have noted did either toleration or separation of church and state, in Milton's mind, extend in principle to the toleration of Catholicism.

Milton's antagonism to Catholicism was life-long, breaking out in his early pamphlets against the prelates. In *The Reason of Church*

Government he associates the bishops with the Catholic organization of the church, and asks why, if Episcopacy is to ascend to a primate, it should not naturally be governed by a pope. He accuses the bishops of using parts of the mass book in their Episcopal services. In *Areopagitica* he attacks censorship as having originated in popery.

Even in his most extreme plea for toleration, *Civil Power in Ecclesiastical Causes*, Milton speaks plainly against tolerating Catholics: "But as for popery and idolatry, why they also may not hence . . . be tolerated, I have much less to say. Their religion the more considered, the less can be acknowledged a religion; but a Roman principality rather, endeavouring to keep up her old universal dominion under a new name, and mere shadow of a catholic religion. . . . Nevertheless, if they ought not to be tolerated, it is for just reason of state, more than of religion . . . Lastly, for idolatry, who knows it not to be evidently against all scripture, both of the Old and the New Testament." [169]

Milton's argument that Catholicism should not be tolerated for state reasons was, as he well knew, the principal seventeenth-century argument not only against Catholic toleration but also against toleration of Protestant sects as well. When applied to Protestant toleration, this was an argument which he himself had more than once refuted. Yet with slight hesitation he ignores all his own pleas for individual liberty in adoption of one's religious creed, all the stinging attacks he himself has made in the past on "forcers of conscience."

Even in *Paradise Lost* Milton gives vent to his antagonism to Catholicism. The symbols of Catholic faith and worship he relegates, it will be remembered, to the Paradise of Fools. There

> might ye see
> Cowles, Hoods and Habits with thir wearers tost
> And fluttered into Raggs, then Reliques, Beads,
> Indulgences, Dispenses, Pardons, Bulls,
> The sport of Winds.[170]

A new significance to Milton's intolerance of Catholics has been attached recently to Milton's description of Pandemonium, lines 710 to 798 of Book I. It is suggested that Milton took his description of Pandemonium from his memory of St. Peter's Church in Rome, and that at the end of Book I he is likening Satan to the Pope, and the hierarchy of angels to the hierarchy of church officials associated with the pope. The following details, it is pointed out, lend themselves to a description of St. Peter's: "Pilasters round," "Doric pillars overlaid with Golden Architrave," "Cornice or Freeze, with bossy Sculptures grav'n," "fretted gold," "arched roof," "Blazing cressets," "porches wide," "pendant . . . lamps." [171] The comparison of the angels with bees upon their entrance into Pandemonium is a further indication that Milton was thinking of Catholicism, inasmuch as the figure of the hive and bees was a familiar one in the Protestant language of intolerance of that period. Moreover, it was not at all unusual to compare the Pope with Satan; Milton himself frequently speaks of the Pope as antichrist. Finally, the last few lines, it is said, especially, "In close recess and secret conclave sat," refer to the secret meetings of the Catholic officials at St. Peter's.

But the most positive denunciation of popery did not come from Milton until a year before his death. His bitterness had, apparently, in his old age increased rather than diminished. *Of True Religion, Heresy, Schism, Toleration; and what best Means may be used against the Growth of Popery* is the title of his shortest pamphlet, only ten pages in length. Milton declares that because heresy is religion arising from tradition and from unwarranted additions to Scripture, there is no heresy except Catholicism; and Catholicism is not to be tolerated by those who study the Bible as the final authority in religion.[172] If the papists pretended only to religious power, there would be less reason for persecuting them; but the Pope claims for himself temporal as well as spiritual dominion, not ceasing to send representatives to turn both Parliament and king to his purposes. But even if their state activities are not dangerous, the exercise of their religion is not to be tolerated either in public or in private: they are idolaters. Still, and here it is apparent that Milton is uneasy, the papists claim that the destruction of the means of worship violates their consciences. No matter, says Milton. Their belief in images and statues is not founded on the Scripture, and therefore their consciences must be wrong! Thus, one by one, Milton disposes of the doubts of those who would tolerate popery. What is more important, he is constantly raising in this last pamphlet his own doubts, and disposing of them, one feels, rather as the Cambridge disputant than as the convincing orator of the *Areo-*

pagitica. He hastens to make an end to his discussion of popery; only one-fourth of the tract is devoted directly to toleration of Catholics. Milton never quite stepped over the dividing line between Protestant toleration and absolute toleration; but for one who had all his life stood near it, and at times wavered upon the brink, he knows that his words scarce carry conviction.

Milton's intolerance of Catholicism reveals a narrowness which, in so lofty an intellect, cannot be said to have been inevitable in his time. As we have shown, Richard Overton in his *Araignement of Mr. Persecution* had made a vigorous, whole-hearted plea for full toleration of Catholics. Roger Williams not only had urged Protestants to tolerate Catholicism, but had suggested that Protestants attend the services of the Catholic Church; in *The Bloody Tenent Yet More Bloody* he recalls John Robinson's high praise of the Christian attributes of earnest Catholics as infinitely preferable to the mechanical, often hypocritical, devotional attitudes of nominal Protestants. To Williams the persecuting fervor was a far more serious error than any Catholic or pagan tenet. "Why," he asks, "should their *Consciences* more then others be oppressed?" [173] The author of *Zeal Examined* (1652) also compares half-hearted Protestants unfavorably with pious Catholics, though, like Milton, he draws the line at an actual toleration. Men as wide apart socially and intellectually as Henry Marten and Gerrard Winstanley favored toleration of Catholics, Marten in an open Parliament, Winstanley in his utopian blueprint. "No man," says Winstanley, "shall be troubled for his judgment or practice in the things of his God, so he live quiet in the Land." [174] The Quakers generally were more tolerant toward Catholics than Milton, being the only sect in 1672 to prefer freedom of themselves and the Catholics to continued persecution of Protestant Nonconformists.[175] In his brief tract, *To All that Professe Christianity* (1661) George Fox, Jr., pleads for mutual tolerance and gentleness, making no exception, as most Protestants did, of the despised Papists. As early as 1644 Christopher Blackwood, like Williams, had pleaded for toleration of the Catholics, with the curious reservation that they be checked should a time ever come when they might outnumber the Protestants. Of less learning and genius than Milton, these men exhibited a compassion and social maturity in their tolerationist views that Milton never attained.

The plight of the Catholics, with an earnest appeal for toleration,

John Austin set forth in *The Christian Moderator* (1651 and 1652).
Austin calls attention to the heartless sequestrations; he estimates
that two-thirds of all the estates of recusants had been seized, and
that some estates worth three hundred pounds annually have been
reduced to sixty. All this the Catholics have suffered for conscience
sake. Like other sincere believers, Catholics meet the tests of tender
conscience, and should not be persecuted: they are men of peaceable, virtuous lives, steady judgments, preferring their faith to their
property, meeting death, "which is no time for dissembling," with
equanimity.[177] Austin proposed to the Committee for Propagation
of the Gospel that no penalty be imposed for differences of opinion
in religion, that no Christian's private worship in his own home be
disturbed, that no person be tried for heresy on the testimony of
one witness, and that no oath be compelled causing a person to forfeit his *"life, liberty, or estate, to swear against his Conscience."* [178]
In moderation of tone, earnestness and sincerity of appeal, unre-
criminatory analysis of Protestant tolerationist contradictions,
Austin pamphlets deserve a place with the most enlightened social
treatises of the period. A passage like the following finds few
parallels in Milton's time:

> Have not the *Papists* understandings as well as we, which our Argu-
> ments may rectifie? have they not souls to save, which our charity may
> gain to heaven? why do we not erect a Committee to purchase souls, as we
> have Contractors to sell Lands? why is there not establisht a Committee of
> *Salvation* . . . where Questions of Religion may be freely discust, and
> the distresses of tender . . . consciences impartially relieved? If men
> dealt mildly . . . surely there would in time grow Society, Commerce,
> and mutuall confidence, and so frequent opportunities of clearer informa-
> tion.[179]

Even Cromwell, whose massacres of the Irish he could scarcely
have initiated against Protestants, was less of a Papist-hater than
Milton. As to the practice of Catholicism in Ireland, Cromwell
felt it necessary to equivocate: "I meddle not with any man's conscience. But if by liberty of conscience, you mean a liberty to exercise the mass, I judge it best to exercise plain dealing and to let
you know where the Parliament of England have power, that will
not be allowed of. As for the people, what thoughts they have in
matters of religion in **their own breasts** I cannot reach, but shall

think it my duty, if they walk honestly and peaceably, not to cause them in the least to suffer for the same." [180] But in England, despite the hostility of the Presbyterian clergy and his own followers, Cromwell lightened the burden of persecution borne by the Catholics. Foreign ambassadors testified to the breadth of Cromwell's leniency. He was opposed to the repressive adjuration bill passed against Catholics in 1657 and as the executive alleviated its effects consistently.[181]

* * *

If there is one element in Milton's personality which, more than any other, increasingly forces itself to the attention of the student, it is his conscious attempt to reason consistently from first principles; and one must admit that he failed less often than a cursory reading of his pamphlets would indicate. Except in his bitterest tracts against Salmasius and More, Milton keeps an inward eye upon the most intelligent of his countrymen and of posterity, anticipating their criticisms, recalling their Cambridge training in logic. From youth to age, when his intolerance of Catholics seems about to give way, his most extreme passion, the efficacy of a subjective approach to truth, aided by the traditional prejudices of his country, holds him in check. The very extremity of his reliance upon individual conscience, a first principle, decides him against letting any one else do otherwise than to determine everything by personal interpretation.

Milton the religious thinker is a striking contradiction to Milton the poet. As a poet Milton was constantly aware of the need of images, of dependence upon traditional poetic devices, of the efficacy of the objective point of view. Master of the classicist art, he thoroughly understood the magic of transporting his reader to the realm of fancy, a realm made real through touch and smell and sound. Yet in religious thinking he was an extreme romanticist. Scorning tradition and hating ritual, he seems to have held in contempt all effort to create periodically amid the bleakness of daily life a world of mystic beauty and spiritual exaltation. Images he despised as idols. The pleasure and need of those who approach religious truth mystically with the aid of images were never apparent to Milton. Radical Protestant that he was, religion was to him an ethical code rather than the art of communion through fusion of sense and spirit. Much as this pronounced individualistic point of view contributed eventually to democratic toleration both of Catholics and Protestants, it was in Milton not mellowed or kindly enough to place him in the ranks of the extreme tolerationists.

LAST APPEAL FOR TOLERATION

Heresy, Schism, and Toleration becomes, the more one studies it, rather a plea for Protestant toleration than an argument against tolerating Catholics. Milton had reasons enough to plead for the cause of the dissenters, thousands of whom, until March 15, 1672, had suffered from the time of the Restoration imprisonment and persecution. On the date mentioned Charles by his own prerogative issued a declaration suspending the penal laws against Non-conformists. But strange as it may seem, these very Non-conformists struggled against acceptance of their liberation.[182] In the first place, it was believed throughout England that Charles was favorable to the Catholics; his declaration would permit their open worship. Secondly, the Puritans and Parliamentarians resented the action of the king in deciding a religious matter, a function properly belonging to Parliament. Through the pressure from Parliament and the Church of England, Charles was forced, in March 1673, to give up his policy of toleration. Moreover, Parliament passed the Test Act, which required every person to worship in the Church of England, and failed to pass a bill for the relief of Protestant dissenters. For the moment Milton had been encouraged to see toleration for the sectaries, but now they are still forbidden the right to open worship. He pleads for them again on the old ground of fourteen years earlier, that the cardinal principle which all Protestants accept is the right of the individual to read and to judge the scriptures. How, then, can any Protestant persecute another Protestant? To do so is to deny the very foundation of Protestantism.[183] Mentioning Lutherans, Calvinists, Anabaptists, Socinians, and Arminians by name, Milton denies that their errors are mortal; he claims for their leaders the utmost sincerity. Sectarianism has benefited, not endangered, Protestantism. "Besides, how unequal, how uncharitable must it needs be, to impose that which his conscience cannot urge him to impose, upon him whose conscience forbids him to obey!" [183] It seems more than once that Milton is using the "No Popery!" cries of his countrymen to turn their minds to intolerance among themselves. Popery may be best overcome by uniting in a solid front, rather than by persecuting each other; by allowing every one to speak his own opinion, by studying the scriptures diligently, by exchange of opinion whereby the false may appear more false and the true more true. Almost three-fourths of the tracts run in this vein, the toleration of Protestants. The intolerance of his countrymen had been his opportunity for speaking to them, not so much on prohibiting Catholicism as on what was much nearer his heart, freedom of conscience among Protestants.

Previously, in 1659, Milton had advanced a strong argument to prove that for Protestants to persecute Protestants is much less reasonable than for Catholics to persecute Protestants. Catholics in other countries do not punish heresies because individually they believe Protestants to be wrong; they persecute because some do not believe as the Church does. They have, therefore, some authority for intolerance, whereas Protestants have nothing but the individual's belief of wrong. How much worse, then, for a Protestant, having no authority except his own judgment, to force the religious beliefs of other Protestants, than it is for a Catholic, having the whole authority of the Church at his back, to refuse freedom of conscience to Protestants. "The papist exacts our belief as to the church due above scripture; and by the church, which is the whole people of God, understands the pope, the general councils, prelatical only, and the surnamed fathers: but the *forcing protestant, though he deny such belief in any church whatsoever,* yet takes it upon himself and his teachers, *of far less authority than to be called the church,* and above scripture believed: which renders his practice both *contrary to his belief,* and far worse than that belief, which he condemns in the papist. By all which, well considered, the more he professes to be a true protestant, the more he hath to answer for his persecuting than a papist." [184]

In perspective, on problems of church-state relationships, Milton assumes a place among the radical fringe of contemporary political thinkers. With extreme Erastians like Hobbes, Milton had nothing in common. Hobbes maintained that the ruler of a country is God's supreme representative, the only lawful interpreter of the Bible, God's infallible mouthpiece.[185] If men judge Scriptures for themselves, they cannot obey their princes.[186] To reach heaven men must obey not only the temporal but also the spiritual laws of the sovereign, who should not divide his religious authority with the church. As in the king men rest their safety, so must they also relinquish to him their consciences.[187] Even the learned Grotius favored a close union of church and state, affirming that a king may rightfully select ministers in order to avoid seditious activities. Once the right of interpretation is granted, a minister in his sermons may hold up his sovereign in contempt.[188] Though the Presbyterians, like Hobbes and Grotius, believed in a close union of church and state, they wanted the state church to maintain its ecclesiastical independence, with the magistrate compelling conformity and financial support, but allowing to the church freedom of democratic organization and criticism of civil procedure. Of the Independents, many like Nye, Sympson, and Owen believed in a state church that would, on the whole, tolerate all dissenters except papists and prelatists. Still further on the left we may place Cromwell and the Levellers, who, though more extreme and insistent tolerationists, were willing to retain the state church to placate public opinion. Winstanley himself favored a peculiar type of commonwealth ministry, responsible for relaying the news of social and economic conditions, explaining the laws of the land, and encouraging scientific and economic discussions among the people, who were free to speak and challenge the ministers at any time; both ministers and people, Winstanley insists, should speak only from observation, not from imagination.[189] Finally, at the outer fringe of the reformers appear men like Vane, Williams, Saltmarsh, and Canne, who demanded both disestablishment and a broad toleration. Among these Milton has a place.

In his advocacy of disestablishment Milton represented a more revolutionary viewpoint than the vast majority of the liberal thinkers of his day. Indeed, even in the twentieth century there has been no strong demand in the Labor Party, for instance, for abolition of the state church. And no widespread protest in the last hundred years has made abolition of tithes a political issue of the importance it assumed during the Puritan Revolution.

As a tolerationist, however, Milton was much less advanced than some of his contemporaries. He would still leave to the magistrate the duty of preventing Catholic worship. He was not so extreme a tolerationist as his friend Roger Williams in far-off Rhode Island, where all worshippers of whatever faith, went unmolested. Nor would he grant that toleration to the Catholics, which the Quakers, among them his friend Thomas Elwood, were willing to see in England. To John Locke, too, Milton must yield place as an advocate of religious freedom; he reasons much more cogently and elastically than Milton, and unhesitatingly extends toleration to Catholics, though curiously enough, he excepts atheists. In Locke's letters on toleration one may find synthesized and refined the important tolerationist arguments of 1640-1660. To these arguments Milton made a substantial contribution; though he gagged at the thought of masses and images, though his "left hand" lacked poise and sureness, he argued better than he knew for the hated papists. To them, one hundred fifty-five years after Milton's death, England extended toleration by statute.

CHAPTER III

RISING SECULAR TONES: THE *AREOPAGITICA*

S THE theological radicals, with increasing intensity, agitated first for the downfall of the prelates and then for toleration of the sects, so they also assumed leadership in the revolutionary political surge. Around the campfires of Cromwell's informal university, as in Lilburne's pamphlets, problems of secular reform gradually loomed uppermost, dissolving theological meanderings, stirring up strange new justifications of democratic concepts from Biblical handbooks, then calling insistently for a resolute stroke of the sword. Into this tide Milton was drawn earlier than most of his contemporaries: for in the *Areopagitica* he struck out boldly for a secular freedom so radical that its principles are repudiated the world over in the twentieth century; yet so fundamentally grounded in elemental justice that no one in thirty decades has attempted seriously to impugn as an ideal the validity of its central thesis: "Give me the liberty to know, to utter, to argue freely according to conscience, above all liberties." A theological radical like Cromwell and Harrison, Milton was, however, less secular in his aims than the Levellers. Cromwell's persistent "I perceived the spirit of the Lord upon me" measures the ideological gulf that separated him and Milton and Goodwin from the Levellers and the Diggers. And Winstanley, who sought a broad release of the poor from the pinch of want, rested his faith at the end on the scientific method and a humanistic interpretation of Jesus' teachings, repudiating all teaching of Heaven and Hell, all knowledge divined or imagined. In him merged the parallel streams of the political and religious radicalism of the Civil War period. In him the social dynamics that had toppled the prelates and conquered the aristocracy found its extreme intellectual application, with few to follow and none to act. In Winstanley one finds crystallized that rationalism that Cardinal Newman anticipated as the logical outcome of the Protestant creed.

Of all the Puritan enthusiasts for toleration, Milton was the only one to agitate for the extension of its principle to the whole field of secular ideas. In the past century printing had become increasingly important as a propaganda weapon. But no one of the oppressed sects, and no aristocratic lover of liberty, had called for freedom of the press and freedom of speech in *all* fields as the *sine qua non* of progress. Raleigh, Eliot, Hampden, Lord Brooke, Williams, Vane, Goodwin, Walwyn, might not one of these have seized upon this liberty as the keystone of the arch of freedom? Milton alone caught the vision, timed with precision his ringing appeal. And no one of his friends, personal or theological, no keen, zealous radical like Overton was fired by Milton's words to a similar bold outburst for open presses. In the rich, vital pamphleteering of the Puritan Revolution the *Areopagitica* stands magnificently alone, like the tower of Big Ben among the diverse structures of Westminster.

Though Milton's divorce pamphlets had provoked bitter, shocked invective, his plea for full liberty of the press, a more dangerous and radical heresy, opening the doors to the most subversive and revolutionary ideas conceivable, brought no more resentment from his enemies than support from his friends. To the men who culled carefully the most scandalous heresies, Paget, Featley, Prynne, Baillie, Edwards, Milton's appeal for a free press was not important enough to mention. Full toleration they denounced scathingly as the highway to atheism and disorder. But they apparently did not recognize in the *Areopagitica* an even wider toleration than any of the Independents had clamored for, a toleration fraught with the sowing of secular explosives. Some of them objected, it is true, to the promiscuous licensing of unorthodox pamphlets; but they did not single out Milton as the outspoken enemy of the censorship principle.

It is possible that the *Areopagitica* evoked no pronounced response because the issue it crystallized was more academic than practical. Every day, if they found not a pliable, willing licenser, men evaded with impunity the laws enforcing censorship. Even before the opening of the Civil War, when censorship had been left largely to the Wardens of the Stationers Company, though Parliament had appointed officials to act as licensers, regulation had largely broken down. In 1642 only 76 books were registered, though

Thomason alone collected over 700 items.[1] In the first six months of 1643 only 35 new publications were licensed, though in this period appeared close to 700 publications. Not all pamphlets required licensing, of course, but the figures indicate sufficiently the gap between requirement and observance. When, aroused by the storm of startling pamphlets and the horrified exclamations of the ministry, Parliament passed its *Ordinance for Printing* on June 14, 1643, it admitted in the *Ordinance* that the existing ordinances for censorship had been nullified.[2] As Milton himself, in the publication of his five prelate tracts, had deliberately disregarded the licenser, so had almost all of his fellow pamphleteers. After the June law was passed, it is true, censorship functioned more effectively, 333 being licensed from July to the end of December, 1643, from a total of around 400 publications collected by Thomason. Among those registered, however, did *not* appear Milton's *Doctrine and Discipline of Divorce*, which came from the press in August, at least six weeks after the passage of the ordinance. In his *Fresh Discovery* Prynne brought to Parliament's attention the unlicensed pamphleteering of Lilburne and Overton, attempting to show how much contempt they had for Parliament's *Ordinance* by quotations from their pamphlets.[3] On Lilburne's demand for open presses, Prynne's marginal comment runs: "Liberty to Print Libels, slanders, invectives against Parliamentary proceedings, is not the Subjects Liberty or priviledge, but his claim and shame." [4] The unlicensed presses mentioned in the ordinance continued to function, though with more hazard to their owners than formerly.

Liberal licensers themselves helped to nullify the censorship ordinance. Edwards called John Bachiler the "Licenser-Generall of the Sectaries Books . . . Man-midwife to bring forth more monsters begotten by the Divell . . . within this three last years then ever were brought into the light in *England* by all the former Licensers the Bishops and their Chaplaines for fourescore years." [5] Bachiler, Edwards complained, had passed books of Saltmarsh, Goodwin, Walwyn, and Web. Such an ignoramus, this Bachiler! Besides, he was not a minister! He knew certainly that Bachiler had altered manuscripts, helping the Independent authors to conceal their dangerous opinions, while actually making them more poisonously effective.[6] Since there were twenty licensers, it was often not difficult for the heretical pamphleteers to find one or two more tolerant or friendly than the rest. In 1649 Theodore Jennings was attacked for having approved *The Vanity of the Present Churches*, in spite of his dissent from some of the sentiments in the pamphlet. Just such a caution John Bachiler used, complains the author, which seemed like giving poison to practice one's skill with antidotes, or attracting rats to poison by scattering a little sugar. *"To passe all at a venture to the Presse, without any notice what it is they* dislike . . . *is* . . . *no better then spirituall murder of souls."* [7]

As usual with Milton, behind the writing of *Areopagitica* lay an impelling personal motive, a motive he does not fully divulge in his own accounts of his pamphleteering. His narrative runs as follows: "Lastly, I wrote my Areopagitica, in order to deliver the press from the restraints with which it was encumbered; that the power of determining what was true and what was false, what ought to be published and what to be suppressed, might no longer be entrusted to a few illiterate and illiberal individuals, who refused their sanction to any work which contained views or sentiments at all above the level of the vulgar superstition." [8] This is an admirable summary of the patriotic ardor and social conscience that sustained Milton in his greatest prose endeavor. But he makes no mention of the ridicule and condemnation heaped upon him by Herbert Palmer in a solemn sermon to both Houses of Parliament, or the resulting surveillance by a Parliamentary committee.

On August 13, 1644, two weeks after the appearance of *The Doctrine and Discipline of Divorce,* on the Extraordinary Day of Humiliation, Mr. Herbert Palmer (*ante,* p. 57) called the attention of Parliament to a divorce heresy, toleration of which would be unthinkable: "of which a wicked book is abroad and uncensored, though deserving to be burnt." [9] On August 24, the Stationers' Company presented a petition (instigated in part by the Westminster Assembly, of which Palmer was a member), complaining about the increase in schism and heresy, and protesting their own displeasure and loss of profit at the increase of unlicensed books.[10] Only two days later the Commons instructed the Committee on Printing to consider the matter of the petition, and "diligently to inquire out" the author of the divorce pamphlet. Though the committee proceeded to business, going so far as to draw up a supplementary printing ordinance, it took no action against Milton, probably brought to a pause by Cromwell's Accommodation motion of September 13. It was this personal injury, aggravated by numerous pamphleteering jibes at his divorce ideas, that canalized Milton's burning intellectual energy on a more broad and secular liberty than he had hitherto espoused.[11]

Milton's mind assumes a new, somewhat unexpected tone quality in *Areopagitica,* a quality hitherto not often apparent except in his finest passages on the nature of marriage. The shadowy cloak of Calvinism, the glasses of theology, the grating accent of Puritanical contumely,—these Milton has thrown aside for a broad humanism fresh as the spirit of Plato's praise of music or Sidney's paeans for poetry. From his reading, from his meditations, his mind has distilled a new richness and a zestful loftiness more Greek than Puritan. His passages on the nature of books, for example, have a timeless and creedless appeal: a good book is the "breath of reason," "the seasoned life of man," the "efficacy and extraction of . . . living intellect," "an immortality," "the precious life-blood of a master-spirit." When a man writes a book, "he summons up all his reason and deliberation to assist him; he searches, meditates." Into this task, "the most consummate act of his fidelity and ripeness" he pours "all his midnight watchings," all the gifts of his genius.[12]

With such a delicate and rare creation a nation should be watchful and tender. Milton is full of praise for that age when "the issue of the brain was no more stifled than the issue of the womb: no envious Juno sat cross-legged over the nativity of any man's intellectual offspring." [13] A book, however monstrous, deserves the gift of life; let no jury condemn it ere it be born into the world. "As good almost kill a man as kill a good book."

The prodigious potency of books Milton does not deny, but the harm they do to fools bears no relation to the merit of their pages. "A wise man, like a good refiner, can gather gold out of the drossiest volume, and . . . a fool will be a fool with the best book, yea, or without book." To restrain fools, let us not hinder the gathering of wisdom. The ripening of a talented person the nation should prefer to the restraint of many vulgar and vicious.[14] Some men were born to be scholarly and studious and creative, not for merely amassing wealth, but for searching out the truth; perhaps to publish books worthy of a perpetual fame.

The ideal seed ground of intellectual growth and national progress was to Milton a free and open clash of wits and ideas. This concept caught up all his enthusiasm, drew from him some of the most poetic passages in *Areopagitica*. The rush and tremor of an idealist upon the verge of realization, looking out upon the inevitable play of righteous forces mounting to triumph, these one can sense on Milton's pages. Much light as we have found, writes Milton, much truth eludes us. Let us use the light to press forward toward further reformation. Not the tumbling of the bishops, nor religious reformation alone, should content us. If "the rule of life both economical and political, be not looked into and reformed, we have looked so long upon the blaze that Zuinglius and Calvin hath beaconed up to us, that we are stark blind." [15] In calling for secular reformation, Milton insists that the need for open debating is more urgent than ever. Only if they flow constantly do the waters of truth stay clear and sweet. Once confined, they stagnate, smelling evilly of conformity and precedent.[16] Let all ideas be propagated, pass through the ferment of discussion, confutation. If the accepted ideas are eternally true, asks Milton, why are we afraid of new ones? It is liberty of speaking and writing that nourishes superior minds. From their criticism is fashioned knowledge itself. When Milton writes of the intellectual ferment of England in transition, he bursts forth in a pacan of patriotic fervor:

The shop of war hath not . . . more anvils and hammers working, to fashion out the plates and instruments of armed justice in defence of beleagured truth, than there be pens and heads . . . sitting by their studious lamps, musing, searching, revolving new notions and ideas wherewith to present, as with their homage and their fealty, the approaching reformation: others as fast reading, trying all things, assenting to the force or reason and convincement. . . .

The people . . . disputing, reasoning, reading, inventing, discoursing . . . things not before discoursed or written of.[17]

Milton appeals to the Parliament not to suppress the fruit of such prolonged and conscientious searching. If the fruit be error, let it sally forth against the truth and break itself to pieces. When all presses are open, and all men free to speak, truth will rise triumphant, itself the most potent censor in the world.[18]

With Milton's ideal of democratic persuasion and debate, realized in the London of 1642 and 1643, the idea of censorship was utterly incompatible. It was especially humiliating to men of spirited patriotism and superior learning, men more and more distrustful of the clerical outlook, who now began to agitate for the removal of secular oppressions, to be now subjected to licensers chosen in part from the Westminster Assembly of Divines. Of this class of unselfish, well-trained men Milton felt that he was representative. In one of the most personal passages of the *Areopagitica* he complains of the indignity censorship imposes upon a talented, upright man of learning, who, though having never given offense by his publications, is not thought "fit to print his mind without a tutor and examiner, lest he should drop a schism, or something of corruption." [19] Is such a person to be thought a youth, who, having escaped the rod of the school master, should now be subject to the *Imprimatur* of a man his intellectual inferior, who perhaps has never written a book himself? To be treated thus as an irresponsible boy, perhaps as a fool or seducer, is a dishonor not only to the sufferer himself, but to all the thinkers and learners of the land. In this and other passages of the *Areopagitica* appears evidence that the censorship ordinance had grievously affronted Milton's proud self-reverence. He could not bear the thought of submitting his divorce tract to the prying eyes and certain rejection of a Presbyterian censor.

The hampering mechanics of censorship, says Milton, even after approval is given, will harass both author and printer. If the author wishes to add passages, as not infrequently happens, perhaps a dozen times in one book, the printer dare not do so without a new *Imprimatur*. Then must the author seek out the same licenser, since a different one could not act, perhaps make several trips to find him at his leisure, meanwhile losing some of his best considered ideas, and perhaps in the end making his book worse rather than better.[20]

On the difficulties of the censor's tasks, and the type of personality required, Milton argues with telling strokes. A man "made judge to sit upon the birth or death of books . . . had need to be . . . above the common measure, both studious, learned, and judicious," [21] though even he could hardly claim, or have bestowed upon him the gift of infallibility. The best type of licenser, being forced to read unselected masses of manuscripts, would find the task unbearably tiresome and boring. The present licensers, indeed, adds

Milton, are already weary of their labors, and give evidence of wishing to be released. If they resign, inferior men are certain to be appointed, officials dictatorial, narrow, negligent, or grasping.[22] The capacity to judge truth and wisdom cannot be limited within twenty minds, however carefully selected. "Truth and understanding are not such wares as to be monopolized and traded in by tickets, and statutes, and standards." [23] Truth is not subject to "tonnaging and poundaging," by even the acutest censor.

The purpose of censorship is to suppress the evil while keeping the good. But, argues Milton, good and evil in books, as in life, are mixed inextricably. To suppress all evil, you must close first the Bible itself, which describes lust gracefully, reveals fully all the arguments of good men for the pleasures of the senses, and contains many passages that the Talmudist thinks too obscene to be read aloud. On many profound questions "it answers dubiously and darkly to the common reader." Next must be forbidden the ancient church fathers: Irenaeus, Epiphanius, and Jerome, who raise up more heresies than they can refute; and Clement's descriptions of pagan obscenities. And the classics of Greece and Rome, which men grant to be masterpieces of wisdom, these too, Milton infers, must be prohibited, their pages being often filled with frankness objectionable to polite society. The books, in short, which are most likely to taint, being distributed in the greatest abundance, are those which "cannot be suppressed without the fall of learning." [24]

Again, if the purpose is to suppress evil, much else must be censored that is now left to each man's discretion. For "evil manners are as perfectly learnt without books a thousand other ways." Games and music, the very instruments themselves, must be inspected; the whispers and songs of lovers, even balconies and windows; dancing and gestures; the repertoires of fiddlers; clothes; companionship; eating; drinking—all these must be censored, the good culled from the evil, the two never to touch again. Anything that a man sees, hears, or does may aptly be called his book. How absurd, how fantastic to attempt a licensing of all morality, manners, life itself! The art of law-making is to know when to persuade only, and when to compel. If God leaves to man the choice of his own food, and the thousand adjustments that frame his destiny, his choosing of books should not be prohibited. To deny him this freedom, but not to close a thousand other doors where evil may enter, is as vain as shutting a park gate to imprison the crows. Moreover, as Bacon has written, "The punishing of wits enhances their authority, and a forbidden writing is thought to be a certain spark of truth, that flies up in the faces of them who seek to tread it out." [25]

Though Milton gives over many pages of his *Areopagitica* to pleas for toleration of the sects, it was his unique achievement to recognize the limitations of religious toleration in an age in which theology colored all public disputes. Calling for economic and political reformation, he anticipated the corresponding need for the open discussion of all secular ideas. Much scripture as he had used in his tractate on divorce, he insisted that marriage is not a sacrament but a civil contract, and the right of divorce a liberty not even contestable by the magistrate. "As this [domestic liberty]," wrote Milton, "seemed to involve three material questions, the conditions of the conjugal tie, the education of the children, and the *free publication of the thoughts,* I made them objects of distinct consideration." [26] In vindicating the right to print freely his ideas on divorce, Milton was not claiming the freedom of a religious sectarian, but the broader liberty of a citizen whose speculations roam from horizon to horizon in the intellectual world: marriage, education, economics, politics, philosophy. His interests, like those of many Independents, were veering rapidly toward a concrete, materialistic realization of a society representing his ideals; and to this end the right to publish freely ideas of every color loomed paramount.

Not the solution for pressing secular problems, such as he was later to propose, but a *medium,* a *method* for settling them, was Milton's unique suggestion. Other writers were to make similar proposals in the struggle for toleration of the sects. In his *Parable of Physitians* Walwyn pleaded for an atmosphere of love and forbearance in the midst of intellectual hostility. In *The Smoke in the Temple* John Saltmarsh offered a remarkable "Design of Reconciliation," a platform of the principles of discussion. Like Walwyn Saltmarsh also urged an attitude of mutual respect and affection. Let us not, he wrote, assume infallibility over each other, use the civil power for our own advantage, rail at or revile each other, call each other unbelievers. Let us have free and open debates. Including a plea for liberty of the press in his platform, Saltmarsh wrote:

Let there be liberty of the *Presse* for *Printing,* to those that are not allowed *Pulpits* for *Preaching;* let that *light* come in at the *window,* which cannot come in at the *doore,* that all may speak and write *one way,* that cannot another; let the *waters* of the *sanctuary* have issue, and spring up *Vallyes* as well as *Mountains.* . .

Let all subscribe their names to what they Print.[27]

In another extreme tolerationist plea, *The Way to the Peace and Settlement of these Nations* (1659) Peter Corneliszoon Plockhoy proposed that a regular assembly of citizens be held in each city and county for discussion of religious problems. Each person attending the forum should be permitted to state his views about the Biblical passages read to the people. In this way, says Plockhoy, when there is opportunity for full discussions, the true interpretations will emerge triumphant.[28] Plockhoy, Saltmarsh, and Walwyn were seeking a method of minimum essentials acceptable to all groups for the settlement of religious controversy. The testimony even of their enemies proves that Walwyn and Saltmarsh were mild and peaceful in conversation, however sharp the philosophical cleavage involved. Walwyn especially recognized the weaknesses of the conversational methods of his day; he found men lacking in the technique of discussion and sought to exemplify in his own disputes the principles he hoped men would follow, claiming always that one may love a person while hating his opinions. Like these tolerationists, Milton saw the need for free and open discussion; unlike them, however, he summoned up the most comprehensive and fundamental arguments for this approach in the settlement of all the nation's difficulties.

Though Milton alone struck out in one bold pamphlet for the primary liberty of freedom of the press, Areopagitican arguments are not wanting in the literature of the period. John Goodwin, for example, wrote that "the setting of Watchmen with authority at the door of the Presse, to keep errors and heresies out of the world, is as weak a project . . . as it would be to set a company of armed men about a house to keep darkness out of it in the night." [29] As light only can dispel darknes, so truth only can disperse errors. Let heresies be freely printed, not forced into hiding from truth-finding critics. To punish a man for his ideas is to lend them plausibility and respect.[30] Like Milton, Goodwin protests against subjecting "all the learning, gifts, parts and abilities of all the worthy men in the Nation, unto the humor and conceit" of a few conforming, unthinking adherents of the *status quo*.[31] Denying that any magistrate has either the right or the insight to appoint a censor, Goodwin derides the concept that any man can exercise infallible judgment in shutting off error or loosing the truth to the minds of men.[32] Another recommendation of the free and open encounter of truth and falsehood is found in *The Beacons Quenched* (1652). The authors, like Milton before them, disclaim any fear of ideological errors so long as presses are open to combat them. They protest against the repression of books containing much good and a little evil.[33] In the army council discussions of 1647 and 1648, wherein the regiments were represented in part by common soldiers, the right of free speech was assumed and for the most part granted by Fairfax and Cromwell. The army debates as reported in *The Clarke Papers* reveal little hesitation of the agitators to speak their minds freely against the sentiments of their commanders. Yet the participants were not altogether satisfied. In a letter to Fairfax Captain John Ingram insisted that those sitting in the councils should be free to speak their judgments *"without check, controule, molestation, or fear of ruine and destruction."* [34] Denial of this freedom is not only the grossest tyranny, nullifying the purpose of all councils.

Since the minority groups are the seekers of change, one expects to hear from them the clearest statements for liberty of the press and the most vehement protests at its denial by the *status quo*. In 1644, when the *Areopagitica* appeared, Milton stood among the most advanced rebels, his divorce tract an object of particular scorn, being unacceptable even to the liberal Independent ministers. From Lilburne, Overton, and Walwyn, who were later to emerge as leaders of the political radicals, to be repressed eventually even by Cromwell, one would also expect a mighty clamoring for liberty of the press; but it was not considered fundamental enough to be made an article in their *Agreement of the People*. Except for the petition of January 18, 1649,[35] they did not devote a whole tract to this ideal, though their incidental protests against restrictions were numerous.

Overton's running attack on Presbyterian censorship in 1645 and 1646 reflects no extended analysis of the problem, no determination to strike for open presses as a primary liberty. On several of the title pages of the Mar-Priest pamphlets Overton smirks at the

Assembly censors with this phrase: "This is Licensed, and printed to Holy Order, but not entered into the Stationers Monopole." The *Nativity of Sir John Presbyter* was licensed, complains Prynne, by "*Rowland Rattle-Priest*, a terrible *Imprimatur*." [36] In *The Araignement of Mr. Persecution*, reviewing the devices of the defendant, Overton singles out censorship as Persecution's masterpiece. The hunters of Persecution were thus brought to a standstill, all being "as fast as *Divel* and the *Presbyters* could make it." When the pursuers appealed without avail for open presses, continues Overton, they printed privately at great danger to themselves, and at length dragged forth Persecution for public condemnation.[37] In defending his country's liberties, wrote Overton, in *Martins Eccho*, he had hazarded his life and property; and the priests wanted his blood.[38] Satirizing the Presbyterians in *A Sacred Decretall*, Overton has them speak as follows: "We bounded the *Presses* within our Presbyterian Compasse, that they could not without hazard of plundering, transgresse our Reverend *Imprimatur*." [39] When the Presbyterians protested against Lilburne's dangerous pamphlets, Overton made a heated defense of his right to speak, demanding to know how any man could be treasonable in appealing to the House of Commons for changing of laws or redress of the people's grievances.[40] In the last sentence of *A Defiance Against All Arbitrary Usurpations* (1646), Overton for the first time reveals his constructive estimate of the value of liberty of the press:

Yea, and this persecuted means of unlicenced Printing hath done more good to the people, then all the bloodie wars; the one tending to rid us quite of all slavery; but the other onely to rid us of one, and involve us into another.

Of all the Leveller comments on press liberty that I have read, this is the most impressive and original. Yet even here Overton shows no considered or organized approach to the topic such as one may find on almost any random page of the *Areopagitica*.

Nor do Lilburne's comments on free presses, striking as some of them are, show any well rounded philosophy of intellectual liberty. Perhaps to him the problem was too academic: even while in prison for long periods he seems never to have experienced difficulty in finding a willing printer, despite all restrictions. In *A Fresh Discovery* Prynne attempted to instigate Parliament against Lilburne for his repeated violations of the licensing ordinance.[41] Lilburne, on the other hand, protested that the Presbyterians had robbed the Independents of their liberty of printing, this while laws were still being debated. Why should the press not be open to all, to Independents alike, as it was at the beginning of the Parliament? Parliament had allowed free presses so that all Englishmen might have that liberty of criticism that the bishops had robbed them of, like the Spanish inquisitors, "by locking it up under the key of an *Imprimatur.*" [42] In the *Preamble* to *Englands Birth-Right* (1645) Lilburne complains that the presses are not equally opened, or petitions freely heard. Moreover the same Hunscott who hunted down dangerous books for the bishops, still breaks into people's houses, as he had into Lilburne's own, gathering up, upon pretence of Parliamentary authority, both old books and new.[43]

But in the *Birth-Right* arguments about a free press Lilburne shows little consistency. While complaining of the broad powers of the Stationers Company to repress liberal pamphlets, he attacks them for allowing libellous and tyrannical ones, particularly the weekly printing of the *Oxford Aulicus;* they even permit printing supplies to be sent to the king, "whereby to Print down both Power of Parliament, and freedome of People." [44] Quoting a passage from *A Just Defence of John Bastwick* (1645) in which Bastwick calls some of the Parliament members *"Ninnyes and Groles,"* Lilburne demands that Parliament punish the licenser responsible for its publication, and require an accounting from Bastwick himself.[45] Thus did Lilburne resort to the tactics of Prynne in arousing Parliament against a personal enemy, meanwhile repudiating the ideal of liberty of the press. To the suppression of *Aulicus,* however, news book of the enemy in time of war, Milton himself would probably have agreed. In the *Areopagitica* he mentions the appearance of the *Aulicus* only to show the practical futility of censorship measures.

Lilburne's more mature notions of freedom of the press appeared in the early months of 1649, when the Levellers were under the suspicious surveillance of the new Commonwealth. In *Englands New Chains Discovered* (February 26) the radicals demand that the presses be open for continuous assaults on treachery and tyranny. This is "a liberty of greatest concernment to the Commonwealth, and which such only as intend a tyrannie are engaged to prohibit." [46] The way to stop criticism is not to shut the mouths of the enemy, but to act for the good of the populace. *The second Part of Englands New-Chaines* (March 24), a much more fiery and provocative pamphlet, contains choleric passages on the repression of printing. The new government, say the authors, has only two fears: one that the Levellers will disclose the treacheries of the leaders; the other, that if the disclosures do appear, the people will believe them. In order to prevent revelations, he continues, they have put strict watch over the press; and to prevent belief in Leveller accusations they have blasted the leaders with scandals. "They may talk of *freedom,*" add the leaders, "but what *freedom* indeed is there, so long as they stop the Presse, which is indeed, and hath been accounted in all *free Nations,* the most essentiall part thereof." [47]

The most complete Leveller appeal for freedom of the press was the petition of January 18, 1649. Though it contains typical Lilburnian arguments, the style appears to be that of Walwyn, from whom we should expect a more philosophical treatment of the topic than Lilburne has presented in any of his known pamphlets. The petitioners complain that Overton, Lilburne, and Larner suffered from censorship in attempting to disclose the approaching tyranny of the army faction, which is now upon them. Meanwhile unlicensed scandalous pamphlets are doing much greater harm than if they had been open for good men to answer. The petitioners recall that unlicensed printing all along has upheld the cause of the army, while the licensing system has done the utmost to destroy it. It was unlicensed printing that won over many people to the army's policies, thus paving the way for its triumph. If you must watch over the press, ask the petitioners, must you not license all private or public discussion and teaching, on all topics? It is the liberty of speaking and writing that appears most essential to freedom. For any bondage may overcome a people when it can say nothing except by permission of censors.[48] "To put the least restraint upon the Press, seems altogether inconsistent with the good of the Common-wealth, and expressly opposite and dangerous to the liberties of the people." [49]

Of the three Leveller leaders Walwyn believed most strongly in triumph of truth in a free and open discussion. In the *Whisper* he had written: "All the war I have made, hath been to get victory on the understandings of men: accompting it a more worthy and profitable labour to beget friends to the cause I loved, rather then to molest mens persons, or confiscate estates." [50] As early as *The Com-*

passionate Samaratane (1644 and 1645) he had spoken out for free presses without castigating, as Milton had, the entire ordinance:

> The Press was to be open and free for all in time of Parliament: *I shall make bold as a* Common *of* England *to lay claime to that* priviledge, *being assured that I write nothing scandalous, or dangerous to the* State, *(which is justly, and upon good grounds prohibited by Your* Ordinance *to that effect) only I humbly desire You to consider whether more was not got from You by that* Ordinance *then You intended . . . it hath by reason of the qualifications* of *the* Licensers *wrought a wrong way, and stopt the mouthes of good men, who must either not write at all, or no more then is sutable to the judgments and interests of the* Licensers.[51]

The *Samaratane* contains arguments strikingly suggestive of *Areopagitica:*

> Truth is not used to feare, or to seeke shifts or stratagems for its advancement! I should rather thinke that they who are assured of her should desire that all mens mouthes should be open, that so errour may discover its foulnes, and trueth become more glorious by a victorious conquest after a fight in open field; they shunne the battell that doubt their strenght . . . Whilest the Press was open no man undertooke the Anabaptists . . . now their adversaries have bound their hands they begin to buffet them; what can they doe else but necessarily ssupect [*sic*] that our Divines have not the truth.[52]

Though Walwyn, like Lilburne, thought in 1646 that Parliament should check the revilers of the Independents,[53] by 1649 new repressions forced an enlargement of his ideal of press liberty. He laments, in *The Fountain of Slaunder,* the degraded condition of a people unable to speak, hold meetings, or debate with Parliament. The people are now "a pittifull mean helplesse thing; as under School-masters being in danger to be whipt and beaten in case they meddle in things without leave and license from their Masters." [54] When the authors of *Walwins Wiles* accused Walwyn of wishing that printing had never been invented, he replied that "printing (if any thing in this age) would preserve us from slavery; and you that know how much I have been against the stopping of the presse, methinks should blush to talk thus." [55] Most intellectual of the Leveller leaders, most conciliatory and impersonal in private conversation, Walwyn had a more profound knowledge than most men of his age of the psychology of persuasion. Understanding the futility of angry affirmations, he habitually probed the weaknesses of superstitious arguments with quiet, unsettling questions. He believed in the full opening of minds by a hospitable hearth. To him there was nothing that created an atmosphere of tolerance and friendship in families or cities or nations "so much as a condescention to the giving, and hearing, and debating of reason." [56] Yet in Walwyn's tracts, as in Lilburne's and Overton's, full arguments for liberty of the press are wanting. Beside the glowing diversity of Areopagitican reasoning, Walwyn's scattered statements, even if we include the petition of January 18, 1649, pale like candle gleams in the noonday sun.

One looks, then, in vain among Milton's liberal contemporaries for a resourceful champion of a free press comparable with Milton himself. At first thought one might be tempted to conclude that the *Areopagitica* had done its work so well that the free press enthusiasts felt no other tract was necessary. Had they felt thus, however, they would have named the *Areopagitica*, quoted from it, defended its arguments, praised its author. Of such recognition I have found no evidence, though, as Masson points out, Lilburne's tracing of censorship to the Spanish Inquisition is some indication that he had at least read Milton's great tract. Though capable of forceful tracts on liberty of the press, Walwyn and Overton, like Lilburne, were busy with more pressing issues; moreover no one of them experienced long delay in getting a pamphlet printed without benefit of licenser. In the last analysis one must grant, too, that there were few men in England of Milton's liberal views qualified to write even feebler *Areopagiticas*. Driven by an imperious will and sustained by a lofty life purpose, Milton had spent many years in preparation for his greatest prose effort. From the time he was sixteen, when he had entered Cambridge, until the age of thirty-six, when he wrote *Areopagitica*, he had lived for thirteen of the twenty years the life of an unhurried student, followed by a year of foreign travel. Not the least of Milton's intellectual advantages was his early revolt against theological dogmatism, coupled with an absorption in the Greek classics, Shakespeare, and Spenser. Only as a humanist escaped from Calvinism could Milton have written the *Areopagitica*. As in *Paradise Lost*, so in *Areopagitica*: it is not the overcoat of theology, but the flesh and bone of Milton's amazing secular knowledge, coupled with his insight into the human soul and its aspirations for fruition, that explain its timeless appeal.

Our concept of the scope of Milton's achievement in writing *Areopagitica* broadens upon comparison with his successors. He anticipated all the objections that three centuries have been able to muster against the liberty of the press. At the same time he exhausted the positive arguments that have sustained a free speech and free press in every democratic country. Locke's essays on toleration yield little meat not already provided by the *Areopagitica*. Mill's "Of the Liberty of Thought and Discussion," though more logical in arrangement, has neither the memorable phrasing nor the originality of the *Areopagitica*. Rather than adding new arguments to Milton's comprehensive-treatment, Mill expands and develops the lines of reasoning already advanced by Milton. "All silencing of discussion," writes Mill, "is an assumption of infallibility." [57] Mill points out that a man who refuses to consider an opinion antagonistic to his own assumes that the certainty of his judgment "is the same thing as *absolute* certainty." This and many other highly stimulating analyses Mill uses to unfold his contention that fallibility is inevitable in the evaluation of ideas. But this generalization, as we know, is inherent in *Areopagitica*, like most of the other arguments in Mill's great essay.

In the *Areopagitica* Milton uses few Biblical quotations; his approach and proofs are broadly humanistic. From his vast knowledge of Greek and Roman literature he drew facts and allusions pertinent to his theme. To learned men of the seventeenth century these were necessary and impressive, though Milton does not mention the enormous differences, from a censorship point of view, between the slow circulation of manuscripts and the prodigious energies of the printing press. Far more fundamental, then as now, than historical authority, were his secular arguments from first principles, philosophical, psychological, utilitarian. The examination of ideas as an educative process for men and nations; the need for new ideas in an age of transition; the mixed influences of environment; the nature of goodness and evil; the inevitability of choice in problems of conduct; the stuff of books; the nature of the creative mood and process; the effect of intellectual restraint on creative minds; the censor's inevitable pretence of infallibility; the shooting power of prohibited ideas; the limitations of the state's power in matters of private conduct; the intellectual insecurity of persecutors; the practical impossibility of censorship enforcement—on these broad grounds Milton rests his case. They give his prose masterpiece a timeless validity, an appeal unhampered by theological bias or environmental peculiarities. Sloughing off the peculiar harshness of Puritanism, while impelled by its noblest influences, Milton rose at one bound into the company of Socrates and Montaigne, his creation destined for universal assent by the world's choice spirits.

In a sense the *Areopagitica* was the most drastically radical tract of its day. What it proposed in reality was a national open mind to the restless tides of progress, the social creativeness of the superior few, the persistent reach toward a more humane existence. It posed a national willingness to examine afresh, to subject to pitiless criticism all traditional ideas, customs, institutions. By its principles England would have engaged in perpetual reformation, change, social experimentation, with the propagandas of reaction and revolution equally free. The socialist tracts of Winstanley, the democratic reforms of the Leveller *Agreement,* the *Oceana* of Harrington, the ideas of Hobbes' *Leviathan* and Milton's own *Readie & Easie Way* would have found throughout England thorough and open-minded consideration. The *Areopagitica* implies, furthermore, the settlement of burning issues by peaceful and democratic means, by the victory of reason's persuasion rather than the imposition of force. In opening to discussion and consequent action any revolutionary plan, Milton was arguing for a principle so far reaching that even he himself was unwilling in practice to accept it: the right to agitate for the overthrow of the dominant political and economic interests. This right, as the Independents themselves discovered, the ruling party will grant only as long as its own propaganda is undoubtedly more powerful and persuasive than that of its enemies. Freedom of the press, like unrestricted suffrage, runs counter to the inevitable pressures of concentrated economic power. The dilemma faced by an enlightened ruling party is thus described by Dr. Johnson, in his *Life of Milton:*

The danger of such unbounded liberty [of the press], and the danger of bounding it, have produced a problem in the science of Government which human understanding seems hitherto unable to solve. If nothing may be published but what civil authority shall have previously approved, power must always be the standard of truth; if every dreamer of innovations may propagate his projects, there can be no settlement; if every murmurer at government may diffuse discontent, there can be no peace; and if every sceptick in theology may teach his follies, there can be no religion.

But Milton, as we know, had no love for settlement, or social tranquillity, or religious faith at the price of gagged mouths and forbidden presses. Disillusionment was far away. In the fall of 1644 he yearned for, he believed in, a better world. Almost within his reach glimmered an English paradise. That paradise he could not describe, but he knew the collective creativeness of his fellow countrymen was equal to the task. Let plans gush forth, tongues speak, presses turn, that not theology alone, but all, all might be transformed and a new England born.

CHAPTER IV

JOHN LILBURNE: AGAINST BISHOPS, AGAINST CROWN

T HE SHIFT from religious protests to political reform may be traced in the pamphlets and statements of the principal radicals of Milton's day. The men branded in *Gangraena* as the most dangerous sectaries, Lilburne, Overton, Walwyn, Burton, Goodwin, Saltmarsh, and Peters, at first embraced no far reaching political objectives: their aim was the purification of the church and the protection of Parliament's prerogatives. With each passing year of the Civil War, however, radical protests mounted and crystallized, the whole structure of English society was examined afresh, and men's thoughts turned inevitably from religious freedom to secular. In this shifting of emphasis, men of decisive theological convictions, like Prynne and Bastwick among the Presbyterians, and Burton and Goodwin and Milton among the liberal Independents, called an abrupt halt to their leftward political swing, became distrustful of more revolutionary malcontents, and justified repressive measures against their former comrades. On the other hand leaders like Lilburne, Walwyn, Overton, and Winstanley, less learned in the Scriptures, more flexible and daring in their interpretations, more worldly and rational in their outlook, pushed forward from one forbidden frontier to another. The secular tendencies of the radicals displayed themselves in their pamphlets and left their political views open to attack from the theological conservatives as atheistical fancies.

The differences in the secularism of the radicals may be accounted for in part by variations in education, occupation, and economic status. Some of the leading apologists for Cromwell's course of action were university men: Milton, Williams, Peters, Goodwin, Ireton, Cromwell himself. Williams, Goodwin, Peters, and Owen were all trained for the ministry. Milton, as we know, had very strong. if unorthodox theological opinions, knew little of

139

problems of the workaday world, lived for many years a life of contemplation, and never engaged in the struggle to earn a living. Of the Leveller leaders, Lilburne had served as a cloth dealer's apprentice and earned his livelihood for a while as a brewer; Walwyn was a merchant, Overton a bookseller, Winstanley a London business man who had lost all he owned. None of these men had attended a university, or studied theology extensively. None actually suffered poverty except Winstanley; and only he of the extremists called for a thoroughgoing economic as well as political revolution.

The early career of John Lilburne affords a striking example of a religious rebel gradually assuming stature as a secular reformer. A gentleman's son, as he tells us, Lilburne after ten years of schooling in Auckland and New Castle was apprenticed by his father to Thomas Hewson, a wholesale cloth dealer of London, who trusted him with large sums of money and responsibility for negotiations at the Exchange.[1] For having assisted with the printing of John Bastwick's *Letany* Lilburne was forced to flee to Holland in 1636, when he was about twenty years old.[2] According to Lilburne's own statement he left his apprenticeship because his master was about to retire from business. In Rotterdam and Amsterdam he read many books which were forbidden in England.[3] Returning to London, Lilburne was arrested January 14, 1637, and committed to the Gatehouse by Sir John Bankes, chancellor to Laud, on the charge of sending scandalous books from Holland to England.[4] After repeated refusals to take the High Commission oath, in which he was supported by Mr. Wharton, an ardent bishop-hating octogenarian, he was brought before the High Commission, where Laud accused him thus: "This fellow . . . hath been one of the notoriousest disperser of Libellous *bookes* that is in the Kingdome, and that is the Father of them all (pointing to old Mr. *Wharton*.)" [5] To the Court Lilburne justified his refusal to take the "ex-officio" oath by its incompatibility with the law of God, the law of nature, the Petition of Right, and the law of the land.[6] The Lords laughed. "My Lords," Lilburne said, "I beseech God . . . to discover . . . unto you the wickednesse and cruelty of the Prelates." [7] On April 18, 1638, having persisted in his obstinate refusals, Lilburne was whipped through the streets from the Fleet to Westminster, receiving from the executioner about two hundred strokes with a corded whip. "I have whipt many a Rogue," said the executioner, as the journey was about to begin, "but now I shall whip an honest man, but be not discouraged . . . it will be soone over." Lilburne counted his ordeal as his marriage with Christ; so great was his exaltation that he did not feel the pain of the whipping. "It is Gods cause," he said, according to his own story, "and for mine owne part I am cheerfull and merry in the Lord." [8] Many sympathetic spectators lined the way and surrounded him at the pillory, where he distributed a few of Bastwick's pamphlets, spoke to the crowd in a fiery fashion, and was finally gagged by the warden. Lilburne's pillory exhortations, as recorded by himself, are a far cry from his later speeches. He glorifies his own sufferings, which he attributes to the persecution of the prelates, and urges the crowd to stand fast against them. Against the Lords of the High Commission he has no complaint; and he shouts at the end, "Let the King live for ever!" [9] Still refractory upon his return to prison, Lilburne was placed in irons, forbidden food other than that of the Poor Man's Box, denied the company of his wife and friends. In May, 1641, it was Cromwell, "my old friend that got me my libertie from the Bishops Captivitie." [10] His sentence was voted by the Commons to be "illegall, and against the Libertie of the subject," also "Bloody, Wicked, Cruill, Barbarous, and Tyrannicall." [11] For a while after his release, Lilburne tells us, he prospered in the brewing business, established with the aid of his uncle's capital.[12] Enlisting when the Civil War broke out, he was made a captain of foot, gained a reputation for courage in action, was captured at Brentford, and tried for treason against the king. Speaking out with his usual boldness at the trial, he would have been executed had not Parliament threatened immediate reprisals, which brought about his release by exchange in 1643. The Earl of Essex gave him three hundred pounds in recognition of his fortitude at the treason trial. On October 7, 1643, he was promoted to the rank of major, and in May, 1644, became a lieutenant colonel in Manchester's dragoons. Finding that he could not enter the New Model without taking the Covenant, he left the army on April 30, 1645.[13]

Thus far, until the age of twenty-nine Lilburne had not manifested any marked political leadership, either intellectual or practical. He had proved, it is true, the tenacity of his opposition to the bishops by the ordeal of torture and imprisonment; he had demonstrated his talents in speaking and pamphleteering, for dramatizing, like Burton and Prynne, his own sufferings for the sake of his cause; and he had won the respect of both Parliamentary and army leaders for his intrepidity in the field. His early pamphlets reflect his fanatic religious zeal, even a desire for martyrdom. His defence before the High Commission combined undaunted carriage with resourceful quick thinking in terms of legal rights, a significant prelude to his many courtroom defences in the years to come; and his insistence on the Petition of Right and the law of the land hint the trend of his future intellectual method. That he had become a zealous Independent we know from his letter to Prynne written January 15, 1645, justifying toleration of the sects and separation of church and state: he does not wish to "joyne the *Ecclesiastical* and *Civill State* together, making the golden Lawes of Christ, to depend upon the leaden Lawes of man." [14] Of the Presbyterians he is extremely fearful: "We are brought into *Egiptian* bonds . . . by the *Blacke-Coates,* who I am affraid, will prove more cruell *Taskmasters* then their dear fathers the *Bishops.*" [15] So far, then, Lilburne was no more secular in outlook than hundreds of other Independents now clamoring for toleration.

In the year 1645, however, Lilburne was driven into a consideration of fundamental political and economic principles, not by the bishops, but by the actions of the House of Commons itself. Twice Prynne contrived to have him brought before the Committee for Examinations, the second time for publishing unlicensed pamphlets; twice he was dismissed unpunished. But on the evidence of King and Bastwick he was accused of having spoken scandalous accusations against Speaker Lenthall.[16] He refused to answer the questions of the Committee on Examinations, until the charge against him was specified, on the ground that he was entitled to such a statement under Magna Charta. Kept in custody, he published an account of his arrest and imprisonment in *The Copy of a Letter from Lieutenant Colonell John Lilburne to a friend* (July 25), in which he challenges the right of the House of Commons to question or punish men in a manner contrary to accepted judicial procedure. For this indiscretion he was promptly shut up in Newgate (August 9), the House ordering that the quarter sessions court should proceed against him. Lilburne complains bitterly that his charge against Speaker Lenthall (of implication in bribery) was not seriously investigated, the informers meanwhile being treated with the utmost suspicion.[17] No further charges were pressed against Lilburne himself; he was released on October 14, 1645.

Nine months of intermittent imprisonment, disillusionment with parliamentary leaders, vain petitioning for arrears, attacks by Prynne and Bastwick, discussions with comrades, had made their mark on Lilburne's thought. His main reaction, however, in *Englands Birth-Right Justified*, was not theorizing so much as vehement protests against concrete evils. In the midst of Reformation existed a clerical monopoly on the printing of Bibles, a monopoly that prohibits many servants and poor people from reading the Bible at all.[18] A monopoly, too, held by the merchant adventurers on the cloth trade with Holland, and the odious monopoly of printing—these old oppressions must be lifted.[19] He complains against the high fees of lawyers, against their writing the laws, for is it not they who first invent evasions? And why are laws still written in Latin, with the Bible now printed in English? For judges Lilburne has only profound distrust. They it was who declared ship money legal, they who under cloak of the King's majesty bought justice wholesale and sold it retail.[20] Lilburne protests too, against the book-hunting beadle Hunscott, whom the bishops used for their tyranny, who still invades men's homes.[21] And still men are seized and imprisoned illegally, as in the days of the bishops. Such are Lilburne's protests, born, as we know, from his own harsh experiences.

Absorbed with concrete problems of his own defence, Lilburne began a closer examination of constitutional documents of generally accepted validity such as Magna Charta and Petition of Right. He was seeking in them justification of his resistance to judicial procedure. In *Englands Birth-Right Justified* appears the result of this seeking, his first important political theorizing, gradually evolved from his study of the traditional charters. Even Parliament's power, he concludes, is limited. The Petition of Right binds Parliament as well as people; therefore Parliament cannot imprison any man without showing cause, or "justly punish any man for walking closely to the knowne and declared Law, though it crosse some pretended Priviledge of theirs. . . . Their power is limited by those that betrust them."[22] To claim that constitutional law binds people but not Parliament is absurd: no people *would be so sottish, as to give such a Power to those whom they choose for their Serv-*

ants." [23] But Lilburne sensed the need for an explicit, comprehensive written constitution, "a plaine platforme agreed on . . . concerning things of so high consequence to all the Commons of *England.*" [24] From such an embryo was to grow the first *Agreement of the People.* Though lacking in the crystallized fullness and colorful language of his later statements, Lilburne's theorizing in *Englands Birth-Right* shows clearly the secular tone of his democratic aims. Already he calls for annual Parliaments.[25]

Innocency and Truth Justified, which appeared January 6, 1646, though it shows no marked development of Lilburne's democratic doctrine, contains further general statements of his creed. Kings, like Parliaments, are subject to the law.[26] A king's possession of his crown is not absolute but conditional upon the safety and freedom of the subjects. He quotes from Henry Parker's *Observations* (1642): "The transcendant aime or pitch of all politiques . . . is the safety of the people, the law of prerogative it selfe, is subservant to this law. . . . Neither can the right of conquest be pleaded to acquit Princes of that which is due to the people as the Authors or ends of all power: for meere force cannot alter the course of nature, or frustrate the tenour of the law . . . there were more reason why the people might justifie force to regain due libertie, then the prince might to subvert the same. And its a shamefull stupiditie in any man to thinke, that our ancestors did not fight more nobly for their free customes and lawes . . . it seems unnaturall to me that any Nation should be bound to contribute its owne inherent puissance, meerly to abet Tyranny, and support Slaverie." [27] This statement anticipates Lilburne's attack on kingship in *Regall Tyrannie* (January, 1647). In 1646, in part through the effective leadership of Lilburne and his followers, the king gradually superseded the bishops and the Presbyterians as the chief barrier to England's liberty. Lilburne's first statements are portents of the heightening secular tone of revolutionary questioning.

Lilburne's struggles of 1646 deepened his rebellion against the constitutional *status quo* and sharpened his skill in the use of ancient documents to buttress his arguments. Prevented by King and Prynne from receiving two thousand pounds awarded him by the Lords, Lilburne in *The Ivst Mans Ivstification* (June 6) returned to his old charges against both King and the Earl of Manchester.[28] When called to account by the Lords for his accusations against

Manchester, Lilburne refused to answer questions except in a written statement, which the Lords at first declined, the clerk attempting to give it back to Lilburne, who rejected it as he was being led away.[29] This statement denied the authority of the House of Lords to try him, a commoner, on any charge whatsoever; he appealed to the House of Commons. Incensed at this attack, the Lords committed Lilburne to Newgate until their further pleasure "for exhibiting a scandalous and contemptuous paper." Five days later (June 16) appeared Lilburne's *Free-Mans Freedome Vindicated,* an uncompromising reaffirmation of his claim that the Lords by Magna Charta may not try a commoner, and that Parliament may not abrogate Magna Charta. Again he accuses Manchester, not only of treason to the state, but also of instigating the Lords to imprison him.[30] In early July, hearing that he was about to be called before the Lords again, Lilburne barricaded the door of his chamber at Newgate, so that the officers were compelled to capture him and carry him away by force. At the bar of the house he refused either to kneel or remove his hat; as the charge against him was read, he stopped his ears with his fingers. After denying again the right of the Lords to try him on any charge, much less imprison him, and accusing them of being false to their oaths, he was led away. An hour later, being brought again into the House, he was sentenced to be fined four thousand pounds, to be imprisoned for seven years, and to be forever incapable of holding any civil or military office; finally, his seditious publications were ordered burned by the hangman.[32] Studying much and agitating ceaselessly, Lilburne spent the rest of the year in prison.

In *Londons Liberty In Chains* Lilburne praises a sixteenth-century collection of London's essential liberties and franchises. Having had the French and Latin translated by a friend, he found after diligent research that the traditional charters assured certain liberties undeniably to free-born Englishmen. Every London freeman, insisted Lilburne, had a right by ancient custom to vote for the mayor and aldermen of London. Yet this right was now being consistently denied.[33] This pamphlet reveals Lilburne's intense intellectual activity in 1646. He was reading the histories of Speed and Daniel, rereading Coke's *Institutes,* extending his method of subverting contemporary legal practices with the constitutional charters. At the same time, however, he was shaping a philosophical superstructure for his democratic ideas, a superstructure that appears fully stated for the first times in the pamphlets of 1646 and early 1647. In *The Free-Mans Freedome* he set down in generalized form his philosophical creed; later it was to appear in *Regall Tyrannie discovered* and in somewhat similar words in Overton's *An Arrow Against All Tyrants:*

God . . . gave man (his meer creature) the soveraignty (under himselfe) over all the rest of his Creatures . . ., and indued him with a rationall soule . . . and thereby created him after his own image . . . the first of which was *Adam,* a male. . . . Woman cal'd *Eve,* which two are the earthly, original fountain . . . of all and every particular and individuall man and woman . . . who are, and were by nature all equall and alike in power, digny [*sic*], authority, and majesty, none of them having (by nature) any authority . . . one over . . . another . . . but meerely by . . . mutuall agreement or consent. . . . And unnaturall, irrationall . . . and tyranicall it is, for any man whatsoever, spirituall or temporall . . . to rule . . . over any sort of men in the world, without their free consent.[34]

A similar statement appears in *Londons Liberty:*

The omnipotent . . . God, creating man . . . in his own Image, (which principally consisted in his reason and understanding) . . . made him Lord over the earth. . . . But made him not Lord, or gave him dominion over the individuals of Mankind, no further then by free consent, or agreement.[35]

From this philosophical basis it was but a step to the doctrine that all political power is inherent in the people:

All lawfull powers reside in the people, for whose good, welfare, and happinesse, all government and just policies were ordained.[36]

The people in generall are the originall sole legislators, and the true fountain, and earthly well-spring of all just power.[37]

Regall Tyrannie discovered (January 6, 1647) combines effectively Lilburne's use of the ancient law with his theory of the social contract to substantiate his democratic doctrine. In this pamphlet his power as a political thinker shows considerable advance. His tracing of the tyranny of king and lords to the conquest of William the Conqueror is a consistent, if one-sided, story, well grounded in reputable sources. To clarify his democratic ideas, he draws together the threads of theory in former pamphlets into a more coherent whole than he has hitherto presented. With his capacity for narrow stubborn resistance to particular injustices, his courage and presence of mind in difficult moments, his skill in dramatizing his own oppressions to inspire mass resentment, he now combined an adequate philosophical method and more effective use of historical sources. And his attention was now riveted almost wholly on secular freedoms.

How strikingly Lilburne emerged in 1646 as leader of the secular radicals is revealed by a comparison of Edwards' three *Gangraena's*. In the original *Gangraena*, which appeared February 26, 1646, Edwards writes much of Lilburne as a headstrong unorthodox religionist, a "darling of the sectaries." He is horrified that a certain Mr. Knowles should have prayed: "Lord, bring thy servant *Lilburne* out of prison, and honour him Lord, for he hath honoured thee." [38] Although he pretends to great piety, Lilburne is reported to be living a loose life, profaning the Sabbath, playing at cards, drinking and tippling. As a judgment of God, Edwards suggests, he had had his eye put out by a pike after writing a letter against Prynne.[39] He has been busy abusing Parliament, scoffing at authority, instigating petitions, all for the sake of money. Though Edwards also records that Lilburne had called for annual Parliaments and claimed that the basic power of any government is in the people,[40] it is evident that these heresies as yet have not assumed marked significance to Edwards, or to the mass of Presbyterians. Likewise in the second *Gangraena* (May 28, 1646) Edwards is still unaware of Lilburne's potentialities as a dangerous political agitator. Absorbed in rebuttals of Saltmarsh, Walwyn, and Goodwin, Edwards mentions Lilburne only to refute defences made by Walwyn and Goodwin, who had denied Lilburne's card-playing practices. He returns to the charge and amplifies it. Admitting that he has erred about Lilburne's total blindness in one eye, he nevertheless affirms that he has seen the wound himself; he hopes, moreover that Lilburne will not lose the eye of his soul in heresies, contempt for the ministry, and maligning of those in authority.[41]

In the third *Gangraena* (December 26, 1646) Edwards strikes at Lilburne with a new and bitter political emphasis. It is now the Lilburne of anarchist principles that he hates and fears, "an Arch-Sectary," a man "highly extolled and magnified by them in many

Pamphlets." Not only has he written against king and lords, laments Edwards; he wants a total overthrow of the House of Lords and the concentration of all power in the Commons, these to be freely elected; he demands a wholesale change in the laws and customs of the realm.[42] Finally Edwards levels against Lilburne and his followers a fearful diatribe:

> How many deaths hath *Lilburne, Overton,* and the rest of their fellowes deserved, who have with so much violence sought the overthrow of the three Estates and the Lawes of the Kingdome . . . to set up an Utopian Anarchie of the promiscuous multitude . . . and if these audacious men and their daring books shall escape without exemplary punishment . . . I do as a Minister pronounce that the plague of God will fall upon the heads of those who are the cause of it.[43]

It is plain that in a year's time, most of which he spent in prison, Lilburne has become to the Presbyterians the *bête noire* of a rising democratic surge they had not for a moment anticipated. To them Reformation meant the establishment of a Presbyterian state church, not the questioning of the traditional rights of kings, lords, or commons. But the Civil War had loosed dynamics not easily to be quelled. Around the imprisoned Lilburne, former apprentice, military hero, fearless pamphleteer, rallied the disenfranchised masses of London, along with the rebellious intellectuals, Overton and Walwyn.

In a remarkable tract pleading Lilburne's cause, *A Remonstrance Of Many Thousand Citizens . . . to their owne House of Commons* (July 7, 1646), one finds pictured unmistakably the rising tide of secular demands. The authors bluntly accuse the conservatives of scheming to persuade the common people to join them in limiting the king's power, this through befriending of the unorthodox ministry influential with the poor, crying up Popery and the bishops, meanwhile maintaining such a grip on Parliament that they can halt the resistance to the king when they have achieved their ends. And though the people, once the movement is under way, will clamor to be "delivered from all kinds of Oppression, both *Spirituall* and *Temporall*, and to be restored . . . to the just liberty of their *Persons* and *Estates*," the dominant party need not fear.[44] But care must be taken, the conservatives have said, lest the House of Commons assume the supreme power; for the power and temporal demands of the common people are even more to be dreaded than the power of the king. If necessary the war against the king must be prolonged so that the people will not dispute about the supreme power. In the meantime Presbyterianism must be established that the clergy may control the people's consciences and keep them loyal to the dominant party. This picture of the Presbyterian strategy, if warped and exaggerated, led the remonstrants to make their demands with wrathful bluntness:

> Have you shoke this Nation like an Earth-quake, to produce no more then this for us; Is it for this, that ye have made so free use . . . both with our Persons & Estates? And doe you . . . conceive us so sottish, as to be contented with such unworthy returnes of our trust and Love? No; it is high time we be plaine with you . . . Wee doe expect . . . that yee *should* in the first place, declare and set forth *King Charles* his wickednesse openly before the world, and withall, to shew the intollerable inconyeniences [*sic*] of having a *Kingly Government* . . . and untill this be done, wee shall not thinke ourselves well dealt withall in this originall of all Oppressions, to wit *Kings*.[45]

The remonstrants further demand that all pretence of necessity for assent by lords or king in the making of laws be forthwith abolished. The Commons are the servants of the people, the supreme representative, accountable only to their masters. Let them free Lilburne and other prisoners arbitrarily imprisoned by the Lords; let them establish complete freedom for "what judgement or way of Worship whatsoever"; [46] let them abolish this intolerable imprisonment for debt; let them set a time for their own dissolution and restore annual parliaments. Finally, the remonstrants complain bitterly about the crowds of poor that beg in the streets for half pennies; but the lords of silks and coaches have no compassion on them, neither do they make any stable provision for their relief.[47]

Stirred by Lilburne's imprisonment and responsive to his democratic propaganda, Richard Overton in 1646 turned aside for the first time from his anti-clerical tolerationist pamphleteering to a consideration of secular freedoms. The satirical soliloquy of the Presbyterian strategists in *A Remonstrance Of Many Thousand Citizens* bears strongly the stamp of Overton's hand, so deftly used in his attacks on the Assembly of Divines. His first signed pamphlet on political liberty, *An Alarum To the House of Lords* (July 31) shows how

completely Lilburne has captured his loyalty; his praise of Lilburne
is idealistic, almost extravagant. For freeing his country, asserts
Overton, Lilburne has suffered and achieved much more than all
the Lords together. Yes, his writings *are* dangerous: dangerous
to arbitrary power in kings, lords, or commons; dangerous to the
clergy, to the court cheats, to monopolists. And how can it be
seditious for a free Englishman unjustly accused and imprisoned to
publish his grievances to the world? Can any one show that his
motives are tyrannical, that *he* is striving for any arbitrary power?[48]
With all that Lilburne has written about the House of Lords Overton fully concurs. "If timely Cautions will not availe with you,"
he warns the Lords, "you must expect to be bridled, for wee are
resolv'd upon our Naturall *Rights* and *Freedoms,* and to be enslaved
to none, how Magnificent soever, with Rotten Titles of Honour." [49]
Undoubtedly Overton knew that his pamphlet would bring reprisals
from the Lords. Arrested in his home a few nights later, haled
before a committee of the Lords, and later brought before the bar
of the House, Overton, like Lilburne, refused to answer or remain
uncovered. On August 11 he was committed to Newgate for printing
scandalous things against the Lords, refusing to answer the speaker,
and using contemptuous words and gestures.[50] Less than a month
later (September 9) appeared *A Defiance Against All Arbitrary
Usurpations,* a tract which, even if only partly his own, reflects
Overton's marked development as a political theorist. Asserting
the natural freedom of the people, he bewails the contented slavery
into which they have fallen through the flattery of the usurping
lords; so befuddled have the masses become that they account it
"their honour to rob themselves, and their posterities, of their just
Birth-rights and Freedoms, to make those domineering Insulters
magnificent and mighty, and themselves and posterities miserable."
He exhorts the people to resist the king and Lords, to acknowledge
no supreme court but the House of Commons; they alone have the
power to try a commoner in criminal cases. Justifying his resistance
to the Lords, Overton adds: "I was not born for my self alone, but
for my neighbor as well . . . and I am resolv'd to discharge the
trust which God hath repos'd in me for the good of others." [51] Overton's imprisonment, like Lilburne's, lent wings to his words; he
dramatized his plight again in *An Arrow Against All Tyrants* (October 12). Under Magna Charta, he insists, the Lords have no right to

judge him or any commoner. As puppet appointees of the king, who has no sovereign power from the people, the lords cannot claim a legislative or a judicial function that the king himself has never rightfully possessed.[52] As Overton had thrown his whole energies into his role as Martin Mar-Priest, scathingly denouncing Presbyterian intolerance, so now he released his biting intelligence into the field of secular reform, turning from philosophical satire to dramatic political protest. The sacrifices of Lilburne had extended his revolutionary spirit and purpose to Richard Overton, a pamphleteering blade even keener and brighter than his own. Their causes merged, the two leaders now claimed thousands of followers among the London lower classes. Soon the army itself was to feel the power of their propaganda.

CHAPTER V

LEVELLER AND INDEPENDENT IN DEBATE

OWHERE in seventeenth-century history does one find the contrast in the mental outlook of the leading revolutionists so clearly illuminated as in the army debates of 1647. In these debates clashed the theories of the property-owning, God-appealing Independents with the more materialistic Levellers: Cromwell and Ireton for compromise with the traditional Constitution, Rainsborough and Wildman for a democratic charter that anticipated American manhood suffrage laws of the 1840's.

For six months the Levellers had engaged in an intensive propaganda campaign among the soldiers and citizenry. When his repeated appeals to the House of Commons had done nothing to effect his release from prison, Lilburne condemned them as tyrannical and threatened to broadside their delinquencies to the people: *"Tyranny* ... is tyranny, exercised by whom soever," he wrote on January 30, 1647, "yea, though it be by members of Parliament. . . . I am now determined . . . if I speedily have not that Justice, which the Law of *England* affords me . . . no longer to wait upon the destructive seasons of prudentiall men: but forthwith to make a formall Appeale to all the Commons of the Kingdome of *England*." [1] A month later, in *The out-cryes of oppressed Commons*, Lilburne and Overton repeated this threat, complaining of the Commons' failure to redress grievances, discuss petitions, of its dividing a hundred thousand pounds of the public's money among its members. By its failure to perform its functions, it is ceasing to be a Parliament, conclude the Leveller leaders; it is therefore returning the kingdom to a state of nature, voiding its own powers. "We for our preservation shall tread in the Parliament steps by *appealing to the People* against them, as they did against the King." [2] From this time forth the Leveller conception that the kingdom was in a state of nature, the government to be re-established only by the mutual consent of the people, was a fundamental tenet argued for in their declarations and conferences, and inherent in the *Agreement of the People*. The impossibility of obtaining such free mutual consent from a majority of Englishmen, justly pointed out by Cromwell, was a fact never openly acknowledged by the Levellers. They judged the consent of the "well-affected" citizenry sufficient.

Notwithstanding their threats against the House, the Levellers in March summarized their grievances in a remarkable petition, so drastic in its demands that the House considered it treasonable and ordered it burned by the hangman. Written perhaps in part by Walwyn, the petition opens in a quiet, complimentary vein, thanking Parliament for its successive measures against ship money, bishops, the High Commission, the Star Chamber. But oppressions still remain "with grievances of the same destructive nature as formerly, though under other notions." [3] The petitioners then list thirteen demands, urging the elimination of veto power in either king or lords; the removal of sentences imposed by the Commons without due process of law; the repeal of compulsive religious ordinances; the abolition of tithes, churches to be supported by voluntary contributions only; the dissolution of the Merchant Adventurers' monopoly; the release of imprisoned debtors "as are altogether unable to pay"; sustenance of the poor; appointment of honest prison keepers; shorter legal procedure; publication of all laws in English; limitation of legal fees; more equitable punishments so that "no mans life may be taken, his body punished, nor his estate forfeited, but upon . . . weighty and considerable causes." [4] So sweeping a program, as Gardiner observes, inimical as it was to the lawyers, the business men, the clergy, in short, to the interests of the most influential London citizens, was more likely to be achieved in three centuries than in a single Parliament.[5] But the Levellers persisted in their attempts to force the social structure and habits of their day into nineteenth-century patterns. Their petitions scorned, their grievances unredressed, they turned to the army for the aid of the sword against Parliament. In *Rash Oaths unwarrantable* (May 31) Lilburne reprinted the famous burned petition, declaring that the Commons had nullified the purpose for which they sat, and comparing them to "devouring Lions and ravening Wolves," who deserve to be utterly destroyed. He would appeal to the Army and the common people to destroy the parliamentary tyrants.

The Army was in a receptive mood for radical propaganda. In its discussions was apparent, as nowhere in England, the explosiveness inherent in the principles of the *Areopagitica*. Now almost three years old, the New Model Army, disciplined and confident, dominated by religious radicals, lived in a ferment of unorthodox religious opinions. A year or two before, Richard Baxter, alarmed by the unsteady notions whirling about, set himself as a kind of unofficial chaplain to combat dangerous tenets. But the task was too difficult. Men with little education, with no training in theology, he found ready to dispute for the most corrupt and silly errors: "sometimes for State Democracy, and sometime for Church Democracy; sometimes against Forms of Prayer, and sometimes against Infant Baptism . . . and sometimes about Free-grace and Free-will, and all the Points of Antinomianism and Arminianism." [6] With growing alarm Baxter listened to the secular applications of corrupt theological doctrines. The king the soldiers took for an enemy, a tyrant, to be killed like any other man. And "what were the Lords of *England* but *William* the Conquerour's Colonels? or the Barons but his Majors? or the Knights but his Captains? They plainly shewed me, that they thought God's Providence would cast the trust of Religion and the Kingdom upon them as Conquerours." [7] An especially dangerous influence in corrupting the soldiers' minds, Baxter found, was the pamphlets of Overton and Lilburne, which were freely dispersed and read by the men in widely separated quarters, where none appeared to contradict them. In argument Baxter found the men passionate and unyielding: "They drowned all Reason in fierceness, and vehemency, and multitude of words." [8] For the dire outcome of such intellectual restlessness Baxter's fears were well grounded. Not only was each man his own Biblical interpreter, to think and preach among his fellows as he pleased; but in an atmosphere of mutual respect he was free to develop individualistic political theories, theories untouched by traditional university patterns, unorthodox, menacing, immature. "Wee are most of us butt young Statesmen," said Allen, in the debate of July 17, 1647, asking for more time to consider the Heads of Proposals.[9] Their ideas slowly crystallizing with the shaping of events, the men finally sensed the crucial importance of the army's role in the drama of England's constitutional upheavals. Of steady, deliberate valor, quick wit at decisive moments, the soldiers of this strange army united an amazing capacity for cohesive action with powers of contemplation and discussion, and a political curiosity unparalleled in military annals.

As early as April, 1647, the soldiers felt a need for expressing their opposition to Parliament through representatives of their own choosing, later called agitators. This may have been done at the instigation of Lilburne himself, upon whose pamphlets the soldiers relied, according to a contemporary letter, as upon statute law.[10] Lilburne was losing faith simultaneously in Cromwell and the "silken Independents" of Goodwin's London congregation.[11] In a letter dated March 25, he accused Cromwell of undermining not only the army's petition but that of the Levellers themselves. If the army disbands before petitioning, he and all his followers will hold Cromwell responsible. In a letter dated July 1 Lilburne claimed credit for organizing the agitators against the opposition of Cromwell and his "fellow Grandees"; he "acted both night and day to settle the Souldiers in a compleat and just posture, by their faithfull agitators, chosen out by common consent from amongst themselves . . . to effect my Liberty, to give a checke to tyranny, and settle the peace and justice of the Kingdome." [12] Again, in *The Iuglers Discovered* (August 21), Lilburne justified his organization of the soldiers, being afraid, he says, to trust the officers further.[13] *Ionah's Cry out of the Whales belly,* consisting mainly of his letters to Cromwell, he had published specifically to warn the private soldiers of the machinations of Cromwell and his officers. In appealing to the common soldiers over the heads of their leaders, Lilburne was not at a loss for theoretical justification: When the army defied Parliament in seizing the king, it ceased to act under Parliament's commission, the soldiers were therefore dissolved "into the originall law of Nature," wherein each soldier was released from military discipline and free to choose representatives to carry out his wishes.[14]

Fearful as they were of the Leveller theories, Cromwell and Ireton found it necessary to placate the radicals as much as possible, meanwhile attempting a settlement of the country by means of an agreement with the king. Thus far they had no thought of eliminating the power of the king or Lords, making them totally subservient to the Commons, much less of appealing to the people, as the source of all power, to agree to a constitution that would limit even the power of the House. Their negotiations with the king showed their desire to return him to the throne under those limitations for which they had engaged. According to the Solemn Engagement signed at New Market June 5, however, no action was to be taken by the army as a whole except by vote of the General Council, in which two soldiers from each regiment were to sit, as well as two commissioned officers.[15] Thus did Cromwell recognize the right of the soldiers to a part in the settlement of the kingdom, the army, through the activities of the agitators, being in a state of mutiny.[16] In their resistance to the extreme demands of the army radicals, he and Ireton slowly and somewhat fearfully yielded point after point, demonstrating much tact and moderation in effecting a united front, meanwhile attempting to retain the traditional constitutional structure.

The Heads of the Proposals as drawn up by Ireton in July, 1647, while providing for biennial Parliaments, more equitable representation according to population, temporary control of the militia by a Council of State, did not eliminate the negative voices of king and Lords.[17] In *Putney Projects* (December 30) Wildman bitingly attacked the Proposals, denying that they represented the sentiments of the soldiers, naming five particulars in which the Proposals were altered in the final draft to give the king more power. Not only had Ireton and Cromwell eliminated the restriction on the king's negative voice; they had reduced the exclusion of royalists from ten years to five, eliminated a provision for extirpation of the bishops as well as one confirming the sale of the bishops' lands.[18] Wildman further pointed out that the control of the militia was prohibited in the Proposals to Charles only, not to his descendants; that the king was not required to swear that he would keep the laws; that the source of authority was not designated as the people themselves but by implication still resided in the king's will.[19] The contradiction in the procedure of the Proposals Wildman summarizes as follows: "The conquered enemy must be petitioned to grant, and confirme the price of the blood of thousands: and an act drawn in this form, YOVR MAJESTIES LOYAL SVBJECTS, *who have subdued your Maiesty by their sword, whose prisoner now you are,* now assembled in Parliament, do HVMBLY PRAY, that it be inacted, &c." [20]

Cromwell and Ireton persisted strenuously in their negotiations with the king notwithstanding the criticism of the Levellers. Even in September, 1647, Ireton told Huntington that the army would purge and purge until Parliament accepted the king; and Cromwell assured the king through Huntington that the army would stand by the Heads of the Proposals.[21] On October 18, five regiments, having elected new agitators, presented to Fairfax *The Case of the Army truly stated,* the original of the first *Agreement of the People.* In it were avowed the theories that all power is inherent in the people; that the free choice of their representatives is the foundation of government; that Parliament itself may not abrogate certain liberties reserved to the people. The power of king and lords was by implication nullified.[22] Thus were crystallized the beliefs of the Levellers, most of which, having grown from concrete circumstances of the imprisonment and court struggles of Lilburne and Overton, had enlisted the support of the discontented soldiers. On October 20, in a three-hour speech in the House, Cromwell disavowed any support of *The Case of the Armie truly stated,* claiming that neither he nor Fairfax nor the principal officers had contributed to it, and urging the immediate re-establishment of monarchy.[23] As late as October 28, in the debates at Putney, Ireton said, "I doe not seeke, or would not seeke, nor will joyne with them that doe seeke the destruction either of Parliament or Kinge." [24] The next day he qualified his position: "If God saw itt good to destroy, nott only Kinge and Lords, butt all distinctions of degrees —nay if itt goe further, to destroy all property . . . if I see the hand of God in itt I hope I shall with quietnesse acquiesce, and submitt to itt, and nott resist itt." [25] On these points, however, so far as the debates reveal, the hand of God touched Ireton only lightly, if at all.

Cromwell's opposition to the *Agreement* as expressed in his extempore speeches of October 28 illuminates the mainsprings of his political reasoning. The elements of the *Agreement,* he said, were new to him; he had not had opportunity to consider them. But it was apparent that it contained "very great alterations of the very Governement of the Kingedome, alterations from that Governement that itt hath bin under, I beleive I may almost say since itt was a Nation." Plausible as it sounded, to adopt it might breed utter confusion. For what was to prevent another group of men, or many groups all for the sake of liberty, from presenting other papers equally plausible, pleading for their validity above all other plans? Too many plans would engender conflict, perhaps break the kingdom asunder into antagonistic states. Then, too, Cromwell continued, they were bound to consider whether or not "the spiritts and temper of the people of this Nation are prepared to receive and to goe on alonge with itt." He anticipated "very great mountaines" in the way of the *Agreement*. Almost any one of them might propose an excellent solution. But was not the likelihood of gaining the people's acceptance a consideration primary to the good or evil of the solution itself? He felt, therefore, that the agitators should show a willingness to make any amendments that "cleare reason" might approve, not insisting peremptorily upon the letter of the *Agreement*.[26]

Cromwell's conservatism and his keen sense of national sentiment are at once apparent in these arguments. He was definitely opposed to a sharp cleavage with the traditional government of the kingdom; he realized that kingship as an institution was deeply reverenced by the masses of the people. True, a time was to come when Cromwell felt Charles' execution necessary; and he had, unlike Essex, insisted upon annihilation of the king's forces. But in late 1647 Cromwell was fearful of new theories of government; he did not understand the democratic intellectual surge that lay behind the presentation of the *Agreement*. He had not followed the trend of the Leveller pamphlets; nor had he been subjected to the long process of theorizing in the position of the underdog that had characterized the lives of Lilburne and Overton. Reaching for national unity, he realized much more clearly than the Levellers the power of the influential classes and the impossibility of gaining their acceptance of such a revolutionary program. And Cromwell's political analyses were based on observation and controlled to some degree by the forces of his social environment. His mysticism, much as it dominated his feeling and speech, did not noticeably affect his opposition to decisive alterations or his insistence on the likelihood of success as a primary criterion.

Both Rainsborough [27] and Wildman replied to Cromwell in a fashion typical of the radical approach to the constitutional problems involved. Neither, it is true, told how they might leap the formidable barrier of public opinion in securing the acceptance of a government so foreign to English traditions. But should the vision of difficulties prevent them, asked Rainsborough, from attempting such a settlement? Though death loomed ahead, and the sea on three sides, a man convinced by conscience should not decline the hazard of advancing. Difficulties indeed! Had they not considered difficulties when the war against the king began? Every man expected them. And the "huge alteration" Cromwell had spoken of he did not fear at all. Many had been the struggles in England between tyrants and honest men, and all the best laws now operative had reduced the power of lords and king. And if the people were dissatisfied with the present order, if they found the laws still unsuitable to free men, why should they not endeavor by all possible means to change them to their advantage? If the *Agreement* was just and right, nothing should deter them from establishing it.[28] Wildman also had been quick to ask that justice, not expediency, be the determining factor in their discussions of the *Agreement*.[29] Like Lilburne and Overton, Wildman and Rainsborough were ready to cry "Justice! Justice!", to tilt with the windmills of the inexorable injustices of generations, without realistically counting the cost. Cromwell, on the other hand, a more practical reformer, wanted a compromise that would not break too sharply with precedent and cleave England further asunder. More logical in application of political theory, possessed of a keener historical sense than Cromwell, the Levellers had less perception than he of the weakness of the masses and the tenacity of class divisions. Neither Cromwell, nor any of his prominent supporters, including Milton, would have agreed fully with Rainsborough's representation of English history as relentless warfare between the commoners and their oppressors. But this is a conception found frequently in Leveller pamphlets; their interpretation of history is one of a simplified class struggle.

After a conciliatory speech by Cromwell, at the end of which he offered to withdraw from the army, even sacrifice his life, before he would hinder a general settlement, Lieutenant-Colonel Goffe suggested an appeal to the Lord for light.[30] As Firth has pointed out, "Cromwell in difficulties generally moved for a Committee; Goffe invariably proposed a prayer-meeting." [31] To the tenets of the *Agreement* Goffe could not agree or disagree, though much of it he thought acceptable. Filled with Fifth-Monarchy phraseology, Goffe's speech of around nine hundred words repeats the word *God* or *Lord* twenty-eight times. He feared that the Lord was withdrawing Himself from them, that He had not manifested Himself so much as formerly. If people walk obstinately against God, He either breaks them in pieces or lets their glory die. Whereupon Goffe added, "I speake itt I hope from a divine impression." [32]

The response to Goffe's proposal illuminates the gulf between Leveller and Independent. Cromwell's support was immediate. He asked, indeed, why they should wait until tomorrow to bring their problems before the Lord. Then he added: "For my parte I shall lay aside all businesse for this businesse, either to convince or be convinc't as God shall please." [33] Likewise praising Goffe's suggestion, Ireton averred that Goffe had never spoken but that he had touched his heart; he confessed that he himself had not walked closely enough with God, and urged every one to "waite uppon God, for the errours, deceits, and weaknesses of his owne heart." [34] Thus far the reaction of the Leveller agitators had been silence only. But when Cromwell suggested that "they should nott meete as two contrary parties, butt as some desirous to satisfie or convince each other," Pettus replied immediately that he had carried out his instructions and could not meet again only to repeat his assent to the *Agreement*. In a vague or half-reported speech another agent (Buffe-Coate) showed some dislike for the idea of a prayer meeting, whereupon Cromwell felt it necessary to defend Goffe's suggestion thus: "I hope wee know God better then to make appearances of Religious Meetings as covers for designs for insinuation amongst you." [35] That the radicals *did* have some such suspicions is inherent in this speech of Cromwell's. It is significant too that Wildman, without referring to the topic of prayer, returned shortly afterward to the problem of whether or not the *Agreement* secured the rights of the people as affirmed in the army declaration of June 14. Nor did Rainsborough seem anxious for a prayer meeting; he spoke for it only briefly and incidentally later in the debate. The attitude of the Levellers, in short, if not one of distrust of the Independent reliance on prayer, was one of indifference. They were concerned, as the speeches of Wildman and Pettus show, with a realistic solution of the problem at hand, the acceptance or rejection of the *Agreement*. Their eagerness for the *Agreement* they derived, not from divine revelation, but from analysis of their own clash with the essential dominant forces of their time.

The debate on manhood suffrage illuminates as no other discussion not only the divergence in Independent and Leveller points of view, but also the intellectual habits of the leading debaters, Ireton, Cromwell, and Rainsborough. Tempers fraying, wits flashing, the burden of pent-up meditations impulsively pouring forth, with now and then the moderating voice of Cromwell, or a caustic interruption by an agitator cutting across the conflict—all these, reported so vividly in the verbatim record, convey the strikingly fundamental nature of the issues, some of them still starkly controversial in the twentieth century.

When the first article of the *Agreement* (providing for manhood suffrage) was read in the October 29 meeting of the General Council, Ireton, speaking in opposition, held persistently to his train of reasoning. To allow every man to vote, he argued, would violate the fundamental constitution of the kingdom, which was property. Time after time Ireton insisted on property as the foundation of English society, and the possession of property as the basis for the right to vote. The source of voting and law-making power was not in the masses at large, but in the land owners: "The originall of power, of making lawes, of determining what shall bee law in the land, does lie in the people that are possess't of the permanent interest in the land." [36] By fixed permanent interest Ireton did not mean necessarily a large holding, but one which according to custom guaranteed a man the franchise, land or buildings worth at least forty shillings a year in rent. If propertyless men (who Colonel Rich said outnumbered the owning class five to one) were allowed to vote, Ireton anticipated that they would elect poor men to office. There was a danger, moreover, that the poor would vote the wealth of the property owners away from them, even destroy all property.[37] Cromwell concurred with Ireton, saying that he had heard no arguments which "in a tittle" answered those of the Commissary General.[38] Also supporting Ireton, Colonel Rich feared that a majority, not necessarily in combustive anarchy, but by orderly legal measures, would destroy property or distribute goods and estates equally. Or might not the poor voters be corrupted by the rich and those tyrants returned to power who could buy the most votes?[39] Thus it was that Ireton and his colleagues analyzed the logical extension of the democratic method. They envisioned far more realistically than the Levellers the irreconcilable conflict between manhood suffrage and concentrated economic power.

Significantly enough, Ireton made no effort to justify his defense of a property-restricted franchise by the law of God or the law of nature. He admitted straightforwardly that justification of one's claim to property by the divine law would be very difficult. "Our property as well as our right of sending Burgesses descends from other things." [40] Upon the phrase "other things" Ireton did not elucidate; he merely reiterated from time to time his definition of property as "the most fundamentall civil Constitution of this Kingedome." The divine law lays down not particulars but general principles, from which principles it is impossible to deduce specific solutions to political problems. Though Ireton declared still again that he was willing to see king, lords, commons, or any human institution destroyed, if he saw the hand of God in the act, he could not consent to any such action otherwise.[41] In all his reasoning about the suffrage, as he himself calls to our attention, Ireton did not look for revelations from God, much as he was accustomed to do so in his daily life. Nor did Cromwell once refer to revelations from God as guiding him on the topic of the franchise. Ireton and Cromwell, to a less extent, it is true, than Goffe and Saltmarsh and Harrison, were God-intoxicated men, sincerely looking for God's direct guidance, often carried away by inspirational fervor. This was the character of the Independent. But in most of their political and military decisions it was the forces of secular training and social environment that carried the day, as in the debates on manhood suffrage. It was intellectual realism that answered, not religious ardor.

In refuting Ireton's arguments, Rainsborough asserted that man's reason, not his property, qualified him to vote. "I doe thinke;" he said, "that the maine cause why Almighty God gave men reason, itt was, that they should make use of that reason . . . Either itt must bee the law of God or the law of man that must prohibite the meanest man in the Kingdome to have this benefitt as well as the greatest. I doe nott finde any thinge in the law of God, that a Lord shall chuse 20 Burgesses, and a Gentleman butt two, or a poore man shall chuse none." [42] The foundation of all law, claimed Rainsborough, was not in property but in the people. Were not people more important than estates? Many soldiers, for instance, who had ventured not only their lives but lost their estates in the war against the king, would return home disqualified from voting. Thus they would lose the use of their reason, so to speak, whereas the men of property would continue to make the laws. "I would faine know," exclaimed Rainsborough, "what the souldier hath fought for all this while? Hee hath fought to inslave himself, to give power to men of riches, men of estates, to make him a perpetuall slave." [43] To Colonel Rich's argument that the poor would vote away the lands of the rich, outnumbering them five to one, Rainsborough replied that with the poor disenfranchised the rich may make the poor their servants and slaves. And when the rich men fall out among themselves, they impress the propertyless citizens into armies to fight for them. [44]

Rainsborough debated with extreme effectiveness, notwithstanding his outbursts of indignation. He took notes on Ireton's comments and attempted to answer him point by point. He was particularly incensed that Ireton should accuse his colleagues of destroying property; the right to hold property, he said, is recognized in the Bible by the commandment, "Thou shalt not steal." Not only did Cromwell and Ireton believe that the champions of manhood suffrage inclined to anarchy, insisted Rainsborough, but they would have liked to make all men believe it, thus confusing the essential issue. To which Cromwell replied, "Noe man sayes that you have a minde to anarchy, butt the consequence of this rule tends to anarchy, must end in anarchy." Then he tried to moderate Rainsborough's anger by saying, "I am confident on't wee should nott bee soe hott one with another." [45] In a later ironical outburst, nevertheless, Rainsborough exclaimed, "Sir I see, that itt is impossible to have liberty butt all propertie must be taken away." [46]

From the debates on the *Agreement* it is evident that Ireton and Cromwell had fallen back on the timeless bulwark of conservative apologists, anticipation of anarchic desolation. How deeply the radical leaders resented this attack, how they struggled to counteract its effects, is revealed not only in Rainsborough's speeches, but also in the pamphlets being distributed among the soldiers. The very day (October 29, 1647) on which Rainsborough spoke, for instance, appeared Wildman's *A Cal To All The Souldiers Of The Armie*. He warned the soldiers against the persuasions of the officers at headquarters: "If yee doe adventure to goe thither, beware that yee be not frighted by the word ANARCHY, unto a love of *Monarchy,* which is but the gilded name for *Tyranny;* for *Anarchy* had never been . . . once mentioned amongst you, had it not been for that wicked end; 'tis an old thred-bare trick of the prophane Court, and doth amongst discreet men shew plainly who is for the Court, & against the liberties [of] the people, who, when soever they positively insist for their just freedomes, are immediatly slap't in the mouthes with these most malignant reproaches, O, yee are for *Anarhchy* [*sic*], yee are against all Government." [47]

Though he spoke only three of four times in the debate on manhood suffrage, Wildman effectively supported the arguments of Rainsborough. The proposal should be judged, he said, not according to its possible consequences, but as to whether it was just and right. He feared that they looked to prophecies rather than to justice. The people had been under slavery and now they were determined upon their freedom. As for the laws they now had, they were tyrannical, having been made by the conquerors of the common people, who had never given their consent to them and consequently were not bound by them. It was not his aim, said Wildman, to uphold these old laws, to go according to custom. Even the history of former days had been written by the privileged classes, who would not allow any other interpretation than their own to be recorded. What they now wanted was a fundamental change, wherein the people would have a voice: "Every person in England hath as cleere a right to Elect his Representative as the greatest person in England." [48]

Sexby, like Rainsborough, spoke of the sacrifices of the poor and of their right to a fuller participation in the affairs of government. Thousands of soldiers with no estates had risked their lives. "I doe thinke," he said, "the poore and meaner of this Kingedome . . . have bin the meanes of the preservation of this Kingedome." [49] These people had a stake in the country, a birthright, as well as the property holders. If they had not such a birthright, which should guarantee them the privilege of selecting their representatives, the soldiers had fought as mere mercenaries. Why should the poor be accused of bringing confusion? This was but a "distrust of providence." Those who supported manhood suffrage were as free from any intention of bringing in anarchy as those who opposed it. He could not for a moment assume that the possession of an estate (regardless of how it had been acquired) made a man capable of choosing his representative. Their stand for manhood suffrage had, he felt, the sanction of the law of God and the law of conscience. In an angry moment Sexby spoke out in condemnation of Ireton and Cromwell: "I am nott sorry to see that which I apprehend is truth, butt I am sorry the Lord hath darkened some soe much as not to see itt." [50]

The 1647 debates of the Levellers with the Independents show the Civil War assuming an aspect that the Independents had never intended to materialize. They had looked first mainly to liberty of conscience and limitation of the king's powers as the main aims of the war. But now, having victory in their grasp, they had to contend with a soldiery aroused by a minority of intellectuals to demand a deeper cleavage with the past. Fearing mutiny and confusion, Ireton and Cromwell compromised with the soldiers' demands, keeping the framing of the army declarations largely in their own hands, slowly becoming convinced that the democratic demands were not without justification, meanwhile attempting a settlement of a modified monarchy through negotiations with Charles. But Ireton and Cromwell were unprepared for the intense surge of democratic agitation carried on by the Levellers and their adherents from March until October. By June the soldiers had forced the adoption of the General Council, but their constitutional demands were only beginning to crystallize. In justly claiming credit for the army declarations, Ireton said, in effect, "Did you want this manhood suffrage in June? Were you not satisfied then with the property restriction as I wrote it for you?" [51] To this Rainsborough made no reply. But the aims of the Levellers, as we have shown, which in the March petition had sought reforms through the House of Commons, had by October crystallized into a constitutional revolution. Backed probably by a majority of the army,[52] certainly by Parliament and the influential classes generally, Cromwell successfully resisted the adoption of the *Agreement*.

The attitude of both Levellers and Independents toward the *Agreement* was colored inevitably by their social and economic status. The Independents were men of the upper middle class, born into families not rich but prosperous, families accustomed to send their sons to Oxford and Cambridge. Cromwell inherited a property which in 1631 he sold for 1800 pounds. In 1642 he subscribed 600 pounds for the conquest of Ireland and 600 pounds for the defense of Parliament.[53] As lieutenant general Cromwell received 2500 pounds annually. In Lilburne's view this was a bribe to keep Cromwell from pressing the House for important reforms.[54] In opposing the *Agreement* Cromwell and Ireton were not, of course, attempting to protect their property holdings. Devoted to their cause, they were unselfishly trying to effect lasting reforms while holding in check immoderate radicalism. But the Ireton arguments on manhood suffrage were those that Royalists or Presbyterians might have advanced with equal validity; socially and economically there was little to distinguish Presbyterian and Independent. In the words of Milton himself, the Independent leaders were "for the most part, men of the better conditions in life, of families not disgraced if not ennobled, of fortunes either ample or moderate." [55] The leaders of the Levellers, on the other hand, though not property-less by any means, sprang from lower social stations. Lilburne, Walwyn and Overton had served as apprentices in London; Rains-borough had early gone to sea; Sexby had joined the army as a private soldier; Prince was a cheesemonger. Of the Leveller spokes-men only Wildman had had any university training. Among the Leveller adherents numbered thousands of soldiers and citizens dis-franchised under the existing qualifications, whereas the Independent followers, by and large, were relatively prosperous.

In their religious views, as the debates show, the views of Leveller and Independent sharply diverged. Sustained by a personal faith, the Independents prayed often, expected divine revelations, believed that God often spoke through them. "Instead of catching occasional glimpses of the Deity through an obscuring veil," wrote Macaulay, "they aspired to gaze full on his intolerable brightness, and to commune with him face to face." With moods of self-abase-ment alternated in the Independent a sense of partnership with God: "He prostrated himself in the dust before his Maker: but he set his foot on the neck of his king." [56] The full fervor of their devotional zeal the Independents directed naturally toward the restraint of passions, the repression of the sex drive, the constant examination of motives, and a consideration of theological dilemmas. In the solution of their social problems, however, except for liberty of conscience, the zeal of the Independents made less effectual contribution. Ireton and Cromwell, as we have shown, made no pretence of connecting their religious zeal with their opposition to the principles of the *Agreement*.

The distrust that the Levellers felt for the zeal for God's direct tutelage is revealed in a statement by Wildman during a debate on the *Agreement*. Much as he reverenced any speech that seemed to bear God's spirit, he said, the truth of that speech had to be demonstrated in some other way than the mere assertion by the speaker that it was God's message. He felt that it was impossible in civil matters to find solutions in the word of God. Then he added this significant statement, typical of the Leveller approach to religious motivation:

I conceive that onely is of God that does appeare to bee like unto God, justice and mercy, to bee meeke and peaceable. I should desire therefore that wee might proceede onelie in that way. If itt please this honourable Councill to consider what is justice and what is mercy, and what is good, and I cannot but conclude that that is of God. Otherwise I cannott thinke that any one doth speake from God when hee sayes [so].[57]

The religion of the Levellers, therefore, sought an outlet in social action, in good works, with a corresponding lack of emphasis on the personal virtues. Time after time Walwyn equated real Christianity and love of one's fellow man. When accused of atheism and lasciviousness by the Independents, Overton wrote:

The businesse is, not how great a sinner I am, but how faithfull and reall to the Common-wealth; that's the matter concerneth my neighbour . . . for my personall sins that are not of Civill cognizance, or wrong unto him, to leave them to God, whose judgment is righteous and just.[58]

The Levellers represented, therefore, the rising tide of secular reform more fully than the Independents. By their opponents the Levellers were labelled atheists and communists; the Independents, hypocrites and Grandees.

CHAPTER VI

HUE AND CRY AFTER WILLIAM WALWYN

ETWEEN four and five on the morning of March 28, 1649, a troop of horse and foot surrounded the house of William Walwyn, awakened and alarmed his family, placed him under arrest, and despite his protests carried him off to Derby House, to await a meeting of the Council of State. Upon his refusal there to answer interrogatories against himself, as to his part in the writing of *The second Part of Englands New-Chaines Discovered* (March 24), he was thrust into prison.[1] To Lilburne this procedure was a familiar experience indeed. But it was Walwyn's first such arrest and first taste of prison life. He attributed it to the malice of the Independents, particularly those of John Goodwin's congregation.

The story of Walwyn's break with Goodwin's followers sheds a searching light both on the mind of Walwyn and the psychology of his Independent enemies. No leader of his day was more secular in his aims, or more devoid of theological predilections, than Walwyn. Yet he was deeply religious. In him were united, as in no other except Winstanley, a revolt against all theology with a radical program of reform. His enemies believed that he, more than Lilburne, was the intellectual leader of the Levellers.[2]

A prosperous silk merchant for seventeen or eighteen years, the father of twenty children, Walwyn was almost fifty years old in 1649. Since 1640 or 1641 he had been engaged in defending the rights of the people, writing a number of pamphlets anonymously and maintaining close association with the Independents in their stand against persecution.[3] Before the New Model, according to his own testimony, he conferred daily with Goodwin, Burton, Peters, and Lilburne.[4] When the Independents were in greatest danger, he defended them, among them the Anabaptist leaders Kiffin and Patience, and Henry Overton, of Goodwin's congregation, who afterward condemned him, Kiffin being one of the signers of *Walwins Wiles*.[5] Even in 1646 he was much respected by Goodwin's followers for writing *A Whisper in the Eare* and *A Word in Season*. To the printing of 10,000 of the latter pamphlet Goodwin's congregation gave 50 shillings.[6] Later in 1646, however, when Walwyn and his followers asked for signers of another petition against persecution, a petition supported by the Brownists and Anabaptists, Goodwin's congregation refused to assist them. The petition, nevertheless, continued in circulation. At a final meeting of the petitioners, at which Walwyn arrived late, some one had so blackened Walwyn's character, that when he arrived the keeper of the petition tore it up in front of the meeting. Walwyn afterward discovered that one Husbands had reported to Cromwell that Walwyn was an atheist and a whoremonger, and that of the Bible he had said, "What do ye tell me of that Idle book?" It was this story that had caused the destruction of the petition and since had circulated throughout the city.[7] Though Husbands in Walwyn's presence retracted his accusation, saying he had mistaken the man, the damage was done. "Aspersions fly faster," concludes Walwyn, "then any man can fetch them back." [8] His strife with Goodwin's congregation had begun.

In 1646 some leading parishioners of Goodwin's church formed a committee to inquire into Walwyn's character. At the conclusion of the investigation, several members of the committee, including one Brandriff, one Weekes, and a Captain Chaplain, were convinced of his integrity; but John Price and others drew up articles against him, which later formed the basis for the charge in *Walwins Wiles*. At a meeting called for the purpose of allowing Walwyn to defend himself, his enemies did not appear.[9] According to Walwyn, Goodwin's people carried bad reports to Cromwell about him. When Walwyn asked Cromwell why he allowed Walwyn to be reproached at his table, why he did not vindicate Walwyn when he was abused, Cromwell replied that he could not believe the scandals about Walwyn, but that they had been brought to him again and again by godly men.[10] Walwyn represents himself as having been on relatively familiar terms with Cromwell, dining with him often, sometimes with John Price, and attempting to persuade Cromwell to cease his negotiations with the king.[11] Were Goodwin's followers intentionally misunderstanding him, endeavoring to blacken his reputation? Walwyn believed so; he felt that *A Declaration of Congregationall Societies* (November 22, 1647) was issued to this end, rather than to vindicate the Independents and the Anabaptists from alleged belief in polygamy and communism.[12] The *Declaration* seriously attacks communism as being unpleasant to God. It would deprive men of the privilege of giving to others, breaking down the distinction between giving and receiving. Each person, declared the Congregations, should provide for his own household. The poor are poor probably because they are lazy. After all, continues the *Declaration*, the Bible affirms the right to possessions, and God has established many fine injunctions on buying and selling practices. God himself has set up differences in ownership.[13]

On the advice of Brandriffe, who in 1647 was still presumably his friend, Walwyn had written *A Still And Soft Voice*. In the human response to the persuasion of reason he had maintained implicit faith. He had been confident that a statement of his beliefs would clear his name and bury forever the aspersions of his enemies. "I . . . am in some hope," he wrote later, "to convert my Adversaries, which hath ever been my aim, equall to my own vindication." [14] *A Still And Soft Voice* describes one of the most remarkable intellectual creeds of Walwyn's generation. A single reading leaves the twentieth-century critic with a conviction of its permanent worth in the history of ideas.

Most professing Christians, says Walwyn, in *A Still And Soft Voice* are superstitious, clinging blindly to the religion imposed upon them by their environment and education, zealous of traditional opinions and customs. Such men are not truly religious at all, being "utterly ignorant of the cleare Heavenly brightnesse, inherent, in pure and undefiled Religion." [15] One of the identifying works of the superstitious Christian is his persecutions, revilings, abuses of other men; by killing and destroying them, the superstitious Christian in his zeal for vulgar notions believes he is being of service to God and the truth. And if any one in a reasonable and affectionate manner attempts to lay open their errors, and asks how they know there is a God, or that the Scriptures are his word, "their common answer is, *doe you deny them: it seemes you doe? otherwise why doe you aske such questions?* if they offer to proove by some common received argument: and you shew the weakenesse thereof: they'le goe nigh to tell you to your face, and report for certaine behind your back, to all they know . . . that you are an Athiest, that you deny there is a God . . . nor doe they hate any sort of men so much, as those who are *inquisitive after knowledge* . . . And thus ignorance becomes . . . Judge of knowledge: and the most grosse and slothfull; comptroller of the most active in Religion." [16] Such men are staunchly opposed to trying ideas. By their disdain of the poor, says Walwyn, you may know them, too. For the souls of the poor the superstitious man is much concerned; he will curse him "out of the Nation, if he can not course [curse] him *into his opinion:* and all upon pretence of doing God service and for the good of his soule." [17] But, says Walwyn,

As for his body . . . thats no part of his care, hee is not so hasty to runn into his poore neighbours house, to see what is wanting there, hee may ly upon a bed, or no bed, covering or no covering, be starved through cold and hunger, over burthened with labour, be sick, lame or diseased . . . he may through want and necessity goe into what prison he will, and ly and rott and starve there: and these kind of Religious people are not halfe so much moved at it, as if he goe to another Church or congregation, then what they approove: and if hee doe so, upstarts their zeale; and after him, watch, spy, accuse and informe: and all for the good of his soule: and for the Glory of God.[18]

Then, too, the personality of the superstitious man betrays him. Never spiritually secure, he tries to assure himself by trampling upon others, constantly alert for blasphemy, suspicious, spiteful, easily roused to anger.

The truly religious man finds as yet very little company in the world.[19] Unbound by tradition or custom, he tests all ideas with his reason; whether old or new he examines them fearlessly. But deeds of compassion and love, rather than tenets, justify the name of Christian. Walwyn calls for "more of the *deeds of Christians,* and fewer of the arguments." [20] A Christian should feed the hungry, clothe the naked, visit the sick, the fatherless, the imprisoned, according to the example of Jesus. Such a faith "will empty the fullest Baggs: and pluck downe the highest plumes." [21] Again and again Walwyn emphasizes the social compulsion of the gospel of love as the true test of a Christian spirit. All the rest is but sounding brass or a tinkling cymbal. Let the Independents sell all their uncertainties and vanities for the dominating principle of love: let them succor the poor and raise the helpless.[22] Governments, too, should be subject to the same Christian sympathy. "One main end of Government," he writes, is "to provide, that those who refuse not labour, should eat comfortably," especially in so fruitful a land as England.[23] In his personal relationships the truly religious man shows courtesy and forbearance, never hesitating to reveal his thoughts for the benefit of others, welcoming all opinions, never allowing dislike of an idea to culminate in personal antagonism.[24] But because he is willing to examine all ideas, the truly religious man must expect to be misunderstood. In the technique of discussion men are generally weak; and his superstitious friends, Walwyn says, when he wished to help them, perverted his ideas and with their reports injured his reputation.[25]

Walwyn's amazing credo, written probably early in 1647, brought no open criticism from Goodwin's people. One of them, in fact, congratulated him upon bringing out such a valuable tract. Walwyn felt that his statement had been acceptable to the Independents, with whom he continued to cooperate in various petitions. In the one of March, 1647, a large number of Independents at first engaged; when it was discovered before being presented and burned by the hangman, however, the leaders among them, Walwyn says, "stood aloof, and look'd on" while a number of the rank and file continued to ply the Commons. During 1647 and 1648, according to Walwyn's account, he and the men of Goodwin's church were on good terms, though sometimes differing on political action and church principles.[26] Goodwin's men were troubled that Walwyn could not ally himself with their church, but Walwyn, though standing firmly for each church's right to its own creed, felt that he could not conscientiously join any. On one occasion after a cup of beer and sugar at Walwyn's home, Mr. Lamb, a linen draper, asked him about his church opinions. After hearing Walwyn's discourse, Lamb appeared satisfied, but added, "O, Mr *Walwyn*, that you had a good opinion of Churches." [27] When Walwyn criticised Goodwin's sermons, saying that he spent too much time in making plain things difficult, that he sometimes confused his audiences, Goodwin's parishioners were displeased. Brandriff would ask, "Well, what shall we say? where can we hear better?" [28] Walwyn's criticism of Goodwin's tracts not only heightened the resentment of the congregation but cost him Goodwin's friendship.[29]

Walwyn relates two incidents that typified in his mind the character-blackening methods of Goodwin's followers. Late in 1647, in a chance street conversation Walwyn learned that his friend Major West had just heard him denounced at the Lord Mayors as a dangerous communist and anarchist:

He looks upon me somewhat ghastly, saying, what are you here? yes, said I, why not? why, saies he, being at my Lord Mayors, you were there said to be the most dangerous, ill-conditioned man alive; that you seek to have the City destroyed; that you would have no Government, and all things common . . . saies I, who is it that avouches this? why, saies he, *Henry Brandriffe,* who saies, he knows it to be true, and that he hath kept you company this seven years, of purpose to discover you.[30]

Upon another occasion, while Walwyn was lingering in a book shop, he was observed by Richard Price (uncle of one of his accusers in *Walwins Wiles*), who afterward denounced Walwyn to the bookseller as a drunkard and whoremaster, adding that he painted his face! When the bookseller reported this to Walwyn, he accosted Price, as his custom was, for an explanation of his conduct. Price assured him that he had not repeated the charges seriously, but would not divulge to Walwyn the name of the original accuser. For fifteen years, Walwyn said, he had lived in one neighborhood, Garlick Hill. Had Price inquired about his character from any of his neighbors? Was there no way by which slanderers could be called to account in the Goodwin's congregation? Price only assured him that no one seriously believed the reports.[31]

Walwyn was convinced that Goodwin's followers, and not Cromwell or the army leaders, were responsible for his arrest as the author of *The second Part of Englands New-Chaines Discovered*. It was they who had repeatedly carried aspersions to Cromwell, with whom he had talked frequently on the best of terms. In March he had twice been warned in letters of plots to imprison him.[32] On April 2, only four or five days after Walwyn's imprisonment in the Tower, appeared a petition designed, in Walwyn's view, to *rivet* him in.[33] Titled *The Humble Petition . . . Of Several Churches . . . in London, commonly (though falsly) called Anabaptists*, it avows that the petitioners had no part in framing or promoting *The second Part of Englands New-Chaines*, which they had openly opposed when it had been read in their meetings. The petitioners disclaim any intention of interfering with the civil power, regretting that their meetings "should be perverted to any sinister ends, or earthly respects whatsoever, whereby the spiritual seed of the Word should be stifled or hindered." [34] Here was a curious repudiation of the right of social action by the churches, a repudiation reminiscent of *A Declaration of Congregationall Societies*. In the seventeenth century church pressure in civil reform was a practice far more commonly accepted in England than it was to be three centuries later. *The Humble Petition* points, therefore, to a rejection of the secular aims heretofore avowed by some of the Independents, a sharp divergence from the Leveller creed, and a corresponding increase in emphasis on evangelistic religion. Yet at the very end of the petition appears a plea for relief of oppressions, coupled with a strong request that Parliament proceed to enforce penalties for drunkenness, whoredom, and cheating.[35] The latter article Walwyn felt his enemies had inserted further to blacken his reputation. The leader of the petitioners was William Kiffin, wealthy Anabaptist merchant and minister, friend of Goodwin, and one of the authors of *Walwins Wiles*. Overton also accused Kiffin of negotiating with the leaders of London congregations to promote the petition for the purpose of turning the religious people against the Leveller leaders.[36] Not his personal sins but his civil faithfulness, adds Overton, should concern his enemies.[37] Thus revolved still another ancient political device, whispers of scandal true or false choking inevitably considerations of social conduct. To the Independents, even to men of Cromwell's broad intelligence, social sinning was an elusive concept; when whoredom and adultery resounded, deeds of civic righteousness gasped and died. Walwyn and Overton reversed these values, but they stood little chance of impressing so secular a view upon the church-going citizens of London. The leaders of Goodwin's congregation, on the other hand, knew how potent would be their attack on Walwyn's personal habits and religious opinions.

Though still in prison, the leading Levellers, including Walwyn, continued their agitation. On April 4 appeared *A Picture of the Councel of State*, with biting denunciations from Lilburne, Prince, and Overton. Did Walwyn draw back from joining his comrades in so stinging a tirade? Lilburne was surprised to see Walwyn under arrest that morning of March 28; Walwyn had not, he says, engaged with them actively for several months.[38] After two weeks in prison, however, Walwyn joined with his three friends in *A Manifestation* (April 14), a calm, dignified statement of Leveller principles, somewhat defensive in tone, renunciatory of all intention of leveling estates or abolishing government. "Though Tyranny is so excessively bad, yet of the two extreames, Confusion is the worst." [39] On May 1 appeared their final edition of the *Agreement*, in which they again disavow communism, and urge their friends to consider the reasons for the campaign of lies against them.[40] The *Agreement* calls for annual parliaments, manhood suffrage (excepting servants, paupers, and Royalist soldiers), abolition of tithes, abolition of the excise, free trade, restriction of capital punishment.[41]

The attacks on the imprisoned Walwyn by Goodwin's parishioners culminated May 10 in the persuasive and enlightening pamphlet, *Walwins Wiles*. The authors' portrait of Walwyn, though exaggerated for propagandistic effect, has an authenticity confirmed by Walwyn's own pamphlets. To discredit Walwyn they resort to the name-calling technique of Edwards' *Gangraena*, trusting that their readers, like Edwards', will be horrified at the mere relation of Walwyn's ideas as dramatized by personal episodes. Avoiding a frontal barrage against the popular Lilburne, the authors first attempt to establish Walwyn as the brains of the Leveller movement: the subtle framer and manager of their petitions; the smooth beguiler and persuader, more crafty than his colleagues; the writer of their *Manifestation* in that "devout, specious, meek, self-denying" manner; the real author of the treasonable *Second Part of Englands New-Chaines Discovered.*[42]

A dangerous man, this Walwyn: consider his irreligious nature, his praise of the pagan classics, his pulling down the authority of the Bible, his many doubting questions, such as, "How can you prove the Scriptures to be the Word of God?" Often he has remarked that surely God would not punish a man eternally for a short time of sinning. God is gracious and good to men, and not without a sense of humor: *"I hope God is a merry old man, and will make a good companion when I am dead."* [43] And has Walwyn not asserted that Hell exists only on this earth, as man's conscience? That there is more wit in Lucian than in all the Bible? That the *Canticles* are nothing but a song about one of Solomon's whores? [44] Why, this Walwyn has even scoffed at prayer, saying,

What a silly thing it is for a man to drop down upon his knees, and hold up his hands, and lift up his eyes, and mumble over a few words for half an hour, or an hour together, as if this did please God, when all this while he might have been doing that which is good in it self, releeving the poor, judging the cause of the fatherless.[45]

He is wont, too, to abuse the ministry roundly, saying that they would let the poor starve to death rather than succor them; even the Papists and the heathen themselves have warmer hearts for the afflicted. To destroy the church he would even abolish tithes. It is not surprising that so scandalous a man should have justified suicide, probably having caused the death of a credulous woman who listened to his sophistry and then killed herself.[46]

Not content with ridiculing religion, continues *Wiles*, Walwyn has seduced and corrupted the poor people by his constant talk of inequalities, speaking thus:

What an inequitable thing it is for one man to have thousands, and another want bread, and that the pleasure of God is, that all men should have enough, and not that one man should abound in this Worlds good . . . and another man of far better deserts, not to be worth two pence.[47]

For Walwyn's part he could wish for no hedges, ditches, or fences in the whole nation; and it would never be well until all things were owned in common. Upon being reminded that this would destroy all government, this dangerous fellow declared that there would be much less need for Government, for thievery and covetousness would then disappear. The difficulty of effecting a revolution, he said, is much less than men suppose: "a very few diligent and valiant spirits may turn the world upside down, if they observe their seasons, and . . . with life and courage engage accordingly." [48] Had not Walwyn criticised Cromwell, Ireton, Harrison? And might not Walwyn have been responsible for the plot of the agitators to kill Cromwell? Thus does Price picture his enemy: a heretic, probably an atheist; but worst of all, a communist, a revolutionary plotter.[49]

So able and convincing a pamphlet as *Walwins Wiles* the Levellers could not allow to pass unchallenged. The first response, however, which probably represented the views of the Leveller agitators generally, seems to have been impelled by personal loyalty to Walwyn himself. *The Charity of Church-Men* (May 28), by Walwyn's friend Henry Brooke, does much to illuminate the campaign against Walwyn by the Independents. When men in authority, says Brooke, wish to divert men's minds from their burdens, what more effectual weapon than to discredit the champions of the people? And what renders a man more odious than to accuse him of atheism and communism? For by atheism are the religious people much antagonized; and by communism, the rich. Such charges the bishops and the Presbyterians had found efficacious indeed. That Walwyn is guiltless on both counts, adds Brooke, his whole life and conversation testify. But to blacken Walwyn his accusers have misquoted him, used parts of his speeches here and there, perverted his meaning. As for atheism, after living eight years in Walwyn's household, Brooke is convinced that Walwyn lives according to the teachings of Scriptures more fully than any one he knows; never has he heard Walwyn speak an angry word.[50] "It is not," writes Brooke, "an habit of Speaking . . . nor an Ability to Dispute or Discuss a point in Controversie, that truly denominates a man . . . [a Christian]; but the inward sweetness and calmness of Spirit, that Christianity prescribes; and which indeed, is more eminent in M. *Walwyn*, then I have known it in any man." [51] To lift the poor from their misery Walwyn had never proposed to pull down the rich. He had insisted, rather, that the commonwealth could be so ordered that every one willing to labor might have a comfortable living for his family.[52]

In defending Walwyn, Brooke bluntly attacks Goodwin and his church, calling Goodwin a timeserver who varies his doctrines according to the ideas of the victorious party. Whereas Goodwin had formerly argued, says Brooke, that the king was not accountable to any earthly court, now he maintains for the abolition of kingship itself. Bitterly Brooke inveighs against the Independents as the recipients of worldly favors. How saintly they are! To them every heart must bow, every head incline. Already they have high hopes of being large possessors, and "justle out other men as profane, worldly irreligious." [53]

The Fountain of Slaunder Discovered, Walwyn's first apology, though it appeared twenty days after *Walwins Wiles,* makes no mention of the enemy broadside. Walwyn wrote much of it before the appearance of *Wiles,*[54] well aware of the forces that had managed his imprisonment, and convinced that his pen was match for the whispering campaign against him. Tuned, except for autobiographical passages, to a philosophical pitch, somewhat after the fashion of *A Still And Soft Voice, The Fountain of Slaunder* makes no accusations against the members of Goodwin's congregation, attempts no vindication by episodic narration. Walwyn reminds the Independents that all progressive thinkers have been persecuted, the Presbyterians by the bishops, the Independents by the Presbyterians, and now the Levellers by the Independents. When the Independents were in gravest danger, he had defended them; they well remember his *Word in Season*. Walwyn protests against the strategy of answering a man's arguments for the public good by calling him *heretic, blasphemer, atheist*:

> Let a man with never so much discretion and fidelity, make known a publique grievance, or an imminent danger, and propose never so many effectual means for redresse and prevention, yet if one of these subtil Politicians, or their Agents, can have opportunity to buz into the ears of those that are concerned, that the proposer art an Heretique, a Blasphemer, an Atheist, a denier of God and Scriptures; or, which is worse to most rich men, that he is a Leveller, and would have all things common: then out upon him, away with such a fellow from off the earth; better perish then be preserved by so prophane a person: and in the mean time, who so seemingly pious, meek and religious as the asperser?[55]

Such persecutors deny the Scripture more literally than any heretic; for do they not reject from their hearts the spirit of brotherly love? Walwyn is convinced, however, that superstitious persecution and theological dross are yielding gradually to a religion of tolerance and reason.

In *Walwyns Just Defence*, which probably appeared in July or August,[56] Walwyn describes his relations with Goodwin's congregation with great care, using a roughly chronological sequence that reached back to episodes of 1642 or 1643. He attempts to show how the writers of *Wiles* have misinterpreted both his speech and his actions, meanwhile posing as his friends and repeatedly accepting his hospitality. To his love for the classics, so denounced in *Wiles*, Walwyn devotes long passages, pointing out that all university men have read Lucian, and that great Bible leaders such as Moses and Paul knew the learning of the Egyptians or the Greeks. The heathen had more charity then than the Independents now, claims Walwyn. He quotes from Montaigne's "On the Christian Religion," and recommends his essay on cannibals: "And what now shall I say? Go to this honest Papist, or to these innocent *Cannibals*, ye Independent Churches, to learn civility, humanity, simplicity of heart; yea, charity and Christianity." [57] If the Independents will hate riches, which Montaigne had termed "The Parcimony of our Fore-Fathers," and love the poor, that will make them more truly Christian than all their vain doctrines. As for "turning the world upside down" that he will leave to the Independents. The *Agreement* shows that he never worked for communism; he has favored only such reforms as will enable every man who will labor a comfortable subsistence.[58]

Walwyn's characterization of Goodwin's people, in which he resorts finally to the scandal-mongering tactics of his enemies, throws into sharp relief the reasons for his animosity. Whereas the true church has always been persecuted, their church now yearns for prosperity and favors. If not, why are they now so strong for the tithes they used to condemn so utterly? Now their steps lead to honors, not to prisons; and now as saints with the power of the sword in their hands, they intend to judge and rule the nation. But their saintliness, claims Walwyn, is flabby and hollow. How could Christians set their names to such an attack as *Walwins Wiles* before even speaking to their victim about the charges? Is it Christian for Goodwin, who knows the falsity of the charges against Walwyn, to remain silent while members of his congregation carry on a campaign of scandal? But in such matters the congregation sticks together, with their unified lying bearing down all opposition.[59] And all the while they are

solemn in their countenances, so frequent and so formall in their devotions, so sad at others chearfulnesse, so watchfull over others tripping, so censorious over others failings . . . bespeaking them in effect. . . . I am holyer then thou; it being a great scruple amongst many of them, the lawfulnesse of playing at Cards, or the like recreation, as being a vain expence of time.[60]

Some of these seeming Christians are usurers, claims Walwyn. Lacy and Lamb have some hundreds of pounds in the excise, which yield them good interest. And Taylor had written a letter to the Commissioner of Excise, asking him to be lenient, that he had friends who would speak for him. "These relations," remarks Walwyn, "are the

tenter-hooks, upon which all oppressions hang." [61] Their seeming
godliness is merely a show to gain reputation. Observe them behind
the scenes, when they are sure of being watched only by their
friends: then they will jeer, and laugh, and play, and tell foolish
jokes and tales, as other men; they will even laugh at each others'
expense, as to how long, for example, various ones had not held
marital intercourse.[62] All these things he had seen and heard himself, says Walwyn, when they pretended to be his friends, but were
in reality plotting to undo him and his family. Of Goodwin's people
Walwyn makes one final request: that they wear upon their hats or
coats, at those times when they are determined to be frank and
truthful, some conspicuous token of their intentions. Thus only can
an honest man put their trust in them.

The publication of *Walwyns Just Defence* brought no reply
either from Kiffin and Price or from John Goodwin himself. Walwyn
remained in prison until November 8, 1649, when, Lilburne having
been acquitted of treason to the Commonwealth for his writing
The second Part of Englands New-Chaines, the four Leveller leaders
were released.[63]

The truth of the charges and counter charges in the strife between Walwyn and Goodwin's congregation is of less significance to
us than the cleavage in social and religious outlook. To Walwyn
emphasis on observance of the Sabbath, playing of games, sins of the
flesh, attendance at church, prayer, doctrinal theories, were all faint,
inconsequential overtones sometimes more harmful than beneficial
to the practice of true Christianity. As an "antinomian" Walwyn
rested all faith in the Gospel of love, especially in the concern for the
material, secular welfare of his fellows. For the destiny of their souls
he cared little; for their immediate release from poverty, ignorance,
prison, governmental oppressions, he was ready to work without
stint or reward. Walwyn's agitation for applied Christianity in terms
of concrete political and economic reforms ran counter to the religious psychology of the leading Independents, though Independency had sowed the seeds from which the Leveller party rose. Lilburne, Overton, and Walwyn, as we have seen, first pamphleteered
as religious rebels allied in aims with the Independents. In fewer
than four years, however, the three men swerved sharply into revo-

lutionary secular reform, casting their lot with the disenfranchised lower middle class, breaking sharply at the end with the more prosperous Independents. Of the three men Lilburne was the most effective orator, the most fearless of consequences, a political leader in whom theoretical justification followed practical resistance of immediate oppressions; Overton as the most brilliant stylist dealt the most telling strokes in wit and satire against the enemy; Walwyn was the most contemplative, the best informed, the most mature theoretician. His demands for economic, as contrasted with political, reforms, loom more consistent and decisive than those of Overton and Lilburne.

CHAPTER VII

SWORDS FOR A KINGLESS ENGLAND

WHEN Algernon Sidney, in the discussions preceding the execution of Charles, insisted that the High Court of Justice could not try any man legally, much less a king, Cromwell turned on him fiercely: "I tell you," he exclaimed, "we will cut off his head with the Crown upon it." [1] This blunt resolution, shared by thousands of his fellow soldiers, deepened by each day's bitterness of the second Civil War, had crystallized in Cromwell's mind within the past thirteen months. In those months the determination of the Army Independents, heedless of tradition, scornful of public sentiment and parliamentary majorities, had been focused on bringing the king to justice. Against them, self-styled agents of God's vengeance, representers of the people, royalist and Presbyterian presses had turned in vain. Now, masters by the power of the sword, the Independents hoped to destroy, not only Charles himself, but the very institutions of kingship and lords.

Only an intense ferment of agitation could have opened the minds of even the tradition-hating army democrats to the desperate design of trying the king as a traitor. More conservative, Cromwell was certainly one of the last among his officers to yield to the persuasion of the Levellers, who anticipated, in 1646 and 1647, all the arguments that the Independents were to use in 1648 and 1649 to justify the accountability of kings. In turn the Levellers were indebted to the pamphleteers of 1642-43, who had sown the seed of democratic authority required to uphold the cause of Parliament against a king. Of these writers Philip Hunton was one of the most temperate and persuasive. In *A Treatise of Monarchy* (1643), possibly the most judiciously reasoned of all the kingship tracts of the period, Hunton asserted the right of the people to resist even an absolute monarchy, claimed that all monarchy had gained power originally by consent of the people, but denied that the people might lawfully either try a king for his misdemeanors or do violence to his person.[2] In his proposals for reconciliation between Charles and Parliament, Hunton recommended that the Parliament should prosecute the war no further than to secure its constitutional privileges; that royalist members should be readmitted without penalty; that Charles should appoint as counsellors and commanders of the militia only those approved by the Commons; and finally, that Charles should suspend his negative voice upon laws passed by majorities in Lords and Commons.[3] But hotter heads were seething with more extreme ideas. In those days Prynne himself was among the comrades of the left. Volume after volume, heavy with authorities, struck the democratic note that returned to plague him in 1649: the pre-eminence of law, the superiority of Parliament and people, the king's accountability, the nation's right to depose tyrants! [4] But the real *provocateur* was Henry Parker.[5] More outspokenly democratic than Prynne, Parker appealed to first principles, affirming that the freedom and safety of the people are by "the Charter of nature" superior to the prerogatives of kings; that kings are invested with power only for the benefit of the people; that toward the people kings should, in Christian humility, bear themselves not as lords but as brothers.[6] The fierce pamphleteering arguments engendered by Parker's sallies laid the basis for the growth of democratic doubts of kingship itself. One finds in Lilburne's *Innocency and Truth Justified* long passages[7] quoted with high approval from Parker's *Observations upon some of his Majesties late Answers* (1642). These passages are especially significant because they are among the first of Lilburne's long theoretical political statements. Until 1645, as we have shown, Lilburne had met the concrete evils of his own persecutions without showing marked development as a political theoretician. With Overton and Walwyn he was now to agitate for wider political liberties than he had hitherto envisioned. To this agitation Parker's ideas lent indispensable aid. But the Levellers were ready to attack kingship and lords with a bold bluntness and revolutionary implications that Parker eventually found unacceptable.

The Leveller attack on king and lords rose in crescendo in 1646, when Lilburne was in the midst of his struggles with the upper house. In the *Ivst Mans Ivstification* (June 6) Lilburne struck out at William the Conqueror and his laws, an approach that the

Levellers were to recur to again and again. *A Remonstrance Of Many Thousand Citizens* (July 7) contains the first Leveller broadside against kingship as an institution. The authors attack kings as the "originall of all oppressions"; they propose that Charles' crimes be displayed to all the world "to show the intolerable inconyeniences of having a *Kingly Government"*; they castigate the king's claim to a negative voice and deplore the superstitious reverence of the people for the trappings of monarchy. It is kings that have held the English people in bondage, beginning with the Conqueror and his tyrannical laws. How ridiculous to think that a nation cannot be happy without a king! [8]

In *Regall Tyrannie* (January 6, 1647) the Levellers stated comprehensively their case against England's kingship. In no other tract does the democratic philosophy that Milton was later to champion appear so fully documented or solidly reasoned. So completely, too, does *Regall Tyrannie* anticipate Milton's arguments that it is difficult not to take for granted that it lay on his desk as he wrote *The Tenure* and *A Defence of the People of England*. Only by mutual consent of the people, in whom lies the supreme power, may any power be delegated to a ruler; which power, not used for their benefit, must return to its original possessors. Recounting the tyrannies of the Conqueror, who had distributed the land to his nobles, set up courts to collect taxes, had the laws written in French "so the poor miserable people might be gulled, and cheated, undone and destroyed," [9] Lilburne deplores the centuries of accumulated oppressions originating in the conquest and concludes his castigation of the Norman monarchy with a stinging thrust: "From how *wicked, bloudy, triviall, base, and tyrannical a Fountain our gratious Soveraignes, and most excellent majesties of England* have sprung." [10] Charles, maintains Lilburne, has broken his contract; therefore the authority which he possessed has now returned to the people. The lords are equally heinous, being created by the king to help him plunder the English people; nor did prelates and lords sit at all in the earliest English parliaments.[11]

Losing confidence in the Commons in the spring of 1647, Lilburne resolved, as we have related, to intensify his propaganda among the army rank and file. To the army he and his colleagues now turned as the only likely saviours of the people's rights. In this campaign of propaganda, carried on vigilantly by the agitators,

Regall Tyrannie must have had an important place, reinforced as it was by succeeding Leveller tracts. The petition of March, 1647, demanded the abolition of the negative voices of king and lords. How long and earnestly soldiers and officers revolved this issue in their discussions of the summer and fall of 1647 we know by the debates of the *Clarke Papers*. In these debates we find, not the preliminary thinking of the radicals, but conclusions and arguments evolved from prolonged discussions. They were much better prepared to defend, than Cromwell and Ireton to refute, the extreme democratic theory. Thousands of soldiers, won over by Leveller agitation, demanded the cessation of all negotiations with Charles and the annihilation of all kingly and lordly power. It was this sentiment in the army that finally impelled the officers to bring Charles to justice and make England a commonwealth.

Of the many decisions forcing the trial and execution of Charles I, that of Cromwell was the most important, yet to historians has been the most puzzling of all to unravel. As late as October 20, 1647, he had made a three-hour speech in the House of Commons urging the restoration of monarchy; and we have seen how marked was his opposition in the Council debates to the "great alterations" proposed by the Levellers. Though on November 6 Cromwell had consented to a debate on the king's authority, on the 8th he again declared against the "anarchical" tendencies of the *Agreement*.[12] On November 11, when Harrison burst out in a meeting of the Committee of Officers that the king was "a Man of Bloud," and that despite all Engagements they should prosecute him accordingly, Cromwell cited Biblical cases to prove that not all murderers should be punished. Both Ireton and Cowling supported Cromwell, Cowling adding that they cared little for the king's person if they could remove "his usurping power in the law." [13] Against Cromwell's support of kingship the radicals' anger mounted daily: the army rumbled with threats of mutiny, quelled momentarily at Corkbush Field on November 15, when Cromwell for the first time resorted to court martial and execution to stem the agitation of radical ideas. The first hint of a change of front was a comment by Ireton on November 18 or 19, when Ireton, according to Huntington, remarked that, some agreement now being likely between the king and Parliament, he hoped "we might with a safe conscience fight against them both." [14] By November 28 Cromwell had swung over to the Leveller position; having resolved, for reasons that to this day escape the light of certainty, to break off all negotiations with Charles. According to Orrery, afterwards one of Cromwell's most intimate friends, Cromwell said in 1649 that he and Ireton had intercepted a letter showing Charles' preference for the Scots as his supporters: "finding we were not likely to have an tolerable terms from the King, we immediately, from that time forward, resolved his ruin." [15] This proof of Charles' perfidy may have been only the culmination of Cromwell's growing distrust of the king, who would not have hesitated, once he gained power through their hands, to reject an alliance with such unbending Roundheads as Cromwell and Ireton.

It is doubtful that the slow growth of political convictions, rather than the exigencies of the moment, determined Cromwell's decision to ruin Charles. Unlike Ireton, upon whom he depended to write the army manifestoes, Cromwell had little grasp of political theory. But his understanding of the play of forces was seldom wanting. According to Berkeley's informer, an officer in the General Council, the most pressing necessity with Cromwell was the unification of the army. Representatives of two-thirds of the army had assured him that notwithstanding the execution of the mutineer the Levellers were determined to swing all the troops to their convictions, or, that failing, to divide the army and destroy their opposers, allying themselves with any who would assist. Facing such a momentous danger, Cromwell and Ireton, partly through the influence of Hugh Peters, resolved that "if we cannot bring the Army to our sense, we must go to theirs." [16] Only with a unified army could Cromwell hope to cope with the rising royalist sentiment, the threatenings of the Scots, the hostile Parliament. Only by an alliance with the leftists could he achieve an even temporary harmony within the ranks. Yet that alliance both the Levellers and the Independents knew to be unstable: the army debates had revealed to each too wide a cleavage to be bridged by the Independents, though Cromwell was able, even a year later, to convince the Levellers that the officers intended to establish the government on the basis of the *Agreement*. The Independents, on the other hand, could not have hoped for compromise from Lilburne, Overton, and Walwyn, though they were to secure the defection of Wildman and Sexby.

In the months that followed, when the Independent sentiment against Charles was crystallizing into a determined policy, Crom-

well's opposition to kingship undoubtedly deepened. Toward the
end of December, at a prayer meeting of the officers, it was resolved that "the King should be prosecuted for his Life as a Criminal Person" to which resolution Parliament should be very gradually reconciled.[17] On January 3, when Sir Thomas Wroth moved "to
lay him [Charles] by, and settle the Kingdom without him: He
cared not what Form of Government they set up, so it were not
by Kings and Devils," exclaiming that "*Bedlam* was appointed for
Mad-Men, and *Tophet* for Kings," Cromwell followed Ireton in
warmly supporting the motion.[18] "The King was a Man of great
parts, and great understanding . . . ," said Cromwell, according to
Clarendon, "but . . . he was so great a dissembler, and so false a
Man, that he was not to be trusted." [19] Parliament should no longer
"teach the People . . . to expect Safety and Government from an
obstinate Man, whose Heart God had hardened." [20] He was in favor
of settling the Kingdom without "having any farther recourse to
the King." [21] The motion of No Addresses being carried, such a
motion as Cromwell had opposed, and Rainsborough favored, on
November 5, the officers of the army almost immediately sent forth
a whole-hearted declaration of approval, affirming that their actions
toward the king had demonstrated their desire to protect his rights
so far as consistent with the public welfare. In the debates from
February 5 to 11, Cromwell upheld with great energy the Declaration of the Commons justifying their Vote of No Addresses, on
February 11 making "a severe invective against monarchial government." [22] The Declaration is a weak defense of the Commons'
actions, resting upon no broad social principles such as the army
or Leveller manifestoes, but reviewing the king's misdemeanors, even
his supposed indifference to his father's death.[23] So complete, nevertheless, was Cromwell's approval that he asked Selden's expulsion
for moving the omission of the Buckingham story from the Declaration. Discussions with the republicans Marten and Ludlow, both
very skeptical of Cromwell's intentions, may have heightened his
opposition to kingship as an institution. To them, as to many
others, he listened, drawing out their opinions, rarely committing
himself with any save enigmatic statements; an immature wrestler
with ideas, but master of practical psychology, master of men
and timer of action. The famous prayer meeting at Windsor at the
end of March confirmed Cromwell's pledge "to call Charles Stuart,

that man of blood, to an account for that blood he had shed, and mischief he had done to his utmost, against the Lord's Cause and People in these poor Nations." [24] Whether this prayer meeting, or the one in late December, had any real influence on Cromwell's final resolution to prosecute the king as a criminal may be reasonably doubted. The resolution once made, however, Cromwell's deep religious earnestness, like that of his officers and men, allowed no doubts of the justice of his cause. His spirit calm, his will inflexible, he now swept away all obstacles to Charles' execution.

The ironic twist to Cromwell's position was that he and the Independents had gradually adopted one plank in the platform of the despised Levellers, who as early as July, 1646, in *A Remonstrance Of Many Thousand Citizens,* had condemned the Commons for entreating the king "to returne to his Kingly Office and Parliament, as if . . . hee were a God, without whose presence, all must fall to ruine, or as if it were impossible for any Nation to be happy without a King." [25] Repeatedly the agitators had urged Cromwell to break off negotiations with the king, to settle the kingdom by making the Commons supreme, without negative voice of king or lords. Them he had resisted, even to the use of court-martial and execution. Ludlow condemned his execution of the soldier at Corkbush Field, saying that "when an agreement with the king was carried on by other hands, he could countenance the army in opposition to the Parliament; yet now the bargain for the peoples liberty being driven on by himself, he opposed those who laboured to obstruct it, pretending his so doing to be only in order to keep the army in subjection to the parliament." [26] After the Vote of No Addresses Ludlow and two others were sent to release the eleven mutineers, who "had been imprisoned by the army, for attempting to bring about that which they themselves were now doing." [27]

Even after Cromwell had decided to break with Charles, and urged upon Parliament the Vote of No Addresses, the propaganda of the Levellers vehemently attacked his motives and emphasized his continued support of the House of Lords. This propaganda further prepared the way for a revolutionary assault on king and lords, forcing Cromwell at the end into a more radical position than he conscientiously could accept. In *The Grand Plea* (October 26, 1647) Lilburne had launched another broadside against the Lords as merely the creatures of the king, not impowered to try commoners or meddle with their estates. The present House of Lords, claimed Lilburne, were the creatures of Cromwell; hence he continued to support them, though several years earlier he had been "the greatest Anti Lord . . . I conversed with in *England*." [28] In *The peoples Prerogative* Lilburne stressed the subordination of kingly power to the will of the people, repeating in his "Proeme" some of the more abstract ideas of *Regall Tyrannie*. At the same time he attempted to show that Cromwell's desertion of the king was based, not on conviction, but on the expediency of preserving his own power.[29] In *A Whip for the House of Lords*, while berating *"the present swaying tyrants, the Grandees in the Army, and their confederates in the two Houses,"* Lilburne follows the lead of Wildman's *Putney Projects* in showing the inconsistency of fighting a war against the king in the king's name, forcing people to take oaths to preserve his person; this is "riddle upon riddle." [30] As the king fundamentally has no legislative power, he cannot confer any upon the Lords. Lilburne recalls the Leveller petition of March, 1647, which had demanded the elimination of negative voices of king and lords; this petition "struck at the very root of all that tyranny" in a much more emphatic way than the Vote of No Addresses.[31] Until the Independents pluck up by the roots the power of the Lords, Lilburne says, he will not believe that they really intend to set free the English people.

Meanwhile the royalists pamphleteered unremittingly for restoration of the king, their cause supported by the war weariness felt by all classes. Comparatively meagre crops in 1647 and 1648, accompanied by rising commodity prices, accentuated the oppressive economic burdens imposed by an army that demanded arrears while refusing to disband. Clarendon's testimony to "a universal discontent and murmuring . . . a detestation both of Parliament and Army, and a most passionate desire that all their follies and madness might be forgotten in restoring the King to all they had taken from him" is substantiated by the pamphlets and petitions of the time.[32] The army was hated and feared, and the king favored, adds Clarendon, by three groups of Charles' former enemies: officers and soldiers forced out of the army at the organization of the New Model, the gentry and nobility replaced in offices of public trust by men of inferior social standing, and the numerous and vociferous Presbyterians.[33] In late February or March, 1648, Hyde himself had written a long pamphlet against the Commons' Declaration justifying their Vote of No Addresses. Admitting that unjust kings may bring oppressions upon the people, which the Lord suffers as judgment for their wickedness, Hyde maintained that wicked kings were more supportable than the confusion inevitable upon their removal. Would any of the king's opposers deny the prerogative of a father, or husband to command his children, his wife and servants? And is it not piety in them to obey the father and master? Yet these same men cannot understand the necessity for a kingly prerogative. Hyde glances with hopefulness upon the army. It is still in their power to restore the king, who would be obliged to reward their fidelity if they so acted. "Let us prostrate ourselves," exhorted Hyde, "at the feet of our abused Soveraign. . . . *Because the Lord hath loved his people, he hath made thee King over them;* To a profane, dissolute, and licentious people, he hath given the most pious and temperate King, to recover & reform them by his example." [34] "The kingdom generally desires their King," wrote one royalist, "and the people grows . . . unquiet, but they are so afraid of a new war as they will hardly stir." [35] Another in February, 1648, had written as follows: "You endeavour still to seperate, whom God hath conjoyned, our King, and us, His Subjects. . . . We will not have you raign over us, we will not have the Laws of England changed. The Head of the Law is the King." [36] The anonymous author of *Great Britans Vote* (March 27) complained bitterly against the Levellers, rebels, and sectaries: "Now like cursed Vipers they endeavour to gnaw out the way to their resolved upon *Democracy* through the Bowels of their Father *Monarchy*." [37] As bees serve their king with unquestioning obedience, watching over him tenderly in sickness, carrying him on their wings in his old age, so should Christians uphold their monarch's dignity and honor. On April 10 the author (Marchmont Nedham?) of *A New discovery of Old England* thus epitomized the struggle against kingship:

The Counsell of Warre begets those orders in private which the Country must Father in publike. . . . Spight of all contradiction, a match must be struck between *Reformation* and *Independency*, I feare while the Nuptials are celebrating, their borther [*sic*] *Presbyterians* . . . will endeavour a rape. And then like *Cadmus* . . . enemies, those twin prodigies will by mutuall execution open a passage through their own bowels for injured Majesty to reascend the throan. . . . The *Independent* craftily cedes to the *Presbyterian,* and while he seems by easie compliance to give ground destroys his pursuer. . . . The *Crown* we all know is at stake, for which the Souldiers and the States are casting lots.[38]

How decisive was the surge of popular sentiment to the cause of royalty appeared from demonstrations in the eastern counties, which in 1642 had most strenuously opposed the king. On May 4 two thousand men of Essex, said to speak the minds of 30,000 people, presented a petition for the restoration of the king and the disbanding of the army. On May 16 a similar band from Surrey paraded through the streets shouting, "For God and King Charles!" and "An old King and a new Parliament!" at the very door of the Commons; whereupon soldiers dispersed them in a bloody melee, several petitioners losing their lives and over a hundred suffering wounds.[39] On May 27, in a mutiny inspired, according to Clarendon, by the common seamen, six ships of the fleet proclaimed their allegiance to the king.[40] The tide of royalist enthusiasm had mounted high.

In the midst of popular enthusiasm for the king's cause, even after Fairfax' successful campaign in Kent and Essex, royalist exhorters intensified their appeals to Parliament and people. "Are you not ashamed," asked the author of *An Eye-Salve For The City of London* (May 29), "to see the spirit of Courage and Loyalty, moving so cheerfully in the Country round about you, for the restoring of His Sacred Majesty . . . and you to sit still and say nothing, nor put to the least of your fingers to set it forward? . . . Have you no regard of the miseries and oppressions of your pious and gracious King, trampled upon by base and unworthy vassals . . . ? . . . Are the eyes of the whole Kingdome opened, and are you onely incurably blind?" Representing Charles as ready to forgive all his enemies and all the errors of his people, the pamphleteer concludes with this challenge to the city: "If *Fairfax* be King, serve him: If CHARLES be King, restore Him." [41] In *The Independent's Loyalty* (June? 1648) Richard Osborne brought to the king's cause a wit as sharp and caustic, if less sustained, than that of Richard Overton. *"And now my Lord the King* is in danger every hour," he wrote, "to be murthered or poysoned; shall wee now give our eye lidds any rest? . . . *Curse yee Meroz . . .* curse her bitterly, for not helping him; and if we cannot afford to helpe him, for the Oathes wee have made . . . yet let us rescue our Lawes, Liberties, and Estates; and our owne soules which will otherwise . . . certainly . . . perish with him." [42] Osborne tried to arouse the people against Cromwell and Peters by showing their contempt for majesty. Upon his first meeting with the king near Cambridge, asserts Osborne, Cromwell had declared: *"This Man is not fit to reigne."* [43] On another occasion Cromwell had exclaimed: *"Are the People so mad upon a King, they shall have a May-pole for their King, as soone as him again."* An even more heinous remark Osborne ascribes to Peters: *"The King was the only grievance now left . . . it was of noe difficultie to remove him, he was but a dead dogg already."* [43]

On June 27 Sir John Maynard, recently readmitted to his seat in the Commons, urged his colleagues to consider the murmuring and complaining of the people, their concern for the safety of the king, their discontent at being deprived of him.[44] On the same day the Mayor, Aldermen, and Commons of London petitioned for a personal treaty with the king. The mariners and masters of ships plying the Thames on June 29 urged haste upon Parliament in the restoration of the king, bemoaning the long continuation of standing armies, the falling off of trade; and asserting that most, if not all, the seamen of England desired a personal treaty with Charles.[45] If in 1642 the middle class had been determined to curb the power of the king, they were now much more incensed against the political power of the army, believing the king on any terms to be the lesser evil. In a bitter Commons debate on July 3, when Thomas Scot asserted "he that draws his Sword upon the King, must throw his Scabbard into the Fire," he was told that "the Generality of the People . . . were resolved to be no longer made Fuel to that Fire wherein those Salamanders live; nor any longer feed those Horse-Leeches the Army, their engaged Party and Servants, with their own Blood and Marrow." [46] When Vane and Mildmay insisted that Charles' manifest perfidy made reliance upon his word impossible, Sir Symonds D'Ewes summarized the state of affairs as follows:

Mr. Speaker, If you know not in what Condition you are, give me Leave in a Word to tell you:——Your Silver is clipped; your Gold shipped; your ships are revolted; yourselves contemned; your *Scots* Friends enraged against you; and the Affections of the City and Kingdom quite alienated from you. Judge then whether you are not in a low Condition, and also if it be not high Time to endeavour a speedy Settlement and Reconcilement with his Majesty.[47]

In *A Letter to the Earle of Manchester* (July 5) a royalist rebuked the Lords for not effecting a personal treaty, insisting that the kingdom would never be content until Charles was restored and all points of controversy between him and his people resolved in open debate.[48]

Thus the royalists wholeheartedly, the Presbyterians somewhat uneasily, agitated for reconciliation with the king; and with them joined the sentiment of all classes. The views of the army, like those of the Levellers, were a political anomaly created by the intense agitation of the radicals. The royalist sympathies of the common seamen form a curious contrast with the democratic fervor of the New Model soldiery, a fervor born of ceaseless discussion and justified by glorious victories. There is every indication that Cromwell and Ireton recognized how small a minority of the population the sentiment of the army represented. Notwithstanding common opposition, however, Cromwell and Ireton determined to force their will upon the country, sustained as they were by a conviction of the justice of their cause. They were unwilling, nevertheless, both from conviction and the dictates of expediency, to accept the political implications of the destruction of kingship and lords, even as the Levellers were unwilling to accept the economic corollaries of manhood suffrage.

Meanwhile Independent leaders and pamphleteers outside the army argued vigorously against the return of the king. As early as March, 1647, the staunch republican Marten had anticipated his execution in a jesting manner: "I wish the King may have two chaplains, as I desire to prepare him for heaven." [49] On April 21, when the Commons resolved to send the Newcastle Propositions to the king again, Marten spoke his mind: "The man to whom these propositions shall be sent ought rather to come to the bar . . . than to be sent to any more." [50] Opposed by Cromwell and Vane, Marten had proposed a vote of no addresses in September, 1647. When the Vote of No Addresses finally passed, Marten wrote *The Independency Of England Endeavored to be maintained,* justifying the Parliament's action, caustically rebuking the Scots for "asserting

the same Cause which we have been all this while confuting with
out Swords," and calling for a resolution of the war by full conquest,
rather than "daube up a rotten compromise with my adversary." [51]
Not in the orders of a commander or laws imposed by a conqueror,
but in laws made by the people or their deputies lay that liberty,
wrote Marten, more precious to him than all other possessions. A
month later (Feb. 7, 1648), in *The Parliaments Proceedings justified,* Marten was even more outspoken. Despite all concessions, he
wrote, Charles is "to this day set in his heart, upon being either
an absolute Tyrant over us, or no King." [52] In treating with the
king, do not speak of equality; for the king represents but himself and his family, whereas Parliament acts for two nations. If the
Scots are so concerned about his absence from Parliament, why do
they not "imploy all this earnestness in procuring to themselves the
blessing of His company"? [53] Late in March Marten exhorted the
House to proceed with dethroning the king. Like the Levellers,
however, Marten was more concerned with the kind of government
to follow than he was with abolition of kingship. About Cromwell's
intentions he had long had doubts; of the long negotiations with
Charles he was especially suspicious, and even considered with
Rainsborough impeachment proceedings against Cromwell.[54]

Other Independent apologists followed the lead of Cromwell
and the army in their prosecution of the king, issuing pamphlets in
justification of the army's threats against Parliament, and deploring the dominant and vociferous royalist sentiment. In his *Pulpit
Incendiary* John Price resorted to the tactics of Thomas Edwards,
recording in horrified accents the prayers for a traitor king. One
Mr. Witham had prayed thus: "Lord advance the King, put the
Crown AGAIN upon his Head, and the Scepter into his Hands,"
but the army in Witham's prayers was "like a Beast spoken of by
the Prophet *Daniel,* which had ten hornes." [55] John Hare, in *England's Proper and onely way* (January 24, 1648) called upon his
countrymen to renounce the pretended title of conquest claimed by
English kings from the time of the Norman invasion:

The Title and Effects of this . . . Conquest are a yoke of Captivity,
unto which while we continue our fond and needlesse Submission, we
renounce Honour, Freedom and all absolute Right to anything but just
shame and oppression, being thereby in the quality of profest Captive
Bondslaves unto the heyres of the Duke of *Normandy* and wearing the

open livery of that Posession; And although we enjoy a mitigation of our Slavery by Charters, yet are those Charters revokable at the Kings pleasure.[56]

In *A Declaration Of some Proceedings of Lt. Col. John Lilburn* (February 14, 1648), which Lilburne attributes to Fiennes or Gualter Frost, the author maintains that only an absolute tyranny would satisfy the king, being unwilling to rule according to any will or law but his own.

In *New Propositions From The Armie* (October 24, 1648), the London Independents issued an official declaration of their support of the army's policies. Assuming, as Milton was to do, that the Army represented the will of the people, the authors claim that "the Lawes of God, Man, and Nature justifie the people in opposing, fighting against, and imprisoning of *Kings,* who act contrary to their Oaths, and the trust imposed on them by the people." The same transcendent laws, continue the declarers significantly, justify opposition to Parliament, which acts merely as the agents of the people (shades of the Levellers!), and should not betray their trust. The king and his faction are "drunk with the bloud of Saints, and have confest themselves guilty of the bloud of three hundred thousand soules that have perished by war in the three *Kingdoms.*" The Independents still desire to be governed by a king, but by one who acknowledges the supremacy of the laws. If he break these laws, he should be no more immune to punishment than the lowliest commoner. The writers quote with approval the last communications from the army (October 23), which demand that the king be not enthroned until he be cleared of the charges against him, the *"shedding and imbruing his hands in the innocent bloud of his people."* [57]

The long army *Remonstrance* presented to Parliament November 20, 1648, revealed fully for the first time the inflexible resolution of Cromwell and his officers to force the trial and execution of Charles. There one finds stated with amazing fullness and no little persuasiveness the arguments that had crystallized in dozens of councils and prayer meetings, most of them synthesized in Ireton's temperate phrasing. Though somewhat stilted and verbose, the *Declaration* is the most able of Independent tracts justifying the army's resolute course of action. "Before God had so clearly given his double Judgment against him in the Cause, or delivered him into your Hands for yours," said the officers, addressing Parliament, "or while Affairs stood in some equal Balance," a settlement with the king, assuming suitable assurances, might have been feasible.[58] But not now. The king must be tried as a traitor, as the "capital and grand Author of our Troubles." [59] Throughout his reign Charles has sought to make himself absolute, seeking an arbitrary power, "without limit from, or Account to, any on Earth," over Parliament, people, laws, property, consciences.[60] To effect this aim he has twice raised armies against the people of his kingdoms; and now when defeated, knowing the people are weary of war, he dangles before them the "Golden Bate" of peace, with concessions and assurances, to gain his throne again.[61] Like Wildman before him, in *Putney Projects*, Ireton shows the inconsistency of requesting a conquered king to resume his supreme place, and grant the people those rights, as emanations of his will, which they have wrung from him on the battlefield. It is true that the army itself sought to treat with the king, in the midst of temptations now happily overcome; not however to strengthen the army, but to prevent others from strengthening themselves. If you set up the king, say the officers, what can you expect from him but further tyranny, breach of promises, revenge upon his eminent enemies, or another bloody war to protect our liberties? Only by the Norman Conquest, with its heritage of arrogant laws, can kings claim dictatorial prerogatives. "If therefore our Kings claim by right of Conquest, God hath given you the same against them," delivering the people from their bondage to their ancient liberties.[62] The Declaration says, in effect: "Proceed to judgment, not only of the king but his principal colleagues. Sequester his estates. Brand his children also incapable of ruling. Show what kings of the future may expect if they attempt a like tyranny again."

It is difficult to doubt the sincerity of the political philosophy that animated the *Declaration*. Though Ireton and Cromwell still distrusted the people, and had no real sympathy for the democratic aims of the Levellers, recognizing, indeed, in the *Declaration*, that mass sentiment was with the king, they had veered sharply to the left in their opposition to kingship and lords. Now they upheld the abolition of the power of both king and lords, an abolition they had frankly dreaded twelve months before. Did Ireton swerve first to this conviction, **and Cromwell follow?** Cromwell's own impressions, even in his letters to Hammond, he veiled, deliberately or not, with shadowy religious utterances. In his November 25 letter to Hammond he asks whether "this Army be not a lawful power, called by God to oppose and fight against the King upon some stated grounds; and being in power to such ends, may not oppose one name of authority [i.e., the Parliament] . . . as well as another . . . ?" Though he wishes the *Declaration* might have been postponed until after the treaty with the king, he will "trust to rejoice in the will of the Lord." [63] If Cromwell wholly approved the *Declaration*, he viewed it through the glasses of a religious mystic. Cromwell was in a sense a religious fascist who adopted without wholly believing the radical democratic ideas of his time to topple the king from his throne. Though upon occasion, as Burnet reveals, Cromwell argued upon the nature of kingship from such sources as Mariana and Buchanan,[64] his beliefs had not sprung from prolonged study of political theory. But now he had made his decision. If Ireton and his fellow officers had also at times used more extreme language than their convictions warranted, they were now utterly convinced that the king must be brought to judgment.

A curious supporter of the army's prosecution of the king appeared in the Fifth Monarchy mystic, William Sedgewick. On December 11 Sedgewick came forth with a sharp rebuke to the army and a staunch defence of the king. In his offers of peace, maintained Sedgewick, the king had shown "a fatherly and large spirit," comprehending the needs and opinions of all factions; whereas the army considered only its own resolutions.[65] The people have a right to live under a great sovereign, to serve and honor him, to identify themselves with his authority. In *The Spirituall Madman*, which appeared on December 20, Sedgewick eulogized the king as follows: "We have now a King in whom we can confide, as in *God;* now the LORD lives in him, tis impiety and wickednesse to have a thought of distrust concerning him; the *sure justice and righteousnesse* of God inhabits in the Throne, as its proper place." [66] The king could not have wished for a more unquestioning devotee. Yet only three days later, on December 23, Sedgewick reversed his stand completely, acknowledging that he had done injustice to the army's intentions. As God had lived in the bosom of the king, explained Sedgewick, and then passed into the Parliament, so now He has lodged in the ranks of the army. And as the people had formerly trusted all their power to the king, and then to the Parliament, so now they are represented in the army, which is *"the most excellent, agreeable to God . . . fittest for the present worke, and mother of other powers."* [67] With as much fervor as he had formerly lauded the king as God's instrument, he now eulogized the army, identifying it with the true interests of the people. Now any one aware of the curious contradictions of Fifth Monarchy psychology, from which Milton and Cromwell were by no means free, will hesitate to condemn Sedgewick of insincerity or timeserving. Men like Cromwell and Sedgewick were unafraid to change their minds suddenly, to appear inconsistent: God directed them. Had Sedgewick wished to gain an office, he would not have condemned the army after the *Remonstrance* appeared. Or having changed his mind, he would have attempted to show, as Goodwin was to do, some real correspondency between his old beliefs and his new. It is extremely doubtful if the idea of gain in any form entered the mind of William Sedgewick in his sudden change of front.

After Pride's Purge, on December 6 and 7, when the Commons became in reality an expression of the army's will, Independent speeches and pamphlets anticipated frankly the king's trial and execution. On December 22, in a sermon at St. Margaret's, Hugh Peters compared Moses' leading the children out of Egypt to Fairfax and his army delivering the people of England from the bondage of monarchy, an institution that the army was to root up also in surrounding countries. [68] On December 23 the more radical members of the House mentioned the king by name as the greatest delinquent of all, whom they should proceed to judge. Whereupon Cromwell, according to Walker, "when it was first moved in the House of Commons to proceed capitally against the King . . . stood up and said, That if any Man moved this upon Design, he should think him the greatest Traitor in the World; but since Providence and Necessity had cast them upon it, he should pray God to bless their Councils, though he was not provided on the sudden to give them Advice." [69] In a pamphlet appearing December 24, William Erbery called for a destruction of all oppressions, including monarchy, by a rule of the army saints. [70] On January 1, without a dissenting vote, the Commons declared it treasonable for the king to have waged war against the Parliament, and ordered the erection of a high court of justice. On the same day appeared

A New-Years Gift, signed by Rushworth and purporting to represent the views of Fairfax and his officers, demanding that no king be admitted to the throne thereafter except by election of the House of Commons; such an elective king to repudiate, however, any claim to veto power.[71] On January 2, John Goodwin sent out his *Right And Might well met,* justifying with somewhat torturous circumlocution the army's purge, denying that the will of the people should interfere with coercive actions for their own welfare. As a skilled sailor at sea is justified in assuming command when the captain is out of his senses, writes Goodwin, quoting Prynne's story against him, so a Parliament, or even particular men, are justified in turning kings, assuming royal prerogatives.[72] When taunted by Nethersole for his *Anti-Cavalierisme* (1642) passage claiming immunity for kings from any human violence whatsoever, Goodwin defended himself in *The Unrighteous Judge* (January 25).[73] Instead of frankly admitting a change in belief Goodwin attempted lamely to reconcile statements separated by seven tumultuous years, asserting that by *violence* he had meant assassination or poisoning, not capital punishment following a legal trial.[74]

In neither quantity nor dynamic persuasiveness could the Independent pamphlets of December and January compare with the flood of Royalist protests. The Leveller leaders, their pens laid momentarily aside, looked with deep distrust upon the very drama they had urged upon the army eighteen months before; their biting, ringing phrases they could not spin for these new tyrants, the Grandees. But on January 12 and 15 supporters of Independency sent forth pamphlets that might have been written by Levellers convinced of the officers' sincere devotion to the democratic cause. The king in a tyrannical manner has attempted to undermine the safety of the people, wrote John Redingstone in *Plain English* (January 12). He is now "wholly elapsed in his splendor, dignity, honour . . . and stands guilty of all the precious blood . . . of millions of People in these three Kingdomes. . . . God makes no distinction of King or Beggar, he is no Respecter of persons." [75] Having poisoned everything he has touched, his eminence enhancing his persuasiveness and consequent destructiveness, the king is now an enemy of the people. Let the people now be divorced from him, secured against him and his adherents forever. *The Peoples Right Briefly Asserted* (January 15), even more democratic in tone than

Plain English, anticipated many of the arguments of Milton's *Tenure;* indeed, save for the relative calmness of the style, one would be tempted to stamp it as Milton's own, so closely does it follow his reasoning:

The Body of a People, represented in a Convention of elected Estates, have a true and lawful power to despose of things at pleasure, for their own Safety and Security . . . that Kings are constituted for the Peoples good, not the People made for the Kings pleasure, is a thing granted by all rational men.

That therefore Kings have been, and justly may be layd aside, or otherwise censured . . . Historians will give Examples in all Kingdoms. . . .

The People never lost, nor gave away their supream Power of making Election, when need required. . . .

Whoever considereth that Kings and all Governors were instituted for the peoples happiness, and made by their consent . . . and because Kings, as men, may stray from their right way, and fail of their Duty; therefore Laws were made for a Bridle to them: which were indeed no Bridle, if there were no power to apply them, and see the execution done. . . .

That private men should be enabled by the law to sue the *Prince* for a small quantity of Land or Goods: and yet that Representative Body of the whole *People* have not power to lay the Law against him for *Parricide, massacring of the People,* and Treason [is an absurdity not to be countenanced]. . . .

The *Law* is more powerful then the *King,* as being the Governor and Moderator of his lusts and actions: But the whole Body of the people are more powerful then the *Law,* as being the Parent of it. For the *People* make the Law, and have power when they see cause, to abrogate or establish it. Therefore seeing that the *Law* is above the *King,* and the *People* above the *Law:* it is concluded as a thing out of question, by *Buchanan, Iunius,* and many others, that the *People* of right have power to call in question, and punish a *King* for transgressing the *Law.* . . .

The *Parliament* of *England,* if they had a lawful power to proceed in this war, have also a just power to dispose of that Victory which God hath put into their hands, as they shall think best for the future security of the whole people, whom they represent.[76]

In *The Peoples Right* appear most of Milton's positive arguments, as well as his questionable assumptions. The author assumes, as Milton was to do, that the will of the people is represented by Parliament, which five weeks before had been purged of a hundred members sympathetic to kingship. Like Milton, too, the author avoids a justification of military interference in civil affairs.

On January 15 the Commons issued a Declaration justifying Pride's Purge and their own determination to bring the king to judgment. Like most manifestoes of the Independents, the Declaration points to the army's victories as certain proof of God's approbation: "We hereupon despairing of any good Return of Justice from the King, did appeal unto the Great God of Heaven and Earth for the same; who, after four Years Wars, did give a clear and apparent Sentence on our Side, by delivering into our Hands all the Castles, Towns, and Persons of our Opposites, even of the King himself." [77] An obstinate king, haughty and tyrannical, making war on his own subjects, still unwilling to abolish Episcopacy, too deceptive and treacherous to keep any agreement: this man the purged members would have placed again on the throne, ready "to decline the Cause of the People, and to assert that of the King's; betraying thereby our own Cause, and justifying his." [78] Are the king's honor and safety of more importance than the welfare of millions of people represented by Parliament? Is the blood of the army martyrs, and that of thousands of innocent people, to be valued at less than the blood of a few guilty malignants, however eminent their titles? The very end of the *Declaration* avows the hostility of the Rump to the whole institution of kingship, however benevolent the incumbent: "We are resolved, by God's Assistance . . . so to settle the Peace of the Kingdom, by the Authority of Parliament, in a more happy Way, than can be expected from the best of Kings." [79]

Despite such declarations, the country was profoundly shocked by the unprecedented Independent design of trying the king. As Cromwell and his colleagues demonstrated daily their unflinching resolution to effect their ends, despite uneasy waverings among the party itself, the spontaneous royalist protests burst all restraints, all fears of reprisals. In his reply to the Army *Remonstrance* of November 20, *A Plea for The King and Kingdome,* Marchmont Nedham placed his finger on the untenable basic assumption that Milton was to uphold in *The Tenure:* that the Independents represented the people, that "their *Interest* is the only *Interest* of the *People*." [80] The four bills presented to Charles at Carisbrooke Castle Nedham called the *four dethroning Bills*. As for the Independent scheme to try and execute the king:

> never was such damnable doctrine vented before in the World: For, the Persons of *Soveraign Princes* have ever been held sacred . . . in no *History* can we finde a *Parallel* for this, that ever the rage of Rebels extended so far. . . . What *Court* shall their King be tryed in? who shall be his *Peeres?* what Form of *Processe* shall be made? who shall give *Sentence?* what eyes dare be so impious to behold the *execution?*[81]

In *Independency Stript and Whipt*[82] (by Richard Osborne?) a satirist as able as Nedham flayed unsparingly the aims of the army leaders. Aghast that the Independents regard it lawful to proceed against the king as against the lowliest subject, the author asserts that Christians must honor the king as God's vicegerent, even though he be a haughty tyrant. Let us not be enslaved, exhorts the author; let us thrust aside the chains that the Independents seek to bind us with. All they lack to make them masters of all is the king's life, and this by a law not yet made. As now ministers pray for the king at their peril, shortly it will be treason "to pray to any other God then *Cromwell* or that Devil *Ireton.*" [83] The Independents intend to foist upon the people a tyrannical government, grasping to their pockets the riches of the kingdom: "they extreamely love to have our coffers and consciences too at their command . . . they hold the best weapon the best evidence, the strongest arme the surest title." [83] The surge of royalist patriotism, which, however unintellectual, represented in the large the sentiment of all classes, was intensified by the hatred of the Independent minority:

> An *Independent* is an incarnate *Devil*, spawn'd by a *broaken rib of Adam*, a holy Sister in the height of *Zeale*, his *Syre* is . . . *Lucifer the Prince of darknesse*, the first *Independent* that ever was: He was a Souldier from his *Cradle*. . . . The *Independent* doubtless is a *Saint* if the *Devill* be one . . . he hates a *Church* more then a *monster* doth a *looking-glasse*, but a *Tub* fits his *devotion* to a haire, where he can *pray*, or rather *prate* by the *spirit*, two houres at least *extempore* against the *King* and *State*. . . . He hates the Lords Prayer and thankes God he hath forgot it.[84]

The anonymous outburst *Heare, heare, heare, heare* (December 14, 1648) invoked God's punishment on the Independent tyrants, accusing them of wanting the king's life that his inheritance might be theirs, and of molding the Parliament to do their will.

No ordinary royalist, battle-scarred William Prynne in December and January stood forth bluntly for reconciliation with Charles. In his long speech in the Commons on December 4, parts of which for Prynne are amazingly persuasive rhetoric, he cited his sufferings and eight years imprisonment at the hands of king and prelates; loss of large sums of money for his anti-royalist beliefs without any recompense by Parliament, so much as public thanks; the sincerity of his support, he never having asked or received any office or preferment. More than any other man, Prynne insisted, he had written and spoken against arbitrary power of king and prelates; and were they to be restored to their former tyrannical prerogatives, he would stand to suffer as much as any of his countrymen.[85] All this time he had sought, not to depose Charles or divert from him the affections of the people, but to make him sensible of his accountability to Parliament, and particularly of his errors against religion. And now the king had yielded in all essential points to Parliament's power; holding himself ready to recall all declarations against Parliament; to acknowledge the justice of the war against him; to secure the lives of all well-affected persons; to settle the militia in Parliament's hand for a period of twenty years, final disposition to be negotiated with Parliament; to ratify all acts under the new Great Seal of the present Parliament; to yield to Parliament's discretion in the appointment of all judges, all chief officers of the government for a period of twenty years; to confirm London's traditional rights and charters; to revoke all titles he had conferred since the opening of the war; to renounce all power of conferring titles except by consent of the Commons, thus guaranteeing the Kingdom against sudden strengthening of the king's power in the House of Lords; to approve the abolition of all popish superstitions and innovations in the church; to approve the abolition of all archbishops, chancellors, deans and chapters, archdeacons, canons, etc., insisting only on the power of the bishops' ordination and their right to their estates, and even the power of ordination to be suspended for three years. Even then, added Prynne, only by act of Parliament could the power of ordination be allowed again to the bishops; so that the power of bishops would be perpetually abrogated should Parliament fail to act.[86] All these concessions, asserted

Prynne, represented a transference of power from king to Parliament more substantial and far reaching than ever achieved in the history of England. What greater security could they wish? To Prynne the argument that Charles could not be trusted to carry out his agreements carried no weight at all: "If all he hath granted were still in his own Power to dissolve or recall at Pleasure, this Argument were material; but since he hath put all our desired Security into our Hands alone . . . the Objection in but weak, and recoils upon ourselves, that we dare not trust ourselves with our own Safety." [87]

No other writer of the day opened so fully as Prynne the implications of the concessions made by Charles; and in retrospect we must grant now, as the Presbyterian majority did then, the solidity of his arguments. They represented grounds for settlement more lasting than Cromwell's. The Revolution of 1688 was to justify the principles, not of the Independents, but of the Presbyterians whom Prynne represented. In Prynne was embodied that persecuting zeal, that narrowest of Puritan attitudes, that the liberal Independents could not stomach; and a Presbyterian state church was as hateful to them as the Anglican. In Prynne, too, lived a remnant of that superstitious reverence for kingship that Milton was to despise as unchristian. "No Protestant Kingdome . . .," wrote Prynne in *A Breife Memento* (January 4, 1649) "ever yet defiled their hands . . . with the . . . blood of any of their Kings, . . . much lesse of a *protestant King* . . . of a temperate and sober life, as the King is." [88] In his political and historical arguments, however, Prynne was on safer ground than the Independents. He recognized the importance of making the House of Commons an increasingly powerful instrument of secular reform, achieving a transfer of power from the king and aristocracy to the flourishing middle class. He visualized the dangers of army interference. "We all sit here," Prynne had declared, "freely to speak our own Minds, not the Army's Pleasure; to follow our own Consciences and Judgments, not their imperious Dictates; to satisfy the whole Kingdom, and those who have intrusted us and sent hither, whose Representatives and Servants we are, not the Army's." [89] In toppling the king from his throne the Independents overleaped the evolutionary processes of fifteen or twenty decades, achieving their ends at the expense of Parliamentary freedom, without building, as the Levellers wished to do, a supporting substructure of democratic reforms. Prynne placed his finger on the weakness of the Independent methods when he wrote: "You now meet, and sit under armed force and violence of a *mutinous* Army, who have leavyed Warre against the Houses to dissolve them." [90]

Undaunted, like Prynne, by the shadows of Independent swords, forty-seven Presbyterian ministers of London on January 18 issued a manifesto on behalf of the king and against the army. It was outbursts of Presbyterian ministers, according to Milton, that impelled him to write *The Tenure of Kings and Magistrates*. Lacking in the persuasive and astute analysis of the conflict that one finds in the earlier sections of Prynne's long speech, *A Serious and Faithfull Representation* makes no substantial contribution to the defense of Charles. When the Presbyterians took up arms, asserted the ministers, they had no thought "to do violence to the Person of the KING, or devest him of his Regal Authority. . . . Much lesse was it their purpose to subvert and overthrow the whole frame and fundamentall constitution of the Government of the Kingdome, or to give power and authority . . . whatsoever so to do." [91] Rather than attempting to persuade the army not to bring the king to judgment, the ministers avowed their unanimous opposition to the army's arbitrary imprisonment of king and Parliament members, recommendation of *The Agreement of the People*, and "opening a door to desperate and damnable Errors and Heresies." As soon as they touch the religious issue, the breaking of the Covenant, the great Diana of toleration, the writing of the forty-seven, like that of Prynne on the same topic, deteriorates to platitudinous, pious thinness. "How is Religion made to stink by reason of your miscarriages," they complained, "and like to become a scorn and a reproach in all the Christian world? How are the faces of Gods faithful servants covered with shame, and their hearts filled with sorrow and grief by reason thereof?" [92] Indignantly the ministers rejected all overtures from the army officers. Narrow and bigoted as they were, the Presbyterian ministers were the most influential leaders of the London middle class. In the years that followed Cromwell attempted unsuccessfully to reconcile them to the Independent regime.

In *Might Overcoming Right* (January 18) John Geree seconded the manifesto of the forty-seven with much more effective reasoning than his colleagues could muster. Contrasting the tyrannical measures of the king with those of the Independents, Geree reminded his antagonist Goodwin that the king had imprisoned but five Parliament members, whereas the army imprisoned over forty and secluded more than a hundred.[93] The king, moreover, was the supreme civil officer, whereas the army had no authority whatever. And he "was easily reduc'd from his errour, and relinquisht it, and assured them [the Commons] of tendernesse of priviledge for future; you avow the Armies act, and they persist in their force." [93] "Will you depose our King," asked another royalist, "before you have set up another King, or agreed about one, to set all the Land together by the eares, and the longest sword take all?" [94] If the king intended tyranny, do not the Independents plan an oligarchical rule? They who believe so much in liberty of conscience will not even allow a free and open debate in a full Parliament. It was this criticism of the inevitable harsh measures of their benevolent fascism that the Independent apologists found hardest to combat. As Geree pointed out, they had sworn to maintain the privileges of Parliament, the essence of which was freedom from violence in the speaking of their consciences. Yet the Independents had destroyed the very privileges that they had formerly considered most inalienable.

During his trial, which opened on January 20, Charles defended his own cause with courage and deftness. When the charge of treason was read, and Bradshaw commanded that he answer, Charles spoke as follows:

I would know by what Power I am called hither: I was, not long ago, in the *Isle* of *Wight* . . . there I entred into a Treaty with both Houses of Parliament, with as much Publick Faith as 'tis possible to be had of any People in the World. I treated there with a number of Honourable Lords and Gentlemen, and treated honestly and uprightly; I cannot say but they did very nobly with me: We were upon a Conclusion of the Treaty. Now I would know by what Authority, I mean lawful; (there are many unlawful Authorities in the World; Thieves and Robbers by the Highways:) But I would know by what Authority I was brought from hence . . . when I know by what lawful Authority, I shall answer.[95]

In challenging the jurisdiction of the court, Charles attacked the procedure of the Independents at its weakest point. To bring him to trial, they had purged the House of Commons of his adherents and ignored the negative of the House of Lords. Weeks before, when first informed of the army's resolution to bring him to judgment, Charles had asked, "Whereas, by the Letter of the Law, all Persons charged to offend against the Law ought to be tried by their Peers or Equals; what the Law is, if the Person questioned be without a Peer?" [96] But now Charles struck at a much more valid inconsistency, the lack of full Parliamentary authority for the erection of the High Court of Justice. On the second day of the trial Charles refused again to plead either guilty or not guilty, protesting against the legality of the court, and denying that a king may be tried "by any superiour Jurisdiction on Earth." [97] Bradshaw professed that the people and the House of Commons had the right to try him. When, asked Charles, had the House of Commons ever served as a court? And as for the people, though he would not grant that they had any authority over him, he stoutly maintained, in a protestation he was not permitted to read in court, that not one man in ten had even been questioned on bringing him to judgment. *"I speak not for my own Right alone,"* Charles declared, *"as* I *am* your King, *but also for the true Liberty of all* My Subjects. . . . *Nor . . . do* I *forget the* Privileges *of* both Houses *of* Parliament, *which this Day's Proceedings do . . . violate. . . . The Higher House is totally excluded; and for the House of Commons, it is too well known that the Major Part of them are detained or deterred from sitting."* [98]

Coerced into silence by Bradshaw's repeated interruptions, Charles did not for a moment show anger or confusion. Indeed nothing in his life became him so much as his conduct during the days before his execution. His dignity in a hostile court, his fearless, courteous defence, his stiff adherence to his principles while death beckoned in the offing, the sincerity of his private devotions, his brave carriage on the Whitehall scaffold, his quiet, unflinching demeanor before the fatal stroke—all stirred to admiration even the hearts of his enemies, drowned momentarily the remembrance of his professed accountability to none but God, his persecution of the Puritans, his persistent wars on Parliament's armies. For the cause of Charles and royalist despotism, his last days wrought more magic than he had mustered during all the years of his reign.

CHAPTER VIII

TYRANTS AND MEN OF DESTINY

To STUDENTS of Milton's politics, his philosophy of leadership assumes a profound and illuminating significance. The conception of a leader holding his position by virtue of his superior integrity alone dwelt in his mind persistently from youth to old age. It sustained his rejection of Charles I; it confirmed his acceptance of Cromwell and his proposal of a perpetual senate in *The Readie & Easie Way;* it emboldened his denunciation of kingship in 1660; and finally, this conception wove itself inextricably into his pattern of action for *Paradise Lost.*

The rapid growth of Milton's republican notions, however early in his youth the germs for them had been planted, are revealed by the notes in the *Commonplace Book.* As Professor Hanford's brilliant study shows, one finds foreshadowed there with unexpected fullness some of the ideas Milton was to expand in *The Tenure, Eikonoklastes, The Defence,* and *The Readie & Easie Way.* One of his earliest references to monarchy is a decidedly hostile one: "Severus Sulpicius says that the name of king has always been hateful to free peoples, and he condemns the willingness of the Hebrews to exchange liberty for slavery." [1] After the Civil War opened, Milton's notes on kings grow more numerous and insistently inimical. He praises the French for electing Robert to replace Charles the Simple, for "preferring a new king who was an able man to a hereditary fool and idiot." [2] He derides the term "lords" for kings and adds: "Kings scarcely know themselves as mortals." [3] After 1649 he is ready to write a still more stinging attack. He quotes Machiavelli: "Against a bad ruler there is no remedy but the sword. To cure the ills of the people, words are sufficient; to cure those of the ruler, the sword is necessary." [4] From his youth somewhat hostile to kingship as an institution, Milton thus privately recorded his growing antagonism with the passing of the tumultuous revolutionary years. Suitable for inferior men, yes; but not for free aspiring spirits like himself.

A. *The Tenure* vs. CHARLES I

In his early pamphlets against the prelates, however, Milton looks upon monarchy with traditional English satisfaction. It is the kind of government best suited to the interests of Christian people; that which destroys Christianity, he urges, proves inimical to the monarch, and the reverse is equally true.[5] "God forbid," he writes, that we should sever the true interests of either the monarch or monarchy from those of Christianity; their aims and well-being are mutual. No government, not even that of Sparta or Rome, has shown itself more just, more "divinely and harmoniously tuned" than England's monarchy.

One accustomed, nevertheless, to the many qualifying clauses of Milton's prose, finds even in his most enthusiastic praise of monarchy the suggestion, inserted as though the reader had taken it for granted, that the monarch to whom he refers is one who has the full approval of the people.[6] In March, 1642, when it had become apparent that Charles would resist parliamentary sovereignty by force of arms, Milton, still favorable to monarchy, hastened to warn against tyranny in the state.[7] Nevertheless, he still showed his old affection for the monarch by attributing his tyrannical attitude, not to his own perverseness, but to the king's pretended friends, the prelates. Like Midas, the prelates, tyrants in religion, touch the king only to make him a tyrant. Yes, yes, Milton admitted halfheartedly, the king is anointed of the Lord.[8] But while smearing the king with their stinking flatteries, the prelates poison his lifeblood. Thus, though still a royalist at the age of thirty-four, Milton voiced uneasily his dread of arbitrary rule.

From 1642 to 1649 Milton made no public statements about his belief in monarchy. He was still less secular in his aims, at least less interested in the general democratic implications of the war than John Goodwin, whose *Anti-Cavalierisme* (1642) called upon Protestants to support the authority of the people. But Milton could not have escaped the impact of the intense controversy over Parker's *Observations,* or the Hunton-Ferne arguments over kingly authority, or the weighty tomes of Prynne himself. To Prynne, in fact, Milton later paid oblique respect. Though he does not mention kingship in *Areopagitica,* this pamphlet shows how sharply Milton had veered to the left, already calling for both economic and political reformation. If, as the evidence seems to indicate, Milton was fairly well acquainted with Richard Overton, he must have read with keen interest some of the Leveller tracts of 1646 and 1647. By 1649 his opinions had crystallized, influenced undoubtedly not only by the democratic pamphleteers, but also by his admiration for Independent principles and Cromwell's victorious legions. His sonnet to Fairfax in September, 1648, shows how devoutly he hoped for the victory of the anti-monarchical army. The name of Fairfax, wrote Milton, fills Europe's monarchs with amazement; even "remotest kings" tremble with fear. To Milton the Independent army was a symbol: kingship itself was now on the defensive.

Though Lilburne and the Levellers had favored army interference with Parliament in 1647, they staunchly opposed the voiding of constitutional rights in the trial of the king. Only by an *Agreement* signed by the people before the Independents acted to try the king could the purging of Parliament be established as the will of the people; on this the Levellers insisted, not being willing to grant that only a comparatively few of the people would have signed the *Agreement* without compulsion. Lilburne himself had been tried too often by courts he refused to recognize to be unsympathetic to the king's position at the trial. "The way of tryall by 12. sworn men of the Neighborhood is infringed," he wrote, "all liberty of exception against the tryers, is over-ruled by a Court consisting of persons pickt and chosen in an un-usual way; the practice whereof we cannot allow of, though against open and notorious enemies." [9] Later he granted the power of the House of Commons to set up a court of justice, provided that none of the members of the Commons took places on the court. In this analysis Lilburne was following his usual insistence on the separation of powers: Parliament had a right to make the laws, not to execute them.[10] In an interview with Hugh Peters, reported to have taken place on May 25, 1649, Lilburne declared that he would "rather desire to live in Turkie under the great Turk, then in *England* under your Religious Masters at White-hall and Westminster." [11] Predicting the return of the monarchy, he added that he would rather live under a limited kingship than under a tyranny.

Of all the protests against Charles' trial and execution Milton resented most bitterly those of his old enemies, the Presbyterian ministers. We have already glanced at *A Serious and Faithfull Representation,* which forty-seven of them, speaking for London congregations, had issued on January 18. It was the signal for the crystallization of Presbyterian sentiment. Hundreds of Presbyterian ministers rushed into print to support their London brethren; their protests in sermons and pamphlets poured forth weeks after the king's execution. On January 27, three days before the fatal stroke, appeared *The Humble Advice and Earnest Desires of certain well-affected Ministers . . . of Oxon, and . . . Northampton* protesting "all proceedings against his Majesties Crown and Life." [12] Simultaneously a much more peremptory pamphlet, *A Vindication of the Ministers of the Gospel,* exhorted the people to hold fast to the Covenant, condemned utterly "that which is so much feared to be now in agitation, *the taking away the life of the King."* To the same purpose, on the same day, petitioned thousands of Presbyterian supporters.[14] On January 29 the Westminster Assembly of Divines, among them Milton's most horrified critics, pleaded that the life of the king might be spared.[15] The vain efforts of the Presbyterians only heightened their allegiance to Charles; and his martyrlike execution confirmed their devotion. A few days later, entitling his sermon *The Devilish Conspiracy, Hellish Treason,* John Warner compared Charles to Christ, the Jews to the Independents. "Let this be remembred, . . ." he urged, *"He must die for the People* . . . for our Laws and Liberties; and so is become by his death your Martyr, your Sacrifice, and your Saviour." [16]

Resentment against these Presbyterian outbursts provided Milton with the impetus to expose the inconsistencies of their position. He sent forth *The Tenure* February 13, 1649, four days after the instantly popular *Eikon Basilike.* As later incorporated in *Defensio Secunda,* Milton's own explanation runs as follows:

Nor did I write anything on the prerogative of the crown, till the king, voted an enemy by the parliament, and vanquished in the field, was summoned before the tribunal which condemned him to lose his head. But when, at length, some presbyterian ministers, who had formerly been the most bitter enemies to Charles, became jealous of the growth of the independents, and of their ascendancy in the parliament, most tumultuously clamoured against the sentence, and did all in their power to prevent the execution. . . . I thought that it became me to oppose such a glaring falsehood; and accordingly, without any immediate or personal application to Charles, I shewed, in an abstract consideration of the question, what might lawfully be done against tyrants.[17]

In the opening pages of *The Tenure,* as in the closing,[18] Milton berates the new royalism of the Presbyterians; much more than one-third of the pamphlet he gives over to flaying their desertion of the parliamentary cause. Had they not broken their allegiance to the king, set up Parliament as the supreme authority against him, fought him in battle, imprisoned him, diverted his revenues to other uses, refused to treat with him? In so doing had they not in fact deposed, "unkinged the king?" [19] Yet now they have halted. With victory in their grasp, many slaveries lifted, they not only refuse to pluck out the root of all the common miseries, but denounce those who would accept the final and most important duty of bringing the king to justice. "He who but erewhile in their pulpits was a cursed tyrant," exclaimed Milton, "an enemy to God and saints, laden with all the innocent blood spilt in three kingdoms . . . is now, though nothing penitent or altered in his first principles, a lawful magistrate, a sovereign lord, the Lord's anointed, not to be touched, though by themselves imprisoned." [20] Now the Presbyterians contend for customs, precedents, "their gibberish laws . . . the badge of their ancient slavery," to prevent the execution of judgment upon their chief enemy.[21]

Milton was now directing to the Presbyterians the same arguments of inconsistency that the Levellers had so forcefully advanced to Cromwell and Ireton in the fall of 1647. While the Independent army leaders, influenced by radical propaganda and dictates of expediency, had accepted the consequences of Wildman's reasoning, the Presbyterians were too deeply rooted in conservative traditions to make the sharp break with the past proposed by the victorious Independent army. And their royalism was of sterner and older stuff than Milton painted it in *The Tenure.* Herbert Palmer's *Scripture and Reason* (1643), for example, which Milton quotes at length to show how the Presbyterians had justified the war by exalting the rights of people and Parliament over those of the king, asserts that kings are anointed of God, and that men may not take away their crowns.[22] The Presbyterians did not suddenly lose their early democratic fervor in 1648; they began to exalt the king again with the rise of the Independents in 1644 and 1645: them the

Presbyterians held in deeper dread than the legions of the king, as shown so plainly in Edwards' *Gangraenas* of 1646 and 1647. I have not read a single Presbyterian sermon or pamphlet of the period that calls the king "a cursed tyrant." As Prynne (whom Milton places scornfully among the "apostate scarecrows") had said in *A Breife Memento,* Parliament over a hundred times, in various declarations, had disclaimed their intention of doing *"the least hurt, injury, or violence to the Kings person, Crowne, Dignity, or posterity."* [23] This was Presbyterian sentiment, now doubly reinforced by the prospect of military dictatorship. The Presbyterians were guilty, it is true, of inconsistency. By warring with the king, they had set loose democratic forces, proclaimed democratic principles, which, when logically extended by Independents, Levellers, and Diggers, they looked upon with extreme horror. The Presbyterians had changed little, especially the ministers; but the active, receptive minds of the day, of which Milton was one, inevitably threw off, like old clothes, the traditional social patterns of their generation.

Aside from exposing the fallacies of the Presbyterians, Milton's main purpose in *The Tenure* is to prove that a tyrant guilty of his countrymen's blood may be brought to judgment, not by established authorities only, but by "whose hand soever is found . . . sufficient to avenge the effusion, and so great a deluge of innocent blood." [24] This is God's intent, to execute justice upon evil doers, whether by ordinary or extraordinary measures. Thus does Milton claim God's approval for the execution of Charles. This argument had been the favorite approach of the royalists in justifying absolutism; and Cromwell as dictator of England was to use it with a frequency that alarmed even his officers.

But Milton himself, sincere as he was, was not content with such unpersuasive rhetoric. He boldly championed the most democratic dogmas that the Levellers had made popular among the common soldiers, dogmas now incorporated by the officers themselves into an *Agreement of the People*. Like Lilburne in *The Free-Mans Freedome* and *Regall Tyrannie,* Milton assumes that man was originally free, "being the image and resemblance of God himself," and possessing the inalienable right of self-government. The outcropping of kingship in the earliest societies Milton attributes to the need of the people themselves, who, having fallen to quarreling and fighting after Adam's transgression, placed one in authority over all for the welfare of the community. The mainspring of his argument here is that it was the people who gave the king power to rule over them; it was they who set up Parliaments and suggested counsellors for the king, their power being likewise derivative.[25] Power thus residing in the people as a natural right, it follows that the king has no right to regard himself as lord by divine right or to claim his sovereignty by inheritance. Can any one maintain that the authority of a whole people is inferior to that of a single man, that the people were created for the king, not he for the people? To uphold such a principle, asserts Milton, would be "treason against the dignity of mankind." Thus Milton condemns absolutism unreservedly: "To say kings are accountable to none but God, is the overturning of all law and government." [26]

Since a king, then, is raised to eminence only for the good of the people, and by their authority, Milton sees no reason why they may not depose him at will. To depose even a good king is within their province, "merely by the liberty of freeborn men to be governed as seems to them best." And against a tyrant men may lawfully act as they would "against a common pest and destroyer of mankind." [27] Would we not destroy a foreign king making war against us? asks Milton. With how much greater justice may we pull down a tyrant within our own land, a tyrant who has broken his pledges to people and parliament, waged war against his subjects for seven years, denounced all accountability to the nation! The very blood of the slaughtered Christians cries out for vengeance against such a king.

Having so forcefully enunciated the right of the people to depose Charles, Milton does not attempt to show that the people as a whole really favored the execution. To have maintained such a position, quite imperative for his argument, was manifestly impossible even to as ardent an Independent as Milton. When Charles was charged in court with treason "in behalf of the Commons assembled in Parliament and the good people of England," Lady Fairfax had cried out, "It is a lie; not half, nor a quarter of the people of England." [28] Lady Fairfax spoke a truth even the Independents did not attempt to refute. Yet on January 4 the Commons had issued a declaration voicing the very democratic doctrine Milton was to proclaim in *The Tenure*, declaring the people the source of all power, the House of Commons the supreme representative of the people, and repudiating the negative voices of king and lords.[29] The Independents, though a decisive minority, unhesitatingly advanced the arguments of the Levellers' *Remonstrance Of Many Thousand Citizens*. Milton had followed the leftward sweep of the army officers to a justification of regicide by democratic principles. It was an untenable position that he was to attempt to resolve in later tracts.

Nor does Milton pursue in *The Tenure* his original proposition, stated on the title page, that "any, who have the Power" may "call to Account a Tyrant, or wicked King, and after due Conviction . . . depose, and put him to death, if the ordinary Magistrate have neglected, or denied to do it." To have expanded this argument would have involved justification of Pride's Purge and emphasis on the army as the instrument of God's justice *in spite of* the wishes of the people. Or, if Milton had assumed that army was justified as God's instrument because it represented more Englishmen than Parliament itself, he would have been faced with the task of proving the army's democratic principles overwhelmingly popular. Neither line of argument could he have followed with telling conviction. Indeed, in writing *The Tenure* Milton was confronted, like the Independent party itself, with the dilemma of justifying at once military coercion and democratic ideology. Milton chose to strike for the rights of the people without applying his principle realistically to the execution of Charles.

None of Milton's fellow-apologists for the Independent cause spoke more convincingly than he, however, of the origin and function of kingship, and the inherent right of self-government. In *Right And Might well met* Goodwin had claimed the right of the army to act the part of a paternalistic physician in time of crisis, concerned more with the welfare of the people than with their consent to the measures used. He had pointed, too, to the impracticality of securing the consent of the people to such an extreme procedure without jeopardizing the cause. As Milton was to do later, Goodwin argued finally that a corrupt and depraved people forfeit their right of self-government.[30] Though he quoted *The Tenure* with much approval in his *Obstructors to Justice* (May 30, 1649), Goodwin made little attempt to lend the army's actions a democratic sanction.[31] Joseph Warr's *The Privliedges* [sic] *of the People* (February 5) and Canne's *The Golden Rule* (February 16) are more in tune with the reasoning of *The Tenure*. "True *Majesty*," wrote Warr, "is in the spirit and consists in the Divine *Image* of *God* in the *minde*, which the Princes of the World comming short off, have supplyed its defect with outward badges of *Fleshly honour;* which are but the *Empty shews* and *carnall appearances* . . . But weake as they are, they have dazled our eyes." [32] Like any other men, maintained Warr, kings are accountable to the law. Canne in less temperate language asserted the right of the people to punish tyrants, calling the trial and execution of the king a "proceeding . . . so legal, it shall live and remain upon record to the perpetual honor of our *English State*, who took no dark or doubtful way . . . but went in the open and plain path of Justice, Reason, Law, and Religion." [33] Kings are not masters, but ministers and servants of the people; nor, insisted Canne, may the people give up their authority to a monarch. Whatever his claims, they retain their inherent freedom; when they set up a king they do not make themselves his slaves. But Canne's pamphlets, like those of Goodwin, overflow with Biblical references that sharply reduced their persuasiveness among even their theology-conscious contemporaries. Though in his second edition of *The Tenure* (February 15, 1650) Milton added long passages from Protestant divines sustaining his arguments for the accountability of kings, his appeal in both additions is in the main humanistic and secular. He appeals more frequently to Aristotle than to the Bible. Indeed for a similar sustained analysis of the origin and nature of government such as one finds in *The Tenure* one must turn to the Leveller pamphlets, notably *Regall Tyrannie*.

In *The Tenure* Milton attempted both to attack the most influential enemies of the Independents and at the same time recapitulate the basic political theory on which his party in large measure relied. Lesser minds than Milton found sufficient satisfaction in exposing the vulnerable position of the Presbyterians. In *An Answer to the London Ministers Letter* (January 27) Samuel Richardson bluntly justified the Independent procedure by the iron law of necessity, exalting it above both the law of the land and the precepts of the Bible. The contest between the king and the Independents Richardson described as a struggle for existence, comparing procedure of the Independents to a man killing his enemy in self-defence.[34] "It is not wise mens parts to cry up the ends, and decry the means, how to suppresse tyranny . . . ," wrote another apologist. "Theory and Practise are two things, one may better make a *Utopia,* then manage a Commonwealth." [35] In *Clerico-Classicum* (February 18) John Price berated the Presbyterians as now praying for the king against whom they had instigated the kingdom to fight. In the second civil war, maintained Price, the Presbyterians had preached and prayed against the army of the Parliament. If the king is considered the father of his country, runs Price's argument, he has murdered his children and therefore deserves a more ignominious death than a common murderer. Like all the Independent writers, Price pointed to the glorious victories of the army as proof of God's favor on their cause: sixteen thousand had destroyed armies totaling one hundred thousand men. With the Lord's help one Independent soldier had beaten off ten enemies, and two had scattered a hundred.[36] The army apologist of *The City Ministers Unmasked* (March 5) accused the Presbyterians of first inciting war against the king because they had hoped to profit by the sequestering of the bishops' lands.[37] But none of these tirades against the Presbyterians was as sustained or devastatingly effective as the anti-Presbyterian outbursts of Milton's *Tenure.*

The *Tenure* was written, Milton afterward explained, "rather to reconcile the minds of the people to the event, than to discuss the legitimacy of that particular sentence." [38] It is doubtful that Milton held this, or any one, purpose, consistently in mind during the days or weeks he busied himself with *The Tenure.* To view this tract as an effort at reconciliation is to stamp Milton as the weakest psychologist among the Puritan pamphleteers and *The Tenure* as a miserable failure. The officers themselves, recognizing the strength of the Presbyterian ministers, had made overtures to them before the trial of Charles, even as after the execution the new Commonwealth tried persistently to win their good will. But in *The Tenure* Milton made no effort to placate the Presbyterians, to assure them that their ministerial rights would be respected, that the army officers intended no persecution of Presbyterian conscience, that the property rights of the influential Presbyterian laymen would be as secure as ever. Rather, bitingly hostile to his old enemies, Milton promulgated in *The Tenure* the very political theories they most bitterly feared and resented. In his *History of*

Independency (August, 1649) the Presbyterian Clement Walker scoffed at *The Tenure*, asking why, according to Milton's theory, it would not be "lawful to put to death wicked *Cromwells*, Councels of State"; and accusing the Independents of having planned the overthrow of monarchy from the beginning of the war.[39]

As a conciliatory gesture Henry Robinson's *A Short Discourse Between Monarchical and Aristocratical Government* (which appeared probably in March or April) was the only tract of distinct merit among the Independent sallies; and as an analysis of the shift in power it is more realistic than *The Tenure*. The king, claimed Robinson, had been the main cause of all the nation's misery, had corrupted all his associates. Only by the desperate remedy of removing him could the nation hope for peace in such a dire emergency. Was not the welfare of the nation worth "such a *Royal Sacrifice*"? Kingship had no divine approval; rather it bore "the stamp of dislike from God." And it had always been hostile to Presbyterianism. A people might choose to live under any type of government they preferred. The present government, asserted Robinson, was not a democracy, but rather "a middle *State* between *Popular Anarchy* and *Prerogative Tyranny*, whereby men are freed from the necessary *exorbitancies of both*." [40] He warned his readers that the country was in danger of drifting toward a "Levelling Confusion," or suffering again under a worse tyranny than they had endured under Charles. Thus did Robinson attempt to assure the Presbyterians that the Independents intended no radical democratic reforms, cajoling them into a support of the Commonwealth as the alternative to dangerous extremes. Finally, he urged all citizens "to be as conscientious in avoyding way of making new Divisions, as we are in remembering former Miscarriages," and appealed to their patriotism: "We are now . . . on a new Foundation . . . and want nothing to make us the happiest *Nation* under the Sun." [41] Robinson's analysis of the state of affairs was strikingly accurate. The Independents were an aristocratic group who wanted religious and intellectual rather than political or economic liberty, though they had gained power with the aid of the extreme democratic convictions of the army radicals. When Robinson's pamphlet appeared they had already broken with the Leveller leaders, and were shortly to imprison them. Once in power, the Independents rejected the consequences of their democratic manifestoes, and invited the support of the prosperous middle classes, of whom the Presbyterian ministry were the most influential representatives.

B. *Eikon Basilike* AND MILTON'S REPLY

All Independent pamphleteers, even the temperate Robinson, were helpless to combat the popularity of the *Eikon Basilike.* First distributed the day after Charles' burial, offering to a stunned people a pious, martyr-like account of his conflict with Parliament, each chapter of the story followed by his prayerful meditations, it instantly fired the popular imagination, passed from hand to hand, was run off the presses in dozens of new editions. Through the *Eikon* the whole literate population was invited to share the king's secret thoughts; these expressed with a dignity, meekness, and undoubted sincerity that impressively recalled his bearing in the days preceding his execution. As in the trial, the Charles of the *Eikon* showed a constant affection for his people and zeal for their liberties; he had been willing, he said, to relinquish some of his traditional powers if recompensed by the love of his subjects; he assumed their good will for him: "I had the Charity to interpret, that most part of My Subjects fought against My supposed Errours, not My Person; and intended to mend Me, not to end Me. . . . I am too conscious of My own Affections toward the generality of My people, to suspect theirs to Me . . . I had rather prevent My peoples ruine then Rule over them; nor am I so ambitious of that Dominion which is but My Right, as of their happinesse." [42] Charles denied that he could be held responsible for the blood of the slain thousands: "For the hazards of Warre are equall, nor doth the Cannon know any respect of Persons." [43] In his meditations on death Charles prayed, according to the *Eikon,* in the following manner: *"Thou madest thy Sonne a Saviour to many, that Crucified Him, while at once he suffered by them, and yet willingly . . . O let the voice of his bloud be heard for My Murtherers, louder than the cry of mine against them."* [44] Charles' prayers for his enemies, phrased in more felicitous language than any Puritan writer could muster, his parting advice to his son, his repentance over Strafford's sentence, his appeal for sympathy as a godly king in the shadow of execution—all these served to make the appeal of the *Eikon* irresistible to the multitude of king-revering Englishmen. The writer, probably Dr. John Gauden, touched the well-springs of English psychology more deftly and surely than any contemporary pamphleteer, making the *Eikon* the most effective propaganda tract of Milton's generation.

Yet the royal apology itself shows why war against Charles was inevitable; and between the lines one reads, too, that given the Independent psychology this man's head would inevitably topple. His very virtues confirmed in his own mind, and obscured in others, his determined despotism.[45] Charles was a sincere absolutist with no real understanding of the democratic aspirations of the rising middle classes; he naively expected feudal loyalty from the new Bible-reading, individualistic capitalists. Parliament's resistance to his will he dismissed in the *Eikon* as "those sparks which some mens distempers . . . studied to kindle," which resistance he hoped to break by ruling for many years without Parliament! The tumultuous disorders of civil war he attributed in part to the sins of the people, urging God to make them repent! *"Rebuke those beasts of the people,"* he prayed, *"and deliver Me from the rudenesse and strivings of the multitude."* [46] Charles' devotion to the bishops as the support of his kingly authority showed his complete incapacity for coming to terms with the spirit of the Reformation. The younger Charles he warned that "the Devill of Rebellion, doth commonly turn himself into an Angell of Reformation." [47] In the seven years of Civil War Charles had learned nothing. At the beginning he had not understood the political demands of the Presbyterian bourgeoisie; as the war progressed he remained blithely unaware of the intense social ferment at work among the New Model soldiers, the Leveller mass meetings, the Independent and Anabaptist congregations. That kingly favors held no charms for Cromwell and Ireton were to him incomprehensible. The gestures of a belligerent democratic surge, Cromwell's failure to kneel and kiss his hand, Lilburne's hat-wearing in the House of Lords, were lost upon Charles. If by 1648 the Presbyterians wished reconciliation with the king at almost any cost, they acted rather from fear of the Independent radicals than from relinquishment of their original purposes. If the Independents and Levellers represented constitutional patterns born too soon, Charles spoke for the declining power of English feudalism, to be curbed finally in 1688.

No very substantial reply to *Eikon Basilike* appeared until August 26, when an anonymous Independent sent forth *Eikon*

Alethine. The shrill tones of the opening pages are a confession of the author's despair. How is it that a dead king calls up the fervent devotion of men once his bitter enemies? *"What is in this Booke,"* asks the author, *"which hath not been in Messages and Declarations . . . by the late King . . . ? You beheld those unchanged; why should this Gorgon so metamorphize you? . . . Let not a Goose quill make you all Ganders, and a sound of words bewitch you, whom drums and trumpets could not affright."* [48] Like those of Milton, though not so brilliant or complete, the arguments of the *Alethine* against the king's arbitrary power, against his definition of tumults, against his reasons for quarreling with Parliament, strike the reader as sensible and sound, the very reasons advanced by all parliamentary defenders in 1642. But against the "Sophistry flashing with Rhetoricke" of the *Basilike,* particularly the images of the martyred king at his prayers, the appeals of the *Alethine* were wholly ineffectual. Moreover, no amount of reasoning by internal evidence, rather skilfully advanced in the *Alethine,* that the king was not the real author, could shake the credulity of the masses. To the *Alethine* doubts that a king under stress could have written such flowing sentences, the royalist *Eikon He Piste* replied: "Are not these fine pick-axes to pick the brains out of a dead mans skull? Was it not enough to take away his Life, Crown and Dignity . . . but you must throw dirt upon his Grave, Blots upon his Writings . . . poyson his Memory that is so precious with all good men . . . ?" [49]

But Milton was preparing a more formidable tract than the *Alethine* in *Eikonoklastes* (October 6, 1649). Using a chapter-by-chapter rebuttal that admitted of few statesmanlike passages, Milton fastened doggedly upon every theoretical weakness of *Eikon Basilike.* What Charles dismisses time after time as *tumults* Milton describes as the just complaints and forceful reforms of "this iron flail, the people." The Star-Chamber; the High Commission; the dissolution of Parliaments; the public theft of private possessions, claimed as crown land or forest land; the tyrannical bishops— against these bitter evils the people protested in vain. And the king called them *tumults!* Never once did he yield willingly to the demands of his Parliament and people; step by step he opposed their petitions, calling Parliaments only to get money for himself, defending tyrannical courts, bishops, ship money to the bitter end.[50] Returning again and again to the attack, Milton scornfully refutes the king's claim to a conscientious negative voice. He denies that the law gives the king such a preposterous power, a power that in one man's hands may defeat the will of a whole nation. Rather it is "an absurd and reasonless custom, begotten and grown up either from the flattery of basest times, or the usurpation of immoderate princes." [51] How absurd to call Parliaments, to debate measures carried by majorities, if one voice may finally nullify all! By such a rejection the king in effect may make the law, subjecting the whole people to his whims. Though Charles claims a conscientious right to judge, he has denied this same right to the multitudes of his countrymen.

Acute as Milton's disputations were, the *Eikonoklastes* as an answer to *Eikon Basilike* was an utter failure. Whereas the *Eikon Basilike* fell on a seed ground created by centuries of patriotic, superstitious reverence for kingship, appealed to hearts with sympathy from the unanswerable pulpit of the dead, *Eikonoklastes* spoke tardily to the cold, the intellectual, the skeptical among the unpersuaded. To the winning, understandable pleas of a martyred king for personal justification, Milton opposed a biting analysis of the political record and unfamiliar theorizing. ",I did not insult over fallen majesty, as is pretended," wrote Milton later, "I only preferred queen Truth to king Charles." [52] Realizing, as he says, that his enemies would thus accuse him, Milton sincerely attempted to avoid insulting personalities. But his scoffing at the king's prayers, stolen or not from the *Arcadia,* and his pictures of the king's guards as "the ragged infantry of stews and brothels"—such sallies diverted his readers from his solid political reasoning. Of the total effect of *Eikonoklastes* Gardiner has written the surest estimate I know: "In such a case mere negative criticism avails but little. What was needed was the development of a higher loyalty to the nation in the place of the lower loyalty to the King, and the quickening of a sense of the exuberant vitality of the collective life of the people in the place of devotion to the head of the national organization. Time had been when Milton had struck that key, and gazed on a vision of a 'noble and puissant nation rousing herself like a strong man after sleep and shaking her invincible locks.' He could not speak in that strain of a Commonwealth supporting itself on an armed force." [53]

Milton's conception of kingship shows considerable development in *Eikonoklastes*. His prolonged study of Charles' record, however negative in effect the consequent analysis, produced a few passages of statesmanlike merit, though nothing comparable in style to his best prose. Thus does Milton summarize the limitations of the king's power under the English constitution:

For every commonwealth is in general defined, a society sufficient of itself, in all things conducible to well-being and commodious life. Any of which requisite things, if it cannot have without the gift and favour of a single person, or without leave of his private reason or his conscience, it cannot be thought sufficient of itself, and by consequence no common-wealth, nor free; but a multitude of vassals in the possession and domain of one absolute lord, and wholly obnoxious to his will. If the king have power to give or deny anything to his parliament, he must do it as a person several from them, or as one greater: neither of which will be allowed him: not to be considered severally from them; for as the king of England can do no wrong, so neither can he do right but in his courts and by his courts; and what is legally done in them, shall be deemed the king's assent, though he as a several person shall judge or endeavour the contrary; so that indeed without his courts, or against them, he is no king. If therefore he obtrude upon us any public mischief, or withhold from us any general good, which is wrong in the highest degree, he must do it as a tyrant, not as a king of England, by the known maxims of our law. Neither can he, as one greater, give aught to the parliament which is not in their own power, but he must be greater also than the kingdom which they represent: so that to honour him with the giving part was a mere civility, and may be well termed the courtesy of England, not the king's due.[54]

Although constitutional monarchy was still agreeable to Milton, we find in *Eikonoklastes* a growing aversion to any monarch at all. He breaks out plainly to ask why the nation should not hope to be governed better without a king; all their past misery has sprung either from the king's actions, or from their resistance against him. In Chapter XVII, "Of the Differences in point of Church Government," Milton remarks that the interests of kings and those of the church of God have always clashed with each other; for whereas Christianity has favored liberty and equality, kings have abhorred them. A people of true virtue and honor does not need a king. And a people wanting to be governed by a man like Charles are "not fit for that liberty which they cried out and bellowed for, but fitter to be led back again into their old servitude, like a sort of clamouring and fighting brutes." [55] Through *Eikonoklastes* runs a tone of personal antagonism to Charles I. Surprised at the strength of that English reverence for kingship which would uphold even a tyrant, the exasperated Milton finds himself striking at Charles as a symbol of monarchy itself. In one of the most striking passages of *Eikonoklastes,* Milton thus epitomizes the weakness of kingship:

> Indeed, if the race of kings were eminently the best of men, as the breed of Tutbury is of horses, it would in reason then be their part only to command, ours always to obey. But kings by generation no way excelling others, and most commonly not being the wisest or the worthiest by far of whom they claim to have the governing; that we should yield them subjection to our own ruin, or hold of them the right of our common safety . . . we may be sure was never the intent of God, whose ways are just and equal; never the intent of nature, whose works are also regular; never of any people not wholly barbarous, whom prudence, or no more but human sense, would have better guided when they first created kings, than so to nullify and tread to dirt the rest of mankind, by exalting one person and his lineage without other merit looked after, but the mere contingency of a begetting, into an absolute and uncontrollable dominion over them and their posterity.[56]

C. The *Defence:* New Justification of Regicide

A Defence of the People of England (December 31, 1650) shows a considerable broadening and deepening of Milton's conception of kingship. Prolonged study of the subject, not only from his old authors of the *Commonplace Book,* but also of Salmasius' own sources, is evident in every chapter. For the first time we have an enlargement of Milton's belief that the true king is one superior to all his subjects in virtue and wisdom. "I confess," wrote Milton, "many eminent and famous men have extolled monarchy; but it has always been upon this supposition, that the prince was a very excellent person, and one that of all others deserved best to reign." [57] For any other to be exalted "is not fitting or decent." By the law of nature "no man . . . has right to be king, unless he excel all others in wisdom and courage." [58] Thus it was, claims Milton, in the earliest societies, in the Greek city states, and in the best governments of Rome. This idea of leadership, now for the first time expanded, had as we have shown dwelt with Milton from youth. Inherited from Plato and Aristotle and his broad reading of the pagan classics, modified by Christian doctrine, this concept of a leader maintaining his place by general acceptance of his superior wisdom took firmer root in Milton's mind than any other political principle.

Again and again Milton affirms that he is not attacking kings in the true sense, but tyrants. He refers to Aristotle's old definition, that a tyrant is one who strives not for the welfare of the whole people, as a just king should, but only for his own selfish ends.[59] In the words of Aristotle: "The perversion of kingship is tyranny . . . as the tyrant considers his own interest, and the king the interest of his subjects; for a king is not a king unless he is self-sufficient and superior to his subjects in all that is good." [60] As in this instance, Aristotle is constantly a primary source for Milton's political opinions. At the end of the *Defence* Milton writes that he has maintained the "common rights of the people against the unjust domination of kings, not out of any hatred to kings, but tyrants." [61] Kings may be honest; tyrants are inevitably rogues. Later Milton wrote that a tyrant is a vicious slave, totally mastered by his own evil passions and subservient to the most depraved elements of the population. God himself commanded that tyrants be put to death.[62]

Nevertheless, in the *Defence* as in *Eikonoklastes*, Milton reveals a growing distrust of the whole institution of monarchy. A commonwealth, he writes, is a more perfect form of government than a monarchy; God was reluctant to permit the Hebrews to have a king. "Christians either must have no king at all; or if they have, that king must be the people's servant. Absolute lordship and Christianity are inconsistent." [63] Whatever vices the English have acquired, Milton affirms, "they have learnt them under a kingly government." [64] The most flourishing free governments of the world have not been monarchies, but commonwealths. The more virtuous, liberty-loving a people the less they have need of a king:

How much better is it, and more becoming yourselves, if you desire riches, liberty, peace, and empire, to obtain them assuredly by your own virtue, industry, prudence, and valour, than to long after and hope for them in vain under the rule of a king? They who are of opinion that these things cannot be compassed but under a king, and a lord, it cannot well be expressed how mean, how base, I do not say, how unworthy, thoughts they have of themselves.[65]

This passage appears near the end of the *Defence,* in Milton's address to his countrymen. In his attempt to reconcile them to the new government, he pictures kingship as inconsistent with the new spirit of self-confidence created by a thriving political reformation.

With voluminous proofs and diverse reasoning Milton expands in the *Defence* his *Tenure* argument that the authority of the people is superior to that of kings. Freedom to choose their own government is inherent in the very nature of the creation, and further enlarged by teaching of Christ. "If one should consider attentively the countenance of a man," writes Milton, "and inquire after whose image so noble a creature were framed, would not any one that heard him presently make answer, that he was made after the image of God himself? Being therefore peculiarly God's own . . . we are entirely free by nature." [66] He quotes from Plato, Aristotle, Aeschylus, Sophocles, Euripides, Cicero, Tacitus, Livy, to prove the accountability of the rulers to the people of Greece and Rome. From English history he cites the elective kings of the Saxons, the judgments of Bracton, Fleta, and Sir Thomas Smith, contending that English kings have ruled only by the authority and consent of the people. If a king fail to use honestly and fairly the power entrusted to him by the people, they may not only recall that power into their own hands, maintains Milton, but also punish the king for his derelictions. If, in England, "the meanest man in the kingdom may even in inferior courts have the benefit of the law against the king himself . . . how much more consonant to justice . . . in case the king oppress all his people, there should be such as have authority not only to restrain him . . . but to judge and punish him!" [67] And Milton cites the time-worn catch-all of the democratic reformers: the safety of the people is the supreme law.

The power having been lodged originally in the people, it is inevitable that positive law and parliament, both products of the people's will, are superior to the will of the king. Finding, Milton had related in *The Tenure,* that the early kings had used unjustly the power that the people had delegated to them, nations established laws to limit the authority of their rulers. But even this did not always hold the king in check; whereupon the custom had grown up of contracting with him to obey the laws only so long as he himself obeyed them.[68] The king's oath is an acknowledgement of the law's superiority to his will: "Will you grant those just laws, which the people shall choose?" The king answers, "I will." [69] If (and it is from this position that Milton attacks the theory of the divine right of kings) kings are responsible to no one but God, why do they swear to obey the laws of the land when they accept their crowns? If we grant that law is above the king, it is none the less true that the institution that makes the laws, parliament, is also superior in authority. Milton readily yields to Salmasius that the king has made the earls and barons of the House of Lords, who have been swayed by his desires, for which reason the new commonwealth has abolished the function of the upper house: "We have done well to take care that for the future they shall not be judges of a free people." [70] But from earliest Saxon days the common people had been represented in the councils of wise men, from which had sprung the power of the House of Commons. Before lords or bishops were represented in Parliament, the king dealt with the Commons only. In them, not in the hands of king or lords, has always resided the delegated power of the nation. Salmasius' taunt that the nation could provide no peers to try the king Milton dismisses thus: "There are none but who are peers good enough for him, and proper enough to pronounce the sentence of death upon him judicially." [71] The law itself cannot be supreme unless power resides in the Commons to execute it, if the need arise, against the king himself.

Milton had attempted to justify the king's trial and execution in a short passage of *Eikonoklastes;* he treats them at length in *A Defence of the People of England*. Commenting on a passage in *Eikon Basilike* in which the author regrets that the king's enemies should have been both his accusers and judges, Milton had agreed that it was a sad event, but had denied that the king therefore should not have been judged at all. To deny the legality of the proceedings is a mere excuse; it is the same plea that may be brought forward at the resurrection, when the saints will both judge and accuse! [72] Fourteen months later, in the *Defence*, Milton justifies the revolution and execution of the king as sanctioned by the law of nature and God: "whatever things are for the universal good of the whole state . . . are . . . lawful and just." [73] As for the purging of Parliament, making way for the king's trial, Milton claims that those secluded were the allies of the king "in their minds and counsels." Of the army Milton asks: "Ought they, therefore, to have been wanting to the nation, and not provide for its safety, because the infection had spread itself even in their own house?" The position of the Independents, continues Milton, was desperate. Having fought so valiantly for the country's liberty, were they now to give themselves up and be destroyed by their enemies? Necessity decreed that they act to preserve themselves.[74] As nature taught men to give up force for the rule of law, so nature now teaches, when a tyrant has subverted the law, to resort again to force and violence.[75]

Milton is no more content in the *Defence* than in *The Tenure*, however, to rest the case of the new commonwealth on a broad appeal of necessity, or the authorization of God and nature. His main thesis is the democratic basis for social action, the approval of the people and its representatives for the regicide. He attempts, therefore, to color the execution with the approval of legality. Charles was condemned to die by the "supreme council of the kingdom." [76] He asks Salmasius if it is not more just to prosecute the king by law, to bring him into a court of justice, and if the law condemn him to put him to death as he deserves, than to assassinate him without trial. The regicides he justifies as having acted lawfully and openly rather than having attempted to evade the scrutiny of the nation. Milton even declares it *was* the people who excluded the lords from Parliament; the soldiers who did it were a great part of the people, and they "did it with the consent, and at the desire, of almost all the rest of the people, and not without the authority of Parliament neither." [77] Furthermore, it was the people who drove out the Commons; that is, Milton continues simply, if the most statesmanlike part of the Parliament, having the true liberties of the people at heart, drove out the majority who were willing to become slaves, may it not be said that the people drove them out? Thus it is that Milton defends the execution of Charles as an act of the people.

Though he reasons from a premise which was then accepted as true by many of the foremost statesmen, i.e., that the people have a right to change their form of government, we cannot now, any more than Sir Harry Vane could then, accept Milton's conclusion that

Charles I was legally executed. Perhaps Charles deserved it for his crimes, which Milton has enumerated in *Eikonoklastes* and in the twelfth chapter of the *Defence*. He had levied illegal taxes; he had treacherously encouraged the Irish to fall upon the English inhabitants; he had compelled men to worship according to the superstitious prelatical liturgy; he had put his will above the law of the land; he had taken arms against Parliament and had slain his own people. But even granting that Charles deserved death for his deeds, and that, as Gardiner observes, there could be no peaceful settlement of the country as long as he lived, he was, we must admit, tried and condemned by men who were his sworn enemies either in Parliament or in the field. Not a full Parliament representative of the people, but a body purged of royalist sympathizers by military power, had set up the tribunal which tried the king. Officers of the army directly urged the court to convict Charles. So little constitutional basis did the trial have that even the distinguished lawyers and judges most sympathetic to the Independents, among them Bulstrode Whitelock, refused to serve as the lord president of the court.[78] The inexperienced Bradshaw treated Charles not as a defendant, but as an already convicted traitor; repeatedly he interrupted the prisoner, refusing him permission to state his reasons for denying the jurisdiction of the court. No one reading a verbatim record of the trial can conclude that the Independents permitted the king even a semblance of the constitutional privileges of a prisoner. Cromwell himself made no effort to assume for the trial a constitutional authenticity.

But throughout his pamphlets on this subject Milton assumes that the court of sixty judges represented the nation, was the nation, and therefore had proceeded impartially according to the laws of the land. The "better and wiser men" of the Commons "in conjunction with the greater or the better part of the people," says Milton, "I should not scruple to call by the name of, and take them for, all the people." [79] To Salmasius' charge that not one Englishman in a hundred thousand consented to the condemnation of Charles, Milton answers that if that preponderance of the nation opposed it, why did they allow it to be done? And the number of the Commons that voted for the condemnation was more than the usual quorum necessary for the transaction of the most weighty affairs of state. True, he had written in *The Tenure*, there was no precedent for a

Protestant nation's putting a king to death. But this is not to be seriously considered; the Parliament and military council will create a precedent. "It argues the more wisdom, virtue, and magnanimity, that they know themselves able to be a precedent to others." [80] When he felt that his justification of legality was breaking down, Milton unhesitatingly applied the principle of cosmic justice. The machinery of justice was not with him an important consideration in his judgment of Charles' trial. Charles deserved to die; the machinery of his condemnation is of relatively little importance; it was merely an instrument to execute God's judgment. [81]

Despite his high motive, therefore, Milton not only justified an illegal action but renounced the democratic principle; namely, the right of the people to determine the actions of its government, the same right for which he has repeatedly argued. It mattered not to Milton that the Presbyterian Parliament, roughly representative of the people, gave way to a military force. They were natural slaves, the people were slaves by nature, who did not want to take the great step toward liberty of abolishing the kingship and of executing a tyrant. They being natural slaves, there was no need to heed them, to prohibit the valorous and liberty-loving from grasping their freedom. "On our side was the army, whose fidelity, moderation, and courage were sufficiently known. It being in our power by their means to retain our liberty, our state, our common safety, do you think we had not been fools to have lost all by our negligence and folly?" [82]

Milton would not grant the right of a people to be governed by a tyrant. When the English people clamored for a king, at that moment, Milton felt, coercion by the enlightened few was entirely justified. It was coercion on the side of progress. It was coercion on behalf of the *ultimate* state of public opinion, as he hints in *Defensio Secunda*: "Those who excel in prudence, in experience, in industry, and courage, however few they may be, will, in my opinion, finally constitute the majority, and everywhere have the ascendant." [83]

Milton and the Independents had fought their way to that formidable wall which separates the Old from the New: the stupidity of the people. Not until the people, throughout the length and breadth of the land, had by the slow growth of political intelligence removed the stones one by one could the nation cross haltingly over the wall. But there was Cromwell's army, the most powerful in

Europe, a great battering ram, as it were, before the barrier; the men of the army had fought their way within reach of that liberty which their countrymen, too deeply rooted in tradition, feared because to them it was incomprehensible. The sword was on the side of immediate liberty. So the Independents battered their way through the wall; the deed was done, but the nation did not cross over. It remained behind fearful, ignorant, to await the return of kingship. To the Independents it mattered not that the people as a whole could not pass from kingship to a republic. Liberty was to them more fundamental than democracy, that democracy toward which Lilburne and the Levellers had reached so strenuously. And liberty was impossible so long as the king lived.

D. Embattled Milton in the Royalist Whirlwind

We have traced in the preceding pages the development of Milton's conception of the ruler as the agent of the people, subject to the laws of the land, and as such liable to prosecution and even condemnation to death for his misdeeds. If we have analyzed the situation accurately, these beliefs, enhanced by the anticipation of immediate liberty, especially disestablishment and freedom of speech, together with his conviction that the praying Independent army leaders were instruments of God's justice, caused Milton to justify the plainly illegal trial and condemnation of Charles I. Our problem now, passing by for the moment the nine years of Milton's relationship to Cromwell, is to discover in the pamphlets of 1660 the crystallization of his earlier beliefs concerning monarchs.

On May 7, 1659, after the dissolution of Richard Cromwell's Parliament by the disaffected army officers, forty-two members of the old Rump Parliament which Oliver had turned out on April 20, 1653, met at Westminster. They had come at the request of the officers themselves, who needed a Parliament badly. Less than six months later, however, the army officers, finding that the Rumpers were as determined as ever to subordinate military to civil authority, stationed soldiers before the doors of the House and refused to let Parliament meet. Before its dissolution, the Rump had debated the issue of a constitution which would satisfy the demands of the Parliament and of the army for a republic.

That the country then needed, and was afterward to need, some kind of generally-accepted authority, was evident from the "ruptures of the commonwealth." In less than a year and a half, from September 4, 1658 to March 16, 1660, Richard assumed the Protectorate—and abdicated; Richard's Parliament dissolved; the army officers brought together the Rump which Cromwell had dissolved six years before; Lambert dissolved the Restored Rump; Monk championed the Rump and restored it a third time; Monk invited the secluded Presbyterian members to take their places in Parliament; the Parliament of the secluded members called a new Parliament which proved predominantly royalist and brought about the restoration of Charles II. The despair of the Commonwealth supporters during this period is nowhere more strikingly expressed than in the words of Hugh Peters (May 10, 1659): *"The authority of the best Parliament . . . trampled upon . . . nothing set up in their place, an Enemy at the door, a penurious souldiery, thousands of poor perishing that by this time might have been payd, Widows and Orphans already dying in the streets. Trade gone, Private souldiers grown Masters, Law, and Gospel dying, the whole Protestant—cause . . . totterring."* [84] Sensing vindication of his long struggle against the Independents, Prynne on May 13 pointed with pride to the confusion: "I shall therefore earnestly desire all persions ingaged in this *whorish, bastard old Cause,* now seriously and sadly to consider, how their often forcing Ruptures, of the Houses, Members, Privileges of Parliament; their absurd, frequent new-modelling of our Government, Parliaments, according to their own whymsical fancies . . . have produced these deplorable effects." [85]

Meanwhile the restoration of kingship loomed as an issue of explosive repercussions. Ten years of army dominance had only strengthened the nation's allegiance to the monarchy. On June 2 appeared *A Word To Purpose: Or A Parthian Dart,* ridiculing both the army and the Parliament as media of establishing a government, and calling for the traditional kingship. On July 22 John Fell sent forth his *Interest of England Stated,* urging the Presbyterians to restore Charles as the only means of saving themselves from the radicals. Presbyterian ministers in Lancashire, as Nedham expressed it, were "blowing the trumpet to rebellion . . . for the Interest of C. Stuart." [86] With each passing month of confusion, the adherents of the king spoke forth more boldly; and commonwealth supporters, divided among themselves, tried in vain to hold in check the running tide of royalist sentiment. "A Great part of the Nation," wrote Nedham in *Interest Will Not Lie* (August 12), "may be said to be Neuters . . . but would fain have Peace, and no Taxes, and are possessed with a phantasie, that there is no way to procure the one, or be rid of the other, but by letting in Charls Stuart." [87]

These are vain hopes, urged Nedham, if only because of the vast charges for the royal court. And proponents of the Good Old Cause, united at least against this common enemy, pamphleteered vigorously against the institution of kingship. *"Kingly Government is a kind of Scourge,"* wrote a pious republican; *"and, at best, an allay of the* freedome *of a people; a* sacred *thing esteem'd, of difficult* accesse, *Idolatrously* adored, *an occasion of great* superfluity *excesse and vanity, unsuitable to this day that is upon us."* [88] In a proposal for a settlement by *The Agreement of the People* (September 22), the author, like Milton, urged the avoidance of "a double evil . . . absolute monarchy, and persecution for conscience." [89] On September 28 a Harrington sympathizer, William Sprigg, distributed *A Modest Plea For An Equal Common-Wealth*, in which he painted a black picture of piety and tyranny rolled together in one princely personality. "If a Prince be invested with the least Punctilio of the Soveraigntie," wrote another agrarian reformer, "it is exceeding vain to imagine, that he should not naturally aspire to the top of it." [90] While condemning each other, both the army officers and the spokesmen of the Rump denounced any rule by a single person. In *A True Relation Of The State of the Case* (October 11), the Rump apologist warned against generals as potential dictators: "The *Officers* of the *Army* cry all, they are not for, but against *A single person*, we wonder men are so voyd of *sence;* is not he that is *Generall of an Army, a Prince?"* [91] The officers, on the other hand, in *The Army's Plea* (October 24) pointed to their long record of unselfish devotion to the cause of the common people against oppression both by king and Parliament.

In the course of this tumultuous pamphleteering, Milton seeking, like a number of patriots of all parties, a constitution to fit his country's need, and perceiving that the restoration of kingship was near at hand unless there was some immediate solution, wrote two letters and two pamphlets which express his final and unqualified renunciation of kingship. In *A Letter to a Friend Concerning the Ruptures of the Commonwealth,* dated Octo-

ber 20, Milton suggests a form of government based on two principles: toleration of all beliefs except Catholicism, and denial of
any single person's rule. It is clear from this statement that he dis-
likes not only kings, but protectors and military dictators as well.
The years of Oliver's Protectorate have by no means convinced
Milton that even a naturally superior ruler can give the liberty his
soul demands. On March 3 appeared *The Readie & Easie Way To
Establish A Free Commonwealth, And The Excellence thereof,
Compar'd with The inconveniences and dangers of readmitting kingship in this nation.* The very title plainly tells his stand: he will
have no king at all now, limited or unlimited in power. Reviewing
the work of the Rump Parliament for the advance of liberty, and
justifying the condemnation of the king by the law of nature, Milton exhorts his fellow-countrymen not to give themselves back into
slavery, but to create a commonwealth which will function without
a king. If we return to kingship, says Milton, we shall soon find the
prelates assuming their old authority over our consciences; we shall
have to fight step by step all over again for each liberty we possess;
we shall lose Scotland, which no king could ever conquer; we shall
lose the most glorious of all governments, a free commonwealth.
Moreover we shall have a ruler uplifted, not by true merit, but by
artificial and false distinctions, to a costly and disgraceful eminence.
Not only must we then bow down to him in a manner contrary to
the teachings of Christ, but we must furnish him with expensive
trappings, clothes, attendants (in whom the court will breed an
unnatural servile spirit), money with which to debauch the youth
of the land in masques and revels. How weak and foolish to place
the hope of happiness in a king! If he lives, and is a good king,
he can do no more than a man could do; if he dies, there is commotion and disorder in the kingdom. In a commonwealth an officer
can be replaced quietly, without disturbance; but in a kingdom all is
turmoil. Further, Milton continues, by acknowledging a man lord
and master, we give over our freedom and become his vassals. After
having fought so gloriously for ten or twelve years to overturn
tyranny, then to set it up again! Finally, it is well to remember that
kings are natural enemies to freedom of thought and speech.
Whereas, in a commonwealth, the people may set up schools
throughout the land, leading the young forward to intellectual
achievements and true virtue, in a kingdom the monarch will use

his influence against education; for the aim of monarchs is to keep the people in a servile state, ignorant and callous.

Meanwhile the royalists, growing bolder week by week, anticipated with high enthusiasm the coming of Charles and the death of the Good Old Cause. As yet no one knew that the wary Monk himself, while preserving every appearance of allegiance to Parliament, had already joined the ranks of the king. On December 30 he had written to the king of his long determined resolution to use his military power to restore the monarchy. "I humbly conceive," said Monk to Charles, "I had never a better opportunity of doing my country service, (in freeing them from their *Egyptian* bondage, as I may term it,) and in restoring the Crown to the right owner thereof; which if possible to be done, shall be done with as much care, safety, and diligence, as God shall enable me." [92] On February 2 (1660) *A Coffin For The Good Old Cause* warned that monarchy was the alternative to bold, decisive action. "Sirs," exhorts the author, "your Vessel's leaky, and your Pump too little; carreen her quickly, or you sink past all recovery." [93] *No Drol, But A Rational Account* (February 14) spoke to the same purpose. On February 20, when at Monk's insistence the secluded members of the Long Parliament were reinstated at Westminster, the nation took another long step toward a restored kingship. The self-dissolution of the new Parliament (March 13) together with the call for a full and free Parliament to sit April 25, was the signal for unrestrained royalist outbursts. "The Kings Authority is *Jure Divino*," affirmed *The Case Stated Touching the Soveraign's Prerogative* (March 24), "he is set over us by God himself, he hath not his Reign or Crown by our favour; for, sayes God, *By me Kings Reign*." [94] The next day at Mercer's Chapel Matthew Griffith preached the sermon that Milton was to read with the deepest hatred, *The Fear Of God And The King*. "All they that *fight* against *God*, and his *Annointed*," proclaimed Griffith, ". . . have the *brand* of Gods *indignation fastned* so much the *deeper* in their *flesh*. . . . The *two Arch-enemies* of all *rule* and *government*, [are] the *Anabaptisticall Independents*, and . . . the *Nonsensicall Quakers*." In *The Samaritan Revived* Griffith had written: "Without the restitution of *King Charles* to his native rights, we can in reason look for no solid settlement of Religion, or Law, Liberty or Property, Peace or Plenty, Honour or Safety." [95] On April 2 an extreme royalist in *The Grand Rebels*

Detected reminded the country of the anti-monarchical misdeeds of the Presbyterians: "A Monarchy they are for, but it must be a limited Monarchy; a King they are for, but they must rule him, and the people too." [96]

Sensing in Milton the most fearless and outspoken antagonist of the inevitable Restoration, royalist pamphleteers, L'Estrange in the lead, heaped bitter satire upon his head. On March 16, in his *Be Merry And Wise, Or A Seasonable Word,* he taunted Milton thus:

I could only wish his *Excellency* [Monck] had been a little civiller to Mr. *Milton;* for, just as he had finished his *Model of a Commonwealth* directing in these very terms, the *Choyce* MEN NOT ADDICTED TO A SINGLE PERSON, OR HOUSE OF LORDS, AND THE WORK IS DONE. *In come the secluded Members, and spoyl his Project.* To this *admirable discovery,* he subjoyns a *suitable Proposition* in favour of the *late sitting Members,* and this is it; having premised the *Abilities* and *Honesty, desirable in Ministers of State,* he recommends the *Rumpers* to us as so *Qualified; advises us to Quit that fond Opinion of successive Parliaments;* and suffer the Persons then in Power, *to perpetuate themselves under the name of a Grand, or General Counsell,* and to rule *us,* and our *Heirs* for ever.[97]

The Character of the Rump (March 17) singled out Milton as the "goose-quill champion" of the Rumpers, "an old heretic both in religion and manners, that by his will would shake off his governors as he doth his wives, four in a fortnight." [98] A parasite of tyrants, now angry because the nation will not accept his new Commonwealth, the author continues, Milton is so individualistic that he will insist on being carried to execution in a wheelbarrow! And Nedham will be his scaffold mate. On April 3, in *Treason Arraigned,* L'Estrange returned to the attack, suspecting Milton of being the author of *Plain English,* which had appeared near the end of March: "It is a *Piece,* drawn by no *Fool,* and it deserves a serious *Answer.* —By the *Design;* —the *Subject;* —*Malice,* and the *stile;* I should suspect it for a *Blot* of the same *Pen* that wrote ICONOCLASTES. *It runs foule;—tends to Tumult*—and, not content, Barely to *Applaud the Murther of the King, the excrable Author . . . vomits upon his Ashes."* [99] The purpose of *Plain English* L'Estrange summarizes as follows:

'Tis too *Malicious*, for a *private Passion;* and too *Dangerous*, for one that writes not, either for *Bread*, or *Life*. Take it in *gross; 'tis an Alarm to all the Phanatiques in England*. . . .

Oh for *Tom. Scots* sake; for *Haslerigs* sake, for *Robinson, Holland, Mildmay, Mounson, Corbet, Atkins, Vane, Livesey, Skippon, Milton, Tichbourn, Ireton, Gourden, Lechmore, Blagrave, Bare-bones, Nedhams* sake, and to conclude; for all the rest of our *Impenitent* Brethrens sakes, Help a company of poor *Rebellious Devils;* that only for *Murthering* their *Prince, destroying three Glorious Nations, Breaking* the *Bonds* of *Faith* both with *God* and *Men*.[100]

In *No Blinde Guides* (April 20) L'Estrange again singled out Milton as the only surviving commonwealth pamphleteer worthy of his royalist talents. This time he addressed Milton directly, accusing him of league with Satan: "Come, come, Sir; lay the Devil aside; do not proceed with so much malice and against knowledge. Act like a man, that a good Christian may pray for you. Was it not you that scribbled a justification of the murder of the King against Salmasius?" [101] As in *Be Merry and Wise* L'Estrange taunts Milton for his inconsistency: "What will become . . . of YOUR STANDING COUNCIL? *If no certain form of Government can bind our posterity* (as you affirm) Then is it free at any time for the People to *assemble,* and *Tumult,* under the colour of a new *Choyce*." [102] Even after the Restoration L'Estrange continued to berate the blind rear guard of the Good Old Cause, reprinting some of his old attacks in *L'Estrange His Apology* (June 6) and adding a final thrust: "And yet they would not leave their Pamphleting. Particularly *Milton* put forth a bawling piece against Dr. *Griffith*." [103]

The longest and most serious reply to Milton's last warning against monarchy was *The Dignity of Kingship Asserted*, by G. S., "a Lover of Loyalty." Dated March 29 (though it did not appear until May), the tract was prefaced by a long dedication to Charles II in which Milton's old attacks on kingship are pilloried as blackest treason. Unlike the writer of *The Censure*, G. S. is a man of little philosophical insight. Following the method of Thomas Edwards, he rests his case on horrified accents, making almost no attempt to grapple with Milton's central arguments. The following outburst is typical:

This MURTHER I say, and these VILLANIES, were defended, justyfied, nay extolled, and commended by one Mr. JOHN MILTON, in

answer to the learned SALMASIUS . . . he did so bespatter the white
Robes of your ROYAL FATHERS spotless life . . . with the dirty
filth of his satirical pen, that to the vulgar, and those who read his books
with prejudice, he represented him, a most debauched vitious man . . .
a bloudy TYRANT, and an inplacable [sic] Enemy of all his good
SUBJECTS.[104]

And now that the Commonwealth is tottering, and the Rumpers
still trying to frustrate the universal yearning for majesty's return,

Mr. MILTON comes on the Stage in post hast, and . . . would easily
delude an INCONSIDERATE READER into a BELIEF, First, THAT THE GOV-
ERNMENT OF A Republique IS IN IT SELF, INCOMPARABLY TO BE PRE-
FERRED BEFORE Kingship, WHETHER WE RESPECT men as men, or as
Christians. But Secondly, as the Case stands with us, he would strike
us into a fear, namely, THAT TO READMIT YOUR MAJESTY, IS UNSAFE,
AND HAZARDABLE, AT THE BEST, AND MAY PROVE DANGEROUS AND RUINOUS
TO ALL.[105]

G. S. taunts Milton with the illegality of the Rump, points to its
imposition of heavy taxes, its unconstitutional trial of the king.
But he descends easily from ideas to personal vilifications, in
which as always, Milton's divorce ideas make the sharpest weapon,
and the epithet "Atheist!" is sure to find a place:

While you held your *obligation* to your *Wife*, which as your learned
doctrine of *divorce* testifies, was an *insufferable yoak* . . . I may imagine
you, likewise to be so poor spirited as to fear an *Oath* . . . and so farre
to reverence *Authority*, as not to dare to bark at the highest thereof, to
wit *Majesty*. But since you grew so wise, as to throw aside your *Wife*
because your *waspish spirit* could not agree with her qualities, and your
Crooked phantasy could not be brought to take delight in her, you then
grew so free, that . . . you could take the *Christian Liberty*, to turn a
Libertine at large, or in plain termes an *Atheist*, and as for your *Allegiance*, you found your self so free set from it, that you could without
remorse discharge your filth at, and vomit forth your poyson against
majesty.[106]

The author of *The Dignity of Kingship* feels a curious inferiority to Milton. For this reason, he confesses, he has not signed
his name, preferring that his arguments should be read before his
name be compared with that of his antagonist. In several places
he mentions Milton's superior literary skill and reputation:

I am not ignorant of the *ability* of Mr. *Milton,* whom the *Rump* (which was well stored with men of *pregnant* although *pernicious* Wits) made choyce of, before others, to write *their* Defense against *Salmasius.*

Allowing then Mr. *Milton* all the advantages which an *acute wit, ready invention, much reading,* and *copious expression* will give him, I shall only trust to the *goodnesse* of the *Cause.*[107]

Of all the outbursts against the unflinching Milton, in the last shattering weeks of the Good Old Cause, *The Censure of the Rota Upon . . . The Ready and Easie Way* (March 26) is the most comprehensive and intellectual. From these pages speaks no ranting, bombastic L'Estrange, no uneasy G. S., but a man in range and method akin to Hobbes. The author uses a rapier, not a bludgeon; a worthy philosophical antagonist to the commonwealth spokesman, he shows how thoroughly he understands and hates all that Milton represents. The author castigates the democratic declaimers of Greece and Rome, from whom, he says, Milton has derived his ideas and whom he imitates in rousing up the rabble. He challenges Milton's knowledge of commonwealth constitutions. "You admire Common-wealths in generall, and cry down Kingship . . . ," asserts the author, "vainly supposing all slavery to be in the Gouernment of a single Person, and nothing but liberty in that of many. . . . You believe liberty is safer under an Arbitrary unlimited power by virtue of the name Commonwealth, then under any other Government how jvst or restrain'd soever if it be but cal'd Kingship." [108] In his governmental notions Milton never descends to particulars; his head is always in the clouds. "You fight . . . also with the flat of your hand like a Retorician, and never Contract the Logicall fist." [108] To the revolutionary implications of Milton's religious individualism the author points with fear and derision. In Milton's view "The Church of Christ ought to have no Head upon Earth, but the Monster of many heads, the multitude, who are the onely supream Judges of all matters that concern him . . . All Christian Lawes . . . ought to be subject to every Man's will and humor, (which you call his best light)." But this, maintains *The Censure,* is the "readie and easie way to root out Religion . . . giving License, and encouragement to all manner of Frenzies, that pretend to new discoveries in matters of faith." [109] Not fair enough to admit Milton's sincere devotion to his fanatic principles, the author attacks his "Canting with signall Assistances from Heaven, and answering Condescensions: The most impious Mahometan Doctrine . . . such as will serve as well to justifie any prosperous villany amongst men." [110] The appeal to God to the modern student is certainly one of Milton's weaknesses as a political theorist; and *The Censure* unerringly touched several thin links in his political reasoning. But the author falls into insurmountable difficulties himself when he attempts to inspire a superstitious reverence for the dead Charles and justify repression of the sects. On these issues Milton emerges triumphant from the shrewd pages of *The Censure*.

In the midst of royalist pamphleteering, already facing execution in the minds of his enthusiastic enemies, Milton held doggedly to his position, lifting his voice yet twice again against the onrushing tide of monarchy. His first target was Dr. Griffith and his sermon, *The Fear of God and the King*. In *Brief Notes on a Sermon*, which appeared sometime in April, Milton derides the preacher's praise of a king as the anointed agent of God. Quoting Scripture with more facility than his antagonist, Milton demonstrates that the "Touch not my anointed" of *Psalms* cv. 15, refers not to the actions of the people, but to the actions of the king; then he returns to his old story of God's unwillingness to grant the Hebrews a king. When Dr. Griffith begins to speak of the king as the highest power according to the fundamental laws of the land, Milton's contempt for him mounts; here is another minister meddling in law and government. Kingship, Milton insists, has been abolished by the law of the land. There is no validity in the argument that it was not a representative Parliament which passed the law; no Parliament is full so long as many counties are not represented, or so long as members are absent. Any group of men sitting as Parliament may represent the people as long as they have at heart the welfare of the nation. Kingship having been abolished, the nation had a right to choose its own government; now it should refuse to admit kingship and tyranny. Yet, and this is the only reference to elective kingship in the 1660 pamphlets, if the people must condemn themselves to thraldom, would it not be better to choose one of our own number who deserves our loyalty and support? Milton concludes by reaffirming what he has stated so often: the will of the king is subordinate to law, to Parliament, and to the people.

Still the blind enemy of kings had not lost confidence in the persuasiveness of his voice. Again he stood forth against the onrushing tide. When the Restoration was not more than three weeks away, all his old charges against monarchy appeared in more bitter language than ever in the second edition of *The Readie & Easie Way*. Anticipating the return of Charles II, Milton strikes back in this second edition at the royalist pamphleteers who have ridiculed him, reiterating with furious scorn what people may expect if they invite the king to return: a tyrant more sure of himself than ever, taunting the very people who have set him on the throne; great sums of money for the upkeep of the king's person and the new prelaty; indictment, confiscation of property, and revenge for personal wrongs; the Presbyterians themselves repudiated by the king; disfavor and contempt for all but known royalists.

In his final and unqualified rejection of kingship, whether limited in power or not, Milton stands foremost among the leaders of seventeenth-century radicalism. In his earlier pamphleteering years a constitutional monarchist, he had accepted the dictator Cromwell, not because Cromwell had the approbation of the people, but because he saw in Cromwell both an instrument of God, about to provide freedom of speech and conscience, and a natural king, one who by nature deserved to rule less virtuous people. As the years passed, however, Milton became convinced that the personal interests of any single person are likely to conflict with religious liberty, for which he cared most, and with the will of republican supporters. He grew to hate any single person rule, not because he thought it was antagonistic to the will of the masses, but because it was incompatible with the will of a large number of free men like himself, men capable of governing both themselves and others. Although his condemnation of single rule did not spring from his confidence in the people, it is only fair to say that he had aspirations for their development into men who would be too virtuous and high-minded to submit to kingship. His contention in *The Readie & Easie Way* that universal education would develop a spirit of freedom too strong to admit of monarchy is proof of this statement. Aside from his republicanism, however, and aside from his conception of himself as representative of a large class of people far more worthy than the king to rule, Milton objected to the ostentation and artificial distinctions of kingship because he thought them inconsistent with Christianity. No one endowed with Christian liberty, and remembering the example of Christ, can so little estimate his worth, in Milton's opinion, as to bow to any one. "And what government comes nearer to this precept of Christ, than a free commonwealth; wherein they who are greatest, are perpetual servants and drudges to the public . . . neglect their own affairs, yet are not elevated above their brethen; live soberly in their families, walk the street as other men, may be spoken to freely, familiarly, friendly, without adoration?" [111]

It is in the spirit of these lines that Milton struck a note which largely prohibited the outcropping of kingship in America in the following century, and has led to the gradual abolition of kingly power throughout Europe. After two hundred and eighty years, a remnant of English kingship yet remains, no hindrance, apparently, to the "evolution of democracy." But in 1660, two weeks before the Restoration, no man in all England strove more fiercely or openly than Milton for the abolition of monarchy.

In sharp extremity Milton's courage burst into a flame which still shines brightly over the centuries. Alone and fearless, the prospect of England lost driving him impetuously on amid whirling fears and premonitions, he was so intent upon staying the tide that he gave no heed to the solitary nature of his position. For the republicans had fled: Haselrig, Scot, Ludlow, Neville, Vane, Nedham—all of them. Drawing and quartering, and the waving of head-heavy pikes, might come for them, soon enough, they knew, without defying the inevitable. Some had suddenly gone over to the royalist ranks or were hastening to surrender. Milton alone, blind and defiant, remained to defend the commonwealth.

E. MILTON AND CROMWELL; NATURAL KINGSHIP

No one has ever discovered with any certainty the exact relationship which existed between Cromwell and Milton. Milton is not mentioned in any of Cromwell's letters or speeches. According to Masson, they may have shaken hands for the first time in March 20, 1649, the day of Milton's induction into the office of Latin Secretary.[112] In the four years that preceded Pride's Purge, Milton was often present in the Council of State; Cromwell, however, during this period was often absent on military duties. When Cromwell dissolved the Council of State the day following Pride's Purge, Milton adhered to him rather than to the Council. But whether or not, in the years that followed, Cromwell called Milton to Whitehall to dictate to him messages of state, or whether Cromwell at any time asked Milton's advice about foreign or internal policies, is speculation. Even if Cromwell preferred Milton, a minor official, to his Secretary Thurloe, Milton's blindness would have prevented his taking down dictation word for word. It is Masson's conjecture that Milton received from Thurloe, from the Council itself while in session, or from Cromwell the substance of the message to be written. Milton would then write the letter in English, return it to Cromwell or to the Council for corrections, and finally write out, or dictate to his amanuensis, the Latin draft. There remains, however, no actual trace of oral or written communication between the two men.

Although Milton had furiously condemned Charles I as a tyrant, at the critical moment of April 20, 1653, when Cromwell dissolved the Rump and made himself a dictator of greater power than Charles I had ever possessed, Milton not only supported him but eulogized him as the saviour of England's liberties.

There are a number of reasons brought forth for Milton's having rejected his friends of the Rump in favor of one-man arbitrary rule. His own words showing his position and his sympathy for Cromwell's act are as follows: "But when you saw that the business was artfully procrastinated, that every one was more intent on his own selfish interest than on the public good, that the people complained of the disappointments which they had experienced, and the fallacious promises by which they had been gulled, that they were the dupes of a few overbearing individuals, you put an end to their domination." [113] In this statement Milton is referring to the generally accepted though not proved belief that the Rump, after having postponed its dissolution in the interest of a more representative Parliament for over two years, had attempted to perpetuate itself in a bill calling for new parliamentary elections.[114] Milton evidently believed that Cromwell was justified in putting an end to such a procedure. Another factor in Milton's acceptance of Cromwell was his desire, as we have said, for liberty of speech and conscience rather than for representative government. The kind of government was to him a matter of indifference as long as man's spiritual nature was not shackled by forced obedience to a state church, and as his intellectual freedom was not stifled by censorship of the press. We cannot doubt that Milton wanted this liberty for all the people, and that he believed Cromwell capable of granting liberty and upholding it. Cromwell, ruling for the welfare of all the people, and not for his own selfish ends, was no tyrant in Aristotle's sense, but one who by nature deserved to rule. Although, Milton admits, such a government is not an ideal government, it is the only one that can give liberty until the people are better fitted to rule themselves.[115] We find still a further reason for Milton's support of Cromwell in his many statements that Cromwell acted in accordance with God's will: "We all willingly yield the palm of sovereignty to your unrivalled ability and virtue, except the few . . . who do not know that nothing in the world is more pleasing to God . . . than that the supreme power should be vested in the best and the wisest of men." [116] To doubt the Protector almost shows a lack of confidence in God himself.[117]

Why, we may inquire, did Milton believe Cromwell an instrument of God? Nothing is more typical of Milton's mental processes than his seeking for a manifestation of God's justice; he wrote *Paradise Lost* to justify the judgments of Jehovah. Then there were Cromwell's own declarations of his alliance with God, of his furthering God's cause. "*If* my calling be from God," exclaimed the Protector, "and my testimony from the People—God and the people shall take it from me, else I will not part with it." [118] And again, "Perceiving the spirit of God so strong upon me, I would no longer consult flesh and blood." [119] If these sentences now seem impossibly egotistic, it is well to remember that to thousands of seventeenth-century people, including Milton, Cromwell was simply speaking what was to them quite evident: God *was* on his side. When a man knelt and prayed before every battle, gleaned his watchwords from the Bible, sent his soldiers into battle singing psalms, praised God after every victory, and suffered no signal defeat, it was only too clear that that man carried with him the power of God.

Milton supported Cromwell, therefore, because he believed Cromwell's charges against Parliament justified, because he saw in Cromwell an authority which not only gave order and stability but also provided the liberty which he wanted most, because he thought Cromwell to be the wisest and best man taking his place as rightful ruler, and because he believed Cromwell an instrument of God's power and justice.

To Milton Cromwell was as much a rational fulfilment of the law of nature as Charles I had been a violation of it. Milton answers Salmasius at length on the question of who has a right to rule by the law of nature. No one will doubt that a ruler should, by the law of nature, govern for the welfare of all the people and not for his own interest. Consequently, Milton continues, the needs and desires of the people are superior to those of the king; he has no right to oppress them. It is true that people in ancient times selected kings to rule over them for the welfare of all, but what kind of men were they? They were the most virtuous and courageous; nothing was more agreeable to the law of nature than that they should rule. But nothing, Milton insists, is more absurd than to maintain that an hereditary or naturally inferior king rules by the law of nature, "For nature appoints that wise men should govern fools, not that wicked men should rule over good men, fools over wise men; and consequently they that take the government out of such men's hands, act according to the law of nature." [120] Charles had been, Milton thought, a tyrant to whom no one was bound by the law of nature; he was naturally an inferior man, neither wise nor disinterested. Cromwell, on the other hand, fitted Milton's formula; he had taken over the reins of government in the interest of all the people; he was fitted by nature to be their ruler, having first learned to govern himself, and having proved himself superior in courage and in magnanimity.

It is a consistent and fundamental part of Milton's political philosophy that the more virtuous should govern the less virtuous. In *Defensio Secunda* he declares that Cromwell and the Independents deserve the superiority which they have acquired, for they excel all others in civil prudence, courage, and industry. Nothing more accords with the law of nature than that virtue and wisdom in the persons of men should rule over those less fitted to govern themselves. It matters not that the Independents do not represent a majority of the people; not numbers should rule but that which is just and right. In *The Readie & Easie Way* Milton refers directly to Aristotle's account of the origin of kingship. The king was one who by his superior virtue was elevated by the people to rule over them, but later, having used his power unjustly, he was by the people deprived of his power.[121] They, having grown in virtue, put aside their kings and established free commonwealths. Thus it was that the first kings ruled because they deserved to rule, because they possessed superior virtue. In *The Readie & Easie Way* Milton pleads for a free commonwealth, not in order that the people may govern for themselves, but in order that the people may submit to those of the nation who, being superior and free from inner tyranny, are fitted to rule. Even in *Paradise Lost* we find an illustration of this theory in Milton's portrayal of Satan: one of Satan's chief sins is that he has rebelled against a just aristocracy of virtue, rather than finding his place (his place as determined by his character) in the actual government of Heaven. Milton's belief in a civil aristocracy of virtue, it is not difficult to see, arose from the fusion in his mind of Old Testament theocracy and Aristotelian law of nature. He is convinced, he tells Salmasius, that the law of God does exactly agree with the law of nature. The belief that the spiritually superior should hold the reins of government, whether or not by the suffrage of the people, is really the core of Milton's political philosophy. Applied to the ruler it was quite as definitely the cause of his rejecting Charles as it was the reason for his supporting Oliver Cromwell.

Time came, however, when Milton discovered that not even the virtuous dictator Cromwell could rule for the welfare of all, despite his sincere desire to do so. He had strengthened, not abolished, the established church;[122] he had imprisoned or removed from office those republicans whom Milton knew and trusted as equals capable of governing themselves—Vane, Harrison, Bradshaw, Overton; he had established a censorship of the press; he had assumed kingly dignities and had conferred knighthoods; he had been suspected of desiring the kingship itself. All these actions could not have failed to be disagreeable to Milton, despite his confidence in the Protector; and we know how plainly he had addressed Cromwell in 1654 on the question of disestablishment. There is little doubt that had Cromwell lived, Milton would have continued to support him; but now that Cromwell was dead, Milton was not at all sure that he would be willing to raise even another Cromwell to supreme power. The pamphlets of 1660 ring with denunciations of rule by a "single person." There is only the slightest hint that he will accept even an elective monarch. On the other hand his frequent praise of the ability of the English to govern themselves, the special praise he had reserved in 1659 for the Restored Rump, the apparently cordial relationship which had not ceased to exist between him and the staunch republicans whom Cromwell had suppressed—all point to Milton's conviction of Cromwell's partial failure, to his admission that the most virtuous and enlightened despot may find it impossible to establish true liberty.

If, in *The Readie & Easie Way*, Milton wanted a perpetual oligarchy in place of a virtuous single person, it cannot be said that he was false to his principle of a virtuous aristocracy in civil affairs. For he visualized his perpetual senate as a company of the country's finest spirits, those who by nature deserved to rule their fellows, not the artificial or hereditary nobility of the nation. Throughout his life Milton was a bitter enemy of false distinctions. Nobility was to him a matter of character, not of titles or of heredity. In response to Salmasius' taunt in 1651, he had written: "Others, whose ancestors were not noble, have taken a course to attain true nobility by their own industry and virtue, and are not inferior to men of the noblest descent." [123] Like Aristotle, from whom he derived so many of his political conceptions, Milton stood for real distinctions, not artificial ones. He believed, nevertheless, that the real distinctions should be recognized by giving the influential civil positions to those who possessed the greatest virtue.

The inconsistency of Milton's demand for the spiritually superior man in the office of ruler lies in his confusion of personal morality with statesmanship. If a man fears God superlatively, if he proves that he is the nation's greatest leader in time of war, if he is entirely incorruptible, Milton's conclusion is that he should rule all others. But the dictatorship of Cromwell proved to Milton that this is not always true. Cromwell had all the qualities which Milton believed a nation's leader should have; yet his very superiority in the field contributed to his failure as a statesman, and his decrees (such as prohibiting the use of carriages on Sunday) prevented his making the Commonwealth government a popular one. However true it may be that rulers should be virtuous, it is equally important that they understand government, that they be able to start the people on the road to partial liberty, that they do not attempt to take away the personal liberty of the people by forcing on them their own codes of morality. Oliver Cromwell was a far more religious, probably a far more virtuous man than George Washington; but he lacked Washington's statesmanship; he did not have the foresight to have some one elected in his own place and thus safely initiate the precedent of elective rulers. Whereas the Puritans, Milton in the lead, pushed further than any of their predecessors toward the separation of church and state, they failed to separate morality from the state. They failed to recognize that personal morality is as much a matter of individual conscience as religion, and as such should be reserved to the individual and not to the state. Milton, attempting unconsciously to reconcile Old Testament ethics and the political beliefs of Aristotle, gave an undue emphasis to the ruler's sins of the flesh or lack of them, to the ruler's skill or deficiency in war; and not enough emphasis to the ruler's constitutional foresight, his tact in winning the people, his sense of historical evolution.

CHAPTER IX

TWO REBELS AND THE MULTITUDE

A. To the Execution of Charles I

THROUGHOUT the early pamphlets on church government Milton again and again manifests confidence in the native intelligence and moral worth of his countrymen. The Englishman is, he declares in *The Reason of Church Government,* naturally religious; with the patient nurture of the church, the English nation might become known to the world as leaders in piety and honesty.[1] In *An Apology for Smectymnuus* Milton affirms that there is nothing in church government beyond the intelligence of the meanest of his countrymen. There are only three abilities necessary to fit him to be a proper judge, for example, of his own minister. The first is to read the Bible; the second is to acquaint himself with the personal life of the minister in question; and the third is to lead a Christian life himself. Milton denies that any one of these achievements exceeds "the capacity of a plain artisan. And what reason then is there left, wherefore he should be denied his voice in the election of his minister, as not thought a competent discerner?" [2] Thus Milton stoutly defends the "rude multitude," presenting their manual skills in favorable comparison with the intellectual ignorance of their critics. "No, my matriculated confutant," he concludes, "there will not want in *any congregation of this island . . . divers plain and solid men,* that have learned by the experience of a good conscience, what it is to be well taught, who will soon look through and through both the lofty nakedness of your Latinizing barbarian, and the finical goosery of your neat sermon actor." [3]

Much the same sentiment underlies the patriotic fervor of the *Areopagitica.* Milton calls upon Parliament to consider the nature of the people whom they govern; the English are "a nation not slow and dull, but of quick, ingenious, and piercing spirit; acute to invent, subtile and sinewy to discourse, not beneath the reach of any point the highest that human capacity can soar to." [4] He beholds all England at work in the "reforming of reformation itself," all men striving to release truth, studiously pondering, inventing, helpful to each other. His hopes for the English people soar as he writes. With their natural intelligence, their willingness to learn, their quick pursuit of the principles of true freedom, they may yet, with statesmanlike guidance, become a nation of Greater Men, partakers in the divinity of their Master.[5] Then follow the famous lines: "Methinks I see in my mind a noble and puissant nation rousing herself like a strong man after sleep, and shaking her invincible locks: methinks I see her as an eagle mewing her mighty youth, and kindling her undazzled eyes at the full midday beam; purging and unscaling her long-abused sight at the fountain itself of heavenly radiance."

Thus far, especially in his attacks on the prelates, Milton had given voice to the overwhelming sentiment of the English nation. For if the practice proposed in the *Areopagitica* did not follow governmental tradition, its spirit of free inquiry was an inheritance more deeply than ever imbedded in English hearts by the Reformation and Laud's persecutions. There appeared as yet no great gulf between the desire of the people for political reformation and that of Milton. Their destructive aims were identical, and Milton felt that they all had the capacity for following a true leader to the heights of freedom; he sensed that he himself represented their aspirations. But such a sympathetic unity of purpose had now not long to exist. Already, by his advocacy of Independency in the *Areopagitica*, Milton had withdrawn himself from the state church traditions of the people, leaped ahead of them into the freer air of a larger liberty. As yet, however, he was not aware how few of them were ready to follow him.

Milton's resentment following the outburst of criticism which greeted his later divorce tracts, although it seems to have been directed mainly at the Presbyterian intellectuals who, he thought, should have known better, was partially aimed at the ignorant masses who misunderstood him. In the preface to *Tetrachordon*, which appeared in March, 1645, Milton vigorously attacks Mr. Herbert Palmer, the Presbyterian divine who has condemned his

"wicked book" in a sermon before the Parliament; in opening
passages of *Colasterion,* published the same day as *Tetrachordon,*
he lashes out at the licenser Caryl, at Palmer again, and at William
Prynne. In neither this pamphlet nor in *Tetrachordon* is there any
direct reference to the people themselves. But in the sonnets which
followed these treatises,[6] Milton shows a dissatisfaction not merely
with the Presbyterian ministers, but with his countrymen as a whole:

> I did but prompt the age to quit their clogs
>> By the known rules of ancient Liberty.
>> When straight a barbarous noise environs me
>> Of owls and cuckoos, asses, apes and dogs; . . .
>> But this is got by casting pearl to hogs,
> That bawl for freedom in their senseless mood,
>> And still revolt when truth would make them free.
>> Licence they mean when they cry Liberty.[7]

Despite his arraignment of the multitude's misinterpretation of
his idea of domestic liberty, Milton had by no means lost confidence
in their desire and capacity for political reformation when *The
Tenure of Kings and Magistrates* appeared four years later. Assuming in parts of this pamphlet that the people are moving toward
liberty and want to depose the tyrant Charles, Milton proclaims on
page after page their inherent right to do so. Kings are but the
agents of the people, placed in eminence by them originally to
secure a common justice.[8] "And to him that shall consider well,
why among free persons one man by civil right should bear authority
and jurisdiction over another, no other end or reason can be
imaginable." [9] He deplores the inconsistency of those who declare,
as the English do, that they are a free people, and then admit that
they do not have the power to remove their supreme magistrate
or abolish his office; this kind of freedom is merely a fancied or
pictured one, potent only to cheat children, not thinking men. We
are slaves, indeed, he continues, as long as we lack the authority
to govern ourselves, or to dispose of those whom we place in
power. For such authority is "the root and source of all liberty." [10]
Granted the people have such decision in the matter of electing
or removing a supreme governor from office, though he be a just

and righteous one, how much greater then is it their responsibility and just right to depose one who reigns tyrannically.

The philosophical foundation for Milton's thesis in *The Tenure of Kings and Magistrates* that the power of government is inherent in the people, was his belief that man is born, not a slave needing a master, as Hobbes [11] and Filmer [12] were to picture him, but a spirit made in God's image, endowed by Him with free will, and therefore free from any earthly government to which he does not consent. That is, having a free will, man is free not only to choose between good and evil in his personal life, but free to choose what government he likes best, free to elect rulers for the common welfare. "All men naturally were born free, being the image and resemblance of God himself, and were, by privilege above all the creatures born to command, and not to obey." [13] Man has a free will, either for spiritual or political choice. But it is well to analyze carefully what Milton means by the use of such free will applied to political action. For the distinguishing element of Milton's political philosophy, that which at once removes it from the extreme democratic feeling of the time and stamps it as peculiarly Puritan, is this: he believed that the right to free choice in politics hinges upon the correct use of one's free will in his religious and moral life. That is, if a man of his own free will chooses good and not evil, then he should, as a virtuous man, have a voice in the government; if, however, he rejects the good, thereby becoming a slave to his passions, he has no right whatever either to a vote or an office; he has lost his birthright of helping to determine the kind of government under which he shall live. "It usually happens," he writes in *Defensio Secunda* (I, 298), "by the appointment, and as it were retributive justice, of the Deity, that that people which cannot govern themselves, and moderate their passions, but crouch under the slavery of their lusts, should be delivered up to the sway of those whom they abhor, and made to submit to an involuntary servitude." Always, of course, there remains the possibility that a man who has chosen evil will by the help of God free himself from his inward tyranny; until that time, however, his political free will is abrogated.

Like Milton, Lilburne believed in the natural freedom of man. In *The Free-Mans Freedome Vindicated*, he states the underlying principle of his political faith, parts of which we have quoted previously:

God, the absolute Soveraign Lord and King, of all things in heaven and earth, the originall fountain, and cause of all causes, who is circumscribed, governed and limited by no rules . . . gave man (his meer creature) the soveraignty (under himselfe) over all the rest of his Creatures . . . and indued him with a rationall soule, or understanding, and thereby created him after his own image . . . the first of which was *Adam,* a male, or man, made out of the dust or clay, . . . Woman cal'd *Eve,* which two are the earthly, original fountain, as begetters and bringers forth of all and every particular and individuall man and woman, . . . who are, and were by nature all equall and alike in power, digniy [*sic*], authority and majesty, none of them having (by nature) any authority dominion or majesteriall power, one over or above another, neither have they, or can they exercise any, but meerely by institution, or donation, that is to say, by mutuall agreement or consent . . . for the good benefit and comfort each of other . . . and unnaturall, irrationall, sinfull, wicked, unjust, divelish, and tyranicall it is, for any man whatsoever, spirituall or temporall, Cleargy-man or Layman, to appropriate and assume unto himselfe, a power, authority and jurisdiction, to rule, govern, or raign over any sort of men in the world, without their free consent. . . .[14]

From my Cock-loft in the Presse yard Newgate.
June 19. 1646

per me Iohn Lilburne.

From this rather remarkable statement, which Lilburne some months later inserted almost verbatim in *Regall Tyrannie discovered,* we may understand how closely Milton's thought in *The Tenure of Kings and Magistrates* parallels that of his contemporary. Their views on the natural freedom of man are identical: that *spirit* of man was made in God's image; therefore man was and is endowed with natural worth and dignity, and is not to be subjected to any one of his fellows without a delegation of the power inherent in himself. Lilburne never receded from this belief; he never in theory struck away this political birthright because the people had chosen to be slaves from within; politically, no matter how sinful, they still retained the heritage of choosing their own government. But Milton, as we know, if not expressly in *The Tenure,* always made the right of political self-government contingent upon a man's ability to govern himself. Lilburne consistently opposed the dissolution or purging of the Long Parliament unless it be by agreement of the people, whereby a new and representative parliament would be summoned; he likewise declared that the king's trial was illegal unless carried out by representatives of the people.[15] But Milton repeatedly denied the democratic principle he proposes in *The Tenure* by justifying the execution of Charles.

In passing we may note in Lilburne's basic proposition two democratic suggestions with which Milton would not have concurred; both of which, in fact, he repudiated in *Christian Doctrine*. Adam and Eve, Lilburne says, are the progenitors of all men and women. These men and women "are, and were by nature, all equall and alike in power, digny [sic], authority and majesty." Whether or not Lilburne would have carried his statement to its logical political conclusion, he here puts women equal to men in majesty and worth; he makes them politically equal in authority. Lilburne further implies that all men at birth are equal in divine resemblance. But Milton consistently placed woman under the government of man, she being by nature inferior to him, and we know already his proneness to believe that the innate spiritual capacity of one man is greater than that of another: "For, as will be shown hereafter, there are some remnants of the divine image left in man, the union of which in one individual renders him more fit and disposed for the kingdom of God than another." [16]

Why, one may ask, if Milton believed that only spiritual freemen should be political freemen, does he champion the birthright of the English people, knowing that many of them are sinners? When he wrote *The Tenure*, partly during the king's trial and partly after the execution, Milton was not sure how the people themselves felt about the impending abolition of kingship, despite the clamor of the Presbyterian ministers in and about London. He wrote *The Tenure*, as we have noted, "rather to reconcile the minds of the people to the event, than to discuss the legitimacy of that particular sentence." [17] Though he feared in his heart that the cry of the people would be against the act, he still hoped for their approbation, which to him would have been proof of their spiritual redemption: "But God, as we have cause to trust, will put other thoughts into the people . . . will incline them to hearken . . . to the voice of our supreme magistracy, calling us to liberty, and the flourishing deeds of a reformed commonwealth." For the past seven years the English people had been passing through a fruitful period, Milton thought, of true spiritual reformation. Might not many of them have freed themselves during this time from inner tyranny and now be prepared to take an active part in the government? Hence the conflicting tone in *The Tenure* concerning the people, apparent, for example, in the following sentences:

The power of kings and magistrates . . . is committed to them in trust from the people to the common good of them all, in whom the power yet remains fundamentally, and cannot be taken from them, without a violation of their natural birthright.[19]

Most men . . . through sloth or inconstancy, and weakness of spirit, either fainting ere their own pretences, though never so just, be half attained, or through an inbred falsehood and wickedness, betray, ofttimes to destruction to themselves, men of noblest temper joined with them.[20]

In the first of these sentences Milton appears unmistakably the democrat; but in the second he shows how his belief in the people is qualified by his fear for their moral constancy. *The Tenure*, in fact, opens upon this note of distrust:

If men within themselves would be governed by reason, and not generally give up their understanding to a double tyranny, of custom from without, and blind affections within, they would discern better what it is to favour and uphold the tyrant of a nation. But, being slaves within doors, no wonder that they strive so much to have the public state conformably governed to the inward vicious rules by which they govern themselves.[21]

Thus, even at the time of his writing, Milton was caught between a motive and a growing opinion: the motive was to attempt to swing the minds of the people into an approval of the execution, joined with a hope that his previous faith in the spiritual reformation of the English people would be justified by their realization of a new political liberty; his growing opinion conflicting with this hope and motive was his fear that the Presbyterian ministers against whom he directed his pamphlet represented the preponderant sentiment of the people. Despite his faith that the nation is still capable of spiritual growth, and notwithstanding his abstract thesis for their birthright, Milton's fear is stronger than his hope. He confesses in the following lines that he has little hope of convincing the whole nation that the tyrannicide was just:

But who in particular is a tyrant. . . . I leave to the magistrates, at least to the *uprighter sort* of them, and *of the people,* though in number *less by many,* in whom faction least hath prevailed above the law of nature and right reason, to judge as they find cause.[22]

Retracing briefly our six years' history of Milton's references to the people, we find his confidence in them, at first extended even to the "plain artisan," and reaching an enthusiastic faith in the *Areopagitica,* gradually thereafter lessening as he found himself diverging from the masses in his religious and political liberalism. Contributory to his lowering confidence was the reception of his divorce pamphlets, which had heightened his conviction that "none can love freedom heartily but good men." We find in *The Tenure* at once his real conviction that the power of government is inherent in the people, his hope that the people will seize the tyrannicide as a step toward further political liberty, and his underlying conviction that after all the people are yet too sinful to have a voice in the government. The hope that Milton still had for the moral and intellectual perception of the people he expresses best in the following passage of *The Tenure:*

But God, as we have cause to trust, will put other thoughts into the people, and turn them from giving ear or heed to these mercenary noise-makers, of whose fury and false prophecies we have enough experience; and from murmurs of the new discord will incline them to hearken rather with erected minds to the voice of our supreme magistracy, calling us to liberty, and the flourishing deeds of a reformed commonwealth.[23]

How little this hope was realized we know; with the overwhelming approval of the *Eikon Basilike,* Milton's fears were to deepen into a certainty.

B. From 1649 to the Restoration

The *Eikonoklastes* was a futile effort to answer the English love of kingship strengthened by Charles' execution and fanned into a flame by the *Eikon Basilike.* In *Eikonoklastes* Milton breaks forth in bitter denunciation of the ignorant multitude's failure to look upon the tyrannicide as an act of justice whereby they were released from the bondage of tyranny. "The people," he exclaims, "exhorbitant and excessive in all their motions, are prone ofttimes not to a religious only, but to a civil kind of idolatry, in idolizing their kings: though never more mistaken in the object of their worship. . . . Now, with a besotted and degenerate baseness of spirit, except some few who yet retain in them the old English fortitude and love of freedom, . . . the rest, imbastardized from the ancient nobleness of their ancestors, are ready to fall flat, and give adoration to the image and memory of this man, who hath offered at more cunning fetches to undermine our liberties, and put tyranny into an art, than any British king before him." [24] Deploring the inconsistency of an "ingrateful and perverse" generation, Milton declares that the people first prayed to be delivered from their king, and now cry as loud against those men who have destroyed the tyrant for them. If the whole nation will be so ignorant and obstinate as to condemn the destruction of a tyrant, he sees not why anyone should blame those who would not sacrifice their liberty for being so few in number. He is glad, in fact, that virtue yet remains in this few to resist the superstitious ignorance of the masses; it is a "high honor done us from God, and a special mark of his favour."

We find this appeal to God as a final arbiter, rather than to the people, and the reading of God's express wishes into the political actions of his earthly saints, often as pronounced in Milton's pamphlets as they are in Cromwell's speeches. In *The Tenure* Milton gives credit for the parliamentary victory to "God and a good cause." It is God who had delivered Charles into the hands of the Independents. Furthermore, since it is God's intention to execute judgment upon evil doers, if ordinary measures fail to bring them to punishment, then any unusual method, such as the army has used in trying and condemning Charles, is the express carrying out of God's will and therefore legal. Milton even denies that anyone has a right to resist such extraordinary measures to bring the king to justice. In *Observations on the Articles of Peace with the Irish Rebels* he calls the king's trial and execution "that noble and impartial piece of justice, wherein the hand of God appeared so evidently on our side." [25]

Pausing for a moment to reflect upon Milton's interpretation of God's will as determining changes in government, we need hardly point out its radical inconsistency with the principal thesis of *The Tenure*, or its divergence from Lilburne's main theory. In *The Tenure* Milton repeatedly asserts the right of the people to deter-

mine their own kind of government, even as he was to do again in
A Defence of the English People. He even maintains that God
himself would not deny this privilege to the people of Israel; though
God was fully aware of the disastrous consequences of kingship,
he looked upon their wishes in the matter as part of an inalienable
right which he did not wish to repudiate. Yet Milton, when the cry
was raised that the act was done without the consent of the people,
and that Charles was beheaded against their express wishes, denies
them the right which he had hitherto declared theirs only: he
declares that God may change the government of a people against
their will, that God had actually acted through the pious minority
in opposition to the will of the "mad multitude." In 1649, when the
tide turned to a commonwealth government through the "effectual
might" of Cromwell's sword, it was by favor of "God and the
parliament;" but in 1660, when the pendulum was to swing the
other way through sheer pressure from the nation, it was not to
be in his mind God's will that would return England to bondage,
but the servile adoration of the people. For Milton, the people under
God rightfully did not possess free will in 1649; but in 1660, their
free will intact, they were to choose evil and suffer thraldom as a
consequence. Such was Milton's reasoning; theocrat that he was,
it was his peculiarly Puritan habit to reason politically from God
downward to humanity, rather than from humanity to God.

Lilburne, on the other hand, founded his political philosophy,
not so much upon abstract justice, or the will of God, as upon the
will of the people as expressed in positive law or agreement among
themselves. To him there was no other way by which the form of
government might be changed legally except by an agreement of
the people. In the fall of 1648, when disagreements between the
Presbyterian Parliament and the Independent army made some
kind of break inevitable, Lilburne and his followers stoutly opposed
any military coercion of a legally representative body such as the
Long Parliament was. The substance of his plan, as he states it
in the second edition of *Legal Fundamental Liberties,* was to call
a new Parliament, not by the action of the king, as was usual, but
by an *Agreement of the People.* Just how this *Agreement* was to be
drawn up and ratified by the voters Lilburne explains in the following manner (p. 34):

1. That some persons be chosen by the Army to represent the whole Body: And that the well-affected in every County (if it may be) chuse some persons to represent them: And these to meet at Head-Quarters.
2. That those persons ought not to exercise any Legislative power, but onely to draw up the foundations of a just Government, and to propound them to the well-affected people in every County to be agreed to: Which Agreement ought to be above Law; and therefore the bounds, limits, and extent of the peoples Legislative Deputies in Parliament, contained in the Agreement to be drawn up into a formall contract, to be mutually signed by the well-affected people and their said Deputies upon the dayes of their Elections respectively.
3. To prevent confusion, the Parliament (if it be possible) may not be by force immediatly dissolved; but that the day of its dissolution be inserted in the Agreement, by vertue whereof it shall be dissolved.

Although this plan was approved by Cromwell and Ireton,[26] the Levellers and the army officers would not agree upon the content of the *Agreement* itself, "our principall difference lying in his [27] desire in the too strict restraining *Liberty of Conscience,* and in keeping a power in the Parliament to *punish where no visible Law is transgressed.*" [28] After this disagreement Colonel Harrison in a conversation with Lilburne explained the necessity of immediate action to prevent a treaty between Parliament and the king; whereupon Lilburne proposed that a committee of sixteen be selected by the army, the Parliament, the Independents, and the Levellers, to draw up the *Agreement* at once, without waiting to call the representatives specified in sections 1 and 2 of the proposition quoted above.[29] He and his followers still resisted any purging *"without giving some good security to the Nation for the future settlement of their Liberties and Freedoms, especially in frequent, free, and successive Representatives."* [30] According to Lilburne's story, Ireton absolutely agreed to the plan of placing the framing of the *Agreement* in the hands of the sixteen men selected, no appeal to be made from their decision.[31] When, however, the *Agreement* had been drawn up by the committee and presented to the Council of Officers, they began to debate its provisions and pass upon them.[32] Seeing this traitorous action, Lilburne says, "I took my leave of them." [33] With his associates, Walwyn, Prince, and Overton, he published the *Agreement* as framed by the committee of sixteen, in order that all might know the difference between it and the one finally agreed upon by the officers. But the purpose of the Levellers was defeated; there was no agreement of the people that Parliament should be dissolved and a new representative called; the army purged the Long Parliament without any civil authority, and the period of military domination had begun.

Nor did Lilburne's championship of the people as the sole ultimate legislative power, as the only authority whereby a change of government could be effected, cease with the execution of the king. *Legal Fundamental Liberties* was not written until four months after the king's death, when Lilburne was a prisoner in the Tower as a Commonwealth offender.[34] During this time he had repeatedly denied the legality of the Rump's authority; he declared that "those company of men at *Westminster,* that gave Commission to the High Court of Justice, to try and behead the King; *etc.* were no more a Parliament by Law, nor a Representative of the people, by the rules of Justice and Reason, then such a company of men are a Parliament or Representative of the people, that a company of armed Theeves, chuse, and set apart to try, judg, condemn, hang, or behead any man, that they please."[35] Now, continues Lilburne, the army having taken away two of the three estates, (lords and kings), upon which all English government had been founded and continued, *"the end both in reason and Law of the peoples trust is ceased,* (and no way in equity, justice, or reason, can there now be found to set up a Common-wealth; but by a new Parliament chosen by an agreement mutually made amongst the free people of England, who have power enough inherent in them, to alter their Government at their pleasure)."[36]

We have explained Lilburne's position at some length for the purpose of showing how fundamentally Milton differed from this extreme democrat in his political thinking. They strove for the same basic human privileges; they both appeal often to "the light of reason" and "the law of nature," i.e., to their innate sense of absolute justice and truth; they reason from the common premise that man is originally a free political agent. But in the struggle for realization of justice, Lilburne, unlike Milton, felt the necessity for coming to terms with traditional methods. He was aware, too, that English law·had set many more precedents for fundamental freedoms and privileges than was commonly supposed; he quotes from Sir Edward Coke, the Petition of Right, Sir Andrew Horne, the laws of Edward III, the statutes of Richard II, Henry VI, etc. Milton, on the other hand, scorning tradition, facing forward, his spirit aflame with a reforming Christianity questing for ultimate truth, visualized no constitutional obstacles. Imperiously he bade his countrymen forthwith bridge the chasm between the old world and the new. Theologian and classicist that he was, Milton knew relatively little about English law; it was "norman gibbrish" to him. Whereas Milton, then, would have taken a short-cut to liberty by means of an enlightened arbitrary power, Lilburne would have built his government, however slowly, from the people upward. And he would have founded his revolutionary program in part upon those governmental precedents, English customs, and written laws for which Milton had such profound contempt.

The most pronounced difference between the two men lies, however, in their attitude toward the people. Lilburne was in his day probably the most popular man in all England; great throngs attended the trials wherein he pleaded for his liberty, and when he was acquitted of treason to the Commonwealth in October, 1649, the tumultuous cheers in the Guild Hall continued for a half-hour.[37] Lilburne had rubbed shoulders with all classes of people, both in the army and among the London populace; the enthusiasm with which they greeted his proclamations of their privileges only increased his confidence in them. But Milton, by nature a social and spiritual aristocrat, had never mingled with the people. How little he knew of carpenters, inn keepers, millers, or country squires! His life-long isolation from the masses served only to increase his distrust of their ignorant clamorings, his distaste for their sinful manners. *Eikonoklastes,* written during the year of Milton's greatest contempt for the multitude, at a time when Lilburne's faith was greatest, ends in the following manner:

an inconstant, irrational, and image-doting rabble; that like a credulous and hapless herd, begotten to servility, and enchanted with these popular institutes of tyranny, subscribed with a new device of the king's picture at his prayers, hold out both their ears with such delight and ravishment to be stigmatized and bored through, in witness of their own voluntary and beloved baseness. The rest, whom perhaps ignorance without malice, or some error, less than fatal, hath for the time misled, on this side sorcery or obduration, may find the grace and good guidance, to bethink themselves and recover.[38]

A Defence of the People of England, in which Milton attempts both to justify the change of government in the minds of Europeans and to crystallize public sentiment for the Commonwealth, has much the same argument and conflict of thought which we found in *The Tenure of Kings and Magistrates.* Although Milton repeatedly asserts his basic principle that the people have a right to choose their own government when they will, that they may set up and depose kings, whether tyrants or not, he then proceeds to justify in no uncertain terms a violation of this principle by an admitted minority of the people. In the preface Milton declares that it would be unfortunate indeed if the God-granted reason of man did not furnish more arguments for delivering them from tyrants, for making them, "as much as the nature of the thing will bear," equal to each other, than it could discover for tyrannical oppression. He has, therefore, not the slightest doubt of his ability to demolish his adversary's structure.[39] Reaffirming his old statement that God has granted liberty to all nations of erecting what governments they will,[40] Milton thinks it preposterous that no remedy should be left them in the event that a tyrant should gain power over them.[41] "The king is for the people, and consequently the people superior to him: which being allowed, it is impossible that princes should have any right to oppress or enslave the people; that the inferior should have a right to tyrannize over the superior." [42] Replying to Salmasius' argument from the law of nature, Milton arrives at the same conclusion: "You see, the closer we keep to nature, the more evidently does the people's power appear to be above that of the prince." [43]

This is a purely democratic principle, and the foundation of the argument for which the *Defence* is justly remembered. But it is in the application of the principle to the revolution of 1649 that Milton denies the will of the people should be considered. When Salmasius asks, "Was it the people that cut off part of the house of commons, forcing some away?" Milton answers in the following words: "Yes, I say, it was the people. For whatever the better and sounder part of the senate did, in which the true power of the people resided, why may not the people be said to have done it?" [44] He then praises the soldiers of the Independent army for "repelling the tumultuary violence of the citizens and mechanics of London, who, like that rabble that appeared before Clodius, had but little before beset the very parliament-house." Notwithstanding, therefore, his declarations of the inherent power of the people to determine their government, majorities in actual practice Milton counted as nothing. When Salmasius calls the common people "blind and brutish, ignorant in the art of governing," and asserts that there is "nothing more empty, more vain, more inconstant, more uncertain than they," Milton agrees with him concerning the masses of the poor: "It is true . . . of the rabble." He then defends the "middle sort" of the common people, "amongst whom the most prudent men, and the most skilful in affairs, are generally found; others are most commonly diverted either by luxury and plenty, or by want and poverty, from virtue, and the study of government." [45] It is evident from this that Milton would have disregarded not only the will of the many poor, but the will of the few rich and noble. In a word, he would have reserved the power to a large minority of the people, the upper middle class, men like himself, wherein lay the strength of the Puritan cause. It is this class of men Milton thinks of when he writes, "but where men are equals, as in all governments very many are, they ought to have an equal interest in the government, and hold it by turns." [46]

By 1654, when Cromwell's personal rule, together with the legislative efforts of the Rump and the Barebones Parliament, had failed to satisfy not only Englishmen of the lower and upper classes, but such men as Milton himself admired most, he was ready to voice his discontent even with the chosen few. He advises Cromwell and his associates, in that last exhortation in *Defensio Secunda*, to repeal old laws, rather than make so many new ones, to refrain from prohibiting "innocent freedoms," to permit greater freedom of discussion, to refrain from questionable means of increasing the revenue, to direct their energies more to the redressing of grievances than to the increasing of naval and military armaments, to avoid imitation of royalist vanities.[47] Part of this advice is inserted in his address to the people, beginning, "For it is of no little consequence, O citizens, by what principles you are governed." But a careful reading of the passage reveals that Milton was directing it only to the party in power; he is disappointed with the chosen few. "War has made many great whom peace makes small." [48]

It is to Englishmen of all classes, however, especially to the masses of the poor, that Milton speaks in the last fearful passages.

If their complaint is that Cromwell and his associates are tyrants, they will find that no man is free from tyranny until he has struck down the tyrant of his own ungoverned passions. Tyrants may come and go, but until that tyranny within is removed there will be no real freedom. Milton, for one, will not "vindicate the right of unrestrained suffrage" to those who have not first freed themselves from spiritual thraldom. And it is quite evident that in his opinion the masses have not yet achieved this inner liberty. Were they allowed to vote, they would not elect to Parliament men of virtue and wisdom; instead they would "exalt the vilest miscreants from our taverns and our brothels, from our towns and villages, to the rank and dignity of senators." [49] To Milton it is self-evident that bad men would elect bad men to office; and why should any government be trusted to those with whom individuals would not trust their money, or the "management of . . . private concerns"? Because, therefore, the ignorant and sinful masses would elect unprincipled politicians to office, they should have no voice in the government; they have lost their political liberty by being unable to govern themselves. "It is not agreeable to the nature of things that such persons ever should be free." [50] "You, therefore," Milton continues, "who wish to remain free, either instantly be wise, or, as soon as possible, cease to be fools. . . . Unless you spare no pains to effect this, you must be judged unfit, both by God and mankind, to be entrusted with the possession of liberty and the administration of the government; but will rather, like a nation in a state of pupillage, want some active and courageous guardian to undertake the management of your affairs." [51]

Thus the same man who, in his earliest pamphlets (and even years later in *The Likeliest Means*), believed the humblest person capable of choosing his minister, did not think him fit to select his political representative. Milton would have placed a character qualification on the suffrage; and there is no evidence that he would have eliminated, as the Levellers wished to do, the property qualification. He did not believe, it is true, that government by an "active and courageous guardian" was the ideal way; he hoped, he expected the time to come when the nation would no longer be "in a state of pupillage," but would be fitted to govern itself.[52] Perfection of character and through it political liberty, might come in time.[53]

About six years after the appearance of *Defensio Secunda*, when the Commonwealth was toppling, Milton published *The Readie & Easie Way,* a tract which showed more clearly than ever his profound distrust of the common people. After arguing for his perpetual Parliament, he declares point blank against "a licentious and unbridled democracy." To give full power to the people tends to destroy them rather than uplift them.[54] It is a fact, too, that in the past no assemblies have so much inclined toward despotic and unreasonable power as those elected by the people.[55] It is necessary, Milton concludes, to keep a balance of authority between the multitude and the few chosen statesmen.[56] Again he denies the principle of majority rule: "Most voices ought not always to prevail, where main matters are in question." [57]

Evidently writing in hurry and anger, Milton then makes his most drastic denial of the people's will. He declares that the majority of the people "have both in reason, and the trial of just battle, lost the right of . . . election what the government shall be." [58] Referring to the defeat of the king by Cromwell's forces, Milton, seeing that the vast sentiment of the nation now demands kingship again, would substitute for this sentiment the mediaeval method of decision—a battle in which it was thought God gave the victory to the righteous. As for those who have not lost the right to choose their government, he continues, can any one be certain that the greater part of this minority want the king again? But even if these do want the king to return Milton refuses *them* even the right of choosing: "which if the greater part value not, but will degenerately forego, is it just or reasonable, that most voices against the main end of government . . . enslave the less number that would be free?" [59] It is more just, in his opinion, that a few should compel the many to partake of liberty than for the many to compel the few to give it up. The right of the few, Milton concludes, to maintain their freedom against the whole nation, if need be, is inviolable.

Milton's distrust of the masses continued to the end of his days. *Paradise Lost* is essentially undemocratic in tone. One finds there praise of proportioned, not mathematical, equality; one is aware that Milton's theme is justification of God's judgment, not sympathy for man's sinful actions in the face of inexorable environmental determinants. What we may think of as his final estimate is found in *Paradise Regained* in the words of Christ (III, 49–59):

And what the people but a herd confus'd,
A miscellaneous rabble, who extol
Things vulgar, & well weigh'd, scarce worth the praise,
They praise and they admire they know not what;
And know not whom, but as one leads the other;
And what delight to be by such extoll'd,
To live upon thir tongues and be thir talk,
Of whom to be disprais'd were no small praise?

Concluding our analysis of Milton's attitude toward the people, we must not fail to state again that Milton, much as he distrusted the democratic methods of the Levellers, was one with them in many of the reforms they hoped to achieve.[60] In order to show wherein Milton strongly supported the ends of the extreme democrats, although differing fundamentally from them in the vehicle of reform, we quote in Whitelock's abridged form the entire thirty articles of the third *Agreement of the People,* published in May, 1649, by Lilburne, Walwyn, Prince, and Overton:[61]

1. The supreme authority of this nation to be a representative of four hundred.
2. That two hundred be an house, and the major voice concluding to the nation.
3. All public officers to be capable of subjection, those of salary not to be members.
4. No members of one representative to be chosen of the next.
5. This parliament to end the first Wednesday in August, 1649.
6. If this omit to order it, that the people proceed to elections.
7. A new representative to be the next day after this is dissolved.
8. The next and future parliaments, each to stand for one whole year.
9. The power to be without the consent of any.
10. They not to make laws to compel in matters of religion.
11. None to be compelled to fight by sea or land against his conscience.
12. None to be questioned concerning the wars, but in pursuance to authority.
13. All privileges of any person from courts of justice to be null.
14. Not to give judgment against any, where no law was provided before.
15. Not to depend longer upon the uncertain inclination of parliament.
16. None to be punished for refusing to answer against themselves.
17. No appeal after six months after the end of representatives.

18. None to be exempted for beyond sea trade where others are free.
19. No excise or custom to be above four months after next parliament.
20. Men's persons not to be imprisoned for debt, nor their estates free.
21. Men's lives not to be taken away but for murder, or the like.
22. Men upon trials for life, liberty, etc., to have witnesses heard.
23. Tithes not to continue longer than the next representative.
24. Every parish to choose their own minister, and to force none to pay.
25. Conviction for life, liberty, etc., to be by twelve neighbors sworn.
26. None to be exempted from offices for his religion only.
27. The people in all counties to choose all their public officers.
28. Future representatives to justify all debts, arrears, etc.
29. No forces to be raised but by the representatives in being.
30. This agreement not to be nulled, no estates levelled, nor all things common.

That for which Milton fought hardest and longest, religious liberty, is inherent in this *Agreement*. Article 10 forbids the Parliament to require people to attend any church or take any religious oath; Article 23 prohibits the continuation of tithes; Article 24 provides for the election of all ministers by the individual congregations; Article 26 provides that there shall be no discrimination against office seekers merely for the sake of their religion. How near all this was to Milton's heart we need not say. But there is more. In 1660, as we shall show in a later chapter, Milton, despite his recommendation of a perpetual senate elected by approximately a fourth of the voting population, provided in his proposed Commonwealth for a popular assembly in each county; that is, an assembly elected by those who could meet the usual property-qualification. Article 27 of the *Agreement* would accomplish the same end. In *Defensio Secunda* Milton complains against military domination and questionable methods of taxation. Articles 9, 12, 19, and 29 would have guaranteed the people against both forms of tyranny. Hence we conclude that Milton would have arrived as quickly as the Levellers, perhaps even more quickly, at the feet of the goddess liberty. Unlike the Levellers, however, he would have placed liberty above democracy; he never for a moment believed that the greatest liberty to the greatest number can come only through democratic methods; he would have driven straight to his goal, despising and rejecting the will of the multitude.

NOTE A. "THE PEOPLE" IN THE PAMPHLETS OF 1648-49

The phrase "the people" as used by the various political parties of Milton's day carried strikingly different meanings. To the Presbyterians "the people" usually meant the substantial citizens who dominated the professional and economic life of the nation. To the Independents "the people" were often the pious, liberal minority bent upon attaining freedom despite opposition of the ignorant majority. The Levellers used the term "the people" to designate especially the disenfranchised members of the lower middle class. To the Diggers "the people" meant the laboring half of the population. Usually by "the people" each group meant "the people who really count." Only a few pamphleteers attempted an objective analysis of population divisions.

Thorold Rogers estimates the population of England during the Civil War at around four millions. If we accept Gregory King's classifications of half a century later, the aristocracy and their dependents, comprising the main royalist support, may have numbered .6 of 1% of the people. The esquires and gentlemen (2%) were divided mainly between the king and the Presbyterians, although many of the Independent leaders, including Cromwell himself, were of the gentleman class. To the Presbyterian strength the office holders, lawyers, clergymen, merchants, farmers, freeholders, and naval officers (in all about 40%) contributed most heavily, although many of the farmers and freeholders (over 20%) were traditionally loyal to the king. The Independents drew their leaders from gentlemen, prosperous business men, and liberal clergy; their supporters from the military officers, common soldiers, and shopkeepers. The Presbyterians of London, judging by the relative number of congregations, outnumbered the Independents eight or ten to one. At the time of Charles' execution the Independents could hardly have numbered more than 150,000 or 200,000 active supporters in all England. The Levellers drew almost all their active adherents from tradesmen, shopkeepers, apprentices, skilled workers, and common soldiers, who numbered as classes about 5% of the population; Lilburne and his colleagues could count, of course, on some assistance from unskilled urban workers. The Levellers probably outnumbered the Independents; certainly they could command more coherent mass support. Half the population, however, was composed of servants, laborers, common seamen, cottagers, paupers, vagrants, who showed little political awareness or independence. They had no leaders except Gerrard Winstanley, who did not begin his agitation until 1648; and then he drew to him probably fewer than a hundred followers. The mass of manual workers, lacking any acute consciousness of their interests as a class, were probably divided according to the persuasions of their employers, who were largely royalists or Presbyterians.

The factions of 1648 I have found nowhere more objectively analyzed quantitatively than in the remarkable anonymous tract *Certain Considerations Touching The Present Factions In The Kings Dominions* (1648). The key passage follows (pp. 2-3): "I esteeme all the remnant of *Royalists* who remained in the House of Commons when the King went away, to be of the *Presbyterian* perswasion, as it is most favourable to Monarchy: . . . in the City of London . . . without question, much of the supernumerary part are *Presbyters,* and are awed only by the activity of the *Independent* Faction; who working by Authority of Parliament, with whom they correspond daily, are made to serve them, though not to love them. The rest of the Kingdom are generally *Presbyterian;* not so much, I suppose, because their names are upon the Covenant Roll . . . as because they find the oppression of Warre, and a headless Government: and that Monarchy is more favoured by the Covenant: which they remember to have been less grievous, and not so perpetuall, as the Government on foot is like to prove: For Kings may die, or their humours change. As for the Townes and Corporations, many of them have nests of *Sectaries,* yet they are not all *Independents:* though they all hope for Liberty from them; and so by fighting with them against all others, they suppose they fight for themselves . . . they are not a considerable part of the Inhabitants; and all that can runne to defend the common Cause (as they call it) in the *Armies.* . . . The *Royalists* make a distressed company of Noble-men, Gentle-men and others, who having engaged their Estates and Credits to compound with the Parliament, are all retired to a private life, to eat the bread of carefulnesse; expecting Gods good houre for their restauration: who are beaten out of all their defences, but that of a good Conscience, which remaines impregnable." Until this year, claims the author, Lilburne's conception that the supreme power of the land is in the House of Commons was "never heard of." He infers that the number of Levellers was relatively few.

Another royalist in *The Parliament Arraigned* made an interesting attempt to represent public sentiment in dramatic form. He skillfully characterizes men from several classes, bringing together at the trial of Parliament a rich man, a poor man, a patient man, an enslaved man, a loyal man, etc. Here are some typical excerpts (pp. 20, 21, 23):

Mr. Richman. . . . 'Tis High Treason for any but an Independent to be rich in these Days.

Poor Man. Alas! I am undone by . . . a Company of the Zaints . . . took away my Bald Mare . . . pressed away my Zon *Dick.* . . .

Innocent-Man. . . . I have lost Three Sons in this unnatural War, and yet never could understand for what we fight . . .

Patient-Man. I am sure, Neighbours, I paid all Taxes, Impositions . . . Sessments, Subsidies . . . Free Quarter . . . Contributions . . . Plate, Men, Horse, Armes. . . . I am sure I am quite undone. . . .

Enslaved-Man. . . . Every lousy Rascal in the Army shall command our Persons, and Purses; so the Devil rides the Army, the Army rides the Parliament, the Parliament rides the People, and they, like patient Asses, must undergo all the Burden, or else be Imprisoned, Sequestered, Plundered, Taxed.

Most royalists (and to a lesser degree the Presbyterians) regarded the masses of laborers, artisans, and apprentices as a multitude condemned forever to social and intellectual inferiority. *A Full Answer To The Levellers Petition* (September 19, 1648) denounced the Leveller assumption that all authority is from the people. In such an atheistical creed (p. 4) "every word hath its poison." The people, in which term the author apparently includes not only the laboring half of the population but also many of the rising commercial classes, rightfully have no power at all. But the Levellers would (p. 13) "make *Kings, Queens, Princes, Dukes, Earles, and Lords,* with themselves fellowes at football, and equall unto the poorest Peasant." *The Mad Dog Rebellion* (1648) struck a similar note, deploring the resolution of the Independents to pull down the rich, the eloquent, the old, the honest, and reduce all to the level of knaves and fools. A Presbyterian manifesto, *The Paper Called the Agreement* (March 6, 1649), denounced the Leveller claim of democratic authority, claiming that the *Agreement* portended anarchy, a society (p. 4) "without distinction or order." In *The Anarchy of a Limited Monarchy* (1648) Robert Filmer took the position that government existed only to represent the social and intellectual elite; king and lords, therefore, were the most fundamental props of the kingdom. The Commons, maintained Filmer (p. 14), "onely represent a part of the lower or inferior part of the body of the People, which are the Free-holders worth 40s. by the year, and the Commons or Free-men of Cities and Burroughs." In asserting that the Commons did not represent the masses of the people, Filmer was on safe ground. The freeholders and freemen, he insisted, were not one-fourth or even one-tenth of the common people of the kingdom. Filmer later criticized with astute accuracy Milton's use of the phrase, "the people," in *Observations Concerning the Originall of Government* (1652).

A curious Independent conception of the people appeared in William Sedgewick's *A second view of the Army Remonstrance*. In the men of the army, claimed Sedgewick, had been distilled the most admirable social and personal attributes of the English people (p. 11): "They are the heart and life of the people, men in whom appeares strong and lively affections for publique good." Like Milton, he preferred to think of the people as the virtuous few deserving the free air of a commonwealth government. The army (p. 13) "are rightly and truly *the people*, not in a *grosse heape*, or in a *heavy, dull body*, but in a *selected, choice* way: They are the people in *virtue, spirit* and *power*, gathered up into *heart* and *union* . . . The people, in grosse, being a monster, an unweildy, rude bulke of no use; but here they are gathered together into one pure, excellent life, and so usefull and active for their good and safety. The cleare understanding of this will be a great meanes to compose the dis-affections of people to them, and to draw their hearts to them in love, being *themselves* formd by God into this body, and that now their interest lies as truly in the Army, as ever it did in King or Parliament. . . . The Army are the *People* gathered and united into a most *excellent* and *divine forme*." Such a passage demonstrates the incompatibility of Leveller democratic ideas and the religious fascism of the Independents. Essentially men like Sedgewick, Cromwell, and Milton in their attitude toward the masses combined snobbishness with fear, translating into interpretations of God's will the political opinions inherent in the forces of their environment. They were sincerely convinced that God spoke through them. The Levellers' psychology was utterly at variance with mysticism of this type. Walwyn and Overton had sloughed off any conviction of partnership with a personal God they may have possessed. Though Lilburne lived under conviction of God's presence with him, he in practice dissociated this conviction from his analysis of social problems. The Levellers' confidence in the disenfranchised men of the lower middle classes sprang from their long association with them.

NOTE B. "THE PEOPLE" VS. THE OFFICERS: LEVELLER VIEW

Nowhere in England was the social struggle of the day more realistically waged than in the army. As we have seen, the Levellers made a successful attempt in 1647 to organize the common soldiers into a political party that could make its will felt with the officers. Eventually the officers broke to pieces the organization of the soldiers.

The Levellers looked upon the Independents as betrayers of the democratic cause. In the army, according to their view, the officers had gradually gained the ascendancy, usurping the authority of the common soldiers in the General Council. *The Hunting of the Foxes* (March 21, 1649) is a brilliant anaylsis of Independent strategy. Nowhere else appears a diagnosis of the fundamental conflict between the authoritarian organization of the army and the attempt of the Levellers to forge it into a democratic instrument to express the civil wishes of the majority. Though the Engagement had provided for a democratic General Council in which officers and soldiers were to have equal votes in the settlement of the army's civil proposals, Cromwell and Ireton disliked the presence of common soldiers (p. 2): "This was a thing favoured too much of the peoples authority and power, and therefore inconsistent with the transaction of their lordly Interest." It was plainly inconsistent, too, we may add, with army discipline and procedure; Cromwell probably adjusted himself more flexibly to the scheme than most army commanders could have done. According to *The Hunting of the Foxes,* Cromwell and Ireton gradually forced the common soldiers from the General Council and replaced them with officers whose power was derived not from the men but from the generals (p. 2), "like so many patentee Lords in the high Court of Parliament, deriving their title from the will of their General, as the other did theirs, from the will of the King. . . . Here was (when at this perfection) as absolute a *Monarchy,* and as absolute a *Prerogative Court* over the Army, as *Commoners,* as ever there was over the Common-wealth." According to the authors' interpretation, then, the political organization of the army had gradually taken the form of a dictatorship corresponding to the kingly dictatorship against which they had engaged to fight.

Finding the *Agreement* popular with the army, the authors continue, the officers announced their approval of its premises (pp. 7-9): "And this was drest out in such taking Saint-like language, as the religious people might best be surprised . . . they call Fasts (a certain fore-runner of mischief among them) cry, and howl, and bedew their cheeks with the tears of hypocrisie and deceit, confess their iniquity and abomination in declining the cause of the people, and tampering with the King; and humbly, as in the presence of the all-seeing God, acknowledge the way of *an Agreement of the People,* to be the way to our Peace and Freedom; and even then . . . proceed even to death, imprisonment or cashierment of all such in the Army as promoted or owned that Agreement; and to fan and cull such Asserters of the Peoples Freedoms out of the Army, they proceed to disband 20. out of a Troop, by which the honest party of the Souldiery was very much weakned, and all the promoters of Freedom discouraged, and the people struck into desperation; which gave rise unto a second war. . . . But the same . . . being over, they finding the old affections of the Souldiers not yet quenched or much cooled . . . they . . . formalize again, and to keep the honest party in suspense . . . they then as a cloke, take up the way of an Agreement again, to present themselves amiable unto us; and a great pudder they make in their Councel about an Agreement, and one they brought forth, but such a one as was most abhorred by such as most sought after the way of an Agreement . . . till they in the mean time so far effected their business, as to the introduction of an absolute platforme of Tyranie, long since hatched by *Ireton* . . . there is a King to succeed . . . O *Cromwel! Whither art thou aspiring?*"

The five authors of *The Hunting*, together with three other troopers, had on March 1 laid a petition before the Council of Officers protesting abridgment of the right of petition and insisting on their responsibility for *Englands New Chains*. For this avowal of Leveller principles they were court-martialed on March 3 and sentenced to ride their horses backward before their regiments, have their swords broken over their heads, and be dismissed from the army in disgrace (Gardiner, *Commonwealth*, I, 35-36). In *The Hunting* the soldiers refer to their sentence as follows (pp. 11-12): "Who would have thought to have seen Souldiers (by their Order) to ride with their faces toward their Horse tailes, to have their Swords broken over their Heads, and to be casheered, and that for Petitioning, and claming their just right and title to the same?"

The *Hunting* soldiers felt that the cause of the people was worse off in the hands of the Independents than under the rule of the king (p. 14): "The King to his death stood upon this principle, That he was accomptable to none but God; that he was above the Parliament, and above the People. And now to whom will these be accomptable? to none on Earth. . . . Are they not above the Parliament? they have even a Negative voice thereover . . . we were before ruled by King, Lords, and Commons; now by a General, a Court Martial, and House of Commons; and we pray you what is the difference?"

To the Levellers the people were the masses of the disenfranchised lower middle class, though they wanted their political reforms to be extended to the unskilled laborers. The Levellers wanted freedom of speech and freedom of economic enterprise for all. After the Independent army had assumed power Walwyn wrote (*The Fountain of Slaunder*, p. 19), "The people is a pittiful mean helplesse thing; as under School-masters being in danger to be whipt and beaten in case they meddle without leave and license from their masters." In the original discussions of the *Agreement* the Levellers, as we have seen, had demanded manhood suffrage; but in the last editions of the *Agreement* the provision was made that servants and beggars should not vote, nor those receiving alms. Though Walwyn had a special concern for the poverty-stricken of the working class, there is no evidence that the Levellers agitated very extensively for the economic betterment of laborers, cottagers, or servants. The leaders hastened to repudiate the program of the Diggers, saying that it was (*A Manifestation*, p. 5) "the utmost of our aime that the Common-wealth be reduced to such a passe that every man may with as much security as may be enjoy his propriety." There is no reason to doubt the sincerity of this statement. Though the Levellers worked for the formation of a political democracy, they limited its economic implications to the extension of unhampered competition, a principle that benefited mainly the restless groups of the lower middle class.

CHAPTER X

CHAMPION AND DETRACTOR OF PARLIAMENTS

T HE STORY or Milton's reactions to parliamentary rule is one of mingled faith, despair, restored confidence, and fearful hope. During that early Revolutionary period of 1642-46, when the Long Parliament steadily pushed forward those reforms which to Milton seemed paramount, his confidence in that body was complete. It was only when their financial methods grew notoriously corrupt, when he himself suffered pecuniary loss by their inconsiderate confiscation of royalist property, that he began to doubt the wisdom of the legislative body which ruled the land. His doubts were verified when, after welcoming the purging of the Long Parliament, he saw the Rumpers themselves go the way of dishonest inefficiency. Only after the disheartening career of Cromwell, in those turbulent months preceding the Restoration, did Milton again place his hope in any kind of Parliament. Not that his confidence in that body was restored: he appealed to Parliament in those latter days only because it had the machinery most likely to provide stability and preservation of reforms already accomplished.

Tracing the record of these twenty years of Milton's association with Parliament, I have found one conviction inescapable: Milton cared not one jot whether the Parliament which he lauded or condemned was representative, whether it was appointed or elected, whether it was legal or illegal. What concerned him was whether or not, in his opinion, the Parliament which had assumed power was acting for the public welfare, was securing the liberties which he held so dear. Thus Parliament was to him any group strong enough to maintain order and courageous enough to legislate fearlessly. Once this point of view is understood, one may read the record of Milton's relations to Parliament with some understanding of his apparent loss of faith in republican government.

273

A. MILTON AND THE LONG PARLIAMENT

The history of Milton's opinions of the Long Parliament divides itself naturally into two periods. The first is those years from 1642 to 1646, when Milton heartily approved the steps Parliament was taking to restore the rights of that body to their full validity, to destroy the power of the bishops, and to suppress the army of the king. The second period covers roughly the years 1646 to 1649, although previous to the year 1646 Milton had begun staunchly to support the minority or Independent party in Parliament. During these years Milton not only began to look upon the Long Parliament as a Presbyterian body attempting to coerce conscience, but from personal contact with sequestration had become bitterly resentful of its rule and convinced of its unfitness to govern.

Apology for Smectymnuus, published early in 1642, shows how thoroughly at that time (still a Presbyterian), Milton approved of the Long Parliament membership and legislative efforts. In the midst of the vituperative language which he has been showering upon his opponent for defending Charles' High Commission court, Milton pauses "to touch upon a smoother string" in praise of the Parliamentarians. They are the kind of men in whom he has the most confidence, certain in judgment, ripe in wisdom, strong in virtue and unselfish love of country. For the most part men of noble descent, they have renounced lives of rich idleness, by reason of their innate virtue and God's grace, to follow in the footsteps of the most illustrious of their ancestors. Escaping from the superstition of the universities to which they were sent, and unmoved by hopes of political preferment in a corrupt church, they have united, says Milton, in parliamentary endeavor to repulse religious tyranny and reform the land. Nor have they failed to win the respect of all classes: they have listened not only to complaints of workers but even to those of women.[1] Thus Milton concludes his eulogy; he is still heartily in sympathy with all that Parliament has done. Absorbed with the destruction of their common enemy, Presbyterians and Independents have not yet parted company.

In the following summer, 1643, Milton dedicated to Parliament his first divorce tract, *The Doctrine and Discipline of Divorce.* Throughout his address to Parliament which precedes the divorce discussion itself, Milton pleads vehemently for an open-minded consideration of his views, however startling they may at first appear. Custom and tradition having continued the greatest helps to error, he bids them unhesitatingly to champion truth now as they have done in the past, not allowing themselves to be intimidated by the "draff of men" who will, he foresees, ridicule their efforts. To seek out truth and translate it into law is their responsibility; they are sitting to redress grievances, and he, John Milton, has one which is of the utmost concern to all England:

A civil, an indifferent, a sometime dissuaded law of marriage, must be forced upon us to fulfil, not only without charity but against her. No place in heaven or earth, except hell, where charity may not enter; yet marriage . . . will not admit now either of charity or mercy. . . . Advise ye well, supreme senate, if charity be thus excluded and expulsed, how ye will defend the untainted honour of your actions and proceedings. He who marries, intends as little to conspire his own ruin, as he that swears allegiance: and as the whole people is in proportion to an ill government, so is one man to an ill marriage.[2]

Thus he exhorts them, declaring that nothing is of more concern to the commonwealth, no tyranny of more distress, than domestic unhappiness; no true reformation is possible so long as no reform takes place to eliminate this unhappiness. Consider, he urges, all the evidence; read over again the scriptures; consult men of liberal views and learned opinions whatever their occupations, and fear not to let each man weigh the truth for himself, not relying altogether on the "narrow intellectuals." Once the truth is determined, Parliament should not fear to act, and act speedily, to repeal the laws forbidding divorce. There will be less prostitution, less adultery, and more sober living in the commonwealth. Again he urges their haste, and signs himself the "Honourer and Attendant of their noble Worth and Virtues."

Milton's next important notice of Parliament was his address in *The Judgment of Martin Bucer Concerning Divorce*, which appeared in July, 1644. His hopes for a favorable hearing from Parliament remained undiminished; but from the Assembly of Divines he had heard only contempt for his new heresy. True, they had not yet openly preached against him; but that was soon to come. That their sharp private criticism had taken effect without deterring Milton appears from the dedication itself. In place of the line "To the Parliament of England with the Assembly," followed by the quo-

tation "Every scribe instructed in the kingdom of heaven is like
the master of a house, which bringeth out of his treasury new things
and old," Milton has substituted the words "To the Parliament of
England," followed by, "Art thou a teacher of Israel and knowest
not these things?" After reiterating all his former arguments,
dwelling especially on happy marriage as the foundation of reformation, Milton praises Parliament anew, confident, he says, that no
governing body will sooner consider that which is generous and
noble, or beyond the grasp of the masses. He trusts that they will
not be bound either by precedent or by those who, while rebuking
others for following tradition, are the most bound by it themselves.[3]
This time there is no complimentary close, but only his plain signa-
ture. At the end of the pamphlet itself Milton writes in an uneasy
vein, wondering whether or not after gaining so much liberty we
shall allow further liberties quite as vital to be trampled under.
Finally, warning against ignorance and church slavery, he calls
upon Parliament to "inform themselves rightly in the midst of an
unprincipled age."

Milton's next address to Parliament is the familiar one of November, 1644, in the *Areopagitica*. So intent is the orator upon his
address to Parliament, and so vital is the connection between them
and his objection to their licensing order, that he gives full emphasis
to his exhortation by placing it, not in a preface, but in the body
of the speech itself. He has, he declares, praised them in the past
either for actual accomplishments or for what reformation he
thought them capable of. Now he hopes they will be convinced of
his loyalty and sincerity if he tells them without fear how they
might improve upon what they have done, doubting not that they
will be more pleased with honest advice than with flattery. Lest
he seem presumptuous, he refers them to those Parliaments of old
which have listened with respect to the advice of single persons;
as, for instance, when Isocrates addressed the assembly of Athens,
advising them to alter their democratic government. If the English
Parliament is more illustrious even than those which had listened
previously to men not members of their assemblies, he prays to be
thought not unduly inferior to the orators who have advised them.
And now the time has come for his advice: Parliament should reconsider the law it has recently passed to license and regulate
printing.

There is definitely more confidence in Milton's plea to Parliament for a free press than there is in his renewed demand for divorce laws five months later. On March 4, 1645, appeared *Tetrachordon* with a prefatory address to Parliament. Although every one knows, he says in opening, that Parliament has been instigated to censure his *Doctrine and Discipline of Divorce*,[4] he has found no order of Parliament which attempts to disgrace or hinder the work of the author. Milton still has a great deal of confidence in Parliament's fairness and in those calm judgments which would prevent rash or hasty decisions; for their services to the nation he feels inexhaustible gratitude. As to the sermon, however, which Herbert Palmer had preached to Parliament concerning his previous tract, he has nothing but scorn. To Palmer's charge that the book ought to be burnt, that, further, it was an insult to Parliament to dedicate it to them, Milton replies in vehement self-defence. He again upholds the divorce theories of Bucer, who, he suggests, should now be as highly honored by the present Parliament as he was by the Parliament of Edward VI. Milton insists that he has dedicated his book to Parliament because of his loyalty to them and his regard for their personal integrity, and for the same reason he now dedicates to them expositions of scripture to prove his theories. His demand for revision of the divorce laws is more imperious than ever. He urges immediate and thorough investigation, not by the divines, but by Parliament itself.

And then it is, at the very end of this *Tetrachordon* address to Parliament, that Milton not only shows his impatience with the Long Parliament, but anticipates the military control of the Independents:

And perhaps in time to come, others will know how to esteem what is not every day put into their hands, when they have marked events, and better weighed how hurtful and unwise it is, to hide a secret and pernicious rupture under the ill counsel of a bashful silence.[5]

Following this passage, lest he be thought distrustful, Milton announces that he might be named among the foremost who pray "that the fate of England may tarry for no other deliverers." It is plain from this that he believes there will be other deliverers if Parliament hesitates to write into positive law what is just and right. To any of Milton's readers the rising power of Cromwell's army and the news which was already abroad of its dissatisfaction with the Presbyterian Parliament, were sufficient testimony of whom Milton was thinking when he wrote "other deliverers."

For five months, since November, 1644, Milton had been outspokenly an Independent. It was inevitable, therefore, much as he sincerely admired the reforms of the Long Parliament, that he should side with the Independent army in its increasingly strained relations with the government. The army's hate for all religious coercion mounted steadily. Parliament was equally antagonistic towards toleration; all England must be brought into the Presbyterian state church. We know enough of Milton's stand on the separation of church and state to conclude without hesitation that his hopes for reformation leaned more and more towards Cromwell's army and to the Independents in Parliament rather than to the predominant Presbyterian majority.

Milton wrote nothing about Parliament from March, 1645, until the spring or summer of 1646, when he composed *On the New Forcers of Conscience under the Long Parliament.*[6] In this sonnet he praises Parliament as the power which is likely to curb Presbyterianism:

> That so the Parliament
> May with their wholsom and preventive Shears
> Clip your Phylacteries, though bauk your Ears,
> And succour our just Fears.

It is evident from these lines that this Parliament is not the same strongly Presbyterian body to which Milton had appealed in his pamphlets of 1642-45. In January, 1646, the Presbyterian party in Parliament had reached its greatest power,[7] but by the time Milton wrote the lines we have quoted, in the spring or summer of 1646, the growing number of Independents in the House of Commons was beginning to make its influence felt. Since August, 1645, when it was apparent that the Parliamentary army would soon control all England, the House of Commons had issued writs of election to fill the vacancies made in 1642, when the Royalists had fled with their king. All the new men were Parliamentarians, either Presbyterian or Independent, but by far the more numerous were the Independents, many of them by this time famous officers in Cromwell's army. Joining with the Erastians, that is, with Parliament members who believed that the Presbyterian church government should be subject to strict parliamentary control, the Independents made their influence felt almost immediately. On April 21, the Commons adopted a resolution rebuking the Assembly of Divines for petitioning against the parliamentary ordinance of March 14 which provided for parliamentary supervision of the church government. This rebuke was drawn up by Haselrig, Marten, Vane, and Selden; it declared that the Assembly had no right to censure or even to discuss acts of Parliament already passed, or to decide whether a law passed by Parliament agreed or disagreed with the Bible; unless, that is, the Assembly was required to render a decision by order of Parliament.[8] It was resolved, moreover, that Parliament only could decide what toleration was to be granted to those not accepting Presbyterianism. Finally, the same committee which had drawn up the rebuke presented to the Assembly with the approval of the Commons a series of nine questions, the first of which was significant enough: "Whether the Parochial and Congregational Elderships appointed by Ordinance of Parliament, or any other Congregational or Presbyterial Elderships, are *jure divino*, and by the will and appointment of Jesus Christ; and whether any particular church government is *jure divino* and what that government is?" [9] From these enactments it was apparent that there was a growing antagonism in Parliament to Presbyterianism. With the arrival of more Cromwellian officers in May, 1646, Parliament became that liberal body that Milton was thinking of when he spoke of "their wholsom and preventive shears."

During the following year, however, from May, 1646, to May, 1647, events served to restore to the Presbyterians the domination of Parliament which they seemed to have lost in the spring of 1646. The king having escaped to the protection of the Scottish army May 5, the Scots retained possession of him until September, and offered to establish his power in England if he would adopt the Presbyterian faith. The Presbyterians in Parliament, with the Scottish army at their backs, were in a stronger position than before to make a peace with the king favorable to their cause of complete conformity to Presbyterianism; and weak members, seeing the strength of the king's position, veered round again to the Presbyterian party.[10] Then there was the question of the army and the continued heavy taxation for its upkeep. Public opinion strongly backed the Presbyterians in their anxiety to disband their enemies, the army Independents.[11] This public opinion had found expression in the newer members of the Commons, who were definitely more Presbyterian than the earlier Recruiters.[12] In February, 1647, the Presbyterian majority in the Commons, supported by the Lords, who had always been overwhelmingly Presbyterian, took the initiative in the struggle—a struggle between Parliament on the one hand, supported by the wishes of the people, and Cromwell's army on the other, maintained by a hitherto unknown fervor for religious liberty. The army refused to be disbanded without pay, refused to relinquish the right to strike for a political liberty visualized but not achieved, refused to return home to be forced into Presbyterian worship. Nothwithstanding the army's strength as a political force, Parliament ordered it to be disbanded on February 19, 1647, by a majority of ten votes, 158-148.[13] That Milton did not want this army disbanded can be no matter for doubt. All his subsequent political actions demonstrated where his sympathies had lain at that critical moment.

When we see that Milton, much as he sincerely admired the reform efforts of the Long Parliament, sided with the Independent army in its antagonism to Parliament, we are afforded some explanation for his silence during those critical years preceding Pride's Purge. Parliament was quite as averse to toleration as the army was to intolerance; it passed motions that no officer should take command in the new army unless he should accept the Covenant and conform to the established church, and further, that no one should become an officer who was also a member of the House of Commons.[14] Such being the case, Milton's hopes, as we have said, leaned more and more to Cromwell's army for reformation in England, and less and less toward the predominantly Presbyterian Parliament. His praise of Parliament, however, during the years 1642-45, was a thing all England remembered. Even as late as 1646, when the Independent members had dominated Parliament long enough to force a rebuke of the Westminster Assembly, Milton had voiced his old faith in the Long Parliament. Clearly, he could not now retract his eulogies, or nullify them by detractions. His only recourse was either to remain silent or to write his criticism in a form which would not be made public at that time: his inconsistency would have become the target of his enemies' shafts. He could no more speak openly against Parliament, a body which contained many Independent statesmen, than he could afterward rebuke Cromwell during the years 1654-58. During those years he could not sincerely praise Cromwell as he had of old; yet he could not consistently criticise him for not separating church and state. So to the public he remained silent, as he did in the matter of the Long Parliament from the spring of 1646 to February, 1649.

There is another motive, however, for Milton's silence, which we must take cognizance of. Despite his partisanship, it remains a matter of record that Milton never openly invited the antagonism of the ruling power, whether that of Charles I, the Long Parliament, Cromwell, the Rump, or Charles II. We find his justification for so doing in *Christian Doctrine:* "That it may be the part of prudence to obey even the commands of a tyrant in lawful things, or, more properly, to comply with the necessity of the time for the sake of public peace, as well as of personal safety, I am far from denying." [15] His whole sympathy with the army sectaries, and his disappointment with the Long Parliament as the main instrument of freedom, Milton could hardly announce openly, whether or not he was influenced by the thought of the Long Parliament's constables and the needless weakening of his frail body by imprisonment. It is hardly necessary to add that his silence on this occasion cannot be interpreted as an indication of physical fear.

Though he remained publicly silent there is evidence that Milton's estimate of the Long Parliament changed almost completely from 1646 to 1649. It was not alone the Presbyterian intolerance which influenced him, but the corrupt practices in which Parliament, regardless of religious parties, was involved. Such evidence of Milton's changed attitude we find in his sonnet *On the Lord Gen. Fairfax at the seige of Colchester,* written about August 27, 1648, when Colchester surrendered. His last word concerning Parliament, written two years previously in his sonnet *On the New Forcers of Conscience,* had been complimentary. Now, however, he has so far lost hope in Parliament that he appeals to Fairfax as a possible leader strong enough to quiet the prevailing disorder and banish the corruption:

> Oh! yet a nobler task awaits thy hand;—
> For what can War but endless war still breed?

Till truth and right from violence be freed,
And public faith cleared from the shameful brand
Of public fraud. In vain doth Valour bleed
While Avarice and Rapine share the land.[16]

It is apparent that Milton believes Parliament too dishonest in its dealings with the public to be the instrument of reformation. Military victories being useless so long as the legislators rob and cheat the people, Milton is already willing to transfer his allegiance from them to a man who is strong enough to create order and provide freedom of conscience. Parliament is no longer that body which Milton himself had "extolled as our greatest deliverers."

With this sonnet in mind it is easier for us to understand the long tirade against the Long Parliament with which Milton prefaced Book III of his History of Britain. Written apparently at the height of his dissatisfaction,[17] his denunciation is a scathing one. In one long paragraph, the fourth of Book III, Milton accuses the members of delaying justice, making decisions through favor and spite, placing on committees unqualified outsiders who betrayed the commonwealth, yielding themselves to unprincipled leaders, passing increasingly heavy taxes, neglecting to repeal bad laws, bestowing gifts and preferred offices among themselves, permitting their agents to sequester property while the owners were being passed from one committee to another without satisfaction, and confiscating property of enemies which really belonged to friends of Parliament by reason of indebtedness.[18] They have received huge sums of money from the people, as well as much of the church wealth, without rendering any account of it to the people. Until lately they have had the loyalty of the people, but by their conduct they have not only unfitted themselves to provide liberty, but have unfitted the people themselves to understand or absorb it. Thus he denounces them, and although he makes plain that a minority of Parliament are both good and wise, it is clear that he intends his accusations not as an indictment of the Presbyterians alone but as an indictment of the entire Parliament. If he had singled out the Presbyterians as the majority part responsible for dishonesty and corruption, his attack would be consistent with his pronounced antagonism to them expressed in the sonnet of 1646. But he does not point out that their misdeeds continued in spite of the efforts of the minority party, the

Independents, to preserve the honor of the state. Rather he includes the Independents in his denunciation, thereby reversing the attitude which he had assumed toward Parliament from 1642 to 1646.

From personal experience with sequestrations, to which he devotes about half of the long paragraph summing up his grievances against the existing government, Milton had had quite enough cause to be dissatisfied with the financial methods of the Long Parliament. In June, 1646, Richard Powell, Milton's royalist father-in-law, and his family had left their Forest Hills home outside the city of Oxford and had taken refuge in the city during its siege by the parliamentary army. On June 16, three confiscators, appointed by the Committee of Parliamentary Sequestrations for the County of Oxford, took an inventory of the personal property in the Forest Hills home of Mr. Powell, together with a record of farm animals, carts, coaches, etc., and sold them to one Matthew Appletree for 335 pounds, the true value of the goods being eight to nine hundred pounds.[19] Appletree was a dealer from London who followed the parliamentary army from place to place to seek bargains in confiscated property. It is rather significant that a Thomas Appletree, evidently a relative to Matthew, was a member of the Oxford County Committee which directed the sequestrators to dispose of Richard Powell's property on the Forest Hills estate. The sequestration had taken place before Mr. Powell had had an opportunity to seek some compensation for his estate according to the provisions of the Treaty of the Surrender of Oxford, and according to Parliament's avowed policy.

What is more important for us, the immediate result of the sequestration was the removal of Mr. Powell and his family to the London house of his son-in-law, John Milton. Once established there he immediately set about to petition Parliament for some sort of settlement. But he was thoroughly disappointed. On July 16, 1646, the Commons granted to the inhabitants of Banbury lumber valued at three hundred pounds, belonging to Mr. Powell, "a Malignant," and directed that it be used by the town of Banbury to repair the church and jail.[20] Any lumber remaining after these repairs the Commons voted to be given to "well-affected" persons for the rebuilding of their private homes. But more was yet to come. Three months after Mr. Powell had petitioned the

Goldsmiths' Hall Committee for leave to compound, he sent to the Committee the "Particular of Real and Personal Estate," which was to be the basis of the compounding. This account of his financial affairs showed him to have more debts than his properties were worth. Yet the Committee, refusing to recognize his debts, and ignoring Mr. Powell's claim for illegal confiscation, judged him to have an income of ninety pounds a year and fined him the amount of two years' income, 180 pounds.

Such was the parliamentary justice in which Milton was directly interested; for Mr. Powell owed Milton three hundred pounds of the old indebtedness to the senior Milton, and had given him nothing of the one thousand pounds marriage portion promised him at the time of his marriage to Mary Powell. Was Milton not thinking of this injustice when he wrote, "Thus were their friends confiscate with their enemies . . . nor were we happier creditors to what we called the state, than to them who were sequestered as the state's enemies"? [21]

I have given a detailed account of Mr. Powell's dealings with Parliament to show how closely Milton himself was concerned in them, and to present his association with the Powells as a partial explanation for his so bitterly denouncing the Long Parliament. By the "ravening seizure of innumerable thieves in office," by Parliament's "sequestrators and subcommittees abroad," the Powell family had been forced from its home. Such a seizure could not have occurred "without secret compliance, if not compact with some superiours able to bear them out." Not only Mr. Powell, but Milton's brother Christopher, a royalist whom Parliament had also treated rather severely, had been "tossed up and down after miserable attendance from one committee to another with petitions in their hands," in an attempt to secure a settlement. Through Parliament's sequestrations Milton had become one of these "bereaved after of their just debts by greedy sequestrations." He who had praised Parliament so often was now deprived of that which was rightfully due him from Mr. Powell's estate by officers of the same Parliament. Face to face with the actual political machinery of the new government, Milton was impelled to rebuke its practice as vehemently as he had formerly eulogized its principles. For the passing of the Long Parliament, Milton held no regrets. Pride's Purge he hailed with satisfaction.

B. MILTON AND THE RUMP

Milton's support of the Rump was immediate and unqualified. Throughout *The Tenure of Kings and Magistrates* he assumes that the Rump is just as truly the Parliament of England as the Long Parliament he had lauded in 1644. In *Observations on the Articles of Peace,* published May 16, 1649, Milton again declares his approval of the Rump as the real Parliament of England, asserting that they put to death the king "justly and undauntedly, as became the Parliament of England." To Ormond's charge that in all ages the three estates, king, lords, and commons have made up the Parliaments, Milton replies with *his* definition of a Parliament: "A parliament signifies no more than the supreme and general council of a nation, consisting of whomsoever chosen and assembled for the public good." [22] He does not reply to Ormond's charge that the House contains but a small number of the former Parliament; as Masson says, he is "judiciously silent on that point." Answering the Belfast Presbytery in the same pamphlet, however, Milton stoutly defends the expulsion of a large number of Presbyterians from Parliament: "No question but it is as good and necessary to expel rotten members out of the house, as to banish delinquents out of the land: and the reason holds as well in forty as in five." [23] They were not privileged to sit there, he insists, to vote the king (author of England's miseries) back into power again.

In *A Defence of the People of England,* Milton again champions the Rumpers. In reply to Salmasius' question whether or not it was the people who forced some members out of the House of Commons, Milton declares that it was indeed the people acting through the few in Parliament who remained faithful to the people's cause: "What if the greater part of the senate should choose to be slaves, or to expose the government to sale, ought not the lesser number to interpose, and endeavor to retain their liberty, if it be in their power?" [24] In such vein does Milton support a Parliament which was legally and constitutionally no Parliament at all. The Rump was in reality the Independent party of the Long Parliament sustained in office by the Independent army.

Nothing could be more convincing proof of Milton's lack of dependence on democratic methods than his unqualified approval of the Rump Parliament. In direct contrast to the stand of Lilburne and the Levellers, his concern was the wielding of parliamentary power for righteous reform, not the orderly and constitutional acquisition of that power.

It is not surprising, then, that Milton should have been willing, four years later, to substitute the dictator Cromwell for the Rump Parliament as a vehicle of reform. The Rump had, it is true, made effective advance in reformation: It had abolished kingship and the House of Lords, and it had been courageous enough to initiate the trial and execution of Charles I. But for one reform, dear to Milton's heart, the Rump seemed less and less enthusiastic. Its Committee for the Propagation of the Gospel, in March 1652, proposed what was in reality a modified state church; a committee of ministers and laymen was to be appointed in every county to examine those who wished to enter the service of the state as paid ministers; all people were to be required to attend public worship except those who could not conscientiously do so; all people who dissented from the state church were to give notice to the magistrates of their projected meetings; no persons were to be allowed to preach against any of the "Fifteen Christian Fundamentals" suggested by the ministers.[25] How averse Milton was to any such plan we already know, and Cromwell at that time strenuously opposed several of the proposals. From Cromwell's former stand for full toleration, and from his statement before the Committee Milton had good reason to believe not only that Cromwell favored toleration, but that he might yet stand for complete separation of church and state. In March, 1652, Milton looked to Cromwell, and not to the Rump, as that "effectual might" which might yet provide religious freedom:

> yet much remaines
> To conquer still; peace hath her victories
> No less renown'd then warr; new foes aries
> Threatning to bind our soules with secular chaines:
> Helpe us to save free Conscience from the paw
> Of Hireling wolves whose Gospell is their maw.[26]

A year later, in March 1653, the Rump passed resolutions for the maintenance of a modified state church as proposed by the ministers. Milton lent his approval to the dissolution of the Rump (in April) partly, then, because it was only by this act that the state church could be abolished, perhaps not to be set up again.

C. Milton and the Barebones Parliament

Milton was losing faith in Parliaments. After an auspicious beginning the Long Parliament had given him an insight into the capacity of popular government for corruption in time of war, and had embittered him because of its predominant Presbyterianism. Likewise the Rump, men for the most part after his own heart, following the most glorious of acts, the judgment of the king, the abolition of monarchy and the House of Lords, and the re-establishment of the country's finances, had gone the way of the Long Parliament into intolerance and inefficiency.

Even the Barebones Parliament failed to stir Milton from his loyalty to Oliver. The "Saints" whom Oliver had called to legislate as a Parliament Milton surely watched with interest; for he was in principle, if anything, a Fifth Monarchy man; that is, he believed in the temporal rule of Christ's godly representatives here on earth. Those reforms for which he had longed seemed about to be realized. On August 24, 1653, the Parliament passed an act declaring that the state would recognize only those marriages performed by a justice of the peace;[27] on December 6 a motion was passed to abolish patronage. The radical "Saints" to a man favored the abolition of tithes, the abolition of a state church, the abolition of a state ministry, in short the complete separation of church and state.[28] Though for a while their program seemed capable of realization (they were ceaselessly active and regular in attendance), the radicals ultimately failed to pass their wishes into law. Slightly outnumbered by their opponents and opposed by Cromwell, they were finally completely frustrated when the conservative members left Parliament in a body and refused to serve longer.[29] But what was Milton's estimate of the Parliament which had seemed most inclined to grant the religious liberty he so ardently championed? "They meet; but do nothing; and, having wearied themselves by their mutual dissentions, and fully exposed their incapacity to the observation of the country, they consent to a voluntary dissolution."[30] Such was Milton's conclusion in 1654. The godliest men were no more fit rulers than their less pious predecessors. Only

Cromwell had strength. Parliaments had become weak and ineffectual.

D. MILTON AND THE RESTORED RUMP

With the passing of Cromwell, however, the growing confusion led Milton to appeal again to Parliament as the hope of stability and reform. Like the pamphlets of 1642-45, those of 1659 ring with "supreme council!" and "supreme senate!" On January 27, 1659, Richard Cromwell's "free and full" Parliament had met at Westminster. On February 16 Milton dedicated to this Parliament *A Treatise of Civil Power in Ecclesiastical Causes.* Declaring that he feels certain Parliament will not only preserve but extend the liberty of conscience already possessed, he knows they will recognize that "it is not lawful for any power on earth to compel in matters of religion." They will, he is positive, have one advantage if they wish to separate church and state: many men who are already persuaded this should be done are among their number. From some of these, sitting with them in council, he has heard excellent distinctions between religious and civil authority. Despite his allegiance to the dictator Cromwell and his simultaneous rejection of his republican friends, it is evident that Milton now hopes that they will receive his personal plea with favorable consideration.

But the republicans in Richard's parliament, being much in the minority, could do nothing for the re-establishment of the republic (which lay nearest their hearts), much less for the disestablishment of the church. Baffled, they sought aid from the very arm of strength which had scattered them once and was to scatter them twice again. To overcome the supporters of the Protectorate they combined with the army officers to force a dissolution. Then by agreement with the officers they called together forty-two members of the Rump dissolved by Oliver in 1653. The Restored Rump met on May 7, 1659, two weeks after Richard's Parliament had fallen. Though this Parliament partially fulfilled Milton's hopes by proceeding immediately to consider the question of disestablishment, on June 27 they voted to continue tithes for church support. Milton continued in his official capacity and wrote two state letters for the Restored Rump; that he was welcomed back into the ranks of the republicans we know from a letter written to him by Moses

Wall, dated May 26, 1659: "But I was uncertain whether your relation to the Court (though I think that a Commonwealth was more friendly to you than a Court) had not clouded your former light; but your last book[31] resolved that doubt." [32]

The Rump being now restored as the supreme power in England, Milton dedicated to them in August his *Considerations Touching the Likeliest Means to Remove Hirelings Out of the Church.* Owing to their protection, he writes, he has for the past eighteen years been permitted to "assert the just rights and freedoms both of church and state." So much did they approve his efforts that they had charged him to write *A Defence of the People of England.* It is only natural then, he continues, that he should address to them (who had freed the land of both prelacy and monarchy) a plea for yet greater liberty. Next to God these men are, indeed, "the authors and best patrons of religious liberty that ever these islands brought forth." With such unstinted praise Milton addresses them, reassured, it would seem, not only of their regard for him, but also of their superior statesmanship.

Then follows that much-debated passage: "The care of whose peace and safety, after a short but scandalous night of interruption, is now again, by a new dawning of God's miraculous providence among us, resolved upon your shoulders." [33] Masson believes that the words "short but scandalous night of interruption" apply to the two-weeks dictatorship which intervened between the fall of Richard's Parliament and the restoration of the Rump. Smart, on the contrary, infers that the phrase applies to Cromwell's rule.[34] Masson points out that Cromwell's dictatorship had not been "short" and that Milton could not have been so inconsistent as to call it "scandalous." Yet, as Smart remarks, his eulogy of the Rump cannot be reconciled with his approval of their dissolution six years before. As he had shifted his hopes from the Rump to Cromwell, so now something has occurred to turn him from belief in Cromwell to belief in the Rump again. Milton seems to imply that the Rumpers, when they were pushing forward toward true liberty, were interrupted by Cromwell, and that now they are ready to push forward again. Knowing Milton's predilection for consistency, one wonders if he purposely left the passage capable of either interpretation. When, however, he continues his praise of the republicans, naming them the "authors, assertors, and now *recoverers* of our

liberty," he clearly indicates that he regards the Rumpers as deliverers from Cromwell and his military tyranny. Further proof that
Milton in 1659 felt that the Rump had been tyrannized over by
Cromwell in 1653 we find in *A Letter to a Friend Concerning the
Ruptures of the Commonwealth,* dated October 20, 1659. In this
letter Milton declares that he is overjoyed to find that the army has
shown the "fruits of their repentance" by "restoring the famous old
parliament, *which they had without just authority dissolved.*"[35] Here
is rather conclusive evidence that Cromwell had come to appear in
his eyes somewhat of a tyrant, and that the Rump, after all, had deserved his support in their struggle against military dictatorship. We
can hardly escape the conviction, then, that the "short but scandalous night of interruption" was that period when Cromwell ruled by
military domination alone.

In his praise of the Rump Milton takes pains, it is curious to
note, to show why they should think his a fitting voice to confound
their enemies. In the past they selected him to preserve the cause of
the Commonwealth, and their own reputations, in the eyes of the
whole world. Nor, he continues, are they now sorry they did so.
Because of his past services, then, he believes there should be no
hesitation in trusting him again, not to defend their policies in
Europe, but to defend them against weaker opposition in their own
country. Then follows his urgent request for them to consider his
plan to remove hirelings out of the church. With a feeling of assurance that his own pamphlets will prepare the way for their actions,
he entrusts to them the task of delivering the English people from
the "oppressions of a simonious decimating clergy."

Milton's plea had, however, no more effect on the Rump than
his former pamphlet had had on Richard's Parliament. Having continued the state church, the Rump for the present appeared in no
hurry, despite many petitions like those of Milton, to reconsider
their position. Furthermore, they were hastening to put themselves
out of power again. Demonstrating their republican determination
of old, they soon refused to treat with the army officers on equal
terms; on October 12 they cashiered Lambert, Desborough, Berry,
and six other officers. Lambert, acting for the army, promptly
responded by disbanding the Rump.

It was then that Milton, at the request of a friend, passed his
opinion of the affairs of the Commonwealth and offered his solution,

as it were, in embryo. The *Letter to a Friend* was written October 20, 1659, one week after Lambert's *coup d'état*. In this letter Milton inveighs bitterly against the army, regretting that they should now dissolve the Parliament which they themselves had re-established, and justifying the Rump's cashiering procedure on the ground that the Rump had not acted until it was known that the army intended to use force against Parliament.[36] He does not utterly censure Lambert's act, not knowing the exact cause thereof, but he believes that other nations will think that army dishonorable which formerly wrought so much for England's liberty. In all Europe, he continues, the military is subordinate to the civil power; that the civil should be superior is agreeable to the light of nature, and to all the laws of human society. "How dishonorable to the name of God, that his fear and the power of his knowledge in an army professing to be his, should not work that obedience, that fidelity, to their supreme magistrates, that levied them and paid them." [37]

(We cannot refrain here from pointing out how contradictory is this condemnation, applying as it does to the army's dissolution of an assembly in no way representative, to Milton's justification of the same army's dissolution of the 1640 representative Long Parliament. Thirsting for political justice, Milton kept his eye steadily fixed on the end of government he desired. The means to that end was no consideration with him. Nor is there any evidence that he ever fully visualized the thousand tight threads that make of one piece, if not of one color, traditions, public opinion, positive law, and permanent reform. It was only when the method of governmental control seemed to restrict liberty that he questioned its validity.)

The state being now in anarchy, Milton says in *A Letter to a Friend*, the first action must be to secure a senate or general council to preserve peace, levy taxes, and represent the country in foreign relations. If the Rumpers are to be called back, and it is plain that Milton would like them to be, there will not be wanting men to mediate between them and the army. If the army does not want the Rump again, then the only resource is for the army to call a Parliament of its own choosing, members of which, in Milton's opinion, should be allowed to sit only on condition that they stand for renunciation of kingship and liberty of conscience. Whichever method be followed, Milton continues, the army committee of officers and the Parliament should bind each other by oath not to desert their mutual cause; they should solemnly agree to uphold each other and to abjure a single person as long as they continue alive. That is, he believes a Parliament chosen either way would be capable and worthy of continuing indefinitely in office they being bound to support the army and the army being bound during life to stand by the Parliament. Here is the proposal in Milton's own words: "that the army be kept up, and all these officers in their places *during life,* and so likewise *parliament* or counsellors of state; which will be in no way unjust, considering their merits on either side, in council or in field." [38]

It is precisely this same scheme for a perpetual senate, without, however, mention of a mutual oath, that Milton enlarged upon four months later in his *Readie & Easie Way.* The Rumpers, having been re-established by Monk in their old power, had decided on February 4 to fill up the House to the number of four hundred members; they were determined, however, that these men should be staunch republicans by defining their qualifications in advance. This is the body of men whom Milton proposes to continue in power indefinitely, men of sturdy commonwealth convictions, likely enough to continue the hated state church; but, on the other hand, men who will grant at least partial liberty of conscience and unqualifiedly abjure kingship. Milton's motives are apparent: he wants to make permanent the power of the extreme republicans; he wants to continue it until such a time as monarchy will be thought of no more. Then will the Commonwealth have had a number of years in which to establish itself, when the people will have become "satisfied and delighted with the decent order, ease, and benefit thereof."

There are several passages in this first edition of *The Readie & Easie Way* which show how sturdily Milton supported the Rump as a body which should perpetuate itself. He declares that "God hath . . . wonderfully now a third time brought together our old Patriots, the first Assertours of our religious and civil rights." [39] In his opinion their small number is no reason for the rabble's reproaching them; rather they should be honored as the "remainder of those faithfull worthies, who at first freed us from tyrannie, and have continu'd ever since through all changes constant to thir trust; which they have declar'd, as they may most justly and truly, that no other way they can discharge, no other way secure and confirme the peoples libertie, *but by setling them in a free Commonwealth.*" [40] Milton refers here to the unwillingness of the Rump to dissolve itself or even to fill up the House. One of their number, Sir Harry Vane, we know to have favored a perpetuation of the Rump's authority, and Vane was too prominent a leader to have stood alone in his opinion.

It can hardly be denied that the motives of the Rump, like those of Milton, were at bottom unselfish. Now for a third time, with the aid of the army, they had proved themselves energetic legislators for toleration and republicanism. They were a nineteenth-century body of men governing seventeenth-century England. No one knew better than they that they were not in the least representative; but, on the other hand, no one knew better than they that their dissolution would mean the return of monarchy and all its antagonism to the liberty of the very people who condemned them. Hence their desire to continue in power, and Milton was one with them: "And the government being now in so many faithful hands, next under God, so able, especially filling up their number, as they intend, and abundantly sufficient so happily to govern us, why should the nation so little know thir own interest as to seek change, to deliver themselves up to meer titles and vanities, to persons untri'd, unknown, necessitous, implacable, and every way to be suspected: to whose power when we are once made subject, not all these our Patriots nor all the wisdom or force of the well affected joind with them can deliver us again from most certain miserie and thraldom." [41] While it is true that Milton and the Rump wanted liberty for themselves more than they wanted liberty for the many, they had at heart the welfare of their country.

Although Milton wrote the body of the first edition of *The Readie & Easie Way* before February 21, when the Presbyterian secluded members were admitted, he published it, with an explanatory preface, on March 3. Why he was still willing after February 21 to make his proposal public, now that he could no longer hope for the Rump with additional members of like convictions to be continued in power, appears from the preface itself. He finds that Parliament is still strongly favorable to the Commonwealth: "Yet not a little rejoicing to hear declar'd, the resolution of all those who are now in power, . . . tending to the establishment of a free Commonwealth, and to remove if it is possible, this unsound humour of returning to old bondage, instilld of late by some deceivers, and nourished from bad principles and fals apprehensions among too many of the people, I thought best not to suppress what I had written, hoping it may perhaps (the Parlament now sitting more full and frequent) be now much more useful than before: yet submitting what hath reference to the state of things as they then stood, to present constitutions; and so the same end be persu'd, not insisting on this or that means to obtain it." [42] From the admission of the Presbyterian members, Milton knew that there could not now be that liberty of conscience for which he had hoped; but there still remained the hope that this Parliament, two-thirds Presbyterian, and one-third the valiant old Rumpers who still retained their seats, would in some way frustrate the restoration of kingship, especially as long as General Monk held out for the Commonwealth. Hence Milton decided to send out after all his proposal for a perpetual senate. Originally a device by which he thought the extreme republicans, by the aid of the army, could continue indefinitely in power, his plan had now become his last refuge in the path of onrushing monarchy. Even a perpetual senate of Presbyterians would be better than an hereditary line of monarchs, and a Presbyterian state church more agreeable than the hated prelates.

The Parliament of the Secluded Members had decided, however, not to discuss the question of a new constitution, but to call a full and free Parliament to meet on April 25 for this purpose.[43] Every one knew that unless something were done to elect only men favorable to the Commonwealth, the new Parliament would be overwhelmingly royalist in sentiment. To prevent such a Parliament from taking their seats, Milton apparently hoped that a direct appeal to General Monk would have an influence; perhaps a letter would show him the way by which a Commonwealth Parliament could be assured. Accordingly, some time in late March or early April,[44] Milton sent a letter to Monk entitled, *The Present Means and Brief Delineation of a Free Commonwealth, Easy to Be Put in Practice and that Without Delay*. In order that the members of the new Parliament may be "such as are already firm, or inclinable to constitute a free commonwealth,". Milton proposes that Monk call up to him immediately the "chief gentlemen out of every county," and explain to them the necessity of continuing the Commonwealth. Then, he continues, let Monk put into the hands of these men the temporary possession of the government. These men will return by Monk's instructions to their various towns and cities and cause to be elected "by such at least of the people who are rightly qualified, a standing council in every city and great town." They are also to cause to be elected members of the perpetual Parliament or Grand Council, as Milton prefers it should be called, these members "to be engaged for a commonwealth." In this manner Milton hopes that by having the supervision of elections placed directly in the hands of Monk's representatives, a Grand Council loyal to the Commonwealth will be chosen; whereas, if the elections are left to local jurisdiction without any pressure from Monk for Commonwealth men only, a royalist Parliament is only too certain. There is no record that Monk ever made any comment on this letter to any of his friends, or to Milton himself.

No reply from Monk forthcoming, and Milton's enemies mean-while spreading forth all manner of abuse of his perpetual Parlia-ment, there was now no one except the people to whom Milton could appeal on behalf of the Commonwealth. How little he could expect from the rank and file of his countrymen! Yet he grasped even this straw of hope: "advise we now the people." Hastily revising the first edition of *The Readie & Easie Way*, here adding passages to prove the efficacy of his perpetual Parliament (now to him symbolical of republican government), and here removing passages or phrases applicable to religious liberty, now no longer possible, Milton sent forth his last Commonwealth plea less than ten days before the new Parliament was to meet at Westminster. But the people had their hearts set upon a king. How little they had heeded the blind Milton's warning and advice appeared soon after. In the words of Ludlow: "The nominal House of Commons, tho called by a Commonwealth writ in the name of the Keepers of the Liberties of England, passed a vote, 'That the government of the nation should be by King, Lords, and Commons, and that Charles Stuart should be proclaimed King of England.' "

Such was the end of Milton's relations to the Parliaments from 1640 to 1660. In these tempestuous twenty years Milton had seen his hopes for England glow, fade, and finally darken into tragic gloom. The grasping by his countrymen for the pottage of kingship, their total disregard of "The Good Old Cause" and all that it

symbolized to him, the enveloping certainty of their servile ignorance—these were the drops which distilled the tragedy of his life.

The words of Milton which best interpret his conception of
Parliament as a governing body are these: "So the same end be
persu'd, [I am] not insisting upon this or that means to obtain
it." Such sentiment is typical of Milton's political temperament.
It offers some explanation for his successively appealing to the Long
Parliament, to the Rump, to Cromwell, to the Rump again, to
General Monk and finally to the Long Parliament a second time.
Parliament was to him any group of patriotic men working for the
liberties he cherished and strong enough to be recognized as legislators. Nothing could have been further removed from extreme
democratic seventeenth-century theory than the means by which
he hoped to achieve liberty; yet the liberty itself, notably liberty
of speech and conscience, was inherent in the Leveller doctrine.

Milton's conception of Parliament was, then, in no wise democratic by seventeenth-century standards. His perpetual Parliament,
in particular, was a more aristocratic body than the most avowed
royalist would have cared to see established. On the other hand,
it should not be forgotten that in urging as his final conviction
the transfer of all authority from king to Parliament Milton was
advocating a principle which was to become fixed in the tradition
of English democracy. And his valiant stand for this principle in
the face of that immediately powerful but ultimately weak English
monarchy remains a landmark in the history of republicanism.

CHAPTER XI

UTOPIA BORN OF CRISIS

A. THE PERPETUAL SENATE

A CLOSE study of *The Readie & Easie Way,* the pamphlets which preceded it, and the historical situation which called it forth, presents indisputable evidence that Milton's proposed commonwealth was not his ideal commonwealth. It was fused in the cauldron of his boiling hopes and fears as a practical solution of a pressing national problem. Milton disclaims, in fact, the idea that his proposal should be classed among the "exotic models." The way he suggests is "plain, easy, and open before us"; and this fact he urges as the principal reason for its adoption. His plan is not one that requires encumbrances, new terms, or new forms.

Even Milton's perpetual senate grew more from the exigencies of the moment than from his study of Greek and Roman models or from his reading of *Franco-Gallia.* In our discussion of Milton's relations to Parliament we have attempted to show how his desire for a permanent council was identified originally with his desire to see the Rump continued in power. Of the five Parliaments which had met from 1640 to 1659, the Rump appeared to Milton to be the only one which had the courage, energy, or conviction enough to reform England as he thought it should be reformed. They, at least, had taken some steps toward religious liberty, inflexibly subordinated the military to the civil rule, defied even Cromwell, legislated with their backs to the wall against both the army and the undoubted will of the majority of laymen. Furthermore Milton knew he was not alone in favoring the continuation of the Rump or some form of permanent council. Sir Harry Vane, in whom he had unlimited confidence, had proposed exactly such a plan in his tract, *A Healing Question propounded and resolved, . . . with a Desire to apply Balsome to the Wound before it becomes incurable.* [1] Moreover, from the Rump's unwillingness to dissolve during the

297

years 1649–53, it was clear that Sir Harry was not the only one among their number who wished to continue their power as long as possible; they felt, and with some reason, that they had proved themselves more capable and energetic than the unwieldy Long Parliament. But not only that. They knew that once they relinquished their power, there could be but one of two results. Either the military under Cromwell would rule entirely, or the preponderant sentiment of the nation would return the kingship were a full Parliament called. Though Milton's proposal for a permanent council became his last refuge against the Restoration, it originally sprang, therefore, from the necessity in his and in other minds of maintaining the revolutionary program known as "the Good Old Cause."

There had been, according to John Lilburne, a movement afoot as early as 1649 to continue the Rump indefinitely in power. In *The Legal Fundamental Liberties of the People of England,* he writes: "And in my observations and discourses at westminster, I apparently found it to be as I feared, their maine endeavors being closely carryed on to *perpetuate this Parliament forever* . . . to govern this declared Free Nation arbitrarily." [2] In the first edition of this same pamphlet, Lilburne declares that he refused to support "so unjust and illegal a fabrick as I judged an everlasting Parliament . . . to be." [3] He quotes from the army's own declarations against any perpetual Parliament; they had pledged themselves to oppose any attempt to "engross that power for perpetuity into the hands of any particular persons, or party whatsoever." From this evidence it is clear Milton's perpetual Parliament may have been seriously projected eleven years before he proposed it. It is also clear how strenuously this constitutional radical opposed the measures Milton wanted to see adopted.

Milton begins his defence of a perpetual senate by citing the need of every government of a "general council of ablest men, chosen by the people to consult of public affairs from time to time for the public good." [4] In such a council the people would place the sovereign power; and although Milton does not make plain how the people under his plan of government would take back the sovereign power, he insists that it would be only delegated to the council, not lodged in them permanently. Milton then defines the powers which he would have his council possess. They should have control of the army and navy. Subject to the approval of inspectors from the various local assemblies, they should levy and expend the public moneys, and make civil laws not reserved to the action of these assemblies. They should have charge of all foreign relations, including declarations of war and treaties of peace. They should regulate commerce. Finally, they should select from their own number a council of state.

Then it is that Milton brings forth his reasons for granting life tenure to the members of this council. In the first place, their business is continuous and frequently urgent; a general council should be "ready always to prevent or answer all occasions." By having the same men continually at the helm of state, the country would be sure of skilful and able legislators. "The ship of the commonwealth is always under sail; they sit at the stern, and if they steer well, what need is there to change them, it being rather dangerous?" [5] Recalling to his readers that kingship is counted more admirable because of its steady continuance in office, Milton shows how, from this point of view, a perpetual council would be much more satisfactory than kingship. For whereas the death of a king often may result in dangerous changes, that of a senate would breed no such commotion; the commonwealth would continue in its course undisturbed. Here it is evident that Milton is trying to meet the demand of the whole nation for stability and permanency, stability and permanency which at that time seemed far more important than their particular rights or representation in Parliament. Milton knew, further, that to the country as a whole the king was a symbol for an unchanging government, under which, whether or not it was the desirable kind of government, they could live with some sense of security. The permanent council will, he hopes, replace the kingship in their minds as a symbol of governmental permanence. Having given theoretical reasons for its likely success, Milton cites historical examples of his perpetual senate. The Sanhedrin among the Jews, the Areopagus among the Greeks, and the Senate among the Romans, had all consisted of members chosen for life. Such are Milton's positive arguments. He has anticipated, however, some objections to his plan.

These objections Milton proceeds somewhat unsuccessfully to answer. The first is the need for the traditional succession of Parliaments. Milton does not see what can be gained by them: "they are

much likelier continually to unsettle rather than to settle a free
government, to breed commotions, changes, novelties, and uncertainties, to bring neglect upon present affairs and opportunities,
while all minds are in suspense with expectation of a new assembly,
and the assembly, for a good space, taken up with the new settling
of itself." [6] Moreover, there is always the spectacle of one Parliament changing or nullifying what the previous Parliament has done:
"till all law be lost in the multitude of clashing statutes." Nor can
Milton accept the proposal of rotation. In the first edition of *The
Readie & Easie Way,* he somewhat hesitatingly yields, it is true, to
Harrington's theory of "partial rotation," by which a third of the
senators would give up their offices annually to be replaced by new
representatives. But in the second edition Milton casts aside even
partial rotation as "having too much affinity with the wheel of
Fortune." And he is absolute in his renunciation of any national
popular assembly to act as a curb on the aristocratic one he has
proposed. This had been Harrington's proposal in *Oceana,* and Milton admits that such assemblies had sprung up in the ancient countries almost side by side with the perpetual senates. But rather than
helping the people, Milton insists, these assemblies are likely to
bring their country to ruin. He then points to the example of the
Roman populace, which, once being granted the tribunes, grasped
more and more power from the senate until they had prepared
themselves for tyranny under Scylla. To have an assembly of a
thousand men, a third of them rotating annually, as Harrington
proposed, would be, continues Milton, to set up a cumbrous and
unmanageable legislative body. It would be so large that the members could not discuss any question thoroughly; and it would be
likely to disagree with the perpetual senate. "The much better way
doubtless will be . . . to defer the changing or circumscribing of
our senate."

B. THE FRANCHISE

Milton's conception of the franchise which should prevail in
electing his original national senate shows further how much he
feared the voices of the many. A number of citizens "who are
rightly qualified" should nominate as many candidates as they wish
for the parliamentary offices. Then a smaller number of citizens "of
a better breeding" than the original large number, should choose

from the first group a second group of candidates. After a third or fourth repetition of this process, the sifting both of voters and of candidates, the exact number would remain to fill up the seats of the senate. The following graphic representation may serve to clarify it:

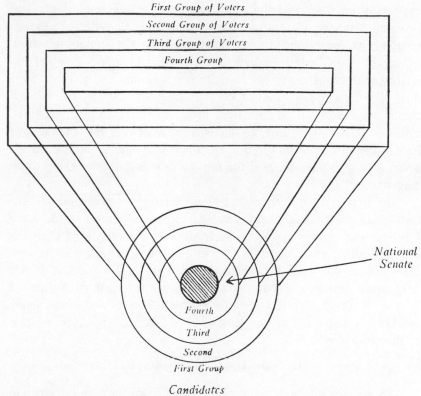

Candidates

Milton does not specify how he would choose the second, third, or fourth groups of voters. He simply states that the second group should be "others of a better breeding." Thus, as the graph indicates, Milton would have allowed the first selection of candidates to be made by the entire voting population of his time (those possessing personal or real property to the value of two hundred pounds or more); but the final selection of Parliament members from the third group of candidates would have been reserved to approximately one-fourth of the voting population. In the same ratio the final group of Parliament members would have been approximately one-fourth of the original list of candidates.

The whole plan is highly theoretical and impractical. Unlike the perpetual senate, Milton's idea of the franchise seems to have had no relation to current affairs, but was derived from Plato's *Laws*. According to Plato, the franchise should be limited to those having a record of military service. These men nominate as many candidates as they wish by engraving their names on tablets and bringing them to a central place of voting. The three hundred nominees whose names appear most often on the tablets are then again voted on by all soldiers, each elector bringing a tablet inscribed with the name of his favorite nominee among the three hundred. The hundred nominees receiving the most votes by this second choice are then reduced to a final group of thirty-seven by a third choosing: "The third time, he that wishes shall vote for whomsoever he wishes out of the hundred . . . Then they shall test the thirty-seven men who have secured the most votes, and declare them to be magistrates." [7]

The important difference between Plato's plan and that of Milton lies in the selection of voters; for whereas Milton would have three or four classes of voters, each of a "better breeding" than the one preceding, Plato permits the whole voting population to vote three times. We need hardly conclude that Plato's method is not only more democratic but decidedly more practical than that of Milton. Nothing of political import which Milton wrote so clearly reflects his disregard of constitutional procedure as his conception of the franchise.

C. THE LOCAL ASSEMBLIES

While rejecting both a popular assembly and a popular election of his aristocratic senate, Milton makes an important concession to democratic sentiment in his proposal of local assemblies. The assemblies in the counties are to be elected, not by any limited ballot, but by the full number of voters. They are to make "their own judicial laws, or use those that are, and execute them by their elected judicatures and judges without appeal, in all things of civil government between man and man." [8] Whether Milton would have permitted these local assemblies, in preference to the perpetual senate, decide upon such fundamental matters as freedom of speech and rejection of tithes, Milton does not disclose. He implies, however, that they would have considerable voice in such problems by giving the majority of the sixty assemblies the important power of rejecting or ratifying any widely-significant laws passed by the national senate.[9] This is important from a democratic point of view, inasmuch as the senate would thereby be forced to submit only laws applicable to all classes, and not laws favorable to one particular group.

Though Milton probably felt that he had to make some concession to the masses, we should be unfair to conclude that his primary assemblies were only a concession and not an integral part of his proposed republic. It is, in fact, too important a cog in the machine to have been considered by him an appendage. All laws "that shall be made, or any of great concernment to public liberty" are to be submitted to the county legislatures for approval. Although Milton unfortunately does not amplify his notion of such laws, we know already the principal subjects he deemed to be without the realm of the magistrates. But not only the emphasis Milton gives to his assemblies shows he felt a real need for them; his whole spirit of individualism led him to desire a more decentralized government. We know from his experience with the Long Parliament how much he resented their sending committees to far-off counties; their abolition is, in fact, the first advantage he called to mind in the establishment of the primary assemblies: they would "henceforth quite annihilate the odious power and name of committees." Furthermore, we know how oppressive had been Cromwell's military rule of England through his major-generals, and how plainly Milton had objected to the increase of naval and military forces. Not only had he objected to the increase in the central power through stronger armies, but he had deplored the increase in laws, particularly those laws prohibiting "innocent freedoms." Add to this evidence Milton's conviction that for such men as he believed himself to be, that is, for those in whom Christ had implanted Himself, there should be effective no civil law whatever, and we may readily see why he was willing, even at this period of his most pronounced distrust, to give more power and freedom to local self-government. And in so far as he advanced the cause of decentralization, we may safely say that his conception of local assemblies contributed to democratic theory.

We find, then, Milton's political convictions of 1660 in a measure finding expression in his proposed commonwealth. In the local assemblies we discover both a necessary concession to the popular vote and his naturally strong predilection for local and individual freedom; in the franchise as he proposes it appears his profound distrust of the masses and their ability to select political leaders wisely; and in the perpetual senate we discover at once his life-long belief that power should be lodged in the hands of the virtuous few and his complete departure from any form of single person rule. In a *Letter to a Friend* Milton had proposed as an integral part of his model the provision that neither the legislature nor the army might obstruct liberty of conscience or attempt to restore kingship. But such a constitutional provision reserving to the people certain inalienable rights does not appear in *The Readie & Easie Way*. We see, therefore, how little Milton was affected by the Leveller con-stitutional doctrine, that defining of powers and guaranteeing of basic privileges which was to become the instrument of government in America and in most democratic countries. Nor was he, as we shall see, sympathetic with the basic reforms of that most famous seventeenth-century model, Harrington's *Oceana*.

D. HARRINGTON AND MILTON

Like Milton, Harrington was sincerely attempting to serve his country in writing *Oceana,* not merely to propose an impossible utopia. This is evident, not only from the model itself, and from the history of its printing, but from Harrington's recognition of Crom-well as the principal agent through whom his government might be realized. When *Oceana* was being printed, Toland relates, it was seized by Cromwell's officers and taken to Whitehall. Harrington, as a last resort, applied to Cromwell's daughter, Lady Claypole, who "acted the part of a Princess very naturally, obliging all persons with her civility, and frequently interceding for the unhappy." [10] Having amused the Princess' three-year-old daughter while waiting for her in the antechamber, Harrington playfully threatened Lady Claypole with the theft of her daughter in revenge for a similar transgression against him. When Harrington explained that the child of his brain, *Oceana,* had been stolen by her father, the princess promised not only to intercede for Harrington, but to ac-quaint her father with Harrington's design to dedicate *Oceana* to England's Protector. Lady Claypole kept her promise, and *Oceana* was published.

But Harrington's dedication of *Oceana* to Cromwell was only a fragment of Cromwell's real significance in Harrington's model. It was through Cromwell that the whole scheme was to be put into operation. It was by Cromwell's power that Harrington proposed a Council of Legislators be established, their doors open to all suggestions, their avowed purpose being to construct a constitution for the commonwealth.[11] This having been done, and the result being Harrington's own model, it was through Cromwell's power that the new government was to be inaugurated. Harrington then visualized an enthusiastic reception of his government by the people of England. And so great was their enthusiasm for the man who initiated it, Cromwell himself, that the Senate is to elect him Lord Strategus for life. His imagination flying still further into the future, Harrington foresaw the immeasurable glory to encircle Cromwell at the end of his fruitful life. He even prophesied a colossal equestrian statue of Cromwell, to be set up on the piazza of Westminster Hall inscribed with glowing predictions of Cromwell's immortal fame.[12] Such compliments, however, and the honor not only of being the efficient cause, but the sole ruler of the new commonwealth for life, did not appeal to the Protector. For having read *Oceana*, he declared that "the Gentleman had like to trapan him out of his Power, but that what he got by the Sword he would not quit for a little paper Shot: adding in his usual cant, that he approv'd the Government of a single Person as little as any of 'em, but that he was forc'd to take upon him the Office of a High Constable, to preserve the Peace among the several Partys in the Nation." [13]

Having considered the place of Harrington's model in the trend of events during the Protectorate, and the place Harrington hoped it would assume,[14] let us briefly examine *Oceana* itself. By Harrington's plan the ten thousand parishes of England were to be divided into one hundred hundreds, these in turn to be separated into fifty tribes, corresponding roughly to the sixty English counties.[15] This being done, all the people were to be divided first according to their age; all men over thirty were to be citizens eligible to vote and hold office; men between eighteen and thirty were not to vote, but were to serve their country by devoting part of their time to military training.[16] Citizens over thirty were further divided according to their wealth; those having property or positions yielding an income of one hundred pounds a year were to be classified as the horse, by reason of their assembling in military fashion on horseback; those not possessing the specified amount of property were to be called the foot.[17] The horse were the property owners; the foot were the large number of citizens possessing little or no fixed wealth.

Harrington's popular assembly was to be elected in the following manner. The horse of the fifty tribes were to elect through their officers three deputies to the assembly from each tribe, making a total of 150 members annually elected by the property owners. The foot were to elect four members from each tribe, or total of two hundred a year. Thus both horse and foot would elect annually 350 representatives. In three years there would be, therefore, a representative assembly of 1050 members. But at the time of the fourth annual election, the 350 members elected the first year would come to the end of their three-year term, and thus make way for the fourth group to be elected. This popular assembly, according to Harrington, thus operating on a rotation basis, would have no power whatever of initiating laws; but it would have the *sole* power of ratification or rejection of any laws the senate should propose.

Harrington's senate, the mainspring of the commonwealth, was to be selected by property owners and composed of property owners alone. The horse of the fifty tribes were to elect annually two knights from each of the tribes to sit in the senate; in three years this body, therefore, would have been composed of three hundred members. In the fourth year the hundred members elected the first year would have retired to give place to the regularly elected senators. The senate thus would have followed the same plan of rotation used by the assembly. By Harrington's plan it would have had the sole power of suggesting laws, but none whatever of approving them. In addition to the power of initiating laws, the senate would also have had the power of electing the executive officers; the six most important of these officers were to be the Lord Strategus, the Lord Orator, the First Censor, the Second Censor, the Third Commissioner of the Seal, and the Third Commissioner of the Treasury. The first four of these offices were to be annual and the last two triennial; thus the most important executive officers, corresponding to the two Roman consuls, were to be elected annually by the senate.

These six executive officers, called by Harrington the Signiory, would be by virtue of their offices also members of the various

Councils (Religion, War, Trade, and Provosts), these councils to be perpetuated by the rotation plan, four or five being elected each year.[18] Harrington had, we may conclude, given the power of executing the laws to the Signiory, that of proposing them to the senate, and that of approving them to the national assembly. From this brief analysis of Harrington's method, let us turn to certain provisions and principles which were, we know, of particular interest to Milton.

Harrington's primary principle, in verification of which he cites voluminous proofs from Greek, Roman, Spartan, and Venetian history, is that government should be a mixture of monarchy, aristocracy, and democracy, else it will perish.[19] If the three orders are not blended, he says, then the particular order in power, be it the one, the few, or the many, will take advantage of the other two orders to deprive them of their land.[20] If, Harrington continues, one of the orders acquires in this manner more than one-half of the country's land, the government is doomed to downfall by rebellion. Every government should, therefore, keep the land so distributed that no one class owns more than one-half of the total land. To this end he proposes in *Oceana* his famous Agrarian law:

An equal *Agrarian* is a perpetual Law establishing and preserving the balance of Dominion by such a distribution, that no one Man or number of Men, within the compass of the Few or *Aristocracy*, can com to over power the whole People by their possessions in Lands.[21]

Corollaries to this law are Harrington's suggestions that no man should give any of his children lands on which the annual revenue exceeds two thousand pounds; that no man be permitted to purchase lands which with those he already possesses would yield more than this same revenue; that "if a man has a daughter, or Daughters, except she be an Heiress, or they be Heiresses, he shall not leave or give to any one of them in Marriage, or otherwise, for her portion, above the value of one thousand five hundred Pounds in Lands, Goods, Monys"; [22] and finally, that the surplus in the national treasury be used to buy for orphan girls tracts of land so that it might be further distributed.[23] Such an Agrarian law would have blotted out primogeniture with one stroke; and Harrington argues closely that this traditional method of inheritance was unfair to the commonwealth.[24] He declares, moreover, that the Agrarian would discourage the wretched custom of marrying for money.[25] We may conclude that Harrington expected the Agrarian to distribute wealth in the form of land, in order that people of all classes may have the means of subsistence, content of mind, and loyalty to their country.[26]

The Agrarian law is one of the two fundamentally democratic provisions of *Oceana;* the rotation plan, inherent, of course, in democratic constitutions such as that of the United States, is the other. Both of these, however, Milton rejects in *The Readie & Easie Way.* The Agrarian law, he declares, dismissing it rather summarily, was "never successful, but the cause rather of sedition, save where it began reasonably with first possession." [27] Further, it is not practicable. Milton implies that it would bring about a "perilous . . . injurious alteration or circumscription of men's lands and properties." [28] He denies that in a commonwealth such as he proposes one man or a few can acquire enough lands to "need the hedge of an Agrarian law." [29] Harrington's second design, that of rotation, did, as we have seen, receive some approbation from Milton in the first edition of *The Readie & Easie Way;* but in the second, he strikes it out as leaving too much to chance. It would lose for the commonwealth some of her most trusted counsellors, and substitute for them "raw, inexperienced, and otherwise affected" men. Thus he dismisses both rotation and the Agrarian law, the two elements of *Oceana* most closely allied to democratic theory.

Whether Milton would have accepted these devices under ordinary circumstances, when the country was not in such dire peril, we have no means of knowing.

There is evidence, however, that the exigencies of the moment were the determining factor in his repudiation of Harrington's democratic devices. Knowing that elections will mean the return of royalists to Parliament, he objects to the rotation plan: it will bring in "otherwise affected" men. As we know from his first edition, he did not object to rotation drastically as a method of election. But it would leave too much to chance; that is, it might permit the return of monarchy, and Milton was writing feverishly to preserve the commonwealth. Expediency was also a factor with Milton in his repudiation of the Agrarian law. He objected to it because it would disturb the balance of ownership throughout the land. It was too complicated and perilous to consider amid such confusion. It was a far too radical departure from custom, a departure which he might have accepted, along with rotation, in a more peaceful period. Not a time to be concerned with ideal governments: the times pleaded desperately for action.

Despite his rejection of Harrington's democratic devices, and notwithstanding their diverging views of ancient democracy (whereas Harrington was sympathetic with the lower orders, Milton had little use for men like the Gracchi, heroes of plebeian Rome and promulgators of a democratic Agrarian law), the two men fully agreed in a number of essentials. Like Milton, Harrington would have had each congregation elect its own minister; he would have granted liberty of conscience to all Protestants; he held some men unfit to be free; he believed liberty and not democracy the main end of government; he felt that the few wise should have the most power; he would have given the preponderance of power to an aristocratic senate; he believed that government exists only by contract, that the will of the people is the supreme law, and that men are born free by the law of nature. Both Harrington and Milton provided for a universal system of education, though Harrington is more definite: he would have required all to attend school to the age of fifteen, the expense if necessary being borne by the state. Both men felt the need of an aristocracy, but Harrington's aristocracy, unlike Milton's, was frankly an aristocracy of wealth. Even here, however, the two men did not separate widely; for although Milton scorned wealth as a criterion of aristocracy, he was not unaware that men of virtue more often than not are men of property also. The beliefs of the two men are, therefore, strikingly similar: both were classicists who believed that the welfare of the many should be trusted to the superior few.

It was in the application of their theories, rather than in fundamentals, that the two men differed. Harrington, the cool historical analyst, had traced the rebellions of Greece and Rome to their roots. He saw first that one of the principal destroyers of governments had been long tenure of power not answerable to the will of the people; to overcome this obstacle he proposed Venice's remedy, rotation. But a far more common source of revolution he knew to have been economic inequality; and for this he proposed the Roman remedy, the Agrarian law. Harrington was one of the first of English constitutional thinkers to identify governmental stability with an equitable distribution of wealth, and to propose a means of correlating them. Milton, on the other hand, had too little knowledge either of political science or of economics successfully to apply the political lessons of antiquity to English politics of his own time.

_____

To recapitulate: Of Milton's three principal provisions for a commonwealth (a highly-aristocratic perpetual senate, a severely limited franchise, and popular local assemblies) the first two, the franchise and the senate, are definitely less democratic than their counterparts in *Oceana*; only the popular assemblies, when compared with Harrington's representative body of one thousand, approach a corresponding recognition of the people's will. Moreover, Milton's repudiation of both the Agrarian law and rotation was a blow at Harrington's inherently democratic hypothesis which tends to heighten the aristocratic tone of *The Readie & Easie Way*. More momentarily practical to set in motion than Harrington's cumbersome mobilizing of horse and foot citizens, it certainly was. But from the standpoint of radical political theory we can only conclude with Toland that it is definitely inferior to Harrington's model.

Neither Milton nor Harrington, however, used the constitutional methods of extreme seventeenth-century democracy. Though the Levellers were scattered by 1660, and produced none of the "exotic models" of the pre-Restoration months, they had in the years 1647–49 initiated a principle and a provision which were to become integral parts of American and English governments respectively. The principle, which is inherent in the American constitution, was to define those rights so inalienable to the individual citizen that no government, local or national could amend or destroy them. Though Harrington's *Oceana* suggests a number of personal liberties, it does not secure them constitutionally against legislative interference. The Leveller provision we mention is that of a single representative house elected by manhood suffrage. A glance at the present English government, with its single representative assembly elected not only by manhood but by womanhood suffrage as well, indicates the modernity of the Leveller legislative doctrine. In the history, therefore, of both English and American democratic constitutionalism, the names of both Milton and Harrington must give place and precedence to those of Lilburne, Overton, Prince, and Walwyn.

CHAPTER XII

WINSTANLEY, MILTON, AND LILBURNE
ON ECONOMIC CHANGE

E ACH radical and revolutionary group of Milton's England was striving for those privileges that the old order had failed to provide for its members. The Presbyterian gentry sought to supersede the king's power with their own, to set up a constitutional monarchy in which ecclesiastically Presbyterianism would rule. More individualistic in matters of conscience, Milton and the Independents envisioned a church without tithes or bishops or secular compulsion, and a state free from the domination of king and nobility. The Levellers, representing large sections of the lower middle class, the apprentices, the artisans, the soldiers who had risen from the ranks, demanded all this and more: they insisted upon a drastic extension of the franchise and a constitutional guarantee of those personal liberties which, roughly speaking, now appear in the American Bill of Rights. Well fed, well housed, and well clothed these groups in the main must have been; in their manifestoes we find no demands for jobs, few complaints of landlords robbing the poor, no revelations of masters mistreating their apprentices. Possessing a substantial degree of economic security, the parties of the center and left-of-center sought those spiritual, intellectual, and political privileges denied to them under Charles and James. Renowned and powerful were their leaders: Cromwell, Bradshaw, Lilburne, Milton, Ludlow, Vane.

For at least half of England's 4,000,000 inhabitants, however, according to the eminent historian, Thorold Rogers,[1] the query, "What shall we eat, wherewithal shall we be clothed?" wanted an answer more insistently than any other, theological, political, or domestic. The *Moderate* for April 17-24, 1649, states that 16,000 families in Westmoreland County "have not bread to put in their mouths." "We are in Wellinborrow in one Parish 1169 persons that receive Alms," runs another contemporary account. "But as yet we see nothing is done, nor any man that goeth about it; we have spent all we have . . . our wives and children cry for bread, our lives are a burden to us, divers of us having 5.6.7.8.9. in Family, and we cannot get bread for one of them by our labor; rich mens hearts are hardened." [2] And Winstanley complains: "At this very day poor people are forced to work in some places at 4, 5, and 6 pence a day; in other places for 8, 10, and 12 pence a day." [3] Such were the wages while mutton, beef, and pork sold for three pence a pound, butter six pence, cheese two pence halfpenny, hens a shilling each, eggs four to five pence a dozen, salt eight and nine pence a pound. While the average laborer at ten, twelve, or fifteen pence a day could not have earned more than fifteen or sixteen pounds a year, his bare expenses amounted to eighteen or nineteen pounds:

Cottage and garden	24s a year
Food	£ 9, 1s a year
Fuel	26s a year
Clothing	£ 6, 9s a year
Tools	15s a year

Total, £18,15s

At best, then, the laborer was frequently unable to gain a comfortable subsistence. His real economic lot may be further clarified by comparing the income of this class with that of other occupations. A lord received 2800 pounds, a bishop 1300, a knight 650, a country gentleman 280, a merchant 400, a lawyer 140, a free-hold farmer 50, and an artisan 40. Writing in 1696 Gregory King estimated that in 1688 laborers, servants, cottagers, paupers, and common soldiers and seamen comprised half the population and received 9,000,000 pounds, or about one-fifth of the total national yearly income.[5] During the Civil War the proportion returned to the laborers could not have exceeded this percentage. What intensified the complaints of the poor during this time was the scanty harvests of the 1640's, bringing with them, during 1648, 1649, and 1650 the highest prices of the century. Despite increase in earnings of as much as 50%, real wages fell: economic security for the great mass of agricultural workers was shifting and uncertain.

True it was, indeed, that thousands of this multitude of laborers, a "herd confused" as Milton could have called them, fought loyally for the king without questioning the inevitability of their economic lot; and thousands more fought for Cromwell without hoping that higher wages would follow the abolition of kingship. True, too, that the mass of them were ignorant, inarticulate, content perforce with the hardships bequeathed them.

A few leaders did rise, however, to demand for the laborers what the old order had failed to provide for them, that is, access to the natural wealth of the land. And the greatest of these leaders, ejected spontaneously from the turmoil of discontent, was Gerrard Winstanley, an unlearned man, a man of little popularity or notice in the newspapers of the day, a man of no oratorical or military talent such as Lilburne possessed, a man whose petition Cromwell thought too inconsequential even to acknowledge. With all his might Winstanley strove for the economic liberation of the agricultural masses; without this freedom the reforms of Lilburne and Cromwell and Milton were to him as chaff whirled by the wind. Attacking the *Agreement* principles, Winstanley wrote:

A thing called *An Agreement of the People* . . . is too low and too shallow to free us at all. . . . What stock . . . is provided for the *poor, fatherless, widows*, and *impoverished people*? And what advancement of encouragement for the *laboring* and *industrious*, as to take off their burthens, is there?[6]

In like terms Winstanley's associates declared: "*England* is not a Free People, till the Poor that have no Land, have a free allowance to dig and labour the Commons." [7]

Though Winstanley was at one with Milton and Lilburne in his hatred of kingship, the king was to him always associated with the economic privileges secured to the rich from generation to generation since the time of William the Conqueror. To destroy the king without destroying these vested interests was to Winstanley no reformation at all. The Norman William, his theory runs, turned the English out of their lands, gave them to his favorites, granted control of the common land to his nobles, thus requiring the poor to pay for the use of it, had the law written in French, and required the English to pay fees to lawyers; so the Conqueror perpetuated the whole harassing system of landholding.[8] "These are some of the *Norman* Laws and Burthens, which if removed, it would be much ease and quiet to this Nation." [9] In *Light shining in Buckingham-shire* he exclaims:

Oh why are you so mad as to cry up a King? It is he and his Court and Patentee men, as Majors, Aldermen, and such creatures, that like Cormorants devoure what you should enjoy, and set up Whipping-posts and Correcting-houses to enslave you. Tis rich men that oppresse you, saith *James*.[10]

Sharing Milton's antipathy toward the established church, Winstanley bitterly denounced the "tything priests." It is they "who keep the people in blindness . . . preferring a wicked man in the place of a God, as they did *Charls Stuart*." [11] When one of the orthodox ministers actively opposed the efforts of the Diggers to take possession of the common land, "he forgets," cried Winstanley, "his Master Christ, that is persecuted in naked, hungry, and houseless members." [12] Blinding the people with the glories of Heaven, meanwhile living comfortably on a hundred pounds a year, the clergy so befuddle their parishioners that they do not demand an economic realization of Christ's teachings. "This," concludes Winstanley, "is the filthy Dreamer, and the Cloud without rain." [13] But what if a poor man, not daring to steal, says to the minister, "We that work most have least comfort in the earth, and they that work not at all, enjoy all; contrary to the Scripture which saith, *The poor and meek shall inherit the earth*"? [14] Then, exclaims Winstanley, the priest stops his mouth and tells him that by that verse was meant the inward satisfactions that the poor are to have in heaven. Thus he berates the clergymen, scoffing at their hypocrisy, taunting them with having a Heaven both here and hereafter. Why may not the poor, as well as the priests, have Heaven here on earth in the form of a decent subsistence, and Heaven hereafter too, since God is no respecter of persons? [15] Unfair as much of Winstanley's condemnation of the clergy may have been, these words after nearly three centuries assume an emphasis that gives us pause. Here, whatever its faults, was a mind fearlessly at work, doubting all precedent, submitting to no intellectual tradition, driving resolutely toward basic realities.

From the Scriptures alone Winstanley derived his fundamental economic principle (and here he parts completely from Milton, Lilburne, and Cromwell) that the earth should be made a *"common*

Treasury of livelihood to whole mankind, without respect of persons." [16] In the beginning God intended his creation to be enjoyed by all; but certain teachers and rulers hedged in much of the land, took it for themselves, and thus made other people their servants and slaves. Subsequently, through more buying and selling and expropriation, the will of God has been further frustrated. To own the land in common is to realize, therefore, the Creator's dream for man's happiness:

If ever the Creation be restored, this is the way which lies in this Two fold power:

First, *Community of Mankind,* which is comprised in the unity of spirit of Love, which is called Christ in you, or the Law writen in the heart, leading mankind into all truth, and to be of one heart and one mind.

The Second is *Community of the Earth,* for the quiet livelihood in food and raiment without using force, or restraining one another: These two Communities, or rather one in two branches, is the true Levelling which Christ will work at his more glorious appearance; for Jesus Christ the Saviour of all men, is the greatest, first, and truest Leveller that ever was spoke of in the world.

Therefore you rulers of *England,* be not ashamed not afraid of Levellers, hate them not, Christ comes to you riding upon these clouds.[17]

Time after time Winstanley returns to his conception of Jesus as an exponent of economic freedom, pointing out that the early Christians were communists, and claiming that the scriptural promise of the poor inheriting the earth is "really and materially to be fulfilled." To give the land to the poor "is the work of the true Saviour to doe, who is the true and faithful Leveller even the Spirit and power of universall love." [18] Laugh and jeer as you will at the name Leveller, cries Winstanley, "I tell you Jesus Christ . . . is the head *Leveller.*" [19] Could it possibly be, he asks bitterly, that the Creator is a "respector of persons, delighting in the comfortable Livelihood of some, and rejoycing in the miserable povertie and straits of others?" [20]

His mind "not at rest, because nothing was acted," Winstanley, accompanied by four followers, went to St. George's Hill, near Cobham in Surrey, on Sunday, April 1, 1649, and began to dig the ground, planting parsnips, carrots, and beans.[21] Within five days the number of the Diggers had increased to more than twenty; within six months, despite persecutions, their numbers were to

mount at times to fifty. On April 19, upon complaint of Henry
Sanders of Walton-upon-Thames, Parliament asked General Fairfax to disperse the Diggers. When, only a few days later, Winstanley and his fellow-Digger Everard appeared before Fairfax,
they stoutly defended their course of action, declaring that they
would disturb no man's property, but would "meddle with what was
common and untilled." [22] Upon being asked why they refused to
take off their hats in the General's presence, they said, "Because
he was but their fellow creature." Having heard them with courtesy
and respect, Fairfax was enough interested in their project to visit
them at their work about five weeks later.

In the meantime, however, persecutions had begun. Twice the
Diggers were attacked by mobs, one of which carried them to the
Walton church and there beat them; their houses were pulled down
and burned; their spades and hoes were cut to pieces; their cattle
were beaten with clubs; their corn was dug up; five of their number were kept five weeks in prison; they were attacked and beaten
a third time by men in women's clothing.[23] On April 28 *A Modest
Narrative of Intelligence* erroneously reported the Diggers' "new
Creation utterly destroyed, and by the Country people thereabouts
they are driven away, and as seekers gone a seeking." [24] The Diggers held on, though few in number, through the autumn and spring
months. "And now," wrote Winstanley, on January 1, 1650, "those
Diggers that remain, have made little Hutches to lie in like Calf-
cribs, and are cheerful; taking the spoyling of their Goods
patiently." [25]

Continuing resolute in their undertaking, the Diggers in 1649
and the spring of 1650 issued appeal after appeal for the realization
of economic as well as political reformation. On June 9 they delivered a letter to Lord Fairfax reasserting their position and protesting against harsh treatment by a Captain Stravie quartered at
Cobham. On July 11 appeared their *Appeal to the House of Commons*, protesting their arrest for trespassing at the instigation of
Thomas Lord Wenman and again demanding the common land for
all the poor people of England. And "if this freedome be not granted
quietly, you will pull the blood of cries of the poor oppressed upon
your heads." [26] No response forthcoming either from Fairfax or
the Commons, Winstanley on August 26 addressed a stirring appeal
to London and the army. It opens thus:

I am one of thy sons by freedome, and I do truly love thy peace; while I had an estate in thee, I was free to offer my Mite into thy publike Treasury Guild-hall . . . but by thy cheating sons in the theeving art of buying and selling . . . I was beaten out both of estate and trade, and forced to accept of the good will of friends crediting of me, to live a Countrey-life. . . . And London, nay England, look to thy freedom, I'le assure thee, thou art very neere to be cheated of it, and if thou lost it now after all thy boasting, truly thy posterity will curse thee.[27]

Again there was no response. After four months of silence still undeterred, Winstanley published another manifesto, *A New-yeers Gift for the Parliament and Armie,* which is probably his most effective protest against the economic order of his day. *"England* is a Prison," he writes bitterly, "the variety of subtilities in the Laws preserved by the Sword, are bolts, bars, and doors of the prison; the Lawyers are the Jaylors, and poor men are the prisoners." [28] Now that the king has been destroyed, Winstanley sees no reason why the lands which he has inherited should not immediately be turned over to the poor; this is the very marrow of the Parliament's cause. How can you effect any substantial reformation, he demands, if you destroy the king and yet not remove all those kingly privileges which have for generations oppressed the poor? [29] "Can the Turkish Bashaws hold their slaves in more bondage than these Gospelprofessing Lords of the Manors do their poor tenants? and is not this the Kingly power? O you Rulers of *England,* I pay [*sic*] see that your own acts be obeyed, and let the oppressed go free." [30] Finally, on March 26 Winstanley issued *An Appeal to all Englishmen,* a tract more triumphant and hopeful in tone than any of the Diggers' manifestoes. "Behold, behold, all *Englishmen,* The Land of *England* now is your free Inheritance: all *Kingly* and Lordly entanglements are declared against . . . The *Norman* power is beaten in the field, and his head is cut off." [31] Winstanley extends greetings to two other Digger colonies, one in Wellingborough, Northamptonshire, and one in Cox Hall, Kent; he is confident that, Parliament, London, and the army having ignored the Diggers' pleas, emancipation may be grasped by the poor themselves. Pitifully weak indeed, with no material resources and few leaders, the Diggers at the end of March, 1650, had gained their greatest momentum as a revolutionary movement. Henceforth they were too discouraged to effect even sporadic organization.

In the meantime slight notice had been given to the Diggers in the newspapers. The Digger movement lacked even momentarily the popularity that the political Levellers possessed; nor was Winstanley in any sense the dominating public figure that Lilburne was. As one might expect, however, the learned men of the time scoffed banteringly at the feeble socialist experiment. One editor wrote as follows:

> Their wives turn them out to graze on Saint *George's* hill with their fellow creatures . . . till all things be as common as themselves. Propriety is with them (its their own term) a disturbing Devil . . . these men were begotten as Frogs . . . had they been of *Adam,* they had had Passions, and then of necessity Laws . . . but do not say that I winde these men into a transcendency of folly, for in truth Nature hath saved me the labour.[32]

Another editor, however, commented favorably upon the sober life and conversation of the Diggers, and took them seriously enough to argue for property ownership as a necessary evil, the consequence of Adam's first sin! [33] In an endeavor to blacken the Diggers' reputation, their enemies accused them of owning women in common;[34] so that Winstanley was impelled to write, in February, 1650, an attack on licentiousness in general and community of women in particular.[35]

Despite repeated rebuffs, Winstanley continued to struggle for the realization of economic reformation until the spring of 1652. Like Milton, when no help was forthcoming from one authority, he appealed to another, this time to Cromwell himself. By the summer of 1650 he had drawn up detailed blueprints of his ideal commonwealth; and in February 1652, when the disorders had somewhat subsided, he presented them to Oliver. In the dedicatory epistle we discover Winstanley's biting disappointment with the turn of events; his whole state of mind in fact is evident in those burning admonitions; only two courses, he warns Cromwell, now lie open:

> Either set the land free to the oppressed Commoners, who assisted you, and payd the Army their wages: and then you will fulfil the Scriptures and you own Engagements and so take possession of your deserved Honor.
>
> Or . . . remove the Conquerors Power out of the Kings hand into

other mens, maintaining the old Laws still: And then your Wisdom and Honor is blasted forever; and you will either lose your self, or lay the Foundation of greater Slavery to posterity then you ever knew.[36]

This is plain language, but Winstanley was desperate, and his message would out. An inner voice had constantly tormented him, warning him, he says, not to bury his talent in the earth; now he presents his plan if only to quiet his spirit. Though kings are abolished, the old grievances remain: tithes, fines, heriots, the established church, the old Norman laws upheld by the same lawyers. And the poor are kept poor still. Now how can the poor be succored?

Winstanley's proposal is a communistic state without buying and selling, without money, without tithes, without hereditary titles, without inequality of income. To be governed democratically by suffrage of all men over twenty, including drunkards and sinful people, the commonwealth is to gather all classes under its wing, even after a brief period, the royalists. Parliament members, in fact all officials of the commonwealth, are to be chosen annually; for Winstanley has a pronounced dread of much power residing long in the same hands. To abolish old oppressive laws, to order the planting and reaping of the crops, and the gathering of them into communal storehouses, where each may go and secure freely what he needs; to establish a suitable postal system; to raise an army: these shall be the duties of the Parliament. Each parish is to elect three overseers, a peacemaker, a master technician, a master of the storehouses. Each family is to bring the products of its labor into the common store; no one, claims Winstanley, will lack abundant food and clothing. Anticipating the inevitable query, "And are you going to feed the idle people too?" Winstanley makes the following provisions. An idle person is first to be admonished by the overseer, then, after a month of recalcitrance, to be whipped; if he still persists in idleness, he is to lose his freedom for one year and to serve under the taskmaster, or jailer. In spite of his hatred of priests, Winstanley would allow a kind of state church to continue in his ideal England. The ministers would, however, be elected annually; they would be required to learn a trade as other workers, to work for the same wages as other men; and their function would be to lecture on philosophical, scientific, and historical as well as religious subjects, man's struggle for economic freedom to be emphasized.[37] Such in brief was the "socialist effusion" which, in the words of Gardiner, "was too far removed from the actual world to move Cromwell either to approval or indignation." [38]

After Cromwell's silent rejection Winstanley apparently ceased to hope for the realization of his dream. No more ringing appeals for the common ownership of land flowed from his pen. Whether he maintained the rationalistic spirit of *The Law of Freedom,* or sought refuge in the mysticism of his earlier years, as Lilburne was to do, is uncertain. In *The Saints Paradise* he had written: "I have no riches, no certain dwelling place, no way to get a subsistence, I am crossed in all, I have no cordiall friend, no succour from men." [39] Unembittered, he had judged his sufferings to be but the tempering of his spirit. So all must suffer "before they lie down quietly in the lap of Providence." [40] If Winstanley continued to meet adversity in the last years of his life, the spirit of all his writings gives assurance that he met it with the utmost equanimity.

Although Winstanley's career and ideals differed drastically from those of Lilburne and Milton, the three men reveal a few marked similarities. At heart deeply religious, each of the three found himself a theological rebel before he struck out against the economic or political conventions of the time. All three strenuously opposed the established church. By 1644 an Independent, Milton's religious views veered more and more toward an extreme individualism difficult to classify; he was at one with Winstanley in his hatred of a professional ministry; he, too, urged that one who preached should labor at a trade or profession. Long before he adopted Leveller views, Lilburne was a hater not only of Episcopalian but also of Presbyterian doctrine. Edwards records in horrified accents that a certain Mr. Knowles had prayed for Lilburne's release from prison.[41] Rebels in religion, Lilburne, Milton, and Winstanley held certain political convictions in common. Each hated tithes, each hated kingship and nobility, each wanted to see England a republic.

The differences among the three reformers are, of course, more striking than their similarities. Understanding more fully than either Winstanley or Milton the evolution of English law and the tenacity of English legal traditions, Lilburne favored the adoption of a new constitution based upon the consent of the people. To Milton, however, the laws were "norman gibbrish," and to Winstanley they were weighted with so much economic tyranny that to abolish them utterly would have been a happy Christian duty. Far separated, too, were these three radicals in their attitude toward war. Whereas both Milton and Lilburne accepted the Puritan belief that war can be a Christian enterprise,[42] Winstanley, who has sometimes been called the source of Quakerism, was a sincere pacifist: "Iesus Christ was Gods annointed not because he conquered with a Sword of iron, but because he conquered by love." [43] Then, too, whereas Milton and Lilburne were strongly nationalistic, Winstanley leaned to internationalism: "Not only this Common, or Heath should be taken in and Manured by the People, but all the Commons and waste Ground in . . . the whole world." [44]

Finally, in their philosophy of economic reform, our main concern in this chapter, Milton and Lilburne were as sharply hostile to Winstanley as they were to the political views of the royalists. Though all three men sprang from the middle class, only Winstanley had known actual want or had been forced through privation into intimate observation of the laborer's economic plight. Lilburne's family was fairly prosperous. That he was not, however, vulgarly indifferent to the plight of the poor is evident from the following passage from one of his printed letters:

Many of them [the House of Commons] take to themselves 3 l. 10 s. a week and some of them more, and other great Places worth 500 l. 1000 l. 1500 l. 2000 l. and more *per annum,* and live in . . . great pompe . . . and many poor Widdows & Fatherlesse children . . . crying at their door, Bread, Bread, and ready to curse them all to their faces.[45]

Lilburne and the Levellers, sympathetic toward the poor as they were, sought no fundamental change in the economic order. Fearing a military dictatorship, they had striven to enlist the aid of Cromwell's officers and men in establishing a constitutional republic. Failing in that, the Levellers heatedly continued their agitation, their leaders sending forth pamphlets from prison; scarcely a newspaper appeared in 1649 without some mention of Lilburne and the Levellers. But they hastened to repudiate any alliance with the feeble communist movement on St. George's Hill. On April 16, 1649, only two weeks after the first digging, Lilburne with his colleagues published a tract in which he rejected the philosophy of the Diggers as "most injurious, unlesse there did precede an universall assent thereunto from all and every one of the People." He continues: "The Community amongst the primitive Christians, was *Voluntary*, not *Coactive*. . . . We profess therefore that we never had it in our thoughts to Level mens estates." [46] In the May 1, 1649, *Agreement of the People* the clause was inserted that Parliament is to have no power to "level mens Estates, destroy Propriety, or to make all things Common," [47] a provision that was incorporated in the *Agreement* which appeared July 23, 1649.[48] On June 2 appeared *The Discoverer;* a tract written to discredit the Levellers, it charged them with holding socialistic tenets. To this charge Lilburne replied briefly in *The Legall Fundamentall Liberties,* which appeared on June 18. In neither of these repudiations of Digger doctrine does Lilburne, we must add, speak of the Diggers harshly or satirically. His sympathy for them as people is suggested in the words *"all the erronious tenents of the poor Diggers at George hill."* [49] But his rejection of socialism is decisive and complete. Nor have I been able to find in Lilburne's pamphlets any concrete proposals for economic reform except a provision incorporated in one of the *Agreements* that interest above six percent be prohibited.[50] This provision is not inserted in the later *Agreements.*

How far removed Milton himself was from Winstanley's position it is scarcely necessary to say. No pacifist, and no internationalist, Milton was far indeed from being a socialist. True, in his youth he had written the following:

> If every just man that now pines with want
> Had but a moderate and beseeming share
> Of that which lewdly-pamper'd Luxury
> Now heaps upon som few with vast excess,
> Nature's full blessings would be well dispenc't
> In unsuperfluous eeven proportion.[51]

That this sentiment was not, however, an integral part of Milton's political philosophy may be surmised from the fact that he does not repeat it in any of his tracts. The only later reference to the scattering of fortunes that I have been able to find, is the decisively hostile one of *The Readie & Easie Way*. His own plan, he writes, "requires no perilous, no injurious alteration or circumscription of men's lands and properties [as Harrington's model would]." [52] If, he adds, the temporal and spiritual lords in accordance with his proposal are extirpated, "no man or number of men can attain to such wealth or vast possession, as will need the hedge of an agrarian law." From this statement, and from his old outbursts against the ostentatious wealth of the prelates, we know that Milton was no believer in great wealth settled in a few families. And he himself cared little for money except as a means to that leisure which a poet and a thinker, living a life of "spare temperance," requires. Unwilling he proclaimed himself, however, to disturb the fundamental practices of the economic order, even to that extent advocated by Harrington.

An explanation of this unwillingness, not far to seek, is this: Milton could not comprehend the problems of the worker because he himself from birth to death had not suffered economic want. So well had his father provided for his needs that he enjoyed not only seven years of uninterrupted study at Cambridge, but also five years of detached study at Horton.[53] Not requiring employment during his middle years in order to sustain his family, he spent even the fourteen years after the Restoration in comparative comfort. Though Milton suffered heavy losses in 1660, in his late years he possessed 1500 pounds in money variously invested, yielding approximately 100 pounds annually. When one compares this with the ten, fifteen, or twenty pounds annual income of the agricultural laborer, he is instantly aware of the gulf in living standards separating the daily life of John Milton from that of the working classes. Unlike Winstanley, who accepted the charitable hospitality of his friends in the country after being impoverished by the "cheating sons" of London, Milton was never forced into an examination of the laborer's struggle for daily bread. A city man, he had seldom if ever rubbed shoulders with the peasants, nor were his cultured associates concerned a whit more than he with the burdens of the poor. Only a petition now and then, or an isolated cry from a Winstanley, brought them to the public eye.

Many of Winstanley's theories even today being pointedly controversial, it is difficult to evaluate his position among seventeenth century radicals. That he was a man of no immediate influence, that he exerted no political pressure, that the great men of the time considered him a queer, deluded visionary—of these things we may be certain. In the "evolution of democracy," however, to use Professor Charles Firth's term, Winstanley's ideas naturally place themselves in the twentieth century and beyond, whereas those of Milton and Lilburne, in the main, fall logically into nineteenth century patterns. Milton represented the enlightened members of the upper middle class, Lilburne the disenfranchised lower middle class. Winstanley alone spoke for the servants, the laborers, the economically dispossessed, the "herd confused" at the bottom of the social scale. Since democratic governments are today concerning themselves to a greater degree than ever before with the material welfare of the working classes, we may conclude that Winstanley anticipated the trend of democracy more fully and more specifically than any other seventeenth-century radical, Milton and Lilburne included. Unlike any other leader of this tumultuous period, Winstanley recognized the limitations of political democracy as the end of all radical effort. To him the test of true reformation was a change in the whole economic order, an actual redistribution of income effected by a governmental agency that would prevent income again being concentrated in the hands of a few. Visionary and impractical as Winstanley undoubtedly was, as a spokesman for extreme democracy in an age of seething theories he has made for himself a secure and respected place among the honored great of England's rebels and reformers.

CHAPTER XIII

MILTON AS A DEMOCRATIC REFORMER

A. MILTON'S INDIVIDUALISM AS A FACTOR IN REFORM

IN THE preceding chapters we have attempted to portray Milton as one who fought valiantly for the liberty of his equals, scorning England's masses in attaining his goal. But if he loved liberty and not democracy, he was, as we have partially demonstrated, striving for ends in many ways identical with democratic achievement. In the course of English history the permanent liberties to which Milton consecrated a third of his life have followed, and not preceded, the rise of popular power. Cromwell, enlightened despot that he was, had not provided liberty, and Milton's proposed senate could have been no more successful. Had Milton lived he might have turned as a last resort to the masses so frequently an object of his patrician contempt. For it was in part through the pressure of relatively popular Parliaments, stirred to action by the tyranny of James II, that the *Toleration Act* and the *Bill of Rights* established in 1689 a large degree both of liberty of conscience and freedom of speech. And it was this same Bill of Rights which permanently established constitutional government in England, banishing forever those kingly presumptions which Milton had so berated in *The Tenure* and in his first *Defence*. Though the king and his peers still remain in England, it has been the ever-spreading franchise which has reduced their power to a mere social representation of a dead political order. England's significant advances toward what Milton considered liberty, toward, for example a system of education which he thought would spread "much more knowledge and civility, yea, religion through all parts of the land" —have been taken, not by the beneficent few, but by that full House of Commons which Milton so feared during his life. The heights upon which Milton planted the flag of liberty have been stormed, not by the few well-armed, but by a host numerous enough to retain lasting possession of them. In each succeeding century greater throngs of Englishmen, led often by aristocrats of Milton's type, have reached for those basic privileges which Milton demanded during his life. Aims substantially democratic and Milton's liberty have fused into one. And in thus having planted the flag, however contemptuous he may have been of the ill-bred army to follow, Milton is entitled to consideration as a democratic reformer.

If Milton did contribute to that stream of liberal action which historically has been a part of democratic reform, what were the elements of his personality and his philosophy which made him a radical and engendered his conception of liberty?

The most significant element, certainly, was the Christian individualism which filled his soul. In the tide of Reformation from Luther to Calvin to Knox to Cartright to Brown and Roger Williams and finally, to almost complete rationalism in men like Richard Overton, there had been a constant shift from acceptance of truth by authority to an unaided personal interpretation of the Bible. In the introduction to this study we attempted to trace the steps by which this increasing reliance on individual authority had affected politics and finally penetrated governmental machinery in Rhode Island. On this path of individualism Milton travelled far to the left, from Presbyterianism and Independency to a belief in no church and no priest whatever. Accepting for his religious convictions no authority except his own interpretation of the Bible, Milton, like his contemporaries, had soon learned to accept no authority in politics except that which to him seemed just and right.

Milton's reliance on his own judgment both in politics and religion led him utterly to reject custom and tradition. In *Christian Doctrine* he writes the following: "We are expressly forbidden to pay any regard to human traditions, whether written or unwritten. . . . Neither can we trust implicitly in matters of this nature to the opinions of our forefathers, or of antiquity." [1] In his *Animadversions Upon The Remonstrant's Defence,* Milton had, many years before, deplored the same dependence upon antiquity which he scores in *Christian Doctrine*. There being so many of the ancients, he says, it is impossible to read them all in one's life and achieve thus a comprehensive view of their quantitative stand on any one subject. Moreover, it is not difficult to find pronounced differences among those classical writers and church fathers whom one does consult. "Why do we therefore stand worshipping and admiring this unactive and lifeless Colussus?" he asks. For Milton there could be only one ultimate authority, his own insight. Much as he weighed the evidence forged on the anvils of other thinkers, and despite his borrowings from them, he denied they should determine his final judgment. Fully as he uses authorities in such a tract as the *Defence,* he declares that he uses them, not because they are needed to prove what the reason of men can comprehend, but because the use of authorities was the foolish custom of his age. He cited preceding thinkers only to rout his opponents by the accepted controversial methods of the day. For himself he would face the future and find truth anew.

Scorning tradition, facing forward, and his spirit aflame with a reforming Christianity questing for ultimate truth, Milton could find no rest until he had thrown himself into the conflict to make all clear to his countrymen. There must be no delay: even as man can conceive liberty with his reason, driving straight to his goal intellectually, so he should decisively and directly in the political world make his dreams come true. That Milton felt himself to be an instrument of this great cause, that he consciously regarded himself as a reformer is clear from his own words in *The Reason of Church Government* and from that famous autobiographical passage in *Defensio Secunda:*

I saw that a way was opening for the establishment of real liberty; that the foundation was laying for the deliverance of man from the yoke of slavery and superstition; that the principles of religion, . . . the first objects of our care, would exert a salutary influence on the manners and constitution of the republic; and as I had from my youth studied the distinction between religious and civil rights I perceived that if I . . . wished to be of use, I ought at least not to be wanting to my country, to my church, and to so many of my fellow-Christians, in a crisis of so much danger; I therefore determined to relinquish the other pursuits in which I was engaged, and transfer the whole force of my talents and my industry to this one important object.[2]

No one can doubt the sincerity of this passage; it shows forth the lofty soul of one who has looked across the narrow but immeasurably deep gulf separating the world that is from the world that might be; a soul so driven by the clarity of his vision that he imperiously bids his countrymen forthwith bridge the chasm. Nor can one dismiss the human sympathy which prompted Milton's profound eagerness to engage for his countrymen in the struggle; to picture for them the world that might be, that they might also desire and achieve the freedom he possessed from tradition, custom, and blind superstition. Much as Milton despised the ignorance of the masses, it can never be said that he did not aspire in his heart for their inhabiting that more ideal world which he believed possible of realization.

B. THE LAW OF NATURE

Another factor in Milton's reforming philosophy which we may set down as contributing to the spread of democratic doctrine is his conception of the law of nature. For Milton consistently assumed that the law of nature was a code of abstract justice superior to the law of the state; by the law of nature individuals had reserved to them certain just privileges which the state had no right to abrogate. This assumption was, of course, inherent in the *Agreements of the People* promulgated by the Levellers. It had been in the seventeenth and preceding centuries a constant authority for democratic reform.

In order fully to understand Milton's conception of the law of nature, let us briefly examine his sources. The first, as recorded in his *Commonplace Book,* was Justinian: *De jure naturali, gentium, et civili statuant jurisperiti: vide* Justinian. institut. 1.1. tit. 2.[3] Turning to the earlier portions of the *Institutes,* we find the Roman distinctions between the law of nature and the law of nations. The law of nature to Justinian was substantially the Stoic conception of a reasonable sense of abstract justice not always obeyed by mankind but recognized by it. Justinian points out, for example, that both captivity and servitude are "contrary to the law of nature; for by that law, all men are born free." [4] The law of nations, on the other hand, is customs universally accepted but not always agreeable to the law of nature. There is the plain statement in the *Institutes* that slavery is the acknowledged practice under the law of nations, but contrary to natural right. Thus Justinian among the later Roman law-givers accepted the law of nature as a principle of pervading justice which it is not always possible to translate into civil law because of the pressure of tradition and international custom. That Milton was familiar with this conception is evident from his reference to Justinian in the *Commonplace Book.*

Another source of Milton's conception of the law of nature is Cicero's *Philippics,* to which he refers directly in *A Defence of the People of England.* Identifying the law of God with the law of nature, he writes: "The most ancient laws that are known to us were formerly ascribed to God as their author. For the law, says Cicero in his Philippics, is no other than a rule of well-grounded reason, derived from God himself, enjoining whatever is just and right, and forbidding the contrary." [5] Cicero's actual words run as follows: "For law is nothing else but a principle of right derived from the will of the Gods, commanding what is honest, forbidding the contrary." [6] Cicero's more complete definition, to which Milton does not, so far as I know, directly refer, is found in the *Laws.* Cicero calls law "the highest reason, implanted in Nature, which commands what ought to be done and forbids the opposite." He writes also that law is "the mind and reason of intelligent man, the standard by which Justice and Injustice are measured. . . . But in determining what Justice is, let us begin with that supreme Law which had its origin before any written law existed or any state had been established." Cicero denies that the first duty of man is to obey written laws rather than the law of nature; he points to the discrepancy which often exists between what is really just and what the written law and judicial decisions accept as just. Justice in reality does not exist at all unless it exists in nature.

Besides Justinian and Cicero, Milton refers to Aristotle as a source for the theory of the law of nature. Aristotle had, however, no well-defined notion of the law of nature such as Cicero possessed; Cicero's law of nature was, in fact, foreign to his whole philosophic method. Whereas Cicero postulated a state of nature in which each man is endowed with reason, therefore free with his brothers from any arbitrary law of rule, Aristotle recognized no such ideal community. He did not accept the belief that each man is gifted with innate reason. Instead he looked about him to find that men were, by nature, unequal in reason and virtue. To Aristotle the law of nature was not the individual's sense of abstract justice, but that code which men accepted universally as being just and right. As in nature, Aristotle says, the soul governs the body and the mind the appetite, this rule being beneficent both to the soul and to the body, to the mind and to the appetite, so always the superior nature should govern the inferior. The excellence of some men consists in their physical strength, not in their spiritual power: "they are slaves by nature, and it is advantageous to them to be always under government." [7] It is of course true, Aristotle holds, that a number of men in every state are by nature equal in spiritual excellence; these men should not in justice rule their equals arbitrarily, but should hold the government by turns. But inferiors should submit to their betters. It is by this code that he justifies slavery; according to his belief a large number of men are not by the law of nature free at all. Unlike Cicero, Justinian, Hooker, Grotius, Locke, and Milton himself, Aristotle did not recognize man's natural liberty.

Although Milton was familiar with the sources of natural law, he does not at any time present his conception of it in any such orderly fashion as Hooker had done, or as Locke afterward accomplished so fully in his *Second Treatise of Government*. At one time we see him influenced by Cicero's conception of the law of nature; at another, by Aristotle's; at another by nothing except his own sense of justice, his own opinions. What further complicates the problem of Milton's concept of the law of nature is the fact that he regarded it as identical with the law of God.[8] This being true, he did not pause to trace the theory historically, but sought from the Bible and from his own mind his conception of right and wrong; whatever agreed with his interpretation of the Bible became for him the law of nature. The result of these conflicting sources is that Milton's law of nature is now one thing, now another; it presents a mixture of Stoicism, Aristotelianism, and Christianity.

It is evident that Milton's idea of the law of nature is often substantially Cicero's own. Like Cicero, Milton looks upon natural law as the rule of abstract justice which should dominate human intercourse in a state of nature, that is, in a community wherein all acted according to their innate sense of what is reasonable and just. Milton sees nature, then, as a state of being agreeable to conscience. The Lady in *Comus*, for instance, rebukes Comus for thinking that "her children should be riotous with her abundance," declaring that nature's abundance is meant only for those who "live according to her sober laws, and holy dictate of spare Temperance." As in the Lady what is natural is reasonable, so in Comus what seems to

Milton unreasonable, i.e., Comus' revelling in the physical charms of nature for their own sake, is unnatural. In *Paradise Lost*, it is likewise plain that Milton looks upon Satan and upon all evil as unnatural. Like Cicero, and unlike Hobbes, Milton believed that according to the law of nature, man is inherently good and free from outward restraint.

In proclaiming man's inherent freedom, goodness, and innate capacity for reasoning, Milton is like Cicero, Justinian, Hooker, and Grotius. But here Milton leaves the law of nature and turns to Christian justice. Man is free from government without consent only so long as he governs himself rationally. If with his free will he makes himself a slave to his passions, if he rejects Christ and the Gospel, then he is no longer free politically, and his consent is not needed to establish over him an arbitrary government. But for Hooker and Locke, by the law of nature this would not be true, nor would it be true for Lilburne. For by the name of nature, in their opinion, a man is free during the whole of his life, unless he actually transgresses the law of the land. Again it is Milton's peculiar emphasis on sin which removes him from the extreme democratic theory as embodied in the law of nature. By the law of nature, in Milton's opinion, men are born free, but having rejected God, they may rightfully be subject to a tyrant against their will.

It is not difficult to perceive how Milton's idea that a sinner loses his freedom approaches Aristotle's theory of the law of nature. By combining free will with Cicero's theory of the law of nature Milton arrives at Aristotle's pagan conception of natural inequality. For Milton it was a man's own free will which made him a slave politically as well as spiritually; for Aristotle it was a man's inherent nature. Aristotle, having no illusions, looked about him to find men bound and unequal. They were to yield, therefore, to their superiors by nature, to subject themselves to wiser men than they. Milton, with infinite hopes for his fellow-men, believing that they all might be free and partially equal only by accepting God, looked about him to find that most men did not deserve political freedom. Their sins were too great. So he, like Aristotle, though for a different reason, decided that men must yield in the commonwealth to their spiritual betters. "For nothing," he exclaims in *Defensio Secunda*, "is more agreeable to the order of nature, or more for the interest of mankind, than that the less should yield to the greater, not in numbers, but in wisdom and in virtue." [9] And again, in the *Defence:* "For nature appoints that wise men should govern fools, not that wicked men should rule over good men, fools over wise men." [10] It is needless to say that Milton here speaks of Aristotle's conception of natural slavery, not of that natural law which provides that every man, no matter how wicked, can be governed only by his consent. How both Milton and Aristotle would have scoffed at Locke's statement that majority rule accords with the law of nature! We see, then, how Milton accepts Aristotle's theory of the law of nature: he combined a rather harsh notion of free will with the more liberal concept of natural law to make an Aristotelian political truism.

We may say that in his practical politics Milton relied upon Aristotle and the theory of inner tyranny; in theory, he gathered his hopes for mankind partly from the more liberal view of the law of nature. In his belief that there exists a code of abstract justice to all written law superior, that this justice may be understood through both man's reason and God's revelation, that any positive law which transgresses the law of nature may be abrogated, that all men are born free, that by the law of nature certain liberties are inalienable, Milton accepts the democratic concept of the law of nature. One who accepts this concept refuses to acknowledge things as they are, but looks forward to the realization of an ideal state. But such an ideal was incapable of realization in actual politics. Milton saw inequality on every hand, concluded with Aristotle that there would always be the ignorant who should be subjected to wiser men, found his countrymen chained by sin and tradition, and in such a mood demanded an aristocracy. It is proportioned equality, not any democratic hope, which Milton advocates in *Paradise Lost.* The world as it existed was more convincing than his aspirations for the freedom of mankind.

C. Milton and Ireton

In order to understand why Milton's more liberal theory of the law of nature places him among the democratic reformers of the seventeenth century, let us turn for a moment to Ireton's theory of the law of nature. On October 26, 1647, when the Levellers were debating with Ireton on the question of manhood suffrage, Col. Rainsborough declared that in his opinion no man in England, however poor, was bound to put himself under the government unless he had a voice in it; that "every man born in England cannot, ought nott, neither by the law of God nor the law of nature, to bee exempted from the choice of those who . . . make the lawes, for him to live under, and for him, for ought I know, to loose his life under." [11] As we know, Ireton replied to this that no man had such a right unless he owned some "fixed interest" in the country. For property, he continued, was the constitution of England, and no man had any natural rights except those which the country granted him. An Englishman's birth rights did not include the privilege of voting; they included, it was true, freedom of the highways, the right to breathe English air, the right to remain in England, and the right to protection under English laws. But according to the Leveller law of nature, he continued, a man had a right to take whatever "goods hee sees: . . . Hee hath a freedom to the land, [to take] the ground, to exercise itt, till itt; he hath the [same] freedome to anything that any one doth account himself to have a propriety in." [12] Thus pushing the theory of the law of nature to the extreme in order to show its inherent weakness, Ireton attempted to prove to the officers that an extended application of the law of nature would break down the laws of the land and throw the country into disorder. For Ireton, who understood perfectly the implications of the law of nature, there were no natural rights except those granted by the state to the individual. It was only in obedience to the civil laws (enjoined, he insisted, by God himself) that men might live together in harmony. The civil constitution of England, the franchise itself, being based on property holdings, there could be no breaking away toward an unknown justice without dire consequences.

Ireton's whole view of the law of nature was foreign to Milton's philosophy. Whereas Ireton would have placed the rights of the state, though admittedly unjust, over the rights of the individual, Milton never ceased to insist upon the supremacy of the individual's privileges over positive law. Ireton as a lawyer had the greatest respect for written law, but Milton, as we know, had none at all. To Ireton it seemed necessary to champion the rights of property against the rights of people, because the rights of property were accepted and fixed in contrast with abstract justice to people bound up in a glibly-mentioned law of nature. But Milton would have scorned such an attitude: to him the rights of the people were ever pre-eminent, and those rights by the law of nature were clear enough to him. Milton would have objected to the Levellers' support of manhood suffrage, not as Ireton did, on the basis of property rights; he would have objected on the ground of character rights, the rights of superior people to choose more burgesses than the less virtuous ones. Standing as Milton did, then, for individual rights above state rights, for human privileges above property privileges, in short for the absolute supremacy of the law of nature to written law, Milton placed himself in direct opposition to Ireton.

In so doing Milton takes his place among those who have faced the future instead of the past, among those who have looked forward to an unrealized just state. For despite the conflict in Milton's classical authorities for the law of nature, despite his propounding of Cicero's theory and application of Aristotle's, and notwithstanding his failure to recognize this conflict or to organize his theory into an organic whole, this concept of the law of nature embodies those principles which place him among the ranks of democratic reformers.

D. Relation Between Positive and Natural Law in Milton's Philosophy

In the preceding sections of this chapter we have tried to demonstrate that Milton's individualism and his conception of the law of nature both led him to favor democratic goals, and that consequently we must recognize his significance in the development of radical political theory. We must not, however, overlook his peculiar limitation as a reformer, i.e., his failure to perceive in the law books of his country not only the basis of tyranny but also the foundation of popular right, the origins of those liberties he hungered for.

In his enthusiasm for reform Milton frequently brushed aside traditions and written laws centuries old without pausing to investigate or consider them as obstacles in his path. Of Milton's proposals in *Means to Remove Hirelings,* Masson writes the following:

No Parliament that England ever saw, not even the Barebones Parliament itself, could have entertained for a moment, with a view to practical legislation, these speculations in all their length and breadth. Disestablishment, Disendowment, Abolition of a Clergy, had been the dream of Anabaptists and Fifth Monarchy men. . . . He sees no difficulties, takes regard of none. It is not with a flesh-and-blood world that he deals, a world of men, and their wives, and their families, and their yearly incomes, and their fixed residences and household belongings. . . . Abolish tithes; provide no substitute; proclaim that, after this day week, or the first day of the next year, not a penny shall be paid to any man by the State for preaching the Gospel, or doing any other act of the ministry: and what then? Why, there would be a flutter of consternation, of course, through some ten or twelve thousand parsonages; ten thousand or twelve thousand clerical gentlemen will stare bewilderedly for a while at their wives' faces.[13]

With Milton it was always so; he thought of reform as an achievement possible with a few strokes of the legislative pen; he did not conceive of English society historically. To him it was not an organism slowly evolving into a more intelligent civilization, applying with slow vigor the principles of liberty to its institutions. He did not see it as a geologist would look upon the earth's past ages, layer upon layer of complex and interwoven formations of rock and clay. Milton was in no wise capable of placing his reforms where alone they could be accepted, at the end, and not in the earlier stages, of a process centuries old. He did not look upon his reforms as the culmination of a slowly-changing order. It was this lack of historical sense which led Milton to discard the written laws as a foundation upon which he might build.

In this respect he was, as we have already suggested, very different from his contemporary John Lilburne. Although not a lawyer, Lilburne possessed a fairly accurate knowledge of English constitutional history, especially of those documents which guarantee certain rights to freeborn Englishmen. Like Algernon Sidney, Lilburne took the stand that certain inalienable rights are not new, that they have been a part of the traditions of the past, but that these rights have from time to time been infringed upon by tyrannical kings, counsellors, bishops, or Parliaments. For this reason Lilburne had the greatest respect for written law. Even when illegal acts might have accomplished the ends he himself sought, he looked upon them with aversion: he stoutly opposed the trial of Charles by the extraordinary tribunal which the Rump appointed. The Rump was not, he contended, a Parliament at all; it had no power to try the king, nor, he insisted, could a full and free Parliament legally have done so. It was only by an *Agreement of the People* changing the established government and vesting the complete power in a single house, that a legal tribunal could be appointed to try the king for his crimes and misdemeanors. In *Regall Tyrannie discovered,* which was published two years before the king's execution, Lilburne had voiced the conviction that the king for his many offenses deserved the death penalty; he was quite as eager as Milton for his dethrone-ment and trial. But he wanted it done legally, with the force of posi-tive law behind it; such an act in his opinion would have become a precedent of the utmost importance, a step toward liberty not to be retraced.

A poet, not a practical statesman, Milton was unable to see in English law a reflection, however dim, of the law of nature. The law was "norman gibbrish" to him. Nor did he understand that reform could come only by making that reflection brighter, not by destroying the old surface and creating the reflection anew on a bright and shining one. In the words of Jesse F. Mack: "Milton and the Puritans failed, at least of their immediate end, because, despite their inspiration, sincerity, enthusiasm, they did not understand the condition under which reform must come. They refused to come to terms with tradition." [14]

Milton is entitled to a place as a democratic reformer because in the course of history the liberties for which he stood have gradu-ally become identified with those reforms demanded and achieved by an increasingly large number of voters. The elements of Milton's political philosophy which gave rise to his conception of liberty and which were inherent in the reform movement are his Christian individualism and his sense of abstract justice as embodied in the law of nature. His weakness as a democratic reformer lies in his inability to perceive the written law to be a necessary foundation for the building of a more ideal England. And this weakness, we should note, this too great dependence on the law of nature, made for his immediate failure as a reformer; whereas his political ideals so far removed from contemporary realization ultimately gave him an important place as a reform agitator.

CHAPTER XIV

JUSTIFICATION: THE WAYS OF GOD

ITH the return of Charles Milton's tower of dreams for England's salvation crumbled to desolate ruins. The England of perpetual reformation, seething with creative fervor, grappling the future with eager arms, a utopia for eleven years on the verge of realization, had now receded irretrievably beyond the horizon. Gone too was the dream of voluntary churches and unpersecuted believers. Alas for the Commonwealth! An England without lords and king, ruled by a company of choicest spirits in plain clothes—all this that but a few short years past stood like a lighthouse to guide a benighted world—had vanished in the enveloping gloom of mass insanity. In the crackling bonfires, the roasting of countless Rumps, the jubilant shouts of his fellow-Londoners, the triumphant pealing of the bells, Milton felt the shattering of those leaping aspirations that had sustained for twenty years his labors for his country. More precious, this new England, than life itself, more precious than that "immortality of fame" that he had foregone so long ago. But now shouts of "The King! The King!" marked the waste of these ripe creative years. At the House of Lords Manchester tendered the affection of the Peers, which Charles accepted with careless ease.[1] The speaker of the Commons bathed his Majesty with obsequious flattery: "You are deservedly the King of hearts . . . to receive from Your People a Crown of hearts . . . 'Tis a sweet Crown . . . perfum'd with nothing but the incense of prayers and praises."[2] In the place of his bright dream this horrible reality of Dagon worshippers, parading the streets and supping at rulers' tables. Lust and flattery and sickly splendor rose grinning and triumphant over the plain commonwealth of the blind man's visions.

How little, in the presence of this catastrophe, his personal safety counted, may be read in the despairing pages of *The Readie & Easie*

337

Way. At no time of his political career was Milton's soul merged with the Good Old Cause so much as in the year of its doom. Though no man might stay to hear him, yet would he speak, though his words might be the last to be uttered for England's freedom: "I was sure I should have spoken only to trees and stones . . . with the prophet, 'O earth, earth, earth!' to tell the very soil itself, what her perverse inhabitants are deaf to." [3] In these lines may be read the most fitting commentary on Milton's identification with the social struggles of his day. To them he had given the deepest hidden energies of his indomitable spirit, beckoning his countrymen toward, as he thought, a more humane and intelligent social order, never for a moment renouncing the community of the quest for happiness. The social success of his fellow men held for Milton an incomparable satisfaction, a satisfaction for which the full expression of his poetic genius could not compensate. But now, even the faint glimmerings of hope that had softened his direst forebodings were submerged in the darkness of the enveloping wave of "epidemic madness." It was this tragedy that distilled in Milton's heart the deepest bitterness of his life.

The deaths of the Independent regicides, vengeance sought, ironically enough, by the pious implacable Presbyterians rather than by the profligate Charles, witnessed to all England the degradation of the Commonwealth. As Harrison was being drawn away on a hurdle to the place of execution, a spectator derided him, saying, "Where is your *Good Old Cause?*" Whereupon Harrison "with a cheerful smile clapt his hand on his breast, and said, *Here it is, and I am going to seale it with my bloud.*" At the scaffold, when the crowd mocked him for his quaking knees, Harrison asserted it was from his many wounds and loss of blood, not from fear, and that his weakness of nerves had lived with him twelve years. *"If I had ten thousand lives,"* he said, *"I could freely and cheerfully lay them down all to witnesse to this matter. . . . By God I have leaped over a Wall, by God I have runn'd through a Troop, and by my God I will go through this death, and he will make it easie to me."* [4] After Harrison was hanged, and pulled down while still alive, the executioner cut away his sex organs, burned his entrails before his eyes, severed his head, and hacked his body into quarters.[5] According to the custom of the day, his captors then set his head upon a pike at Westminster Hall and exposed his quarters on the city gates. It was the morning of October 13, 1660. In such a manner died Carew, Cook, and Peters on October 16, Scot, Clement, Scoop and Jones on the 17th, Hacker and Axtel on the 19th.[6] At Peters' death the crowd was so riotous and his voice so low that the reporter could make no record of his last words. Though the hangman rubbed his bloody hands (from the quartering of Cook's body) before Peters' eyes, he died unterrified, as did all his fellows.[7] Forbidden to express their political beliefs on the scaffold, the Commonwealth men nevertheless attempted to speak their minds despite the sheriff's interruptions. *"It is a very mean and bad Cause,"* said Scot, *"that will not bear the words of a dying man."* [8] Even in his last prayer Scot reminded his hearers of the justice of his cause: *"O Lord,"* he prayed, *"remember the price of Blood, that hath been shed for the purchasing of the Civil and Christian liberties."* [9] But the cruel shouts of the spectators, like the biting interruptions of the judges and the cynical merrymaking of Charles' court, submerged in general contempt any lingering defence of the once powerful commonwealth. "I saw not their execution," wrote Evelyn, "but met their quarters, mangled and cut and reeking, as they were brought from the gallows in baskets on the hurdle. O the marvellous providence of God!" [10] A few months later the bodies of Cromwell, Ireton, and Bradshaw were disinterred from their graves, reburied under the gallows, and their heads set on pikes at Westminster Hall.[10]

The trial and execution of Vane less than two years later must have deepened for Milton inexpressibly the tragedy that had befallen his country. In Vane reposed those ideals of statesmanship that Milton deemed pre-eminent. After Cromwell's failure Milton's confidence in Vane had risen again; and him he certainly visualized as the leader of his perpetual senate. With sufficiently contrite admission of his errors, Vane might have escaped execution; for he had, indeed, refused to be a party to the trial of Charles. To represent his cause unreservedly, however, Vane thrust aside all caution, all hope of reprieve, and spoke with the freedom of a zealot. His court speeches sound in part like declarations from the pen of a less violent Lilburne or the more democratic passages of Milton's *Tenure.* "God doth allow and confer by the very Law of Nature," he asserted, "upon the Community . . . of the People . . . the Liberty by their common Vote . . . to be Assenters or Dissenters [to] what shall apparently be found by them to be for the good or hurt of . .

Society." [11] This freedom of self-government no man can relinquish; it returns to him upon the defection of the ruler, of whose actions he and his fellow citizens are the final judge. In the struggle between king and Parliament Vane insisted that in siding with Parliament he had rightfully defended the liberties of the citizens. "In Quarrels between Subjects and Soveraigns . . ." he added, " 'tis seldom seen, but that Error lies on the Soveraign's part, who is apt to be flattered into the presumptuous exercise of such an absolute Soveraignty . . . as becomes no creature, and exceeds all the bounds of that contract he made with them." [12] With the utterance of such words Vane left his royalist judges no alternative. On June 14, 1662, clad in black suit and cloak and a scarlet waistcoat, he was led forth to Tower Hill, where he showed to the audience such a serene and untroubled countenance "that he rather seemed a looker-on, than the person concerned in the Execution." To prevent his being heard by the multitude, his captors sounded trumpets and snatched his papers from his hands. With what words he was able to speak, Vane defended to the last those principles he had affirmed in court, saying, *"Whereas the Judges have refused to seal with their hands, that they have done; I am come to seal with my Blood, that I have done."* [13] Until the fatal blow Vane's face retained the utmost composure and serenity, and a royalist declared, *"He dyed like a Prince."* [14] Thus was one of Milton's heroes overwhelmed by triumphant royalism. In his most despairing moments he could not have envisioned a more merciless persecution or humiliating defeat of Commonwealth ideals.

The tragedy for Milton was undiminished by any doubts that his sense of social values was unbalanced or inadequate. If he lived to question or deny his analysis of the Revolution's social forces or his definition of its immediate aims, he made no admissions to posterity. Milton was, as we have shown, an unrealistic critic of the democratic forces which he had championed in *The Tenure* and *The Defence.* Unlike Winstanley and Walwyn, he gave scarcely a thought to the economic salvation of England's masses or to the political rights of the disenfranchised. What difference between Commonwealth and monarchy, asked Winstanley, if the plain man under both ate scantily and felt under each the heel of perpetual Norman inequalities? No more than a name and a shadow. Whereas Winstanley wanted earth's substance for all as the fruit of reforma-

By the King.

A PROCLAMATION

For calling in, and suppressing of two Books written by *John Milton;* the one Intituled, *Johannis Miltoni Angli pro Populo Anglicano Defensio, contra Claudii Anonymi aliàs Salmasii, Defensionem Regiam;* and the other in answer to a Book Intituled, *The Pourtraicture of his Sacred Majesty in his Solitude and Sufferings.* And also a third Book Intituled, *The Obstructors of Justice,* written by *John Goodwin.*

CHARLES R.

Whereas John Milton, late of Westminster, in the County of Middlesex, hath Published in Print two several Books. The one Intituled, Johannis Miltoni Angli pro Populo Anglicano Defensio, contra Claudii Anonymi, aliàs Salmasii, Defensionem Regiam. And the other in Answer to a Book Intituled, The Pourtraicture of his Sacred Majesty in his Solitude and Sufferings. In both which are contained sundry Treasonable Passages against Us and Our Government, and most Impious endeavors to justifie the horrid and unmatchable Murther of Our late Dear Father, of Glorious Memory.

And whereas John Goodwin, late of Coleman Street, London, Clerk, hath also published in Print, a Book Intituled, The Obstructors of Justice, written in defence of his said late Majesty. And whereas the said John Milton, and John Goodwin, are both fled, or so obscure themselves, that no endeavors used for their apprehension can take effect, whereby they might be brought to Legal Tryal, and deservedly receive condigne punishment for their Treasons and Offences.

Now to the end that Our good Subjects may not be corrupted in their Judgments, with such wicked and Traitrous principles, as are dispersed and scattered throughout the beforementioned Books, We, upon the motion of the Commons in Parliament now assembled, doe hereby streightly charge and Command, all and every Person and Persons whatsoever, who live in any City, Burrough, or Town Incorporate, within this our Kingdom of England, the Dominion of Wales, and Town of Berwick upon Tweed, in whose hands any of those Books are, or hereafter shall be, That they, upon pain of Our high Displeasure, and the consequence thereof, do forthwith, upon publication of this Our Command, or within Ten days immediately following, deliver, or cause the same to be delivered to the Mayor, Bayliffs, or other chief Officer or Magistrate, in any of the said Cities, Burroughs, or Towns Incorporate, where such person or persons so live; or, if living out of any City, Burrough, or Town Incorporate, then to the next Justice of Peace adjoyning to his or their dwelling, or place of abode; or if living in either of Our Universities, then to the Vice-Chancellor of that University where he or they do reside.

And in default of such voluntary delivery, which We do expect in observance of Our said Command, That then and after the time before limited, expired, the said Chief Magistrate of all and every the said Cities, Burroughs, or Towns Incorporate, the Justices of the Peace in their several Counties, and the Vice-Chancellors of Our said Universities respectively, are hereby Commanded to Seize and Take, all and every the Books aforesaid, in whose hands or possession soever they shall be found, and certifie the names of the Offenders unto Our Privy Councel.

And We do hereby also give special Charge and Command to the said Chief Magistrates, Justices of the Peace, and Vice-Chancellors respectively, That they cause the said Books which shall be so brought unto any of their hands, or seized or taken as aforesaid, by vertue of this Our Proclamation, to be delivered to the respective Sheriffs of those Counties where they respectively live, the first and next Assizes that shall after happen. And the said Sheriffs are hereby also required, in time of holding such Assizes, to cause the same to be publickly burnt by the hand of the Common Hangman.

And We do further streightly charge and Command, That no man hereafter presume to Print, Vend, Sell, or Disperse any the aforesaid Books, upon pain of Our heavy Displeasure, and of such further Punishment, as for their presumption in that behalf, may any way be inflicted upon them by the Laws of this Realm.

Given at Our Court at *Whitehall* the 13th day of *August,* in the Twelfth year of Our Reign, 1660.

LONDON, Printed by *John Bill* and *Christopher Barker*, Printers to the Kings most Excellent Majesty, 1660.

tion, and Lilburne a vote in every fist, Milton wanted the superior moral and intellectual tone of the commonwealth and an end to the degrading subservience of monarchical customs. He stood for the dominance of nature's talented aristocrats over both the insolent assumption of hereditary privilege and the incoherent political gropings of the confused multitude. Only under such tutelage, he thought, might the people cultivate the personal graces and the enlarged civic liberties still hidden in the womb of Christian progress. The fall of the commonwealth symbolized for him the quenching of the reforming fires of twenty years, a defeat of Christianity itself. And by the soaring reach of Milton's spirit we may measure the intensity of his suffering.

How to explain a paradise gone glimmering, the last voices of liberty mocked with drunken hoots, himself hounded and the gibbet beckoning? As Milton revolved again that other dream, "to leave something so written to aftertimes, as they should not willingly let it die," it was inevitable that he should seek the central reason for this tragedy. It was inevitable, too, that both the tone and the ideas of his great epic should reflect not only the intense political thinking of his twenty years of pamphleteering, but also his interpretation of the place of Restoration in the scheme of cosmic justice. To explain the catastrophe, Milton might have drawn upon his knowledge of the ancient commonwealths and his amazing secular grasp of human psychology, analyzing realistically the play of forces: the faulty educational system, the economic maladjustments that persisted through the Commonwealth, the response of the people to Commonwealth piety, the errors of Cromwell and his successors. Ignorance only, not sinfulness, might have been Milton's judgment of the people, had he accepted in 1660 Socrates' definition of virtue. Or had the Reformation led him, as it did Walwyn and Saltmarsh, a step beyond Arminius to the infinite compassion of the Gospels, he could not have looked upon the Restoration as a just punishment of an erring nation. To neither of these patterns in his intellectual background, however, did Milton turn as an explanation for the untimely doom of the Good Old Cause. Rather it was by the harsher strain of Calvinistic coloring, the "retributive justice of the Deity," that Milton interpreted the crashing of his hopes for England's salvation. For eight years cut off from the cheering eyes of kindred spirits, now plunged into a deeper gloom than enveloping blindness, his last sally for liberty lost in the frenzy of idolatrous king-worship, Milton invoked the just penalties of the Old Testament upon his fellow-countrymen. Not Milton the pagan humanist, or Milton the tolerationist, but Milton the stern prophet pronounced judgment upon sinning man in *Paradise Lost*.

The Leadership Principle in *Paradise Lost*

The bitterness and despair of 1660 confirmed and intensified the more aristocratic of Milton's political convictions. Though they had signally failed of recognition by his fellow citizens, he unhesitatingly incorporated them in his greatest artistic achievement. Of these principles the one of most far-reaching implications in Milton's philosophical structure was his conception of the rule of the virtuous. To his analysis of the government of heaven and hell, of the home, and of man himself, Milton applied the leadership principle that he had so persistently championed during the tumultuous pamphleteering years.

The government of heaven, as described by Milton, accords ideally with the pattern of his commonwealth principles. Not, as Satan claims, "upheld by old repute, consent, or custome," but sustained by his perfection of character, God rules over all the aristocracy of Heaven. Though Milton wavers in placing Jesus second to God in power, apparently preferring at times the Trinitarian to the Unitarian position, in Book VIII he unequivocally denies that God's equal exists. God's own claim is as follows:

> For none I know
> Second to mee or like, equal much less.[15]

When the Son is appointed by God to reign as the active head of Heaven's hierarchy, the angelic hosts, though they have had no voice whatever in his selection, pay their homage in joyful song. The Son's divinity entitles him to supreme authority. Similarly, in the descending scale of Heaven's leaders, "Thrones, Dominations, Princedoms, Vertues, Powers," the relative governing power of each official corresponds to the degree of his spiritual perfection. When Satan rebels against bending the knee to authority thus determined, Abdiel sternly rebukes him:

> Unjustly thou deprav'st it with the name
> Of *Servitude* to serve whom God ordains,
> Or Nature; God and Nature bid the same,
> When he who rules is worthiest, and excells
> Them whom he governs.[16]

Nowhere could one find a more exact statement of Milton's philosophy of leadership than in these lines. God at its head, the hierarchy of Heaven wields its power with or without the consent of the governed, secure in its spiritual superiority. The duty of the lesser angels is identical with that of men: They should place themselves under the immediate direction and control of wiser and more virtuous beings, resting content in intelligent obedience.

In Milton's Hell, as in his Heaven, the "worthiest" angels stand pre-eminent. Though Satan has revolted against God's dictatorship, he unhesitatingly assumes absolute sovereignty in Hell, thus ironically recognizing the justice of the proportionate equality of Heaven. Milton writes that Satan was "by merit raised" [17] to the leadership of his fellows. Satan himself claims that he is king through "just right," "the fixed laws of Heaven," "free choice," and the worth of his achievements in council and battle.[18] Contrary to Satan's assertion, the angels of Hell have not exercised "free choice"; no more consent of the governed obtains in Hell than in Heaven. In his claims to natural superiority, however, Satan is fully justified: he possesses supreme courage, intellectual resourcefulness, rhetorical genius, subtle knowledge of passions and jealousies. Gladly the inhabitants of Hell yield themselves to his will:

> He spake: and to confirm his words, out-flew
> Millions of flaming swords.[19]

In Hell, as in Heaven, "great consulting peers" take their places under their ruler according to natural merit. The same gradations of authority and virtue, "Thrones, Dominations, Princedoms, Vertues, Powers," against which Satan strove in Heaven, he instinctively confirms in Hell.

The government of the home, in Milton's opinion, should be organized on the same secure foundation: the more virtuous and intelligent of the pair should rule; the lesser intelligence should submit. Convinced that husbands are almost universally superior to their wives, Milton visualizes man as woman's master in the home. Both outwardly and inwardly, according to Raphael, woman resembles the image of God less than man.[20] Adam is "more wise, more watchful, stronger," than Eve.[21] "My Author and Disposer," Eve says to Adam, "what thou bidst unargu'd I obey; so God ordains." [22] But the most unqualified of Milton's claims to man's dictatorship in marriage is the following one from *Christian Doctrine*:

Marriage therefore gives place to religion; it gives place, as we have seen, to the right of the master; and the right of a husband, as appears from passages of Scripture above quoted . . . *is nearly the same as that of the master.*[23]

This is an extreme statement, and there can be no doubt that Milton's ideal of marriage transcended it; these words evidently represented to him the particular rights of the husband in marriages not ideal. Add to these words, however, Milton's belief that polygamy is sanctioned by Scripture, and one has a still lower estimate, from Milton's point of view, of the wife's privileges. He believed that woman's natural inferiority made the rule of the husband just and inevitable. But there is no reason to believe that in particular marriages Milton would not have advocated a husband's yielding himself to the superior personality of the wife.

Milton's conception of man's government of himself, like his conception of governments in earth, hell, heaven, and home, is colored by the domination of superior virtue and wisdom. Even here his philosophy of leadership obtains: the soul, being compounded of the senses, the passions, and the reason, should yield freely to the government of reason:

> Know that in the Soule
> Are many lesser Faculties that serve
> Reason as chief.[24]

Raphael warns Adam against allowing the "dear delight" of sense to overwhelm love; and love "hath his seat in Reason." [25] Adam is further admonished:

> Take heed least Passion sway
> Thy Judgement to do aught, which else free Will
> Would not admit.[26]

Everywhere Milton extols those who have learned to govern themselves, those in whom the passions and the appetites are subordinate to "Reason as chief." In the words of Jesus:

> He who reigns within himself, and rules
> Passions, Desires, and Fears, is more a King;
> Which every wise and vertuous man attains:
> And who attains not, ill aspires to rule
> Cities of men, or head-strong Multitudes,
> Subject himself to Anarchy within.[27]

To psychology, too, then, as well as to earthly and heavenly governments, Milton applies his fundamental philosophy of leadership.

Believing that "Orders and Degrees jar not with liberty, but well consist," that one's happiness lies in placing himself willingly under the government of reason or superior beings, Milton unhesitatingly ascribed the failures and tragedies of life to violations of his principle of government by the best. When, overcome by her noon-hour hunger and by her passion for equality with Adam,[28] Eve tossed reason from the throne, she incurred life-long despair. When, chivalrously but foolishly, Adam allowed his love for Eve to supersede Reason as master of his soul, he, too, suffered banishment from Eden. Had Satan revolted against a ruler inferior to himself, Milton would have acclaimed him; but since Satan rebelled against One supreme in spiritual attainment, Milton has him undergo eternal pain. So, too, when England thrust aside her reason in favor of her idolatrous passion for kingship, she was destined to bear excruciating national sorrow.

In Milton's judgment of Adam we may trace his analysis of mankind's woes, including the suffering of his fellow-countrymen under a restored monarchy. His analysis combines Aristotle's concept of natural slavery and the Christian doctrine of sin. If one is a sinner, he cannot be governor of himself; therefore he cannot continue in his original freedom; he should not have a voice in the selection of his ruler. Being wicked, man yields easily to the persuasion of wicked tyrants; thus had the English acted when they had accepted Charles. Now they deserve their slavery. God's judgment is upon them. In *The Readie & Easie Way*, it is true, he had for a moment glanced at the environmental determinants of the people's political weaknesses:

To make the people fittest to choose, and the chosen fittest to govern, will be to mend our corrupt and faulty education, to teach the people faith, not without virtue, temperance, modesty, sobriety, parsimony, justice; not to admire wealth or honour; to hate turbulence and ambition; to place every one his private welfare and happiness in the public peace, liberty, and safety.[29]

The implications of this statement are far-reaching indeed and utterly contradictory to Milton's doctrine of free will. Here Milton appears to conclude, with Comenius, that not only secular knowledge but private and social virtues may be inculcated in a widespread plan of education; moreover, that the weaknesses of the citizenry may be traced to the failure of the state to provide appropriate training. For their sinfulness, then, not they but the state has been responsible. Not wilful wrongdoing, but ignorance, has been their curse. To this conclusion Milton might have been led by the secular humanism of his background, which was rich and powerful, or by the charity of the Gospels, which had brightened the pages of his most persuasive tolerationist arguments. But Milton did not venture to extend such a revolutionary concept as his passage on education suggested. It was, after all, only a fragment of his social thinking, struck off the hot anvil of his intense imagination in a moment of crisis. Had he accepted its implications, the very basis of freedom, man's capacity for choosing, would have been obliterated. As a product of his environment, having no choice of his own, Adam would have been a slave with no responsibility for his destiny. After such an assumption justification of God's judgment would have been ridiculous and futile. For the ultimate explanation, then, of man's failure, Milton turned to the theology of Arminius and the righteous judgments of Jehovah.

In *Paradise Lost*, as in the pamphlets, Milton identified sin with political ignorance. Sin meant, in part, refusal to yield unquestioning obedience to a being superior in wisdom; the superiority to be defined by the virtuous ruler or the pious minority, not by the subjects as a whole. Thus Satan's sin was in questioning the judgment of God and revolting against a decree in which he had no voice. Eve's sin also sprang from her questioning of a decree that to her went unexplained and unjustified, a decree against knowledge that Satan was quick to attack with Areopagitican reasoning:

>   Wherein lies
> Th' offence, that Man should thus attain to know? [30]

In Eve, as in Satan, sin was in part a desire to rise closer to God
in power and intelligence, to exalt the godlike in themselves. When
Eve questions whether or not she should tell Adam of the forbidden
fruit, she spoke of her passion for equality:

> And render me more equal, and perhaps,
> A thing not undesireable, sometime
> Superior: for inferior who is free? [31]

To Milton sin meant also the victory of sex over reason: it was a
concept always near the surface of his philosophy, and had an important bearing on his political conclusions. The first sin in heaven,
according to Milton, was Satan's revolt against God's elevation of
Jesus. But while Satan addressed his cohorts for the first time, Sin
came forth from his head in the shape of a lovely woman; and death
was begotten in incest. Similarly, the first fruits of Adam's rejection
of God's decree was a lust painted by Milton as utterly unlike the
joyous delights of first wedded love. To Milton control of sexual
passion was an important element of sound citizenship, really a part
of the "faith . . . virtue, temperance, modesty," which he had extolled as the qualities of intelligent voters in *The Readie & Easie
Way*. Most men, Milton felt, had not yet attained government over
their passions; if permitted to vote they "would soon exalt the
vilest miscreants from our taverns and our brothels . . . to the
rank and dignity of senators." [32] England's acceptance of Charles
had been a defection in character; it was not only the lust of idolatry that impelled their frenzied rejoicings; it was their intemper-
ance, their gluttony, their drunkenness, their rejection of all the
sober virtues typified in the leaders of the Good Old Cause. In
Charles and his cavaliers was mirrored the temper of the people,
the "general defection of a misguided and abused multitude." Upon
such a sinning nation, Milton pronounces his judgment in *Paradise
Lost:*

> Yet somtimes Nations will decline so low
> From vertue, which is reason, that now wrong,
> But Justice, and some fatal curse annext
> Deprives them of their outward libertie,
> Thir inward lost.[33]

Milton's emphasis on sensual appetites as a factor in the loss of Paradise, and man's outward freedom in general, trails behind it the cloak of Calvin, marking the cleavage between the Puritanism of the Independents and that of the Levellers in the interpretation of man's political destiny. To the Leveller leader Richard Overton, as we have seen, personal morality had little or nothing to do with a man's civic intelligence or social action. A drunkard, a profane person, or an adulterer, might be a citizen of high worth, working intelligently for that social justice in which, thought Walwyn and Overton, resided true Christianity. On this point had poised the extreme leftward sweep of the Puritan Revolution: a repudiation of the paramount importance of Puritan virtues for an affirmation of the social Gospel. Compassion for one's fellows, concern for their political and economic freedom, had superseded, as a Christian virtue, all the codes of Moses. To Milton, as to Cromwell, such a civic emphasis was incomprehensible. When Cromwell, in dismissing the Rump in 1653, looked intently at Marten and Wentworth, and said, "Some of you are whoremasters," he gave voice to a political implication wholly acceptable to Milton.[34] When, in the bitterness and despair of the 1660's, he poured the infinitely diverse riches of his mind into the mold of his great epic, the impulse of social compassion was too weak to sustain a comprehension of the multitude's political blunders. In the stern judgments of *Paradise Lost* the boundless charity of the Christ, glimpsed by extremists like Saltmarsh and Walwyn and Roger Williams, flutters helplessly in the offing. Adam's deliberate disobedience to God in eating the apple marks the conflict between the law and the Gospels that one finds in the pages of Milton and all the fellow radicals of his day. The law decreed unquestioning obedience to God's will. But Adam loved Eve more than he feared God's wrath, and for this he was condemned to the loss of Paradise. At such a moment it was not only the charm of Eve that swayed Adam's judgment; it was a sympathy born of crisis for a fellow human in despair. To have acted otherwise would have stamped Adam as an incarnation of relentless Puritanism. Much as Milton sympathized with Adam's chivalry, however, he sincerely approved of God's unhurried judgment upon him.

It may be said that the nature of Milton's judgment of erring man in *Paradise Lost* was the inevitable outcome of his choice of a topic; that it was necessary for him faithfully to reproduce both the outline and the tone of the Biblical story. This is true, however, only in part. The Biblical story is very short; though Milton has not deviated from its broad outline, he expanded it so much that various interpretations were possible, from the extreme Calvinistic viewpoint, which Milton had rejected over fifteen years before, to a deep sympathy for Adam, even justification of man's ways to God. None of the drafts of the epic made twenty years before suggest decisively the sombre judgments of the finished poem. Then, too, Milton's portrayal of Christ in *Paradise Lost* shows his lack of sympathy with the full measure of love and forgiveness that the extreme Puritan revolutionists emphasized in their characterizations.

When Milton did select a New Testament theme, he rejected all those characterizations that may have revealed the compassionate Christ, some of which he had mentioned in his early outlines: "Christus patiens," "Christ bound," "Christ Crucifi'd," "Christ risen." [35] It was to the temptation-resisting Christ, the stern incarnation of reason, rather than to the symbol of human brotherhood, that Milton turned in the last years of his life. The failure of *Paradise Regained* is not one of achievement, but of selection. Its characterization of Jesus disregards the central fascination that inspired the most revolutionary utterances of the Puritan Revolution. In the *white and soules beloved* of Roger Williams, the "head Leveller" of Winstanley, the Christ of *A Still And Soft Voice,* Milton could not place his deepest faith; in Him he could not find sufficient justification for a stern judgment on man's wickedness; in Him lived no bitterness for past calamities, only infinite hope for the future. Though Milton had caught glimpses of this Christ, both the decisive teachings of his youth and the doom of the Commonwealth reinforced in the last years of his life the stern prophetic strain that dominates *Paradise Lost* and *Regained.* Though the prophetic note is softened in *Paradise Lost* by the assurance of man's ultimate progress and salvation, and by the timeless appeal of Milton's humanistic wisdom, his justification of man's punishment obscures the charity Milton might have felt more deeply had the Commonwealth survived.

The identification of personal sin with man's political failures in *Paradise Lost* throws into sharp relief Milton's rich contributions to the progressive thought of the Puritan Revolution. In contrast to the political implications of his great epic, these contributions were secular in the main and humanistic. The timeless arguments for intellectual liberty found in *Areopagitica* transcend all theological creeds; they breathe, indeed, a revolutionary fervor that would open all creeds to pitiless criticism, leaving no institution unchallenged, no social assumption static or secure. Among the hundreds of bright creations struck off in a society straining with conflict, a society aroused to awareness of dynamic forces shattering the traditional molds and tracing patterns of the future, the *Areopagitica* was the unique and unanswerable classic of intellectual freedom. In his prose masterpiece Milton's theology fades into relative insignificance before the prospect of salvation by the collective fearless searching of a whole energetic people. Beside this beckoning utopia man's defeat and God's punishment fade like a pale and horrible dream. In ever widening knowledge, not in absorption with sin, man escapes the bonds of his tradition-ridden world: thus the *Areopagitica*. Where Milton plumbs most deeply the needs of aspiring free men like himself—in his passages on the nature of marriage, the conflict of truth and error, the response to persuasion, artificial distinctions, the sanctity of individual judgment, the nature of reflection, the yearning for sensuous beauty—he speaks as well to the pagan and the Christian, the Puritan and the Catholic. In his justifications of democratic ideals, though he was not consistent or realistic in their application, he spoke best from the riches of his humanistic knowledge, arguing better than he knew for the "miscellaneous rabble" of the Levellers and the Diggers. This humanism, together with his extreme Protestant individualism, drove him away from the royalists and the Presbyterians, justified the toleration and republicanism of the Independents, and sustained the democratic arguments of *The Tenure* and The *Defence*. To go further than this Milton's environment and training and his theological convictions forbade. Here was his place in the Puritan Revolution.

APPENDICES

LIGHT FOR THE BENIGHTED: COMENIUS AND MILTON

O NE of the curious deficiencies in the leadership of the Puritan Revolution was its failure to transform liberal agitation into educational
blueprints, much less actuality. If the democratic ideology propounded by both the Independents and the Levellers was to find justification in social change, a broad extension of free education, by which sons of
their supporters might be trained for public and professional leadership,
was a crying necessity. Only by unstinted broadening of educational opportunities could the Commonwealth have hoped for intelligent democratic
support or a rising mass consciousness of the sources and effects of the
prevailing inequalities and oppressions. Thus only could they have trained
a generation of youth from the poorer classes to uphold the Commonwealth and frustrate the return of kingship. But Cromwell and his followers, unpopular with the upper classes, make no attempt to win the
untutored masses toward the relief of which their agitation was apparently projected. Not only did the Independents make no effort to extend
or establish free schools; even their spokesmen among the pamphleteers
remained relatively indifferent to educational needs. Milton alone among
the Independents proposed even vaguely a school system of liberal dimen-
sions. Nor did the Levellers, except in scattered references, sense the
significance of the educational limitations that stifled the potential
leadership of future democratic surges. Although Walwyn, it is true,
criticized the highly theoretical training of the universities and recommended mastery of the practical arts, sound training in history and
economics, not in technical skills, would have transformed manhood
suffrage into more substantial privileges. Winstanley, as we know, visualized
the whole state ministry performing the functions of secular teachers on a
wholly informal basis; but he seems not to have recognized the place of
intense and systematic training of the whole citizenship for the efficient
functioning even of his utopia.

In his youth Milton had enthusiastically expressed his hope for the
perfection of the human spirit through universal learning: "So, at length,
my hearers, when once universal learning has finished its circles, the soul,

not content with this darksome prison-house, will reach out far and wide
till it shall have filled the world itself, and space beyond that, in the
divine expatiation of its magnitude." [1] Although in this sentence Milton
does not make known his conception of universal learning; although we
do not know merely from these two words whether he would have included both boys and girls, whether he would have carried on his teachings
at the expense of the state, it is evident that he looked upon some such
widespread plan as the most important factor in the perfectibility of
mankind. With a partial historical grasp of human evolution, he unhesitatingly assumed that the time would come when man would have fully
developed through education all the potentialities of his mind and spirit.
Despite the fact that Milton did not conceive of any full democratic plan
of education, and notwithstanding his loss of faith in his countrymen, he
never entirely departed from this youthful belief and hope.

In Milton's day the leading exponent of democratic educational
schemes was the Austro-Slav, John Amos Comenius, friend and teacher
of Samuel Hartlib, and resident of London in the late months of 1641
and spring of 1642. Through Hartlib's indefatigable efforts Comenius'
A Reformation of Schooles, really an English rendering of his *Great
Didactic*, was published in London January 12, 1642, Comenius' notions
were rather widely circulated among the intellectuals of London at the
opening of the Civil War. But they apparently left no mark on the minds
of the leading English liberals; for in the tumultuous years that followed
no Leveller or Independent pamphleteer came forth to demand the privileges for English children that Comenius had set forth as the birthright
of all the world's young. When Hartlib urged Milton to read the ideas
of Comenius, Milton flatly refused, writing to Hartlib as follows: "To
search what modern Januas and Didactics, more than ever I shall read,
have projected, by inclination leads me not." Not that Milton was not
interested in reforming English education. Quite the contrary; he speaks
of the "Reforming of Education . . . for the want whereof this Nation
perishes," and calls for instant action.[2] But for the time being, notwithstanding his youthful dream of universal learning, he closed his mind
to the queer educational notions of the distinguished foreigner.

Milton's *Of Education*, written before the intellectual wrestlings of
the Civil War had really begun, shows no awareness whatever of the
educational needs of the English masses. On the essentially aristocratic
nature of the plan all Milton critics concur. As Masson notes, Milton did
not have in mind *homo* but *vir:* "When he framed his definition of
Education, only one of the sexes was present in his mind; and throughout the whole tract, from first to last, there is not a single recognition of
girl, woman. . . But more than that. Not only is it the education of one

sex only that is discussed in the tract, but it is the education only of a portion of that sex, and of that portion only at particular period of life. There is nothing about the Infant Education, or what we might call the Primary Education, of male children; and there is nothing about the ways and means for the secondary or higher education of any others than those whose parents could pay for such education out of their own resources. In short, the tract is a proposal of a new method for the education of English gentlemen's sons between the ages of twelve and twenty-one." [3] St. John writes that Milton's object was "to create, from among the youth of ampler leisure and fortune, able and accomplished senators, judges, and generals." [4] When considered as suggestions for educational reforms, Milton's measures are, Pattison writes, "ludicrously incommensurable with the evils to be remedied." [5] After this testimony we need not pause on Milton's only systematic treatment of education. It is in no sense democratic; and it is almost as far removed from extreme seventeenth-century theory as the practical English school system of that day was removed from the American system of the present century.

In 1659, however, fifteen years after the appearance of his tract, *Of Education,* Milton incorporated in the *The Likeliest Means to Remove Hirelings Out of the Church* a more democratic education scheme than he had hitherto proposed. Although suggested as a solution of the problem of ministerial education, Milton's plan is one which would have extended to all sorts and conditions of men. He proposes that the public funds be used "to erect in greater number, all over the land, schools, and competent libraries to those schools, where languages and arts may be taught free together, without the needless, unprofitable, and inconvenient removing to another place. So all the land would be soon better civilized, and they who are taught freely at the public cost might have their education given them on this condition, that herewith content, they should not gad for preferment out of their own country, but continue there thankful for what they received freely, bestowing it freely on their own country, without soaring above the meanness wherein they were born." [6]

The following year, in his *Readie & Easie Way,* Milton again discussed briefly such a plan, one which he would have initiated by the various primary assemblies throughout his proposed commonwealth. "They should have here also schools and academies at their own choice, wherein their children may be bred up in their own sight to all learning and noble education; not in grammar only, but in all liberal arts and exercises. That would soon spread much more knowledge and civility, yea, religion, through all parts of the land, by communicating the natural heat of government and culture more distributively to all extreme parts, which now lie numb and neglected; would soon make the nation more industrious, more ingenious at home, more potent, more honorable abroad. To this a free commonwealth will easily assent; (nay, the parliament hath had already some such thing in design;) for of all governments a commonwealth aims most to make the people flourishing, virtuous, noble, and high-spirited." [7] Milton refers in this passage, of course, not to the children of the gentry and nobility so much as to the youth of the middle and lower classes. He wants for them, however, not only elementary schools, but also secondary schools and municipal universities, training "in all the liberal arts and exercises." In the public schools Milton would have separated, throughout the country, the slower from the superior students. In 1654, he had addressed to Cromwell the following plea: "Then, if you make a better provision for the education of our youth than has hitherto been made, if you *prevent the promiscuous instruction* of the docile and the indocile, of the idle and the diligent, at the public cost, but reserve the rewards of learning for the learned, and of merit for the meritorious." [8] It is clear, therefore, that Milton's educational plans would have involved, not a class system of education based upon social privilege, but a class system based upon intellectual merit; the country retaining, meanwhile, the traditional aristocratic superstructure. Milton's scheme is democratic in the sense that it would have permitted youths of humble birth, had their intelligence warranted it, to receive advanced education at the public cost.

Having briefly examined Milton's one definitely-aristocratic and two vaguely-democratic plans of education, let us turn to Comenius' *Great Didactic:*

THE GREAT DIDACTIC

Setting forth

The whole Art of Teaching
all Things to all Men

or

A Certain Inducement to found such Schools in all the Parishes, Towns, and Villages of every Christian Kingdom, that the entire Youth of both Sexes, none being excepted, shall

Quickly, Pleasantly, and Thoroughly

Become learned in the Sciences, pure in Morals, trained to Piety, and in this manner instructed in all things necessary for the present and for the future life.

What Comenius proposes is, then, not only a nation-wide, but a world-wide attempt to educate "all alike, boys and girls, both noble and ignoble, rich and poor," not the children of the "rich or of the powerful only." All having been born, he declares, with the same end in view, namely, that they may be rational men and women, images of their creator, it is just that all should be given an opportunity to acquire wisdom, piety, and virtue sufficient for the successful use of the present life and worthy preparation for the life to come.[9] Since God has so frequently asserted that he is no respecter of persons, Comenius continues, we should be rebuking God himself to deny to any one the culture of the intellect. "Nor do we know to what uses divine providence has destined this or that man; but this is certain, that out of the poorest, the most abject, and the most obscure, He has produced instruments for His glory. Let us, therefore, imitate the sun in the heavens, which lights, warms, and vivifies the whole earth, so that whatever is able to live, to flourish, and to blossom, may do so. In this respect the fervour of all men will increase in proportion to the flame of knowledge that has been kindled. For our love is in direct ratio to our knowledge."[10] Comenius denies that we should withhold training from those who seem naturally dull and stupid. It is these people who especially need the assistance of education; it will serve to rid them of their brutish lack of penetration. These dull people Comenius compares to a sieve which cannot contain liquid, but constantly grows brighter and brighter as water is poured through it. Furthermore, it is undeniable that some intellects, like trees which bear late fruit, do not show promise early, but late in life bear witness to their true capacity. Or, just as weak bodies develop into strong ones, so it is with intellects: "Some develop early, but soon wear out and grow dull, while others, originally stupid, become sharp and penetrating . . . Why, therefore, should we wish that in the garden of letters only one class of intellects, the forward and the active, be tolerated? Let none be excluded unless God has denied him sense and intelligence."[11]

Refusing to confine his plan to boys only, Comenius declares that women are also made in the image of God; that they have attained highly important positions in worldly affairs, having served even as rulers over kingdoms. Why, then, should we refuse to teach them to read and write, or to deny to them books of culture?[12]

And then Comenius answers that "sluggish objection" one yet hears as a legitimate argument against universal learning: "What will result if artisans, rustics, porters, and even women become learned?" They will learn, Comenius replies, to think and choose for themselves, to reconcile labor with philosophical meditation, and, by being able to read the

Bible and other good books, to avoid "that idleness which is so dangerous to flesh and blood." [13] If it be argued that some lack inclination to work, and that to compel them against their will would be useless, Comenius questions any such innate lack of inclination: if students are unwilling it is more often the teacher's fault than that of the student.[14] Such in substance are Comenius' arguments for universal education. His plans for financing it are not so detailed or so complete.

Appealing to the magistrates and rulers at the end of his treatise to put his vast plan into operation, Comenius endeavors to show why they should provide funds freely for the purpose. Money expended for education is much more worth while than money expended for armaments and internal improvements. Yet if some one were to show these rulers how they might fortify all their towns at slight cost, how their rivers might be made navigable, how all the youth might be instructed cheaply in the art of warfare, Comenius has no doubt that the rulers would be highly grateful. But what is far more important, he now offers them his plan for universal learning. If they invest in it, it will bring to them untold benefits far more precious than military or economic advancement. Comenius then quotes Luther's words that for every ducat expended on armaments and buildings, one hundred should be spent in educating one potentially great man. If we are to admit that no expense should be spared in educating one promising youth, asks Comenius, why should we not invest in all young people, reaping immeasurable benefits therefrom? "Stay not," concludes Comenius, "to consider expense." He looks upon money expended for education as money expended for religious purposes, which God will repay a thousandfold. We see, therefore, that there is nothing of budgets or tax rates in Comenius' suggestions. He merely exhorts the rulers to provide whatever money is needed to carry out his vast scheme, to invest in human securities rather than in state buildings and armaments. What is important for us, it is plain that by his plan boys and girls would share alike in the distribution of educational funds.

Whatever his faults as an educator, or whatever the inherent fallacies in democratic theory, it is doubtful whether succeeding centuries have produced a more thoroughgoing educational democrat than Comenius. At a period when only leading thinkers like Roger Ascham and Defoe advocated education for women; when few people on the continent considered the minds of peasants capable of development; when education was largely a private venture reserved for those who could afford it; when no one would have thought possible or desirable a mingling of peasants, artisans, gentry, and nobility in one school, Comenius worked steadily at his intricate educational dream. In spirit a twentieth-century democrat, Comenius believed superlatively in environment, in the infinite intellectual and spiritual capacity of the average person, and in the Christian maxim of spiritual equality. Ambition and will he believed to be acquired rather than inherited. Refusing to acknowledge that any objective judgment can determine a person's fitness for a high calling, Comenius declared it to be the inalienable right of every person, whatever his station, ancestry, color, intelligence, or sex, to such educational environment which would, at the public cost, completely unfold his talents and personality. No passive reformer, Comenius presented to the world a practical plan, in his opinion, whereby his ideals might be realized. It was to the study of this man and these ideals that Milton said, "My inclination leads me not."

Compared with Comenius' *Great Didactic*, what plan of democratic education did Milton present to his countrymen? It cannot be said, of course, that Milton constructed any systematic plan at all. To put it quantitatively, which may be unfair to Milton, he wrote only two paragraphs concerning such a plan, and these he inserted in pamphlets not mainly concerned with education. Compare these paragraphs with the three hundred pages of *Didactic Magna*, and one has a quantitative estimate of Milton's contribution to democratic education compared with that of Comenius.

One searches in vain for evidence that Milton had any inkling of the importance of a secular democratic school system to the achievement of that liberty he so ardently desired. Though theoretically he believed with Comenius in man's perfectibility, he believed in perfectibility mainly through Christ. To Milton spiritual perfection was primary to intellectual achevement; to Comenius the reverse was true. He believed that man grows into the image of God by the process of intellectual training and cultural development. With Milton, all one had to do to achieve Christian liberty, to become spiritually wise, was to throw away one's bad habits and by the aid of God become a virtuous person; Comenius, on the contrary, was firm in his belief that secular education is the only fundamental method by which large numbers of people can achieve virtue. Character being essential to political citizenship, but education not being essential to character, Milton did not conceive the primary need of the nation to be a widespread system of public schools. Milton never seems to have felt that large numbers of young men, much less women, needed the same secular education he possessed to become as devoted to liberty as he was.

But this was not all. Down deep in his heart Milton never felt that large numbers of his countrymen were capable of advanced education, that there would ever be fundamental change in the class-bound educational system of his country. This system of his own land meant "orders and degrees" which "jar not with liberty, but well consist." It meant, too, at least a partial recognition and development of any very evident talent among the poorer classes. Again it was his conception of proportioned equality, his study of Greek and Roman education, which convinced him that there always would be multitudes of the intellectually-incapable whose needs must be sacrificed to the privileges and capacities of the superior few.

First, then, because he felt that religious and not secular instruction was the *primary* need of the nation, and secondly, because he did not believe in a thoroughly democratic mixing of superior and inferior minds in one great system, the inferior minds remaining always inferior, Milton contributed no more than a suggestion of any unified plan for the thorough education of all the people. He was no educational democrat, and his importance in seventeenth-century educational democracy, compared with that of Comenius, is remarkably slight.

In conclusion, we believe that as in politics it was Milton's overemphasis on religion, his Puritan dependence on God to the exclusion of faith in his fellow-man, which prevented his acceptance of a democratic political doctrine, so in education his high Puritan faith in God's miraculous power minimized for him the importance of secular education for the masses. In this, however, Milton was not exceptional among the Puritan reformers. In an age pregnant with panaceas, none of his fellow liberals, whether Independent, Leveller, or Digger, visualized a determined extension of educational privileges as one of the highways to freedom.

NOTES. APPENDIX I

1. Milton's *Exercise VII*, Masson I, 228-29
2. Masson, III, 235
3. Masson, III, 238
4. St. John's note, *Prose Works*, III, 462. Cf. J. H. Hanford, *A Milton Handbook*, p. 72: "The tract offers an essentially aristocratic plan, designed for the training of the sons of gentlemen to leadership in war and peace."
5. Pattison, *Milton*, p. 45
6. *Prose Works*, III, 27
7. *Prose Works*, II, 136
8. *Prose Works*, I, 294 (italics mine)
9. John Amos Comenius, *The Great Didactic*, ed. M. W. Keating (2 v. London: Adam and Charles Black, 1907-10), II, 66, 71
10. *Ibid.*, pp. 66-7
11. Comenius, *op. cit.*, II, 67
12. *Ibid.*, II, 68
13. Comenius, *op. cit.*, II, 69
14. *Ibid.*, II, 87

WILLIAM WALWYN

A STILL AND SOFT VOICE

A Still And Soft Voice appeared in 1647 without name or imprint. Walwyn acknowledged himself the author in his *Just Defence*, saying that he published it to "stand clear in the sight of all men," and that against it he "never yet heard any objection."

The pamphlet anticipates Walwyn's controversy with the Independents and Anabaptists who sided with Cromwell against the Levellers in the early months of 1649. Throwing into bold relief Walwyn's philosophical motivation, *A Still And Soft Voice* also reveals the intellectual cleavage between the relatively pious Independent leaders and the secular Levellers. Through the literature of the Puritan Revolution this cleavage has persistent and far reaching ramifications. In the tolerationist revolt against Presbyterian formulas, in Milton's divorce heresies and the bold appeal of *Areopagitica,* in the pamphlets of Roger Williams, one may trace the same divergence of the orthodox from the traditional interpretation of the Scriptures. It was left to Walwyn, however, to write the classic analysis of the conflict, with a penetration unequaled by his contemporaries except in the pages of Winstanley.

The tract is here reprinted from the copy in the McAlpin Collection of Union Theological Seminary. Spelling and punctuation follow the usage of the original tract. The design of the title page is an imitation, not an exact reproduction, of the original. Pagination of the original tract has been inserted in brackets.

A
STILL AND SOFT VOICE
From the Scriptures,
VVitnessing them to be the
VVord of God.

---

1 Kings. 19. 11. 12.

And he said (to Eliah) come out and stand upon the Mount before the Lord.   And behold the Lord went by, and a mighty strong wind rent the Mountaines and brake the Rocks before the Lord, but the Lord was not in the wind, and after the wind came an Earth-quake, but the Lord was not in the Earth-quake.

And after the Earth-quake came fire, but the Lord was not in the fire, and after the fire came a still and soft voice.   And when Eliah heard it, he covered his face with a Mantle, &c.

Printed in the Yeare, 1647.

A STILL AND SOFT VOICE.

AS he who is arrived to the full age of a man, and seriously considers, the severall passages and progresse of his fore past life: what he did or understood, when he was a child, a youth, a young man; a meere man, or before he came to be advised, and to consider all things by *true rules* of reason: is best able to deale with every one in every age and condition, to shew them their vanity, ignorance and mistakings: and to point them out the path of vertue. Experience making the best Schoole-master in things naturall and morall.

Even so is it in Religion, he only can best judge, advise and counsell others, who hath observed and *most seriously considered* the severall passages and progresse of his owne knowledge in things divine: yet who are so forward to judge and comptrole therein, as meere smatterers and such as have least experience.

I suppose it will be acknowledged, by all experienced Christians, that the greatest number of men and women in the world, are drawne into the consideration and Practice of Religion, by education, and custome of the place where they are bred: and that [3] many never have any other foundation, nor motive to continue therein, then the reputation it brings them: all other religions or wayes of worship being discountenanced and out of credit, such as these are Champions for whats in fashion: ever running with the streame, and crying downe all contrary minded; *Vox populi, Vox dei,* the Major voice (then which nothing is more uncertain in Religion) is to these as the voice of God: and when they are zealous for *vulgar opinions* they thinke they are zealous for God and his truth: when they revile, abuse, and hale men before the Magistrates, and even kill and destroy them, they think they doe God good service: being zealous of the *traditions of the times*: for though truth should be publickly professed: yet to such as hold it only by education and custome: it is in them traditionall, and they are not truly religious; but meere morrall christians: utterly ignorrant of the cleare Heavenly brightnesse, inherent, in pure and undefiled Religion.

But though it be evident, that there are too too many, who hold their religion, on this fraile foundation, yet it is very comfortable to behold, the sincerity of multitudes of good people in our dayes: who; not content to possesse their knowledg in a traditionall way: doe accustome themselves to try and examine all things.

Yet as it is a hard thing unto men, bred so vainly as most men are, to keepe the golden meane, in naturall or morrall Reformations: so is it difficult to preserve from **extreames**, in matters of religion, the reason is, because in our tryalls and examinati[4]ons, we have not that heedfull care, which is absolutely necessary, to free our Judgments from *absurdityes or improper things*: common and uvlgar [*sic*] arguments catching fast hold upon us too suddenly; and so we engage over violently, averring and maintayning without giving due time to our consideration to worke and debate itselfe into necessary conclusions.

The first sort of these religious persons: are deadly enemies to examination and tryall of things, we (say they) are not fit to Judge of these matters *ne sutor ultra crepidam*, is commonly in their mouthes: *the Cobler ought not to goe beyond his last*: what are the learned for, if these high things fall within the compasse of our capacities, why chuse wee wise and juditious men, more able then our selves, but to reforme, and settle Religion: if you draw them into any discourse, and endeavour to shew them their weakenesse, their only aime is how to entrap you, in your words, and if it be possible to make you obnoctious to authority.

If their ignorance and superstition appeare so grosse and palpable, that (in loving tearmes, and for their better information,) you demand how they come to know there is a God, or that the scriptures are the word of God: their common answer is, *doe you deny them: it seemes you doe? otherwise why doe you aske such questions?* if they offer to proove by some common received argument: and you shew the weaknesse thereof: they'le goe nigh to tell you to your face, and report for certaine behind your back, to all they know, or can know, that you are an Athiest, that you deny there is a God, and deny the |5| Scriptures to be the word of God: nor doe they hate any sort of men so much, as those who are *inquisitive after knowledge,* judgeing them as busie bodyes, men of unquiet spirits, that know not when they are well, or when they have sufficient: for their parts, they are constant in one, for the substance; their principles are not of yesterday but of many yeares standing: and the most learned and wise are of their way, and why should not others be as well content as they, is it fit (say they) that every one should follow his owne understanding in the worship of God, wee see what comes of it; when men once forsake the beaten Road (the Kings high way) in Religion, into how many by-pathes, doe they runne, nay, whether would they not runne, if our care were not to hedg and keepe them in.

And thus ignorance becomes many times Judge of knowledge: and the most grosse and slothfull; comptroler of the most active in Religion.

Of this sort of men there are very many; and they are made very much use of by worldly Pollititians, who have found by constant experience, that superstition is the easiest meanes to lead a multitude, this way, or that way as their occasions and purposes may require, and on the contrary, that true Religion is in it selfe as oppsite to their unjust ends, as it is to superstition and therefore if they observe any man who out of the principles of true Religion opposeth their ends; at him they let loose these ignorant and morrall christians, furnish them with reproachfull tales, and falshoods, against him, call him Athiest Infidell, Heritick, Scismatick, any thing: which is as eagerly effected, as wickedly devised: and how to stop these mens mouthes is in my apprehension [6] no lesse a worke then to make white a Blackamore.

Those others who are startled in their consciences, and roused by *the word of God,* out of this worldly way of religion, or running with the streame, it is a hard matter to hold them *to a due pace, in the persute of necessary knowledge* or to keepe them *to a propper Method,* or to obtaine this of them, *that they receive nothing as a truth, which they see admiteth of an obsurdity.*

But having broke loose from the bands *of educated and customary religion,* through necessity of conscience, and being *anew to begin,* they are apt *hastily to take in,* that which is first offered *with any resemblance of truth,* and so in an instant, fall into new entanglements.

For if hast, make wast in any thing, it is in pursute after knowledge: and though every considerate mans experience findeth this a truth: though it be confest by all, that there is nothing of greater concernment to man, then *the truth of his Divine knowledge:* though nothing doth more disturb the minde of man, *then error and mistakeing in religion.*

Yet is there not any thing wherein men: proceed more irregularly, or more impatiently: either they are over rash and sudden or over fearfull, and irresolute: they approach all discourse with prejudice, and a mind distempered, searching nothing throughly or orderly, but content themselves with an overly examination, and (in my apprehention) are not so disingenious in any thing, as in religion: willingly resigning and forfeiting their understandings, and Judgments, at a cheap rate then Esau did his Birthright: and so continue *very long* (not truly religious, [7] but) superstitious men, alwayes amazed: neither remembring what themselves or others speake: he that once opposeth them, hath a Wolfe by the eares, hee can neither speake, nor hold his peace, without damage, they take allthings in the worst sence sigh, lament, pitty, or censure, all that sutes not with their opinion or practice: and talk or report of, any man, any thing that comes in their imaginations; those that come behind them in knowledge; are carnall: those before them desperate And therefore it may be very profitable; that the differences betwene true Religion and superstition, be made knowne *to thesetimes,* more fully than it is, the one being commonly taken for the other.

Now both are best knowne by their effects: for true Religion setleth

a man in peace and rest: makes him like unto the Angels, alwayes praising God and saying Glory to God on High, in earth peace, Good will
towards men, it is ever provided with good intentions and good desires,
maketh the best construction in doubtfull cases, see how true Christian
love is described by the Apostle in the 13. to the Corinths. and that is
the *true* Religious mans Character.

On the contrary, superstition troubleth and makes a man wilde, a
superstitious man suffereth neither God nor man to live in peace, (as
one well observeth from experience) he aprehendeth God, as one anxious,
spiteful, hardly contented easily moved, with difficulty appeased, exam-
ing our actions after the human fashion of a severe Judge, that watcheth
our steps, which hee prooveth true by his manner of serving him, hee
trembleth for feare is never secure, fearing he never doth well, and that
he hath left [8] some thing undone, by omission whereof, all is worth
nothing that he hath done.

But generally now a dayes, (contrary to former tymes) the superstitious mans devotion costs him litle, he hath somuch worldly wit in his
zeale, as to save his purse, hot and fiery against heresie and blasphemy,
(which are titles he freely bestowes on all opinions, contrary to his own,
true or false), he will course his poor neighbour out of all he hath, yea
out of the Nation, if he can not course him *into his opinion*: and all upon
pretence of doing God service and for the good of his soule.

As for his body, or estate, thats no part of his care, hee is not so
hasty to runn into his poore neighbours house, to see what is wanting
there, hee may ly upon a bed, or no bed, covering or no covering, be
starved through cold and hunger, over burthened with labour, be sick,
lame or diseased: and all this troubles not the superstitious mans (nor
the morall Christians) Conscience: he may through want and necessity
goe into what prison he will, and ly and rott and starve there: and these
kind of Religious people are not halfe so much moved at it, as if he goe
to another Church or congregation, then what they approove: if hee doe
so, upstarts their zeale; and after him, watch, spy, accuse and informe:
and all for the good of his soule: and for the Glory of God.

One would not think it were possible man could be so blind, or so
inconsiderate as to immagin, that God would be thus mocked, thus madly
served, contrary to the whole tenor of the Scriptures, but such are the
effects of *educated, customary or superstitious* Religion.

Whist [*sic*] the effects of pure and undefiled Religion, are another
thing: as Feeding the hungry, Cloathing the naked, Visiting the sick, the
Fatherlesse, the Widdowes and Priso[9]ners: and in all things *walking as
becometh the Gospell of Christ*: it will empty the fullest Baggs: and
pluck downe the highest plumes.

And whoever serveth God sincerely in this Religion, shall be knowne by his fruites: his light shall so shine before men, that they seeing *his good Workes,* shall Glorify our Father which is in heaven.

But of these there are few to bee found; and as few that truly labour, to reclaime those many thousands of miserable people that are drencht all their life long in grosse ignorance, and notorious loathsome wickednesse: *Yet there is joy in heaven over one sinner that repenteth, more then for ninety nine just persons that need no repentance:* Why talke wee so much of Christianity, holinesse, and saintship, whilst wee neglect the lost sheep, or the recovery of our brethren from those *Errors* of their wayes.

The plain truth is, this grosse neglect of known duty herein, and the generall eagernesse in the lesse necessary parts of zeale and devotion, manifesteth *the world* is not subdued; that there is little selfe-deniall, little of pure and undefiled Religion as yet in the world: men content themselves with forms of godlinesse, but are regardlesse of the power thereof.

And therefore I have been the lesse troubled in my selfe; for the hard measure I have found: amidst so great a mixture of worldlinesse, ignorance, and superstitious zeale, why should one looke for much ingenuity, these times have but cast an eye towards the *materiall* parts of true Christianity: It is not yet knowne what it is, in its excellency, the end and issue thereof, is too good to bee deserved, or discerned, by a people that are not yet broad awake, they strike him that brings them more light; then they can well endure.

All the evill and reproach I have suffered, hath beene by occasion of my forwardnesse to do others good: my freenesse [10] in discourse, though harmlesse in it selfe, and intended for good, hath been perverted, misconstrued, and made use of to my prejudice.

I accompt nothing more vain, then to discourse meerly for discourse sake, nay, it is painfull and ircksome to me, to heare a discourse that is not really necessary and usefull, nor doe I know, that I have ever purposely set my self to debate any serious matter, slightly or carelessely, though cheerefully.

And my manner is, whatever is in debate, to search it thorowly, being of an opinion, that, what is really true, stands the firmer, for being shaken: like a house that is built upon a rock.

I have been much troubled, to observe men earnestly engage to maintaine the strongest maximes and principles by weak arguments; the weaknesse whereof, I have endevoured to manifest, that I might discover the weaknesse of such practises, and to make it evident, that fundamentall truthes support all things, and need no supporters: *Thou bearest not the root, but the root, thee.*

But this my free dealing (with uncharitable or superstitious people) hath found this evill returne, they have reported me, to deny that there is a God, when I have only denyed the validity of a weak argument, produced to prove that there is a God; it being too too common, to insist upon meere notionall indigested arguments: so also have I been most uncharitably slandered to deny the Scriptures to bee the word of God, because I have opposed insufficient arguments produced to prove them such: and because at the same time I have refused to shew the grounds inducing me to beleeve them.

Now it hath been my lot to be drawne into discourses of this nature for the most part by timerous, scrupulous, people, in whom, I have discovered so much impatience, and discontent, at the shaking of their arguments, that I have not discerned any reason to open my selfe at that time; yet I never [11] parted with any of them, but I alwayes professed that I did believe, both that there is a God, & that the Scriptures are the Word of God, though I judged their grounds not good; and withall, that if they would be so ingenious as to acknowledge the weaknesse of their arguments, I would then shew them my ground of faith; or if at any time they stood in need, I would not be wanting to the uttermost of my power to supply them, but I have seldome found any, who in the heat of contest and prosecution of dispute, have been qualified, to receive, what I had to say, touching this matter, their apprehension and mine being at too great a distance therein.

But I blesse God it is not so ill with me, as some bad minded men desire, nor as some weak and scrupulous men imagin.

And there are some ingenious men, with whom I have daily converst, that know I doe acknowledge and beleeve there is a God, and that the Scriptures are the Word of God.

Yet the testimony of men in this case to mee is little, my owne conscience being as a thousand witnesses.

That there is a God: I did never beleeve through any convincing power I have ever discerned by my utmost consideration of any natural argument or reason I ever heard or read: But it is *an unexpressible power*, that in a forcible manner constraines my understanding to acknowledge and beleeve that there is a God, and so to beleeve that I am fully perswaded there is no *considerat man* in the world but doth believe there is a God.

And, *That the Scriptures are the Word of God*, I shall clearly make the same profession, That I have not beleeved them so to be, by force of any argument I have ever heard or read, I rather find by experience, most, if not all arguments, produced *in prejudice* thereof: (Art, argument, and compulsive [12] power, in this case holding resemblance with the mighty strong *wind*, the *Earth quake* and fire, distracting, terrifying and scorching the minds of men) but I beleeve them through an irresistible perswasive power that from within them (like unto the soft still voyce wherein God was) hath pierced my judgment and affection in such sort, that with aboundance of joy and gladnesse I beleeve, and in beleeving have that *Peace* which passeth all utterance or expression; and which hath appeared unto me after so many sad conflicts of a distracted conscience, and wounded spirit, that it is to me a heaven upon earth: It being now long since, I blesse God, that I can truly say, *My heart is fixed, O God, my heart is fixed, I will sing and give praise:* In other respects, I conceive the most holy upon earth, if they give impartiall eare to this voyce, will finde no cause to boast or to finde fault with others, but as *Eliah* to cover their faces with a mantle.

And truly were it not that too too many *pretenders to Religion,* are over apt to receive false reports (which is a most uncharitable disposition) and over-prone to make the worst construction, which is altogether unchristian, it had beene impossible for any to have abused me in these or any other respects.

But it will be neefull [*sic*] for all such, seriously to lay to heart, *that they ought to do as they would be done unto in all things, that he who seemeth to bee religious and bridles not his tongue, that mans religion is vaine.*

That he who boasteth *to beleeve a God,* and *the Scriptures to be the Word of God,* and glorieth in his ability of exposition thereof: yet applieth it to the discovery of a mote in his brothers eye, rather then a beame in his own: he whose expressions and actions do demonstrate him to say within himselfe, *Lord I thank thee, I am not as other men, extortioners, unjust adulterers, nor as this Publican:* This man who ever he be, is not [13] yet got through the lesson of the Pharisies; *that were wise in their owne eyes, and despised others.*

But it would be much more profitable to society and good neighbourhood that there were a more exact accompt taken by every man of his owne wayes; it is verily thought most men neede not goe abroad for want of work, if either pride, covetousnesse, backbiting, unreasonable jealosy, vanity of minde, dotage upon superfluities: with hard heartedness to the poore: were thought worthy of Reformation.

To be zealous *in lipp service,* or to expresse our devotion, *in censuring of others,* yeelds neither honour to God, nor good to man.

Who were more blinde, then those *who* said *are wee blind, also?* the Angell of the Church of Laodicea, boasted that he was rich, and increased with goods and *had neede for nothing*: and knew not that he was *wretched, and misserable and poor and blind and naked.*

Wee have many now a dayes, who are *doubly unjust* and thinke not of it: they are partiall and favourable in examining and corecting of themselves: and severe towards others, when as they ought to be severe towards themselves: and favourable towards others.

And it is a fault not easily mended: it requires agreater power of true religion to doe it, then the most have as yet attained, if one may judge by the Fruites: and therefore it will be good for every one to neglect that which is behinde, and to presse forward to the marke, for the price of the high Calling of God which is in Jesus Christ: either renounce the Name, or let your practice demonstrate, that you are a Christian.

Hee who greedily receiveth a hard report of his neighbour, is not provided of charitable and loving thoughts as he ought; and if he report any evill, before he be certaine of the [14] truth thereof, hee is a slanderer; and when hee is certaine it is true, if he report it with delight, it argues him of malice.

He who is glad of his neighours defamation, would not be sory at his ruine: a slanderer would be a murderer but for feare: and therefore, every honest vertuous religious man should shun a slanderer, as he would shun a Serpent.

And thus having said enough to free my self from this slander (if religious people will but study ingenuity, which hath been too much wanting amongst them) the whole course of my actions, writings and discourses, evidencing the contrary to all that throughly know me: and this my profession being added to, satisfie those that know me but by hearsay: *I have done*: judging it a small thing to be judged of any, or of mans judgement; *Who art thou that judgest another mans servant, to his owne master, hee standeth or falleth.*

The liberty of my native Country, and the freedome of all consciencious people hath been, and still is pretious in my esteeme: nor shall I be discouraged (by any the unworthy slanders cast upon me) from a just and due prosecution of both, according to my place and calling: I shall make *bold to deceive the deceiver and his instruments therein:* I should be glad to see the Educated and customary morall Christians become Christians indeed, and cease to persecute: I should exceedingly rejoyce to see the superstitious, become really religious, and to see babes; become strong men in Christ, and all bend their endevours to deliver the captive, and set the oppressed free, to reclaime the vicious, and to labour the saving of the lost sheep of the house of *England*: To see Charity abound, and all envy, malice, and worldly mindednesse to cease for ever, and not to be named amongst us, as becommeth *Saints indeed*: to see all men ingenious, loving, friendly and tender-hearted one towards another: but I must neither be silent, nor slothfull till I see it, nor sorow as one with[15]out hope of seeing it: but through evill report, and good report, do my duty? patiently expecting a good issue? laboring in all estates to be content; knowing there is no temptation hath taken hold upon others, but may befall unto me. In the mean time, knowing all terrestriall things to be but vain and transitory, my chiefest comfort is, that I desire to know *Nothing save Jesus Christ and him crucified*: accounting all things as losse and dung that I may be found in Christ, not having my own righteousnesse which is of the Law, but the righteousnesse which is of God in him.

I have no quarrell to any man, either for unbeleefe or misbeleefe, because I judge no man beleeveth any thing, but what he cannot choose but beleeve; it is misery enough to want the comfort of true beleeving, and I judge the most convincing argument that any man can hold forth unto another, to prove himselfe a true sincere beleever, is to practice to *the uttermost* that which his faith binds him unto: more of the *deeds of Christians*, and fewer of the arguments would doe a great deale more good to the establishing of those that stagger: It being not the leaves but the fruit that nourisheth and carrieth the seed with it, Shew me thy faith by thy workes; If I have all faith and have not love, I am as sounding brasse, or as a tinckling cymball, if faith worke, it workes by love: Let us all therefore hence-forth walk in love, even as Christ hath loved, and hath given himselfe an offering and a sacrifice for us: to whom bee glory and dominion for ever. *Amen.* [16]

By WILLIAM WALWYN, *Merchant:*
(*there being a Minister of the same name.*)

FINIS.

GERRARD WINSTANLEY

A WATCH-WORD TO THE CITY OF LONDON

A Watch-Word To The City of London appeared in London, September 10, 1649. Richest of Winstanley's tracts in autobiographical facts, it contains a number of details about the Digger experiment and reflects the main trends of Winstanley's economic ideas. The tract is reprinted from a photostat of the copy in the Thomason Collection of the British Museum. Spelling and punctuation follow the usage of the original tract. The design of the title page is an imitation, not an exact reproduction, of the original.

A
WATCH-WORD
TO
The City of London,
AND THE
ARMIE:

WHEREIN
You may see that Englands freedome,
which should be the result of all our Victories,

is sinking deeper under the Norman power, as appears by
this relation of the unrighteous proceedings of Kingstone-
Court against some of the Diggers at *George*-hill, under colour of
Law; but yet thereby the cause of the Diggers is more brightened
and strengthened: so that every one singly may truly
say what his freedome is, and where it lies.

By *Jerrard Winstanly*.

When these clay-bodies are in grave, and children stand in place,
This shewes we stood for truth and peace, and freedom in our daies;
And true born sons we shall appear of England that's our mother,
No Priests nor Lawyers wiles t'imbrace, their slavery wee'l discover.

LONDON,
Printed for *Giles Calvert* at the Sign of the black Spread-Eagle,
at the West end of *Pauls*, 1649.

To the City of London, *Freedome and Peace desired.*

THOU City of London, I am one of thy sons by freedome, and I do truly love thy peace; while I had an estate in thee, I was free to offer my Mite into thy publike Treasury Guild-hall, for a preservation to thee, and the whole Land; but by thy cheating sons in the theeving art of buying and selling, and by the burdens of, and for the Souldiery in the beginning of the war, I was beaten out both of estate and trade, and forced to accept of the good will of friends crediting of me, to live a Countrey-life, and there likewise by the burthen of Taxes and much Free-quarter, my weak back found the burthen heavier then I could bear; yet in all the passages of these eight yeers troubles I have been willing to lay out what my Talent was, to procure Englands peace inward and outward, and yet all along I have found such as in words have professed the same cause, to be enemies to me. Not a full yeere since, being quiet at my work, my heart was filled with sweet thoughts, and many things were revealed to me which I never read in books, nor heard from the mouth of any flesh, and when I began to speak of them, some people could not bear my words, and amongst those revelations this was one, *That the earth shall be made a common Treasury of livelihood to whole mankind, without respect of persons;* and I had a voice within me bad me declare it all abroad, which I did obey, for I declared it by word of mouth wheresoever I came, then I was made to write a little book called, *The new Law of righteousnesse,* and therein I declared it; yet my mind was not at rest, because nothing was acted, and thoughts run in me, that words and writings were all nothing, and must die, for action is the life of all, and if thou dost not act, thou dost nothing. Within a little time I was made obedient to the word in that particular likewise; for I tooke my spade and went and broke the ground upon *George-hill* in Surrey, thereby declaring freedome to the Creation, and that the earth must be set free from intanglements of Lords and Landlords, and that it shall become a common Treasury to all, as it was first made and given to the sonnes of men: For which doing the Dragon presently casts a flood of water to drown the manchild, even that freedom that now is declared, for the old Norman Prerogative Lord of that Mannour M *Drake,* caused me to be arrested for a trespasse against him, in digging upon that barren Heath, and the unrighteous proceedings of Kingstone Court in this businesse I have here declared to thee, and to the whole land, that you may consider the case that England is in; all men have stood for freedom, thou hast kept fasting daies, and prayed in morning exercises for freedom; thou hast given thanks for victories, because hopes of freedome; plentie of Petitions and promises thereupon have been made for freedome, and now the common enemy is gone, you are all like men in a mist, seeking for freedom, and know not where, nor what it is: and those of the richer sort of you that see it, are ashamed and afraid to owne it, because it comes clothed in a clownish garment, and open to the best language that scoffing *Ishmael* can afford, or that railing *Rabsheka* can speak, or furious *Pharoah* can act against him; for freedom is the man that will turn the world upside downe, therefore, no wonder he hath enemies.

And assure your selves, if you pitch not right now upon the right point of freedome in action, as your Covenant hath it in words, you will wrap up your children in greater slavery than ever you were in: the Word of God is Love, and when all thy actions are done in love to the whole Creation, then thou advancest freedome, and freedome is Christ in you, and Christ among you; bondage is Satan in you, and Satan among you: no true freedom can be established for Englands peace, or prove you faithfull in Covenant, but such a one as hath respect to the poor, as well as the rich; for if thou consent to freedom to the rich in the City and givest freedome to the Freeholders in the Countrey, and to Priests and Lawyers, and Lords of Mannours, and Impropriators, and yet allowest the poor no freedome, thou art then a declared hypocrite, and all thy prayers, fasts, and thanksgivings are, and will be proved an abomination to the Lord, and freedome himselfe will be the poors portion, when thou shalt lie groaning in bondage.

I have declared this truth to the Army and Parliament, and now I have declared it to thee likewise, that none of you that are the fleshly strength of this Land may be left without excuse, for now you have been all spoken to, and because I have obeyed the voice of the Lord in this thing, therefore doe the Free-holders and Lords of Mannours seek to oppresse me in the outward livelihood of the world, but I am in peace. And London, nay England look to thy freedom, I'le assure thee, thou art very neere to be cheated of it, and if thou lose it now after all thy boasting, truly thy posterity will curse thee, for thy unfaithfulnesse to them: every one talks of freedome, but there are but few that act for freedome, and the actors for freedome are oppressed by the talkers and verball professors of freedome; if thou wouldst know what true freedome is, read over this and other my writings, and thou shalt see it lies in the community in spirit, and community in the earthly treasury, and this is Christ the true manchild spread abroad in the Creation, restoring all things into himselfe; and so I leave thee,

August 26. 1649.

Being a free Denizon of thee, and a true lover of thy peace,

Jerrard Winstanly,

A WATCH-WORD TO THE CITY OF LONDON,
AND THE ARMY.

WHEREAS we *Henry Bickerstaffe, Thomas Star,* and *Jerrard Winstanly*, were arrested into Kingstone Court, by *Thomas Wenman, Ralph Verny,* and *Richard Winwood*, for a tresspasse in digging upon George-hill in Surrey, being the rights of Mr. *Drake* the Lord of that Mannour, as they say, we all three did appear the first Court day of our arrest, and demanded of the Court, what was laid to our Charge, and to give answer thereunto our selves: But the answer of your Court was this, that you would not tell us what the Trespasse was, unlesse we would fee an Attorney to speak for us; we told them we were to plead our own cause, for we knew no Lawyer that we could trust with this businesse: we desired a copie of the Declaration, and profered to pay for it; and still you denied us, unlesse we would fee an Attorney. But in conclusion, the Recorder of your Court told us, the cause was not entred; we appeared two Court daies after this, and desired to see the Declaration, and still you denied us, unlesse we will fee an Attorney; so greedy are these Attorneys after money, more then to justifie a righteous cause: we told them we could not fee any, unlesse we would willfully break our Nationall Covenant, which both Parliament and people have taken joyntly together to endeavour a Reformation. And unlesse we would be professed Traytors to this Nation and Common-wealth of England, by upholding the old Norman tyrannicall and destructive Lawes, when they are to be cast out of equity, and reason be the Moderator.

Then seeing you would not suffer us to speak, one of us brought this following writing into your Court, that you might read our answer; because we would acknowledge all righteous proceedings in Law, though some slander us, and say we deny all Law, because we deny the corruption in Law, and endeavour a Reformation in our place and calling, according to that Nationall Covenant: and we know if your Lawes be built upon equity and reason, you ought both to have heard us speak, and read our answer; for that is no righteous Law, whereby to keep a Common-wealth in peace, when one sort shall be suffered to speak, and not another, as you deal with us, to passe sentence and execution upon us, before both sides be heard to speak. [1]

This principle in the forehead of your Laws, foretells destruction to this Common-wealth: for it declares that the Laws that follow such refusall, are selfish and theevish, and full of murder, protecting all that get money by their Laws, and crushing all others.

The writer hereof does require Mr. *Drake*, as he is a Parliament man; therefore a man counted able to speak rationally, to plead this cause of digging with me, and if he shew a just and rationall title, that Lords of Mannours have to the Commons, and that they have a just power from God, to call it their right, shutting out others; then I will write as much against it, as ever I writ for this cause. But if I shew by the Law of Righteousnesse, that the poorest man hath as true a title and just right to the Land, as the richest man, and that undeniably the earth ought to be a common treasury of livelihood for all, without respecting persons: Then I shall require no more of Mr. *Drake*, but that he would justifie our cause of digging, and declare abroad, that the Commons ought to be free to all sorts, and that it is a great trespasse before the Lord God Almighty, for one to hinder another of his liberty to dig the earth, that he might feed and cloath himself with the fruits of his labor therefrom freely, without owning any Landlord, or paying any rent to any person of his own kind.

I sent this following answer to the Arrest, in writing into Kingstone Court: In foure passages, your Court hath gone contrary to the righteousnesse of your own Statute Laws: for first it is mentioned in 36. *Ed.* 3. 15. that no Processe, Warrant, or Arrest should be served, till after the cause was recorded and entred; but your Bailiffe either could not, or would not tell us the cause when he arrested us, and Mr. *Rogers* your Recorder told us the first Court day we appeared, that our cause was not entred.

Secondly, we appeared two other Court daies, and desired a copy of the Declaration, and profered to pay for it, and you denied us. This is contrary to equity and reason, which is the foundation your Lawes are, or should be built upon, if you would have England to be a Commonwealth, and stand in peace.

Thirdly, we desired to plead our own cause, and you denied us, but told us we must fee an Attorney to speak for us, or els you would mark us for default in not appearance. This is contrary to your own Laws likewise, for in 28. *Ed.* 1. 11 chap. there is freedome given to a man to speak for himself, or els he may choose his father, friend or neighbor to plead for him, without the help of any other Lawyer. [2]

Fourthly, you have granted a judgement against us, and are proceeding to an execution, and this is contrary likewise to your own Laws, which say, that no plaint ought to be received, or judgement passed, till the cause be heard, and witnesses present, to testifie the plaint to be true, as Sir *Edward Cook 2.part of Institutes* upon the 29. chap. of *Magna Charta,* fol. 51. 52. 53. The *Mirror of Justice.*

But that all men may see, we are neither ashamed nor afraid, to justifie that cause we are arrested for, neither to refuse to answer to it in a righteous way, therefore we have here delivered this up in writing, and we leave it in your hands, disavowing the proceedings of your Court, because you uphold Prerogative oppression, though the Kingly office be taken away, and the Parliament hath declared England a Common-Wealth; so that Prerogative Laws cannot be in force, unlesse you be besotted by your covetousnesse and envy.

We deny that we have trespassed against those three men, or Mr. *Drake* either, or that we should trespasse against any, if we should dig up, or plow for a livelihood, upon any the wast Land in England, for thereby we break no particular Law made by any Act of Parliament, but only an ancient custome, bred in the strength of Kingly Prerogative, which is that old Law or custome, by which Lords of Mannours lay claime to the Commons, which is of no force now to bind the people of England, since the Kingly power and office was cast out: and the common people, who have cast out the oppressor, by their purse and person, have not authorized any as yet, to give away from them their purchased freedome; and if any assume a power to give away, or withhold this purchased freedome, they are Traytors to this Common-Wealth of England: and if they imprison, oppresse, or put to death any for standing to maintaine the purchased freedome, they are murderers and thieves, and no just rulers.

Therefore in the light of reason and equity, and in the light of the Nationall Covenant, which Parliament and people have taken, with joynt consent: all such Prerogative customes, which by experience we have found to burden the Nation, ought to be cast out, with the Kingly office, and the Land of England now ought to be a free Land, and a common treasury to all her children, otherwise it cannot properly be called a Common-Wealth.

Therefore we justifie our act of digging upon that hill, to make the earth a common treasurie. First, because the earth was made by Almighty God, to be a common treasury of livelihood for whole mankind in all his branches, without respect of persons; and that not any one [3] according to the Word of God (which is love) the pure Law of righteousnesse, ought to be Lord or landlord over another, but whole mankind was made equall, and knit into one body by one spirit of love, which is Christ in you the hope of glory, even all the members of mans body, called the little world, are united into equality of love, to preserve the whole body.

But since the fall of man there from, which came in by the rising up of covetousnesse in the heart of mankind (to which Serpent the man consented) and from thence mankind was called *A-dam*: for this covetousnesse makes mankind to be a stoppage of freedome in the creation, and by this covetous power, one branch of mankind began to lift up himself above another, as *Cain* lifted up himself, and killed his brother *Abel*: and so one branch did kill and steal away the comfortable use of the earth from another, as it is now: the elder brother lives in a continuall theevery, stealing the Land from the younger brother. And the plain truth is, theeves and murderers upheld by preaching witches and deceivers, rule the Nations: and for the present, the Laws and Government of the world, are Laws of darknesse, and the divells Kingdome, for covetousnesse rules all. And the power of the sword over brethren in Armies, in Arrests, in Prisons, in gallows, and in other inferiour torments, inflicted by some upon others, as the oppression of Lords of Mannours, hindring the poore from the use of the common Land, is *Adam* fallen, or *Cain* killing *Abel* to this very day.

And these Prerogative oppressors, are the Adamites & Cainites that walk contrary to the Word of God (which is love) by upholding murder and theft, by Laws which their Fathers made, and which they now justifie; for in the conquests that Kings got, their Ancestors did murder and kill, and steal away the earth, and removed the Land mark from the conquered, and made Laws to imprison, torment, or put to death, all that would adventure to take the Land from them againe, and left both that stoln Land, and murdering Laws to their children, the Lords of Mannours, and Freeholders, who now with violence, do justifie their Fathers wickednesse by holding fast, that which was left them by succession.

For what are all the Laws of the Nations, in this corrupt covetous Government, lifting up one branch of *Adam* mankind above another, the Conqueror, above the conquered, or those that have power above them that are weak, I say what are they, but Laws of murder and theft, yea enmity itself, against the Law of righteousnesse, which is love, which makes people do, as they would be done unto? [4, mispaged as 6]

And so all Kingly power, (in one or many mens hands) raigning by the sword, giving the use of the earth to some of mankind (called by him his Gentry) and denying the free use of the Earth to others, called the younger brothers, or common people, is no other but *Cain* lifted up above *Abel;* the Prerogative Lawes is *Belzebub,* for they are the strength of covetousnesse and bondage in the creation, lifting up one, and casting down another: the Atturneys, and Priests, and Lawyers, and Bayliffs are servants to *Belzebub,* and are Devils; their Prisons, Whips, and Gallows are the torments of this Hell, or government of darknesse; for mind it all along, and you shall see, that covetousnesse and bitter envie gets freedome by these Lawes; But the sincere and meek in spirit, is trod underfoot.

And this is that power, that hath made such havock in the Creation, it is that murderer and Devill that is to be cast out: this power of covetousnesse, is he that does countenance murder and theft in them that maintaines his Kingdom by the sword of Iron, and punishes it in others: and so that which is called a sin in the Common people, if they act such things, is counted no sin in the action of Kings, because the [*sic*] have they [*sic*] power of the sword in their hands, the fear whereof makes people to feare them.

But since this Kingly Office by the Parliament, is cast out of *England*, and *England* by them is declared to be a free State or Common-wealth, we are in the first place thereby set free from those bonds and ties that the Kings laid upon us: Therefore this Tyranny of one over another, as of Lords of Mannors over the Common people, and for people to be forced to hire Lawyers to plead their causes for them, when they are able to plead themselves, ought to be taken away with the Kingly Office, because they are the strength of the Antient Prerogative custom.

Secondly we justifie our digging upon *George's* hill to make the Earth a common Treasury, because all sorts of people have lent assistance of purse and person to cast out the Kingly Office, as being a burden *England* groaned under; therefore those from whom money and blood was received, ought to obtain freedom in the Land to themselves and Posterity, by the Law of contract between Parliament and People.

But all sorts, poor as well as rich, Tenant as well as Landlord, have paid Taxes, Free-quarter, Excise, or adventured their lives, to cast out that Kingly Office.

Therefore, all sorts of people ought to have freedom in the Land of this their nativity, without respecting persons, now the Kingly Office is cast out, by their joynt assistance. And those that doe imprison, oppresse and take away the livelihood of those that rise up to take Possession of this purchased freedome, are Traitors to this Nation, and Enemies to righte[5]ousnesse: And of this number are those men that have arrested, or that may arrest the Diggers, that endeavour to advance freedom; therefore I say all sorts ought to have their freedom.

And that in regard they have not only joyned persons and purses together, but in regard likewise, they took the Nationall Covenant, with joynt consent together, which the Parliament did make, of whom Mr *Drake* that caused us to be arrested was one; which Covenant likewise, the Ministers in their Sermons, most vehemently prest upon the people to take the intent whereof was this, That every one in his severall place and calling, should endeavor the peace, safety and freedom of *England* and that the Parliament should assist the people, and the people the Parliament, and every one that had taken it, should assist those that had taken it, while they were in persuit thereof, as in the sixth Article of the Nationall Covenant.

But now Mr *Drake* that was one that made this Covenant, and the *Surrey* Ministers that took it with great zeal at *Kingstone,* which I was eye witnesse to, and shall be of their hypocrisie therein, have set up a Lecturer at *Cobham* one purpose to drive off the Diggers to forsake the persuit of their Covenant are the most vehement to break Covenant and to hinder them that would keep it, neither entring into peace themselves, nor suffering them that are entring in to enter.

But in regard some of us did dig upon *George's* Hill, thereby to take Possession of that freedom we have recovered out of the hands of the Kingly Office, and thereby endeavour a Reformation in our place and calling according to the Word of God (which is Love:) And while we are in persuit of this our Covenant, we expect both Parliament that made the Covenant, and the Officers of this Court, and Parish Ministers, and Lords of Mannors themselves, and especially Mr *Drake,* to assist us herein, against all that shall oppose us in this righteous work of making the Earth a common Treasury; and not to beat us, imprison us, or take away our estates or lives, unlesse they will wilfully break Covenant with God and man, to please their own covetous froward heart, and thereby declare themselves to be the worst of Devils.

Therefore, in that we doe dig upon that Hill, we do not thereby take away other mens rights, neither do we demand of this Court, or from the Parliament, what is theirs and not ours: But we demand our own to be set free to us and them out of the Tyrannicall oppression of ancient custome of Kingly Prerogative; and let us have no more gods to rule over us, but the King of righteousnesse only.

Therefore as the Free-holders claime a quietnesse and freedom in their inclosures, as it is fit they should have, so we that are younger brothers, or [6] the poore oppressed, we claime our freedome in the Commons, that so elder and younger brother may live quietly and in peace, together freed from the straits of poverty and oppression, in this Land of our nativitie.

Thus we have in writing declared in effect, what we should say, if we had liberty to speak before you, declaring withall, that your Court cannot end this Controversie in that equity and reason of it, which wee stand to maintaine: Therefore we have appealed to the Parliament, who have received our Appeal and promised an Answer, and we wait for it; And we leave this with you, and let Reason and righteousnesse be our Iudge; therefore we hope you will do nothing rashly, but seriously consider of this cause before you proceed to execution upon us.

You say God will blast our work, and you say, you are in the right, and we are in the wrong: Now if you be Christians, as you say you are; Then doe you act love to us, as we doe to you; and let both sides waite with patience on the Lord, to see who he blesses; but if you oppose by violence, arrest us, judge, condemn and execute us, and yet will not suffer us to speak for our selves, but you will force us to give money to our Enemies to speak for us, surely you cannot say your cause is right; but hereby you justifie our cause to be right, because you are the Persecutors of a loving meek spirited people, and so declare that the God you say that will blast us, is covetousnesse, whom you serve by your persecuting power.

Covetous might may overcome rationall right for a time,
But rationall right must conquer covetous might, and that's the life of
mine.

The Law is righteous, just and good, when Reason is the rule,
But who so rules by the fleshly will, declares himself a foole.

Well, this same writing was delivered into their Court, but they cast it away and would not read it, and all was because I would not fee an Atturney; and then the next Court day following, before there was any tryall of our cause, for there was none suffered to speak but the Plaintiffe, they passed a Iudgement, and after that an Execution.

Now their Iury was made of rich Free-holders, and such as stand strongly for the Norman power:. And though our digging upon that barren Common hath done the Common good, yet this Jury brings in damages of ten pounds a man, and the charges of the Plaintiffe in their Court, twenty nine shillings and a peny; and this was their sentence and the passing of the Execution upon us. [7]

And 2 dayes after (for in this case they can end a cause speedily in their Court; but when the Atturney and Lawyers get money they keep a cause depending seven yeares, to the utter undoing of the parties, so unrighteous is the Law, and Lawyers) I say, two dayes after they sent to execute the execution, and they put *Henry Beckarstaffe* in prison, but after three dayes, Mr *Drake* released him again, *Beckarstaffe* not knowing of it till the release came; They seek after *Thomas Star* to imprison his body, who is a poore man not worth ten pounds.

Then they came privately by day to *Gerrard Winstanleys* house, and drove away foure Cowes; I not knowing of it and some of the Lords Tenants rode to the next Town shouting the diggers were conquered, the diggers were conquered. Truly it is an easie thing to beat a man, and cry conquest over him after his hands are tied, as they tyed ours. But if their cause be so good, why will they not suffer us to speak, and let reason and equity, the foundation of righteous Lawes, judge them and us. But strangers made rescue of those Cowes, and drove them astray out of the Bailiffes hands, so that the Bailiffes lost them; but before the Bailiffes had lost the Cowes, I hearing of it went to them and said here is my body, take me that I may come to speak to those *Normans* that have stolne our land from us; and let the Cowes go, for they are none of mine; and after some time, they telling me that they had nothing against my body, it was my goods they were to have; then said I, take my goods, for the Cowes are not mine; and so I went away and left them, being quiet in my heart, and filled with comfort within my self, that the King of righteousnesse would cause this to work for the advancing of his own Cause, which I prefer above estate or livelyhood,

Saying within my heart as I went along, that if I could not get meat to eat, I would feed upon bread, milk and cheese; and if they take the Cowes, that I cannot feed on this, or hereby make a breach between me and him that owns the Cowes, then Ile feed upon bread and beere, till the King of righteousnesse clear up my innocency, and the justice of his own cause: and if this be taken from me for maintaining his Cause, Ile stand still and see what he will doe with me, for as yet I know not.

Saying likewise within my heart as I was walking along, O thou King of righteousnesse shew thy power, and do thy work thy self, and free thy people now from under this heavy bondage of miserie, *Pharaoh* the covetous power. And the answer in my heart was satisfactory, and full of sweet joy and peace: and so I said Father, do what thou wilt, this cause is thine, and thou knowest that the love to righteousnesse makes me do what I do.

I was made to appeal to the Father of life in the speakings of my heart [8] likewise thus: Father thou knowest that what I have writ or spoken, concerning this light, that the earth should be restored and become a common Treasurie for all mankind, without respect of persons, was thy free revelation to me, I never read it in any book, I heard it from no mouth of flesh till I understood it from thy teaching first within me. I did not study nor imagine the conceit of it; self-love to my own particular body does not carry me along in the mannaging of this businesse; but the power of love flowing forth to the liberty and peace of thy whole Creation, to enemies as well as friends: nay towards those that oppresse me, endeavouring to make me a beggar to them. And since I did obey thy voice, to speak and act this truth, I am hated, reproached, and oppressed on evere side. Such as make profession of thee, yet revile me. And though they see I cannot fight with fleshly weapons, yet they will strive with me by that power. And so I see Father, that *England* yet does choose rather to fight with the Sword of Iron, and covetousnesse, then by the Sword of the Spirit which is love: and what thy purpose is with this land, or with my body, I know not; but establish thy power in me, and then do what pleases thee.

These and such like sweet thoughts dwelt upon my heart as I went along, and I feel my self now like a man in a storm, standing under shelter upon a hill in peace, waiting till the storm be over to see the end of it, and of many other things that my eye is fixed upon: But I will let this passe,

And return again to the Dragons Den, or Hornets nest, the selfish murdering fleshly Lawes of this Nation, which hangs some for stealing, and protects others in stealing; Lords of Mannours stole the land from their fellow creatures formerly in the conquests of Kings, and now they have made Lawes to imprison and hang all those that seek to recover the land again out of their thieving murdering hands.

They took away the Cowes which were my livelyhood, and beat them with their clubs, that the Cowes heads and sides did swell, which grieved tender hearts to see: and yet these Cowes never were upon *George* Hill, nor never digged upon that ground, and yet the poore beasts must suffer because they gave milk to feed me, but they were driven away out of those Devills hands the Bailiffes, and were delivered out of hell at that time.

And thus Lords of Mannours, their Bailiffes the true upholders of the *Norman* power, and some Freeholders that doe oppose this publick work, are such as the countrey knowes have beene no friends to that Cause the Parliament declared for, but to the Kingly power; and now if they get the foot fast in the stirrup, they will lift themselves again into the *Norman* saddle; and they do it secretly; for they keep up the *Norman* Lawes, and thereby Traytours to freedome, get into places of Law and power, and by [9] that will enslave *England* more then it was under the Kingly power.

Therefore *England* beware; thou art in danger of being brought under the *Norman* power more then ever. The King *Charles* that was successour to *William* the Conquerour thou hast cast out: and though thy Parliament have declared against the Kingly office, and cast it out, and proclaimed *England* a Common wealth, that is to be a free land for the liberty and livelyhood of all her children;

Yet *William* the Conquerours Army begins to gather into head againe, and the old *Norman* Prerogative Law is the place of their randezvous: for though their chief Captain *Charles* be gone, yet his Colonells, which are Lords of Mannours, his Councellours and Divines, which are our Lawyers and Priests, his inferiour officers and Souldiers, which are the Freeholders, and Land-lords, all which did steal away our Land from us when they killed and murdered our Fathers in that *Norman* conquest: And the

Bailiffes that are slaves to their covetous lusts and all the ignorant bawling women, against our digging for freedome, are the snapsack boyes and the ammunition sluts that follow the *Norman* Camp.

These are all striving to get into a body againe, that they may set up a new *Norman* slaverie over us; and the place of their randezvous, Prerogative power is fenced already about, with a Line of Communication. An act made by a piece of the Parliament to maintain the old Lawes, which if once this Camp be fortified in his full strength, it will cost many a sighing heart, and burdened spirit before it be taken.

And this *Norman* Camp are got into so numerous a body already, that they have appointed their Sutlers to drive away the Cowes which were my livelyhood, and some of them they would sell to make money of to pay the Atturney, *Gilder,* and Lawyers their fees, for denying the diggers our priviledge to plead our own cause; for as it is clearly seen that if we be suffered to speak we shall batter to pieces all the old Lawes, and prove the maintainers of them hypocrites and Traitours to this Common wealth of *England,* and then the Atturneys and Lawyers Trade goes down, and Lords of Mannours must be reckoned equall to other men. And this covetous flesh and blood cannot endure.

And other of the Cows were to be killed to victuall the Camp, that is, to feed those *Normans, Wil Star* & *Ned Sutton,* both Freeholders & others the snapsack boyes, and ammunition drabs that helped to drive away the Cows that they might be encouraged by a belly full of stoln goods to stick the closer to the businesse another time. Or else the price of these Cowes were to pay for the sack and Tobacco which the *Norman* officers of Knights, Gentlemen, and rich Freeholders did spend at the White Lion at *Cobham,* [10] when they met the 24. of *August* 1649, to advise together what course they should take to subdue the diggers; for say they, if the cause of the diggers stand, we shall lose all our honour and titles, and we that have had the glory of the earth shall be of no more account then those slaves our servants and yonger brothers that have been footstools to us and our Fathers ever since the *Norman William* our beloved Generall took this land (not by love) but by a sharp sword, the power by which we stand: and though we own Christ by name, yet we will not do as he did to save enemies, but by our sword we will destroy our enemies, and do we not deserve the price of some of the diggers Cows to pay us for this our good service? And doe not our reverend Ministers tell us that *William* the Conquerour, and the succeeding Kings were Gods annointed? And do not they say that our inclosures which were got by that murdering sword, and given by *William* the Conquerour to our Fathers, and so successively, from them, the land is our inheritance, and that God gave it us, and shall these broken fellows, and beggarly rogues take our rights from us, and have the use of the land equall with us? Thus do these *Norman* Gentlemen comfort their hearts, and support themselves with broken reeds, when they meet toegther in their Counsels.

But stay you *Norman* Gentlemen, let me put in a word amongst you, doth the murderers sword make any man to be Gods anointed? Surely, Iesus Christ was called Gods annointed not because he conquered with a Sword of iron, but because he conquered by love, and the spirit of patience: therefore your Generall was not Gods annointed, as Christ was.

And then the Earth was not made to be the successive inheritance of children of murderers, that had the strongest arm of flesh, and the best sword, that can tread others under foot with a bold brasen forehead under colour of the Law of justice as the *Norman* power does; But it was made for all by the Law of righteousnesse, and he gives the whole Earth to be the inheritance of every single branch of mankind without respect of persons, and he that is filled with the love of this righteous King, doing as he would be done by is a true annointed one.

Therfore, that god whom you serve, and which did intitle you Lords, Knights Gentlemen, and Landlords, is covetousnesse, the god of this world, which alwayes was a murderer, a devil and father of lies, under whose dark governing power, both you and all the nations of the world for the present are under. But the King of righteousnesse or God of love whom I serve, did not call the earth your inheritance, shutting out others, but gave the earth to be a common treasurie to whole mankind (who is the Lord of it) without respect of person. [11]

This power of love, is the King of righteousnesse, the Lord God Almighty that rules the whole Creation in peace, that is the Seed that breaks covetousnesse the Serpents head; he is the restoring power, that is now rising up to change all things into his own nature, he will be your Iudge, for vengance is his; and for any wrong you have done me, as I can tell you of many, yet I have given all matters of judgment and vengance into his hand, and I am sure he will doe right, and discover him that is the true Trespasser, that takes away my rights from me.

And take notice of this, you Lords of Mannors, and Norman Gentry, though you should kill my body or starve me in prison, yet know, that the more you strive, the more troubles you hearts shall be filled with; and doe the worst you can to hinder publick freedom, you shall come off losers in the later end, I meane you shall lose your Kingdom of darknesse, though I lose my livelihood, he [*sic*] poor Cowes that is my living, and should be imprisoned; you have been told this 12 Months agoe, that you should lose ground by striving, and will you not take warning, will you needs shame your selves, to let the poore Diggers take away your

Kingdome from you? surely, the power that is in them, will take the rule and government from you, and give it a people that will make better use of it.

Alas! you poor blind earth mouls, you strive to take away my livelihood, and the liberty of this poor weak frame my body of flesh, which is my house I dwell in for a time; but I strive to cast down your kingdom of darknesse, and to open Hell gates, and to break the Devils bands asunder, wherewith you are tied, that you my Enemies may live in peace, and that is all the harm I would have you to have.

Therefore you Lords of Mannors, you Free-holders, you Norman-Clergy, oppressing Tith-mungers, and you of the Parliament men, that have plaid fast and loose with this poor Nation, for what is past let it goe; hereafter advance freedom and liberty, and pluck up bondage; and sinne no more by Lording it over your Lords and Masters, that set you upon those Parliament Seats, lest worse things befall you then yet hath.

But to return again to Mr *Gilders* advice, the Atturney of *Kingstone* Court, and the proceeding of that Court with the Cowes; you heare how they did judge, condemn and execute me, not suffering me to speak; and though those four Cowes were rescued out of their hands by strangers, not by me; and so by their own Law, they should have looked after the Rescuers, yet contrary to their own Law, they came againe to *Winstanleys* dwelling a fortnight after, and drove away seven Cowes and a Bull in the night time, some of the Cowes being Neighbour's that had hired pasture; and yet the damage which their Norman Iury, and their covetous be-[12] sotted ignorant Atturney Mr *Gilder,* had judged me to pay for a Trespasse in digging upon that barren *George*'s Hill, was but eleven pound nine shillings and a penney charges & all, which they are like never to have of me, for an empty carrier will dance and sing before these Norman theeves and pick-purses: And thus you see they judged and passed sentence upon me but once at their prerogative pleasure, which they call *Englands* Law: but they executed me twice, that they might be sure to kill me. But yet these Cowes likewise are brought home againe, and the heart of my Enemies is put into the pound of vexation because the Cowes are set free. Surely, these Lords of Mannors and the Atturney Mr *Gilder,* that gave advice to Arrest us for digging, have burned their Bibles long agoe, because they have so quite and clean forgotten that Petition in the Lords prayer, *forgive us our trespasses as we forgive them*; for they make this a trespasse against them, for digging upon the wast land of our mother the Land of *England* for a livelihood, when as their Law it self saith, *That the Commons and wasts belong to the poore*.

So that you see the Norman Camp is grown very numerous and big, that they want much beeffe to vituall them, and they are such hungry ones, that they will eat poor lean Cowes, that are little better then skin & bone; and poor Cowes if I keep them in the winter, they are like to be poorer for want of Hay; for before the report of our digging was much known, I bought three Acres of grasse of a Lord of a Mannor, whom I will not here name, because I know the councel of others made him prove fals to me; for when the time came to Mow, I brought mony to pay him before hand; but he answered me, I should not have it, but sold it to another before my face; this was because his Parish Priest, and the *Surrey* Ministers, and sorry ones too they are that have set up a Lecturer at *Cobham* for a little time, to preach down the Diggers, have bid the people neither to buy nor sell with us, but to beat us, imprison us, or banish us; and thereby they prove themselves to be members of the Beast that had two horns, like a Lamb, and yet speak like a Dragon, & so they fulfill that Scripture in *Rev.* 13.16. *that no man might buy and sell, save he that had the mark of the Beast.* Or else surely, they do it on purpose to quicken us to our work, and to drive us to Plant the Commons with all speed as may be.

But though the Cowes were poor, yet they care not, so the skins will but pay the Lawyers and Atturneys *Gilder* his Fees, and the flesh to feed the snapsack boyes, either to eat and make merry with, or else to sell to make money of, to pay those that drive away the Cowes for their paines or charges they have been at, in this 18 weeks striving to beat the Diggers off their work: But the bones will serve the Bailiffs to pick, because their action will be both proved thievery in stealing another mans cattell, and their [13] trespasse very great against the same man, in opening all the Gates round about the ground, where *Winstanley* dwels, and let Hogs and common Cattell into the standing barly and other corn, which the right owner will seek satisfaction for.

So that the fury of this Norman Camp against the Diggers is so great, that they would not only drive away all the Cowes upon the ground, but spoyl the corn too, and when they had done this mischief, the Bayliffes, & the other Norman snapsack boyes went hollowing and shooting, as if they were dancing at a whitson Ale; so glad they are to do mischief to the Diggers, that they might hinder the work of freedome.

And why are they so furious against us? but because we endeavour to dig up their Tythes, their Lawyers Fees, their Prisons, and all that Art and Trade of darknesse, whereby they get money under couller of Law; and to plant the plesant fruit trees of freedom, in the room of that cursed thornbush, the power of the murdering sword; for they say, they doe all they do by the Law of the Land which the Parliament hath confirmed to them by an Act: And if so, Then Souldiers where is the price of your blood? and Countrey-men, and Citizens, Where is the price of your Taxes and Free-quarter? If this be the freedom, you are like to have, to be beaten and not be suffered to say why doe you so, and shall have no remedy, unlesse you will Fee a Lawyer (an Enemy) to plead for you, when you are able to plea your own cause better your self, and save that charge, and have your cause ended sooner and with more peace and quietnesse.

And you zealous Preachers, and professors of the City of *London* and you great Officers and Souldiery of the Army, where are all your Victories over the Cavaliers, that you made such a blaze in the Land, in giving God thanks for, and which you begged in your Fasting dayes, and morning Exercises; Are they all sunck into the Norman power again, and must the old Prerogative Laws stand; what freedom then did you give thanks for? Surely, that you had killed him that rid upon you, that you may get up into his saddle to ride upon others; O thou City, thou Hypocriticall City! thou blindfold drowsie *England,* that sleps and snores in the bed of covetousnesse, awake, awake, the Enemies is upon thy back, he is ready to scale the walls and enter Possession, and wilt thou not look out.

Does not the streames of bondage run in the same river that it did, and with a bigger stream of Norman power; so that if you awaken not betimes, the flood of the Norman Prerogative power, will drown you all; here's more rivers comes into the maine stream, since the storm fell and the waters of fury rises very high, banked in by Laws; and while you are talking and disputing about words, the Norman Souldiers are secretly working among you to advance their power again; and so will take away [14] the benefit of all your victories by a subtile act of intricate Lawes, which the sword in the field could not do against you: and when you have lost that freedom, which you boasted of that you will leave to your posterity, then who must give thanks, you that vapoured in words, or they that lay close in action, waiting to trip up your heels by pollicy, when the sword could not do it.

I tell thee thou *England,* thy battells now are all spirituall. Dragon against the Lamb, and the power of love against the power of covetousnesse; therefore all that will be Souldiers for Christ, the Law of righteousnesse joyn to the Lamb. He that takes the iron sword now shall perish with it, and would you be a strong Land and flourish in beauty, then fight the Lambs battels, and his strength shall be thy walls and bulwarks.

You Knights, Gentlemen, and Freeholders, that sat in councell at the white Lion in *Cobham* to find out who are our backers, and who stirs us up to dig the Commons, Ile tel you plainly who it is, it is love, the King of righteousnes ruling in our hearts, that makes us thus to act that the creation may be set at liberty, and now I have answered your inquirie, do what you can to him and us his servants: And we require you in his name, to let our cause have a publick triall, and do not work any longer in darknesse, set not your Bailiffes and slaves to come by night to steal away the Cowes of poore men under colour of justice, when as the cause was never yet heard in open Court.

He that backs you, and that sets you to work, to deny to us our younger brother the use of the common land, is covetousnesse, which is Beelzebub the greatest, devil so that there is the 2 generalls known, which you & we fight under, the 2 great Princes of light and darknes, bondage and freedom, that does Act all flesh in the great controversies of the world. These are the 2 men that stir in this busines, that is, the wicked man that councels, & backs you to be so envious and furious against us, and the righteous man Christ, that backs and councells us to love you our enemies. And do we not see that *Gebal, Ammon* and *Amaleck,* and all the rabble of the nations, Lords, Knights, Gentlemen, Lawyers, Bailiffes, Priests, and all the *Norman* snapsack boyes, and ammunition women to the old *Norman* Camp do all combine together in the art of unrighteous fury, to drive the poore diggers off from their work, that the name of commmunity [*sic*] and freedome which is Christ, may not be known in earth. Thus I have dealt plainly with you all, and I have not flattered Parliament, Army, City, nor Countrey, but have declared in this, and other writings the whole light of that truth revealed to me by the word of the Lord: and I shall now wait to see his hand to do his own work in what time, and by what instruments he pleases. And I see the poore must first be picked out, and honoured in this work, for they begin to receive the word of righteousnesse, but the rich generally are enemies to true freedome.

> *The work of digging still goes on, and stops not for a rest:*
> *The Cowes were gone, but are return'd, and we are all at rest.* [15]
> *No money's paid, nor never shall, to Lawyer or his man*
> *To plead our cause, for therein wee'll do the best we can.*
> *In* Cobham *on the little Heath our digging there goes on.*
> *And all our friends, they live in love, as if they were but one.*

Thus you Gentlemen, that will have no Law to rule over you, but your Prerogative will must be above Law, and above us that are the yonger brothes [*sic*] in the Land; but if you say, no, your wil shal be subject to Law: then I demand of you Mr *Drake*, Mr *Gilder*, and other the Bailiffes and Officers of *Kingston* Court, why will you arrest us, and trouble us, and say we trespasse against you, and though we came to answer to your arrest, and to plead our own cause, yet contrary to the equity, nay contrary to the bare letter that the Law, as I shewed you before, you denied me that priviledge, but went on and did condemne and execute a forceable power upon body and goods, is not your will here, above Law? do you not hereby uphold the *Norman* conquest?

Mr *Drake,* you are a Parliament man, and was not the beginning of the quarrel between King *Charles* and your House? This the King pleaded to uphold Prerogative, and you were against it, and yet must a Parliament man be the first man to uphold Prerogative, who are but servants to the Nation for the peace and liberty of every one, not conquering Kings to make their wil a Law? did you not promise liberty to the whole Nation, in case the Cavalier party were cast out? and why now wil you seek liberty to your self and Gentry, with the deniall of just liberty and freedome to the common people, that have born the greatest burden?

You have arrested us for digging upon the common Land, you have executed your unrighteous power, in distraining cattel, imprisoning our bodies, and yet our cause was never publickly heard, neither can it be proved that we have broke any Law, that is built upon equity and reason, therfore we wonder where you had your power to rule over us by will, more then we to rule over you by our will. We request you before you go too far, not to let covetousnesse be your Master, trample not others under your feet, under colour of Law, as if none knew equity of Law but you; for we and our estates shall be horns in your eyes, and pricks in your sides, and you may curse that Councell bid you beg our estates, or imprison our persons. But this we request that you would let us have a fair open triall, and do not carry on the course of Law in secret like *Nicodemus* that is afraid to have his businesse come to light; therefore I challenge you once more, seeing you professe your selves Christians, to let us be brought to a trial of our cause; let your ministers plead with us in the scriptures, & let your Lawyers plead with us in the equity & reason of your own Law; and if you prove us transgressours, then we shal lay down our work and acknowledge we have trespassed against you in digging upon the Commons, & then punish us. But if we prove by Scripture & reason, that undeniably the land belongs to one as well as another, then you shal own our work, justifie our cause, & declare that you have done wrong to Christ, who you say is your Lord and master, in abusing us his servants, & your fellow creatures, while we are doing his work. Therefore I knowing you to be men of moderation in outward shew, I desire that your actions towards your fellow creatures may not be like one beast to another, but carry your selves, like man to man; for your procceding [*sic*] in your pretence of law hitherto against us, is both unrighteous, beastly & divelish, and nothing of the spirit of man seen in it. You Atturnies and Lawyers, you say you are ministers of justice, & we know that equity and reason is, or ought to be the foundation of Law; if so, then plead not for mony altogether but stand for universall justice & equity, then you will have peace; otherwise both you with the corrupt Clergy will be cast out as unsavoury salt. [16]

FINIS.

LILBURNE, OVERTON, AND PRINCE

THE SECOND PART OF ENGLANDS NEW-CHAINES
DISCOVERED

The second Part of Englands New-Chaines appeared in London March 24, 1649. Two days later Milton was directed by the Council of State to make a reply to it, but did not obey orders. On March 29 the four Leveller leaders were imprisoned, charged with treason to the Commonwealth. *The second Part of Englands New-Chaines* represents the final disillusionment of the Levellers with the Independent leaders. Recapitulating from the Leveller viewpoint the tactics of the army officers from 1647 to the establishment of the republic, it also restates many of the democratic tenets typical of Leveller manifestoes.

The tract is here reprinted from a photostat of the copy in the McAlpin Collection of Union Theological Seminary. Spelling and punctuation follow the usage of the original tract. The design of the title page is an imitation, not an exact reproduction, of the original.

The second Part

OF

ENGLANDS

New-Chaines

DISCOVERED:

Or a sad Representation of the uncertain
and dangerous condition of the

COMMON-WEALTH:

DIRECTED

To the Supreme Authority of *England*, the
Representors of the People in Parliament assembled.

By severall wel-affected persons inhabiting
the City of *London*, *Westminster*, the Borough of
Southwark, *Hamblets*, and places adjacent,
presenters and approvers of the late
large Petition of the Eleventh of
September. 1648.

And as it is avowed by Lievtenant Colonel
John Lilburn, Mr. *Richard Overton*, and Mr. *Tho. Prince*,
upon perill of their lives; and for which they are
now committed to the Tower as *Traytors*.

London, Printed in the Year, 1649.

TO THE SUPREME AUTHORITY OF *ENGLAND*,

the Representors of the People, in Parliament Assembled.

THE SAD REPRESENTATION

of the uncertain and dangerous Condition of the Common-wealth:
By the Presenters and Approvers of the Large Petition *of the*
11. *of* September, 1648.

F our hearts were not over-charged with the sense of the present miseries and approaching dangers of the Nation, your smal regard to our late serious Apprehensions, would have kept us silent; but the misery, danger, and bondage threatned is so great, imminent, and apparent, that whilst we have breath, and are not violently restrained, we cannot but speak, and even cry aloud, until you hear us, or God be pleased otherwaies to relieve us.

Nor should you in reason be with-held from considering what we present you withal, through any strangeness that appeareth therein; For what was more incredible, than that a Parliament trusted by the people to deliver them from all kinds of oppression, and who made so liberal effusion of their bloud, and waste, of their estates (upon pretense of doing thereof) should yet so soon as they were in power, oppress with the same kind of oppressions, which yet was true in the times of *Hollis* and *Stapletons* faction, and who, (as the King and Bishops had done before) laboured for an Army to back and perpetuate them therein.

Nor were our Petitions then presented (wherein we justly complained of those oppressions, and fore-warned them of the dan[1]ger ensuing) the less considerable for their burning of them by the hand of the common hangman; Nor the Petitioners the more blame-worthy for being reproched with the names of Atheists, Hereticks, and seditious Sectaries (as now with Jesuite, and Leveller) Aspersions being the known marks of corrupt States-men, and usually working no other effect, but the discredit of the Aspersers. Yet were there then many who believed their reports of us, and they were as impatient with us, for our taxing them with their wicked and pernicious designs, as others are now for our presuming to detect them, who are so high in present power and reputation: But it is now evident, that it is possible for our Physitians to bring us into a more dangerous condition than they found us.

And though experience hath made us wofully sensible that nothing is more dangerous to any people than their bearing with unjust, covetous, or ambitious practises in those they trust; Yet did we forbear to interpose our judgements, or to oppose those mens designs, until they had made a large progress toward our bondage, and endeavoured to grasp the power of the Army into their hands, thereby to enforce their tpranny [*sic*] upon us; insomuch that it was almost too late to give check to their wicked intentions: so unwilling were we to believe it possible for men who all along pretended liberty and redress of grievances, to degenerate so soon into the grossest Principles and practises of long setled Tyrannies.

And much more do our Consciences bear us witness of our backwardness to believe any evil intentions in those who not only were most vigorous and successful against the common enemy, but seemed so sensible of the injustice and trechery of that prevalent faction in Parliament, as to engage with the utmost of their might, as if they had really intended to deliver the Nation from that dangerous thraldom, so that we both durst, and did many of us, venture our lives upon their fidelity; Yea so powerful, perswasive, and contentful were their first Engagements, Papers, and Remonstrances, so fraught with self-denying Doctrines, tender regard to the peace of the Nation, and satisfaction to all interests; as even lulled all peaceable People into a sound sleep of security, casting all their care upon the General Councel of the Army, as upon a People they thought could never have the face to decline either those principles, or to neglect the performance of so many en[2]gagements, promises, and protestations, made as in the presence of the all-seeing God, frequently calling upon him, the searcher of all hearts, to bear witness to their integrity and sincerity therein: insomuch that we (who alwaies with some wariness observed them) many times denied our own understandings rather than we would draw hasty conclusions from evident testimonys of their deffection.

But when after they had once sleighted the Adgitators, and discountenanced those Officers and Souldiers, who first engaged against the destructive Votes of Parliament; such as stood firm to their Engagements at New-market, and Triploe Heath: when we saw they not only neglected them, but adhered to persons sent from Parliament and City, in those corrupted times, and fell immediately to plead for Negative Voyces in the King, and Lords; checking and controuling those that opposed: When we understood their General Councels (which according to their engagements ought to have consisted only of two select Commission Officers, and two private Souldiers chosen by every Regiment, with such General Officers as assented to the Engagement, and no other) were nevertheless overgrown with Collonels, Lieut. Collonels, Majors, and others, not chosen; and many of them dissenters from the said Engagement; and that some few eminent persons presumed above measure therein, and in effect overawed and controuled those Councels: and that the contrivance of a Councel of State, was the great engine which those

Councels laboured to bring about: when we found them not only to Court the King, by kissing his hand, and the like, and that a correspondency was held between him and the General Officers, and Agents sent to and fro continually, whereby they came to so neer a close, as that their Proposals were not only received, but corrected and amended by the King, before they were sent to the House, til they became very consistent with his ends and Prerogative: and those Officers so engaged thereby, as to be moved to impatience towards any that spake a sillable against this their trafique and intercourse with him: upon which likewise, they concluded an Agreement with the opposing Citizens of London, without so much as calling the Adgitators to advize thereupon. Seeing, Hearing, and Vnderstanding these things, no marvel if we were staggered in our Beleefe of their integrity.

But that a person so deeply charged as the Earl of Manchester, and other grand self-seekers of this House should be intertained with so great respect, and gaurded to their places in Parliament, [3] and that notwithstanding the prevailing power of the Army, those who had usurped the Authority of the House, and Voted a new warre, were nevertheless permitted to sit and Vote there, and that contrary to the importunate desires of the Agitators, and the Remonstrance of the Army: and then one of the first fruits of this their conjunction was the passing of an Ordinance for Tythes, upon trebble dammages, which the corrupt Clergy had presented (in the absence of the Speaker) to *Pelhams* Parliament; and the burning of Mr *Biddles* Book, by the Common Hangman; and imprisoning his person: and that notwithstanding their glorious March through London, the prerogative Prisoners in the Tower, New-gate, and elsewhere, were utterly neglected, and the Councel of those friends sleighted, who had been instrumental, even to the losse of some, and the hazard of all their lives, to make an easie and unbloudy passage for the Army into Southwark and the City. Vpon observation of these and abundant more particulars, which we could enumerate, we concluded, that the Councels of the Army were not steered as at their first engagement, by the select persons chosen thereunto, nor for the ends in that engagement expressed; but by some other powerfull and over-ruling influences, that intended other matters then were pretended, and that laboured by all possible means to convert the honest endeavours of good men in the Army and else-where, and the happy successs [sic] God had blessed them withall, to the advantage of their Lusts, Pride, and Domination: And as time came on, it more and more appeared, that they intended meerly the establishment of themselves in power and greatnesse, without any regard at all to the peformance of their promises and engagements, or any respect to the faith and credit of the Army, or to the peace and prosperity of the

Common wealth, and that they walked by no rules or principles either of honesty or conscience; but (as meer pollititians, were governed altogether by occasion, and as they saw a possibility of making progress to their designs, which course of theirs they ever termed a waiting upon providence, that with colour of Religion they might deceive the more securely.

Now that this may appear no slander, we entreat that without partiality, their after proceedings may be throughly scan'd: as first, at *Kingston* it was proposed by the Agitators, friends of *London, Southwark,* and the places adjacent, that the Tower, City, and [4] Borough, might be secured by the well-affected Inhabitants, and not by Souldiers, that so trade and traffique might be preserved, which otherwise would be driven away (as it soon after proved) And that it was hoped they intended not to secure any place by Souldiers, when the wel-affected Inhabitants were able to secure it. Which advise proceeded as well from our respects to the City and neighbour places, as upon fears of what we know to be the practise of other Tyrants (and therefore doubted would be exercised by those) namely, the garisoning great Towns, thereby to keep the people, as well in poverty, as in continual aw and subjection.

Which advise, though assented unto by the Agitators, was yet rejected by the grand Officers, and a new Regiment raised, to the further charge of the Common-wealth; the Proposers themselves being dismissed with reproches, and the Agitators thrust out, and not permitted to observe how they were dealt withal.

At which time also its very remarkable with how much height of State they observed the King at *Hampton* Court, visiting him themselves, and permiting thousands of people dayly to visit him, to kiss his hand, and to be healed by him, whereby his party in the City, and every where, were exceedingly animated, his Agents being as familiar at the head-quarters, as at the Court. Then on a sudden, when the House complyed not with their purposes, in all hast, it was to be purged, and thereupon they publish a large Remonstrance, *Aug.* 18. stuffed with publike reasons, to shew the justness and necessity thereof: but the House again complying, through the sight of their Remonstrance, though no whit changed in respect of its corruption; & they finding, if it were purged, it would not be for their design; they make nothing of their former resolution, but continue it in its corrupt condition, and sit with them themselves.

Then they fall to work again about the King and send the propositions of *New-castle* to him, which they knew, and were agreed he should not sign; in the mean time, they so wrought the King by deep promises, and hopes of restauration, as that he inclined much to countenance the Army, gave out words in their favour, and in his answer to the House, prefer'd their Proposals, before the Parliaments Propositions; in lieu thereof, the great ones of the Army themselves, endeavoured the revival of a Treaty, and some of them in the House, were very violent against motions of no more Address, and expressed it was the sense of the Army that further Address should be made, and that except they would make [5] Addresses of another nature to the King, they could not promise them the assistance of the Army; and accordingly they take pains to work every man at the head-quarters; upon which petitions were attempted in the Army, in favour of a Treaty, and some conscientious, but weak people, were drawn to second their design, with a Petition for a Personal Treaty, which they had ready at the House dore.

These strange and mysterious proceedings occasion'd a new face of things in the Army, many of the Officers being much distasted thereat, & whole Regiments chusing new Agents to look after the publike, as fearing things were runing head-long into a most dangerous condition: The far greater number of the Officers, would not by any means indure to hear of the Armies compliance with the King, and the Agents finding all former engagements, promises, and declarations broken, and utterly neglected, and the Common wealth in danger of utter dissolution, produce an *Agreement of the People, upon grounds of Common Right, for uniting of all unprejudiced people therein;* the great Officers very much oppose it a while, as having set up another Interest: but seing the same take with the Army, profess *though at present their judgements could not so far close with it as to act for it, yet they would never oppose it.* Hereupon the whole frame of the design alters, and the matters in projection with them, were how to dis-ingage themselves, and be rid of the King, and how likewise to discountenance and keep under the discerning party in the Army. In order to the first, they cast about how to get the King into the Isle of *Wight,* where they might both easier keep others from him, and the more entirely possess him themselves; and that he might with willingness be hurried thither, they work upon his fear; suggesting to him, that there was an intention in some violent persons to murder him, and perswade him to leave that in a letter, as the cause of his re-move. To make which the more credible, they wrought L. Col. *Hen. Lil-burn* to asperse his brother *John* (who then stood in the way of the great men of the Army) with a base & abhorrid resolution of being one that intended to murder the King; to the proof whereof they would never suffer the Asperser to be brought (though solicited thereunto by a Peti-tion from divers well-affected persons) but instead [sic] thereof, for that perfideous service, they advanced him to the government of *Tinmouth* Castle, above his brother *Robert,* where [6] retaining the leven of his

Apostacy, which the Gen. Officers had laid in him, he suffered the deserved reward of a perfidious traytor.

And though the General Officers enclined him to this revolt themselves, as well by their example, as by countenancing him in the beginning thereof; and though for the same he incurred the extreme displeasure of his Father, and Kindred, yet are both his Father and Kindred by the Officers themselves and their Associates aspersed with the fact, as if tainted with guilt and contamination thereof.

Thus did they kill two birds with one stone, framing a Name for them which of all others is most distasteful to the People, and was therefore most likely to beget a beleef of the pretended assassination.

Where (by the way) we desire it may be observed, that nothwithstanding the word *Leveller* was framed and cast upon all those in the Army (or elsewhere) who are against any kind of Tyranny, whether in King, Parliament, Army, Councel of State, &c. And though it was not so much as beleeved to concern those upon whom they cast it, the inventers having often professed as much, yet have they both themselves and by their Instruments industriously propagated the same, and insinuated both this and other slanders of us into the hearts of all the easy and credulous people they could meet withall.

But to returne, The King thus removed, they judge themselves at good leisure to deal with the Agreers for the People, and so suddainly violent they became in that work, that at the first Randevous neer Ware, they shot a Souldier to death, for pursuing the ends of the Engagement at New-market, and for insisting upon the Agreement for the People: unworthily abused Major *Skott*, a Member of this House, sent him up a prisoner, and accused him and Col. *Rainsborough* for appearing in behalf of the Agreement, and therewithall sent Col. *Ayres*, Major *Cobbet*, Capt. *Bray*, and many others after them prisoners to Windsor, where, as Parties, Judges, and Juries, the Officers did what they would against them, sentencing some to death, others to disgracefull punishments, restraining and releasing at pleasure, and with as much Arbitrarinesse as ever was in the world, and could not be diswaded though Mr *Saltmarsh* and others bore full testimony against the cruelty and injustice thereof. Hereupon at the House they procured at once the imprisonment of five cordial Citizens, for justi[7]fying the Agreement of the People, and requiring Justice for the blood of the Souldier that was shot at Ware, disfranchised them, and under the notion of London Agents forbad their meetings. And when now they thought they had moulded and qualified the Army to their own bent, and had gratified their complying Officers, with the cruelty upon the Levellers, (for so they had stiled all who have manifested any sence of Common Right) and had found that they could be nothing so great, rich, and potent, upon a close with the King, and that it would be impossible for them to hold either Officer or Souldier firm to them, in case of such composure. Hereupon uterly to frustrate his hopes that way, they prevail with the House to Vote no more Addresses; and so vanisht away all their glorious flattery of the King and his Party, and their notorious dissimulation appeared, abusing thereby the Faith of the Army, and making it cleer to all discerning men, that such as could so break with one sort of men, will make no Conscience of keeping faith with any.

Their next work was to new-mould the City, and make it theirs, for which purpose they brought some Regiments of Horse and Foot, to White Hall and the Muse, to the extreme discontent of the City, and provoke them further by keeping their Lord Mayor, and some of their Aldermen in the Tower, without admitting them to a Legal Tryal, though upon Petitions and earnest Desires: at last they were referred to be tryed by the Lords, contrary to the known Law of the Land; but their jurisdiction being disclaimed, after a while they were released without any Tryal at all, their end being accomplisht, which was the terror of the City, and changing the Magistrates thereof, so as should best serve their designes.

About this time also they began to exercise their Marshal power over persons not of the Army, and did sentence Mr *William Thomson* to death at White Hall. And then also they began to new moddel the Army, and for that end, (though the new raised Regiment for the Tower was thought no burthen, yet upon pretence of easing the charge of the Common wealth, the Life-Guard must be disbanded, because consisting of discerning men, faithfull to their Country and former promises, and many others of like principles were pickt out of every Regiment; the designe being by weeding the choisest and best resolved men, to make the Army wholy mercinary, slavish, and the Executioners of a few mens lusts and lawlesse Pleasures. [8]

All which those good men perceiving and resolving thereupon not to be disbanded, according to the Agreement at *New market,* till the ends therein expressed were fully gained, they were enforced thereunto by *Tyrannicall sentences* of *Imprisonment* and Death (though the Officers themselves had formerly refused to disband upon command of *Parliament* upon the same grounds and strength of the same engagement:) By all which 'tis evident, that acording to the *maxime* of *Polititions,* they judge themselves loose where other men are bound; and that *all Obligations* are to them *Transitory* and *Ceremoniall,* and that indeed every thing is good and just only, as *it is conducing to their corrupt and ambitious Interests.*

And thus the most hopefull opportunity that ever *England* had for recovery of our *Freedom,* was spent and consumed, in such their uncertaine, staggering motions, and *Arbitrary, irrational Proceedings,* whereby all partyes became extreamly exasperated, as people that had been meerly mock'd and cheated by fair promises and under the most religious *pretences* &c. Hereby the *Army,* that but few *moneths before,* had been the joy and *hope* of all sorts of *Rationall People,* was made a *byword,* a *hissing,* and a *reproach* to the whole *Nation:* insomuch that those (in hope of their large *good Promises,* and *protests* in their *Declaration,*) who thought nothing *too precious* for them, now grudged them bread, and were ready to stone *them* in all places where they came; Trade fled, Poverty increased, and dicontents [*sic*] abounded, till at length broke out such a *flame,* as no time had ever seen before; and no doubt, was the *proper issue* of such *horrid delusions,* ministering such *matter* for a *generall Rising* and *Revolt,* as all former *Policies* could never attain to, and more threatning the ruine of *the Nation* then all the *former forces* and Stratagems of the Enemies; and which is rightly to be imputed to the unjust, partiall and *perfidious dealings of these men.*

But when they saw what a strange *predicament* they had brought themselves into, and which they would never beleeve, till it was come upon them (no more then now they will) they had before manifested a greater *Obstinacy,* then now they did a serious Repentance (*which yet as the sequell proves, was but counterfeit*) though (*as God knoweth*) we were overjoyed to beleeve it reall: Acknowledging, with the greatest expressions of sorrow, that [9] they had walked by *corrupt Pollitick Principles*; That they had been to blame in Actings against honest men; That the name of *Leveller, Jesuite* or the like reproaches, should never be more heard amongst them, that if ever the Nation be happy, it must be by a conjunction in the *Levellers* Principles, calling upon all, to lay by all *Discontents,* to forget and forgive, and to unite all against the *Common enemy,* and promising with greatest asseverations, That if God, upon our joynt endeavors, should be pleased to deliver us out of this Sea of *danger,* that they would never divide from just *Principles,* nor in the least discountenance honest men as they had done, nor endeavor to set up a party, but cast themselves upon an *agreement of the People* for the future settlement of the *Peace of the Nation:* but how and what performance they have made, that we shall intreat, may be impartially observed in the ensuing story; And for a full and timely proofe of their *Relapse,* & Discovery of their dissimulation; No sooner had they (through Gods blessing and the assistance of their reconciled friends) finished their worke at *Colechester,* but presently they call to question certaine Persons, that had appeared at St. *Albanes* in behalf of Captaine *Reynalds,* chusing rather to forsake the *Service,* then to be commanded by Captaines, that had been violent against them, that had drunke the Kings *Health* upon their knees, and profest they could rather fight against the *Levellers* then *Cavaliers,* and these (according to their old wont) they *sentenc'd to Death,* and soon after release them, as finding or supposing this kinde of Discipline most effectuall, to the breaking and debasing the spirits of the *English.*

And because Col. *Rainsborough* had *ever opposed their unjust Proceedings,* they withdraw him from the *Army,* by a plausible, but onely a *Titular command at sea,* where by the straitness of his Commission, he not having thereby the command of the Shippes or Officers, he could neither restrain their Revolt, nor preserve himself from being expulsed at the Seamans pleasure, out of that employment.

Then upon his return, the *ruling Officers* finding him as inflexible to their ends as formerly, they put him upon that dangerous and unhappy Service before *Pomfret* (nothwithstanding a Commander had been appointed thereunto by the *Committee* of *Yorke*) whether [*sic*] he went with much Reluctancy and discontent, as won[10]dering at the *Cause of his being Design'd thither,* and expressing as much to his *Friends, his sad soul presaging the misfortune, which after befell him.* But that which gives greatest cause of *grief* and *suspect* to his friends, is, that his *Brother* receives no furtherance, but rather, all discouragement that may be in searching after, and prosecuting the causers of that so bloody and inhumane a *Butchery.*

In the *North,* though during the *Service* and Necessities of the *Army,* the *Levellers* (as they are call'd) were countenanc'd, and taken into the *Boosme,* who thereupon (forgetting all former affronts and disrespects) did liberally hazzard their lives, without suspition of *fraud* and *delusion;* Yet the *Necessities* being over, and the enemies subdued, they renew fresh disgraces, and fall into a greater *Odium,* and contempt then ever.

First, *divers Souldiers* for Petitioning in the behalfe of Major *Reynolds,* that he might serve in the room of Major *Huntington,* were therefore rated, and threatned to have their skulles cutt, and some of them struck for so Petitioning; Major *Iohn Cobit,* who *with the extreamest hazard had regain'd* Tinmouth Castle, *where his Superiour Commander had through the dangers thereof refused, was notwithstanding rejected, and a Member of Parliament taken from his duty there,* & *contrary to the* self-denying Ordinance, made Governor *thereof. Major* White, *who in all the desperate services in the* North, *had performed the duty of Lieutenant Colonel, and Major both in the Generalls Regiment, yet because a constant man to his* Promises *and* **Principles**, ***was* refused *the*** Lieftenant

Colonelship, *and a man of a more complying Spirit fetch'd from another Regiment to officiate therein.*

And this was the usage not onely to these Gintlemen, but to all others whether Officers, or souldiers in North *or* South *(for their Counsells were one in both) that did retaine a sense and Resolution to prosecute those good things intimated in their former Ingagements.*

And as before, upon their first great Successe against the City, when now again it justly was expected they should have made use of so notable and unexpected Blessings to the benefit & advantage of the Common-wealth, (as their late repentances, promises and Pretences gave men cause to hope) the event proved, they intended another use thereof, for (having now subdued all their enemies, they proceed with greater confidence to their former purposes, of making themselves absolute masters over the Common-wealth, wherein there yet appeared one main obstacle, and that was an unanimous and universall Resolution in all Well-minded People (especially in that numerous P E O P L E that concurred in the P E T I- T I O N [11] of the *Eleventh* of *September* to center in an *Agreement of the* People, *which if not evaded,* it would be impossible for them) to goe *through* with their Worke: Hereupon againe they cry out for Union, and imploy their *Agents,* to get *meetings,* and *Treaties* with *those* that were most forward for an *Agreement* and contract with them to center in an *Agreement,* and that the matter of *the* Petition of *the Eleventh of September* (as was desired) should be the substance of that *Agreement*: there being no other way then by this yeelding in shew, to amaze this busie watchfull Party, and to keep them quiet, whilst they went on with other pieces of their worke.

For what else hath all the time spent thereabouts produced, but a meere amusing, blinding and deluding all that cordially desired the same, it being (before they left it) so obscur'd and perplext in the sense thereof, so short of what was intended, and so corrupted in many particulars, that those most loath'd it, that most desired it; In the meanetime, whilst they had fixt good Mens eyes and thoughts upon that Worke, they secretly and swiftly prosecute their other Designes, as principall in their purposes, wherein questionlesse they had not had the Assistance of good men, but that it was verily beleeved in shew of driving on their owne Designe; they were really and cordially producing a perfect and complete *Agreement of the People,* as large both in grounds of *freedome,* and redresse of grievances, as the *petition* of the Eleventh of *September,* in the uttermost extent thereof did import.

Many of which Petitioners were not satisfyed but that such an *Agreement of the People* might then have been obtained without any of those **extraordinary** sudden **and** **violent** **Courses** **lately** taken, neither in bringing the *Army* to the City, breaking the House in pieces, or removing the *King* by such an extra judiciall Proceeding & Court of Justice, as had no place in the *English* Government; and did really foresee there would be nothing but abuse in their pretence of an *Agreement of the people;* and that their owne domination, in and by a *Counsel of State,* was the maine thing aimed at, and intended.

The Removing the *King,* the *taking away the House of Lords* the over-awing the House, and reducing it to that passe, that it is become but the Channell through which is conveyed all the Decrees and Determinations of a private Counsell of some few Of[12]ficers, the erecting of their *Court of Iustise,* and their *Counsell of State, The voting of the* People *the supreame Power,* and this House the *Supreame Authority*: all these Particulars, (though many of them in order to *good ends,* have been desired by *wel-affected* People) are yet become (*as they have managed them*) of sole conducement to their ends, and Intents, either by removing such as stood in the way between them and *the power, wealth* or command of the *Common-wealth;* or *by actually possessing and investing them in the same.*

And though all *this was foreseen by us,* yet so *perswasive* were their *insinuations* in *the ears* of many good and *well disposed* People, *both Souldiers* and *others,* that they *have been really carryed away with belief of them, and reliance upon them, and have thought they could not better imploy their time and abilities, then in affording them all furtherance, and assistance that might be.*

So that their onely *fears* remain upon our *Discoveries,* to *prevent which, they use means, that either we might not have opportunity to lay open their Treacheries,* and *Hypocrisies, or not be beleeved if we did it.*

In order to the first, They strictly *stop the* Presse; In order to the second; *They blast us with all the Scandalls,* & *false Reports their* Witt *or* Malice *could invent against us; and so monstrously wicked have they been in this particular, That they have pry'd into all our* Actions, *made use of all our* Acquaintances, & *friendly* Intimacies, *and in conclusion, have onely produced such* Scandalls, *as have been customarily used by former Statesmen, and such, when scan'd and examined, containe both contrariety in themselves, and have not the least ground of Truth, as concerning us.*

By these *Arts* are they new fastened in their Power, till either by opposition from the *enemy,* which they may well expect God will raise against them, as the deserved Recompence of their vile Apostacy; or by the weight and Violence of their *many Injustices* (which in the wicked course they are in) must every day be multiplyed, till they be thrown down from their usurped greatnesse.

They have already lost the Affections of all People, and are only supported by *their present strength;* but when once those good men that hold them up, shall perceive how Instrumentall they are made, contrary to their intentions, in advancing a few [13] lofty and imperious mens *designes;* and how easy it is for them to convert their *abilities & power* to better, and more *common ends* exprest in their former engagements, and which the *complaints of the agrieved people,* and their owne *understandings* can furnish them withall, they will then lament that they have so long been out of the way, and set themselves with the utmost courage & resolution to *free their distressed Country* from the *fears* and *captivity* it now groans under. They may talk of *freedom,* but what *freedom* indeed is there, so long as they stop the Presse, which is indeed, and hath been so accounted in all *free Nations,* the most essentiall part thereof, imploying an *Apostate Iudas* for *executioner* therein, who hath been twice burnt in the hand, a wretched fellow, that even the *Bishops* and *Star-chamber* would have sham'd to own. What *freedom* is there left, when honest & *worthy Souldiers* are sentenc'd and enforc'd to *ryde the horse* with their faces reverst, and *their swords broken over their heads* for but Petitioning and presenting a Letter in *justification of their Liberty therein*: if this be not a new way of breaking the spirits of the *English,* which *Strafford* and *Canterbury* never dreampt of; we know no difference of things. A taste also of *Liberty of Conscience* they have given us in the *Case* of a worthy *Member* of your House; so as we may well judge what is like to follow, if their *Reigne continue.* And as for *Peace,* whilst the *supream Officers of the Army* are supream in your *House,* in the *Councel of State,* and all in all in the *generall Counsell of the Army,* when the *martiall power* is indeed *supream* to the *Civill Authority,* what *Peace* can be expected; we professe we see no *councells* tending to it, but hereof mighty and vast sums of money to be taxed upon the People *per mensem,* as if *warre* were become the only *trade,* or as if the *people* were bound to *maintain Armyes* whether they have trade or no; yea, whether they have bread or no.

And as for *the prosperity of the Nation;* what one thing hath been done that tendeth to it? Nay, hath any thing been done since they were in *power?* but what increaseth the rancor, hatred, and malice, which our late *unhappy differences* have begotten amongst us, as if they had placed their happiness and security in the *totall division of the People,* nothing being offered by them, that hath any face of *reconcilement* in it, nothing of cheerfulnesse or *generall satisfaction,* the mother of *trade & plenty,* that might take away the private *remembrances and destinctions of partyes,* nothing indeed, but what tendeth to implacable *bitternesse of spirit,* the mother of confusion penury, and beggery. [14]

Nay what sense *of the heavy burden of the people* have they manifested of late? hath it not been by their procurement that the Judges their Creatures have a thousand a yeer allow'd to every one of them above the ordinary fees, which were ever esteem'd a heavy *oppression* in themselves? is there any abridgement of the Charge, or length of *time* in *triall* of Causes? are they touch'd with the general *burden* of Tithes, that *canker* of *industry & Tillage?* or with that of *exize,* which out of the bowels of labourers & poor people enriches the Userers, & other Catterpillars of the Comon-wealth: or what have they done to free *trade* from the *intolerable burden of* Customs, except the setting fresh hungry flies upon the *old* sores of the *people?* what one matterial thing did they offer unto you in their late Petition, which you gave them so many thanks for? terming their Desires modest & discreet; when it's evident by the *contents,* they did it only to stop the mouthes of their Souldiers, & to amuze them into a pleasing *dream,* whilst they goe on in their Designe of absolute *domination,* & which should you in the least *oppose,* you would finde their modesty no more towards you, then towards your *excluded* Members: In the mean time, where is their Charge against those Members? or why finde they not who amongst them have conferr'd *offices* upon each other & upon their Creatures & relations? or who they were that gave so large Donations of thousands & hundreds *per an.* whilst the *publick faith* is broken, and Families are ready to starve for emptying themselves to serve the publick necessities; or why discountenance not they al those who have betrayed the *trust* of *feoffes* for Bishops & Delinquents lands? & are purchasers themselves of great Estates for few yeers purchases, the due *value* rightly considered; or why blame they not the L. *chief Iustice,* and L. *chief Baron* for keeping their places, which were conferred on them (and the like on others) by this House, when those *members* sate there, they have excluded? or why finde they not out those *perfidious persons* that have made no Conscience of breaking the *self-denying Ordinance,* and persist therein? or is the reason visible why they have nothing to say against those sorts of men namely, because these are their own, and their creatures cases? Oh wretched *England,* that seeth, and yet suffereth such *intollerable Masters.* What can be expected from such *Officers,* who frequently manifest a thirst after the blood of such *People,* and *Souldiers,* as are most active for the common *freedom, peace & prosperity* of the Common wealth, & against whom they have nothing else to object: or what can be expected from such a *counsell* in *the Army,* as shall agree *that the supream Au*[15]*thority* should be moved to make a *Law,* That *that Counsell of Officers* may have *power* to hang all such *Persons* (though not of the *Army*) as they should judge, were disturbers of the *Army.*

Certainly these things cannot but manifest unto you their very hearts, their inward purposes and Intentions representing visibly before you and all the World, the most dangerous condition, that ever yet this *Nation* hath been in: And if there be any Conscience towards God or man to be found amongst you, the whol series & Progress of this our sad *Representation* is so fully known, and fresh in memory, that it is impossible, but it must work up-upon [sic] all amongst you that are not Co-partners with them in their *Designe,* or are not ingaged (as the Lawyers are) in some corrupt Interest.

But though this long betrayed and miserable Nation should prove so unhappy as that there should not be one found amongst you, to own these known *Truths,* which yet ring in every mans ears, throughout the Land; but through feare, or other vile respects, should shut your eyes against the *light*: it shall be so farre from inducing us, to repent of what we have herein (or in our late Apprehensions) expressed, and set before you, that we shall rejoyce above measure, that we have witnessed to the *Trueth*; and against all those Delusions and perfidious Stratagems lay'd by those men to betray and enslave the Common-wealth, to their owne Pride, Ambition, Lusts, Covetousnesse, and Domination, if not Dukeship, or Kingship; their Creatures discoursing of late, *That the Power must be reduced to One*: What their meaning is, time (*if they be not hindred*) will manifest: but the Premises duly weighed, doth evidence, what ere it be, it will be as bad, as bad possibly can be.

And as we shall not altogether doubt of the appearance of some, in this *Honorable House,* that will consci8onably performe that *Supream Trust* which is really and essentially resident in your integrity; what ever may be suggested to the contrary: (it being not others treachery, nor anyes violence, that can divest you of that Authority:) but if you all should say therein, as God forbid yet we shall not doubt, but that what we have here presented, and published will open the eyes, and raise the hearts of so considerable a number of the *Souldiary* and *People* in all places, and make them so sensible of the bondage and danger threatned, as that these men, this Faction of Officers, shall never be able to goe through with their wicked intentions. [16]

It being an infinite shame that they should be suffered to proceed so farre therein, as they have done, there having beene no party hitherto so inexcusable, for it is possible, if not probable that the King and his party might at first be induced to offend through error of breeding, long custome, and sway of times, (although that excuse neither him nor them.) That *Hollis,* and that party, might at first be drawne into their violence, against people faithfull to the Common wealth through an errornious zeale against supposed Sectaries, and for uniformity in Presbytery (though that also but little extenuates their offence) but neither the one nor the other can be imagined to have transgressed against so evident light. nor against so many and great obligations of love, and great respects from the people as this party hath done; So that the in[t]entions, and endeavours of these men, to enslave the Common-wealth, or their continuing of burthens, without any remorse at the dearnesse of food, and and [sic] utter losse of trade, exceeds in the nature and measure of it, all the wickednesse of both the other parties put together.

And therefore upon due consideration of the premises, and in utter detestation of their most perfidious and treacherous dealing with the Army, Parliament and Common-wealth; we do in behalf of ourselves and all wel-minded people, here before this Honourable House, as in the presence of Almighty God, protest against their breaking the faith of the Army with all parties, their dissolving the Councel of the *Agitators*, and usurping a power of giving forth the sence of the Army to the Parliament and people, also against the shooting of the *S*ouldier to death at *Ware*, and their cruelties exercised on other persons, to the debasing of their spirits, and thereby new moulding of the Army to their owne designes, then playing fast and loose with the King and his party, till they brought a new and dangerous Warre upon the Nation.

We also protest against their dissembled repentances, as in no measure satisfactory for so abominable offences: we also protest against all their late extraordinary Proceedings, in bringing the Army upon the City, (to the ruine of trade) there breaking the House in pieces without charging the Members particularly: And then judging and taking away of mens lives in an extraordinary way, as done for no other end, but to make way for their owne absolute domination: we also protest against the Election and Establishment of those High-Courts of [17] Justice, as unjust in themselves, and of dangerous Presidence in time to come: as likewise against the Councell of State, and putting some of themselves therein contrary to their owne Agreement: we also protest against all other the like meetings of those officers, that on *Thursday* the 22. of *February* last, voted for so bloody a Law, as to hang whom they should judge, disturbed the Army, (as having no power either by such Councels, either to give the sence of the Army, or to judge any Person not of the Army, or to do any thing in reference to the Common-wealth, more then what any, so many fifty Souldiers or persons not of the Army have power and may lawfully do: though all the Generall officers were continually present:) these we protest against, as things unjust abominable and dangerous and declare that our present not seeking for Justice or reliefe therein, shall be no bar against us for the future, when we shall see cause to seek for Justice and reliefe therein.

*A*nd for the truth of our Judgements herein: we should with gladnesse submit unto the determinations of this *H*onourable House, were not their High hand as yet held over you. *A*nd therefore we are enforced to appeale to a new Representive, equally chosen in such like manner, as is exprest in our serious apprehensions lately presented unto you, and do likewise desire that you would encourage the *A*rmy in chusing a Representative, consisting of select Persons, chosen by every Regiment of the *A*rmy, as at the first at *New-market*: and shall humbly pray that you will not any more receive the result of a few officers, as the sence of the *A*rmy, the officers of an *A*rmy having no more power to make Laws for an *A*rmy, then the officers of the Common wealth to make Laws for the People; both of them being constituted only for the Discipline, and Government thereof. We hope you will proceed to further an *A*greement of the People; according to our late desires in our serious *A*pprehensions, and also speedily take in hand and effect those other things therein desired, tending very much to the abrogation of the bondage intended.

Thus have we once more unburdened our hearts before you, and faithfully discharged our duties to our Country, giving timely warning of the most dangerous thraldom and misery that ever threatned this much wasted Nation, and much we doubt not, wil, by wisdom mixt with som honest resolutions, be timely prevented: which we shall exceedingly rejoyce to see, that so after so many yeers of sorrow, the people may at length be comforted, and the Land enjoy her rest; and that all the world may be enforced to confess, That *There is a reward for the righteous,* and *that there is a God that judgeth the earth.* [18]

FINIS.

JOHN SALTMARSH

SHADOWS FLYING AWAY

A selection from John Saltmarsh's pamphlet, *Reasons for Vnitie, Peace, and Love* (1646), the following pages throw light on one of the most important controversies of the seventeenth century. The sharp clash between emphasis on the Gospels and emphasis on the Old Testament is nowhere more sharply delineated than in these passages.

The selection is reprinted from a photostat of the copy in the McAlpin Collection of Union Seminary. Spelling and punctuation follow the usage of the original tract.

To Mr. Gataker.

SIR,

Hope I shall answer all things material in your *Book;* but your *Margin* I shall not meddle with: I observe you commonly in all your books fill that with *things,* and *Authors,* of little value to *Christ crucified*: As in your *last leaf,* where you quote *Sophocles* the Poet, comparing your self to an old pronseing *horse.* I should not rebuke your years, but that I find you *Comical* and *Poetical:* and for my part, I am now ashamed to own those *Raptures,* though I am young, having tasted strains of a more glorious *Spirit:* how much more you that are old, and call your selfe a *Divine,* ought not to have any *fruit in those things.*

I hope I shall be in no more passion with you, than with your Brother of the *Assembly,* Mr. *Lee.* I write to *edifie,* not to *conquer;* nor to teach others, but that we may be all taught of God.

John Saltmarsh.

[A short passage is omitted here.]

Shadows flying away: *Or,*

A Reply to Master GATAKER's Answer to some passages in Master *Saltmarsh* his Book of FREE GRACE.

Master *Gataker.*

(1) That he was traduced by one Master John Saltmarsh, *a man unknown to him, save by one or two Pamphlets, as witnessing to the* Antinomian *party. (2) That he must unbowell and lay open some of the unsound stuff. (3) That some think they have found out a shorter cut to heaven. (4) That my Inferences upon his words are not true, nor as he intended: As if a Protestant with a Papist disputing about the Masse, should say, The Controversie is not concerning the nature of the Sacraments.*

Answer.

To the first, *that you were traduced by me:* Let not *you* and *I* be judge of that: both our Books are abroad; and I have quoted your *words* to the very *leaf* where they are. Your *meaning* I could not come at: the *deep things of the heart* are out of the power of anothers *quotation*.

For my selfe *unknown to you but by two Pamphlets:* I take your sleigtings: I could call your Trearises [*sic*] by a worse name then *Treatises;* for I knew *one* of them some yeers since, *that* of *Lots,* wherein you defended *Cards* and *Dice-playing:* And It had been happy for others as well as my selfe, in my times of vanity had you Printed a [1] Retractation. I believe you strengthned the hands of many to *sin.* I know you love ancient Writers well by your *Margin* and *quotations.* And I pray remember how *Augustine* honoured Truth as much by confessing *Errours* as professing *Truths. What fruit should you and I have of these things whereof we are now ashamed?*

For your *witnessing to the Antinomian partie against your will,* Is that your fault or mine? Nor am I to judge of your reserves, and secret senses, but of *words* and *writings.* Nor is it an Antinomian party I alleadge you to countenance; but a party falsly traduced and supposed so: a Party called *Antinomian* by you, and others, and then writ against: A setting up Hereticks to deceive the world, and then telling the world Such and such are the men. You may make more by this trick, then you finde so.

To the Second, *That you will lay open the unsound stuff:* I shall not be unwilling, I hope, to be told my failings: but I must look to the *stuff* you bring in the room of mine, and intreat others to try the soundnesse of yours. It is not *my* saying that mine is *sound,* will make it better; nor your saying It is *unsound,* can make it worse. *Let every ones work be proved, and then he shall have whereof to boast.*

To your Third, of some *finding out a shorter cut to heaven then some former Divines:* I know not what you mean by *shorter cuts.* The Papists finde a way, they say, to heaven by *works,* some Protestants by *Jesus Christ* and *works,* and others by *Jesus Christ* alone, and make works the praise of that Free grace in *Jesus Christ:* And is that a *shorter cut* then theirs, as you call it? or rather, a clearer revelation of *Truth?* Me thinks your expressions have too much of that which *Solomon* calls *frowardnesse* in old men. Argue, and prove, and bring Scripture as long as you please, but be not too *quarrelsome.* But I shall excuse you in part, because you tell us you are not yet recovered from sicknesse: so as I take this, with otber [*sic*] of your book, as *part or remainders* of your *disease,* rather then your *judgement;* and the infirmity of your *body,* not the strength of your *spirit.* But why chose you not a better time to trie *Truth* in, when you were not so much in the *body?*

To the Fourth, That *nothing lesse was intended by you:* I undertook not to discover your *intents* to the world. You might have done well to have revealed your selfe more at first, that I might not have taken you to be more a friend to Truth then I see you are: *forgive* me this injury, as the Apostle sayes, if I accounted you better then [2] you desire to be. *Love hopeth all things, and believeth all things.* And *Paul* it seems was better perswaded of *Agrippa* then there was cause, and quoted some of the Heathen Poets better then they intended them as it seems I have done with you; that being the greatest thing you lay to my charge.

Master *Gataker*.

(*1*) *That our Antinomian Free grace is not the same with that of the Prophets in the Old Testament, & the Apostles in the New.* (2) *That in saying the Old Testament was rather a draught of a legall dispensation, then an Evangelicall or Gospel one, was to tax the Ministry of the Prophets for no Free-grace.* (3) *That in saying the Ministers now by the qualifications they preach do over-heat Free-grace as poor souls cannot take it, doth make the Prophets Juglers and deluders of the people.*

Answer.

To your first, That *our Antinomian Free grace is not the same with the Prophets and Apostles:* Why doe you tel us of *Antinomian*, of *Prophets* and *Apostles* Free-grace? It is not the free-grace of any of these: Free-grace is of God in Jesus Christ; Prophets and Apostles are but dispensers of it, and Ambassadours of it, and Ministers of it: and yet Ambassadours not in the same habit: the *Prophets* preached Grace in a *rough* and *hairy* garment, or, more *Legally*, the *Apostles* in a more *clear* & bright habit, in the *revelation* of the *mystery* of *Christ.* *The Law was given by Moses, but Grace and truth by Jesus Christ.* I could as easily say Master *Gataker's Free-grace*, and *The Legalists Free-grace*, as he says *Our Antinomian Free-grace*; but such *words* and *reproaches* make neither *you* nor *I* speak *better truth.*

To your Second, That *in saying the Old Testaments strain was rather Legall then Gospel, taxes the Ministerie of the Prophets for no Free grace:* That is according to your Inference onely. Because the *Spirit* sayes the *Law was given by Moses*, therefore will you put upon the *Spirit* that *Moses* taught or gave out nothing but *Law?* Because, I say *The Old Testament was a Legall ministration*, therefore do I say there was no Free-grace in it? or do I not rather say, Therefore it was Free grace Legally dispensed, or preached; or ministred? Would not such Inferences be bad dealing with the *Spirit?* and will it be fair dealing [3] with

me? I wonder you who pretend to write against me, as having not
dealt *justly* with your sense, will deal so *unjustly* with mine, and commit
the same *sin* your self, in the very time of your reproving mine. You
may see what this *Logick* hath brought you to, To deceive your self,
as well as your neighbour. Can you cast out my mote, and behold, a
beam is in your own eye?

I have printed all you quoted: let the Reader judge from this, and
compare it with the rest of my Book.

The whole frame of the Old Testament was a draught if [sic] *Gods
anger at sin.—And God in this time of the Law appeared onely as it were
upon terms and conditions of reconciliation: and all the Worshipe then,
and acts of Worship then, as of Prayer, Fasting, Repentance, &c. went
all this way, according to God under that appearance. And in this strain*
(saith he) *runs all the Ministery of the Prophet too, in their exhortations
to Duty and Worship, as if God were to be appeased, and intreated,
and reconciled, and his love to be had in way of purchase by Duty, and
Doing, and Worshipping: So as under the Law, the efficacy and power
was put as it were wholly upon the Duty and Obedience performed, as
if God upon the doing of such things, was to be brought into terms of
peace, mercy and forgiveness; so as their course and the service then,
was as it were aworking for life and reconciliation.*

Do not these words and terms inserted, *As it were,* and, *in the way,*
and, *as if,* and *as it were,* clear me from such positive and exclusive
assertions of *Free grace* as you wovld make me speak?

To the Third, That *in saying the Preachers with their qualifications
over-heat Free grace, I do by that make the Prophets deluders of the
people,* &c. I Answer: That way of preaching the Prophets used, pressing,
as you say, Repentance, Reformrtion [sic], Humiliation, and with Com-
mination of the Law, &c. was but according to the way, and method,
and strain the *Spirit* taught them under the *Old Testament:* but if the
Prophets should have held forth Jesus Christ under the *New-Testament,*
and when Christ was manifested in the *flesh,* with such *veils* over him,
and so much *Law* over him. as they did before, they had sinned against
the *glory* of that *ministration,* as well as some of you, who bring Christ
back again under the cool shadow of the *Law,* & make that *Sun of
righteousnesse* that he warms not so many with the *love* of him as he
would doe, if ye would let [4] them behold with open face as in a glasse
the glory of the Lord, and if you would give his beams more liberty to
shine upon them; doth not the *ministration of the spirit exceed in glory.*

Nor were the Prophets *deluders of the people then,* because it was the peoples time of *Pupillage,* add being under *Bondage*; they *were shut up under the law till faith came*; they were under *Tutors and Governours till the time appointed:* So as that was *truth* and right dispensation in them to preach so much of the *law,* of *curse* and *judgement, &c.* as they did; and of *Repentance* and *Reformation* in that strain they did: But in ye who pretend to preach *Christ come in the flesh*; ye who pretend to be *Preachers in the Kingdom of God,* and so greater then the greatest *Prophet,* then hee that was more then a *Prophet*; in ye, such preaching were delusion, because it were not as the truth is in Christ, nor according to that *glory* of the *Gospel,* to that *grace revealed,* to that *manifestation of Christ in the flesh,* to that *ministration of glory*; but rather to those *deceitfull workers* the Apostle speaks on, to those that *troubled them with words, subverting their souls,* who preached *Law* and *Gospel, Circumcision* and *Christ.*

Master *Gataker.*

(1) That we gird at those that bid men repent, and be humbled, and be sorry for sins, and pray, &c. as legall teachers. (2) That Christ preached repentance, humiliation, selfe-denyall, conversion, renouncing all in purpose: this is not the same Gospel with that they preach, as in Free-grace, *page* 125. *page* 126. *page* 152. *page* 153. 163. 191. 193.

Answer.

To your first, for our *girding at those that bid men repent, and be humbled, &c, as Legall teachers:* If ye presse *repentance* and *humiliation* legally, why wonder ye at such words as *Legall teachers?* Will ye doe ill and not be told of your faults? must we prophesie smooth things to you, and say ye are able Ministers of the New Testament, when we are perswaded that truth is detained in unrighteousnesse? We blame not any that bid men repent, or be sorry for sin, &c. be humble, &c. if they preach them as Christ and the Apostles did; as *graces* flowing from him, and out of his *fulnesse,* and not as spring[5]ings of their own, and *waters* from their fountains; as if the teachers, like *Moses,* would make men believe they could with such Rods and exhortations, smite upon mens hearts as upon rocks, and bring waters out of them, be they never so hard and stony. Wee agree with you, that *repentance,* and *sorrow for sin,* and *humiliation,* and *self-denyall,* are all to be preached, and shall contend with you who preaches them most, and cleerest: but then, because *John* said Repent, and Christ said Repent, and *Peter* said Repent; are wee to examine the Mystery no farther? Know wee not that the whole *Scripture* in its fulnesse and integrality reveals the whole truth? and must wee not look out, and compare Scripture with Scripture, Spirituall things with Spirituall, and so finding out truth from the degrees, to the glory and fulnesse of it, preach it in the same glory and fulnesse as we find it? We heare Christ preaching before the Spirit was given, *Repent*; and we finde, when the Spirit was given, Christ is said to give *Repentance* to *Israel*, and *forgivenesse of sins*; and shall we not now preach Jesus Christ, and repentance in Jesus Christ the fountain of repentance, the author of repentance, and yet preach repentance, and repentance thus, and repentance in the glory of it more? The Apostle in one place saith, *Believe in the Lord Jesus Christ, and thou shalt be saved;* and in another place, *He is the author and finisher of our Faith*; Shall wee not now preach *Jesus Christ* first? and *Jesus Christ* the *fountain*, and *Jesus Christ* the *authour* of *faith* and *believing* and yet preach *faith*; yea, and thus preach *faith*, faith in the *glory*, faith in the *revelation* of it, faith from *Christ*, and faith in *Christ?*

One Scripture tells us *godly sorrow worketh repentance to salvation, &c.* And another tells us, *They shall look on him whom they have peirced, and they shall mourn for him, &c.* Shall we not now preach *sorrow for sin* took from *Christ*, *Christ* peircing, and wounding, and melting the heart; Christ discovering sin, and *pouring water* upon drie ground? this is sorrow for sinne in the glory of the Gospel.

One Scripture bids, *He that will follow me, let him deny himselfe, & take up his crosse.* Another sayth, It is *he that worketh in us both to will and to doe of his good pleasure*, and *I am able to doe all things through Christ that strengtheneth me.* Shall we not now preach *Christ* our strength, and *Christ* our self-deniall? and is not this *self-denyall* in the *glory* of the Gospel? [6]

So as the difference betwixt us is this; Ye preach Christ and the Gospel, and the graces of the Spirit in the parts as ye finde it: we dare not speak the Mystery so in pieces, so in halfe and quarter revealings; we see such preaching answers not the *fulnesse* of the Mystery, the *riches* of the *Gospel*, the *glory* of the *New Testament:* We finde that in the fulnesse of the New Testament, Christ is set up as a Prince, as a King, as a Lord, as a crown and glory to every grace and gift: nay, he is made not onely *righteousnesse*, but *sanctification* too and so we preach him. Whereas to preach his riches without him, his graces by themselves, single and private; as, *repent,* and *believe,* and *be humbled,* and *deny yourselves,* ye make the gifts lose much of their glory, Christ of his praise, and the Gospel of its fulnesse.

To the Second, of your alleadging my Book in such and such pages, as another Gospel from Christs: I shall print them as you quote them; and with them, I desire these things to be considered, together with the other parts of my Book, and the scope of it, which you have *detained in unrighteousnesse:* All these I freely open to the judgement of all who are spirituall.

Master *Gataker.*

(*1*) *That* John, *Christs, and his Apostles method were all one for matter and manner, for they all preached Faith and Repentance, and yet we are taxed for these things as Legalists by this Author.* (2) John & the rest preached life and salvation upon condition of Faith and Repentance, and Obedience. (3) Where we finde Faith onely preached, it is because we have but the summaries or heads of their Sermons.

Answer.

To the first, that I *tax you for preaching Faith and Repentance, as the Apostles did, and* John *did, as Legalists.* Nay, I tax ye onely because ye preach it not as they did, according to the full revelation of it in the New Testament; but you preach it onely as you finde it in their Summaries, and in the brief narration of their Doctrine; and this you ought not to do, if you will preach according to that glorious analogy of the Gospel: and to this, I shall onely bring in your own words to convince you, and so from *your own mouth condemne you.* You say of the Apostles, Wee have but Summaries of them, [7] as in *Acts* 2.40. and 16.32. and you knowing this, preach onely by their first Methods and Summaries, not looking to the revelation of the mystery, which the Apostle says is now made manifest. And for *Johns manner of Preaching,* his *Preaching* is to be no more an example to you then his *Baptisme.* You know the least in the Kingdom of heaven is greater then he.

To the second, That *Faith, Repentance and Obedience, were condition: of life and salvation.* Why keep you not to the form or *wholsome words* in *Scripture?* Where doth the Scripture call *these* conditions of salvation? They that are Christs, do believe, and repent, and obey; but do they *believe, repent,* and *obey,* that they may be Christs? Hath not God *chosen us in him,* and predestinated us unto the adoption of children in Jesus Christ? But I know you will say, That when the Apostles did believe, repent, and obey, it is by consequence as much as a *condition,* and the same with a *condition.* But I answer: The interpreting the *Spirit* thus in the *letter,* and in *consequence,* hath much darkned the glory of the Gospel. When some of Christs disciples took his words as you do, under a condition, *Except ye eat the flesh of the Son of man,* &c. *the words,* saith he, *that I speak, are spirit.* Consider but what *straits* you bring the *Gospel* into: first, you make life appearing to be had in the *Covenant of Grace,* as at first in the *Covenant of Works*; *Do this, and live*; so *believe. repent, obey and live*; thus runs your *Doctrine:* nor can you with all your distinctions make *Faith* in this consideration lesse then a *work,* and so put *Salvation* upon a *condition* of *works* again. Is this *Free grace?* But you say *Faith* is a gift *freely given* of *God*; and here is *Free grace* still. But I pray, Is this any more *Free grace* respectively to what wee do for life, then the Covenant of works had? All the works wrought in us, then, were freely of God, and of *free gift* too, as *Arminius* well observes in the point of universall grace; and wee wrought onely from a *gift given.* Either place Salvation upon a free bottom, or else you make the *New Covenant* but an *Old Covenant* in new terms; instead of *Do this and live. Believe this and live, repent and live, obey and live:* and all this is for want of revealing the mystery more fully.

To your third, That *where we find Faith onely preached, and so Salvation made short work*; *that it is because we have but the summaries.* I agree with you that we have but the Doctrine of the *Apostles* as *Johns,* of whom it is said, *He spake many other things in his exhortation to the people.* It is true, we have much of what they said, and wee [8] want much; yet we have so much, as may shew us, that according to the *work* of Salvation in us, *Faith* is the *work* which gives most glory to God: *Abraham believed,* it is said, and *gave glory to God*; they that *believe, give glory*; and *Faith* of all the *works* of the *Spirit,* is the glorious Gospel-work, Christ calls it the *work indeed, this is the work that ye believe:* So as the only reason why we hear so much of *Faith* in the Gospel, is not only and meerly as you insinuate, because we have but their Sermons in Summaries, and because of another reason of yours, drawn from the *qualification* of some they Preached to, that had other *gifts,* and not *Faithe.* But because *Faith* is of all Spiritual encreasings in us, the most gloriously working towards *Christ, Faith* goes out, and *Faith* depends, and *Faith* lives in *Christ,* and *Faith* brings down *Christ,* and *Faith opens* the riches, and *Faith believes* home all *strength, comfort, glory, peace, promises.*

And *Faith* hath so much put upon it, as *becomes a stumbling stone, and a rock of offence,* to many: *Justification, imputation of righteousnesse* is put upon *Faith*; Salvation upon *Faith,* as *Christs* blood, is put upon *the Wine*; *the Cup that we blesse, is it not the Communion of the blood of Christ*; and *Christs body* upon the *Bread,* the bread that we *break, is it not the Cummunion of the body of Christ?* and yet neither the *Wine* nor the *Bread,* is his *Blood* or his *Body,* no more then *Faith* is either *Iustification* or *Righteousnesse*; but such a work as goes out most into him, and carries the soul into him who is *Righteousnesse* and *Iustification* to us.

The *word* were no *mystery*, if it were not thus ordered, and things so mingled, that the *Spirit* only could discern and distinguish; Do not the *Papists* stumble at *Works?* And why? because they see not *Faith* for *Works:* And do not others stumble at *Faith?* And why? because they see not *Christ* for *Faith:* Do not some say that the *words, world,* and *all,* and *every man,* makes some stumble at the Election of some, and so conclude *Redemption* for *all.*

Master *Gataker.*

(1) That Christ and his Apostles never Preached Free grace, without conditions and qualifications on our parts, Rom. 8.1. Mar. 5.8, *&c. (2) Christs Blood or Wine is not to be filled out too freely to Dogs and Swine, to sturdy Rogues. (3) That saying, Promises belongs* [9] *to sinners as sinners, not as humbled,* &c. *and all that received him, received him in a sinful condition, is a creeping to Antinomianism. (4) That God may be provoked to wrath by his Children, and* David *and* Peter *made their peace with God by Repentance. (5) That God loves us for his own graces in us; God is as man, and as a Father is angry and chastiseth his for sin. (6) Faith is not a perswasion more or lesse of Christs love, all may have that, men may beleeve too suddenly, as* Simon Magus. *(7) Christ bids us repent, as well as believe; yea, first to repent, we are to try our Faith,* 2 Cor. 13.5. 1 Joh. 4.1. *(8) That he clogs men with conditions of taking and receiving, as well as we of repenting and obeying. (9) The sum of this mans Divinity is, Men may be saved whether they repent or no, whether they beleeve or no.*

Answer.

To the first, *That Christ and his Apostles never preached Free-grace, without conditions.* &c. *on our parts*:

I answer, They *Preached Faith,* and *Repentance,* and *Obedience:* But how? First, in *degrees* of *Revelation,* the Gospel came not all out at once in its glory: they *Preached them,* But how? Not in *parts,* as we have their Doctrine, as you confesse *they Preached them*; but all along in the *New-Testament* there is more of their *glory* and *fulnesse* revealed concerning them; so as the *degrees* of revealing, the *parts* or summaries of their Sermons, the *fuller discovery* in the whole New-Testament, are *those things* you consider not, and they are *the things* we only consider, and so dare not *Preach* the *Gospel* so in *halfs,* in *parts* and *quarters* as you do, and yet will not leeve you do, which is so much worse, *Ye say ye see, and therefore your sin remaineth.*

To the second, *Christs blood is not to be filled out to Rogues and Dogs.*

Take heed you charge not Christ for being with Publicans and Sinners, you may upon this ground say he Preached false Doctrine, because he said, *He came not to call the Righteous, but Sinners.*

What were all of us in our unregenerate condition, sinners or righteous persons? unholy or holy? men of faith or unbeleef? or not rather *dead in trespasses and sins, till quickened with Christ?*

To the third. That saying, *Promises belong to sinners as sinners, and not humbled, &c.* [10]

I pray, To whom doth all promises belong first, but to Christ? and from whom to us, but from Christ? and what are the Elect, and the chosen in him, before they are called or beleeve, but sinners as sinners? Do you look that men should be first whole for the Physician, or Righteous for pardon of sins, or justified for Christ; or rather *sinners, unrighteous, ungodly? While we were yet sinners Christ dyed for us*; He *dyed for the ungodly*: Christ is the *Physitian*, the *Righteousnesse*, the *Sanctification*, and makes them *beloved that were not beloved*, and to *obtain mercy that had not obtained mercy*, and *Saints* who were *sinners*, and *Spiritual* who were *carnal*.

So as we look at Christ and the Promises comming to men in their sins; but those men were beloved of God in Christ, who suffered for sins before; so as they begin not now to be *loved*, but to be made to *love*; *God* begins not to be *reconciled* to them, but they begin to be *reconciled* to him, *The love of God being shed abroad in their hearts by the holy Ghost, which is now given unto them.*

So as we looking at *persons* as *chosen* in *Christ*, and at their *sins*, as born by *Christ* on *his body on the Tree*, we see nothing in persons to hinder them from the Gospel, and offers of grace there, be they never so sinful to *us*, or *themselves*, they are not so to him who hath *chosen* them, no to *him* in whom they are chosen: And this is the mysterie, why *Christ* is offered to *Sinners*, or *Rogues*, or whatsoever you call them, they are, as *touching the Election, beloved for the Fathers sake*: I speak of such to whom *Christ* gives *power* to receive him, and beleeve on him, and *become the Sons of God*; and Christ finds them out in their sins, and visits them *who sit in the Region* and *shadow of death*; and them that are *darknesse*, he makes *light in the Lord.*

To your fourth, *That God may be provoked to wrath by his Children.*

I pray, Can *God* be as the *Son* of *man*? Is there any *variablenesse or shadow of change in him?* Can he love and not love? Doth he *hate persons* or *sins?* Is he said to *chastise* as *Fathers*, otherwise then in expressions after the *manner of men*; because of the *infirmities of our flesh*, must we conceive so of God as of one another? Can he be provoked for sins done away and abolished? Hath Christ taken away all the sin of his? Hath he born all upon his body or no? Speaks he of anger otherwise then by way of *Allusion* and *Allegory?* as a *Father &c*. And is that, *He is a Father* af[11]ter the fashion of men? Or speaks he not in the Old Testament according to the Revelation of himself then, and in the New Testament of himself now, only because our infirmity, and his own manner of appearing which is not yet so; but we may bear him in such expressions, and yet not so in such expressions, but we may see more of him and his love, and the glory of Salvation in other expressions, and not make up such a love as you commonly do of benevolence and complacence.

Did David *and* Peter, *as you say, make up their peace with God by Repentance*: Is there any that makes peace put one Iesus Christ, who makes peace through the blood of his Crosse? Can *Repentance* make *peace?* Or *Obedience* make *peace?* Is there any sacrifice for sin, but that which was *once offered, even he that appeared in the end of the world, to put away sin by the sacrifice of himself? And was not this called by the Apostle, One sacrifice for sins for ever?*

Repentance, Obedience, &c. may make way for the *peace* made already for sin, that is, in such workings of Spirit, the *love* of *God* in the *face* of *Jesus Christ*, may shine upon the *Soul* more freely and fully; and the more the *Spirit* abounds in the fruits of it, the more *joy* and *peace* flows into the *Soul*; and the more the *Soul* looks *Christ* in the *face*, so as peace with God is not *made*, but more *revealed* by the Spirit in obedience and love, *&c*.

To your fifth, *That God loves us for his own graces in us.*

I thought he had loved us too in himself, and from that *love* given Christ for us, and yet loved us in Christ too; can any thing without God, be a cause of Gods love? Doth God love as we love one another, from complexions or features without, or loves he not rather thus? *God is love,* and therefore we are *made,* and *Redeemed,* and *Sanctified*; not because we are *Sanctified,* therefore he loves us; *We love him, because he first loved us*; he loved us, because he loved us, and not because we *love him,* not because of any Spiritual complexion or feature in us; because of his Image upon us, that is but an *earnest* of his love to us, that is only given us because he *loved us*; he *loves us* from his will, not from without: for though we are *like him,* yet we are not *himself,* and he loves us as in *Christ* and *himself*.

Whereas you say, *God is as man, and as a Father*. I hope you mean not as in *himself*, but as in his ways of *speaking* and *appearing* to us, and if so, we are agreed: But your taking things more [12] in the *Letter*, then the *Spirit*, makes your Divinity lesse *Divine*, and your conceptions more like things of men then of *God*: This makes the glory of the Gospel so legal and carnal, when we rise little higher then the bare *Letter* or *Scripture*, not the inspiration by which it came, all Scripture being given by inspiration.

To your sixth, *That Faith is not a perswasion more or lesse of Gods love*, and *that all may have that.*

I pray mistake not, Can all believe from the *Spirit?* Can all be more or lesse spiritually perswaded? Do I speak of any *perswasion* of *Christs love* which is not Spiritual? Deceive not yourself, nor your Reader, nor wrong not your Author; or do I speak of *Faith* abstracted from all *Repentance, Obedience, &c.* why deal ye thus? When you *say men may believe too suddenly*, because I presse men to *believe*, and you instance in *Simon Magus*; Was he blamed for *believing* too *suddenly*, or for *misbelieving?* because he believed the gifts of the *Holy Ghost* were to be bought with money? Can any *believe* too soon? If some misbelieve, or *believe falsly*, what is that to them that truly *believe?* Shall *the unbelief of some make the Faith of God without effect?* God *forbid:* Can *Christ* be too soon a *Saviour* to us? Can the *Fountain* be too soon opened for sin? Can the *riches of Christ* be too soon brought home? *Paul* counts it an honour to be first in *Christ*: *Salute Andronicus and Junia who were in Christ before me*, and the *Church in Priscilla's house, and Epenetus, who were the first fruits of Achaia unto Christ,*

To your seventh, *That Christ bids us repent as well as believe, yea first repent.*

Yea, but will you take the Doctrine of the Gospel from a *part*, or *summary* of it, as you say, and not from the Gospel in its *fulness*, and *glory*, and *Revelation:* Will ye gather Doctrines of Truth, as *Ruth* for a while did *gleanings*, here one *ear of Corn*, and there another; and not rather go to the full sheaf, to Truth in the Harvest and Vintage? Will you pick up *Truth* by pieces and parcels, in *Repentance*, and *Obedience*, and *Self-denial?* and not *reveal* these as *Christ* may be most *glorified*, and the *Saints* most *Sanctified*, and these gifts most *Spiritualized* and improved? Will ye Preach Doctrines as they lie in the *Letter*, or in their *Analogy* and inference of Truth? The Papists Preach Christs very flesh and blood to be in the *Wine*, And why? but because they look but half way to the *demonstration* of *Truth* in the *Spirit*, they shut up *Christ* in one *Notion* and [13] not in *another*, and so loses the *Truth* by revealing it in that *form of words* which is too narrow for it, and too short of the *height*, and *depth*, and *length* of it.

You say, *We are to try our Faith*: So say I too, if you would not pick and choose in my Book, to make *me* some *other* thing then you finde *me*: But you mean, we must try our *Faith* for assurance, as your other words imply; and so far I say too, but you will not hear me speak: But you would have the best *assurance* from *tryal*; but so far I say not as you say, is that the best Spiritual assurance that is from our own Spirits in part, or from Gods alone? from our own *reasoning*, or his *speaking?* Can a Spouse argue better the love of her friend from his Tokens and Bracelets, or from his own *Word*, and *Letter*, and *Seal?*

One of the three that bear witnesse on Earth is the *Spirit*, and in whom, after ye beleeve, ye were sealed with that *Spirit* of *Promise.* Can any *Inference* or *Consequence* drawn from Faith, or Love, or Repentance, or Obedience in us so assure us, as the breathing of Christ himself, *sealing, assuring, perswading, convincing, satisfying*; I will hear what *God the Lord will say, for he will speak peace to his Servants:* A *Saint* had rather hear that voyce, then all its own *Inferences* and *Arguments,* which though they bring somthing to *perswaue* [*sic*], yet they perswade not so answerably *till the voyce speak from that excellent glory.*

To your eigth, *That I clog men with conditions of receiving, as well as you of repenting,* &c.

I answer, I Preach not *Receiving* as a condition, as you do *Repenting.* I preach *Christ* the *Power*, and *Life*, and *Spirit*, that both stands and *knocks*, and yet *opens* the door to himself. I Preach not *Receiving* as a *gift,* or condition given or begun for *Christ,* but *Christ working* all in the *Soul*, and the *Soul* working up to *Christ* by a *power* from himself. And if you would Preach *Repentance* and *Obedience* as no other preceding or previous dispositions, we should agree better in the *Pulpit* then we do in the *Presse.*

To your ninth, *That the sum of my Divinity is, That men may be saved whether they Repent or no, or beleeve or no.*

I answer, Should I say to you, The sum of your Divinity is this, That *Faith*, and *Repentance*, and *Obedience,* are helps with *Christ*, and *conditions* with *Christ* to mans *Salvation*; and that Salvation is not *free,* but *conditional*; the *Covenant* of *Grace* is as it were a [14] *Covenant of Works*? Should I do well in this to upbraid you and those of your way?

Say not then that I think men may be saved that never *repent* nor *beleeve*: Why do you thus set up and counterfet opinions, and then engrave our Names upon them? Could not I piece up your Book so (if I would be unfaithful) as make ye appear as great an Heretick as any whom you thus fancy? because I preach not *Repentance*, or *Faith* as you do; because I make all these as gifts from Gods love in Christ, not as gifts to procure us God, or his *love*, or Christ; because I make all these the fruits of the Spirit, given to such whom Christ hath suffered for, to such whom God hath chosen in him; because I Preach *Faith*, and *Repentance*, and *Obedience*, in that full Revelation in which they are left as in the New-Testament, and not in that scantling of Doctrine, as they are meerly and barely revealed in the History of the *Gospel*, or *Acts* of the *Apostles*, onely where the *Doctrine* is not so much revealed as the *Proctise*, and the Story in Summaries; because we preach thus, therefore we are all *Antinomians*, *Hereticks*, men not *worthy* to live.

Brethren, Must ye *forbid us to Preach, because we follow not with you*? Because we Preach not the *Law* as ye do, nor *Faith* as ye do, nor *Repentance* as ye do; therefore do we not Preach them at all?

We Preach them all, as we are perswaded the *New-Testament* and *Spirit* will warrant us, and as we may make *Christ* to be the *power* of all, and *fulnesse* of all, as we may *exalt* him whom *God* hath *exalted* at his own right hand. And we wish that *ye and all that hear us, were both almost, and altogether as we are,* except in *reproaches.* [15]

CONCLUSION

FROM the 29 Page to the last, all your Replyes amount not to anything of substance, but of quarrelsom and humorous exceptions; and I shall, I hope, redeem my time better then in making a businesse of things that will neither edifie the Writer nor the Reader: There are some things you might (had you pleased) raised up into some Spiritual discourse, as that of Works, *and* Signs *for assurance, &c. But you say of your self (how becoming such a one as you I leave) that* you were like an old Steed which neighs and prances, but is past service; *so as I must take this of your age and infirmity, as a fuller Answer, or Supplement to what you fail in against me.*

There are two or three things more observable then the rest:

1. *That you tax me for saying, That the marks in* Johns *Epistles and* James, are delivered rather as marks for others, then our selves to know us by; *and I affirm it again, not as you say, excluding that other of our* selves, *but as I said, rather* marks *for others, though for both in their* degrees, *and* kindes *of* manifestation.

So in James 2.24. *where he saith,* By Works a man is Justified, not by Faith; *So in* Vers. 18.21. *All which set forth Works a sign to others rather then our selves. So in* 1 John 3.14. Hereby know we, we are passed from death to life, because we love the Brethren; *compared with* Ver. 17.18. *shews, That it is a love working abroad in* manifestation *to the* Brethren; *and yet I exclude not any evidence which the fruits of the* Spirit *carry in them, as in my Book, which yet you alleage to that purpose, after you have been quarrelling so long with it, pulling my Treatise in pieces to make your self work, and then binde it up again after your own fashion.*

For your Story of your Lady, and your fallacy, That she might as well conclude her self damned because she was a [16] sinner, as one that Christ would save because she was a sinner. *And durst you thus sport with a poor* wounded spirit, *that perhaps could see little but* sin *in her self to conclude upon? Know you not that* Christ *came* to call sinners, *to* save sinners? *And durst you make use of your Logick to cast such a mist upon the* promises *to* sinners? *Suppose one should ask you how you gather up your assurance, now you are an old man? how would you account to us? Would you say, Such a measure of Faith, so much Obedience, so much Love to the Brethren, so much Zeal, Prayer, Repentance, and all of unquestionable evidence? But if we should go further, and question you concerning your failings when you. writ in the behalf of* Cards *and* Dice, *of the* Common-prayer-Book; *if we should ask ye of your luxuriancy in* quotations *in your* Books *and* Sermons; *whether all be out of pure* zeal, *no* selfishnesse, *no* vain-glory? *whether all your* Love *was without* bitternesse *to your* brethren *of a diverse judgement, whom you call* Antinomian, *&c. whether you* preached *and* obeyed *all out of love to Jesus Christ, and not* seeking *your own things, not making a* gain *of* godlinesse? *Whether all your* Fastings *and* Repentance *were from true* meltings *of heart,* sound humiliation; *or because the* State *called for it, and constrained it? Whether your* praying *and* preaching *was not much of* Self, *of* Invention, *of* Parts, *of* Art, *of* Learning, *of* seeking praise *from men? Oh! should the. light of the* Spirit *come in in* clearnesse *and* glory *upon your* spirit, *oh! how much of* Self, *of* Hypocrisie, *of* Vanity, *of* Flesh, *of* Corruption, *would appear? how would all be unprofitable? For my part, I cannot be so uncharitable but to wish you a better assurance then what you and your brethren can finde in your owne works or righteousnesse: For,* it is not what we approve, but what God approves is accepted. *And I am perswaded, however you are now loth, it may be to lose reputation by going out of an old* track *of* Divinity, *as* Luther *once; yet when once your* spirit *begins to be unclothed* [17] *of* forms of darknesse, *and* art, *of* self-righteousnes, *and that* you with open face behold the glory of the Lord, *you will cry out,* Wo is me, I am undone; for I have seen the Lord: *and,* Lord depart from me; for I am a sinfull creature: *and,* What went I out to see? *My own unrighteousnesse: or rather,* A reed shaken with the winde. [18]

NOTES

NOTES. INTRODUCTION

Unless otherwise indicated, the pamphlets of the Puritan period referred to here are those in the McAlpin Collection. The Thomason Collection pamphlets are those marked "British Museum."

1. John Haweis, *Sketches of the Reformation* (1844), p. 271
2. *Ibid.*, p. 276
3. W. Cunningham, *The Growth of English Industry and Commerce* (3 v., 1910-1912), II, 165n
4. *Ibid.*, (1st ed., 1882), p. 324n
5. *Walwyns Just Defence* (1649), p. 11. To Hobbes the Presbyterians seemed singularly deficient in charity. "Charity is nothing with them," he wrote, "unless it be charity and liberality to them, and partaking with them in faction." In the *Behemoth* Hobbes shrewdly if maliciously recorded the emphasis in Puritan preaching (*English Works,* ed. Molesworth, 6 v., London, 1840, VI, 195): "They did, indeed, with great earnestness and severity, inveigh often against two sins, carnal lusts and vain swearing; which, without question, was very well done. But the common people were thereby inclined to believe, that nothing else was sin, but that which was forbidden in the third and seventh commandments (for few men do understand by the name of lust any other concupiscence, than that which is forbidden in that seventh commandment; for men are not ordinarily said to lust after another man's cattle, or other goods or possessions): and therefore never made much scruple of the acts of fraud and malice, but endeavored to keep themselves from uncleanness only, or at least from the scandal of it."
6. *Reliquiae Baxterianae* (1696), p. 6
7. *Christian Mans Triall* (1641), p. 19
8. Tawney, Bland, and Brown, *English Economic History; Select Documents* (1914), p. 441
9. *Ibid.*, p. 444
10. *Ibid.*, pp. 465-66
11. R. H. Tawney, *Religion and the Rise of Capitalism* (New York, Harcourt Brace and Co., 1926), p. 237
12. *Clarke Papers* (4 v., 1891-1901), I, 310, 311
13. *Prose Works* (Bohn ed.), II, 127
14. P. 9

15. G. L. Scherger, *Evolution of Modern Liberty* (1904), p. 23
16. Lord Acton, *History of Freedom* (1907), pp. 192-93
17. Quoted by C. Sydney Carter, *The English Church and the Reformation* (London, Longmans, Green and Co., 1925), p. 63
18. G. P. Gooch, *English Democratic Ideas* (Cambridge, 1927), p. 6
19. *Institutes* (tr. John Allen, Philadelphia, 1813), II, 272: "The imposition of hands on the ministers was not the work of the whole multitude but was confined to the pastors."
20. John Knox, *The Historie of the Reformation of the Church of Scotland* (1644), p. 313
21. Knox, *op. cit.*, *A Letter to the Queen Regent*, pp. 92-93
22. Knox, *op. cit.*, *The Admonition*, p. 36
23. L. Elliott-Binns, *The Reformation in England* (London, Duckworth, 1937), p. 32
24. Quoted by Carter, *op. cit.*, p. 64
25. Trevelyan, *History of England* (2d ed. New York, Longmans, Green and Co., 1937), p. 367.
26. Charles Borgeaud, *Rise of Modern Democracy* (1894), pp. 11ff.
27. John Strype, *Annals* (1824), Vol. I, Part 2, pp. 391-92
28. Daniel Neal, *History of the Puritans* (2 v., 1843), I, 95
29. *Ibid.*, I, 99
30. *Ibid.*, I, 99
31. Quotations are from the 4th edition, 1572. No pagination.
32. Benjamin Brook, *Lives of the Puritans* (3 v., 1813), II, 186
33. W. H. Frere and C. E. Douglas, *Puritan Manifestoes* (New York, 1907), p. 92
34. *Ibid.*, p. 93
35. *Ibid.*, p. 124. The word *resemble* in the sentence as reprinted by Frere and Douglas I have changed to *remember*. This is in accordance with the edition n. d. [1572?] found in the McAlpin Collection.
36. *Ibid.*, pp. xviii-xix
37. *The Marprelate Tracts* (edited by William Pierce, London, 1911), pp. 68-71
38. *Ibid.*, p. 248
39. *Ibid.*, p. 79
40. *Ibid.*, p. 246
41. *Letters of Elizabeth to James* (edited by John Bruce, Camden Society Publications, 1849), pp. 63, 64
42. Neal, *op. cit.*, I, 233n
43. Joseph R. Tanner, *Constitutional Documents of the Reign of James I* (Cambridge University Press, 1930)
44. *Ibid.*, p. 72
45. *Ibid.*, p. 276
46. *Ibid.*, pp. 81, 82
47. *Publications of the Narragansett Club* (6 v., Providence, 1866-74), I, 382
48. *The Marprelate Tracts*, p. 118
49. *Ibid.*, p. 238n1, quoted from Strype's *Whitgift*
50. Brook, *op. cit.*, II, 368
51. *Old South Leaflets*, No. 100, pp. 11, 16, 10, 11 (in order of quoting)
52. Benjamin Hanbury, *Historical Memorials* (3 v., 1839-44), I, 34
53. Brook, *op. cit.*, II, 54-55

54. Hanbury, *Memorials*, I, 37
55. *Ibid.*, I, 37n
56. *Ibid.*, I, 54
57. John Strype, *The Life and Acts of John Whitgift* (3 v., 1822), II, 178-81
58. Hanbury, *Memorials*, I, 185
59. *The Works of John Robinson*, edited by Robert Ashton (3 v., 1851), I, xxxiii, xxxiv
60. Hanbury, *Memorials*, I, 179
61. *Ibid.*, I, 248
62. Robinson, *Works*, II, 62
63. *Ibid.*, III, 168
64. Hanbury, *Memorials*, I, 249
65. William Bradford, *History of Plymouth Plantation* (2 v., Boston, Houghton Mifflin Co., 1912), I, 37
66. *Ibid.*, I, 44
67. *Ibid.*, I, 43
68. Robinson, *Works*, I, lxx
69. *Ibid.*, II, 213
70. *Ibid.*, II, 140
71. Bradford, *History*, I, 134
72. Brook, *op. cit.*, II, 36
73. Benjamin Evans, *The Early English Baptists* (2 v., 1862-64), I, 219
74. *Ibid.*, 218
75. *The Works of John Smyth*, ed. W. T. Whitley (2 v., Cambridge, 1915), II, 752
76. *Ibid.*, II, 754
77. *Ibid.*, II, 748
78. Thomas Helwys, *A Short Declaration* (London, Kingsgate Press, 1935), p. 69
79. *Tracts on Liberty of Conscience* (Hanserd Knollys Society, 1846), p. 51
80. *Ibid.*, p. 53
81. *Ibid.*, p. 70
82. *Publications of the Narragansett* Club, III, 62
83. W. T. Whitley, *A History of British Baptists* (London, Charles Griffin and Co., Ltd., 1923), pp. 74, 75; Louise Brown, *The Political Activities of the Baptists and Fifth Monarchy Men* (Washington, 1912), p. 11
84. Whitley, *op. cit.*, p. 76; Evans, *op. cit.*, I, 254-56
85. In *Walwins Wiles* (1649)
86. *Magnalia Christi Americana* (2 v., 1853), I, 69
87. *Ibid.*
88. Thomas Hutchinson, *The History of the Colony and Province of Massachusetts Bay*, ed. L. S. Mayo (3 v., Harvard University Press, 1936), II, 356
89. *Ibid.*, I, 415
90. James Ernst, *Roger Williams* (New York, Macmillan, 1932), p. 63
91. I am here following Dr. Ernst's account of Williams and Knowles' *Memoir*.
92. Bradford, *op. cit.*, I, 161-63
93. James Knowles, *Memoir of Roger Williams* (1834), p. 53
94. *The History of New England*, ed. James Savage (2 v., Boston, 1825), I, 170-71

95. *Publications of the Narragansett Club*, I, 393, 350
96. *Ibid.*, III, 58 (marginal note)
97. *Ibid.*, I, 340
98. *Ibid.*, I, 317
99. Winthrop, *History*, I, 307
100. *Publications of the Narragansett Club*, I, 381
101. *Ibid.*, III, 13
102. *Ibid.*, I, 385
103. *Gods Doings and Mans Duty* (a sermon preached to Parliament and Assembly of Divines April 2, 1645), p. 41
104. *Law of Freedom in a Platform* (1652), pp. 58, 59

NOTES. CHAPTER I

A RADICAL SECTARY IN THE MAKING

1. *Eikon Basilike*, edition published February 9, 1649, pp. 147-48, British Museum C59. a24 (1)
2. *Works* (7 v., 1859), V, 11
3. *Works* (5 v., 1853), V, 613-14
4. David Masson, *The Life of John Milton in Connexion with the History of His Time* (7 v., 1859-1894), II, 196ff.
5. William Haller, *Tracts on Liberty in the Puritan Revolution, 1638-1647* (4 v..) (New York, Columbia University Press, 1934), I, 10
6. *The Letany of Dr. John Bastwicke*, 1637, pp. 2-3, 4, 6
7. *For God and the King*, 1636, preface addressed to the king
8. Benjamin Brook, *The Lives of the Puritans*, III, 50
9. *Ibid.*, III, 49
10. *Ibid.*, III, 50
11. *Ibid.*
12. *Ibid.*
13. *A Narration of the Life of Mr. Henry Burton*, 1643, p. 14
14. *Narration*, p. 41
15. Masson, II, 194ff.
16. Henry Gee and William Hardy, *Documents Illustrative of English Church History* (London and New York, 1896), pp. 537-45
17. February 12, 1641. British Museum 669. f4 (107)
18. 1641, British Museum 669. f4 (138)
19. Masson III, 222. "It was now . . . ," said Pym, "growne common, for ambitious and corrupt men of the Clergie, to abuse the truth of God, and the bond of conscience, preaching downe the lawes and liberties of the Kingdome, pretending Divine authoritie, for an absolute power in the King, to doe what hee would with our persons, and goods, that hath beene often published in Sermons, and printed bookes, and is now the high way to preferment." See *A Speech Delivered in Parliament*, 1641, p. 22. British Museum E198 (35)
20. *Prose Works* (Bohn ed.), I, 257-58
21. *Ibid.*, II, 482

22. *Prose Works*, II, 403-404
23. *Ibid.*, II, 506
24. *Ibid.*, II, 503; cf. I, 480
25. *Ibid.*, II, 373
26. *Ibid.*, II, 402, 403
27. *Ibid.*, II, 378
28. *Ibid.*, II, 495-96
29. *Ibid.*, II, 423
30. *Ibid.*, II, 483
31. *Ibid.*, II, 376, 378, 464
32. *The Apprentices of Londons Petition Presented to the Honourable Court of Parliament . . . in devoting the Prelates, and Lordly Bishops, which insult too much over the whole Clergie. . . . Subscribed, and presented with the Names of above 30000 Apprentices*, 1641
33. *The Parliamentary or Constitutional History of England* (24 v., London, 1751-66), X, 268-73
34. Gee and Hardy, *Documents*, pp. 537ff.
35. *Ibid.*, pp. 555ff.
36. It cannot be said for Milton that he carried on his pamphlet warfare with that forbearance and humility which he says should characterize bishops. Like Cromwell, he thought that a bitter and unlovely means may often be the only effectual way to a noble end, a principle that only the Digger and Quaker pamphleteers were to regard as a violation of their Christian ethics. Interwoven with passages remarkable for their eloquence appear epithets and lip curlings unworthy of Milton's capacious spirit. At the end of *Of Reformation* he consigns the bishops to "the darkest and deepest gulf in hell," to be slaves of the damned, "the most dejected, most underfoot, and downtrodden vassals of perdition." The bishops he calls "ravenous and savage wolves," "tyrannical crew and corporation of imposters"; he speaks of their "bastards and centaurs of spiritual fornications" and of their "inquisitorious and tyrannical duncery." Nothing in the pamphlets of Bishop Hall is comparable to Milton's most savage thrusts. Milton was unable to evaluate some of his opponents as sincere, upright apologists for their cause.
37. *Prose Works*, II, 490
38. William A. Shaw, *A History of the English Church During the Civil Wars and under the Commonwealth* (2 v., London, 1900), I, 197
39. Masson, II, 397
40. *Prose Works*, II, 465
41. *Ibid.*, II, 490
42. *Ibid.*, II, 468
43. Thomas Edwards, *Reasons Against the Independant Government of Particular Churches*, 1641, pp. 23, 4. Katherine Chidley's reply to Edwards, entitled *The Justification of the Independant Churches of Christ*, contains typical arguments of the church radicals in rather striking form: "I affirme, that all the Lords people, that are made Kings and Priests to God, have a free voyce in the Ordinance of Election, therefore they must freely consent before there can be any Ordination." Chidley complains bitterly about the additional burdens thrust on the poor by the Church of England. They charge for burial of poor children two to eight shillings.

For the priest's blessing during pregnancy, even for prayers said over a still born child, the poor must pay fees. See pp. 5, 57, 58.

44. Masson, II, 585ff.

45. British Museum E178 (10)

46. *The Works of John Robinson* (3 v., Boston, 1851), II, 140

47. *A Survay*, 1641, pp. 26, 30

48. *Prose Works*, III, 154

49. *A Discourse Opening the Nature of . . . Episcopacie*, pp. 111-12

50. *Ibid.*, p. 103

51. *Prose Works*, II, 95

52. Samuel R. Gardiner, *History of the Great Civil War* (3 v., London, 1886-91), I, 47

53. Edwards, *Reasons Against the Independant Government of Particular Congregations*, 1641, Epistle Dedicatory

54. *Prose Works*, V, 238

55. Masson, III, 15

56. *Prose Works*, III, 315

57. *John the Baptist . . . or, A Necessity for Liberty of Conscience, as the only means under Heaven to strengthen Children weake in faith*, [1644], p. 101

58. *Queries*, pp. 5-6

59. *The Iniquity of the Late Solemne League*, 1643

60. *Prose Works*, III, 281

61. *Glasse of Gods Providence* (1644), p. 57

62. *Twelve Considerable Serious Questions touching Church Government*, p. 7

63. *Prose Works*, III, 434

64. *Apologeticall Narration*, p. 24

65. *A Reply of two of the Brethren*, pp. 57-58

66. *Theomachia*, p. 35

67. *Independency Examined, Unmasked, Refuted*, 1644, p. 5

68. *Prose Works*, II, 96

69. *Ibid.*, II, 92

70. *Ibid.*, II, 84

71. *Ibid.*

72. *Ibid.*, II, 90

73. *Ibid.*, IV, 454

74. *Ibid.*, IV, 463

75. *Ibid.*, IV, 464

76. *Ibid.*, IV, 225ff.

77. *Ibid.*, IV, 99, 134

78. *Ibid.*, IV, 275-76

79. *Ibid.*, V, 74

80. *Ibid.*, IV, 405

81. *Paradise Lost*, I, 17-23

82. *Prose Works*, IV, 187. E. C. Baldwin, in *P.M.L.A.*, 35, 210ff., has an excellent discussion of Milton's conception of the soul compared with that of Plato. Cf. Milton's Latin Exercise VII, as translated by Masson (I, 227): "This I conceive . . . that the great Maker of the Universe, when he had framed all else fleeting and subject to decay, did mingle with man . . . a certain divine breath, and as it were, part of Himself, immortal

indestructible, free from death and all hurt; which should flutter upward to his native heaven, and return to its proper place and country."

83. *Prose Works*, IV, 327ff.
84. *Paradise Lost*, III, 151; *Paradise Regained*, IV, 197. Cf. Denis Saurat's discussion of Milton's ontology in *Milton, Man and Thinker* (New York, MacVeagh, 1925), pp. 113-34
85. *Prose Works*, II, 485-86
86. *Ibid.*, IV, 59
87. *Paradise Lost*, V, 470ff.
88. *Ibid.*, V. 788-90
89. *Prose Works*, IV, 37
90. *Paradise Lost*, III, 98, 99
91. Cf. article on Arminianism in Hastings' *Encyclopedia of Religion and Ethics*, (1908)
92. *Prose Works*, I, 298
93. *Paradise Lost*, XII, 90-94
94. Theodore Calvin Pease, *The Leveller Movement* (Baltimore, 1916), p. 279
95. Masson, II, 597
96. *Ibid.*, III, 147
97. "The Preface To The Reader"

NOTES. CHAPTER II

TENDER CONSCIENCE AND MAGISTRATES SHADOW

1. Gardiner, *History of the Great Civil War*, II, 218
2. P. 4
3. Gardiner, *Civil War*, III, 39, 42
4. Masson, III, 533ff.
5. *Ibid.*, III, 548
6. *Ibid.*, III, 549
7. *Old Parliamentary History*, XVI, 212-24
8. Masson, III, 600
9. *Ibid.*, III, 613
10. *Old Parliamentary History*, XVIII, 161-238
11. P. 7
12. *The Justification of the Independent Churches*, p. 29
13. *Publications of the Narragansett Club*, III, 172
14. *Ibid.*, III, 95
15. *Ibid.*, III, 182
16. *Ibid.*, III, 11
17. *Reliquae Baxterianae* (London, 1696), p. 57
18. *Ibid.*, p. 50
19. *Old Parliamentary History*, XVI, 218
20. Rushworth, *Historical Collections* (8 v., London, 1721), VII, 860
21. Reprinted in appendix to Gardiner, *Civil War*, Vol. III. Also E 412 (21)
22. *Several Proposals for Peace & Freedom by an Agreement of the People* (December 11, 1648) E 477 (18); 100 A 72 (dated by Lilburne December 15, 1648)

23. E 477 (17), p. 3
24. *Old Parliamentary History*, XVIII, 539; E552 (23), p. 5
25. E323 (2), pp. 122, 125
26. P. 22
27. Pp. 17, 26
28. *Anapologesiates Antapologias*, p. 113
29. Pp. 7-8
30. P. 25
31. P. 24
32. Pp. 11-12
33. *The Bloudy Tenent, Publications of the Narragansett Club*, III, 204
34. Pp. 34-35
35. *Englands Birth-Right* (1645), p. 29
36. *A Whisper in the Eare of Mr. Thomas Edwards* (1646), E328 (2), p. 5
37. *A Word More to Mr. Thomas Edwards* (1646), E328 (20), p. 5
38. Pp. 15, 16
39. *Reliquae Baxterianae* (1696), p. 51
40. C. H. Firth, *Cromwell's Army* (London, 1902), p. 338. Quoted by Firth from Carlyle, *Cromwell*, Letter cxlviii
41. *Ibid.*, p. 334
42. *Reliquiae Baxterianae* (1696), p. 56
43. E261 (5), p. 47
44. P. 657
45. *The Humble Petition Of the Ministers Of the Counties of Suffolke and Essex* (May 29, 1646), E339 (11), p. 1
46. *To the . . . Lords . . . in . . . Parliament: The Humble Remonstrance and Petition of the Lord Major, Aldermen, and Commons* (May 28, 1646), E 339 (1), p. 4
47. Pp. 3, 5, 6
48. Pp. 2, 3, 4, 5, 6
49. P. 24
50. "Epistle Dedicatory," Part I
51. "Epistle Dedicatory," Part I
52. P. 3
53. P. 73
54. *The Difference About Church Government Ended* (1646), p. 3
55. E 355 (22), pp. 52, 53
56. Pp. 24, 29
57. *Poetical Works* (Oxford ed., London, 1930), p. 86
58. Pp. 3, 9, 10
59. P. 3
60. *Prose Works* (Bohn ed.), II, 35
61. *Ibid.*, II, 7 (my italics)
62. *Old Parliamentary History*, XVIII, 497
63. *Ibid.*, XVIII, 534
64. Shaw, *A History of the English Church* (2 v., London, 1900), II, 75
65. *Prose Works*, II, 193
66. *Ibid.*, II, 185
67. *Ibid.*
68. *Ibid.*, II, 193

69. *Prose Works*, II, 184-85
70. *Ibid.*, II, 197
71. *Ibid.*, II, 184
72. *Ibid.*, II, 189, 190
73. Shaw, *op. cit.*, II, 77
74. *Old Parliamentary History*, XIX, 177ff.
75. Masson, IV, 124
76. Shaw, II, 78
77. Masson, IV, 179
78. Cobbett, *Parliamentary History* (5 v., London, 1808), III, 1351
79. Walker, *History of Independency*, Part II (1661), p. 53
80. *The Christian Moderator* (1651), p. 25
81. P. 8
82. *A Warning from the Lord* (1654), E813 (15), p. 7
83. Pp. 131, 132, 133
84. *The Fourth Paper, Presented by Maior Butler* (1652) E658 (9), pp. 20-22;
     The Humble Proposals of Mr. Owen, Mr. Thomas Goodwin (1652),
     E 658 (12)
85. *Old Parliamentary History*, XX, 122-23
86. P. 5
87. *Thirty Queries*, p. 15
88. *The Apologist Condemned*, pp. 21-22
89. James D. Knowles, *Memoir of Roger Williams*, p. 264
90. *Publications of the Narragansett Club*, IV, 317
91. *Ibid.*, IV, 175
92. *Ibid.*, IV, 19
93. *Ibid.*, IV, 524-28
94. P. 17
95. *Poetical Works* (Oxford ed.), p. 88
96. George Sikes, *The Life and Death of Sir Henry Vane* (1662), p. 96
97. Thomas Hutchinson, *The History of the Province of Massachusetts Bay*
     (2 v., 1765-68), I, 55ff.
98. *Ibid.*, II, 483
99. Baillie, *Letters and Journals* (3 v., Edinburgh, 1841), II, 230
100. *Ibid.*, II, 235
101. *Twelve Arguments Drawn out of the Scripture*, p. 6
102. Article on Bidle, *D.N.B.*
103. James Hosmer, *Young Sir Henry Vane* (New York, 1888), p. 369
104. E485 (I), p. 388
105. E879 (5), pp. 7-8
106. Diary of Thomas Burton, Esq. (4 v., 1828), IV, 328-39
107. George Sikes, *The Life and Death of Sir Henry Vane* (1662)
108. Gardiner, *The Constitutional Documents of the Puritan Revolution*
     (Oxford, 1889), p. 324
109. *Prose Works*, I, 290
110. A casual reading of this passage will leave the reader in doubt about the
     identity of "you". But eleven lines above Milton has said that he will
     mention the men "whom you, sir, have admitted to your councils." It is
     evident that he is talking directly to Cromwell.
111. *Prose Works*, I, 293

112. Pp. 41-42
113. Gardiner, *Commonwealth and Protectorate*, II, 277
114. Knowles, *Memoir of Roger Williams*, p. 263
115. Article on Feake, *D.N.B.*
116. Gardiner, *Commonwealth and Protectorate*, II, 254
117. *The New Non-conformist*, postscript, "A short Word" (1654)
118. *A Second Voyce from the Temple* (1653), p. 6
119. Pp. 14, 16, 25, 26, 41
120. *Prose Works*, I, 288
121. *The Readie & Easie Way* (ed. E. M. Clark, New Haven, 1915), p. 35
122. Gardiner, *Commonwealth and Protectorate*, II, 320-24
123. Gardiner, *Documents*, p. 324
124. *Prose Works*, II, 524-25
125. *Ibid.*, II, 526-27
126. *Ibid.*, II, 544
127. *Ibid.*, II, 541
128. *Clarke Papers* (4 v., 1891-1901, ed. C. H. Firth), II, 101
129. *A Sermon Preached To The Parliament, Octob. 13. 1652*
130. *Prose Works*, II, 537-38
131. *The Readie & Easie Way*, ed. Clarke, p. 35
132. John Selden, *Historie of Tithes* (1618), p. 132
133. *Ibid.*, pp. 16, 83
134. *Ibid.*, p. 117
135. *Tracts and Treatises of . . . Wycliffe* (ed. Robert Vaughan, London, 1845), pp. 38, 39, 293
136. Henry Lansdell, *The Sacred Tenth* (2 v., London, 1906), I, 290
137. Shaw, *op. cit.*, II, 254ff.
138. *Aphorisms Political* (1659), E995 (8), pp. 2, 3
139. *An Answer to Severall Petitions . . . for the taking away of Tithes* (1652), E664 (11), p. 4
140. *The Humble Petition Of Many thousands, Gentlemen, Free-holders, and others, of the County of Worcester* (December 22), p. 6
141. *A Gospell Plea . . . For The Lawfulness & Continuance of . . . Tithes* (1653), pp. 11, 15
142. *Ten Considerable Quæries Concerning Tithes* (1659), E767 (2), p. 1
143. *The Case of Ministers Maintenance by Tithes*, pp. 13, 17, 29
144. *The dreadful danger of Sacrilege* (1658), 669 f21 (3)
145. *Englands Birth-Right* (1645), pp. 13, 45
146. *Martin's Eccho* (1645), 18
147. Pp. 11, 12, 13, 26
148. E1380 (3), p. 20
149. *Law of Freedom in a Platform* (1652), E655 (8), pp. 20, 21
150. *A Warning from the Lord* (1654), E813 (15), p. 21
151. *The Journal of George Fox* (ed. Norman Penny, New York, E. P. Dutton Co., 1924), p. 43
152. *The Copie of a Paper Presented to Parliament* (1659), E988 (24), pp. 3, 6
153. E989 (28), pp. 2, 7, 8, 14
154. Pp. 20, 21
155. *Prose Works*, III, 12
156. *Ibid.*, III, 15

157. *Prose Works,* III, 18
158. *Ibid.,* III, 28
159. *Ibid.,* III, 30
160. *Ibid.,* III, 38
161. *Prose Works,* II, 482
162. *Ibid.,* III, 87
163. *Ibid.,* I, 275
164. *Ibid.,* II, 36
165. *Ibid.,* IV, 458-59
166. XII, 508
167. Article on tithes, *Encyclopædia Britannica* (14th ed.) and Selden's *Histoire of Tithes,* p. 243
168. *Prose Works,* III, 41
169. *Ibid.,* II, 532-33
170. III, 489-93
171. II, 714, 715, 717, 726, 728, 762. This interpretation is found in "The Source of Milton's Pandemonium" by Rebecca W. Smith, *Modern Philology,* Nov., 1931.
172. *Prose Works,* II, 510ff. Milton would make only one exception to his rule. Foreigners may worship openly as Catholics being privileged by the law of nations.
173. *Narragansett Club Publications,* IV, 312
174. *Law of Freedom in a Platform* (1652), E655 (8), p. 81
175. Masson, VI, 692
176. *The Storming of Antichrist,* p. 23
177. Part I (1651), p. 7
178. Part II (1652), p. 31. Part III appeared in 1653.
179. Part I, p. 24
180. Firth, *Cromwell* (London, 1900), pp. 267-68
181. I am here following *The Development of Religious Toleration In England* (London, Unwin, 1938), by Dr. W. K. Jordan. On pp. 179-94, Dr. Jordan has an excellent discussion of Cromwell's attitude toward the Catholics.
182. Masson, VI, 691
183. *Prose Works,* II, 512-13
184. *Ibid.,* II, 532 (my italics)
185. *Philosophical Rudiments* (1651), pp. 311, 314
186. *Ibid.,* p. 334
187. *De Corpore Politico* (1652), pp. 67, 52, 131
188. *Of the Authority Of The Highest Powers About Sacred Things* (1651), pp. 9, 15, 37, 215
189. *Law of Freedom,* E655 (8), pp. 55, 56, 57
190. *Works of John Locke* (4 v., London, New York, Ward, Lock and Co., no date), III, 31

NOTES. CHAPTER III

RISING SECULAR TONES: THE *AREOPAGITICA*

1. Masson, III, 268
2. *Ibid.,* 269

3. Masson, III, 433
4. Prynne, *Fresh Discovery*, p. 8
5. *Gangraena*, III, 102
6. *Gangraena*, II, 138, 139
7. "To the Reader," *Church-Levellers* (1649)
8. *Prose Works*, I, 259
9. Masson, III, 263
10. Masson, III, 265
11. Masson, III, 165, 266, 274, 275
12. *Prose Works*, II, 55, 78
13. *Ibid.*, II, 62
14. *Ibid.*, II, 70, 71
15. *Ibid.*, II, 90
16. *Ibid.*, II, 85
17. *Ibid.*, II, 91-92, 93
18. *Ibid.*, II, 94
19. *Ibid.*, II, 78
20. *Ibid.*, II, 79
21. *Ibid.*, II, 76, 77
22. *Ibid.*, II, 77
23. *Ibid.*, II, 81
24. *Ibid.*, II, 69, 70
25. *Ibid.*, II, 73, 66, 85
26. *Ibid.*, I, 258 (italics mine)
27. *The Smoke in the Temple* (1646), p. 3
28. *The Way to the Peace*, pp. 13, 14
29. *A Fresh Discovery of the High-Presbyterian Spirit* (1654), p. 9
30. *Thirty Queries* (1653), p. 7
31. *A Fresh Discovery*, p. 4
32. *Ibid.*, p. 7
33. *The Beacons Quenched*, pp. 7, 13
34. Lilburne, *The peoples Prerogative* (1648), p. 54. A curious reflection of the *Areopagitica* may be found in Cuthbert Sydenham's attack on open presses in *An Anatomy of . . . Lilburn's Spirit and Pamphlets* (1649), p. 1. "Among the Exorbitancies of this last Age," wrote Sydenham, "there is none hath stained the Glory of this Nation more then the multitude of licentious and abusive Pamphlets that continually fly abroad like Atomes in the Air, whereby the Press is made a common strumpet to conceive and bring forth the froth of every idle and wanton fancy, or to vent the malice of every discontented and debaucht spirit: and Books, that were wont to be monuments of the industry and seriousness of mens spirits, and records of the vertues and noble acts of brave men, adorned with Reason and Judgment, and *ordained to be as Embalmings to their names*, are now turned into Pasquils and Libels, stuffed with the rancor and rage of these men, who know no way to recruit their own lost reputation, but by defacing the names of their betters." The words I have italicized above were no doubt suggested to Sydenham by Milton's "embalmed and treasured up on purpose to a life beyond life."
35. British Museum 669 f 13 (73), *To the Commons. The Petition of firm friends to the Parliament*, January 18, 1649. I have had access only to

the long quotation in Dr. William M. Clyde's excellent book, *The Struggle for Freedom of the Press from Caxton to Cromwell* (Oxford University Press, 1934).

36. Prynne, *Fresh Discovery*, p. 28. *The Nativity*, hitherto unnoticed, is, I believe, a genuine Overton pamphlet.
37. Pp. 2, 10
38. P. 19
39. P. 14
40. *Alarum to the House of Lords*, p. 8
41. Pp. 3, 7, 8, 34
42. *Fresh Discovery*, p. 8
43. Pp. 10, 42
44. P. 11
45. P. 27
46. No pagin.
47. Pp. 13, 14
48. Cf. Walwyn's reference to the people as "a pittiful mean helplesse thing" not allowed to speak or debate, in *The Fountain of Slaunder Discovered*, p. 18
49. William M. Clyde, *op. cit.*, pp. 164-65
50. P. 3
51. *The Compassionate Samaritane*, "To the Reader," in Haller's *Tracts on Liberty* (3 v., New York, Columbia University Press, 1934), II, 63
52. *Ibid.*, p. 60, in Haller's *Tracts*, II, 94
53. *A Word More to Mr. Edwards*, p. 12
54. Pp. 18-19
55. *Walwyns Just Defence* (1649), p. 25
56. *Fountain of Slaunder*, p. 18
57. *On Liberty*, etc. (World's Classics edition, Oxford University Press, 1912), p. 24

NOTES. CHAPTER IV

LILBURNE: AGAINST BISHOPS, AGAINST CROWN

1. *Innocency and Truth Justified* (1646), p. 8; *Christian Mans Triall* (1641), p. 2; *Legall Fundamentall Liberties* (second edition), p. 25
2. *D.N.B.*
3. *Christian Mans Triall*, p. 2
4. *Ibid.*, 2, 3
5. *Ibid.*, p. 8
6. *Ibid.*, p. 25
7. *Ibid.*, p. 15
8. *Ibid.*, p. 19
9. *Ibid.*, p. 33
10. *Innocency and Truth Justified*, p. 41
11. *Ibid.*, p. 13
12. *Ibid.*, p. 39
13. *D.N.B.*
14. British Museum E24 (22), p. 4
15. *Ibid.*, p. 2

16. Godwin, *History of the Commonwealth*, II, 19; *Englands Birth-Right Justified*, p. 16. The charge was that Lenthall had transmitted sixty thousand pounds to the King from Sir Basil Brooke, a prisoner suspected of treason. The investigating committee reported Lenthall innocent (Prynne's *The Lyar Confounded* (1645), pp. 28-29).

17. *Englands Birth-Right*, p. 6

18. *Ibid.*, pp. 8, 9, 42

19. *Ibid.*, pp. 9, 10

20. *Ibid.*, pp. 35, 36

21. *Ibid.*, p. 42

22. *Ibid.*, p. 3

23. *Ibid.*, p. 4

24. *Ibid.*, p. 8

25. *Ibid.*, pp. 32, 33

26. *Innocency and Truth*, p. 26

27. *Ibid.*, p. 58

28. Godwin, II, 412

29. *Free-Mans Freedome Vindicated*, pp. 4, 5

30. *Ibid.*, p. 8

31. Godwin, II, 414

32. *Ibid.*, II, 415

33. *Londons Liberty In Chains* (October, 1646), pp. 21, 7, 11

34. Pp. 11-12

35. P. 17

36. *Londons Liberty*, p. 2

37. *Regall Tyrannie*, p. 99. In the various lists that Lilburne gives of his own books, he does not, so far as I have noted, acknowledge either *Regall Tyrannie* or *Englands Birth-Right* as his own, though he often mentions them favorably. He must have collaborated to some extent, however, in the writing of both pamphlets. *Regall Tyrannie* bears less the stamp of his hand than *Englands Birth-Right;* the former is a better organized pamphlet, and more theoretical in substance, than Lilburne had thus far written. The whole fascinating problem of the collaboration of the Leveller leaders is one that needs much investigation.

38. *Gangraena*, I, 40

39. *Ibid.*, 67, 96, 70

40. *Ibid.*, I, 33

41. *Ibid.*, II, 104

42. *Ibid.*, III, 153, 156, 195, 196, 197

43. *Ibid.*, III, 217-18

44. Pp. 8, 9

45. P. 6

46. P. 13

47. Pp. 8, 12, 13, 15, 16, 19, 20. Though the stinging style of the *Remonstrance* no doubt is Overton's, it seems unlikely that he contributed more of the ideas than Walwyn. The *Remonstrance's* denomination of Magna Charta as "a beggerly thing, containing many marks of intollerable bondage" is far more typical of Walwyn than Overton, who several months later inserted praise of Magna Charta in *An Arrow Against All Tyrants*. The economic philosophy of the *Remonstrance*, the insistence on succoring

of the poor, recur much more frequently in Walwyn's tract than in Overton's. Moreover the thought of the *Remonstrance* as a whole is far more mature than that revealed in Overton's first signed political tract, *An Alarum to the House of Lords,* which appeared three weeks after the *Remonstrance.* It is difficult to account for Overton's sudden maturation as a political theorist except as a pupil of Walwyn.

48. Pp. 5, 7, 8
49. P. 6
50. *Defiance Against All Arbitrary Usurpations,* pp. 9, 14, 15, 17, 18
51. *Ibid.,* pp. 2, 5
52. *Ibid.,* p. 12

NOTES. CHAPTER V

LEVELLER AND INDEPENDENT IN DEBATE

1. *Oppressed Mans Oppressions declared,* pp. 24, 26
2. *The out-cryes of oppressed Commons,* p. 14
3. *Rash Oaths unwarrantable* (May 31, 1647), p. 30. It has thus far escaped the notice of scholars that Lilburne reprinted the famous petition in this tract, pp. 29-35.
4. *Ibid.,* pp. 33, 34
5. *Civil War,* III, 74
6. *Reliquiæ Baxterianæ* (1696), p. 53
7. *Ibid.,* p. 51
8. *Ibid.,* p. 54
9. *Clarke Papers,* ed. C. H. Firth (4 v., 1891-1901), I, 213
10. Gardiner, *Civil War,* III, 50, 51
11. *Jonahs Cry* (July 26, 1647), pp. 5, 6
12. *Ibid.,* p. 9
13. P. 3
14. *Jonahs Cry,* p. 13
15. Rushworth, VI, 512
16. See *Clarke Papers,* 1, xxii, xxiv
17. Gardiner, *Constitutional Documents,* 232ff.; Rushworth, VII, 731-36
18. Pp. 14, 15. On one of these charges Ireton spoke as follows (*Clarke Papers,* I, 357): "Butt as to the Kinge wee were clear. There is nott one thinge in the proposalls, nor in what wee declar'd, that doth give the Kinge any negative voice; and therefore that's parte of the scandall amongst others. Wee doe not give the Kinge any negative, wee doe butt take the Kinge as a man with whom wee have bin att a difference, wee propound termes of peace. Wee doe nott demand that hee shall have noe Negative, butt wee doe nott say that hee shall have any."
19. *Putney Projects,* pp. 23, 32, 36
20. *Ibid.,* p. 31
21. Gardiner, *Civil War,* III, 191
22. Pease, *The Leveller Movement,* pp. 203, 205; Gardiner, *Civil War,* III, 214.
23. Gardiner, *Civil War,* III, 217
24. *Clarke Papers,* I, 233
25. *Ibid.,* I, 296

26. *Clarke Papers,* I, 236-40
27. Though Rainsborough was nominally an Independent, his reasoning in the debates is indistinguishable from that of the Leveller leaders. We have therefore treated him as a Leveller leader, though he was not an associate of Lilburne or his colleagues. His funeral, like that of Lockyer, was the signal for a silent marching tribute by thousands of Levellers. Unlike Wildman, whose later life was filled with conspiracies and shifts of allegiance, and Sexby, who possessed no very deep personal integrity, Rainsborough and Lockyer were men of the loftiest motives.
28. *Clarke Papers,* I, 246-47
29. *Ibid.,* I, 240
30. *Ibid.,* I, 253
31. *Ibid.,* I, lxxiv
32. *Ibid.,* I, 253-55
33. *Ibid.,* I, 255
34. *Ibid.,* I, 257
35. *Ibid.,* I, 258
36. *Ibid.,* I, 319
37. *Ibid.,* I, 314
38. *Ibid.,* I, 332
39. *Ibid.,* I, 315
40. *Ibid.,* I, 310-11, 322
41. *Ibid.,* I, 310, 311, 322. Compare Ireton's claim for the recognition of property as protected by the social contract, in which he makes no mention of God's revelations (I, 263).
42. *Ibid.,* I, 304
43. *Ibid.,* I, 325
44. *Ibid.,* I, 320, 326
45. *Ibid.,* I, 309
46. *Ibid.,* I, 325
47. P. 6
48. *Clarke Papers,* I, 318
49. *Ibid.,* I, 323
50. *Ibid.,* I, 330, 329
51. *Ibid.,* I, 333
52. Pease, *op. cit.,* 225
53. *D.N.B.*
54. *Jonahs Cry,* p. 4
55. *Prose Works,* I, 291
56. "Milton and the Puritans"
57. *Clarke Papers,* I, 384
58. *A Picture of the Councel of State* (1649), p. 44

NOTES. CHAPTER VI

HUE AND CRY AFTER WILLIAM WALWYN

1. *Fountain of Slaunder Discovered* (May 30, 1649), pp. 11-13
2. *Walwins Wiles,* by Kiffin and Price (May 10, 1649), p. 5

3. *The Charity of Church-Men,* by Henry Brooke (May 28, 1649), pp. 2, 10, 11
4. *Walwyns Just Defence* (1649), p. 1. This tract, which was not listed by Thomason, appeared probably in late July or early August. Lilburne does not mention this tract in his first edition of *Legall Fundamentall Liberties,* which appeared, according to Thomason, June 18. In the second edition Lilburne characterizes Walwyn as *"my most choise and honest Comrade and Fellow-suff'rer"* and mentions his "two late books, intituled *The Fountain of Slander,* and *Walwyns just Defence"* (page 24). The date of the second edition of *Legall Fundamentall Liberties* is uncertain, but Lilburne says the revised tract was occasioned by the appearance of Prynne's *A Legal Vindication,* which did not appear until July 16.
5. *Defence,* p. 4; *Fountain,* p. 6
6. *Fountain,* p. 7; *Defence,* p. 31
7. *Defence,* pp. 2, 3
8. *Defence,* p. 3
9. *Ibid.*
10. *Defence,* p. 17
11. *Ibid.,* p. 6
12. *Ibid.,* p. 16
13. *Declaration,* pp. 8, 9, 10
14. *Defence,* p. 12
15. Walwyn, *A Still And Soft Voice* (1647), pp. 3, 4, 7, 8
16. *Ibid.,* pp. 5-6
17. *Ibid.,* p. 9
18. *Ibid.*
19. *Ibid.*
20. *Ibid.,* p. 16
21. *Ibid.,* p. 10
22. *Defence,* p. 24
23. *Ibid.*
24. *Voice,* p. 11; *Parable of Physitians* (1646), pp. 15, 16, 38
25. *Voice,* p. 11
26. *Defence,* p. 4. In November, 1648, John Price was one of four Independents chosen to debate the *Agreement* with four Levellers, of whom Walwyn was one. Price, however, sent word to Lilburne and his colleagues that he (Price) would not serve if Walwyn were on the opposing committee, that he "had a prejudice against him." Lilburne replied that Walwyn "had more honesty and integrity in his little finger then John Price had in his body." Nevertheless, after much discussion, Price and Walwyn were both withdrawn from the committees, and the debate was held with three on a side. This story reflects the feeling between Price and Walwyn, with definite antagonism on the part of Price, and emphasizes the part Price played in the writing of *Walwins Wiles. Legall Fundamentall Liberties* (2 ed.) p. 34
27. *Defence,* p. 30
28. *Ibid.,* p. 31
29. *Ibid.*
30. *Ibid.,* p. 7
31. *Ibid.,* p. 14
32. *Fountain,* p. 11

33. *Defence,* p. 17
34. *Ibid.,* p. 5
35. P. 6. Lilburne accused Kiffin of misrepresenting the sentiment of the Anabaptist congregations. *Picture of the Councel of State,* p. 24
36. *Picture of the Councel of State,* p. 36
37. *Ibid.,* p. 44: "The business is, not how great a sinner I am, but how faithfull and reall to the Common-wealth."
38. *Ibid.,* p. 2
39. P. 5
40. Pp. 2, 7
41. Pp. 2, 3, 4, 6
42. Pp. 22, 5, 9
43. P. 11
44. *Wiles,* pp. 7, 11, 9
45. *Ibid.,* p. 10
46. *Ibid.,* pp. 13, 24, 12
47. *Ibid.,* pp. 14-15
48. *Ibid.,* pp. 15, 16
49. *Ibid.,* 17, 18
50. *Charity of Church-Men,* pp. 2, 3, 6, 11
51. *Ibid.,* p. 7
52. *Ibid.,* pp. 7, 8
53. *Ibid.,* pp. 13, 14
54. See *Fountain,* pp. 9, 24
55. *Fountain,* p. 4
56. See note 4. The words on Walwyn's title page refer to *Wiles* as a "late un-christian Pamphlet."
57. *Defence,* p. 11
58. *Ibid,* p. 24
59. *Ibid.,* pp. 16, 32, 31
60. *Ibid.,* p. 32
61. *Ibid.,* p. 33
62. *Ibid.,* pp. 32, 33
63. Gardiner, *Commonwealth and Protectorate,* I, 189

NOTES. CHAPTER VII

SWORDS FOR A KINGLESS ENGLAND

1. Gardiner, *Great Civil War,* III, 569
2. Pp. 9, 19, 16
3. Pp. 78-79
4. *The Treachery and Disloyalty Of Papists* (second edition, enlarged, 1643), pp. 33, 35, 37, 45, 83, 86, 92. This edition contains the first part of *The Soveraigne Power Of Parliaments & Kingdomes.* The *Second Part* (licensed March 28) proclaims on the title page that the *"King hath no absolute Negative Voice in passing publicke Bills of Right and Justice."* The repetitious *Third Part* appeared June 23, the *Fovrth Part* August 28. Lilburne refers to the *Appendix* of the *Fovrth Part* in *Innocency and*

Truth Justified. Prynne quotes widely from most of the sources of English history later used by the Levellers and the Independents to justify the accountability of kings to the people and their representatives.

5. See Professor Haller's able summary of Parker's influence in *Tracts on Liberty*, I, 23-29.

6. *Observations upon some of his Majesties late Answers* (1642), pp. 1, 3, 4; *Jus Populi* (1644), pp. 1, 18, 19; *Jus Regum* (1645), p. 38.

7. Pp. 57ff.

8. Pp. 4, 5, 6, 7, 15

9. P. 15

10. *Ibid.*

11. See pp. 11, 14, 15, 17-25, 42, 97

12. *Clarke Papers*, I, 411

13. *Ibid.*, I, 417, 418

14. *Sundry Reasons Inducing Major Robert Huntington to Lay down his Commission* (August 2, 1648), p. 10

15. Gardiner, *Civil War*, III, 262

16. Berkeley, *Memoirs*, in Maseres, *Select Tracts* (2 v., 1815), II, 385

17. Clarendon, *The History of the Rebellion* (3 v., London, 1707), Vol. III, Part I, p. 93

18. *Old Parliamentary History*, XVI, 491-92

19. *The History of the Rebellion*, Vol. III, Part I, p. 91

20. *Old Parliamentary History*, XVI, 492

21. Gardiner, *Civil War*, III, 288

22. *Ibid.*, III, 298-99

23. *Old Parliamentary History*, XVII, 2-24

24. From Allen's *Narrative* reprinted in part in Carlyle, *Letters and Speeches* (New York, 1846), p. 88

25. P. 5

26. Ludlow, *Memoirs* (London, 1751), p. 86

27. *Ibid.*, p. 91. Lilburne's own explanation of Cromwell's change of front, which he admits was not based on any factual evidence, runs in part as follows (*The peoples Prerogative*, February 17, 1648, pp. 58-59): "But . . . be it known unto thee *O Cromwell*, that *I* will not serve thee . . . or stand in feare of thy tyrannicall power, or that golden or painted Image, the present House of Lords. . . .

As the only meanes to reimpinioante [*sic*] them into the good thoughts of those men, they and their late royall friends lately christned Levellers, and to add strength unto the last, the two chiefe of the Grandees *Cromwell* and *Ireton*, came to the Parliament to heighten them in their votes against the King, because he had forsaken his first love, and would not be content with that price that they would give him, to let them reign and rule under him, the which if he would have taken, no doubt but he might have com'd in to have joyntly with them oppressed and rid the people, but because it may be the *Scots* feared, if he came in by the Grandees of the Army, they and hee might joyn together to chastise them for all . . . old . . . provocations given unto both, and therfore out of meer safety (it may be) to themselves outbid the Grandees to gaine the Kings affection, at which they [the Grandees] are mad, and therefore to preserve their own greatnesse, and to gaine if it be possible, the lost affections of the honest Nown-Substantive Englishmen, they flie high both against him and the Scots, that so they may . . . induce them to joyn with them in a new war . . . without giving or offering unto the people the least valuable consideration for all the blood they have already lost, and are more . . . like to loose upon the ingaging a new warre . . . which for my part *I* doe abhorre†

    † Which is clearly evident, by both their pleading and plotting for the supportation of the Lords usurped Legislative power, which . . . they have no more right to . . . then a thiefe and robber to . . . which he takes by force upon the high way."

28. P. 20 of edition containing *The additional Plea*.
29. See passage under note 27.
30. Pp. 2, 12
31. P. 13
32. Vol. III, Part 1, p. 119
33. *Ibid.*, p. 120
34. *A Full Answer to an Infamous and Trayterous Pamphlet*, pp. 152, 153, 157. Quotation, pp. 187-88
35. Gardiner, *Civil War*, III, 369
36. *The Kingdomes Briefe Answer*, p. 22
37. P. 4
38. Pp. 4-5
39. Gardiner, *Civil War*, III, 372, 375
40. Vol. III, Part 1, p. 136
41. Pp. 1, 14
42. P. 22
43. P. 13
44. *A Speech Spoken*, pp. 4-5
45. *Old Parliamentary History*, XVII, 271
46. *Ibid.*, p. 276
47. *Ibid.*, pp. 278-79
48. P. 20
49. Gardiner, *Civil War*, III, 28
50. *Ibid.*, III, 58
51. P. 15
52. P. 14
53. Pp. 7-8
54. Gardiner, *Civil War*, III, 337, 252
55. Pp. 3, 4
56. P. 4
57. Pp. 1, 2, 3, 6
58. *Old Parliamentary History*, XVIII, 185
59. *Ibid.*, XVIII, 228
60. *Ibid.*, XVIII, 176
61. *Ibid.*, XVIII, 190
62. *Ibid.*, XVIII, 212
63. Wilbur C. Abbott, *The Writings and Speeches of Oliver Cromwell* (2 v., Harvard U. Press, 1937-39), I, 697, 698
64. *History of My Own Time* (ed. Osmund Airy, 2 v. Oxford, 1897), I, 71

65. *Justice upon the Armie Remonstrance*, p. 46
66. P. 11
67. *A second view of the Armie Remonstrance*, p. 6
68. *Old Parliamentary History*, XVIII, 477
69. *Ibid.*, XVIII, 479
70. *The Lord of Hosts*
71. P. 7
72. P. 9
73. See Nethersole's Ό᾽Αυτο-Κατάκριτος. *The Self-Condemned* (January 8), p. 5
74. P. 9
75. Pp. 2-3
76. Pp. 3, 4, 5, 8
77. *Old Parliamentary History*, XVIII, 504-505
78. *Ibid.*, XVIII, 511
79. *Ibid.*, XVIII, 513
80. "To the Commons." This tract was dated by Nedham November 27, 1648.
81. P. 9
82. This tract appeared probably in December or January.
83. P. 13
84. P. 14
85. *Old Parliamentary History*, XVIII, 304-05
86. *Ibid.*, XVIII, 314, 319, 320, 323, 324, 325, 326, 328, 341, 343
87. *Ibid.*, XVIII, 379
88. P. 12
89. *Old Parliamentary History*, XVIII, 375
90. *A Briefe Memento*, p. 11
91. P. 7
92. Pp. 9-10
93. P. 29
94. *The Kingdomes Grand Qvere*, letter dated January 25, 1649
95. *England's Black Tribunal* (fifth edition, London, 1720), p. 8
96. *Old Parliamentary History*, XVIII, 282
97. *England's Black Tribunal*, p. 13
98. *Ibid.*, p. 18

NOTES. CHAPTER VIII

TYRANTS AND MEN OF DESTINY

1. *Works* (18 v., New York, Columbia University Press, 1931-1938), XVIII, 175. The indispensable guide to the *Commonplace Book* is Dr. J. H. Hanford's "The Chronology of Milton's Private Studies," *P.M.L.A.*, 1921, 251-315
2. *Ibid.*, XVIII, 187
3. *Ibid.*, XVIII, 169
4. *Ibid.*, XVIII, 183
5. *Prose Works*, II, 391
6. *Ibid.*, II, 408: "With full approbation and suffrage of the people."
7. *Ibid.*, II, 503
8. *Ibid.*, II, 507

9. *Englands New Chains Discovered,* no pag.
10. *Picture of The Councell of State* (April 27, 1649, second edition), p. 8
11. *A Discourse Betwixt . . . Lilburn . . . and Mr. Hugh Peter,* p. 8. The authenticity of this pamphlet is doubted by Gardiner and asserted by Professor Pease. That Professor Pease's analysis is correct is substantiated by a reference by Lilburne to this tract in a letter to Cornelius Holland dated June 26, 1649, which Lilburne inserted in his *An Impeachment of High Treason Against Oliver Cromwel* (1649) following p. 8. See p. 5 of the letter.
12. British Museum E 540 (12), p. 4
13. British Museum E 540 (11), p. 5
14. British Museum 669. f. 3. (75)
15. Gardiner, *Civil War,* III, 589
16. Pp. 20, 21 (February 4)
17. *Prose Works,* I, 259-60
18. In the second, as in the first, edition. In the second edition, after citing Protestant authorities in justification of bringing the king to trial, Milton closes with an excoriation of the Presbyterian ministers. The first edition closes with the words "zeale of his people" (*Prose Works,* II, 37). The second edition appeared February 15, 1650.
19. *Ibid.,* II, 28, 29, 30, 31
20. *Ibid.,* II, 11, 7
21. *Ibid.,* II, 4. On the guilt of the Presbyterians Hobbes was in full agreement with Milton (*English Works,* VI, 357): "What greater crimes than blasphemy and killing God's anointed; which was done by the hands of the Independents; but by the folly and first treason of the Presbyterians who betrayed and sold him to his murderers?"
22. P. 37. This pamphlet contains curious contradictions between democratic affirmations and assertions of the divine right of kings.
23. P. 5
24. *Prose Works,* II, 8
25. *Ibid.,* II, 9-11
26. *Ibid.,* II, 12-13
27. *Ibid.,* II, 14, 18
28. Gardiner, *Civil War,* III, 572. Clarendon's account makes her say (Vol. III, Part I, p. 255): "No, nor the hundredth part of them."
29. *Declaration of the Commons in Parliament Assembled,* pp. 2, 3
30. British Museum E 536 (28), pp. 14, 15
31. British Museum E 557 (2), pp. 71-95. This is much the longest quotation from Milton's pamphlets used by the writers of the period.
32. British Museum E 541 (12), p. 11
33. P. 36
34. Pp. 2, 3
35. *An Answer to The Cities Representation* (February 7), p. 7
36. Pp. 7, 23, 25, 28, 46
37. P. 13. This pamphlet contains a remarkable passage on law (p. 19): "Since but few Laws among us, are the *pure results* of *right reason* and *equity,* but there is something of *humane darkness,* or *lust,* or *humor,* or *interest* cleaving to them; therefore as men grow up into more *reason,* they may change the Laws which themselves have made; and as succeeding

generations grow up into more *clear* and *refined reason,* then their Ancestors; so may they change . . . *former Laws,* as less suitable to them . . .

Right reason and *equity* carry all Laws in their *bowels,* and will at all times be a *fruitful womb* of them for the peoples good, when the tyranny of *form* is done away: And it is much better for people to go to *Reason* for *Laws,* then to Laws for *Reason.*

Each *generation* can judg better what is for its own good, then their forefathers, who could not foresee what was to fall out in the world.

38. *Prose Works,* I, 260
39. British Museum E 570 (4), pp. 199-200. Walker's comment runs in part as follows: "There is lately come forth a book of *John Meltons* (a Libertine, that thinketh his Wife a Manacle, and his very Garters to be Shackles and Fetters to him; one that (after the Independent fashion) will be tied to no obligation to God or man) wherein he undertaketh to prove, *That it is lawful for any that have power to call to account, Depose, and put to Death wicked Kings, and Tyrants.*"
40. P. 14
41. P. 7
42. British Museum C. 59. a. 24, pp. 123-24
43. *Ibid.,* p. 55
44. *Ibid.,* p. 267
45. Cf. Clarendon's analysis of his character, Vol. III, Part 1, pp. 256-59
46. P. 24
47. P. 235
48. "Epistle to the Reader"
49. P. 7. This tract probably appeared in September, 1649.
50. *Prose Works,* I, 325, 359, 378, 380
51. *Ibid.,* I, 360
52. *Ibid.,* I, 261
53. *Commonwealth and Protectorate,* I, 195-96
54. *Prose Works,* I, 398
55. *Ibid.,* I, 482
56. *Ibid.,* I, 418
57. *Ibid.,* I, 113-14
58. *Ibid.,* I, 111
59. *Ibid.,* I, 200
60. *Ethics,* VIII, xiii (tr. with an analysis and critical notes by J. E. C. Welldon. London, The Macmillan Co., 1920)
61. *Prose Works,* I, 212
62. *Ibid.,* I, 224, 96
63. *Ibid.,* I, 66
64. *Ibid.,* I, 74
65. *Ibid.,* I, 209
66. *Ibid.,* I, 63
67. *Ibid.,* I, 176
68. *Ibid.,* II, 44
69. *Ibid.,* I, 151-53, 165
70. *Ibid.,* I, 170

71. *Prose Works,* I, 177
72. *Ibid.,* I, 492-93
73. *Ibid.,* I, 15
74. *Ibid.,* I, 192
75. *Ibid.,* I, 150
76. *Ibid.,* I, 3
77. *Ibid.,* I, 143
78. Two others who declined to serve were Robert Nicholas and Sir Thomas Widdrington. See article on John Bradshaw in *D.N.B.*
79. *Prose Works,* I, 154
80. *Ibid.,* II, 34
81. *Ibid.,* I, 315, 341
82. *Ibid.,* I, 192
83. *Ibid.,* I, 265
84. Arthur Annesley, *Englands Confusion* (1659), p. 18
85. *The Re-Publicans And Other Spurious Good Old Cause* (1659), p. 15
86. *Interest Will Not Lie* (1659), p. 11
87. *Ibid.,* p. 20
88. Anonymous, *The Cause of God* (1659), "To the Reader"
89. *The Agreement of the People* (1659), p. 12
90. Anonymous, *The Armies Duty,* p. 15
91. P. 11
92. *A Collection of Several Letters And Declarations . . . By General Monck* (1660), p. 2
93. P. 8
94. P. 4
95. British Museum E 1918, pp. 32-33, 106
96. P. 12
97. P. 6
98. Masson, V, 659
99. P. 3
100. Pp. 3, 22
101. Masson, V, 690
102. British Museum E 187 (2), p. 11
103. P. 157
104. British Museum E 1915, Epistle Dedicatory
105. *Ibid.,* Epistle Dedicatory
106. *Ibid.,* pp. 111-12
107. *Ibid.,* pp. 2, 6
108. British Museum E 1019 (5), p.13
109. *Ibid.,* p. 12
110. *Ibid.,* p. 9
111. *Prose Works,* II, 116
112. Masson, IV, 83
113. *Prose Works,* I, 288 (*Defensio Secunda*)
114. Masson, IV, 112
115. *Prose Works,* I, 14
116. *Ibid.,* I, 288
117. *Ibid.,* I, 287
118. *Letters and Speeches* (Carlyle), II, 425

119. *Letters and Speeches*, I, 295
120. *Prose Works*, I, 111
121. Cf. the *Politics*, III, xiv
122. It is noteworthy that Cromwell, at least as a statesman, was more toler-
    ant of Catholics than Milton; yet on the question of disestablishment
    he was much less progressive than Milton.
123. *Prose Works*, I, 16. Cf. I, 111

NOTES. CHAPTER IX

TWO REBELS AND THE MULTITUDE

1. *Prose Works*, II, 470
2. *Ibid.*, III, 154
3. *Ibid.*, III, 155-56 (italics mine)
4. *Ibid.*, II, 90
5. Cf. the following lines (*Prose Works*, II, 93): "For now the time seems
   come, wherein Moses, the great prophet, may sit in heaven rejoicing to
   see that memorable and glorious wish of his fulfilled, when not only our
   seventy elders, but all the Lord's people, are become prophets."
6. Sonnets 11 and 12, *On the detraction which followed upon my writing
   certain treatises.* I have adopted Mr. Hanford's suggestion that Sonnet
   XI, "I did but prompt, etc." was written in 1645 or 1646. Masson (III,
   460) places it between October, 1645, and January, 1646.
7. Smart, *The Sonnets of Milton*, p. 65
8. *Prose Works*, II, 9. As we have shown (in Chapter VII), Milton's arguments in *The Tenure* were anticipated in a remarkable degree two years
   earlier in John Lilburne's *Regall Tyrannie discovered.* The full title of
   his treatise is as follows: *Regall Tyrannie discovered,* or, "A Discourse,
   shewing that all lawfull (approbationall) instituted power by God
   amongst men, is by common agreement, and mutual consent. Which
   power (in the hands of whomsoever) ought alwayes to be exercised for
   the good, benefit, and welfare of the Trusters, and never ought otherwise
   to be administred: Which, whensoever it is, it is justly resistable and
   revokeable; It being against the light of Nature and Reason, and the
   end wherefore God endowed Man with understanding, for any sort or
   generation of men to give so much power into the hands of any man or
   men whatsoever, as to enable them to destroy them, or to suffer such a
   kind of power to be exercised over them, by any man or men, that shal
   assume it unto himself, either by the sword, or any other kind of way."
   On page 99 of this pamphlet occur the following words: "For, first, I must
   shew and prove; *That the people in generall are the originall sole legis-
   laters, and the true fountain, and earthly well-spring of all just power.*"
   (Italics Lilburne's)
9. *Ibid.*, II, 10. Cr. *Regall Tyrannie*, p. 11: "So in the same case amongst the
   Sons of *Men*, that live in mutual society one amongst another in *nature
   and reason*, there is none above, or over another, against mutuall consent
   and agreement . . . becomes a *Soveraign Lord* and *King*."

10. *Prose Works*, II, 33. In showing that God himself would not deprive the people of their inalienable right to select their own governors, Milton uses the identical argument that Lilburne had used in *Regall Tyrannie*, p. 41: "And so man is the free and voluntary author, the Law is the instrument, and God is the establisher of both. . . . Yet so just was the righteous God, that he would not impose them [kings] upon the people of *Israel* against their own wills, and mindes, neither did they rule as Kings, till by the common consent of the people, they chose them, and appointed them to raigne over them." Cf. "The Tenure," *Prose Works,* II, 15: "These words confirm us that the right of choosing, yea of changing their own government, is by the grant of God himself in the people. And therefore when they desired a king, though their changing displeased him, yet he that was himself their king, and rejected by them, would not be a hinderance to what they intended."

11. Thomas Hobbes, *Leviathan* (Oxford, 1909), p. 133: "And therefore, they that are subjects to a Monarch, cannot without his leave cast off Monarchy, and return to the confusion of a disunited Multitude; nor transferre their Person from him that beareth it, to another Man or other Assembly of men: for they are bound, every man to every man, to Own, and be reputed Author of all, that he that already is their Soveraign, shall do, and judge fit to be done."

12. Robert Filmer, *Patriarcha, or the Natural Power of Kings,* printed with *Two Treatises on Civil Government,* by John Locke (London: George Routledge and Sons, 1884), pp. 15-16: "I see not how the children of Adam or any man else can be free from subjection to their parents. And this subjection of children being the fountain of all regal authority, by the ordination of God himself: it follows, that civil power, not only in general is by divine institution, but even the assignment of it specifically to the eldest parents." Also p. 61: "What is hitherto affirmed of the dependency and subjection of the common law to the sovereign prince, the same may be said as well of all statute laws; so that neither of these two kinds of laws are or can be any diminution of that natural power which kings have over their people by right of fatherhood."

13. *Prose Works*, II, 8-9

14. Cf. *Vox Plebis*, p. 4

15. *Legal Fundamental Liberties*, second edition, p. 62: "For I would fain know in law, where Col. Tho. PRIDE *was authorized to chuse the People of England a Parliament; or to purge away at his pleasure by his sword three quarters of four of the House of Commons.*" Cf. the first edition, p. 43: "And therefore I pressed again and again, seeing themselves confess'd all legal Authority in England was broke, that they should stay his tyrall till a new and equal free Representative upon the Agreement of the well-affected people, that had not fought against their Liberties. Rights and Freedoms, could be chosen and sit, and then either try him thereby, or else by their Judges sitting in the Court called Kings Bench."

16. *Prose Works*, IV, 59

17. *Ibid.*, I, 260

18. *Ibid.*, II, 33

19. *Ibid.*, II, 11

20. *Ibid.*, II, 3

21. *Prose Works*, II, 2
22. *Ibid.*, II, 7
23. *Ibid.*, II, 33
24. *Ibid.*, I, 313
25. *Prose Works*, II, 186
26. *Legal Fundamental Liberties* (2d ed.), pp. 34-5
27. Ireton's
28. *Legal Fundamental Liberties* (2d ed.), p. 35
29. *Ibid.*, p. 36
30. *Legal Fundamental Liberties*, (2d ed.), p. 35 (italics Lilburne's)
31. *Ibid.*, p. 37
32. *Ibid.*, p. 39
33. *Ibid.*, p. 39
34. *Legal Fundamental Liberties* was dated by Lilburne June 8, 1649
35. *Legal Fundamental Liberties* (2d ed.), p. 60
36. *Ibid.*, p. 61
37. *The Triall Of Lieut. Collonell John Lilburne*, p. 151: "Which No being pronounced with a loud voice, immediatly the whole multitude of People in the *Hall*, for joy of the Prisoners acquittall gave such a loud and unanimous shout, as is beleeved, was never heard in *Yeeld-hall*, which lasted for about halfe an hour without intermission: which made the Iudges for fear, turne pale, and hange down their heads; but the Prisoner stood silent at the Barre, rather more sad in his countenance then he was before."
38. *Prose Works*, I, 496
39. *Ibid.*, I, 6
40. *Ibid.*, I, 33
41. *Ibid.*, I, 42
42. *Ibid.*, I, 111
43. *Ibid.*, I, 151
44. *Ibid.*, I, 143
45. *Ibid.*, I, 155
46. *Ibid.*, I, 53-54
47. *Ibid.*, I, 294-96
48. *Ibid.*, I, 295
49. *Ibid.*, I, 297
50. *Prose Works*, I, 298
51. *Ibid.*, I, 299
52. *Ibid.*, II, 127. The relation of Milton's plan for a wide-spread system of education, "not in grammar only, but in all liberal arts and exercises," to this statement is obvious.
53. As we have pointed out previously it was Milton's life-long belief that religious and political insight were synonymous. Yet in the seventeenth century, despite the rough correlation between democratic thought and pronounced individualistic religious beliefs, the sectarians who believed least in piety and goodness were often the most democratic in their political convictions. That the Levellers were often thought of as free thinkers is suggested by the fact that Overton and Walwyn were accused of being atheists, though these were false accusations. Conversely, the saints of the Barebones Parliament not only did not believe

in democracy, but proved themselves incapable of any real statesmanship. The most democratic element of the army, though at heart religious, were often singularly irreverent. Masson tells a story from Edward's *Gangraena* to the effect that some soldiers once took a horse into a village church at Hunts, baptised him with due ceremony, and named him *Esau* after his hairy nature! (Masson, III, 526n)

54. *Prose Works*, II, 124

55. *Ibid.*, II, 125

56. From his study of Greek and Roman government, Milton evidently believed that Aristotle's theory of the frequent transition of democracies into tyrannies was just as applicable to England as it had been to Greece and Rome. Cf. the *Politics* (Everyman edition, 1928), p. 153 (V, v).

57. *Prose Works*, II, 112

58. *Ibid.*, II, 132

59. *Ibid.*, II, 132-33

60. On March 26, 1649, Milton was instructed to answer *The second Part of Englands New-Chaines Discovered*, but did not obey orders. That Lilburne had high regard for Milton is now settled by a hitherto unnoticed passage in *As You Were*, written by Lilburne in 1652. Here Lilburne praises Milton for his forthright advice to the new government and quotes him at some length. I have analyzed the implications of this passage in an article forthcoming in *Modern Language Notes*.

61. *Memorials* of the English Affairs from the beginning of the reign of Charles I, etc., by Bulstrode Whitelock (4v. Oxford: University Press, 1853), III, 25-6.

NOTES. CHAPTER X

CHAMPION AND DETRACTOR OF PARLIAMENTS

1. *Prose Works*, III, 149

2. *Ibid.*, III, 176

3. *Ibid.*, III, 85

4. Just what the "hard censure" was is unknown. On December 28, 1644, the Lords ordered Mr. Justice Reeves and Mr. Justice Bacon to examine Milton in the presence of the Stationers. But there is no record that Milton was interviewed by these men or afterward censured by the Lords.

5. *Prose Works*, III, 321

6. Masson (III, 470-71) places this sonnet in "some early month of the year 1646," probably in March. Professor J. H. Hanford, in "The Arrangement and Dates of Milton's Sonnets," (*Modern Philology* XVIII (1921). 475-83) places it in the summer of 1646.

7. Masson, III, 400

8. *Ibid.*, III, 409

9. *Ibid.*, III, 410

10. *Ibid.*, III, 530

11. Gardiner, *History of the Great Civil War*, III, 216

12. Masson, III, 529

13. *Ibid.*, III, 530-31

14. Gardiner, *op. cit.*, III, 220
15. *Prose Works*, V, 156
16. John S. Smart, *The Sonnets of Milton* (Glasgow: Maclehose, Jackson, and Co., 1921), p. 83
17. According to his remarks in *Defensio Secunda*, Milton had completed the first four books at the time of the abolition of monarchy, February, 1649.
18. *Prose Works*, V, 236-37
19. Masson, III, 474-78
20. *Ibid.*, III, 634
21. *Prose Works*, V, 237
22. *Ibid.*, II, 187
23. *Ibid.*, II, 195
24. *Ibid.*, I, 143
25. Masson, IV, 391-92
26. *To the Lord Generall Cromwell*
27. Gardiner, *History of the Commonwealth and Protectorate*, II, 242
28. Louise Brown, *Baptists and Fifth Monarchy Men*, pp. 28-43
29. Masson, IV, 516
30. *Prose Works*, I, 288
31. *Treatise of Civil Power*
32. Quoted by Masson, V, 602
33. *Prose Works*, III, 2
34. Smart, *The Sonnets of Milton*, p. 92
35. *Prose Works*, II, 103. Italics mine.
36. *Ibid.*, II, 103. Milton's judgment was historically accurate. See Masson, V, 490.
37. *Ibid.*, II, 104
38. *Ibid.*, II, 105. Milton was well aware that General Monk might re-establish the Rump. Everybody in England was waiting for further word from this general, who on April 11 had sent tidings to the Rump that he and his army would stand solidly behind them in their quarrel with Lambert and his officers.
39. *The Readie & Easie Way*, ed. E. M. Clark (New Haven: Yale University Press, 1915), p. 13
40. *Ibid.*, p. 20
41. *Ibid.*, pp. 27-28
42. *Ibid.*, p. 9
43. Masson, V, 551
44. Though the letter itself is undated, internal evidence shows it to have been written late in March or early in April rather than "soon after March 3," as Masson assumes.

NOTES. CHAPTER XI

UTOPIA BORN OF CRISIS

1. *Somers Tracts*, VI, 304–15
2. P. 69
3. P. 43

4. *Prose Works*, II, 121
5. *Prose Works*, II, 122
6. *Prose Works*, II, 122
7. *Laws*, (tr. R. G. Bury, New York: Putnam, 1926), I, 401
8. *Prose Works*, II, 135
9. *Prose Works*, II, 135
10. James Harrington, *The Oceana and other Works of James Harrington Esq;*
    Collected, Methodiz'd, and Review'd, with An Exact Account of his
    Life prefixed by John Toland (London: A. Millar, 1787), p. xix
11. Harrington, *op. cit.*, p. 78
12. Part of the inscription is as follows:

GRATA PATRIA   OCEANA

Piae and Perpetuae Memoriae   Pater Patriae
OLPHAUS   MEGALETOR,   Invincible in the Field
Lord Archon and sole Legis-   Immortal in his Fame
lator of   The Greatest of Captains
                                         The Best of Princes
      Who setting the Kingdoms of Earth at Liberty,
      Took the Kingdom of the Heavens by Violence

13. Toland's *Life of Harrington,* in Harrington, op. cit., p. xx
14. The importance of *Oceana* in contemporary politics really began, of course,
    with the death of Cromwell. In 1659, Harrington published at least four
    short models based on *Oceana,* one of which contained seven brief pro-
    posals based on the commonwealths of seven countries. On July 6, 1659,
    Harrington and his friends presented a petition to Parliament for a con-
    sideration of a Harringtonian government. Finally, as late as 1660, Har-
    rington sent forth two other short models similar to his previous ones.
    See Harrington, op. cit., pp. 475, 524, 539, 541, 620, and 621.
15. *Ibid.*, p. 91
16. Harrington, *op. cit.*, pp. 83-4
17. *Ibid.*, p. 84
18. Harrington, *op. cit.*, 123-24
19. Harrington, *op. cit.*, pp. 39-40
20. Cf. his definition of a commonwealth, *op. cit.*, p. 55
21. *Ibid.*, p. 54
22. Harrington, *op. cit.*, p. 102
23. *Ibid.*, p. 222
24. *Ibid.*, p. 108
25. *Ibid.*, p. 109
26. Following is Harrington's definition of a commonwealth (*op. cit.*, p. 55):
    "An equal commonwealth . . . is a Government established upon an
    equal Agrarian, arising into the Superstructures or three Orders, the
    Senate debating and proposing, the People resolving, and the Magis-
    tracy executing by an equal rotation thro the suffrage of the People
    given by Ballot."
27. *Prose Works*, II, 128
28. *Ibid.*, II, 127
29. *Ibid.*, II, 123

NOTES. CHAPTER XII

WINSTANLEY, MILTON, AND LILBURNE ON ECONOMIC CHANGE

1. James E. Thorold Rogers, *Six Centuries of Work and Wages* (2 vols, London: 1884), I, 431.
2. *A Declaration of . . . the Poor Inhabitants of . . . Wellinborrow*, March 12, 1650; British Museum 669 f. 15 (21)
3. *A New-yeers Gift for the Parliament and Armie*, British Museum E587 (6), p. 40
4. James E. Thorold Rogers, *History of Agriculture and Prices in England* (7 vols., Oxford: 1886-1902), V, 829-30
5. *Natural and Political Observations . . . upon the Conditions of England*, British Museum 1137 k27, pp. 48-9
6. *More Light Shining in Buckingham-shire*, British Museum E548 (33), p. 16
7. *The True Levellers Standard Advanced*, British Museum E552 (5), p. 15
8. *An Appeal to the House of Commons*, British Museum E564 (5), pp. 15-16
9. *An Appeal to the House of Commons*, p. 16
10. *Light shining in Buckingham-shire*, British Museum E475 (11), pp. 6-7
11. *More Light Shining in Buckingham-shire*, p. 15
12. *A New-yeers Gift for the Parliament and Armie*, p. 17
13. *Law of Freedom in a Platform*, British Museum E655 (8), p. 62
14. *A New-yeers Gift*, pp. 40-41
15. *An Appeale to all Englishmen*, British Museum 669 f. 15 (23)
16. *A Watch-word to The City of London and the Armie*, British Museum E573 (1), preface
17. *New-yeers Gift*, pp. 37-38
18. *Ibid.*, p. 42
19. *Ibid.*, p. 43
20. *The True Levellers Standard Advanced*, p. 7
21. *Clarke Papers*, II, 209; *New-yeers Gift*, p. 44
22. Whitelocke, *Memorials*, p. 397
23. *New-yeers Gift*, pp. 44-46
24. British Museum E552 (7), p. 32
25. *A New-yeers Gift*, p. 46
26. P. 8
27. *A Watch-word to The City of London and the Armie*, prefatory address
28. P. 10
29. Though he was less concerned with the poor than with the middle class, Sir Harry Vane argued in a similar vein for the uprooting of kingly privileges. See his *A Healing Question propounded and resolved*, E879 (5), p. 5
30. *New-yeers Gift*, p. 17
31. *British Museum* 669 f. 15 (23)
32. *A Modest Narrative of Intelligence*, June 9-16, 1649, British Museum E560 (12), p. 81
33. *The Perfect Weekly Account*, July 18-25, 1649, British Museum E565 (28), p. 552
34. *New-yeers Gift*, p. 16

35. *A Vindication of those . . . called Diggers*, B. M. E1365 (1)
36. *Law of Freedom*, p. 4
37. *Law of Freedom*, pp. 12, 13, 29, 34, 40, 50, 69, 72
38. *History of the Commonwealth and Protectorate*, II, 6
39. British Museum E2137 (1), p. 33
40. *The Saints Paradise*, p. 34
41. British Museum E323 (2), p. 40
42. Cf. *The Souldiers Catechism*, B. M. 8122. b. 15, p. 1:
      Q. *Is it lawfull for Christians to be souldiers?*
      A. Yea doubtlesse: we have Arguments enough to warrant it.
43. *Watchword to the Citie of London and the Armie*, p. 11
44. *The True Levellers Standard Advanced*, p. 16
45. *Copy of a Letter from Lieutenant Colonel John Lilburne, to a friend*, British Museum E296 (5), p. 61
46. *A Manifestation from Lieutenant Col. John Lilburn*, etc., British Museum E550 (25), pp. 4-5
47. British Museum E552 (23), p. 7
48. British Museum 669 f 14 (59)
49. British Museum E 560 (14), p. 75
50. Dated by Lilburne Dec. 15, 1648. British Museum 100A 72, p. 14
51. *Comus*, 768-73. I am indebted to Dr. James H. Hanford's note on this passage in his recent edition of Milton's poetry.
52. *Prose Works*, II, 127
53. Grateful for leisure, Milton realized that it was made possible by the labor of others. *Cf. Prose Works*, II, 475: "Yet ease and leisure was given thee for thy retired thoughts, out of the sweat of other men."

NOTES. CHAPTER XIII

MILTON AS A DEMOCRATIC REFORMER

1. *Prose Works*, IV, 451
2. *Prose Works*, I, 257-58
3. *Commonplace Book*, ed. A. J. Horwood, (rev. ed.) p. 179
4. *Institutes*, ed. Thos. Cooper (3rd ed., New York, 1852), p. 8
5. *Prose Works*, I, 70-71
6. *Philippies*, XI, xii, 28-9 (tr. Ker. London: Heineman, 1926)
7. *Politics*, I, v, tr. Ellis
8. Hooker differentiates between the two. The one is common to all men; the other to Christians.
9. *Prose Works*, I, 265
10. *Ibid.*, I, 111
11. *Clarke Papers*, I, 305
12. It is this very theory that man has a natural right to any land he can use that Locke boldly sets forth in his *Second Essay in Government*.
13. Masson, V, 615-16
14. "Evolution of Milton's Political Thought," *Sewanee Review*, XXX (1922), 196

NOTES. CHAPTER XIV

JUSTIFICATION: THE WAYS OF GOD

1. *The Earl of Manchesters Speech* (May 29, 1660)
2. *The Speech of Sr. Harbottle Grimston* (May 29, 1660), p. 7
3. *Prose Works*, II, 138
4. *The Speeches And Prayers of Some of the late Kings Judges* (1660), pp. 6, 7, 8, 10
5. H. Finch, *An Exact and most Impartial Accompt* (1660), p. 282
6. *Ibid.*, pp. 286-87
7. *The Speeches and Prayers* (1660), p. 62
8. *Ibid.*, p. 69
9. *Ibid.*, pp. 72-73
10. Masson, VI, 97
11. *The Tryal of Sir Henry Vane*, Kt. (1662), British Museum 1418 h. 56, p. 100
12. *Ibid.*, p. 123
13. *Ibid.*, p. 87
14. *Ibid.*, p. 89. The writer adds (pp. 95-96): "No signs of inward fear appeared by any trembling or shaking of his hands, or any other parts of his body, all along on the Scaffold. Yea, an ancient Traveller and curious observer of the demeanor of persons at such publick Executions, did narrowly eye his Countenance to the last breath, and his Head immediately after the separation; he observed that his Countenance did not in the least change: and . . . the Head of this Sufferer lay perfectly still, immediately upon the separation: on which he said to this purpose, That his Death was by the free consent and act of his mind."
15. *Paradise Lost*, VIII, 406-7
16. *Ibid.*, VI, 174-78
17. *Ibid.*, II, 5
18. *Ibid.*, II, 18-24
19. *Ibid.*, I, 663-64
20. *Ibid.*, VIII, 543-44
21. *Ibid.*, IX, 311
22. *Ibid.*, IV, 635-36
23. *Prose Works*, IV, 246 (my italics)
24. *Paradise Lost*, V, 100-3
25. *Ibid.*, VIII, 590-91
26. *Ibid.*, VIII, 635-37
27. *Paradise Regained*, II, 466-71
28. *Paradise Lost*, IX, 821-25
29. *Prose Works*, II, 126
30. *Paradise Lost*, IX, 725-26
31. *Ibid.*, IX, 823-25
32. *Prose Works*, II, 297
33. *Paradise Lost*, XII, 95-101
34. Gardiner, *Commonwealth and Protectorate*, II, 209
35. *Works* (Columbia ed.), XVIII, 240-41

BIBLIOGRAPHY

BIBLIOGRAPHIES

Catalogue of the Pamphlets, Books, Newspapers, and Manuscripts Collected by George Thomason, 2 v. London. 1908.

Gillett, G. R., *Catalogue of the McAlpin Collection of British History and Theology.* 5v. New York, Union Theological Seminary, New York. 1927-30.

Hanford, J. H. *A Milton Handbook.* New York. F. S. Crofts and Co. 1927, 1933, 1939, pp. 401-22 of 1939 edition.

Pease, T. C. *The Leveller Movement.* Washington. American Historical Association. 1916. pp. 365-83.

Stevens, D. H. *A Reference Book in Milton.* Chicago. University of Chicago Press, 1930.

Thompson, E. N. S. *John Milton Topical Bibliography.* New Haven. Yale University Press. 1916.

IMPORTANT REFERENCE BOOKS AND REPRINTED SOURCES

Adams, George H. and Stephens, M. Morse. *Select Documents of English Constitutional History.* New York. Macmillan. 1924.

Aristotle. *Politics.* tr. J. E. C. Welldon, D.D. London. Macmillan. 1923.

Aubrey, J. "Collections for the Life of John Milton." 1681. In W. Godwin: *Lives of Edward and John Phillips.* London. 1815.

Berens, Lewis H. *The Digger Movement in the Days of the Commonwealth.* London. 1906.

Borgeaud, Charles. *Rise of Modern Democracy in Old and New England.* New York. Scribner. 1894.

Brown, Louise. *The Political Activities of the Baptists and Fifth Monarchy Men in England during the Interregnum.* New York. Oxford U. Press. 1912.

Buchanan, George. *Dialogue Concerning the Rights of the Crown of Scotland.* tr. Robert Macfarlan. London. 1799.

Calvin, John. *Institutes of the Christian Religion.* ed. John Allen. Philadelphia. Presbyterian Board of Publication. 1813.

Cicero. *Philippics.* tr. Walter Ker. New York. Putnam. 1926.

Cicero. *De Re Publica, De Legibus.* tr. C. W. Keyes. New York. Putnam. 1926.

Comenius, John Amos. *The Great Didactic.* ed. M. W. Keatinge. 2 v. London. Adam and Charles Black. 1907-10.

Evelyn, John. *Diary and Correspondence.* ed. H. Wheatley. 4 v. London. Bohn. 1899.

Figgis, J. N. *Theory of the Divine Right of Kings.* Cambridge. U. Press. 1922. 2nd edition.

Firth, C. H. *Clarke Papers.* 4 v. Camden Society Publications. 1891-1901.

Firth, C. H. *The Last Years of the Protectorate.* 2 v. London. 1899.

Fuller, Thomas. *Works.* ed. J. S. Brewer. Oxford. 1895.

Gardiner, S. R. *History of England, 1603-42.* 10 v. London. 1883-84.

Gardiner, S. R. *History of the Great Civil War.* 1642-49. London. 4 v. 1886.

Gardiner, S. R. *History of the Commonwealth and Protectorate.* 3 v. London. 1894-1903.

Gardiner, S. R. *Constitutional Documents of the Puritan Revolution.* 1625-1660. Oxford. Clarendon Press. 1899.

Godwin, William. *History of the Commonwealth.* 4 v. London. 1824-28.

Godwin, William. *Lives of Edward and John Phillips.* London. 1815.

Gooch, Geo. P. *English Democratic Ideas of the Seventeenth Century.* Cambridge. University Press. 1927.

Grotius, Hugo. *The Rights of War and Peace.* ed. A. C. Campbell. Washington. Walter Dunne. 1901.

Haller, William H. *Tracts on Liberty in the Puritan Revolution.* 3 v. New York. Columbia University Press. 1934.

Haller, W. H. *The Rise of Puritanism.* New York. Columbia University Press. 1938.

Hanbury, Benjamin. *Historical Memorials relating to the Independents or Congregationalists.* 3 v. London. 1839-44.

Hanford, J. H. *A Milton Handbook.* New York. F. S. Crofts. 1933.

Hanford, J. H. *Studies in Shakespere, Milton, and Donne.* New York. Macmillan. 1925.

Harrington, James. *The Oceana and Other Works* of James Harrington, Esq.; Collected, Methodiz'd, and Review'd, with An Exact Account of his Life prefix'd by John Toland. London. 1785.

Hooker, Richard. *Of Ecclesiastical Polity.* 2 v. Everyman edition. New York. 1907.

Hutchinson, Lucy. *Memoirs of the Life of Colonel Hutchinson.* ed. Rev. Julius Hutchinson. London. Bohn. 1889.

Knox, John. *The History of the Reformation of the Church of Scotland...* Together with some Treatises conducing to the History. London. 1644.

Lactantius. *Works.* tr. William Fletcher. Edinburgh. 1886.

Ludlow, Edmund. *Memoirs.* 2 v. ed. C. H. Firth. Oxford. Clarendon Press. 1894.

Machiavelli, Nicolo. *Works.* tr. Thomas Bedingfield, 1595. 2 v. London. David Nutt. 1905.

Masson, David. *The Life of Milton in Connexion with the History of His Time.* London. 1859-1894. First volume revised 1881. Seven volumes including index.

Milton, John. *The Works of John Milton.* Columbia University edition. 18 v. plus index of two volumes. New York. Columbia University Press. 1931-40.

Milton, John. *The Prose Works of John Milton.* ed. J. A. St. John. 5 v. London. 1848-53. Bohn edition.

Milton, John. *The Poetical Works of John Milton.* ed. H. C. Beeching. London. 1900. Oxford edition.

Milton, John. *A Commonplace Book of John Milton.* ed. Alfred J. Horwood. Revised edition. Camden Society Publications. 1877.

Milton, John. *Of Reformation Touching Church Discipline in England.* ed. Will T. Hale. New Haven. Yale University Press. 1916.

Milton, John. *The Tenure of Kings and Magistrates.* ed. William T. Allison. New Haven. Yale University Press. 1911.

Milton, John. *The Ready and Easy Way to Establish a Free Commonwealth.* ed. Evert M. Clark. New Haven. Yale University Press. 1915.

Neal, Daniel. *History of the Puritans.* ed. John O. Choules. New York. 1871.

Pease, Theodore Calvin. *The Leveller Movement.* Washington. American Historical Association. 1916.

The Parliamentary or Constitutional History of England. 24 v. London. 1751-1766. Cited as *Old Parliamentary History.*

Pepys, S. *The Diary of Samuel Pepys.* ed. H. B. Wheatley. 9 v. Boston. 1892. Volumes 1, 2, and 3.

Phillips, E. *The Life of Milton.* In W. Godwin: *Lives of Edward and John Phillips.* London. 1815.

Plato. *Laws.* tr. R. G. Bury. 2 v. New York. G. P. Putnam's Sons. 1926.

Publications of the Narragansett Club. First Series. 6 v. Providence. 1866-74.

Rushworth, John. *Historical Collections of the Great Civil War.* 8 v. London, 1721.

Saurat, Denis. *Milton, Man and Thinker.* New York. The Dial Press. 1925.

Shaw, William A. *A History of the English Church During the Civil Wars and Under the Commonwealth.* London. Longmans, Green, and Co. 1900.

Smart, John S. *The Sonnets of Milton.* Glasgow. Maclehose, Jackson and Co. 1921.

Smith, Sir Thomas. *De Republica Anglorum.* ed. L. Alston. Cambridge. University Press. 1906.

Somers Tracts. ed. Sir Walter Scott. 13 v. London. 1811. Vol. 6.

Taylor, Jeremy. *Works.* ed. Heber and Eden. 7 v. London. 1859.

Toland, John. *The Life of John Milton with Amyntor;* or a Defense of Milton's Life. London. Printed for John Darby, 1699. Reprinted for A. Millar. 1761.

Thompson, E. N. S. *Essays on Milton.* New Haven. Yale University Press. 1914.

Whitelock, Bulstrode. *Memorials* of the English Affairs from the Beginning of the Reign of Charles the First to the Happy Restoration of Charles the Second. 4 v. Oxford. University Press. 1853.

Woodhouse, A. S. P. *Puritanism and Liberty.* London. J. M. Dent and Sons. 1938.

JOHN LILBURNE

The following list of pamphlets by and about Lilburne is arranged in chronological order. Information has been culled from the pamphlets, from the Thomason and McAlpin Catalogues, from Pease's *The Leveller Movement,* and from Peacock's "John Lilburne: A Bibliography" in *Notes and Queries* for 1888. Though there are errors in both Thomason Catalogue and Peacock title entries, I have had to rely upon them for correct wording and spelling of titles of some pamphlets not available to me for rechecking. For the sake of completeness I have included a number of Lilburne pamphlets not used in this study. On the other hand, all but two editions of *The Agreement of the People,* and most related pamphlets, have been omitted. The "Th" at the end of each item indicates the date of the tract's appearance as recorded by Thomason. Other symbols refer to libraries where the tracts may be found. In this I have followed Peacock in the main. The library symbols are as follows: B.M., British Museum; Bodl., Bodleian; C.C.C., Corpus Christi College, Oxford; G.L., Guildhall Library, London; Linc. College, Lincoln College, Oxford; H., Harvard University Library; McAl., The McAlpin Collection, Union Theological Seminary, New York City.

A Worke Of The Beast Or A Relation of a most vnchristian Censure, Executed upon . . . Lilburne . . . the 18 of Aprill 1638 . . . 1638. [No place or printer. See *Christian Mans Triall,* 1641, for a later edition. 32 pp. B.M., H., McAl.]

Coppy of a Letter written by L.C.L. to one of his special friends when he was in a cruell close imprisonment. [This letter is dated by Lilburne November 11, 1638. As first pointed out by Professor Haller (*The Rise of Puritanism,* p. 434), it was printed by Lilburne for the first time in his *Innocency and Truth Justified,* 1645. It follows p. 76 of the pamphlet. 21 pp. McAl.]

A cry for Justice: Or; An Epistle written by John Lilburn, To all the grave and worthy Citizens of the famous City of London, but especially to the Right honorable Maurice Abbot, Lord Maior thereof, The most miserable and lamentable complaint of that inhumane, barbarous, savage and unparalell'd cruelty and tyranny . . . exercised upon me John Lilburn . . . 1639. [Reprinted by Lilburne on pp. 22-26 of *Picture Of The Councel of State* (second ed.). *The Cry,* according to Lilburne, was printed in Amsterdam in 1639. It is dated at the end "middle of this fifth Month, called *May,* 1639." Lilburne mentions several of his early pamphlets (p. 22): "three severall Books of mine now in print, and published to the view of England, Scotland, Ireland and Holland. They are called *My unjust Censure in the Star-chamber, My Speech at the Pillory,* and *My mournfull Lamentations.* I have not seen them since they were put in print, because the Prelate of Canterbury wrongfully detains well nigh two thousand of them from me: but there are still many thousands of them behinde." On p. 23 Lilburne speaks of "*my Grievous and mournfull Complaint* already published." McAl.]

The Poore mans cry. Wherein is shewed the present miserable estate of mee John Lilburne, close prisoner in the Fleete. . . . Published by a backe friend of the English Popish Prelates 1639. [G.L.]

Come out of her my people or an answer to the question . . . about Hearing the Public Ministers: where it is largely discussed and proved to be sinfull and vnlawfull. Also a Just apologie for the way of Totall Separation. . . . By mee John Lilburne, close prisiner in the Fleete for the Cause of Christ. . . . Anno 1639. [G.L.]

A copy of a letter written by John Lilburne, close prisoner in the wards of the Fleet, which he sent to James Ingram and Henry Hopkins, wardens of the said Fleet, wherein is fully discovered their great cruelty exercised upon his body. [No title. Date at end October 4, 1640. S.K., H.]

The Christian Mans Triall; Or, a Trve Relation of the first apprehension and severall examinations of Iohn Lilburne. . . . The second Edition, with an addition. London, Printed for William Larnar . . . 1641. [Preface by William Kiffin. *A Worke of the Beast* is inserted, pp. 17-38. *A Worke* dated on p. 17, March 12, 1637 [8] 39 pp., B.M., McAl. Th: Dec., 1641]

Examination and Confession of Captaine Lilbourne and Captaine Viviers who were taken at Brainford by his Maj. forces, and had their triall at Oxford on Saturday the tenth . . . December . . . Sent in a letter from Mr. Daniel Felton . . . London, Printed for T. Wright. [1643. G.L., B.M., Th: Dec. 10, 1642]

The Examination . . . of Captaine Lilburne and Viviers . . . 1642. [According to Peacock, this deals with Lilburne's capture by the king's forces. S.K.]

Letter Sent from Captaine Lilbvrne To divers of his friends . . . in London. London, Printed for Iames Rogers, 1643. [8 pp. B.M., Bodl., H., G.L., Th: Jan. 3, 1643]

Speech spoken by Prince Robert to the K . . . wherein is declared the resolution concerning Serg. Maj. Skippon, Col. Browne and Col. Hvrry. . . . Likewise the Heads of a speech, spoken by Captaine Lilbovrne before a Councell of Warre, held at Oxford December 18. Dec. 21. Printed for J. H. and Richard Crosby 1643. [G.L.]

A Copie Of A Letter, Written by . . . Lilburne . . . To Mr. William Prinne Esq. (Upon The Coming Out Of His Last Booke, Intituled Truth triumphing over Falshood, Antiquity over Novelty.) [No place, printer, or date. Dated at end by Lilburne January 7, 1645. 7 pp. B.M., Bodl., G.L., S.K., H. Reprinted in Haller's *Tracts on Liberty.* Th: Jan. 15, 1645]

An Answer to Nine Arguments . . . by T.B. . . . . Written long since by that faithfull Servant of God and his Countrey, John Lilburne . . . London . . . 1645. [B.M., Bodl. Th: Jan. 17, 1645]

Reasons of Lieu. Col. Lilbournes sending his letter to Mr. Prin . . . presented to the . . . committee of Examinations. [No title page. At the end is "Printed 13. June, 1645." B.M., Bodl., G.L., S.K. Th: June 13, 1645]

A more full Relation of the Great Battell fought betweene Sir Tho. Fairfax and Goring. Made in the House of Commons by Lieut. Col Lilbourne. Printed by T. Forcet for Peter Cole. [B.M. Th: July 10, 1645]

The Copy of a Letter, from Lieutenant Colonell John Lilbvrne, to a Friend. [No title page. London, 1645. Three editions appeared in 1645. 24 pp. B.M., Bodl., G.L., S.K., McAl., H. Th: July 25, 1645]

[Note from Peacock: A fragment beginning p. 150. An extract relating to the militia, with a commentary by John Lilburne. A single folio leaf. Probably of the year 1645. B.M., 669.f.10.43. Th: Aug. 30, 1645]

Col. Lilburnes Letter to a Friend published to vindicate his aspersed Reputation. Printed for Peter Cole. [B.M. Th: September 23, 1645]

Englands Birth-Right Justified Against all Arbitrary Usurpation. [1645. No date, printer, or place. Mentioned repeatedly by Lilburne, but not claimed as his own. See *Picture of Councel of State* (both editions), p. 8; *The peoples Prerogative,* pp. 69, 73; *A Whip for the present House of Lords,* pp. 17, 20. 48 pp. B.M., G.L., S.K., McAl. Th: Oct. 10 1645]

Innocency And Truth Justified . . . 1645. [No place, no printer. 76 pp. followed by *The Coppy of a Letter.* Much autobiographical material. G.L., McAl., H. Th: Jan. 6, 1646]

True relation of the material passages of . . . Lilburnes sufferings, as they were . . . proved before the . . . House of Peers . . . 13 . . . Feb. 1645. [No title page. Dated at end, 1645. Peacock's note: "There is another edition, a copy of which is in the B.M., dated 1646." B.M., G.L., S.K. Th: Feb. 13, 1646]

The Ivst Mans Ivstification: or A Letter by way of Plea in Barre; written . . . Lilburne . . . to . . . Justice Reeves. [No place or printer. Dated by Lilburne on p. 16, June 6, 1646. 20 pp. McAl., B.M., G.L., S.K., H. Th: June 6, 1646]

The Free-Mans Freedome Vindicated. [No date, place, or printer. Contains Lilburne's address to the Lords of June 11, 1646, a petition to the Commons dated June 16, 1646, and the "Postscript, containing a generall Proposition," dated June 19, 1646. 12 pp. B.M., McAl. Th: June 16, 1646]

A Copy of a Letter sent by . . . Lilburne to Mr. Wollaston, Keeper of Newgate or his Deputy. 23 June 1646. [B.M. Linc. Coll. Th: June 23, 1646]

Liberty Vindicated against Slavery . . . 1646. [No place or printer. 34 pp. B.M., McAl., H. Th: Aug. 21, 1646]

Londons Liberty In Chains Discovered. And, Published by Lieutenant Colonell John Lilburn, prisoner in the Tower of London, Octob. 1646. [No place or printer. Contains one of Lilburne's first statements of democratic theory (pp. 17 ff) similar to those found in *Free-Mans Freedome* and *Regall Tyrannie*. 72 pp. B.M., McAl., Bodl., S.K., G.L., H. Th: Oct. 1646]

An Anatomy of the Lords Tyranny and iniustice exercised upon Lieut. Col. John Lilburne . . . Delivered in a speech by him, Novem. 6. 1646. before the honorable Committee of the House of Commons. [No place or printer. Dated by Lilburne at the end, November 9, 1646. 23 pp. B.M., McAl., H. Th: Nov. 6, 1646]

The Charters of London, or the second part of Londons Liberty in Chaines Discovered. Printed at London, Decemb. 18. 1646. [B.M., Bodl., G.L., S.K., H. Th: Dec. 18, 1646]

Regall Tyrannie discovered: Or, A Discourse, shewing that all lawfull . . . instituted power by God amongst men, is by common agreement . . . London . . . 1647. [List of Lilburne's pamphlets on pp. 3-5. Those written, the author says, before the Long Parliament, include *The Afflicted Mans Complaint, A Cry for Justice, Epistle to the Prentices of London, Answer to Nine Arguments of T.B.*, and *Epistle to the Wardens of the Fleet*. Though Lilburne often refers to *Regall*, he never directly claims it as his own. See *Council of State* (1st ed.), p. 14; *The peoples Prerogative*, p. 68; *The resolved mans Resolution*, pp. 7, 39; *A Whip for the . . . Lords*, p. 20. The first part of *Regall* was probably written by Overton. 108 pp. B.M., McAl., H. Th: Jan. 6, 1647]

The Oppressed Mans Oppressions declared. [1647. No place, printer, or date. Dated at end by Lilburne January 30, 1646 [7]. 28 pp. B.M., McAl., H. Th: Jan. 30, 1647]

The out-cryes of oppressed Commons. Directed to all the Rationall and understanding men in the Kingdome . . . From . . . Lilburne and . . . Overton . . . Febr. 1647. [No place or printer. Dated on p. 18 "this last of Februa. 1647." 20 pp. B.M., McAl., H. Th: Feb. 28, 1647]

The resolved mans Resolution, to maintain with the last drop of his heart blood, his civill Liberties and freedomes . . . by . . . John Lilburne . . . Aprill 1647. [No printer or place. Dated by Lilburne April 30, 1647. On p. 15 Lilburne mentions as "bookes also then made" his *Christian Mans Triall, Come out of her, my people, The Afflicted Mans Complaint, A Cry for Justice, Epistle to the Apprentices of London, Epistle to the Wardens of the Fleet*. B.M., H., McAl. Th: April 30, 1647]

The Recantation Of . . . John Lilburne . . . Opening, all the Machinations of the Independent Partie . . . 1647. [Lilburne's authorship doubtful. He certainly did not write pp. 6, 7, 8, which satirize Overton at Martin Mar-Priest and contain mention of *Mans Mortallitie* and *Martins Eccho*. I believe these pages were written by Overton. 8 pp. B.M., McAl., H. Th: May 13, 1647]

Rash Oaths unwarrantable . . . 1647. [No place or printer. Dated at end by Lilburne May 31, 1647. It has been hitherto unnoticed that the famous petition of March, 1647, was inserted in this tract, pp. 29-36. 56 pp. B.M., McAl. Th: May 31, 1647]

Ionahs Cry out of the Whales belly: Or, Certaine Epistles writ by Lieu. Coll. Iohn Lilburne, unto . . . Cromwell, and . . . Goodwin. [1647. No printer, place, or date. Letters dated February 13, 1647; March 14, 1647; March 25, 1647; April 10, 1647; June 22, 1647; July 1, 1647; December 9, 1645. The most important of Lilburne's tracts in showing his break with Cromwell and the Independents. 16 pp. B.M., McAl. Th: July 26, 1647]

Two Letters Writ By . . . Lilburne . . . to Col. Henry Martin . . . upon the 13. and 15 of September. 1647. [No place or printer. Dated at end September 18, 1647. Letter to Cromwell on p. 8 contains list of Cromwell's relatives and friends in key army positions. 8 pp. B.M., McAl. Th: Sept. 13, 1647]

The Ivglers Discovered, In two Letters writ by Lievt. Col. John Lilburne . . . the 28. September, 1647. [No printer or place. Letters inserted dated by Lilburne July 22, 1647, and August 21, 1647. Dated by Lilburne at end September 8, 1647. 12 pp. B.M., McAl. Th: Sept. 28, 1647]

The grand Plea of . . . Lilburne . . . before an open Committee of the House of Commons, the twenteth day of October, 1647. [No place or printer. Dated by Lilburne October 26, 1647. 16 pp. B.M., McAl., H. Th: Oct. 20, 1647]

The additional Plea . . . the 28. of October, 1647. [No place or printer. Appeared separately, according to Thomason, on October 28 (E. 412. (11). In a later edition of *The Grand Plea*, it appears on pp. 17-24. B.M., McAl. Separate edition not available at McAlpin. Th: Oct. 28, 1647]

A Cal To All The Souldiers Of The Armie, By The Free People Of England . . . 1647. [8 pp. By John Wildman. McAl. Th: Oct. 29, 1647]

An Agreement Of The People For A firme and present Peace, upon grounds of common-right and freedom; As it was proposed by the Agents of the five Regiments of Horse . . . which have already appeared for the Case, of The Case of the Army truly stated. . . . 1647. [6 pp. The first *Agreement*, the one discussed in the army debates recorded in *Clarke Papers*. B.M., McAl. Th: Nov. 3, 1647]

Plaine Truth without Feare or Flattery: Or A Trve Discovery Of The Unlawfulnesse of the Presbyterian Government . . . by I. L. . . . 1647. [No place or printer. First edition. Not by Lilburne, in my judgment, though by some attributed to him. 22 pp. McAl., H.]

Putney Projects. Or the Old Serpent In a new Forme. . . . 1647. [By John Wildman. McAl., B.M. Th: Dec. 30, 1647]

Truths triumph, Or Treachery anatomized. . . . Iohn Wildman. London. Printed for Ia. Hornish, Feb. 1, 1647[8] [18 pp. McAl., B.M. Th: Jan. 18, 1648]

A Defiance of Tyrants or the Araignment of two Illegal Committees viz. The Close Committee or Lords and Commons appointed to examine the London agents, and the Committee of Plundered Ministers. In two pleas made by Lilburne . . . London Jan. 1648. [B.M., Bodl., G.L., Linc. Coll. Th: Jan. 28, 1648]

The peoples Prerogative and Priviledges, asserted and vindicated, (against all Tyranny whatsoever.) . . . 1647. [No place or printer. Preface dated February 6, 1647 [8]. In addition to some traditional documents of common liberties and Lilburne's own statements, contains protests of soldiers against martial law applied to civil cases. 80 pp. B.M., McAl. Th: Feb. 17, 1648]

A Whip for the present House of Lords, Or The Levellers Levelled . . . an Epistle writ to Mr. Frost . . . By . . . Lilburne . . . Feb. 27. 1647. [No place or printer. In this tract Lilburne accuses Frost of Fiennes of having written *A Declaration Of some Proceedings.* 28 pp. B.M., McAl., H. Th: Feb. 27, 1648]

A Plea, or Protest, Made By William Prynne. . . . Published for the common good of all honest Englishmen, By Lionel Hurbin Gentleman, March 17. 1647. Printed for Iah. Hornish, 1648. [No place. Lilburne refers to this tract in *An Impeachment Of High Treason Against . . . Cromwell,* p. 20, and in *Picture of Councel of State* (2d ed.), p. 7. The passage on p. 4 of *The Plea* seems unmistakably Lilburne's. B.M., McAl. Th: March 16, 1648]

The Prisoners Plea for a Habeas Corpus, or an Epistle writ by . . . Lilburne . . . the 4 of Aprill to the Honourable Mr. W. Lenthall, Speaker of the House of Commons. [No title page. Dated by Lilburne April 4, 1648. B.M., S.K., G.L., H. Th: April 4, 1648. To Harvard copy is appended *Letter to the Apprentices of London,* dated at end by Lilburne May 10, 1639]

The oppressed mans importunate and mournfull cryes to be brought to the Barre of Iustice, or An Epistle writ by . . . Lilburne. [8 pp. No title. Dated April 7, 1648. G.L., H.]

The Prisoners mournful cry against the Iudges of the Kings Bench, or an epistle writ by . . . Lilburne . . . unto Mr. Justice Roll. [No title page. Dated May 1, 1648. B.M., G.L., S.K., H. Th: May 9, 1648]

The Lawes Funerall, Or, An Epistle written by . . . Lilburn. [No title page. Dated by Lilburne May 15, 1648. B.M., G.L., S.K. Th: May 15, 1648]

Englands weeping Spectacle: or, The sad condition of Lievtenant . . . Lilburne . . . 1648. [No place or printer. A sympathetic biographical sketch. 13 pp. B.M., McAl. Th: June 29, 1648]

To every individual Member of the Honourable House of Commons: The Humble Remembrance of . . . John Lilburn . . . September 4. 1648. [No place or printer. 8 pp. B.M., McAl. Th: Sept. 4, 1648]

A Plea for common-right and Freedom. To his excellency, the Lord General Fairfax and the Commission-officers of the Armie . . . as it was presented to his Excellency Decemb. 28. 1648. [Peacock: "and fifteen others, whose names are given"] London. Printed for Ja. and Jo. Moxon for Will Larnar. . . . [1648. B.M., G.L.]

Englands New Chains Discovered; Or The serious apprehensions of a part of the People, in behalf of the Commonwealth . . . By . . . Lilburn, and divers other Citizens of London . . . February 26. 1648 [1649]. [No printer. 15 pp. G.L., McAl., H., B.M. Th: Feb. 26, 1649]

The second Part of Englands New-Chaines Discovered. [No place or printer. Reprinted complete on pp. 399-415 of this book. 18 pp. B.M., Bodl., G.L., S.K., McAl., H. Th: March 24, 1649]

The Picture of The Councel of State, Held forth to the Free People of England By . . . Lilburn . . . Prince . . . and Overton . . . 1649. [No place or printer. Contains stories by the three men of their arrests on March 28.

Lilburne's account dated April 4, Overton's, April 4, and Princes, April 1. Overton mentions three of his tracts, including *Vnhappy Game of Scotch and English,* on p. 36. 54 pp. B.M., McAl., H. Th: April 4, 1649]

The Picture Of The Councel of State, Held forth to the Free people of England . . . The second Edition, with many large Additions by the Authors themselves . . . 1649. [No place or printer. Accounts of Prince and Overton omitted from this edition. Contains letter to Fairfax on Lockyer's behalf dated April 27, 1649. Contains also *A Cry for Justice,* which Lilburne says was printed at Amsterdam in 1639, dated at end "middle of this fifth Month, called *May,* 1639." 28 pp. McAl.]

A Manifestation From . . . Lilburn . . . Walwyn . . . Prince . . . and . . . Overton, (Now Prisoners in the Tower of London) and others, commonly (though unjustly) Styled Levellers . . . 1649. [No place or printer. Dated by the authors April 14, 1649. 8 pp. B.M., McAl., H. Th: April 14, 1649]

An Agreement Of The Free People of England. Tendered as a Peace-Offering to this distressed Nation. By . . . Lilburne . . . Walwyn . . . Prince . . . and Overton . . . May the 1. 1649. [London, Giles Calvert, 1649. Licensed by Mabbott April 30, 1649. 8 pp. B.M., McAl. Th: May 1, 1649]

A Discovrse Betwixt Lieutenant Colonl Iohn Lilburn . . . And Mr. High-Peter: Upon May 25. 1649. London, 1649. [In *Cornelius Holland* Lilburne mentions a second edition of this tract. Lilburne said he set down from memory the conversation and sent it to Mr. Hunt. 8 pp. B.M., McAl., H. Th: May 25, 1649]

The Discoverer. Wherein Is Set Forth . . . the reall Plots . . . of . . . Lilburn . . . Walwyn . . . Prince . . . Overton . . . London; Printed for Mathew Simmons, 1649. [By John Canne. Contains numerous marginal references to Leveller tracts. 48 pp. A "Second Part" of *the Discoverer* (80 pp.) appeared on July 13. McAl., B.M. Th: June 2, 1649]

The Legall Fundamentall Liberties Of the People of England Revived, Asserted, and Vindicated. . . . London . . . 1649. [No printer. Dated by Lilburne June 8, 1649. Contains an address by Lilburne prepared for Committee on Indemnity June 20, 1648. Autobiographical sketch, pp. 20 ff. Account of *Agreement of the People,* pp. 28 ff. List of some of Lilburne's books, pp. 24-27. On pp. 24-25 he mentions *Epistle of Two Sheets of Paper, dated July 25, 1645.* Mentions *Birth-Right* and *Regall Tyrannie,* but does not acknowledge authorship of either. 75 pp. B.M., McAl. Th: June 8, 1649]

The Legal Fundamental Liberties. . . . The second Edition . . . occasioned by the late coming out of Mr. William Prynnes Book . . . Intituled, A Legal Vindication . . . London . . . 1649. [No place. Mentions Walwyn's *Fountain of Slander* and *Just Defence,* p. 25. Autobiographical sketch begins on p. 24. 80[?] pp. B.M., H., McAl. This edition could not have appeared until late July or August]

To all the Affectors and Approvers . . . of the Petition of the eleventh of September 1648, but especially to my true friends . . . usually meeting at the Whalbone in Lothbury, behinde the Royal Exchange, commonly (but most unjustly) stiled Levellers. [No title page. Dated at the end, July 17, 1649. G.L]

A New Bull Bayting, or a match played at the Town Bull of Ely by twelve Mungrills . . . 1649. [August 7. Note by Peacock: "The Ely bull is Oliver

Cromwell. The "mungrills" are Lilburne and his friends." B.M. Th: Aug. 7, 1649]

To His honored Friend, Mr. Cornelius Holland, These. [No date, title, place, printer. On p. 5 of this tract Lilburne mentions a second edition of his discourse with Hugh Peters, a passage which substantiates Pease's assumption that *A Discovrse Betwixt . . . Lilburn . . . and Peter* is a genuine Lilburne product. Copies of this pamphlet in the Guildhall Library and South Kensington Museum, according to Peacock, contain Huntington's *Reasons* and the other principal documents of the *Impeachment*. This pamphlet apparently preceded the *Impeachment*, which appeared on August 10, 1649. S.K., G.L.]

An Impeachment of High Treason Against Oliver Cromwell, and his Son in Law Henry Ireton Esquires . . . London . . . 1649. [No printer. Contains *To His honored Friend, Mr. Cornelius Holland, These*, dated June 26, 1649, by Lilburne. Contains also (pp. 53-61) Huntington's *Sundry Reasons Inducing . . . Huntington To Lay down his Commission.* Lilburne's speech of January 19, 1648 to House of Commons reprinted on pp. 18-45. 58 pp. B.M., McAl. Th: Aug. 10, 1649]

A Preparative To An Hue and Cry After Sir Arthur Haslerig. [No place and printer. Contains letter dated by Lilburne August 18, 1649. *Birth-Right* mentioned on p. 24. 40 pp. B.M., McAl. Th: Aug. 18, 1649]

A Salva Libertate, sent to Collonell Francis West, Lieutenant of the Tower of London, 14 Sept., by . . . Lilburne. [Single sheet. 1648. B.M. Th: Sept. 14, 1648]

An Anatomy Of . . . Lilbvrn's Spirit and Pamphlets . . . London, Printed by John Macock for Francis Tyson . . . 1649. [Attributed to Cuthbert Sydenham. 16 pp. B.M., G.L., McAl. Th: Oct. 16, 1649]

Strength out of Weaknesse, or the finall and absolute plea of . . . Lilburn . . . against the present Ruling Power, sitting at Westminster. Being an epistle writ by him Sep. 30. 1649. [B.M., G.L., S.K. Th: Oct. 19, 1649]

The Innocent mans first proffer. London 1649. [Single sheet, folio, B.M. Th: Oct. 20, 1649]

The Innocent mans second proffer. London October 1649. [Single sheet, folio. B.M. Th: Oct. 22, 1649]

To the Supreme Authority of this Nation, the Commons assembled in Parliament. The humble Petition of divers wel-affected Women . . . In behalf of . . . Lilburn . . . Prince . . . Overton . . . Bray . . . And . . . Sawyer . . . London, 1649. [8 pp. B.M., G.L., McAl. Th: Oct. 23, 1649]

The Triall Of Lieut Collonell John Lilburne, By an extraordinary . . . Commission of Oyear and Terminer at the Guild-Hall . . . Published by Theodorus Verax . . . Printed by Hen. Hils . . . Southwark. [No printer. Short preface by Lilburne dated November 28, 1649. *The Innocent Mans First Proffer* (October 20, 1649) is reprinted on pp. 155-58 of the tract; *The Innocent Mans second Proffer* (October 22, 1649), on p. 161. 168 pp. Note by Peacock: "There are two editions of this trial of the year 1649, which may be distinguished by the name of the title being in the one case Varax, and in the other Verax." It was reprinted in what was called a second edition in octavo in 1710 by "H. Hills, in Black-fryars." B.M., H., McAl., G.L., S.K. Th: Oct. 24, 1649]

The Second Part Of the Triall of Lieut. Col. John Lilburn: By An extraordinary . . . Commission of Oyer and Terminer . . . the 24, 25, 26, of October 1649. . . . London Printed 1649. [Contains a section entitled "Certaine Observations Upon The Triall Of Leiut. Col. . . . Lilburne." In this section is printed a letter from Lilburne to Lenthall dated December 1, 1649. "First Dayes Proceedings" follow "Certaine Observations." 31 pp. B.M., G.L., McAl. Th: Oct. 24, 1649]

Truths Victory over tyrants, being the Tryall of that worthy asserter of his country's freedoms John Lilburne . . . 1649. [November 16, 1649. B.M. E. 579(12)]

Certaine Observations Upon The Tryall Of Lieut. Col. . . . Lilburne. [No title page, place, or printer. Dated at end December 1, 1649, 18 pp. S.K., McAl.]

The Engagement Vindicated & Explained, Or the Reasons Upon which . . . Lilburne, tooke the Engagement . . . London, Printed by John Clowes . . . 1650. [Dated at end by Lilburne, December, 1649. 6 pp. Bodl., S.K., G.L., McAl., H., B.M. Th: Jan. 23, 1650]

To the Supreme Authority, the People assembled in Parliament. The humble Petition of . . . Lilburne; praying that the sum remaining due to him . . . may immediately be ordered to be paid out of the estate of the late Lord Keeper Coventry, March, 1649. [Folio broadside. B.M. Th: March 12, 1650]

A Letter Of Due Censure, and Redargvtion to Lieut. Col. John Lilburne: touching his Triall at Guild-Hall . . . The intent is, to eat away the Patients proud, dead flesh, not to destroy any sincere, sound part . . . London. Printed by Fr. Neile, 1650. [Attributed to Henry Parker. Signed at the end: *H.P.* 41 pp B.M., Bodl., McAl. Th: June 21, 1650]

To every individual member of . . . the parliament of the Commonwealth . . . but more especially to George Thompson, chairman of the committee for regulating the new impost of excise and particularly for that of sope . . . by John Lilburne. London, November 7. 1650. [B.M., Th: Nov. 6, 1650]

To the Supreme Authority, the Parliament of the Commonwealth. The humble Petition of many well affected People . . . in behalfe of the just Liberties of the Common-wealth, highly concerned in the sentence against . . . Lilburne Presented. January 20. 1651. [Society of Antiquaries. Single sheet, folio.]

A Iust Reproof To Haberdashers-Hall. [1651. No place, printer, or date. Dated by Lilburne August 2, 1651. 40 pp. B.M., McAl. Th: July 30, 1651]

The Case Of The Tenants Of The Mannor of Epworth . . . by John Lilburne. [No title. Dated at the end November 18, 1651. Peacock's note: "This tract relates to the controversy regarding the drainage and enclosure of Hatfield Chace and the Isle of Axholme." B.M., S.K., H. Th: Nov. 18, 1651. 7 pp.]

To every individual member of the Supream authority of Parliament . . . by John Lilburne. [London, November, 1651. Peacock's note: "An answer to W. Huntington." B.M. Th: Nov. 26, 1651]

A Declaration of Lieutenant Colonel John Lilburn. 1651. [B.M. Th: Jan. 20, 1652]

Petition for reparing certain wrongs done unto them by John Lilburne. 1651.
[Peacock's note: "that is, David Brown and his family." Single sheet, folio.
B.M. Th: Jan. 22, 1652]

*The dissembling Scot . . . or a vindication of . . . Lilburn . . . from the
Aspersions of David Brown. By Samuel Chidley.* [No place. 1652. Bodl., B.M.
Th: Feb. 1, 1652]

*Lieft. Colonell I. Lilburne his Apologeticall Narration, in reference to his
late illegall and unjust Banishment; directed to the people of the united Provinces.* [Dated:] *From my studie in . . . Amsterdam this present 3 of April
1652.* [English and Dutch in parallel columns. 72 pp. B.M, McAl. Th: April,
1652]

*As You Were Or The Lord General Cromwel and the Grand Officers of the
Armie their Remembrancer . . . May 1652.* [Contains letters from Lilburne
to Cromwell and Kiffin. Hitherto unnoticed passage on Milton is on pp. 15-16.
33 pp. McAl.]

*A Remonstrance Of . . . Lilburn: Concerning The Lawes, Liberties, Privi-
leges . . . Published by a Well-wisher . . . London, for G. Horton, 1652.*
[Quotes Overton with high admiration. 8 pp. B.M., S.K., McAl.]

*The Remonstrance and Declaration of . . . Lilburn concerning the Crown
and Government of the Common-Wealth of England. . . . Sent in a letter to
the King of Scots. . . . London, Printed for George Horton 1652.* [G.L.]

*L. Colonel John Lilburne. Shewing the cause of his long silence, and cessa-
tion from Hostility against Alchemy St. Oliver, with an answer in part to the
pestilent calumniation of Cap. Wendy Oxford. . . . Printed in the Yeare 1653.
In March.* [G.L., B.M. Peacock's note: "The B.M. copy purports to be printed
at Amsterdam." Th: March 27, 1653]

*The Banished mans suit for Protection to his Excellency the Lord Generall
Cromwell, being the humble address of Lieutenant Colonell John Lilburn.
London 1653.* [B.M., Bodl. Th: June 14, 1653]

*A second address directed to . . . the Lord Generall Cromwell and the
right honorable the council of State. . . . The humble petition of John Lilburne.* [June 16, 1653. B.M. Th: June 16, 1653]

A Third address directed to . . . the Lord Generall Cromwell. [Newgate,
June 20, 1653. B.M. Th: June 20, 1653]

*A Defensive Declaration of Lieut. Col. John Lilburn against the unjust
sentence of his banishment by the late Parliament.* [Dated at end, June 22,
1653. G.L., S.K., B.M. Th: June 22, 1653]

*A Jury-Man's Judgement Upon the Case of Lieut. Col. John Lilburn. . . .
That it is as great a wickedness for any . . . to have a hand in his death upon
that Act, as wilfully to murther him.* [1653. No title page. 15 pp. B.M., McAl.
Th: June 22, 1653]

*An Additional Remonstrance to the Valiant and wel-deserving Souldier and
the rest of the Creditors of the Common-wealth . . . with a little friendly
touch to . . . John Lilburne. By Samuel Chidley. Printed for the Author.*
[B.M. Th: June 22, 1653]

To the Parliament of the Commonwealth of England, the humble petition of divers afflicted women in behalf of Mr. J. Lilburne, prisoner in Newgate. London, June 25, 1653. [B.M. Th: June 25, 1653]

The Prisoners Most mournful Cry . . . An Epistle written by John Lilburn . . . July 1. 1653. Unto John Fowke, Lord Maior of London. [7 pp. London, 1653. Bodl., H., S.K., B.M. Th: July 1, 1653]

Lieut. Col. John Lilburnes plea in Law against an act of parliament of the 30 of January 1651. [London, July, 1653. B.M. Th: July 2, 1653]

Lieu. Col. John Lilburn's Plea in Law, Against an Act of Parliament of the 30 of January 1651 . . . The second Edition, much inlarged. . . . [16 pp. H., B.M. Th: July 2, 1653]

The Second Letter from John Lilburn Esquire . . . to John Fowke, Lord Mayor of . . . London. London 1653. [B.M., S.K. Th: July 10, 1653]

Several Informations and Examinations Taken concerning . . . Lilburn Shewing His Apostacy to the Part of Charles Stuart. London, Printed by H. Hils, and for G. Calvert and T. Brewster . . . 1653. [Contains important biographical information. ? pp. B.M., McAl. Th: July 13, 1653]

The Triall of Mr. John Lilburn. . . . At the Sessions of Peace. . . . At Justice-Hall in the Old-Baily . . . 13, 14, 15, and *16 of July, 1653.* [Contains important documents: A statement by Manuel Suarez in answer to Staplehill's charges against Lilburne; a petition to Parliament signed by Lilburne July 12, 1653; several official charges against Lilburne signed by Sadler. 44 pp. B.M. G.L. McAl. Th: July 13, 1653]

The Tryall of . . . Lilburn at the Sessions in the Old Baily, with the new exceptions brought by the said . . . Lilburne. Printed for J. C. [B.M. Th: July 13, 1653]

The Exceptions Of John Lilburne Gent. . . . To A Bill of Indictment Preferred against him . . . 15 day of January, 1651. . . . London, Printed for Richard Moon . . . 1653. [Signed, according to a note at the end, by Lilburne's counsel, John Norbury and John Maynard, and presented to the Lord Mayor and his Court, July 16, 1653. But see pp. 8 and 9 of *The Triall . . . 1653.* 8 pp. B.M., G.L., McAl., II. Th. July 16, 1653]

John Lilburne Anagram. O! I burn in hell. [With an acrostic on the name "John Lilburne"] B.M. Th: July, 1653

The upright mans vindication: or an epistle writ by John Lilburn Gent. Prisoner in Newgate August 1. 1653. unto his friends and late Neighbours and acquaintance at Theobalds in Hartfordshire. . . . [B.M., G.L. Th: Aug. 1, 1653]

The humble and further demand of John Lilburn . . . 13 August 1653. [B.M., Th: Aug. 13, 1653]

The Afflicted Mans Out-Cry against the Injustice and Oppression exercised upon him, or An Epistle of John Lilburn Gent, Prisoner in Newgate 1653 to Mr. Feak, Minister of Christ Church in London. [London, 1653. B.M. Th: Aug. 19, 1653]

The Just Defence of John Lilburn against such as charge him with a Turbulency of Spirit. London, 1653. [No printer. B.M., Bodl. Th: Aug. 25, 1653]

An Hue and Cry after the Fundamental Lawes and Liberties of England. Occasionally written upon the stealing of one of the Grand Asserters of them out of Newgate. Europe! Printed in a year of Melodius Discord. [B.M. Th: September 26, 1653]

The Resurrection of John Lilburne, now a Prisoner in Dover-Castle . . . the second edition, with remarkable Additions by way of appendex. . . . [London, Giles Calvert, 1656. Shows Lilburn's conversion to Quakerism. 22 pp. B.M. McAl. Th: May 16, 1656]

Lilburns Ghost . . . By one who desires no longer life then to serve his Country. London 1659. [B.M. Th: June 22, 1659]

RICHARD OVERTON

The following list, like the others inserted in the bibliography, is not exhaustive. Much work is yet to be done on Overton in identifying his pamphlets and tracing the development of his thought.

New Lambeth Fair newly Consecrated. [1642. Satire in Verse. B.M., H. Th: Jan., 1642]

Articles of High Treason . . . against Cheapside Crosse. [Satire in Verse. 1642. B.M., H. Th: Mar., 1642]

Mans Mortallitie: Or, A Treatise Wherein 'tis proved, both Theologically and Philosophically, that whole Man . . . is a Compound wholly mortall. . . . Amsterdam, Printed by John Canne . . . 1644. [43 pp. B.M., H., McAl. Th: Jan. 19, 1644]

The Araignement Of Mr. Persecution . . . Europe . . . 1645. [Overton claims authorship of this tract in *A Picture of the Councel of State*, p. 26. 45 pp. A second edition is almost identical. McAl (both eds), B.M., H. Th: April 8, 1645]

A sacred Decretall, Or Hue and Cry. From his superlative Holinesse, Sir Symon Synod, for the Apprehension of Reverend Young Martin Mar-Priest. . . . Evrope [1645. No printer or date. 24 pp. B.M., McAl. Th: May 31, 1645]

The Nativity Of Sir John Presbyter. . . . Licensed by Rowland Rattlepriest . . . 1645. [21 pp. McAl. Th: July 2, 1645]

Martins Eccho: Or A Remonstrance . . . [1645. No Place, printer, or date. 20 pp. McAl.]

England's Miserie And Remedie. In A Jvdiciovs Letter from an Utter-Barrister to his speciall Friend, concerning . . . Lilburn's Imprisonment in Newgate, Sept. 1645. [No place, date, or printer. Parts of this pamphlet may have been written by Overton. I doubt that Lilburne wrote any of it. 8 pp. B.M., S.K.McAl. Th: Sept. 14, 1645]

The Ordinance For Tythes Dismounted . . . Evrope . . . 1646. [No printer. 40 pp. B.M., H., McAl. Th: Dec. 29, 1645]

Divine Observations Upon the London-Ministers Letter against Toleration. . . . Evrope . . . 1646. [No printer. 16 pp. B.M., H., McAl. Th: January 6, 1646]

A Remonstrance Of Many Thousand Citizens, and other Free-born People Of England, To their owne House of Commons. . . . 1646. [No place or printer. 20 pp. Reprinted in Haller's *Tracts on Liberty*. Walwyn probably collaborated with Overton in writing this tract. B.M., McAl. Th: July 7, 1646]

An Alarvm To the House of Lords. . . . 1646. [No place or printer. 12 pp. B.M., McAl. Th: July 31, 1646]

A Defiance Against All Arbitrary Usurpations . . . 1646. [No place or printer. 26 pp. Dated by Overton August 26, 1646. B.M., H., McAl. Th: September 9, 1646]

An Arrow Against All Tyrants And Tyrany, shot from the Prison of Newgate into the Prerogative Bowels of the . . . House of Lords . . . Richard Overton . . . 1646. [No place or printer. Dated at end October 12, 1646. 20 pp. B.M. McAl. Th: Oct. 12, 1646]

Vox Plebis, Or, The Peoples Out-cry Against Oppression, Injustice, and Tyranny . . . London . . . 1646. [No printer. Much of this tract was probably written by Overton. 69 pp. B.M. McAl. Th: Nov. 19, 1646]

An Vnhappy Game At Scotch And English. Or, A Full Answer from England to the Papers of Scotland. . . . Edinburgh . . . 1646. [False imprint, Thomason I, 477. Formerly attributed generally to Lilburne, this pamphlet was certainly written by Overton. The authorship is claimed by Overton in *A Picture of the Councel of State,* p. 36. The pamphlet contains analysis of monarchical prerogative that anticipates the arguments of *Regall Tyrannie.* 26 pp. B.M., H., McAl. Th: Nov. 30, 1646]

The Commoners Complaint: Or, A Dreadful Warning From Newgate, to the Commons of England . . . 1646. [No place or printer. Signed at the end by Overton and dated by him February 1, 1647. Reprinted in Haller's *Tracts on Liberty.* 23 pp. B.M. McAl. Th: February 10, 1647]

An Appeale from the Degenerate Representative Body . . . the Commons of England. [B.M. 1647]

To the Supreme Authority . . . the Representors . . . the Petition of . . . Overton. [B.M. Th: March 3, 1649]

Overtons Defyance of the Act of Pardon: or, The Copy of a Letter to the Citizens. [Dated by Overton at end July 2, 1649. 8 pp. B.M., H. Th: July 4, 1649]

The Baiting of the Great Bull of Bashan unfolded . . . By Richard Overton. [B.M. Th: July 16, 1649]

WILLIAM WALWYN

The best guides to Walwyn's works are Pease, *The Leveller Movement,* and Haller, *Tracts on Liberty* (Appendix A, Vol. I). Professor Haller in late years has identified a number of Walwyn's pamphlets, most of which are included in this list.

The Humble Petition of the Brownists, 1641 [B.M. Th: November, 1641. Attributed to Walwyn by Professor Pease]

Some Considerations Tending to the undeceiving those, whose judgements are misinformed by Politique Protestations . . . a necessary Discourse for the present times, concerning the unseasonable difference between the Protestant and the Puritan. [No date, printer, or place. 16 pp. Ascribed to Walwyn by Professor Haller. McAl., B.M. Th: November 10, 1642]

The Power of Love. London, Printed by R. C. for John Sweeting . . . 1643. [51 pp. Reprinted in Haller's *Tracts on Liberty.* B.M. Th: September 19, 1643]

Good Counsell to all those that heartily desire the glory of God [No title page. Thomason catalog: "The pagination begins with page 79. MS note by Thomason: 'This is all of this booke though it begins thus.'" B.M. Th: July 29, 1644]

The Compassionate Samaritan Vnbinding the Conscience, and powring Oyle into the wounds which have been made upon the Separation. . . . The Second Edition, corrected, and enlarged . . . 1644. [No place or printer. 79 pp. A copy of the first edition (83 pp.) is in the Yale University Library. The second edition is reprinted in *Tracts on Liberty.* B.M. Th: January 5, 1645]

A Helpe to the right understanding of a Discourse Concerning Independency. Lately published by William Pryn . . . 1644. [No place, or printer. McAl., B.M. Th: February 6, 1645]

Englands Lamentable Slaverie, Proceeding from the Arbitrarie will, severitie, and Injust[ic]es of Kings. . . . [No printer or place. At end: "Printed *October,* 1645." 8 pp. Reprinted in Haller's *Tracts on Liberty.* B.M. Th: October 11, 1645]

A Whisper In The Eare of Mr. Thomas Edwards . . . By William Walwyn Marchant. . . . [At end:] *London, Printed according to Order, by Thomas Paine, for William Ley . . . 1646.* [15 pp. Reprinted in Haller's *Tracts on Liberty.* McAl., B.M. Th: March 13, 1646]

A Word More To Mr. Thomas Edwards . . . By William Walwyn Marchant. . . . London, Printed by Thomas Paine. 1646. [15 pp. McAl., B.M. Th: May 18, 1646]

A Word in Season: Or Motives to Peace, Accomodation, and Vnity, 'twixt Presbyterian and Independent Brethren. . . . London, Printed for J. Macock. . . . 1646. [8 pp. McAl., B.M., Th: May 18, 1646]

An Antidote Against Mr. Edwards [B.M. Th: June 10, 1646]

The Just man in bonds or . . . John Lilburne close Prisoner in Newgate by order of the Hovse of Lords . . . 23, July 1646. [No title. B.M., G.L., S.K., H. Th: June 23, 1646]

A Pearle in a dovnghill. . . . John Lilbourne in Newgate. [Date at the end: June 1646. Peacock's note: "Other editions, June 19, 1646, and April 30, 1647." B.M., G.L., S.K. Th: June 23, 1646]

A Prediction Of Mr. Edwards His Conversion, and Recantation. By William Walwin. London. Printed by T. P. for G. Whittington and N. Brookes . . . 1646. [B.M. Th: August 11, 1646]

A Parable, Or Consvltation of Physitians Vpon Master Edwards. . . . London, Printed by Thomas Paine, for Giles Calvert. [16 pp. McAl., B.M. Th: October 29, 1646]

A Still And Soft Voice From the Scriptures, Witnessing them to be the Word of God. . . . Printed in the Yeare, 1647. [McAl. Appeared probably in April. See notes on Chapter VI. This tract reprinted on pp. 365-74 of this book.]

Walwins Wiles: Or The Manifestors Manifested . . . Lilburn . . . Walwin . . . Overton . . . Prince. Discovering themselves to be Englands new Chains. . . . April 23. 1649. . . . London, Printed for H.C. and L.L. [Attributed to John Price and William Kiffin in Thomason and D.N.B. 32 pp. B.M., McAl., H. Th: May 10, 1649]

The Fountain Of Slaunder Discovered. By William Walwyn, Merchant. . . . London, Printed by H. Hils, and are to be sold by W. Larnar. . . . M.DC.XLIX. [26 pp. McAl., B.M. Th: May 30, 1649]

The Charity Of Church-Men: Or, A Vindication of Mr William Walwyn Merchant, from the aspersions plentifully cast upon him in . . . Walwyns Wiles. By H. B. Med. a friend to Truth, his country and Mr Walwyn. . . . London, Printed by H. Hils, and are to be sold by W. Larnar. . . . M.DC.XLIX. [14 pp. McAl. On June 25 appeared another pamphlet by Brooke, *The Craftsmen's Craft*]

Walwyns Jvst Defence Against The Aspertions Cast Upon Him . . . By William Walwyn. . . . London, Printed by H. Hils, for W. Larnar. . . . M.DC.XLIX. [34 pp. McAl., H. Appeared probably in late July or early August. See notes on Chapter VI.]

Juries justified: Or, A Word Of Correction To Mr. Henry Robinson; For His seven Objections against the Trial of Causes, by Juries of twelve men. By William Walwyn. . . . London, Printed by Robert Wood. . . . 1651. [14 pp. H., McAl.]

GERRARD WINSTANLEY

The following list of Digger pamphlets, though not exhaustive, is representative of Digger history and Winstanley's main ideas. Students of Winstanley are indebted to Lewis H. Berens' *The Digger Movement in the Days of the Commonwealth* (London, 1906) for the first important exposition of Winstanley's thought; it contains the first fairly complete Digger bibliography. I have gleaned information from photostatic copies of the pamphlets in my possession. A number of the pamphlets are in the Seligman Collection of Columbia University.

The Mysterie Of God Concerning the whole Creation, Mankinde. To Be Made known to every man and woman. . . . By Ierrard Winstanley . . . 1648. [67 pp. B.M.]

The Saints Paradise: Or, The Fathers Teaching the only satisfaction to waiting Souls. . . . By Jerrard Winstanley. . . . London, Printed for G. Calvert. [No date, but probably 1648. Marked by Thomason "July". Another edition of this tract is in the Seligman Collection at Columbia University. 134 pp. H., B.M.]

The Breaking of the Day of God. . . . London. Printed in the year 1649. [Epistle dedicatory dated May 20, 1648. B.M., H.]

Truth Lifting up its Head above Scandals. . . . By Gerrard Winstanly. . . . London . . . 1649. [No printer. Address to Cambridge and Oxford men among the ministers at the beginning dated by Winstanley October 16, 1648. 77 pp. Two pages of verses at the end of the tract. B.M.]

Light shining in Buckingham-Shire, Or, A Discovery of the main ground; Originall Cause of all the Slavery in the World, but cheifly in England . . . 1648. [No printer or place. 13 pp. B.M., H. Th: December 5, 1648]

The New Law Of Righteousness Budding forth, in restoring the whole Creation. . . . By Gerrard Winstanley. . . . 1649. [120 pp. Copies in Jesus College, Oxford, and Seligman Collection of Columbia University]

Fire In The Bush. The Spirit Bvrning, Not ConSuming, but purging Mankinde. . . . By Jerrard Winstanly. . . . London, Printed for Giles Calvert . . . 1650. [77 pp. At the end is printed "A Vindication Of Those, Whose endeavors is only to make the Earth a common treasury, called Diggers. Or, Some Reasons given by them against the immodierate use of creatures, or the excessive community of women called Ranting, or rather Renting." The "Vindication" is signed at the end by Winstanley and dated February 20, 1649. Bodl.]

A Declaration From The Poor oppressed People Of England. . . . 1649. [No printer or place. 8 pp. Signed by forty-five Diggers, Winstanley first. B.M., March, 1649]

A Vindication Of Those . . . called Diggers. Or, Some reasons given by them against the immoderate use of creatures, or the excessive community of women called Ranting; or rather Renting. [9 pp. Signed by Winstanley at the end and dated March 4, 1649. B.M. Th: March 20, 1649]

A Declaration Of The Wel-Affected In the County of Buckinghamshire. Being A Representation of the middle sort of Men within the three Chilterne Hundreds of Disbrough, Burnum, and Stoke, and part of Alisbury Hundred, whereby they Declare their Resolution and Intentions, with a Removall of their Grievances . . . 1649. [8 pp. No place or printer. An unsigned Digger protest. B.M. Th: May 10, 1649]

More Light Shining in Buckingham-shire: Being A Declaration of the state and condition that all Men are in by Right. . . . The second part. . . . London . . . 1649. [No printer. 16 pp. B.M. Th: March 30, 1649]

The Declaration and Standard Of the Levellers of England; Delivered in a Speech to his Excellency the Lord Gen. Fairfax, on Friday last at White-Hall, by Mr. Everard, a late Member of the Army, and his Prophesie in reference thereunto. . . . London, for G. Lawrenson, April 23, 1649. [6 pp. An account of the interview of Winstanley and Everard with Fairfax. Not written by a Digger partisan. B.M.]

The Speeches Of The Lord Generall Fairfax, And the Officers of the Armie To The Diggers at St. Georges Hill in Surry, and the Diggers severall Answers and Replies thereunto. . . . London: Printed for R.W. MDCXLIX. [Contains a few paragraphs about the Diggers and several other unrelated news items. B.M. Th: May 31, 1649]

A Perfect Diurnall Of Some Proceedings. . . . Licensed by the Secretary of the Army under His Excellency the Lord Fairfax. From Munday April 1. to Munday April 8. 1649. London, Printed for F. Leach, and E. Griffin in the Old-baily. [Contains a public letter from the Diggers warning against unauthorized collections of funds to assist them. B.M.]

A Letter To The Lord Fairfax, And His Councell of War. . . . By Jerrard Winstanly. . . . London: Printed for Giles Calvert . . . 1649. [13 pp. B.M. Th: June 13, 1649]

A Declaration of The bloudie and unchristian acting of William Star and John Taylor Of Walton, With divers men in Womens apparell. . . . London, Printed for Giles Calvert . . . 1649. [14 pp. B.M. Th: June 22, 1649]

An Appeal To the House of Commons, Desiring their Answer: Whether the Common-people shall have the quiet enjoyment of the Commons and Waste

Land; Or whether they shall be under the will of Lords of Mannors still. . . . *By Gerrard Winstanly, Iohn Barker, and Thomas Star, In the name of all the poor oppressed.* . . . *1649.* [No place or printer. 19 pp. G.L., B.M. Th: July 11, 1649]

A Watch-Word To The City of London, And The Armie: . . . *By Jerrard Winstanly.* . . . *London, Printed for Giles Calvert.* . . . *1649.* [16 pp. Reprinted complete on pp. 377-96 of this volume. G.L., B.M. Th: September 10, 1649]

A Mite Cast Into The Common Treasury. . . . *Robert Coster.* [No place or printer. 5 pp. B.M. Th: December 18, 1649]

A New-yeers Gift For The Parliament And Armie: Shewing, What the Kingly Power is; And that the Cause of those They call Diggers Is the life and marrow of that Cause the Parliament hath Declared for, and the Army Fought for. . . . *By Jerrard Winstanley.* . . . *London, Printed for Giles Calvert, 1650.* [49 pp. B.M. Th: January 1, 1650]

The Diggers Mirth, Or, Certain Verses composed and fitted to Tunes, for the delight and recreation of all those who Dig, or own that Work, in the Commonwealth of England. Wherein is shewed how the Kingly power doth still Reign in severall sorts of Men. . . . *London* . . . *1650.* [No printer. 16 pp. B.M. Th: April 4, 1650]

An Humble Request To The Ministers of both Universities And To All Lawyers in every Inns-a-Court. To Consider of the Scriptures and points of Law . . . *to give a rational and christian Answer, whereby the difference may be composed* . . . *between the poor men of England* . . . *And The Lords of Mannours that trouble them.* . . . *By Gerard Winstanley.* . . . *London, Printed by J.C.* . . . *1650.* [Prefatory address dated by Winstanley April 9, 1650. 16 pp. S.K.]

The True Levellers Standard Advanced: Or, The State of Community opened, and Presented to the Sons of Men. By [names of fifteen Diggers, Winstanley and Everard first] *Beginning to Plant and Manure the Waste Land upon George-Hill.* . . . *London.* . . . *MDCXLIX.* [23 pp. A selection from this pamphlet is reprinted in Woodhouse, *Puritanism and Liberty* (London: J. M. Dent and Sons, 1938). B.M., H. Th: April 26, 1650]

A Declaration of the Grounds and Reasons why we the Poor Inhabitants of the Town of Wellinborrow, in the County of Northampton, have begun and give consent to dig up, manure and sow Corn upon the Common, and waste ground. . . . *London, Printed for Giles Calvert, 1650.* [Single sheet. Signed by nine men, Winstanley not among them. B.M. Th: March 12, 1650]

An Appeale to all Englishmen, to judge between Bondage and Freedome, sent from those that began to digge upon George Hill in Surrey; but now are carrying on, that publick work upon the little Heath in the Parish of Cobham. . . . [Single sheet. Dated March 26, 1650. Signed by Winstanley and twenty-four others. B.M., H.]

The Law Of Freedom in a Platform . . . *by Gerrard Winstanley.* . . . *Printed for the Author and are to be sold by Giles Calvert* . . . [London, 1652. Epistle dedicatory to Cromwell dated November 5, 1650. 89 pp. G.L., Bodl. B.M., H. Th: February 20, 1652]

INDEX

487